Art in the World

Second Edition

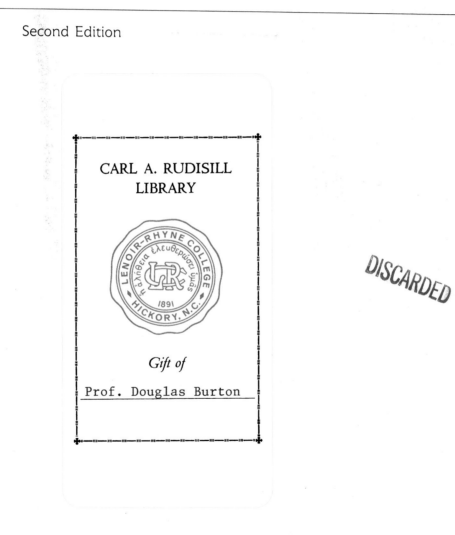
Cover: Frank Lloyd Wright. The Solomon R. Guggenheim Museum, New York. 1956–59. Photograph © Jake Rajs.

Art in the World

Second Edition

STELLA PANDELL RUSSELL
Nassau Community College

HOLT, RINEHART AND WINSTON
New York   Chicago   San Francisco   Philadelphia   Montreal   Toronto
London   Sydney   Tokyo   Mexico City   Rio de Janeiro   Madrid

Publisher Susan Katz
Editor Karen Dubno
Picture Editor Joan Scafarello
Picture Researcher Sybille Millard
Senior Project Editor Françoise Bartlett
Art Director and Cover Designer Lou Scardino
Production Manager Nancy Myers
Design and layout Caliber Design Planning

Composition and camera work York Graphic Services
Color separations The Lehigh Press, Inc.
Printing and binding Von Hoffmann Press

For Janna, Jonathan, Loriann
and their father, George

Library of Congress Cataloging in Publication Data

Russell, Stella Pandell.
  Art in the world.

  Bibliography: p. 332
  Includes index.
  1. Art appreciation. I. Title.
N7477.R87 1983   701'.1   83-8394

ISBN 0-03-061976-9

CBS COLLEGE PUBLISHING
Holt, Rinehart and Winston
The Dryden Press
Saunders College Publishing

Preface

Art in the World is an introduction to art appreciation—intended to provide a foundation in the basic concepts, materials, and processes of the visual arts—as well as a brief history of art. Through analysis of examples drawn from the art of the past and the present, it assists the student in recognizing the universal qualities in human aesthetic response and the special differences that define every culture. Although many fine books are available for study, none is as clearly written or provides as broad a coverage of these major areas.

Besides fulfilling this need, *Art in the World,* second edition, focuses on areas too often given insufficient attention in other texts.

1. Contemporary Art For most students, the art of our own time is difficult to understand, let alone appreciate. For this reason, an entire section of the text is devoted to 20th-century art and its roots in the art of the Age of Revolution. Whenever appropriate, modern and traditional works of art are compared and contrasted.

2. Applied Arts Another emphasis of this text is to treat the decorative arts and the arts of industry with the same respect accorded the fine arts of painting, sculpture, and architecture. It is in these functional arts, after all, where most of us have daily contact and experience. If this book can help the reader to appreciate the value and beauty in well-made objects of everyday use, much will have been accomplished.

3. Non-Western and Minority Arts A separate chapter in the history section is devoted to non-Western art and its influence on the Western world. In addition, examples of non-Western art are discussed and illustrated within the context of specific media whenever contrast with Western traditions would be instructive. There is also a section on the black-American artist expanded from the previous edition and an entirely new section on Feminist art. In addition, early minority contributions have been integrated within the body of the other sections of the text.

Art is inspired by living. In the years since *Art in the World* was first published, living artists with their unique ability to invent images that illuminate our world have continued to add to the body of art. Changes in the contemporary visual arts have therefore required a number of substantial adjustments to the text and illustrations of the first edition. Parts I and II have been painstakingly revised and expanded to present a comprehensive survey of media and process. Chapter 2, "Exploring the Artist's Language," is vastly increased. Because of the modern focus on duplicate images, Chapter 4, "Printmaking," has been added so that printing processes may be analyzed and contrasted with the mass reproductions which surround us. The new interest in handmade paper is reflected in a section on the papermaking process, and the print workshop movement is introduced. In Chapter 5, "Arts of the Lens," the sections on television and film, including the role of the director, have been expanded. Occupying more of our interests and time, the photographic arts are examined with particular reference as an American phenomenon. Additionally, in response to our increasing concern about the depletion of energy sources, Chapter 10,

"Environmental Design," includes a discussion of ecological balance and solar energy, contrasting age-old solutions with modern answers.

While these changes make the second edition of *Art in the World* more relevant to the concerns of today's students, considerable effort has been made to retain a simple, flexible organization, adaptable to many teaching styles and approaches. Part I introduces the visual arts and the nature of appreciation and explores the basic elements and principles of art. Part II, a more leisurely adventure in process, materials, and methods used to produce the various art forms, moves in a logical progression from the two-dimensional to the three-dimensional media. Parts III and IV provide a chronological history of art beginning with the Stone Age and continuing down to the most recent styles and trends of the 1980s, with a glimpse of the future world of art. These main divisions may be taken up in any order to suit the needs of the instructor and students.

Art in the World, second edition, has a new 8 by 10 inch format that permits the more than 400 illustrations, 19 in color, to be reproduced much larger than previously. It is also printed on higher-quality paper to achieve greater clarity of detail and a fuller range of values. With the exception of the color plates, the illustrations appear in close proximity to the textual discussion, usually on the same or facing page. To foster comprehension of complex subject matter, important terms are highlighted in boldface and defined the first time they appear in the text. Each chapter ends with several art activities and research exercises that can provide deeper learning opportunities to interested students. Concluding the book are a glossary of terms to clarify the artist's vocabulary and an annotated bibliography, arranged by chapter, to help students prepare papers or pursue topics of interest in greater depth.

It is hoped that *Art in the World,* second edition, will prove a valuable guide to the world of art, and that students will find stimulation for the continuing experience of art in their own world and will learn to understand and perhaps enjoy art in whatever form it appears.

Acknowledgments

Many able professionals, artists, teachers, students, and friends helped in the revision of this book. The author wishes to thank them all and to offer particular thanks to the following teachers who read the various drafts of the manuscript and made useful suggestions: Lloyd Benjamin, University of Arkansas; Marion Brown, University of Wisconsin at Madison; Barbara Curlee, Northeast Mississippi Junior College; Helen Duff, Delaware State College; Whitney Engeran, Indiana State University; John Linn, Henderson State University; Donald Parks, Delaware State College; Jill Peterson, University of Portland; Jane Mayo Roos, Hunter College; and Norman Whitefield, Abilene Christian University.

Many thanks are also due a multitude of museums, galleries, private collectors, agencies, and businesses. And, of course, a warm acknowledgment goes to all the artists of the present and past whose works are reproduced in this text.

I wish again to thank Gordon Ekholm for all he has taught me, for his guiding eye for many long years. I am especially indebted to my editor, Karen Dubno, for her advice and labor during the writing of this edition; Françoise Bartlett, for her project editorial skills, which turned a manuscript into a book; and picture editor Joan Scafarello and picture researcher Sybille Millard for their persistence in organizing and locating illustrations. Acknowledgment is also due Lou Scardino for supervising the design and layout and Nancy Myers for ensuring quality production and printing. A special thanks to Chancellor Clifton Wharton for his singular encouragement in what proved to be a demanding process of revision.

S.P.R.

Oyster Bay, N.Y.
August 1983

Contents

PART III Art in Society 159

Art in the World

Second Edition

PART I

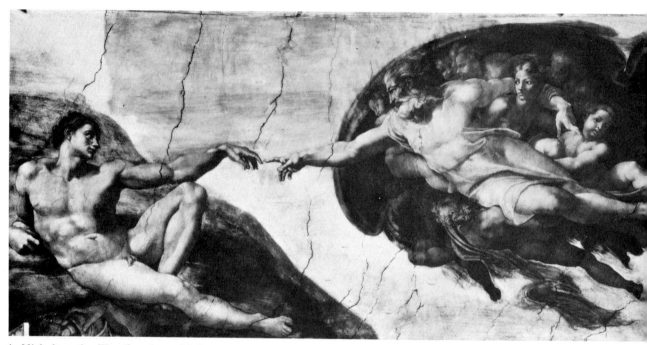

1. Michelangelo. *The Creation of Adam,*
detail of Sistine Chapel ceiling. 1511.
Fresco, 45 × 130′ (13.71 × 39 m).
Vatican, Rome.

The Visual Arts

What is art? A key to existence, perhaps? Robert Browning said, "Art remains the one way possible of speaking truth." Exploring what and how and why artists create can be a way to extend our own awareness beyond ordinary consciousness.

We expect to find art when we visit great museums of painting and sculpture, such as the Solomon R. Guggenheim Museum in New York City, but who has not heard the term *art* applied to such varied fields as literature, theater, dance, and music? These areas are all considered branches of the humanities as distinguished from the sciences.

One element common to all these forms of art is skill, but when we speak of the arts, we usually mean much more than skill. We expect art to provide us with unique experiences that affect our senses in special ways. Art may convey a message that moves us deeply or awakens us to new insights. Art also reminds us of feelings all people share but few can express as profoundly as the artist. Great art stretches our awareness of how special we can be. For instance, while we all marvel at the creation of life, not many of us can represent the act of creation with the impact Michelangelo (1475–1564) achieved in his fresco *The Creation of Adam* on the ceiling of the Sistine Chapel in Rome (Fig. 1).

We cannot hope to discuss all the areas of art in this book. We will not be concerned with the art of literature, which depends on words, nor with the **performing arts,** which are fleeting experiences of music, dance, and drama designed to be heard or seen as sequential events. Although dance and drama have visual elements, their foundation is the human body; they leave nothing material behind them but costumes and stage props. We must confine ourselves to the **visual arts,** which consist of works created primarily to be seen.

Works of art are not simple objects. A painting, a church, or a vase is a complex phenomenon concerned with beauty, often utility, psychological fulfillment, and sometimes, revelation. For many, art also represents cultural attainment, social status, and even a form of investment. For all these reasons, society has supported the visual arts for thousands of years. In the ancient past there was an unspoken "contract" between the community and its artists. In modern times, artists have worked through private commission for the art patron, or have prepared work for sale to the general public.

In this book we will review the different areas of the visual arts and the history of the arts of various peoples. As a preliminary to our study, in Part I we will attempt to discover something about creativity and our response to it. We will also explore the basic elements common to all the visual arts, such as line and color, and the principles of composition, such as unity, balance, rhythm, and proportion.

1 Creation and Response

*Cold exactitude is not art; ingenious artifice,
when it pleases or when it expresses,
is art itself.*

EUGÈNE DELACROIX

Art has been with us since our beginnings in communal living. From the first stick figures hesitantly drawn in sand and the earliest animals painted and carved on stone (Fig. 2) until today, people have reacted to the world by making **images.** Most of their images have far outlasted the societies for which they were created and first enjoyed.

The ancient Romans called these images *arti,* a word they defined as "skills." Artists were skilled workers who were trained in painting, carving, building, pottery making, and other crafts. Two thousand years later we look at ancient works of art and realize that although they may have required skill, it is their beauty that attracts us. In addition, such works show us how others once lived. Art reveals what was important to every society and is the gift people leave behind.

Art still touches us today in many aspects of our lives—in our homes, on the job, and at play. We evolve our art, perhaps, from what we perceive of the order in nature, yet

2. Paleolithic cave painting.
c. 15,000–10,000 B.C. Approximately life size. Lascaux (Dordogne), France.

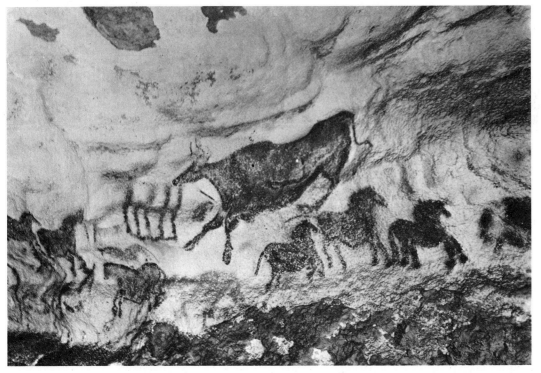

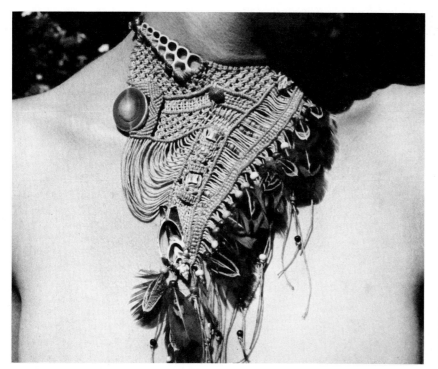

3. Janna Russell. *Peace with Feathers*. 1979. Beige waxed linen cord with horn section, bone, sliced shells, and feathers. Collection the author.

we are apt to think of art as something mysterious or complex that only an artist, scholar, or critic can fully understand.

In the West it has been convenient to divide the visual arts into two categories. The **fine arts,** or **major arts,** are considered by many to be primarily concerned with beauty. We include under the term drawing, painting, printmaking, sculpture, architecture, photography, and new art forms involving light, laser beams, and computers. The **functional, decorative,** or **minor arts** are concerned with utility. They include printing, ceramics, textiles, furniture, jewelry, and metalwork, both as handcrafts and as industries.

It is important to emphasize that this division, which developed after the Renaissance and especially at the time of the Industrial Revolution in the 19th century, is a useful way to classify the enormous variety of visual arts; it is not a system of ranking them. Few artists today believe that painting, for example, is more worthy of our attention than fine jewelry. The goal of Janna Russell (b. 1955) in her fiber art (Fig. 3) differs little from that of most artists who work on canvas or paper.

> I strive to achieve a sense of motion arrested in balance, combining textures which yield a unified form greater than its parts. The materials of *Peace with Feathers* are drawn from the shifting shoreline. The tensions of knots and slivered shells echo the sea's endless movements and changes.

The decorative arts are often as impressive as the fine arts for beauty, skill, and the message they offer. Today all the arts are a part of our lives when we are open to see them.

Creativity

Many people believe that artists create from personal experience. They are convinced by the unhappy life story of the Dutch painter Vincent van Gogh (1853–1890) that art often reflects high emotion or stress. Some may even believe that art is created a little like a pearl, erupting from deep-seated feelings in extraordinary ways. It is true that some artists may produce their work under situations of severe personal demand and others as the mood strikes them through trial and error, but just as many work well at scheduled hours in the studio. Whatever way creativity occurs, few artists produce inspiring art objects such as van Gogh's *Starry Night* without it (Fig. 4).

All of us share in the impulse to create, although not to the same degree. It is born in the child and frequently stifled by pragmatic demands from the adult world. Certainly the child who dresses in her mother's clothes plays out a creative fantasy just as the Dutch artist M. C. Escher's (1898–1972) print of *Drawing Hands* reflects creativity endlessly (Fig. 5). If you have ever held an audience spellbound with a story or grown a garden that draws admiring attention or drawn images you really cannot remember seeing, then you have been close to inspiration—and to the exhilaration that comes from creating something where nothing existed before.

Sometimes creativity, or artistic invention, is clearly expressed, as in Michelangelo's *The Creation of Adam* (Fig. 1); at other times it is less evident, as in Josef Albers' (1888–1976) *Homage to the Square* (Pl. 1, p. 21). Albers took the square, traditionally considered to be a perfectly balanced geometric form, and presented it in a new way

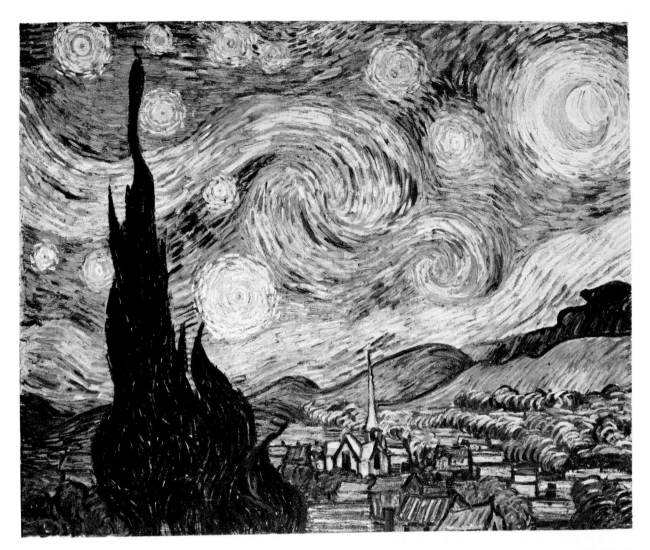

above: 4. Vincent van Gogh. *The Starry Night.*
1889. Oil on canvas, 29 × 36¼″ (74 × 92 cm).
Museum of Modern Art, New York
(acquired through the Lillie P. Bliss Bequest).

right: 5. M. C. Escher. *Drawing Hands.*
1948. Lithograph. 11¼ × 13⅜″ (29 × 34 cm).
Escher Foundation, Gemeentemuseum,
The Hague.

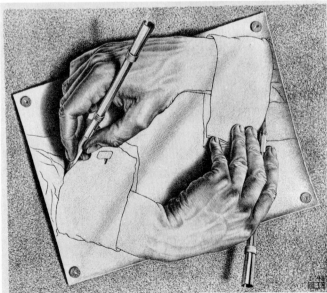

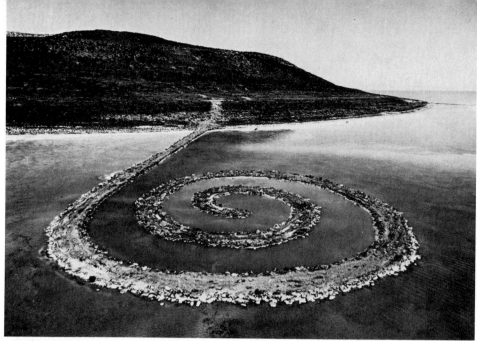

6. Robert Smithson. *Spiral Jetty.*
1970. Black rock, salt crystals, earth, and red water (algae);
coil 1500' (457.2 m) long, 15' (4.57 m) wide. Great Salt Lake, Utah.

characterized by subtle color relationships. Each of these works takes a common theme—creation and the square—and expresses it in an uncommon, creative way. Thus art reveals universal *and* special experiences.

In the 20th century many artists, searching for unique expression, have tried to free themselves creatively from the confines of traditional forms of art. Some artworks, for example, share the characteristics of both painting and sculpture. Robert Smithson (1938–1973) rejected the long-held notion that sculpture is produced only in the artist's studio. Like the Japanese, whose carefully sculptured gardens are living, changing, natural designs, he used the natural elements of earth and water in his startling earth sculpture *Spiral Jetty* (Fig. 6). An important feature of this large-scale, public sculpture was change through erosion, since the action of the water eventually left nothing of the work but a photographic record of its existence. When we can be open to experiencing art without trying to establish its category or separate it from daily life and nature, we are more likely to enjoy creativity in places we never expected it to be.

Meaning

Many people today have grown accustomed to think that the sole purpose of art is to give pleasure by being beautiful. Yet the fundamental goal of much art, especially in the past, was not to achieve beauty but to convey meaning, to express important ideas and feelings through arresting images. As Pablo Picasso (1881–1973) once said, "Art is not for interior decoration."

There are many kinds of meaning in art. They reflect the fact that art as an expression of thought or emotion is also a response to the world that nurtured the artist. One kind of meaning is the practical role art often plays in society. The specific purpose it serves and the form it takes reflect the values and concepts of beauty in different times and places. Painting on cave walls in prehistoric Europe was a magico-religious ritual that arose out of the need of a hunting society to ensure a plentiful supply of game (Fig. 2). Most civilized societies have required artists to glorify the society's gods and heroes in sculpture, painting, and architecture. In the commercial society of the 20th century, much art is in the form of printed matter or television and is used to promote the sale of goods and services.

Another kind of meaning, sometimes closely related to the practical purpose of art, is symbolism. If we are aware of the meaning of religious, political, or other symbols, we will better understand and enjoy a work of art. We may need to study Islamic art to know that Islamic artists often incorporated Arabic sayings from the Koran into their designs, as in the border of this 19th-century Persian prayer rug (Fig. 7). Symbols used in much 20th-century art are probably the easiest for us to follow because they derive chiefly from contemporary society.

Knowing what a car means to many Americans, we do not find it hard to decipher some of the messages conveyed in James Rosenquist's (b. 1933) *I Love You with My Ford* (Fig. 8). Through advertising we have been persuaded that success in love and possession of "wheels" are closely allied. In the Islamic rug, symbolism was used to strengthen the believer's faith. In the Rosenquist work, symbolism is a

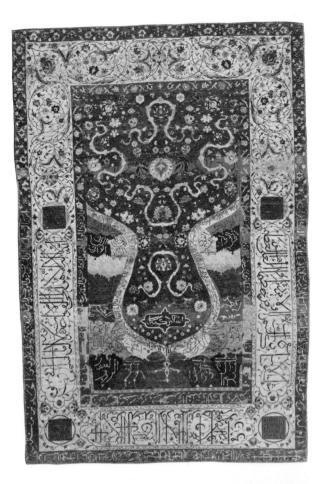

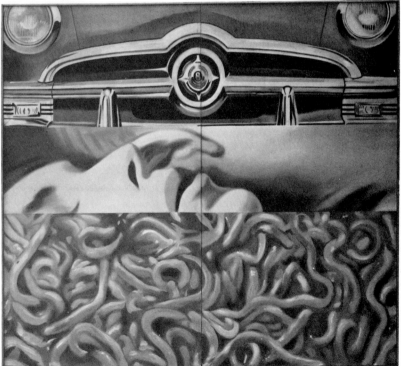

left: 7. Prayer rug. North Persian (probably Tabriz). 19th century. Wool, 5′3½″ × 3′6⅛″ (1.61 × 1.07 m). Metropolitan Museum of Art, New York (Mr. and Mrs. Isaac D. Fletcher Collection; Bequest of Isaac D. Fletcher, 1917).

below: 8. James Rosenquist. *I Love You with My Ford.* 1961. Oil on canvas, 7′1¼″ × 7′11⅝″ (2.14 × 2.43 m). Moderna Museet, Stockholm.

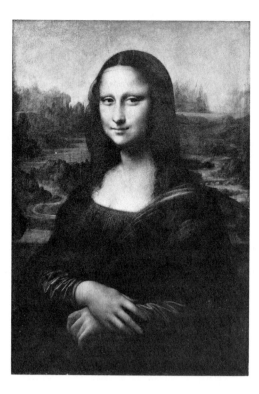

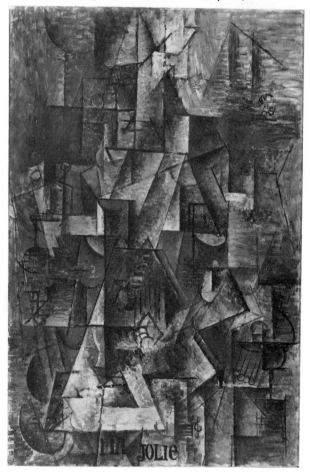

means of commenting on a society in which advertising shapes popular tastes.

On a more personal level, meaning in art is to be found in the individual approach of the artist. Because everyone observes the world differently, each work of art is unique—a reflection of the artist's perceptions, insights, and experience. For instance, a favorite theme of artists, most of whom have been men, has been women. An artist's approach to that theme reflects both the period and his or her own orientation, as you can see in Leonardo da Vinci's (1452–1519) *Mona Lisa* (Fig. 9) and Picasso's *"Ma Jolie"* (Fig. 10). A quite different treatment of the same theme is Marie Guillemine Benoist's (1768–1826) *Portrait of a Negress* (Fig. 11). Although the artist sensitively records her subject's graceful form, long neck, and full breasts, she emphasizes not bodily features but her subject's quiet dignity and reserve.

To express an individual point of view, an artist consciously selects certain aspects of the world, eliminates others, adds some items, and exaggerates others. In addition to choosing the subject, the artist also adopts materials, colors, and shapes to communicate a particular perception, shaping an image into a full artistic statement. Were it possible to clone nature without change the result would not be art. It is the artist's creative translation of subject or materials that produces significant work.

The night sky, which all of us see and usually ignore, becomes a vehicle of emotional and aesthetic release for van Gogh. His excited perception is communicated to us by his exaggerated swirling shapes and tense brush strokes (Fig. 4). The tiny village sleeps beneath the turbulence of nature, unaware that both the sun and the moon have joined the stars to illuminate the heavens. As observers, we are filled with awe at the extraordinary event.

The Observer's Response

Responsiveness is necessary to an appreciation of art. If we do not react to a work of art, it might as well never have existed for us. The more we learn about the meaning of art

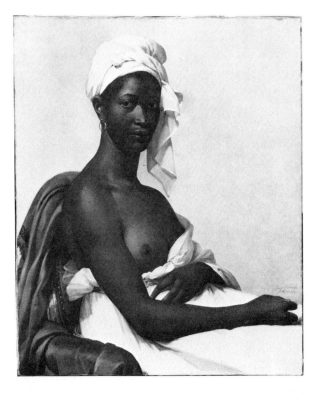

to its society and the artist, the more sensitive and discerning our responses can become.

Emotional Response We can also respond on an emotional level. Art can shock, disturb, or horrify us as well as soothe, delight, or excite us. For example, we may stand in a great cathedral and be overwhelmed with religious exaltation. Or we may be shocked by Artemesia Gentileschi's (c. 1597–c. 1651) depiction in pitiless detail of Judith's ferocious beheading of Holofernes (Fig. 12). The work is unique in the violence of the killing, the fury of the artist, and the horror we feel observing the scene.

All art, however, need not move us quite so intensely. We may open a magazine and enjoy the illustrations and the pleasing display lettering or type without being conscious of the graphic design. We may savor a fine dinner and be less aware of the design and quality of the porcelain, silver, and crystal. We may enjoy in a palatial home the attractive groupings of furniture and subtle relationships of colors and textures. These reactions, though of a lesser nature, are also emotional responses to artistic expressions.

In developing an appreciation of art, such reactions are important for they imply sensitivity. Whether you love or hate an artwork initially is really less important than that

above: 11. Marie Guillemine Benoist.
Portrait of a Negress. 1880. Oil on canvas,
31⅝ × 25¾" (81 × 65 cm). Louvre, Paris.

right: 12, Artemisia Gentileschi.
Judith Beheading Holofernes.
c. 1620. Oil on canvas, 5'11" × 5'8"
(1.80 × 1.72 m). Uffizi, Florence.

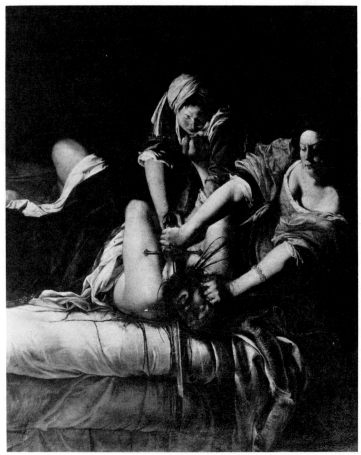

you try to accept it. It takes little effort to react pleasurably to paintings of colorful flowers or brilliant sunsets, yet many of us find difficulty in appreciating other works of art. Many viewers may be confused by much art that does not seem to record natural phenomena. Could it be that such works deal only with fractured aspects of today's complex society? For example, try to see and experience fully the interwoven web of colors and shapes created by Jackson Pollock (Pl. 2, p. 21). His great paintings are like gardens, designed, however, not for a stroll but for a visual refuge from the real world and its problems. By following the many-colored paths, we experience visual therapy and are refreshed. Pollock's infatuation with color and his delight in the overlay of pulsations of paint can become our own vehicles of sensation.

Perceptual Awareness Some understanding of the way the human eye and brain react to visual stimuli may help us achieve enriched responses. The 20th-century British author Aldous Huxley defines the art of seeing as three processes, occurring almost simultaneously: sensing, selecting, and perceiving.

Sensing is an instinctual response of the eyes and the nervous system. As the eye scans a crowd of people, it receives details of shape and color, light and dark. The physiological process takes care of sending these impulses to the brain.

Selecting is the process of focusing intensely on one part of the total visual field. From the huge number of stimuli the eye takes in, the brain chooses those that have meaning for the brain.

Perceiving gives meaning and significance to the whole act of seeing. Our perceptions are influenced by past experiences, knowledge, emotions, and expectations. What we finally say we "see" is the result of the combination of these influences.

Past experiences affect our perceptions to a greater extent than we realize. We may see what our observations have led us to expect rather than what is really there. Psychiatry informs us that we often project our inner emotions onto people and objects around us. The drawing of a poet's ideas of flowers and trees by Leonard Baskin (b. 1922) is a result of just such a projection (Fig. 13).

Aesthetic Response Full appreciation of a work of art demands more than understanding its meaning or responding to the emotions expressed by the artist. The aesthetic satisfactions that our eyes, bodies, or hands receive from the art object itself also expand our appreciation. These responses may range from the pleasure we derive from a particular grouping of colors in a painting to the exhilaration we experience passing through an impressive building or the tactile satisfaction we feel in handling a well-designed piece of silver (Fig. 14). In each of these situations, the aesthetic response comes from an interaction between the art object and the observer.

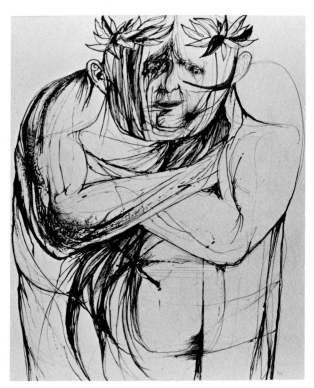

13. Leonard Baskin. *Poet Laureate*. 1954. Ink drawing, 29 × 23" (74 × 58 cm). Kennedy Galleries, New York.

14. Henning Koppel. Pitcher. 1952. Silver; height 11¼" (29 cm), diameter at largest part 19¼" (49 cm).

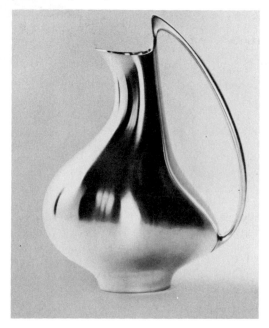

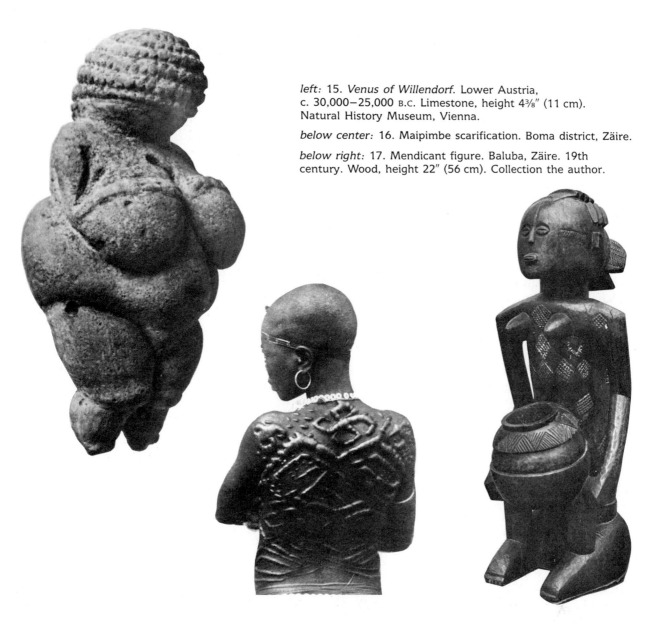

The word **aesthetic** refers to a sense of what seems beautiful to us. Surprisingly, notions of beauty are determined not so much by what we instinctively feel but what is commonly accepted by the culture in which we live. Thus, we must make an effort to put ourselves into the world in which the artist lived. If we know something about what people felt, thought, and experienced during a particular historical period, we can better understand their aesthetic.

Some experiences—particularly birth, love, and death—are universal. When art deals with these themes, we usually have less trouble responding to it. But even these emotions are experienced differently in certain cultures, so some knowledge of social and religious attitudes can heighten our aesthetic responses. For example, prehistoric peoples were deeply concerned with survival through perpetuation of the race. The *Venus of Willendorf* (Fig. 15) may have been considered beautiful 22,000 years ago, but it is more likely that she was revered as a fertility symbol. Her enormous breasts and swollen belly reinforce her role as Earth Mother. Her generous proportions outweigh her small size.

There is no doubt that concepts of beauty change and will continue to fluctuate from culture to culture and throughout history. An African woman from Zäire evoked an aesthetic response from her community because it considered the intricate scarification decorating her back a mark of beauty (Fig. 16). If we did not know of her willingness to undergo pain to be made "beautiful," we would have only a superficial understanding of her scarification designs and those seen on most African sculptures as well (Fig. 17).

Quite different is the concept of ideal beauty in the West in the 1950s. At that time the blonde film actress Marilyn Monroe was surely a favorite symbol of femininity in the United States and possibly the world. If a single image of Marilyn was created to please, then consider the fifty identical pictures of her (Fig. 18) presented in one work by Andy Warhol (b. 1930). Warhol focused our attention on the mass media, which use multiple imagery and tantalizing packaging to promote a product, person, or point of view. By using in the title *Diptych,* the word for a two-paneled work such as a medieval altarpiece, Warhol suggests that an advertising aesthetic has replaced the religious orientation of other ages. We may contrast Marilyn Monroe with other portraits of women in this text to note further the changing concepts of feminine beauty in Western culture.

Intelligent appreciation of art, then, requires an understanding of its meaning, response to the artist's vision or emotion, and sensitivity to the work's aesthetic in its historical context.

Evaluation and Criticism

We are accustomed to making judgments in every phase of life. We use our critical skills in making choices—size, color, style, or quantity; what to eat, what to wear, where to vacation. Aesthetic judgments originate from similar demands; they involve a process quite distinct from, yet linked to, art appreciation. They are not simply determining what we like.

The question of value in art is complex. While there are no absolute standards for deciding if a work of art is beautiful or appraising its quality, every evaluation depends on the experience and education of the judge, not just on his or her instincts. We may be helped in making evaluations by drawing on the experience and insights of professionals in art such as critics. They often tend to agree in their opinion of a particular work. In making an evaluation critics generally consider the following points. One concern is the individuality of the work. Has the artist observed even a familiar aspect of the world from a unique point of view that has resulted in an arresting image? Another concern is the artist's choice and use of medium. Does a watercolor, for example, reveal freshness of hues and perhaps transparent layers of colors and the crisp highlights of unpainted paper? A third consideration is whether an art statement in its subject, materials, or approach illuminates its era. Finally, many critics evaluate art primarily on the basis of the artist's vocabulary—whether he or she has successfully fused the various elements of design.

Critics may reach similar conclusions, possibly because their standards of judgment are derived from similar educational backgrounds. Whatever the reason, the influence of art criticism upon many of today's artists cannot be ignored. Trends in art can be affected by art critics and galleries.

The livelihood of an artist is tenuous at best. Encouragement in competition, presentation in a gallery, recognition by a critic, and finally purchase by an art collector can make the difference between bare survival and success. The whole circle of activities that revolves around the actual creation of art is also affected by art criticism. Collectors, patrons, galleries and museums, art periodicals and newspapers, reproduction services, auction houses, art appraisal services, to name but a few, depend upon the professional critic for objective opinions.

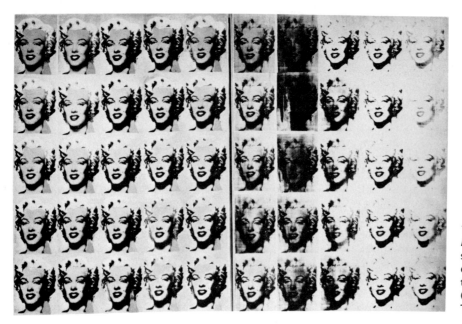

18. Andy Warhol. *Marilyn, Diptych.* 1962. Acrylic screen print on canvas, 6'9" × 9'6" (2.06 × 2.90 m); two panels, each 6'9" × 4'9" (2.06 × 1.45 m). Tate Gallery, London.

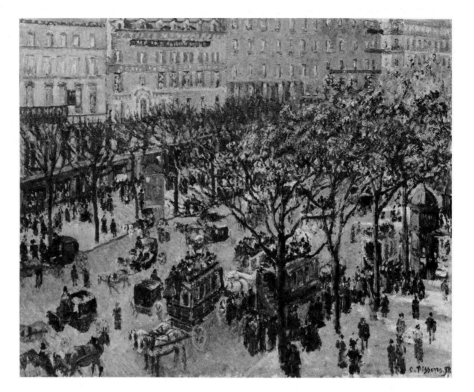

19. Camille Pissarro. *Boulevard des Italiens, Morning, Sunlight.* 1897. Oil on canvas, 28⅞ × 36¼″ (73 × 92 cm). National Gallery of Art, Washington, D.C. (Chester Dale Collection, 1962).

To be sure, many artists believe they are the people best qualified to evaluate works of art since their direct involvement with the process has expanded their awareness of the problems and the solutions. Professional art critics, however, argue that detachment is more important. Critics have usually studied art history in depth, are familiar with materials and processes, and have demonstrated skill in reviewing a wide range of art objectively.

A critic's viewpoint is helpful when it provides a fresh interpretation of a work of art. Often a critic's knowledge of art methods and aesthetic tools will reveal new facets of the work. Some art is so startling that we are unable to accept the work as art without the critic's help. The critic clarifies the artist's message, helping us to look at unfamiliar images with more tolerant vision.

Critics, however, are not infallible. Some have been known to change their minds, while others are unwilling to accept new ideas. Today we find pleasing *Boulevard des Italiens* (Fig. 19) painted by Camille Pissarro (1830–1903). Nothing about it disturbs or surprises us for we have seen many similar views of city streets. But when it was created in 1862, most critics condemned Pissarro for his lack of sensitivity to real painterly concerns. They complained that *Boulevard des Italiens* was like a "slice of life" without redeeming creative contributions from the artist. Even the perspective, such as a bird might see from a lofty studio window, was considered a weakness by the critics.

If evaluation requires more professional knowledge than most of us have, all of us can develop appreciation, given time and a willingness to be involved.

We may conclude that while we can learn from a critic's comments, they should never serve as the only criterion for evaluation or for controlling our appreciation. Our own unfolding exposure to art will lead to value judgments like those of professionals. As with all skills, the trip that leads to informed judgments and deep appreciation must be taken alone by an individual who is sensitive to the work of art and the spirit that produced it. Ultimately, the most important effect of art is what the artist says directly to each individual observer.

Experiencing art can provide great joy and reveal discoveries about ourselves, our society, and, above all, our relationship to our world. Many people find contemporary art enjoyable and fascinating, yet others find it bewildering, unskillful, and even ugly. Its variety echoes the complexity of today's world and the differences in artists' reactions to it. We do not all like the same things. Nor do we all have the same tolerance for the new, the disturbing, or the disagreeable. In many situations what the artist is revealing about our society and ourselves may be unwelcome. But if we shut our eyes to everything that seems unpleasant or difficult to understand, if we refuse to expand our horizons or to look at art with a sense of adventure, we will surely lose the opportunity to profit from an artist's message. Certainly in such a situation a pioneering artist will suffer, but the greater loss is likely to be our own. Our encounter with art can be made satisfying if we learn *how* the artist creates by exploring the simple art materials and activities that follow—noting basic elements like line or color, and art principles, such as unity and balance.

EXERCISES AND ACTIVITIES

1. Since exposure to art tends to expand our artistic horizons, visit your school and public libraries to become familiar with their art books and art magazines. Which collection is most comprehensive? Determine the strengths of each art collection for future reference.

2. Some universal themes have occupied artists from prehistoric times through today. List some of these themes that you find illustrated in this or other books.

3. Attend an art exhibit in a local gallery or museum. Write a one-page review, explaining why you do or do not like certain pieces of art. How has the artist individualized his or her personal art statement, that is, created a work that is memorable for you?

4. If possible, locate an art critic's review of the same exhibit. What appear to be the criteria the critic has used on which to base his or her comments? Write your own review.

5. What psychological, emotional, and aesthetic factors do you feel are involved in the appreciation of art? Can you explain why some masterpieces seem to have universal appeal?

6. Picasso's "*Ma Jolie*" and Leonardo's *Mona Lisa* are both portraits of women and masterworks. Discuss how they differ and cite some historical factors that may explain these differences.

7. Find five artworks in this book that have been inspired at least in part by the natural environment. Which appear to be duplications of nature? Which works reinterpret or abstract details from nature?

8. To experience how varying viewpoints affect your perception of a subject, set up a still-life arrangement of four or five objects. Make a simple drawing of it from three different points, noting the resulting changes that you see in the shapes, lines, and arrangements of the objects.

2 Exploring the Artist's Language

Art is human intelligence playing over the natural scene, ingeniously affecting it toward the fulfillment of human purposes.

ARISTOTLE

The search for knowledge has pulled us high above the earth, far below its crust, and deep beneath the sea. From the dawn of human awareness on earth, we have reacted to this world in conscious and unconscious ways, some of which are termed art. In fact, observations of the natural environment and of human experiences within it have been the inspiration for most art for thousands of years. Artists select, summarize, and then interpret what they have perceived. In reworking their responses, they transform ideas into art. Commenting on his work, Paul Klee (1879–1940) observed that the artist is like "the trunk of the tree, gathering vitality from the soil, from the depth (the unconscious), and transmitting it to the crown of the tree, which is beauty."

Inspiration

Most artists call the process of creativity simply inspiration. Scientists have defined four stages. Probably we all explore this process at one time or another.

1. fooling around: intake of data, examination of tools and materials, unformed ideas, curiosity
2. gestation: conscious and subconscious realignment of disorganized insights, time out
3. inspiration: flashes of intuition and intimation of solutions, excitement
4. verification: conscious, organized evolution and culmination of project

Artistic experiment for its own sake is simply not enough. Nor is invention itself the goal of every artist. The process of creativity with inspiration leads to significant contribution—the masterpiece at the end of the road. Television and the film industry often portray artists as if they were driven by creative urges when, in fact, few awaken of a morning with the conviction that they will produce a work of art before the day is out. Most artists are committed to spending time in the studio, sometimes on a scheduled basis, where ideas, perhaps perceived at another time and place, can be reworked into art.

Picasso explained the process simply when he said, "I do not seek, I find." *Bull's Head* (Fig. 20) probably evolved from an idle observation of a discarded bicycle. With a flash of inspiration, the elements were hastily reconstituted into a witty, sculptural expression of a primal motif in Western art, the bull. We are in turn delighted with the unexpected origin of the new form.

Human beings seem to have a need for clarity, order, and, finally, full understanding. Artists in particular search for order and ultimate truth, often with the diligence we

20. Pablo Picasso. *Bull's Head.*
1943. Bronze, height 16″ (41 cm).
Galerie Louise Leiris, Paris.

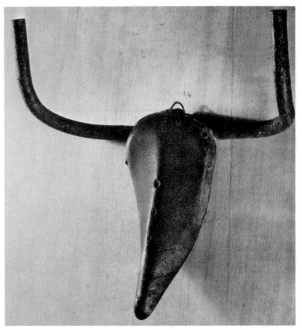

associate with the scientist. During the Renaissance, Leonardo da Vinci recorded thousands of exploratory details of anatomy, botany, and mechanics. His notions of ballistics certainly predated modern projectiles. He also examined human physiology by studying such things as bone formations and the human head.

Usually, however, the artist's purpose is not so much to echo nature as to know nature well enough to feel free to comment in the language of art. Artistic inspiration transforms the world through skilled use of shape and mass, line, light and shade, color, and texture. The artist may abstract from nature and reinterpret it to give us heightened aesthetic experiences.

Form and Content

We can tell the same story many ways. When we retell an anecdote, we consciously select some details and omit others depending upon our audience. In a work of art the theme or story is the **content** and the way it is told is the **form.** When Picasso, aroused by the Spanish Civil War, prepared for the great mural *Guernica,* his preliminary drawings of the bull took many forms (Fig. 21), and the content was somewhat altered in the final configuration (Fig. 22).

The bull is probably the oldest subject of art in Western civilization. Appearing even earlier than images of humans, the bull can be traced from Paleolithic times in the Lascaux Caves in France (Fig. 2) to a triumphal culmination in *Guernica.* The bull is perhaps a symbol of persecuted innocence or of insensate, brute force (even in the bullring). The bull's form is balanced by the figure in the burning building on the right. Although Picasso seems to relate the bull and the victims of the destroyed town of Guernica to the misery of war-torn Spain, he never gave us an explanation of the painting, believing that art tells its own story. His

studies for the bull, the only stable element of the composition, reveal many changes in form from a Classical image to the final enigmatic countenance of the bull, quietly dominating the composition. The horror of Guernica's story remained the same throughout the many changes in its presentation.

Sometimes an artist must be adventurous and creative to lead us into his or her vision. Sometimes artists present us with visual statements based on the familiar world in new, disturbing contexts. It takes courage to depart from

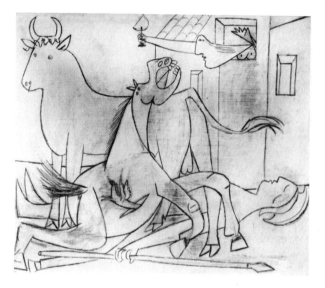

above: 21. Pablo Picasso. Study for *Guernica.* 1937. Pencil on gesso on wood, 25⅜ × 21¹⁄₁₆″ (65 × 54 cm). Prado, Madrid.

below: 22. Pablo Picasso. *Guernica.* 1937. Oil on canvas, 25′5¾″ × 11′5½″ (3.49 × 7.77 m). Prado, Madrid.

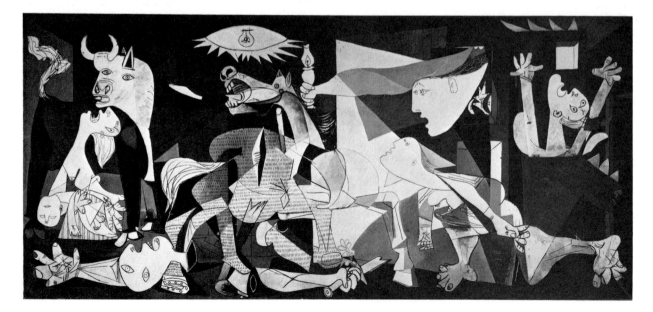

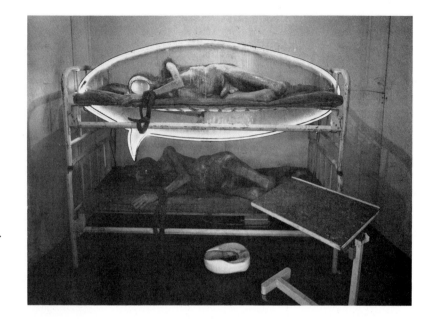

right: 23. Edward Kienholz.
The State Hospital, detail. 1966.
Mixed media, 8 × 12 × 10′
(2.44 × 3.66 × 3.05 m).
Moderna Museet, Stockholm.
(© Edward Kienholz.)

below: 24. William Hogarth.
In Bedlam, from *The Rake's Progress.*
c. 1734. Engraving,
24½ × 29½″ (62 × 75 cm).
Metropolitan Museum of Art,
New York
(Harris Brisbane Dick Fund, 1932).

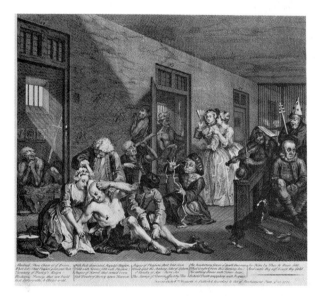

horror appear in this victim of modern civilization with mottled, leathery skin stretched over his living skeleton. The duplicate upper figure, set off in cartoon style by neon tubing, may represent the old man's imagined self, lit up like a fish for all to see. The head of the lower figure has been replaced by a bowl in which a live fish darts fitfully. *The State Hospital* suggests to most of us loss of personal status. Have you ever felt stripped of identity by institutions, which assign you a bed and number for their convenience? As part of hospital inventory, your samples are extracted for endless record keeping. Kienholz dramatizes the plight of the elderly and the infirm who struggle for self-worth within the anonymity of a public institution when few opportunities for pride remain. Contrast the different forms yet related content of these two works, both concerned with the weaknesses of society. Is today's artist more powerful because the language of art has changed to satisfy a new age? Surely, both works have achieved the artists' intention of eliciting strong responses from their viewers.

Style and Subject

Closely related to form and content are style and subject. Most people look at a work of art for the theme represented, say a landscape or a portrait. Although the subject may be considered the most obvious element of the work, full appreciation demands much more than recognition of images. The viewer must go past the obvious subject to consider form and style. **Style** is the characteristic approach an artist takes to a theme. Artists consciously and subconsciously choose to work in a certain way according to what they wish to express and in doing so reveal different personal styles. Thus the work of well-known artists can often be identified as easily as the FBI distinguishes fingerprints.

tradition to upset visual conventions, but by tossing away preconceptions, the artist can often bring us a new reality with new symbols and a fresh point of view.

In *The State Hospital* (Fig. 23), Edward Kienholz (b. 1927) has assumed the mantle of social concern worn in the 18th century by William Hogarth (1697–1764). Both artists force us to confront an unpleasant scene behind the façade of a public institution. Hogarth's print of Bedlam, London's insane asylum (Fig. 24), clearly reveals the degeneration of a nobleman, strait-jacketed after debauchery, and a fitting end, in Hogarth's view, to the evils of excess—food, drink, and sex. Kienholz's view of a cell block is more indirect. At first, we view the tableau with curiosity, until we realize the old man is chained to his cot. Details of

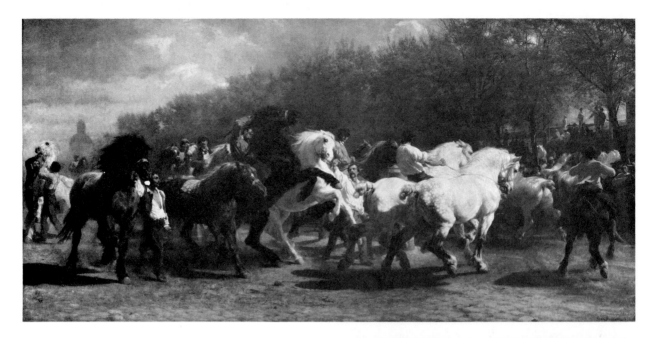

above: 25. Rosa Bonheur. *The Horse Fair.* 1853—55.
Oil on canvas, 8'1/4" × 16'7½" (2.44 × 5.07 m).
Metropolitan Museum of Art, New York
(gift of Cornelius Vanderbilt, 1887).

right: 26. Romare Bearden. *The Prevalence of Ritual: Baptism.* 1964. Synthetic polymer paint and pencil on paperboard, 9⅛ × 12" (23.2 × 30.5 cm).
Hirshhorn Museum and Sculpture Garden,
Smithsonian Institution, Washington, D.C.

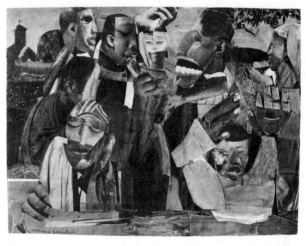

Art experts can quickly identify an artist's style in works they have never seen before.

As an example of personal style, consider Rosa Bonheur (1822–1899), whose forceful approach projected the artistic strength she needed to compete early in the 19th-century art world then dominated by men. She chose active subjects in energy-charged compositions. *The Horse Fair* (Fig. 25) typifies her style; vitality; skill in texture and color; and, above all, sure knowledge of complex composition, involving rhythmic interpenetration of space.

Romare Bearden (b. 1914), in contrast, developed his use of photomontage in a uniquely personal style. His work characteristically involves assembled pieces of photographs and paint arranged in Cubist-inspired compositions of urban blacks. The vitality of his art is based upon the contrasting shapes and textures of his figures and their unexpected sizes, which are rarely faithful to reality (Fig. 26). An impossible seascape may be glimpsed through a bedroom window while utensils and other objects within violate gravity, floating in the orderly disorder of a room that cannot quite be believed.

Style is also, however, more than a personal approach. It is a way of treating a subject that may be shared by many artists who belong to a particular historical period or cultural region or who have a similar point of view. Thus, subject matter may be representational, abstract, or non-objective, depending upon how faithful the artist is to the appearances of the real world.

Representational art reproduces the world we know with minimal change from the appearance of things in everyday experiences. Clearly, Piet Mondrian's (1877–1944) early landscape painting of 1906 was dominated by a large tree hanging over an isolated farmhouse (Fig. 27). The style is representational and direct. Yet, as we examine enlarged details, we note his early concern with the pattern created by the tree's branches and his emphasis upon the horizontal and vertical divisions of the shingles.

Abstract art alters the view of a real world, retaining only the essence of a thing or an idea, while freely changing qualities of the original. Mondrian's first interest in the tree he undertook to paint appears to have been gradually expanded to focus upon the spaces trapped by the tree's

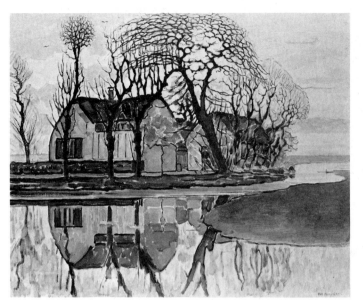

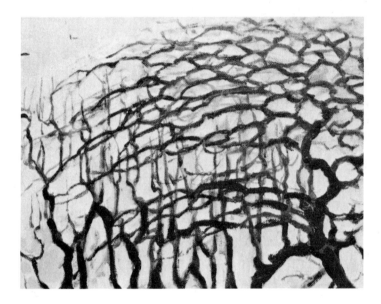

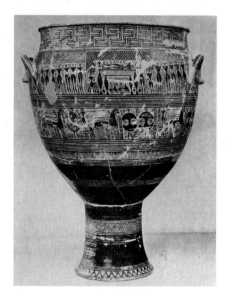

left: 27. Piet Mondrian. *Farm Near Duivendrecht.* 1906. Oil on canvas, 34 × 42¾″ (86 × 109 cm). Collection Dr. and Mrs. Isaac Schoenberg, Swarthmore, Pa.

below left: 28. Detail of Figure 27.

below right: 29. Dipylon vase, with funeral scenes. Attic, 8th century B.C. Terracotta, height 40½″ (103 cm). Metropolitan Museum of Art, New York (Rogers Fund, 1914).

branches, which primarily form a horizontal and vertical pattern (Fig. 28). The detail of branches appears to have been an early step that led to his eventual total concentration upon the whole tree and then on horizontal and vertical design.

Nonrepresentational art, also called **nonobjective** or **nonfigurative art,** depicts no recognizable object or clear reference to the real world. Had we not studied Mondrian's early work, tracing the evolution of his nonobjective compositions, we would be unaware that what became his lifelong preoccupation, the "essential plastic means of art"—line and color free from any particular subject—may have been originally inspired by a farmhouse, a tree, and its branches (Pl. 3, p. 22). Nonobjective art usually presents an aesthetically pleasing design, involving line, color, value,

shape, and texture, some of the visual elements we will examine next.

The Visual Elements

Artists use certain basic components both consciously and unconsciously to develop a work fully. Though these elements are fundamental to all the visual arts and other arts as well, the manner in which each artist organizes them is unique.

An ancient Greek vase and a contemporary painting seem worlds apart in their inspiration, function, and material composition, yet they are related in that each uses some of the basic elements of art. The Greek vase (Fig. 29), an early grave marker from the Dipylon cemetery in Ath-

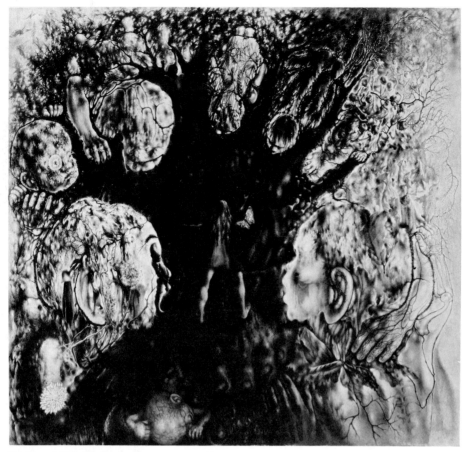

30. Pavel Tchelitchew.
Hide-and-Seek. 1940–42. Oil on canvas, 6'6½" × 7'¾"
(1.99 × 2.15). Museum of Modern Art, New York
(Mrs. Simon Guggenheim Fund).

ens, has been decorated with an orderly composition of horizontal lines confining tiny figural and geometric motifs. The allover design is flat, without reference to three-dimensional space. The small figures, rhythmically repeated, form a textural pattern of evenly balanced dark and light values. The geometric decoration painted on the red clay is typical of early pottery. The key design at the lip of the vase identifies the work as Greek.

In contrast, Pavel Tchelitchew's (1898–1957) surrealistic, mid-20th–century painting *Hide-and-Seek* (Fig. 30) is comprised of brilliant, highly imaginative figurative images, typical of the artist's style, with color the only additional element to those already described. The vivid reds and yellows advance from the cold blues of the background. A multiplicity of lines in this work suggests a vast, pulsating circulatory system as the basic texture. The irregular foreground shapes, varying in size, are massed around the small child almost hidden in the dark shadows at the center. Amorphous human forms emerge mysteriously from the depths of the painting. In the game of "hide and seek," perhaps the child imagines her worst fears of the unknown. In both the vase and the painting, line, shape,

value, texture (and color) have been organized to provide powerful aesthetic experiences.

Line We may begin to communicate what we see through **line,** the basis of most drawing and much painting. A moving point forms a line. A speeding arrow and the light of a moving flashlight demonstrate lines formed by connecting moving points in space. Line may consist of actual marks, drawn with pencil, pen, or brush, or it can refer to the outside of a shape. In paintings, lines often occur by contrast; lines may be drawn, but also the edges formed by contrasts of light and shadow or of different colors and shapes suggest lines. Whether it can actually be seen or is only implied, line undoubtedly is one of the artist's most eloquent tools, enclosing space, suggesting mass or volume, and creating a feeling of movement. Lines may vary from thick to thin to convey shape. Where light falls on the contours of an object, the outlines may be lightly drawn. Where the shadow is deepest, thicker lines can suggest and provide emphasis, while grouped lines create illusions of volume and shadow.

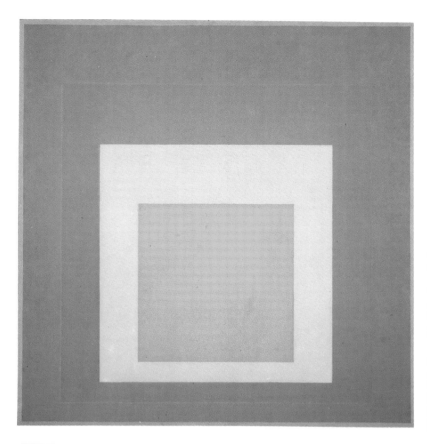

left: Plate 1. Josef Albers.
*Homage to the Square:
"Ascending."* 1953.
Oil on composition board,
43½" (110 cm) square.
Whitney Museum of American Art,
New York.

below: Plate 2. Jackson Pollock.
Number 1. 1948.
Oil on canvas,
5'8" × 8'8" (1.73 × 2.64 m).
Museum of Modern Art,
New York (purchase).

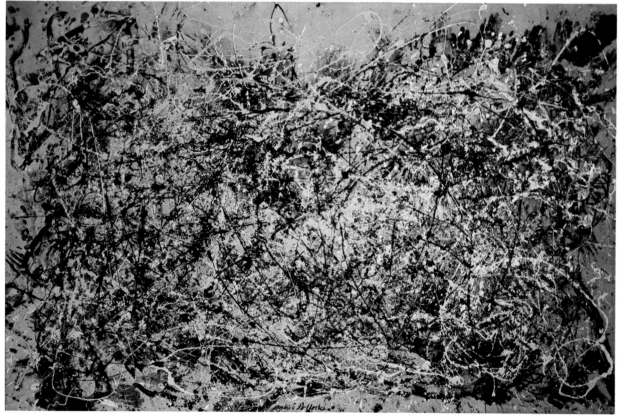

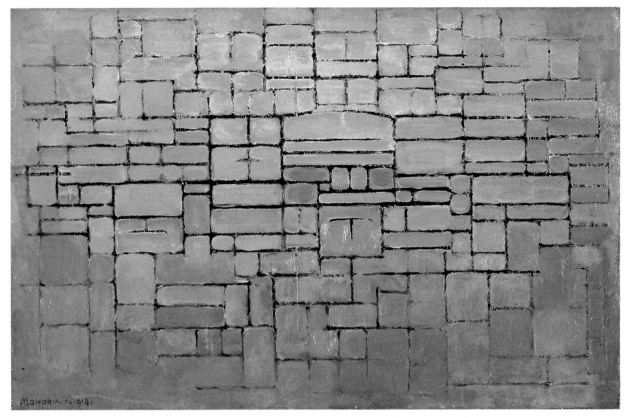

Plate 3. Piet Mondrian. *Composition, V.* 1914. Oil on panel, 21⅝ × 33⅝" (55 × 85 cm).
Museum of Modern Art, New York (Sidney and Harriet Janis Collection).

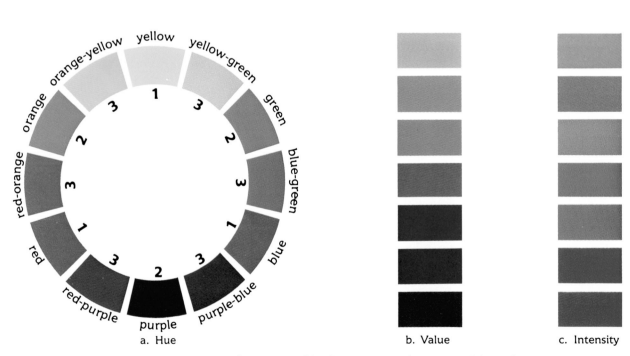

Plate 4. The major elements of color: hue (as expressed in the color wheel), value, and intensity.

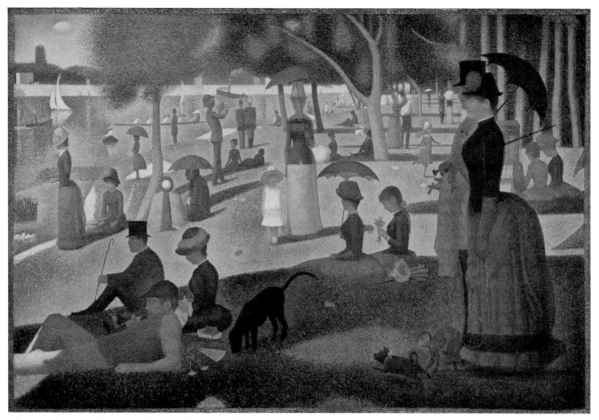

above: Plate 5. Georges Seurat. *Sunday Afternoon on the Island of La Grande Jatte.* 1884–86. Oil on canvas, 6'9" × 10'¼" (2.06 × 3.05 m). Art Institute of Chicago (Helen Birch Bartlett Memorial Collection).

below: Plate 6. Seurat, *Sunday Afternoon on the Island of La Grande Jatte* (detail).

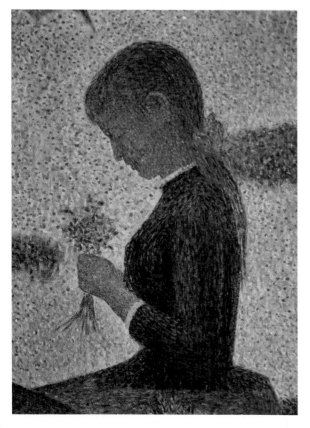

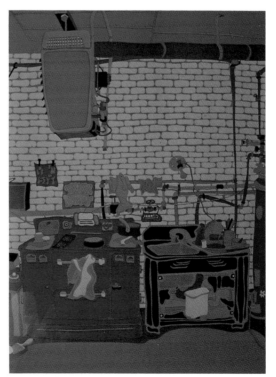

Plate 7. Clayton Pond.
The Kitchen in My Studio. 1970.
Serigraph, 30 × 40" (76 × 107 cm).
Nassau Community College, Garden City, N.Y.

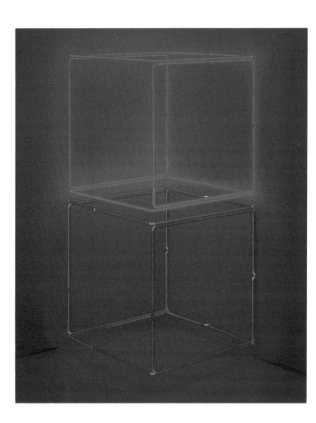

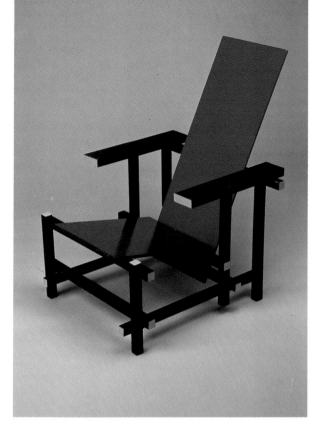

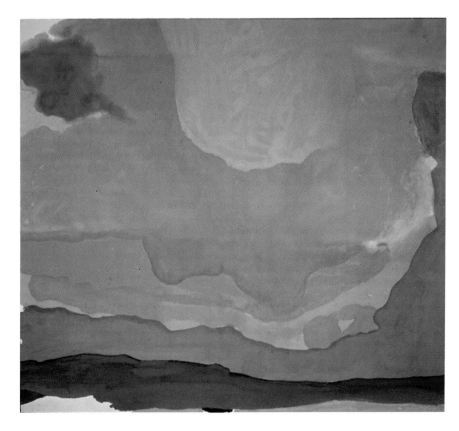

above left: Plate 8.
Stephen Antonakos.
*Red Box over Blue Box,
Inside Corner Neon.* 1973.
Neon tubes, 4′1¾″ × 2′ × 2′
(1.26 × 0.61 × 0.61 m).
La Jolla (Calif.) Museum
of Contemporary Art.

left: Plate 9.
Helen Frankenthaler.
Flood. 1967.
Synthetic polymer on canvas,
10′4″ × 11′8″ (3.15 × 3.56 m).
Whitney Museum
of American Art, New York
(gift of the Friends
of the Whitney Museum
of American Art).

above right: Plate 10.
Gerrit Rietveld.
Red-Blue Chair. 1918.
Wood; height 33⅞″ (86 cm),
width 24¼″ (64 cm),
seat height 12½″ (33 cm).
Stedelijk Museum, Amsterdam.

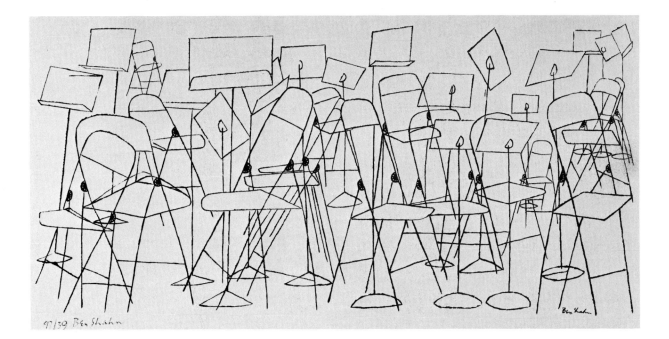

above: 31. Ben Shahn. *Silent Music.*
1950. Serigraph, 17⅛ × 35⅛" (44 × 89 cm).
Museum of Modern Art, New York (purchase).

right: 32. Sesshu. *Landscape.* Muromachi Period,
c. 1500. Hanging scroll, ink on paper;
30⅜ × 10⅝" (77 × 27 cm). Seattle Art Museum
(Eugene Fuller Memorial Collection).

Line also has the potential to convey emotion, and in this role it is one of the artist's most valuable tools. Line may be drawn forcefully (with strong, thick strokes), nervously (with uneven, broken strokes), or smoothly (with stable, consistent strokes) to create a mood or express a personality. In *Poet Laureate* (Fig. 13), Baskin uses short, jerky lines to suggest the poet's restless thoughts. The pools of india ink on the paper emphasize emotional depths, while irregular lines in the features create torment. In contrast, Ben Shahn (1898–1969) in *Silent Music* (Fig. 31) uses an action line. This method is derived from the games children play in making a drawing without lifting the tool from the paper to assure continuity of line and the communication of a sense of action.

Line is basic not only to drawing and most painting but also to **calligraphy,** the art of decorative fine line, as in handwriting. Calligraphy has existed for centuries in the Orient, where calligraphy and painting are intimately related. The processes are produced with the same brushes and similar brush strokes and are frequently found in the same work of art. A high degree of such linear control can be found in examples of both Western and Eastern art. If we compare the ink work in Baskin's drawing of the poet (Fig. 13) with Sesshu's (1420–1506) *Landscape* (Fig. 32), we can see that both subjects, though quite different in

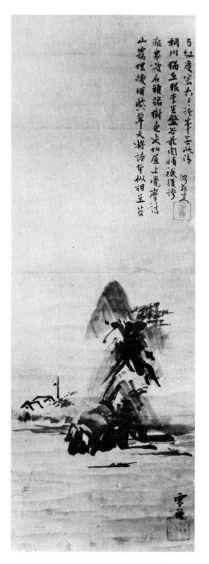

25

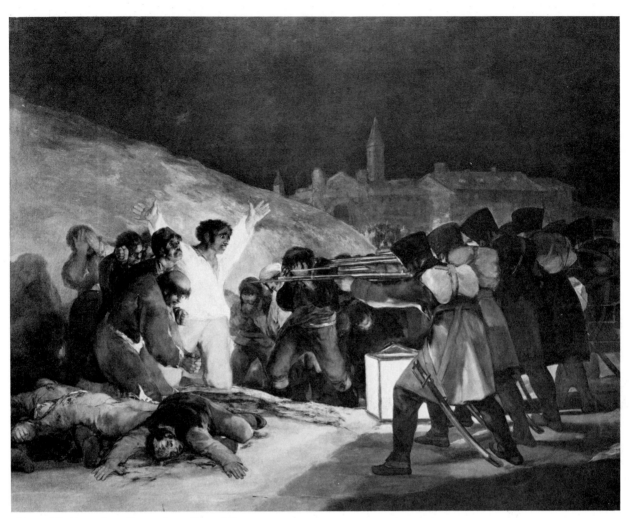

above: 33. Francisco Goya. *Execution of the Madrileños on May 3, 1808.*
1814. Oil on canvas, 8′8¾″ × 11′3¾″
(2.66 × 3.45 m). Prado, Madrid.

right: 34. Diagram of Figure 33.

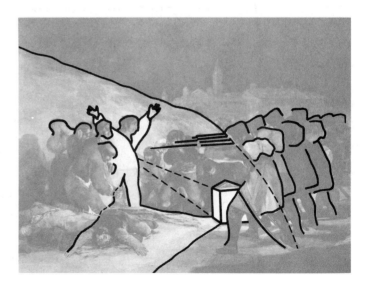

style, are represented with a minimum of strokes and with emphatic lines, which produce an effect of vigor. Closer examination of the Japanese painting reveals also little difference in linear approach between the painted message and the landscape.

Another kind of line is seen in the painting *Execution of the Madrileños on May 3, 1808* (Fig. 33) by Francisco Josè de Goya y Lucientes (1746–1828). Here the contours of various shapes produce or imply lines that serve to guide the viewer to the central theme: the brutal execution of hostages randomly chosen by the French troops of Napoleon occupying Madrid, in reprisal for the uprising of an unruly Spanish mob the day before. The directional lines are so strong that we can diagram them (Fig. 34). The contour of the hill leads us down through the body of the principal soldier, then up through the saber at his waist to

the rifles pointing at the civilian with arms outstretched—as if on an invisible cross. You may find many other contour lines that reinforce this movement to focus our attention on the drama. Although the linear element is rarely so easy to see, it exists in most works of art.

Line can be also followed in three-dimensional works of art, suggested by the silhouette of a figure, the upward thrust of a vault, or the long horizontal edge of a building. For example, the clear-cut shapes of the Great Pyramids (Fig. 35) present a strong, simple geometry of linear planes, which dominate the Egyptian desert and are visible for many miles. They represent, perhaps, the most familiar triangular silhouettes of all time.

In contrast, recent advances in our knowledge of optical laws have led to a complex new use of line in which images shift depending upon the viewer's angle of vision. In the

35. The Sphinx (c. 2540–2514 B.C.) and the pyramid of Cheops (c. 2590–2568 B.C.). Giza.

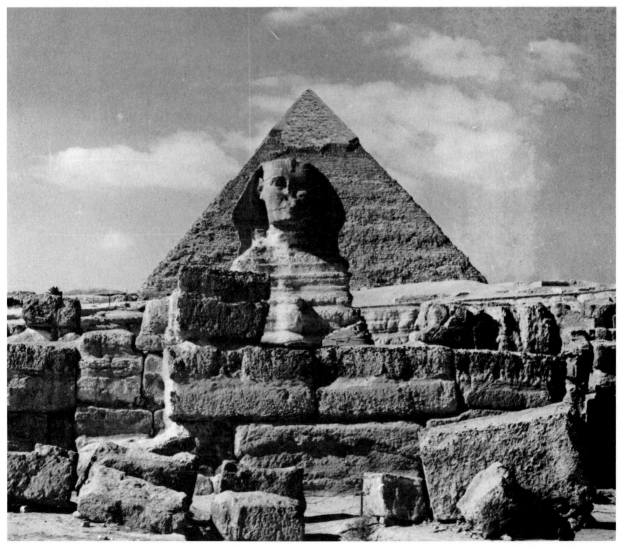

hands of an artist such as Bridget Riley (b. 1931), repetitious lines of precisely equal weight, equally spaced, create visual illusions that seem to advance and retreat as we observe the work (Fig. 36).

Shape and Mass In painting, and sometimes in drawing, any area enclosed by a line is usually perceived as a whole entity or **shape,** set apart from its surroundings. Shape can also be made to stand out through the use of strong contrasts in color, value, or texture. Shapes can be geometric or organic, symmetrical or asymmetrical, related to known objects or nonobjective. Artists may use

shape, like line, to express different moods. The playful shapes in the whimsical mobile (Fig. 37) by Alexander Calder (1898–1979) create a gay mood and are reminiscent of a school of fish in formation. A truly original artist, Calder has created highly intellectual and controlled works, which delight us with the variety of movements of the abstract organic shapes as they interplay when the entire piece is set in motion (Fig. 38). Many artists such as Calder evolve distinctive vocabularies of shapes they often repeat.

To the novice in art, shape is always easy to see. Few beginners, however, take the time really to look at the space around the shapes, which is generally ignored as

36. Bridget Riley. *Current.* 1964.
Synthetic polymer paint on composition board, 4′10⅜″ (1.48 m) square. Museum of Modern Art, New York (Philip Johnson Fund).

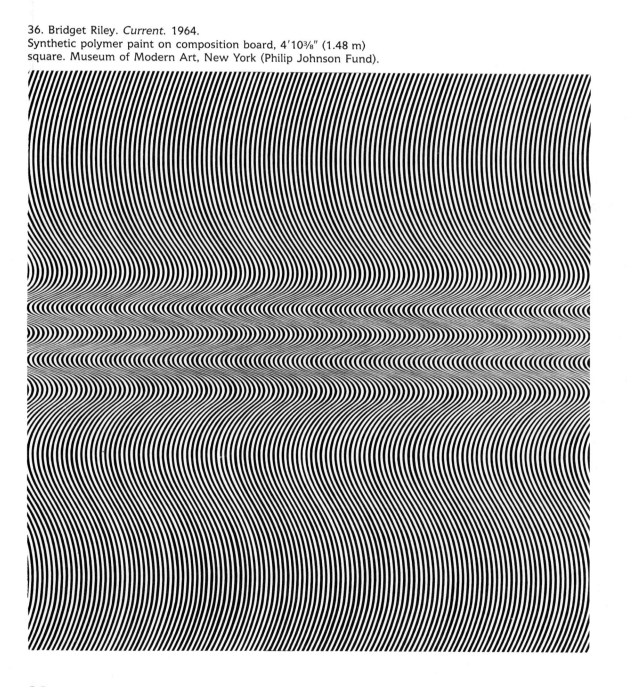

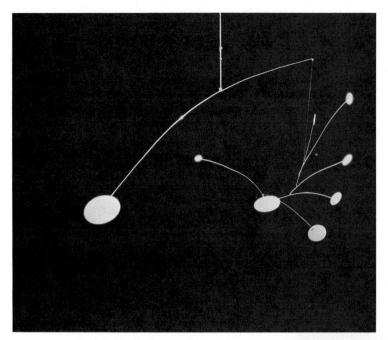

left: 37. Alexander Calder. *Hanging Mobile*. 1936. Aluminum and steel wire, width c. 28″ (71 cm). Collection Mrs. Meric Callery, New York.

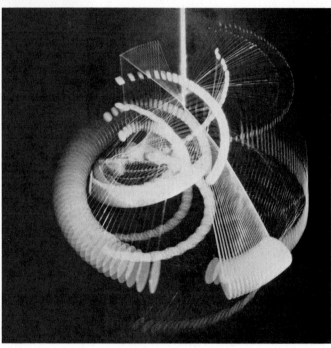

38. Stroboscopic photograph of Alexander Calder's *Hanging Mobile* (Fig. 37) in motion.

mere background. Many times, however, these same areas, called **negative space,** are as important to the artwork as the positive shapes we usually see first. Artists manipulate relationships of the figure to its ground to increase visual excitement and to take advantage of the different ways all of us perceive shapes in space.

The term "shape" usually refers to defined areas in a painting or drawing, while **mass** is used more often in discussions of sculpture and architecture. However, the term "mass" may also occasionally be applied to paintings where the artist has concentrated upon the illusion of mass. During the Renaissance, many artists tested the newly discovered principles of geometry and linear perspective and produced more solid-looking forms on a two-dimensional surface than had been seen for a thousand years. In addition, many artists used heavy shadows in their paintings to exaggerate the appearance of three-dimensional weight. For example, the draperies massed in shadow on the left in the painting *The Artist in His Studio* by Jan Vermeer (1632–1675) form a strong contrast with the artist's model positioned in the bright central area (Fig. 39). The woman creates a focal point, which ties together the geometric shapes of the furniture and the room.

Mass can also be emphasized, as in the pyramids of Egypt, which were built to ensure a comfortable immortality for the pharaohs (Fig. 35). The sense of mass may be reduced or denied altogether by creating perforations, or openings, in a structure. A Gothic cathedral like St.-Denis

39. Jan Vermeer. *The Artist in His Studio.*
c. 1665–70. Oil on canvas, 47¼ × 39⅜" (120 × 100 cm).
Kunsthistorisches Museum, Vienna.

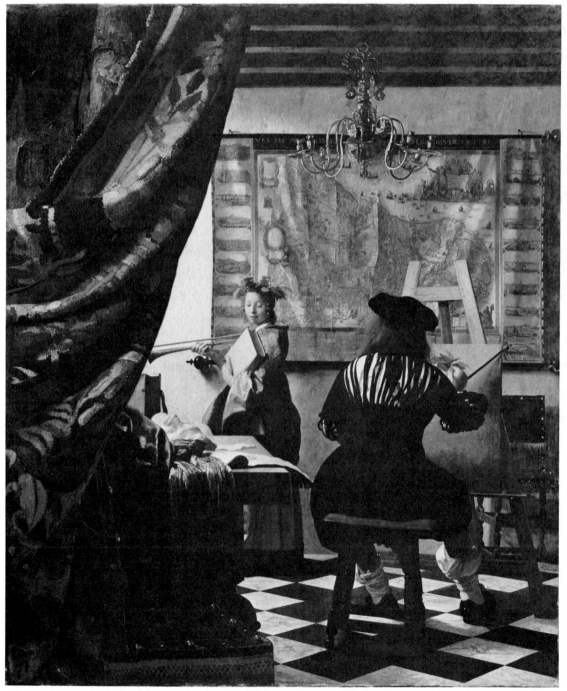

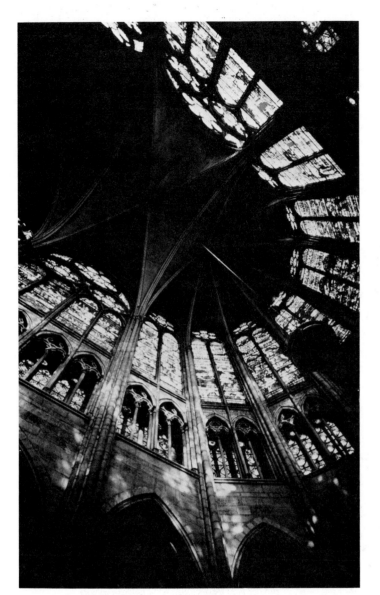

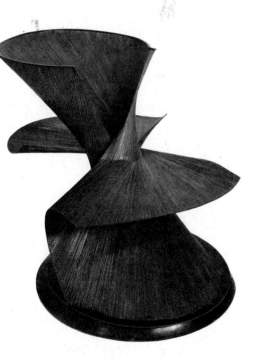

above: 40. Interior, abbey church of
St.-Denis, Paris. 1144.

right: 41. Antoine Pevsner. *Developable Column.*
1942. Brass and oxidized bronze; height 20¾″
(53 cm), diameter of base 19⅜″ (49 cm).
Museum of Modern Art, New York (purchase).

(Fig. 40), an expression of spiritual aspirations toward heaven, appears light and fragile. Glass windows fill the spaces between structural supports, and the cathedral's strong vertical lines, just as those of the *Developable Column* (Fig. 41) by Antoine Pevsner (1886–1962), imply a weight light enough to rise into the air. Pevsner's column was designed to simulate a force twisting upward. The emphatic silhouette of the sculpture plunges through space, while the heavy mass of the Sphinx appears stable, eternal, and static.

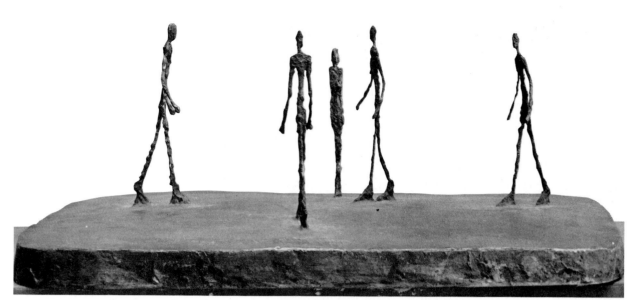

above: 42. Alberto Giacometti. *City Square.*
1949. Bronze; base 25 × 17″ (64 × 43 cm), height of
tallest figure 8″ (20 cm).
Pierre Matisse Gallery, New York.

below: 43. Nadar (Gaspard Felix Tournachon). *Sarah Bernhardt.*
1859. Photograph. International Museum of Photography,
George Eastman House, Rochester, N.Y.

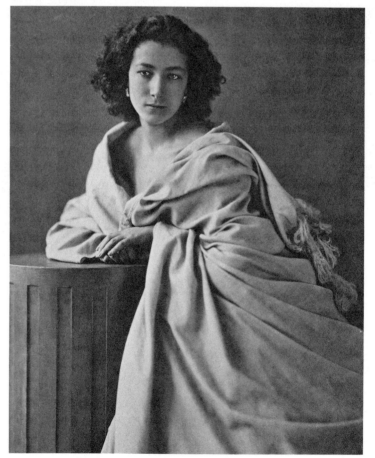

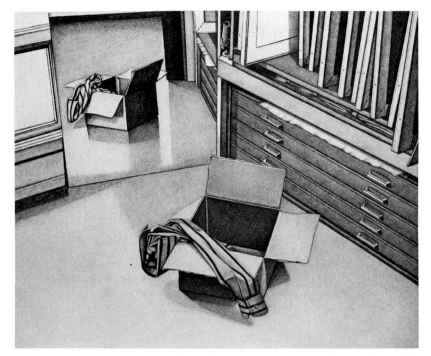

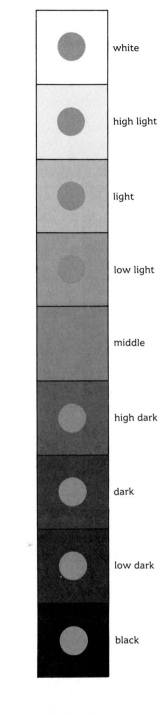

above: 44. Helen Meyrowitz. *Interiors, Composition #6.* 1978. Conté crayon on gesso, 22 × 28″ (56 × 71 cm). Collection the artist.

right: 45. The gray scale shows variations in value from white to black. The circles in the centers are all middle value, although they seem different against lighter or darker backgrounds.

white

high light

light

low light

middle

high dark

dark

low dark

black

Paradoxically, the long, open figures by Alberto Giacometti (1901–1966) in *City Square* (Fig. 42) utilize so little solid material that we become as aware of the space the figures occupy as the mass of matter that forms them. Such works investigate relationships of positive and negative space, as well as of mass. Giacometti is known for his attenuated figures—thin masses corroded by time. The indistinctness of the details and their apparent lack of weight suggest a spiritual isolation that projects loneliness.

Value The degree of lightness or darkness of a surface is referred to as its **value.** As applied to the visual arts value can range from the darkest to the very palest tones or from pure black through shades of gray to pure white. Variations and contrasts in values form an effective ploy whether the artist is working with colors or black and white. For example, a portrait of *Sarah Bernhardt* (Fig. 43) demonstrates a full range of values, from white to black; the strongest contrasts of tone (the lightest and the darkest elements) are placed near the center of the photograph for dramatic emphasis. On the other hand, in the conté crayon drawing of *Interiors, Composition #6* (Fig. 44) by Helen Meyrowitz (b. 1929), we find a somewhat different treatment of tones.

Although pure white and intense black values exist together in this work, the total effect is generally soft, because most of the picture is made up of delicate gradations of medium to dark tones.

A value-gradation scale helps us to understand how we perceive tones (Fig. 45). Even when tones are identical in value, they may appear quite different when the value of their surrounding tone is changed (Pl. 4b, p. 22). The phenomenon is evident not only with black and white, and grays, but also when color is involved. Josef Albers spent a lifetime exploring subtle color relationships and frequently used colors of similar value to produce very different effects (Pl. 1, p. 21).

Variations in values can be used like line to guide the viewer's eye or to give a sense of movement. For example, an area of sharp contrast in a painting will attract our attention. Three or four such areas, if related in a composition, may cause our eye to travel from one to another, giving a sense of movement. Values are often used to create an emotional response. Sharply contrasting colors or blacks and whites can express dramatic tension or excitement. The portrait of the *Mona Lisa* by Leonardo (Fig. 9) produces a dramatic emotional impact not only because the range of values is wide but also because the artist has effectively used lighting to focus on our center of interest. However, the areas of dark shadows in Leonardo's paintings are equally important. They are never voids of darkness but instead suggest details that our imaginations can enlarge upon. Light values, on the other hand, with few contrasts can give a hazy or mystic feeling to a composition.

Only with illumination by natural or artificial light to create highlights and shadows is it possible to represent form. As light changes, the entire character of the subject may be revealed or concealed. Whether we observe the geometric shapes of cylinder, sphere, and cube, or the human figure, the artist can emphasize shape and mass by manipulating tones of value.

The use of light and dark in a painting to represent the effect of light and shadow in nature is called **chiaroscuro,** an Italian word meaning "light and dark." This method of using light and shadow to reveal the modeling of three-dimensional forms was common to Western painting from the Renaissance to the 19th century. Leonardo developed a smokelike haze called **sfumato** to envelop his forms, resulting in transitions from light to dark so gradual as to be imperceptible (Fig. 9). In this technique, light seems to come from a source within the painting, creating soft contours.

Though Western painters have used value relationships for many effects, until recently they have been preoccupied with how contrasting values and light patterns play over solid objects to create the illusion of three-dimensional form on a flat surface. Oriental artists have also made use of value changes but not for the purpose of creating an illusion of space. The patterns formed by light and dark shapes can evoke moods and emotions designed to lead the viewer away from the reality of the here and now toward spirituality. Art works executed with limited gradations of tones such as Sesshu's *Landscape* (Fig. 32) are keyed to values that tend to heighten mood. Images limited to light shades are termed **high key** and are associated with areas of intense light such as beach scenes or scrubbed-clean sites such as hospitals. **Low key** locales typically include night views of streets and intimate bars.

Color Perhaps the most effective of all the art elements available to the artist is **color,** that which we perceive when our eyes sense light reflected from an object. Artists have used color from earliest times, generally reproducing the natural color, or **local color,** they saw. The science of color has developed more slowly. Although the Greeks as early as 400 B.C. realized that the apparent color of an object changes with the color of light that falls on it, it was not until the mid-17th century that the English mathematician Sir Isaac Newton discovered that white light passed through a prism is broken into a whole spectrum, or scale, of colors (Fig. 46).

Newton deduced from this discovery that white is actually a mixture of all colors. The prism fragments the light, breaking it into component color rays. When we see a rainbow with violet at one edge, moving step by step through the spectrum to red at the other, we are seeing an

46. A ray of white light projected through a prism separates into the hues of the rainbow.

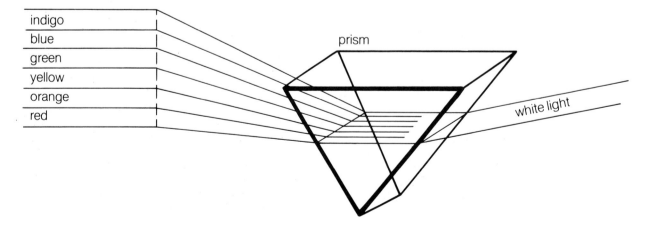

example of the same phenomenon. In this situation, however, instead of being fragmented by a prism, the sunlight is broken apart as it passes through the raindrops. On the other hand, Newton also discovered that when various quantities of red, blue, and green light rays are projected onto a single area, they combine to form white light. These three colors of light—red, blue, and green—are therefore known as the **additive primary colors.** When white light is projected through the **subtractive primary colors**—cyan (blue), magenta, and yellow—onto a single surface, all color is subtracted from the white light, resulting in black.

The colors, or **hues,** of the spectrum are produced by light rays, while artists' colors come from substances called **pigments.** Pigments absorb certain light rays and reflect others. Blue pigment, for example, will absorb almost all but the blue rays. Blue paint will therefore reflect the blue waves and we will see blue. No pigment can produce as pure a color as the prism, so no paints have ever achieved the brilliance of light, nor are they standardized. For example, one pure alizarin crimson (deep red) pigment may reflect more yellow rays than another red pigment. To make the problem of standardization even more difficult, colors look different under different kinds of illumination.

The color wheel is made up of the main colors in the spectrum plus other colors achieved by mixing the main colors. The twelve colors on the wheel (Pl. 4a, p. 22) can be divided into three groups: **primary,** those colors that cannot be produced by intermixing other hues; **secondary,** combinations of primaries; and **tertiary,** or intermediaries. The three primary hues are blue, yellow, and red. The artist can use mixtures of these three colors to create all other colors on the color wheel. By mixing two primary hues, ideally, secondary hues are produced, although the proportions of each may vary with the pigments. The three secondary colors are created in this way: blue mixed with yellow yields green; blue mixed with red becomes violet; and red plus yellow makes orange. There are six tertiary colors, each a result of mixing a primary color with a nearby secondary color. Thus, red and orange make red-orange, yellow and orange produce yellow-orange, and blue and violet yield blue-violet, and so on.

Complementary colors are those that appear opposite each other on the color wheel. For example, blue and orange are complementary colors; so are red and green. Adjacent colors on the color wheel, such as blue and blue-green, are called **analogous** colors.

Each color varies in value, which ranges from light to dark, just as uncolored values may range from white through a series of grays to black (Fig. 45). A very light blue, for example, is high on the value scale and is called a **tint,** while a dark, low value of blue is called a **shade** (Pl. 4b, p. 22). We may note that color values and hues appear quite different depending upon the local values and hues around them.

Intensity, or **saturation,** refers to the purity of a color. A pure blue, as it appears in the color wheel and as near the spectrum blue as possible, is said to have a full intensity, or saturation. Color complements neutralize the intensity of each other when they are combined in varied amounts; when mixed in equal amounts they create a neutral gray, but pigment impurities often make this gray difficult to achieve (Pl. 4c, p. 22). The addition of shades of gray will also neutralize color intensity.

The three major elements of color may be summarized as follows:

1. Hue: an identifiable color on the color wheel and the spectrum; a specified wavelength of spectrum color
   a. primary hues: red, yellow, blue
   b. secondary hues: green, orange, violet
   c. tertiary hues: yellow-green, blue-violet, and so on
2. Value: the degree of lightness or darkness of a color
3. Intensity or saturation: the degree of purity of a hue; ideally, a pure hue reflects no other color rays

Artists achieve infinite color variations by mixing colored pigments with one another and with black and white. Even more vibrant colors than pigment mixtures seem to occur when dots of pure color are placed next to one another. These then appear to the viewer, from some distance, to be blended. This practice of optical color mixture was introduced by Impressionists in the 19th century. Georges Seurat (1851–1891) advanced these techniques further when he restricted his **pallette,** the pigments he chose to use, mainly to the color primaries, applying tiny dots of color in a method he called **Pointillism.** Examination of a detail of *La Grande Jatte* (Pls. 5, 6, p. 23) reveals a dot pattern surprisingly similar to modern four-color printing. Seurat used no black for shadows.

Artists make use of color schemes, or arrangements of certain colors, to produce special effects. In a color scheme where complementary colors are used next to each other, the effect will be one of strong contrast and emotional excitement. An analogous scheme made up of colors close to one another on the wheel has a subdued physical or emotional effect. Schemes with light colors, or tints, evoke different emotional responses than those with dark colors.

These emotional reactions appear to be almost universal—some colors depress us while others lighten our spirits. There is a sense of joy in *The Kitchen in My Studio* (Pl. 7, p. 23) by Clayton Pond (b. 1941) with its variations of reds and other bright colors. Psychologists believe that the satisfactions most of us associate with these hot colors ultimately go back to the pleasures given to us from the warmth of a fire on a wintry night or by the sun itself.

Color can be used symbolically as well as emotionally. The Virgin Mary, Queen of Heaven, is traditionally shown in a blue cloak because the color has come to symbolize heaven. Unlike emotional responses to color, however, symbolic color varies from culture to culture. For example, a particular color may symbolize mourning in one culture and joy in another. When complementary colors are placed side by side, they seem to intensify one another's hue, a fact known as **simultaneous contrast.** If, however, a neutral gray shape is placed on a yellow background, the gray appears violet, a phenomenon called **successive contrast.** There are many other optical effects like these we have come to recognize, but none so familiar as rubbing our eyes and seeing flashes of color. No one is entirely sure why these phenomena occur, only that our view of color is linked to the retina of the human eye as well as to the effects of the light.

Impressionist painters tried to duplicate the usual effect of sunlight on us by placing small brush strokes of contrasting colors next to each other (Pl. 5, p. 23). Vibrations in the eye from these painted colors heightened the effect of dancing light. Today's artists are using light itself as a medium. Neon sculptures by Steven Antonakos (b. 1926) extend our concepts of what our future environment may be like (Pl. 8, p. 24). While colors are almost always dependent upon existent light to create hues, under certain other conditions, special color effects can occur. For instance, after staring fixedly at the red shape in Pond's *The Sink in My Studio* (Pl. 7, p. 23), when you shift your eyes quickly to a white surface, the complementary color to red, a definite green, will appear. This visual phenomenon is called **afterimage.**

Reducing color to its elemental characteristics, Mondrian sometimes simplified his paintings to the primary hues. Working in this way, he used colors at full intensity, and the apparent differences in their distance from the viewer come from the different sizes of the color areas and their relative warmth and coolness. Large areas appear closer, small ones farther away. Warm colors—red, yellow, and orange, colors we associate with the sun—are dominant, tending to move forward toward the eye. Cool colors—violets, blues, and greens, like icy waters—tend to recede from the viewer. It sometimes surprises a beginner studying art to realize that Mondrian often spent months determining slight differences in color areas. His works are so orchestrated that one cannot imagine any alteration to one area that would not have to be matched with corresponding changes in the others to balance the effect.

Because of the great number of visual effects that can be achieved through color and because of its effect upon our emotions, and even well-being, color is an expressive device of endless excitement and visual variety. Although we think of color as the particular concern of the painter, it is essential to designers in other areas of art such as interiors, fashion, advertising, and theater.

Texture The surface quality of an object, or its **texture,** appeals to our senses of both touch and sight. Nature is lavish with surfaces, which artists sometimes try to duplicate or even exaggerate in their work. Such textures, however, are not real—not tactile. They are only implied. On the other hand, a close look at an orange skin or other rough surface reveals true hills and valleys, which compare with the surface of the moon. Paint may be applied to suggest the smoothness of human skin or of a river-polished rock. The sculptor grinds and polishes stone to simulate the sheen of satin. Rough, smooth and shining, dull, hard, and soft textures are contrasted to increase the expressiveness of shapes and to avoid monotony. Infatuation with texture and with the tactile quality of oil paint has driven some artists to pile on pigment, creating frenzied surfaces, as in van Gogh's *Starry Night* (Fig. 4). Often painters achieve a desired effect though the addition of actual textures such as we see in Georges Braque's (1882–1963) collage of newspaper cutouts and painted surfaces, a medium invented in the 20th century (Fig. 47).

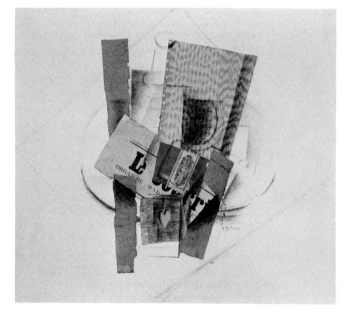

47. Georges Braque. *Le Courrier.*
1913. Collage, 20 × 22½″
(51 × 57 cm).
Philadelphia Museum of Art
(A. E. Gallatin Collection).

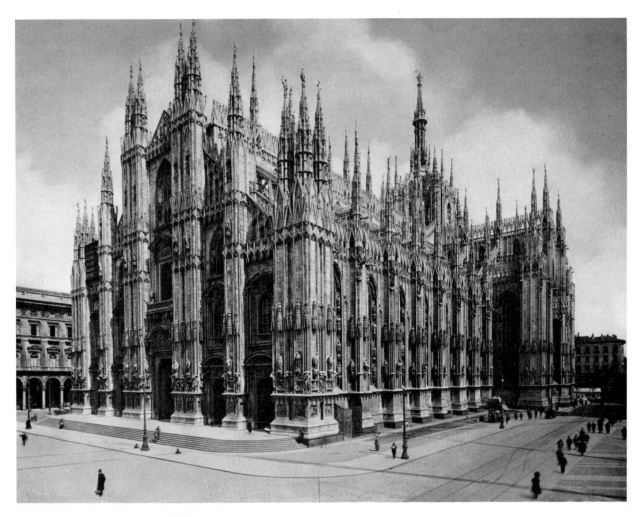

48. Milan Cathedral. Begun 1368.

Many artists have forsaken traditional use of brush and paint to create new tactile effects. Abstract Expressionists in the 20th century worked with heavy, irregular strokes as they became involved with the physical process of painting, following the lead of Pollock, who poured paint from the can directly onto prepared but unstretched canvas (Pl. 2, p. 21). Such surfaces reveal unusual textures. Helen Frankenthaler (b. 1928), in contrast, has chosen to work upon unstretched canvas surfaces that are not coated with a primer like gesso (plaster) in the technique traditional since the Renaissance. Therefore, her paints sink into unprimed canvas, creating pools of deep color. The variations in dye surfaces of *Flood* (Pl. 9, p. 24) were achieved by sponging thinned acrylic dyes onto the vast canvas areas.

Since the period of the Impressionists, sculptors also have been moving away from the traditional smooth surfaces of well-worked materials. Auguste Rodin (1840–1917) was said to have worked by flickering candlelight, slowly moved over his models, in order to simulate the effect of broken light sought by the Impressionists. In the 20th century, Giacometti's roughened sculptural surfaces intrigue us, perhaps, because they suggest the erosion of time (Fig. 42). Unusual effects also occur when layers of fine strings are laid in textural patterns of surprising complexity, all produced within the limitations of an inch or two of space. Such art is unique to our time.

As much concerned with texture as are the other arts, architecture is also dependent upon varieties of materials, such as glass, slate, marble, brick, and wood, to provide us with pleasing surfaces. The huge Gothic cathedral of Milan (Fig. 48), one of the largest in the world, was designed with setbacks and carved details that create pockets of shadows and highlights to add textural interest to what might otherwise have been a large, monotonous area. The various setbacks of structural parts and the open stonework on the façade of the cathedral are typical of the Gothic style, as are the sculpture in high niches and the carved decoration over the roof, which can be seen only by the birds or, perhaps, God.

Space and Perspective A sense of space depends on what occupies it. The layperson sees space as emptiness.

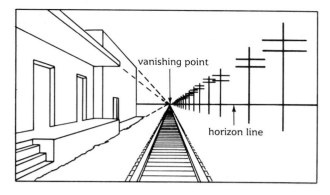

left: 49. One-point perspective.

below: 50. Two-point perspective with multiple vanishing points.

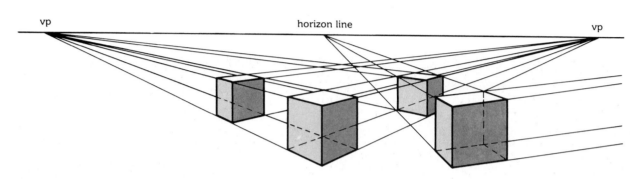

The artist regards space as a challenging arena in which to arrange forms and colors. The visual arts are often known as spatial arts because their elements are arranged in space. In distinction, the arts of theater, dance, music, and poetry are temporal arts, comprehended in sequences of time.

In two-dimensional art forms, such as drawing, painting, prints, and photography, the artist often wishes to create an illusion of three-dimensional space, or depth. Images are rendered upon a two-dimensional surface, as in Vermeer's *The Artist in His Studio* (Fig. 39), through the device of **perspective,** to make them appear to vary in distance from the viewer. When we think of the term "perspective" we usually mean **linear perspective,** an inheritance of the Italian Renaissance that has influenced our way of creating and looking at art for centuries. In linear perspective the artist uses lines either implied or actual, to give an illusion of great depth on a flat surface. The main rules of linear perspective follow:

1. All objects appear to grow smaller the farther away from the viewer they are.
2. Parallel lines receding into the distance appear to converge. The point at which they seem to meet is called the **vanishing point.** Horizontal parallel lines cannot converge.
3. In **one-point perspective** the viewer appears to be looking at the object from directly in front of it, and all nonfrontal sets of parallel lines, if extended, meet at one vanishing point (VP) (Fig. 49).

4. In **two-point perspective** the viewer appears to be looking at the object from an angle so that no side is frontal; this must involve two vanishing points, one for *each set* of parallel lines receding in space. Objects viewed at different angles have their own vanishing points, which result in multiple vanishing points on the horizon line (Fig. 50).
5. Vanishing points are positioned along an imaginary line called the **horizon line**—generally, our eye level from level ground. Parallel lines above the horizon appear to converge down toward it. Parallel lines below the horizon appear to converge up toward it.
6. The horizon line may be arbitrarily raised or lowered by the artist to make the objects appear below (a bird's eye view) or above (a worm's eye view) the viewer's eye.
7. Round and irregularly shaped forms that do not have parallel sides are viewed in perspective as if enclosed in regularly shaped blocks (Fig. 51).

Leonardo's *The Last Supper* (Fig. 52) is a classic example of one-point perspective, as the diagram (Fig. 53) shows. The painting occupies the upper end wall of a long room. The lines of the walls, ceiling, and table in the painting continue the lines of the room and converge from above and below the imaginary horizon line toward a single point behind the frontal figure of Christ. His divine calm at the center of the painting thus becomes its focal point and is in

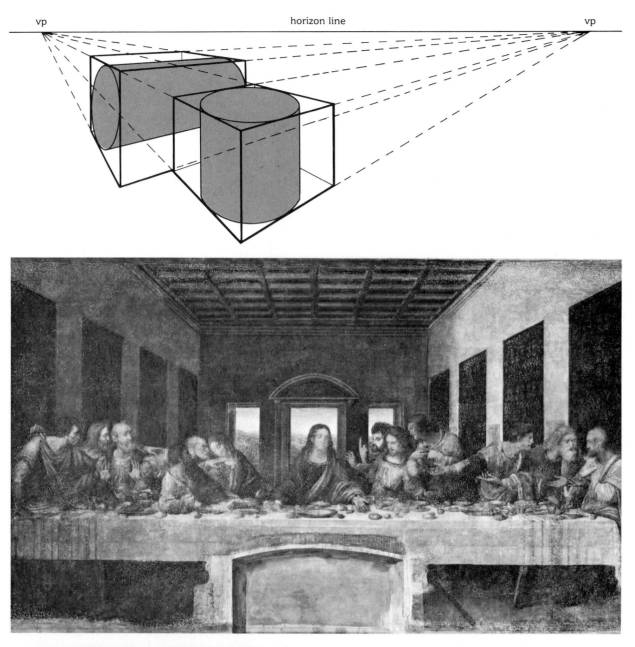

vp   horizon line   vp

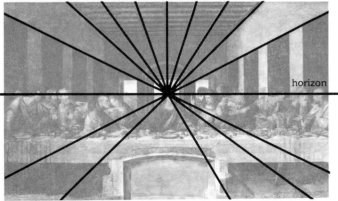

horizon

top: 51. Two-point perspective for round objects.

above: 52. Leonardo da Vinci. *The Last Supper.* 1495−98. Fresco, 14′5″ × 28′1⁄4″ (4.39 × 8.61 m). Refectory, Sta. Maria della Grazie, Milan.

left: 53. Diagram of Figure 52, showing one-point perspective.

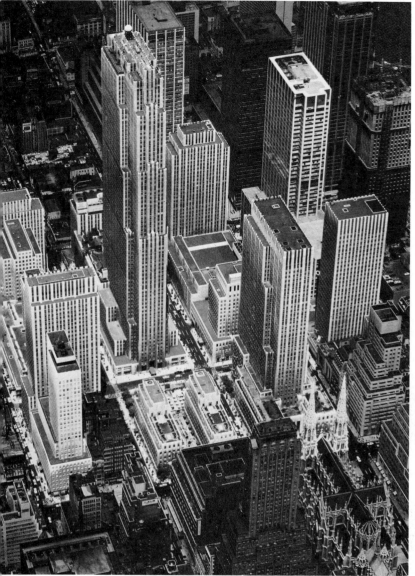

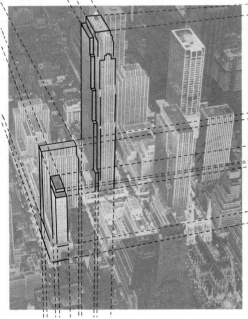

above: 54. Rockefeller Center. Photograph.

right: 55. Diagram of Figure 54, showing three-point perspective.

dramatic contrast with the writhing, agitated forms of the disciples to his left and right.

The system of perspective at work in the photograph of Rockefeller Center (Fig. 54) is a relatively recent extension of linear perspective brought to our consciousness by the camera and our ability to view tall structures from great heights, or, as in this case, from an aerial view. In this dense composition one vanishing point lies far below the base of the buildings; two others are outside the image on a horizon line far above the photograph, emphasizing the endlessness of urban centers (Fig. 55). This system is known as **three-point perspective.**

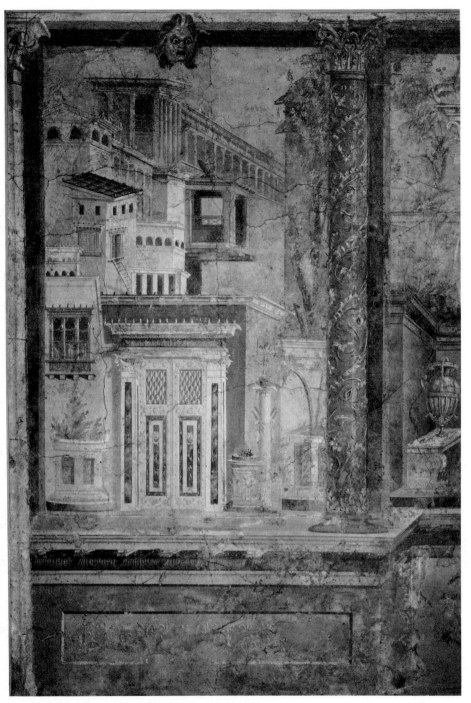

56. Architectural painting from the cubiculum wall
at a villa at Boscoreale, Italy.
1st century B.C. Metropolitan Museum of Art,
New York (Rogers Fund, 1903).

The Romans had only elementary knowledge of linear perspective. Then artists reported their surroundings from many **viewing positions,** or **vantage points,** which they combined into one single rendering with resultant inconsistencies in perspective (Fig. 56). After the Renaissance artists learned to confine their drawing to a single veiwing position.

Many contemporary artists choose to ignore linear perspective or may combine it with other methods of producing spatial effects. The Cubists, for instance, rejected the rules of linear perspective altogether. In *Three Musicians* (Fig. 57), Picasso used several vantage points and aspects of each figure, assembled with flat, overlapping shapes. He was not concerned with creating an illusion of three-dimensional reality on the flat surface of the painting any more than were Egyptian painters, who combined front, top, and side views in order to depict the clearest views of an object (Fig. 58). The most important figures were shown very large, while wives, servants, and children were much reduced. This tradition developed from the dominance of the pharoah in Egyptian society, not from any lack of artists' ability to place figures in space. Unusual or emotional experiences of space can be found in many other cultures where art is not concerned with three-dimensional representations of the real world.

Another form of perspective is known as **atmospheric perspective,** or **aerial perspective.** It involves the use of cool colors and light values to make objects appear more distant. In a distant view individual parts merge, colors are less intense, and details seem diffused as a result of air and sunlight. Artists attempt to reproduce these effects to create a sense of deep space in painting (Fig. 9).

As with two-dimensional space, every civilization has occupied three-dimensional space differently. For example, in ancient Egypt great horizontal expanses of desert were blocked by huge temple complexes approached by vast walkways. In order to cover vast areas and create interior space, Egyptian architects used forests of mammoth columns to support flat stone roofs. Later in medieval Europe, the cathedral was at the heart of the medieval city and very

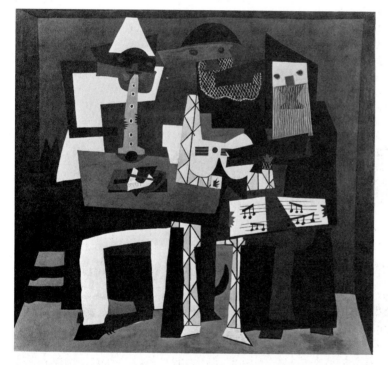

left: 57. Pablo Picasso. *Three Musicians.* 1921. Oil on canvas, 6′7″ × 7′3¾″ (2.01 × 2.23 m). Museum of Modern Art, New York (Mrs. Simon Guggenheim Fund).

below: 58. Fowling scene. Copy in tempera of wall paintings from the tomb of Khum-Hotep, Beni Hasan. Twelfth Dynasty, c. 1900 B.C. Metropolitan Museum of Art, New York.

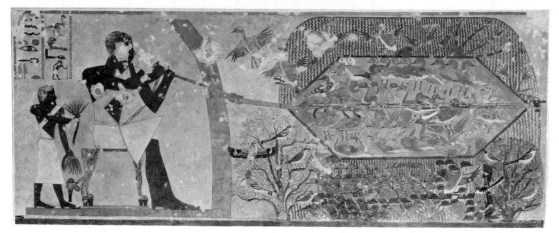

often positioned on a high ground, where it dominated the living and working spaces clustered on three sides. Gothic builders used fewer columns, strengthened, as we shall see, by buttresses, to support vaulted roofs over huge interior spaces. Contrast the sense of the slivers of space between columns in the hypostyle hall of the Great Temple at Karnak (Fig. 59) with the soaring interior space of St.-Denis Cathedral (Fig. 40).

Compare these uses of space with the concentrated space of many major cities today, crowding boxlike skyscrapers together in a comparatively small area. Interior space is divided into numerous floors or storeys, each further subdivided into tiny cubicles. Some urban communities are blighted with industrial plants and wastelands of burned and abandoned tenements. They are often empty at night and inaccessible to commuters during a failure of electric power. Berenice Abbott captured the essence of a modern city in her striking photograph (Fig. 54), taken at night. The photograph, however, softens the rigid geometry of the skyscrapers and, through its intricate pattern of light, suggests limitless possibilities for visual exploration.

Like architecture, sculpture and all other three-dimensional arts are designed in relationship to the space they occupy. Since ancient times, sculpture has been a solid form dominating space from a central position. Many contemporary sculptors, however, emphasize space, which they enclose within the design of their work as, perhaps, a reflection of our preoccupation with the space age. Giacometti's *City Square* (Fig. 42) appears to focus on the alienation of people in today's society by isolating the figures in a space that seems too large for their elongated bodies. As a result, they are lost in an urban environment that discourages human contacts.

Time and Motion Artists have always recognized that paintings are illusionistic splinters of time. Some artists, however, have been interested in implying the passage of time in a single work. When the Florentine painter Masaccio (1401–1428) told the story of *The Tribute Money* (Fig. 60) he created an illusion of passing time by repeating the life-size figure of St. Peter three times to illustrate the three-

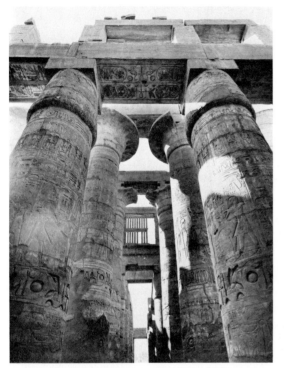

above: 59. Temple at Karnak. 1350–1205 B.C.

below: 60. Masaccio. *The Tribute Money.* c. 1427. Fresco, 8'4" × 19'8" (2.54 × 5.9 m). Brancacci Chapel, Church of Sta. Maria del Carmine, Florence.

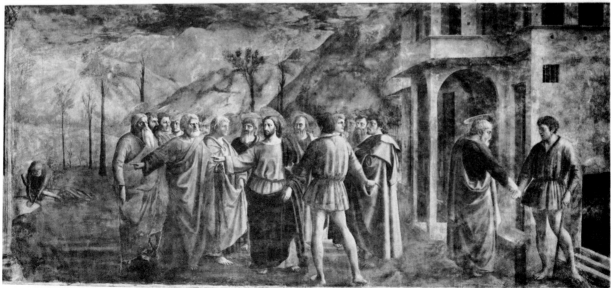

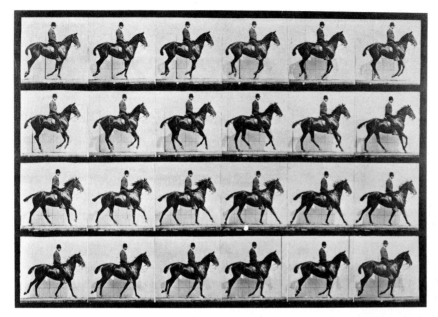

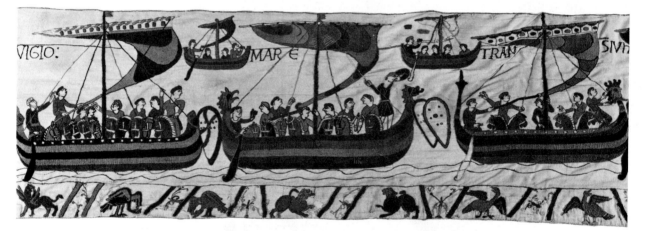

part event that was painted at the viewer's eye level. First, we see St. Peter with the tax collector (right); then we observe him extracting a coin from a fish's mouth (left); finally we can see the payment of the tribute (center). Despite its sequential arrangement, *The Tribute Money* appears unified because of its orderly composition and its repeated colors and figures.

The photographic advances of Eadweard Muybridge (1830–1904), which inspired the invention of the motion picture camera, involved a series of 24 frames to be projected at speed, producing an illusion of time through motion (Fig. 61). In fact, we will learn how the marvel of the motion picture can manipulate time, contracting and expanding a timed experience. With the development of television, it has become possible to transmit images as they occur in the real world. The video synthesizer can mix past and present time in order to create the desired psychological and educational effect.

Motion has always fascinated people. Accordingly, there have been many allusions to motion in the static images of two-dimensional painting and drawing. Even the prehistoric representation of the leaping antelope on a wall in the Lascaux caves (Fig. 2) is portrayed with front and rear legs spaced for the forward plunge into space. Subsequent artists have attempted whole battle scenes, depicting men and animals in violent motion, as in the *Bayeux Tapestry* (c. 1080), which immortalized the Battle of Hastings (Fig. 62). In the desire to portray the correct sequence of events, the artist decorated a very long strip of linen with thousands of carefully embroidered soldiers, horses, and other figures. The features of the major characters are repeated to permit us to follow the action. In the 20th century, concurrent with the invention of cinematography, many artists combined multiple images to demonstrate the changes in position of a moving object.

Few illusionistic works, however, ever created the furor

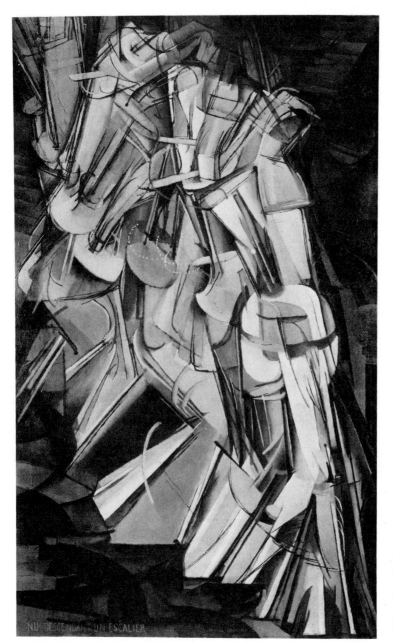

63. Marcel Duchamp.
*Nude Descending a
Staircase* (*No. 2*).
1912. Oil on canvas,
4'10" × 2'11"
(1.47 × 0.89 m). Philadelphia
Museum of Art (Louise and
Walter Arensberg Collection).

of *Nude Descending a Staircase* (*No. 2*) (Fig. 63) by Marcel Duchamp (1887–1968). In the vast 1913 Armory Show in New York comprising 1100 pieces of art, this painting of a technological Venus figure in motion is said to have moved U.S. President Theodore Roosevelt to comment, "Explosion in a shingle factory!"

Recent styles in art have approached the illusion of movement by means of nonobjective designs. Some works, such as Bridget Riley's *Current* (Fig. 36), produce the effects of changing images as the position of the viewer is altered. Although many optical paintings are simple, repet-

itive patterns of distinct, often geometric shapes, after prolonged scrutiny of the works, hard edges blur and colors vibrate, appearing to ripple before our eyes. Some works executed in fluorescent paints produce heightened visual experiences when viewed under black-light illumination.

Today, numbers of artists are exploring other time-motion dimensions of the visual arts. The hypnotic effect of moving bodies of water accounts for our delight in fountains. In some fountains, computers coordinate musically activated changes of light with changes in the flow of waters. The earth's rotation, the sway of branches in the

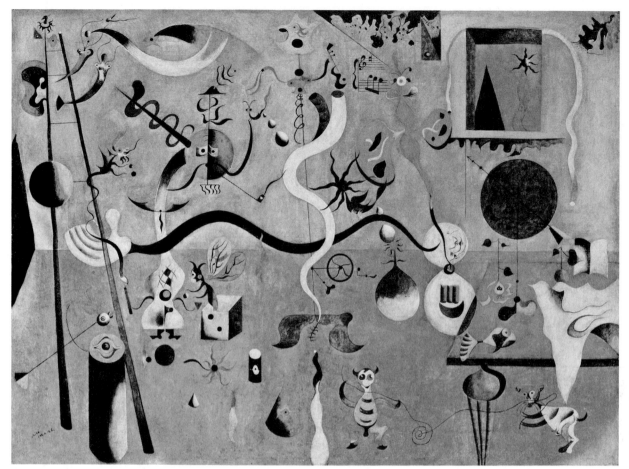

64. Joan Miró. *Carnival of Harlequin.*
1924–25. Oil on canvas, 26 × 36⅝"
(66 × 93 cm). Albright-Knox Art Gallery,
Buffalo, N.Y.

wind, or the turbulence of waves breaking upon a beach perhaps account for Alexander Calder's first notions of mobile art, an invention of the 20th century. Although the motions of the sun, fire, and steam-propelled machines have been noted since Leonardo's early preoccupation with motion in the 1400s, Calder's wind sculptures were revolutionary (Fig. 37). These kinetic works appear deceptively simple. Many of the pieces rotate on separate axes and coordinate also with the larger movements of the whole sculpture, apparent in the photograph showing the mobile in motion (Fig. 38). In essence, motion in art is an evocation of motion in life and is a desirable part of human experience.

Principles of Design

The order of the universe has given us a basic appreciation of **design** and a need to create an orderly, harmonious existence. Natural designs inspire created designs. The vis-

ual arts are made up of elements organized into combinations. These arrangements, whether spontaneous or planned, are termed **composition.** Up to this point, we have been discussing the technical language of the artist dealing with those areas of concern unique to the visual arts. We are now ready to examine the language the artist uses in reference to composition, which is common to all the arts, visual and performing. That language includes words for principles basic not only to most of the arts but also to many other of life's experiences—unity and variety; rhythm; balance; proportion and scale; and thrust, dominance, and subordination.

Unity and Variety Visual **unity** (oneness) occurs through the interrelationship of all parts of an artwork so that they fit together in a recognizable order. This order may be simple or highly complex. A composition can be related and unified by repeating and echoing certain shapes, masses, colors, or lines, as, for example, the curved lines repeated in Riley's *Current* (Fig. 36) and the processions of columns in the Temple of Karnak (Fig. 59). In these works the repetition and interrelationship of the parts give pleasure and satisfaction by creating unity.

Sometimes a work of art may appear to the inexperienced eye to have little unity, as in *Carnival of Harlequin* (Fig. 64) by Joan Miró (b. 1893). The apparent disorganization adds to its sense of fantasy, yet the repetition of similar shapes, colors, and lines produces a composition that holds together. The contrast between the way different elements are represented, as well as the differences between the elements themselves, provides variety within the basic unity.

Rhythm   A basic element of life is **rhythm.** It is created through the regular repetition of natural phenomena, such as waves pounding on the shore or a regular heartbeat, whose rhythmic pattern can be seen in a cardiogram. The natural rhythms of the tides, the phases of the moon, and the turning of the earth all suggest the rhythm of regular repetition. In the visual arts, rhythm is produced by the regular repetition of similar lines, shapes, colors, or textures. Our eyes quite naturally follow the pattern of repeats. Marcel Duchamp created a sense of flowing rhythm in *Nude Descending a Staircase* (*No. 2*) (Fig. 63) by repeating shapes of the body as it moves down the stairs. The female form has been reduced to machined parts, reflecting the technological interest of many early 20th-century artists, but it has rarely been expressed more dramatically. Even the colors, muted grays and browns, remind us of the machine. Rhythm appears similarly in the repeated forms of the Temple of Karnak (Fig. 59), and we are comfortable with their regularity. These are obvious examples of rhythm in art. A more subtle design appears in Michelangelo's *The Creation of Adam* (Fig. 1), in which the lines of Adam's listless, still lifeless body are echoed but not exactly repeated in the vital, life-giving lines of God's figure.

Balance   A sense of **balance** exists in all of us, and we are disturbed when our equilibrium is threatened. A teetering tightrope walker creates extremes of tension in the audience. In the same way, although the Leaning Tower of Pisa is famous for its imbalance, few of us are comfortable climbing its ascending ramp. When we experience works of art, that same need for balance is involved.

Balance results from the unified relationship of two opposing forces. When almost equal shapes or masses are evenly distributed in a work of art, it is said to have formal balance. An example of informal balance may be seen in Miró's painting (Fig. 64), while in some of Mondrian's work, geometric areas of color are balanced against white space.

Exhibiting yet another kind of balance, Calder's mobiles fascinate us with their ever-changing but totally balanced relationships. His subtle organic shapes move animatedly through space to create a vital rhythm (Figs. 37, 38).

Proportion and Scale   In art, as in mathematics, science, or cooking, **proportion** refers to the relationship of the parts to each other and to the whole. Greek civilization was particularly concerned with proportion, both in human actions and in art. This attitude is revealed in the remarkably subtle relationships of each small part of their designs to every other part. The Greeks refined the sense of proportions into a principle called the Golden Section, which they applied to their temples and most other artworks (Fig. 65).

According to this rule, a small part relates to a larger part as that larger part relates to the whole; that is, $a:b = b:a + b$. This ratio was likely derived unconsciously from natural laws we have only recently understood. Science has verified that this year's growth of a mollusk (or indeed any living form) relates to last year's increase as that amount relates to the whole.

Scale in art refers to size, that is, to the relative measurements of the viewer and the work. For instance, when we consider **miniatures,** which are small paintings or objects, we anticipate works that can be held in the hand. Most paintings and wall hangings are perhaps 2 to 5 feet (0.61 to 1.52 meters) wide, enough to serve as a focal point of decoration in the average building. On the other hand, artists of the New York School of the 1950s overwhelmed their viewers with monumental works, planned essentially to surround their viewers with painted environments. Consider that Jackson Pollock's *Number 1* (Pl. 2, p. 21) is close to 6 by 9 feet (1.73 by 2.64 meters). This is as large as a whole wall in many homes and decidedly oversize for most.

People have often been concerned with the proportionate relationships of the parts of the body; the Greeks developed an idealized scale that served as a canon of beauty for a thousand years. Scale also intrigued Leonardo, who declared: "Man is the measure of all things." He placed the human figure as a unit of measurement in the center of the

65. The Golden Section.

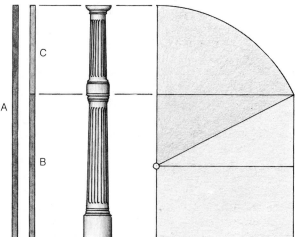

66. Leonardo da Vinci. *Study of Human Proportions According to Vitruvius.* c. 1485–90. Pen and ink, 13½ × 9¾″ (34 × 25 cm). Accademia, Venice.

most perfect geometric shapes of his day, the circle and the square (Fig. 66).

Some rules of human proportion can be set with considerable accuracy. A child's head is larger in relation to the rest of the body than is that of an adult. In teaching figure drawing, an instructor may suggest that students measure a figure's proportions in relation to the head. The average adult is about seven to eight head-lengths tall. Sometimes artists change human proportions for expressive purposes. The fashion artist may draw a figure whose proportions measure twelve heads, while a painter elongates figures to suggest spirituality. In contrast, Classical Greek sculptures adhered to the proportions set forth by Polykleitos in a book called *The Canon.* The figure considered ideal measured seven head-lengths tall.

Human proportion also affects architecture and furniture design. In contemporary design, the **module,** or core unit, is based on dimensions and ratios derived from the human body. Similarities in proportions from one person to another have permitted fashion designers to standardize clothing. Modern, mass-produced plywood or plastic furnishings are also designed to suit average proportions. The scale of a building in relation to the size of the human figure has much to do with its emotional impact. For example, the immense size of many churches and public buildings dwarfs the individual's sense of importance. When the artist tampers with predictable proportions in order to create a desired Surrealistic effect, the viewer experiences a discomfort that often gives way to fascination.

Thrust, Dominance, and Subordination   Directional, linear forces are created in the basic structure of a work of art. Vertical and horizontal lines suggest growth and repose, respectively, because they refer to natural states. Diagonal lines repeat the direction of driving snow or rain and consequently suggest lines of action to us. **Thrust** is created by the most dominant linear force within the work of art. Thrust is always directed (connected) to the focal point of the work, those aspects that are emphasized in the composition. Unless unimportant parts are subordinated, confusion results. For example, in order to direct attention to his model in *The Artist in His Studio* (Fig. 39), Vermeer places the greatest contrasts in light and dark and the largest shapes near her figure. The thrust of the draperies echoes her pose and helps to frame her effectively. By subordinating all other forms through their reduced size and limited value contrasts, Vermeer assures the dominance of the model.

We have seen that sensitivity to design, inspired by the natural world, is as old as humanity. The veining of a leaf and the pattern of annual growth of a tree suggest designs of variety and complexity. Similar curved, spiral, wavelike, and animal designs based on nature are found everywhere in the world. Whether we view the decoration on a clay pot or analyze the complex plan of a building, we note a universal awareness of structure and order.

In our further studies of the visual arts, we will try to identify the devices used by all artists to achieve satisfying designs.

EXERCISES AND ACTIVITIES

1. Select two to six works reproduced in this book to analyze on the basis of the artists' use of any or all of the following terms: line, shape, mass, value, color, texture. Find works that illustrate unity and variety; rhythm; and thrust, dominance, and subordination.
2. Cover a sheet of paper with lines, using pencil, chalk, charcoal, pen and ink, and paint. Vary the thickness, length, direction, and spacing of the lines. Notice how the lines produce different effects.
3. Inside of small squares draw groups of lines that express joy, sorrow, excitement, humor, confusion, tension, or other emotions. Analyze which kinds of lines express each emotion best.
4. Linear perspective has been used by painters to create the effect of three dimensions on a two-dimensional surface. To understand how artists use this method, place some solid objects, such as books, on a table. Try to see where the horizon line and vanishing points lie and make a simple drawing of the objects in perspective.
5. The traditional color wheel places the primary, secondary, and tertiary colors in a certain relationship. Using poster paints, mix these colors, paint them on pieces of paper, and paste them in the order shown on the color wheel (Pl. 4a, p. 22).
6. Take two complementary colors and mix them, producing a series of equal steps from one color to the other. Mix as neutral a gray in the middle as is possible with your pigments (Pl. 4c, p. 22).
7. Set up a simple still life. Look at it to see how you might express a personal feeling by varying the colors. Choose two of the types of color schemes listed below and create two small color compositions to express your feelings.
   a. strongly constrasting values and hues
   b. analogous hues and values
   c. cool colors with warm accents
   d. warm colors with black and white accents
   e. opposite colors with black and white accents
   f. monochromatic color with a wide value range
8. The way in which varying types of shapes are combined produces different effects. To see how artists use shape as an expressive tool, draw groups of shapes inside small rectangles. Draw one arrangement that is balanced, another that suggests chaos.
9. Mass is used in the three-dimensional arts of sculpture and architecture. The illusion of mass is also often created in painting. Using clay, wood, or cardboard, make two compositions in which mass is used to create (a) a calm, quiet effect and (b) an exciting effect of tension. Or, paint two compositions creating the illusion of mass and producing these same effects.
10. Using chalk and sheets of newsprint, make rubbings of actual textures. Cut and paste these on a flat surface to create an interesting composition.

PART II

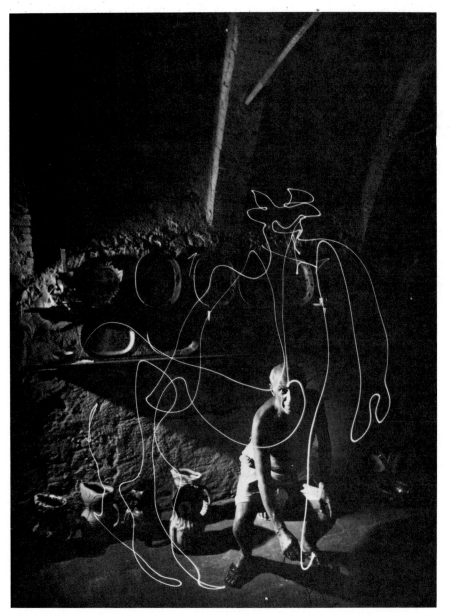

67. Gjon Mili. A centaur
drawn with light.
Pablo Picasso at
the Madoura Pottery,
Vallauris, France. 1949.

Media and Techniques

All the visual arts communicate some level of human experience, expressed in a wide range of media. In the next few chapters we will examine the fine arts—painting and drawing; the other two-dimensional graphic arts of printmaking and photography; and sculpture. We will also study the applied arts—decorative arts made by hand and design for industry. We will conclude this section with chapters on architecture and environmental design, which are both fine arts and applied arts.

All these media depend on the same visual elements and principles of design we have explored in Chapter 2, but each has unique characteristics and potential depending on the materials used. These include traditional materials, such as stone, wood, clay, and paper and new materials developed in the 20th century, such as polyresins, gases, color film, and electric light. Some artists work in only one medium; others, like Picasso, try many. Painting, carving, etching, weaving, potting, even light, his final experiments with a new technique (Fig. 67)—there is scarcely a medium which he has not explored. The traditional distinctions among media and techniques are being eroded by many 20th-century artists, who work in mixed media. By examining each medium in turn, moving from two-dimensional process to three-, we will be prepared to understand and enjoy art wherever we find it.

3 Drawing, Painting, and Mixed Media

It is not enough for a painter to be a clever crafts-man; he must love to "caress" his canvas too.

PIERRE AUGUSTE RENOIR

Drawing, painting, and mixed media—each of these arts has its particular characteristics, yet all share similarities. What related skills do they require?

Traditionally, the creation of an image upon a flat surface through the application of some kind of coloring material has been the common element in all these arts. Whether they are produced by drawing on parchment or on paper, or by painting on plaster walls, wood, or canvas panels, these images have all appeared on flat surfaces. Artists have translated individual visions to a working surface by using brushes, pens, and assorted graphic tools. New techniques and materials, however, have changed the visual forms of these arts, for the changing world has led artists to search for new methods to express their ideas.

For that reason, we will find it impossible to separate fully the study of materials and techniques from the study of form. When we investigate the contemporary art world, we will discover that while many artists continue with familiar methods and materials, many are experimenting with industrially developed techniques and other new methods of creating images on two-dimensional surfaces.

Still others are rejecting the limitations of flat surfaces altogether. Such trends confirm that demarcations between the arts have broken down. Sculptured forms appear on paintings; paint is used on sculpture; and some graphic expressions are three-dimensional. Time and sound enter into many art experiences, and the viewer often becomes a participant in a staged environment. We will examine these newer concepts of art in greater detail later. At this point, let us study some of the many technical processes used to create images on flat surfaces.

Drawing

Of all the art skills, drawing has always been the most basic. Have you ever doodled at the telephone or picked up a stick at the beach and drawn with it in the sand? Undoubtedly, some of our ancestors reached for pieces of burnt wood, idly rubbed them on rocks, and discovered a way to make images. Today, artists have a choice of many materials with which to draw.

Drawing provides the underlying structure of many painted works. The lively images painted on the walls and ceilings of prehistoric caves depend on the contour of drawn lines to express the action of the charging animals (Fig. 2). Earth pigments were used to fill the spaces between the lines with shaded color. Many scenes on the walls of Egyptian tombs were first drawn on with heavy outlines and then filled in with flat color (Fig. 58). Thousands of pottery jugs and drinking vessels throughout the Greek world were decorated with brush drawings outlining flat areas. The monks who decorated early medieval manuscripts usually outlined the complex, intertwined designs with a pen or brush before filling them in with color. A cross page from the Lindisfarne Gospels (Fig. 68) is a complex linear delight, revealing fantastic monsters whose birdlike heads and clawed feet interlace with snake-like bodies.

Drawings also exist independently and fall into three groups: (1) notes or sketches made for the artist's information, (2) drawings that are completed artworks, and (3) drawings that serve as plans or studies for other works. The third category includes studies for paintings, prints, sculptures, architecture, the decorative arts, and the industrial arts. Artists and designers make rough sketches for their final works much as writers jot down ideas and notes.

Such early studies, through which artists try out ideas in pencil, conté crayon, or pen, determining how to draw this part of a figure, or how this shape combines with that one, are apt to be planned only for personal use. Many artists' sketchbooks are full of studies like these. Leonardo's sketchbooks are well known, although he wrote his verbal observations from right to left in order to keep his discoveries somewhat secret. When Michelangelo was commissioned

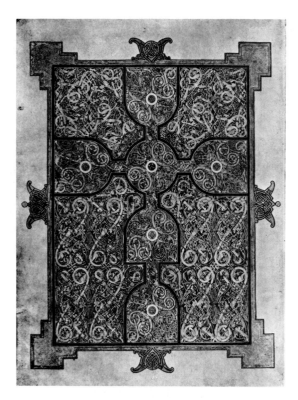

papyrus with carbon ink, the ancient Chinese used ink on silk scrolls, and Western manuscript illuminators drew with ink on vellum made from animal skins. Paper is believed to have been developed in China around A.D. 100 and brought to Europe with the spread of Islamic culture. By the 15th century, paper was manufactured in Europe, offering a wider choice of drawing surfaces and techniques. Ink was brushed onto the paper with hair brushes or stroked on with a bamboo or quill pen. Depending on the materials and techniques used, artists could produce a wide variety of effects, ranging from broad brushstrokes to delicate pen lines. By studying their ink drawings, we can see how artists such as Goya and Rembrandt van Rijn (1606–1669) worked out the dramatic light and shadow in their prints and paintings.

Rembrandt's study for *The Sortie of Captain Frans Banning Cocq's Company of the Civic Guard,* familiarly known

left: 68. Cross page from the Lindisfarne Gospels. Late 7th century. Manuscript illumination, 13 × 9½″ (33 × 24 cm). British Museum, London.

below: 69. Michelangelo. Studies for the Libyan Sibyl. Red chalk on paper, 11⅜ × 8⅜″ (29 × 21 cm). Metropolitan Museum of Art, New York (purchase, 1924, Joseph Pulitzer Bequest).

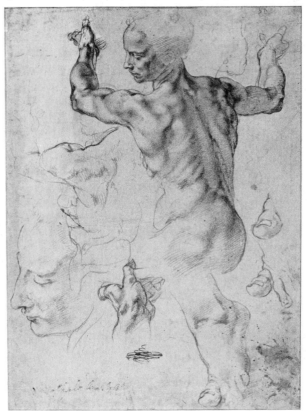

to paint the ceiling of the Sistine Chapel, he doubtlessly prepared for that complicated project with considerable thought before he ever put chalk to paper. There are, in fact, few of his drawings still extant, but each is a record of search and discovery. Michelangelo's sketches for the Libyan Sibyl reveal careful observation and concern for accurate rendering of anatomy (Fig. 69). Those parts of the human form that presented problems to him, such as the big toe of the left foot, he drew three times, observing it from three different viewpoints. While he must have anticipated that the ceiling would receive considerable attention from Pope Julius II, who had commissioned it, Michelangelo would have been much surprised at the affection the world has since given those very private, preliminary drawings.

Working from sketchbook notations, artists, especially in the Renaissance, often created a preparatory full-scale drawing of the intended work called a **cartoon**. Once approved, the cartoon guided the artist in creating the **mural** or other work planned.

Architects and designers also use preliminary drawings to develop their ideas and communicate them to clients. Plans for buildings; sketches for furniture, utensils, or clothes; rough layouts for books and advertisements—all depend upon drawing in one way or another.

Ink The artist's basic, fluid drawing medium, ink, has been in use for thousands of years. The Egyptians drew on

as *The Night Watch,* was rendered in **wash** (diluted tones of ink) and demonstrates how solid blacks in the background were contrasted with thin lines and with the infinite range of diluted inked grays in the figures. It will be interesting to compare the wash study (Fig. 70) with the completed painting (Fig. 71). Although the composition involving many figures is much the same in both works, the mass confusion in the study has been reduced in the finished work by reserving the light values for the focal points of the painting, that is, Captain Cocq and the young girl. The nonessential, detailed remainder of the work has been largely subdued in shadow.

The variety of tones possible with wash is well demonstrated in Sesshu's *Landscape* (Fig. 32). Also typical of Chinese and Japanese paintings is the vertical composition depicting an imagined idyllic sea and landscape. While our

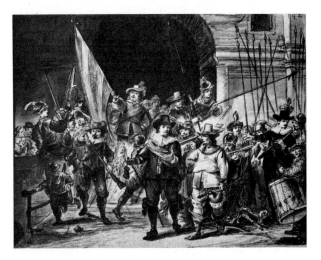

above: 70. Drawing after *The Sortie of Captain Frans Banning Cocq's Company of the Civic Guard* by an unknown artist. Wash drawing, 12′2″ × 14′7″ (3.71 × 4.45 m). Rijksmuseum, Amsterdam.

below: 71. Rembrandt. *The Sortie of Captain Frans Banning Cocq's Company of the Civic Guard.* 1642. Oil on canvas, 12′2″ × 14′7″ (3.71 × 4.45 m). Rijksmuseum, Amsterdam.

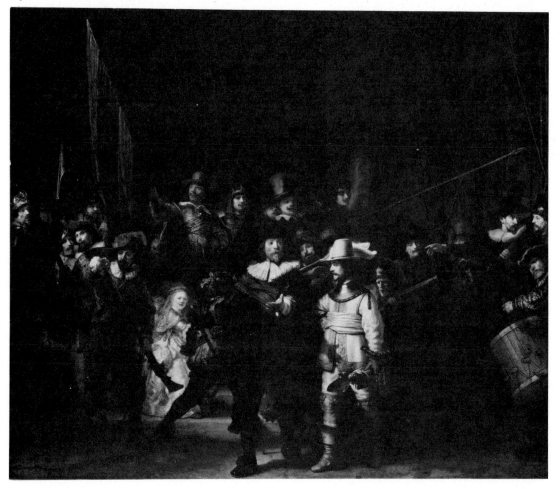

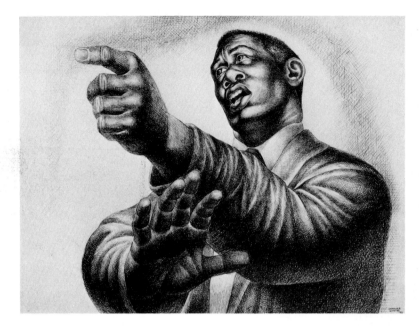

eyes journey upward from the lower right of the work, delicate details of gray shrubs lead us to the mountain at the top. These grays are particularly characteristic of Oriental drawings, which are washed onto silk or paper with subtle tone gradations. Here, again, we find an instance where the distinction between drawing and painting disappears.

Pure (undiluted) ink is used when the artist wishes to make a strong statement that can be quickly understood. The classic pen drawing by Ben Shahn of *Silent Music* (Fig. 31) was commissioned by CBS during a musicians' strike and commanded half a page in *The New York Times.* Shahn's brilliant use of line captivates our eyes, while we follow the path he has laid out for us, threading our way through the orchestra pit. CBS resolved its differences with the musicians almost immediately, but the charm of Shahn's drawing lives on.

Pen and ink with bister (brownish) wash produces another variation of delicate transparent effects and eloquent varied line.

Tones of gray can also be achieved by building up fine, parallel, dark lines in pencil, ink, or chalk in a process known as **hatching**. By crossing the parallel lines in another direction, cross-hatching produces deeper and solid tones, as in the powerful *Preacher* (Fig. 72) by Charles White (1918–1979). The white highlight areas and light grays are almost devoid of inked lines. The enlarged left arm and foreshortened right arm emphasize the preacher's dramatic and dynamic arm movements in his exhortations to the congregation.

While most of us are familiar with the detailed study for Dürer's *Praying Hands* (Fig. 73), we are less aware that we are viewing only a preliminary drawing for a much larger work, *The Assumption,* which few of us know. Artists, it

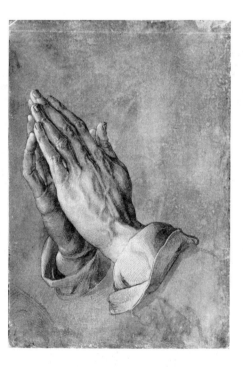

seems, cannot always predict what will attract the public's fancy. The study of reverent hands is meticulously rendered in a technique quite common in the Renaissance but rarely used today. Dürer used blue paper as the base for the drawing; then he slowly built up highlights with opaque Chinese white paint, while at the same time, he applied dilutions of ink (wash) for the shaded areas and pure ink for the deepest tones. The beauty of the drawing has commended it for study through the years both as inspiration for occasions of worship and as a model for imitations.

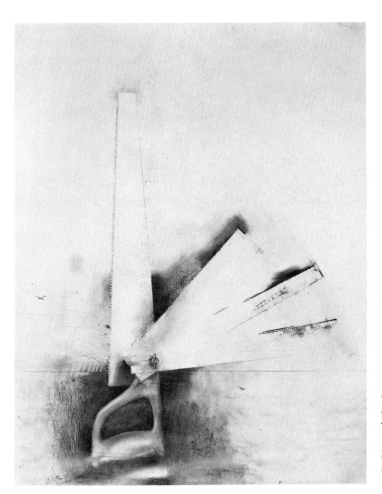

74. Jim Dine. *5-Bladed Saw,*
from Series of Seven
Tool Drawings.
1973. Charcoal and graphite,
25⅝ × 19⅞" (65 × 51 cm).
Museum of Modern Art,
New York (purchase).

Chalk, Charcoal, and Crayon   Chalk, suspended in a binder such as gum arabic and pressed into sticks, became a popular drawing material in the Renaissance. It was available in black, white, and in shades of red and brown. Then, as now, it is a versatile material. It can be sharpened to a reasonably fine point, can be used bluntly, or can even be rubbed on its side across the paper to cover large areas. Chalk can be used strongly and vigorously or lightly and delicately. Many chalk drawings by the greatest artists of the Renaissance still exist. In them, we can see, for example, how Leonardo studied a series of heads or Michelangelo worked out the twist of a body or, as seen earlier, the detail of a foot (Fig. 69). Although this drawing was rendered on a sheet of paper small enough to fit into a modern type-writer, the study was large enough to lead Michelangelo to the life-size figure we know so well. We are brought very close to the creative inspiration of these great Renaissance masters when we view the studies they made for their major works.

Charcoal has come a long way from the crumbled pieces our distant ancestors salvaged from the ashes of a fire to the convenient, prepared stick, made from hard, close-grained wood, now available. Artists find charcoal an easy material with which to work because they can quickly develop with it a wide range of different tones. It is especially useful in drawing large areas of light and shade, or, if sharpened with sandpaper, charcoal may be used for linear drawings, or smudged and rubbed into the paper, can create soft, hazy effects. Traditionally, a popular way to use charcoal was to draw with it on gray textured paper, adding white chalk highlights. Charcoal is limited because it smears easily. Consequently, charcoal drawings must be protected with a sprayed fixative to prevent them from damage. Jim Dine (b. 1935), in an untitled series for a special exhibition of drawings for the Museum of Modern Art, rendered seven tools (Fig. 74), using a combination of charcoal and graphite pencil to produce extraordinary drawings. The blurred, rubbed tones of the charcoal serve as a soft contrast for his impeccable pencil detail.

Wax crayons have an advantage over charcoal in that they do not smear or rub off paper so easily. Crayon is useful for drawing large areas of light and shade. With crayon, the artist can create rich, shining darks, or, if handled lightly, soft mid-tones as well. Conté crayon is a highly compressed pigment with binder that can be used like chalk, producing effects like lithographic crayon, in which

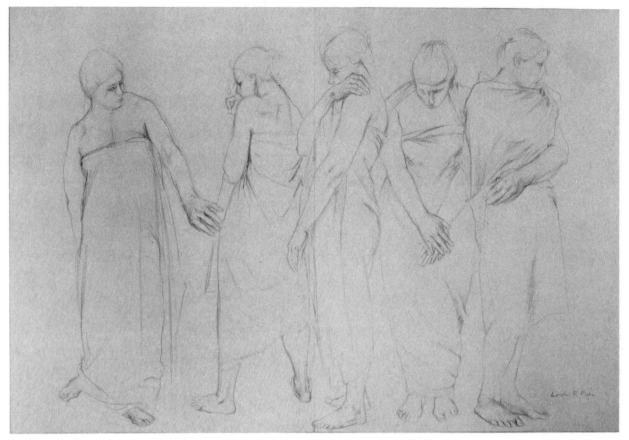

75. Leonda Finke. *Survivors,* study for a frieze.
1980. Silverpoint, 36 × 24″ (91 × 61 cm).
Collection Adrienne and Arthur Bloch.

velvety shadows contrast with brilliant whites. When conté is applied to a gesso surface, variations of tone are almost unlimited if the artist has patience to build up values slowly, with painstaking effort. Drawings by Helen Meyrowitz in conté (Fig. 44) are starkly realistic and as black and white studies, minutely render reflections of the artist's studio. The *Interiors* series demonstrates her preoccupation with confined space and her query, "Can objects of personal meaning such as articles of clothing carry the sense of a human presence, even in its absence, in that little space?"

Pencil Before the lead pencil was invented, artists used silver-tipped tools to draw delicate lines on paper coated with white or tinted pigment. Through oxidation, as the **silverpoint** slowly travels over the surface, the line tarnishes, darkening to a delicate gray. Such lines cannot be erased. Modulated tones are developed from many individual parallel strokes. Silverpoint drawings such as those by Leonda Finke (b. 1922) result in works of refinement and sensitivity. In her frieze of *Survivors* (Fig. 75), the line has a remarkable sensitivity to form and suggests light and dark in small areas. The small cross-hatchings lend some solidity to the figures while they define their contours.

The earliest pencils were lead points in a holder, but by the 18th century, the graphite pencil had widely replaced lead. Its wood-encased point creates lines that can be thin and hard or smudgy and soft. Today, pencils remain a prime medium. They range in grades from the soft 6B to the hard, fine 9H. Pencil does not smear as readily as chalk or charcoal. Though it is particularly suitable for small sketches and detailed drawings, it can serve for larger drawings, provided the artist has unlimited time and patience to work on that scale. Pencil is particularly effective in the hands of Robert Carter (b. 1938). His themes are generally concerned with black culture; lovingly handled, they are based upon recollections or uniquely imagined forms (Fig. 76). The delicacy of the tones is applied and slowly built up with so long and fine a point that any excess pressure would instantly destroy it, yet huge areas of ground are effectively covered. His drawings are sometimes 6 feet high (1.8 meters).

New Combinations of Drawing Materials and Techniques Today many drawing methods are used in untraditional ways to produce varied effects. Ink and chalk

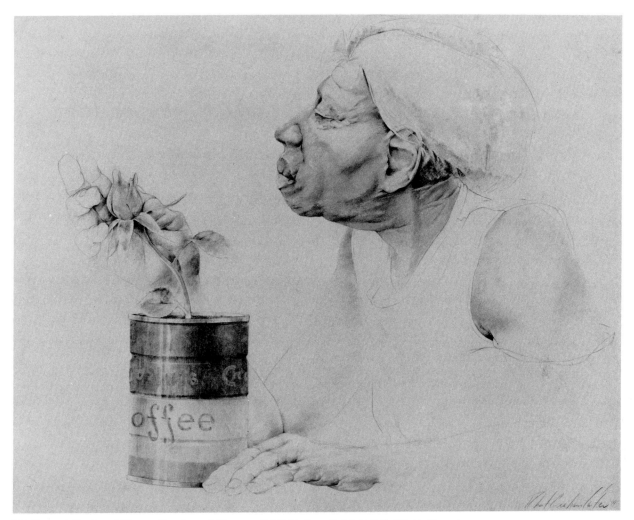

76. Robert Carter. *"Mama She Loved Flowers."* 1979. Pencil, 18 × 24" (46 × 61 cm).
Collection the artist.

drawings may have bits of photographs or magazine reproductions pasted on them. Pencil drawings may be combined with commercial overlays of printed dot patterns just like the screen used to reproduce photographs and artwork for magazines and newspapers. Some artists blow fine mists of paint and ink onto paper with airbrushes; many others draw with the same brushes with which they paint. It is difficult to say at which point drawing ceases and painting begins. These new methods have given artists freedom to express new ideas, so that drawing continues to serve as a base for all who work in the visual arts.

Painting

The most memorable of the artist's media is, perhaps, painting. In painting, color is usually the first consideration, basic to most painted works. Drawings are sometimes colored, but paintings hardly exist without differentiation of color as the avenue for developing all the other elements. As we have learned, a painting need not be pleasing to be aesthetically moving. The subject matter or emotional content may produce sensations of horror, while the composition and other elements of design are aesthetically organized.

Paint consists of **pigment** (dry coloring material) suspended in a **vehicle**, or mixing agent, which is a liquid made up of a binder (a sticky material) and a solvent (thinner). Various kinds of paint—oil, tempera, watercolor, and the paint used in fresco—differ in the vehicle, the surface to be covered, and the technique of application.

Pigments are made from both organic and inorganic substances. Traditional organic sources for pigments which occur naturally include charcoal (black), a kind of beetle (red), the urine of cows fed on mango leaves (yellow), and a vast variety of plants (indigo blue). In recent times, an important synthetic organic source is coal tars. Among the organic pigment sources are natural earths, which produce yellow ocher and raw and burnt umber, and minerals such as zinc (white), cadmium (yellow), and cobalt (blue). In the Middle Ages ground lapis lazuli, a semiprecious stone, produced a beautiful blue, which was so costly that it was often reserved for images of sacred figures, such as the Virgin Mary's cloak. Today many inorganic pigments are artificially made.

In the past, artists ground their own pigments and mixed them with the appropriate vehicle. Paleolithic painters mixed charcoal and earth colors with animal fat to paint the walls of caves (Fig. 2). In the ancient and medieval world, artists mixed pigments with such binders as gum arabic, egg, beeswax, or lime and water to paint the walls of tombs and houses or the pages of books. The dryness of the Egyptian climate and the sealing of the tombs have combined to keep Egyptian painting fresh through thousands of years (Fig. 58). Most 20th-century artists use commercially prepared paints in which the pigment and vehicle are already mixed. If, however, artists wish to mix their own paints, dry pigments are still available.

Fresco The Italian term **fresco**, meaning "fresh," is the technique of painting on freshly plastered walls. The artist usually prepares a full-size drawing, or cartoon, and transfers the outline to the wet-plastered wall surface. Then he or she quickly brushes on pigments mixed with water. As the wall dries, the pigments form a strong, extremely durable surface. Indeed, the colors quite literally become part of the wall.

Because the pigment must be brushed on when the plaster is wet, only enough plaster is applied to cover an area that can be painted in one day. If you look closely at a frescoed wall, you can often see lines where one day's plastering stopped and the next began. Usually the artist tries to conceal these lines by planning them to fall along the edges of the shapes in the painting.

This technique on wet plaster is also called **buon fresco** ("true fresco") to distinguish it from **fresco secco**, in which pigments mixed with a binder are applied to plaster that has already dried. *Fresco secco* is less durable and brilliant than *buon fresco*.

Fresco secco was used by many early peoples to make murals. As far as we know, the earliest true frescoes were painted on the walls of the famous palace of King Minos in Knossos, Crete. The representation of figures leaping over a bull (Fig. 77) formed the basis for the later Greek legend of the Minotaur. The whole series inspired later murals on the Greek mainland, but Crete's slender-waisted athletes dominate a fun-loving way of life, unique among frescoes in the ancient world.

Fresco was an important technique in the Greek, Roman, medieval, and Renaissance periods and reached a peak in the Renaissance with such works as the Sistine Chapel ceiling by Michelangelo. The artist's care in preparing and plastering the wall affects the durability of a fresco.

77. *Bull Leaping,* reconstruction of fresco in the Palace of Minos, Knossos, Crete. c. 1500 B.C. 34 × 63″ (86 × 160 cm.) The University Museum, University of Pennsylvania, Philadelphia.

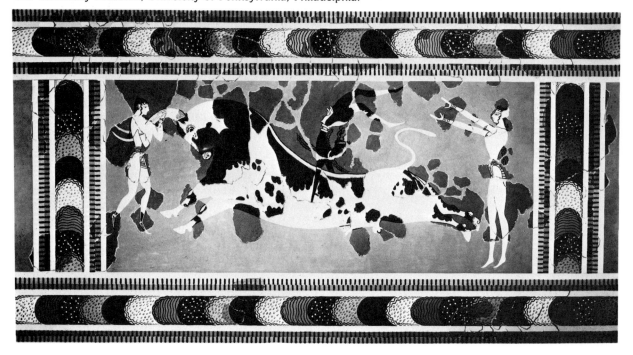

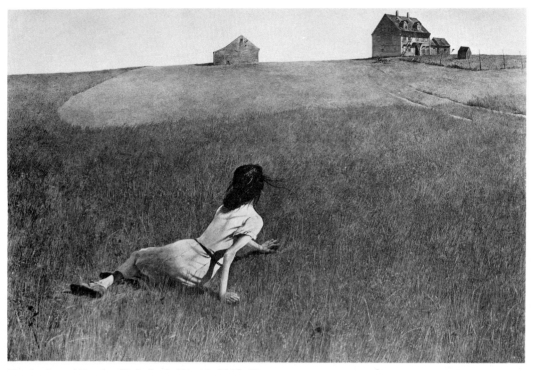

78. Andrew Wyeth. *Christina's World.* 1948. Tempera on gesso panel, 32¼ × 47¾" (82 × 121 cm). Museum of Modern Art, New York (purchase).

Because Leonardo worked slowly with great attention to detail, he experimented with new, slow-drying vehicles. Consequently, his famous *The Last Supper* (Fig. 52) in the monastery refectory of Sta. Maria delle Grazie in Milan began flaking off the wall even during his lifetime.

Little used in succeeding centuries, fresco was revived in the early 20th century by Mexican painters. Revolutionary figures in *The Modern Migration of the Spirit* by José Clemente Orozco (1883–1949) were painted in the same basic technique that Michelangelo used, though the artists differed in the ways they chose to evoke emotional response. Fresco is still used, chiefly for murals in public buildings, but it is an exacting technique far less common than it once was.

Tempera When you hear the term **tempera,** you probably think of the jars of poster paint you used in grade school. Actually, these paints are **gouache,** or watercolor paint made opaque with the addition of white, not true temperas, which depend upon egg yolk, gum, or casein as the binding material. Applied to a properly prepared surface called a **ground,** egg tempera is very durable. The most suitable surface is wood. A wood panel is first coated with a ground of **gesso,** a mixture of white pigment (chalk, plaster, or white clay) and animal glue. Perfect preparation of the gesso is important. Incorrectly mixed gesso can cause cracks to develop all over the painting. After the

ground is prepared, dry pigments are mixed with egg yolks and water and then applied to the absorbent gesso. Sometimes the egg yolks are mixed to create an emulsion with oil and varnishes. During the Middle Ages, this method of painting with egg tempera was widely used for household and church altar paintings on wood called **polyptychs** if many-paneled and **diptychs** if double-paneled. Later painters used tempera on canvas, which proved to be far less durable.

Tempera paintings can be built up by painting layer over layer. Early artists slowly built up dark and light values over an under painting of umber pigment. Brilliance and crispness are characteristic of tempera paintings. Colors dry quickly, and repainting over underpainted layers, when the artist wishes to alter the original concept, is simple. Although the technique fell into disuse when painting with oils was introduced, many contemporary illustrators continue to use tempera. A few painters, such as Andrew Wyeth (b. 1917), choose tempera because of the opportunities it offers for precision. By overpainting several layers of varying tones, for instance, Wyeth retains our interest in the very broad foreground area of *Christina's World* (Fig. 78). By selectively etching with a knife blade various surface pigments he achieves finely detailed blades of grass. The expanse of grass is particularly important in this work because it emphasizes Christina's physical problems in reaching the distant house.

79. J. M. W. Turner. *Venice: From the Giudecca Looking East, Sunrise.* 1819. Watercolor, 8¾ × 11¼″ (22 × 29 cm). British Museum, London.

Watercolor **Watercolor** paints are made of pigments and binder such as glue, egg white, or gum arabic, which can be diluted with water. Washed over a white surface, which shows through the pigments, watercolors produce paintings of distinctive freshness, clarity, and transparency—qualities that can be easily lost if the painting becomes overworked. Watercolor has been used in the West since Classical times, and almost all medieval manuscripts were executed with watercolor or gouache. The Lindisfarne Gospels (Fig. 68) demonstrate the delicacy and fine detail possible with watercolor.

Watercolor paintings using nonfading pigments on good-quality paper or silk are remarkably permanent, as can be judged from examination of many Oriental works, treasured for centuries. Sesshu's *Landscape* (Fig. 32), depicting the Oriental love of nature, demonstrates the vitality of watercolor despite a lifespan of almost five hundred years. The basic pigment used is lampblack mixed with glue, although Oriental artists also used colored pigments. Years of training prepared the artist to use the brush skillfully and expressively. Unlike most Western painting, color was never used to give an illusion of reality. Eastern traditions required that paintings be quickly executed so that both the theme and calligraphic identification are not only handled with the same tools and materials but fulfill the artist's original concept in minimal time. Suggestion, therefore, has always been more desirable than faithfully detailed representation.

In the West, for some time after oils became popular, watercolor was restricted primarily to sketches. It is a quick, spontaneous technique, which lends itself well to the notes an artist might make as the study for an oil painting. In the 18th century, watercolor was revived as an important art

medium. Joseph Mallord William Turner (1775–1851) created misty paintings in watercolor, which were forerunners of later Impressionist works. His view of Venice (Fig. 79) at sunrise is certainly very close to 19th-century Impressionism. Even though the variety of effects possible with watercolor does not measure up to the potential of oils, artists have used the medium in different ways to serve their purposes.

Thinly diluted watercolor is also used in wash drawings to provide a wide range of tones. Wash works well with line drawing. **Gouache**, watercolors mixed with some form of white pigment, is opaque, and therefore light is not reflected from the white paper beneath the paint. Because of its opacity, gouache can be reworked more than watercolor. However, since all the colors have been mixed with white, the range of values is limited. *Going Home* (Fig. 80) by Jacob Lawrence (b. 1917) is a witty summary of day's end on the subway. The highly stylized character of Lawrence's technique and themes, concentrating on his Afro-American heritage, work well with the gouache medium, which depends upon strong accents of solid tone to carry the thrust of works. The rhythmic repetition of vertical seats and diagonally positioned passengers reinforces the message of returning home after a day's work, utterly exhausted.

Oil **Oil paints** consist of a mixture of dry pigments with oil and sometimes varnishes diluted with turpentine. Developed in Flanders in the 14th century and gradually refined, oil painting was an outgrowth of the commercial developments of that period. Trade with many parts of the world brought new materials to Europe, including those from which oils and varnishes could be extracted. The transition

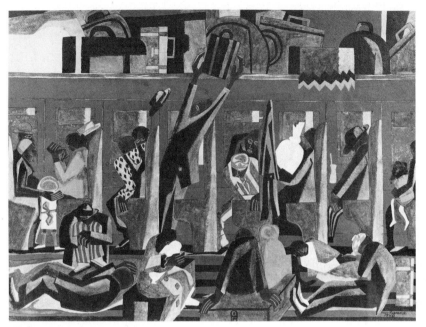

above: 80. Jacob Lawrence. *Going Home.*
1946. Gouache, 21½ × 29½" (55 × 75cm).
Collection IBM Corporation.

below: 81. Hans Holbein the Younger. *Sir Brian Tuke.*
c. 1527. Oil on wood panel, 19⅜ × 15¼"
(49 × 39 cm). National Gallery of Art,
Washington, D.C. (Andrew Mellon Collection, 1937).

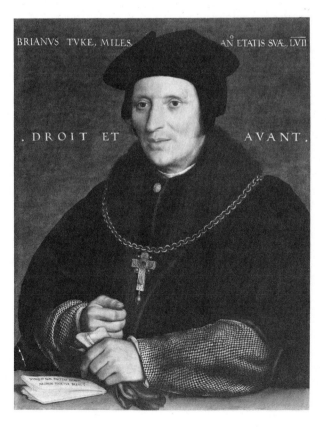

from tempera to oil was slow. Oil paint was first used for transparent glazes over a tempera underpainting on gesso-covered wood panels. Solid form was modeled with tempera, and the final painting was completed with thin oil glazes. The Renaissance practice of layering thin, semi-transparent glazes of warm and cool colors on top of each other imparted a rich glow and depth to the painting. In *Sir Brian Tuke* (Fig. 81), Hans Holbein the Younger (1497–1543) displays consummate skill in capturing human expression and great technical brilliance in rendering details of clothing and the textures of fabrics. These are painstakingly painted with oil glazes, which make the surfaces glow like enamel.

By the 16th century, in Italy, linen canvas gradually replaced wooden panels as the preferred surface for oil paint, since fabric was light in weight, less costly, and easy to prime with gesso or with glue, white pigment, and oil. Although oil paint on canvas is not as durable as fresco or tempera on wood, other advantages led to oil becoming the major choice of artists in the Western world for centuries. Oil dries slowly and can be reworked for a long time. It can be applied in thin glazes over underpainting, or it can be put on in thick layers with a brush or palette knife. Oil allows a wide range of tones from light to dark. Thin, transparent, dark shadows can be contrasted with thickly applied highlights, a combination that was unobtainable with earlier methods of painting.

Rembrandt made full use of this quality of oil paint in his contrast of deep, mysterious shadows and concentrated brilliant light areas, particularly evident in *The Night Watch* (Fig. 71). Oil paint, in the hands of a master such as Frans Hals (1580–1666), can also be used to suggest spontaneity. Like all of Hals's work, the under drawing of *The Bohemian Girl* (Fig. 82) is precise and carefully painted; only in finishing it did Hals apply fluid fine strokes that appear deceptively casual, much like the candid photographs of the 20th century.

Later painters, instead of using underpainting and glazes, applied the paint directly to canvas with free brush strokes. For example, the Impressionists created an effect of vibrant light by placing small, thick strokes of complementary colors next to one another, as in Seurat's work (Pl. 5, p. 23). Cézanne also practiced this technique. His *Still Life* (Fig. 83) is a careful attempt to direct the viewer's conscious attention to the changing volumes of the fruit and cloth by shifting tones, plane to plane, instead of transcribing a literal, photographic surface. This deliberate counterbalancing of changing tones to suggest mass led directly to Cubism in the early 20th century.

Oil paint can also be applied heavily as *impasto*, a technique preferred by some painters, van Gogh in particular,

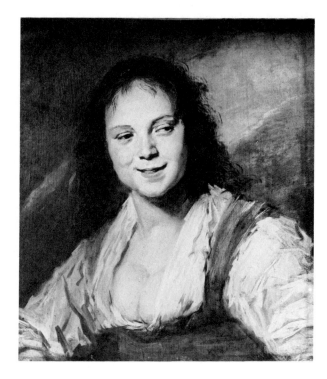

above: 82. Frans Hals. *The Bohemian Girl.* 1628–30. Oil on canvas, 22⅞ × 20½" (58 × 54 cm). Louvre, Paris.

below: 83. Paul Cézanne. *Still Life with Peppermint Bottle.* c. 1894. Oil on canvas, 26 × 32⅜" (66 × 82 cm). National Gallery of Art, Washington, D.C. (Chester Dale Collection, 1962).

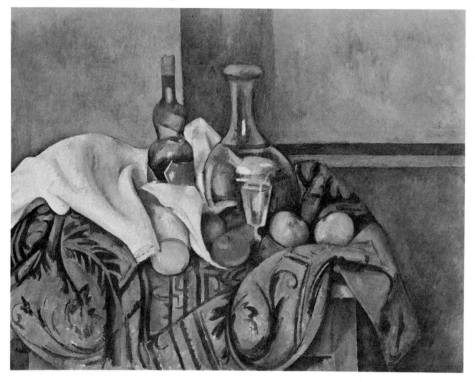

who used a palette knife to spread the thick paint. Observing a van Gogh oil painting (Fig. 4) becomes almost a tactual experience.

With this change to direct techniques, painters generally became less concerned with the precise craft of painting than with the immediate effect produced. Many carelessly painted works from the 18th and 19th centuries are cracking. Very heavy paint is likely to crack when it is not properly applied, and some colors will darken and bleed into each other. Many artists, including Rembrandt and, three hundred years later, Albert Pinkham Ryder (1847–1919), applied so many layers resulting in such thick paint that the solid, substantial-looking images become crisscrossed with countless fine cracks. Yet the variety of styles and techniques possible with oil account for its great popularity.

Pastels In their present form of pure pigment and a minimum of gum binder compressed into sticks, **pastels** date back about two hundred years. Pastel painting depends more on broad areas of color for its effects than it does on drawn outlines. Because the colors are not mixed with egg

84. Edgar Degas. *After the Bath: Woman Drying Her Feet.* c. 1890. Charcoal and pastel on cardboard, 22⅜ × 16″ (57 × 41 cm). Art Institute of Chicago (gift of Mrs. Potter Palmer).

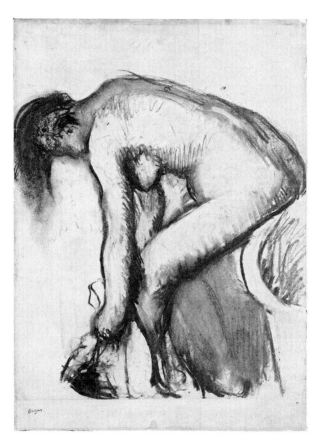

or oil they do not suffer from darkening or from other effects of age. When these nonfading colors are used on high-grade paper, the result is one of the most permanent types of painting. It will rub off, however, unless it is protected by glass or by a fixative spray. Because of its brilliant color and freshness of application, pastel appealed to Impressionist painters, who sought to capture momentary effects. During the latter part of his life, Edgar Degas (1834–1917) confined most of his painting to pastels, for the ease of achieving broad tones with them as well as for their effect of spontaneity. Many of his studies, such as *After the Bath* (Fig. 84), are intimate glimpses of women at work or at ease.

Acrylics and Other New Materials In their search for new ways to respond to inner emotions and the outer world and to achieve permanent color effects, many artists investigate new materials and techniques. Sometimes restricted access to traditional materials leads an artist to new materials, with which he or she may develop an original approach to art. For example, Jackson Pollock (Pl. 2, p. 21) confided that he used oil-based house paints and metallic enamels for his canvases because he could not afford artists' oils. The fluidity of inexpensive paints from the hardware store, however, led him to experiment by pouring, dribbling, and flinging his paints onto canvas laid out on the floor. Such a process would have been impossible with oils from tubes brushed on to a canvas set on an easel.

New, synthetic polymers have given artists probably the greatest shift in materials and techniques since the evolution of oils five hundred years ago. The most popular synthetic paints today are the acrylic and pyroxlin paints, in which pigments are suspended in a polymer vehicle, producing opaque or transparent films. These paints have greater durability than oils and can be used on a wide range of surfaces. They are thinned with water yet are resistant to water once they are dried. As a synthetic, these paints are inert and will not change color or affect the surface upon which they are applied. In addition, acrylics are brilliant and can be used as transparent glazes, or they can be built up in thick impasto surfaces. Thin-glazed areas can be contrasted with heavily painted textures. Since acrylic dries rapidly, it can be worked over in a matter of minutes, and many layers of paint can be built up. Acrylics can be directly laid on canvas that has not been primed, thereby permitting the paints to sink into the fibers of the cloth. For instance, *Flood* by Helen Frankenthaler demonstrates the luminosity of acrylics, when applied as dyes on the canvas. The huge areas involved literally surround the viewer with color (Pl. 9, p. 24).

The brilliance and vividness of synthetic paints account for their popularity in Optical Art, as in Bridget Riley's work (Fig. 36). The viscosity of barely thinned acrylics permits the paint to be poured and blended in highly personalized ways. While Morris Louis (1912–1962) never described his methods, it is apparent that he poured on his colors and then, setting the canvas on end, let gravity pull the paint

85. Morris Louis. *Tet*. 1958. Synthetic polymer on canvas,
3'9" × 12'9" (1.14 × 3.89 m). Whitney Museum of American Art, New York
(gift of the Friends of the Whitney Museum of American Art).

down, as in *Tet* (Fig. 85). With further thinning, acrylics can be used in airbrushes. This small tool, barely larger than a ball-point pen, is a refined, small-scale paint sprayer, capable of producing effects ranging from fine lines to broad sprays. Intended for the commercial world of photo retouching and illustration, the airbrush has become a favorite of many artists who, influenced by Pop Art, rework images from advertising art. Many of the Photo Realists of the 1970s also take advantage of the airbrush to create detailed acrylic works, frequently derived in some way from original photographs.

New Ideas, New Images

For many centuries, artists were concerned with how to paint the illusion of three dimensions on a two-dimensional surface. The Greeks and Romans used a limited form of linear perspective, which Renaissance painters developed into a science. Leonardo, Dürer, and Leone Battista Alberti (1407–1472) wrote treatises on the scientific aspects of painting, and rules were established. Leonardo observed:

> The first requisite of painting is that the bodies which it represents should appear in relief, and that the scenes which surround them with effects of distance should seem to enter into the plane in which the picture is pro-

duced by three parts of perspective; namely the diminution in the distinctness of the form of bodies; the diminution in their size; and the diminution in their color.

Alberti, a Renaissance architect, also wrote a treatise on painting, saying that painters "have no other aim but to make the shape of things seen appear on the surface of the picture not otherwise than if this surface were of transparent glass."

Mixed Media

In addition to experimenting with new paints and techniques, artists in the 20th century have also incorporated new kinds of materials into their paintings. Before 1920 Cubist painters in Paris such as Picasso and Braque (Fig. 47) were pasting scraps of printed paper and fabric onto their painted canvases. They called these works **collages**, from the French word for "paste" or "glue." Many artists today combine a variety of materials—metal, fabric, wood, sand, string, and words or images photoprinted on paper, plastic, or canvas—with the painted surface to make **assemblages**, from the French word for "gathering together." The English term is **combine art**. These materials, along with three-dimensional, **ready-made** objects, are glued, stapled, nailed, or even welded onto paintings. Sometimes the shadows cast by the solid objects are painted onto the canvas to push further the *trompe l'oeil* ("trick the eye") effect. Robert Rauschenberg's (b. 1925) *Pantomime* (Fig. 86) is a combine work of canvas, dripping paint, and a real electric fan (trailing its wires) to accelerate the process of drying the paint. That process is a kind of charade, which is the theme of the work.

86. Robert Rauschenberg. *Pantomime.* 1961. Combine painting, 7 × 5′ (2.13 × 1.52 m). Courtesy Leo Castelli Gallery, New York.

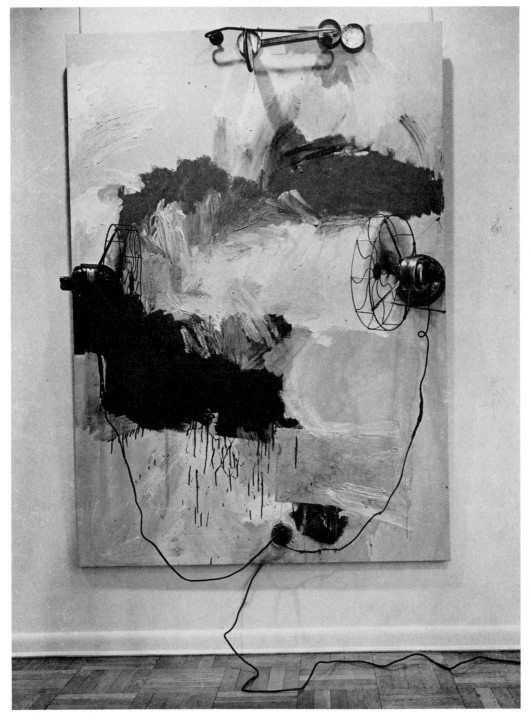

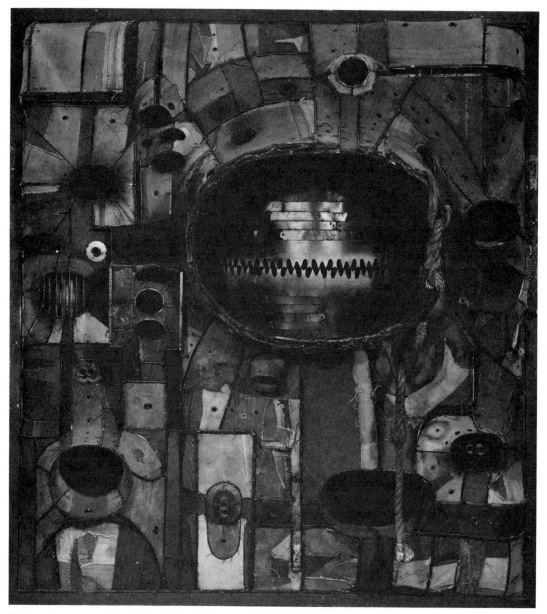

87. Lee Bontecou. *Untitled*. 1961. Welded metal and canvas,
6′ × 5′6¼″ × 2′2″ (1.83 × 1.68 × 0.66 m).
Whitney Museum of American Art, New York.

Other artists use three-dimensional canvases. Lee Bontecou (b. 1931), for example, experiments with stretched canvas over three-dimensional armatures (Fig. 87). In her fascination for hollows and openings she brings actual space into the painting, instead of creating an illusion of space with paint. Are these works sculptures or paintings? The frequently used term in today's art world is **mixed media**, a convenient way to get around the problem of how to classify much contemporary art.

Synthetic paints, new techniques, and mixed media have not replaced traditional materials and techniques; rather, they have greatly expanded the artist's possibilities for expression. The great diversity that results is also a product of the changing concepts of subject matter, approach, and role of the artist that have characterized art since the late 19th century (see Chapter 16), freeing it from many traditional restrictions. Yet does this diversity not also echo an ambiguity in our society? Artists, as in all periods, whatever materials they use, help us to understand our own time.

EXERCISES AND ACTIVITIES

1. Contrast Rembrandt's sketch for *The Night Watch* with the finished oil painting. How do you account for the differences in approaches between the two works?
2. Contrast any three drawing techniques in regard to the medium and the expressive opportunities each offers. Use specific examples of artworks to clarify your statements.
3. In the same way, compare any three painting techniques.
4. Since different drawing materials vary in flexibility, use several media, such as pencil, pen and ink, crayon, and poster paints, to create a full range of values from black to white. Arrange them in small squares in nine equal steps to determine the differences in effect and the difficulty of creating tone with some media.
5. Each drawing medium is capable of producing distinctive textures, which may be expressively manipulated by the artist. Divide a large sheet of drawing paper into rectangles. Find a texture in your environment that pleases you and try to copy it in pencil, crayon, ink, or paint. Using the same media, create new textures.
6. Colors make a direct appeal to the emotions and have come to be associated with various feelings. Select a black and white photograph or reproduction that conveys a specific mood to you. Using any medium, make a simple composition based on the photograph, using a color scheme that expresses the mood.
7. The color of a subject may be modified by the artist in many different ways in order to express a personal feeling or emotion. Set up a still life and draw it in simple outline form. Fill in the outlines, using any three contrasting colors at full intensity, widely separated on the color wheel. Repeat the same grouping in an analogous color scheme and note the difference in effect.
8. Create a mixed-media composition using a combination of at least three techniques and materials.

4 Printmaking

[When making a print] You are performing on a stage. You can be heavy, you can be light—an accent here, an accent there. What you do alone today, thousands of people will see tomorrow.

TATYANA GROSMAN

In our multimedia world we are bombarded daily with thousands of images—printed, photographic, and electronic. From the moment we open the morning mail to the last page we read before extinguishing the lights at bedtime, we have probably made our way past more printed images in a day than our ancestors faced in a lifetime. Messages, once written by hand before carbon copies, can today be duplicated almost endlessly by machine. Words and pictures are printed on countless packages, posters, soup cans, and magazines. Even works of art, once unique objects viewed by a handful, or reproduced in a limited number of original prints, can today through mechanized techniques be duplicated millions of times. Andy Warhol's use of repeated images of bottles of Coca Cola or the faces of Marilyn Monroe reflects our involvement with multiple images (Fig. 18). It makes sense to try to understand and differentiate among the kinds of printed images we see.

Though the dependency of our society upon the printed image is a recent phenomenon, the process of printing is ancient. **Printing** may be defined as transferring an inked image from a "master" surface to another surface, a method by which we can reproduce the same image many times. Printing has existed since the earliest days in Egypt, China, and India. A process that was first developed to repeat textile designs, printing was soon applied also to paper.

Papermaking

Early surfaces for writing were papyrus scrolls invented in Egypt, clay tablets produced in Mesopotamia, and vellum scrolls and sheets used in the West. All these were less convenient than scrolls and sheets of paper, made by the Chinese about A.D. 100. The Chinese adapted to paper-making the skills they had already developed in forming felt cloth. A hand-beaten mash of plant and rag fibers and water was put through a sieve, called a mold. As the water drained off, a sheet of vegetal felt was deposited in the mold. Such sheets, dried and sized with fish glue or soft rice paste to prevent fibers from absorbing ink, were translucent when held up to the light, like most modern book paper.

They were of two kinds. **Wove** paper, possibly so called from the cloth that covered the first molds, revealed virtually no pattern when held to the light. **Laid** paper was thick and thin as a result of fibers lodging unevenly in the strips and spaces of the bamboo grid that formed later molds. Against the light it revealed a pattern of closely spaced horizontal lines and widely spaced verticals corresponding to the structure of the grid. These basic differences in paper have been continued in the wove and laid papers of today. The tough, smooth, cheap sheets of paper produced by the Chinese provided ideal printing sufaces.

When papermaking spread from China to Spain by about 1150, European printers of cloth extended their skills to papermaking. Italians used animal glue for sizing and substituted water-powered hammers for hand beating. About 1300 they made the first watermarks, simple crosses pressed into the damp paper to identify the kind or the paper mill. Increased stocks of paper stimulated the use of printing, which in turn created a market for more paper. Eventually papermaking became a large-scale, mechanized industry.

In the 20th century, papermaking, like other skills lost since preindustrial times, has been restored as a handcraft that can reach the level of art. The artist Douglass Morse Howell (b. 1906) has dedicated a lifetime to papermaking and achieved a reputation that spans continents. His papers are works of art in themselves, and his workshop is a showplace of inventive art with paper (Fig. 88). Howell's work with other pioneers has spawned a new generation of papermakers such as Coco Gordon (b. 1938) who enjoy the challenge of working with textural, handmade papers. Many find the paper itself is their goal, without embellishment by printing.

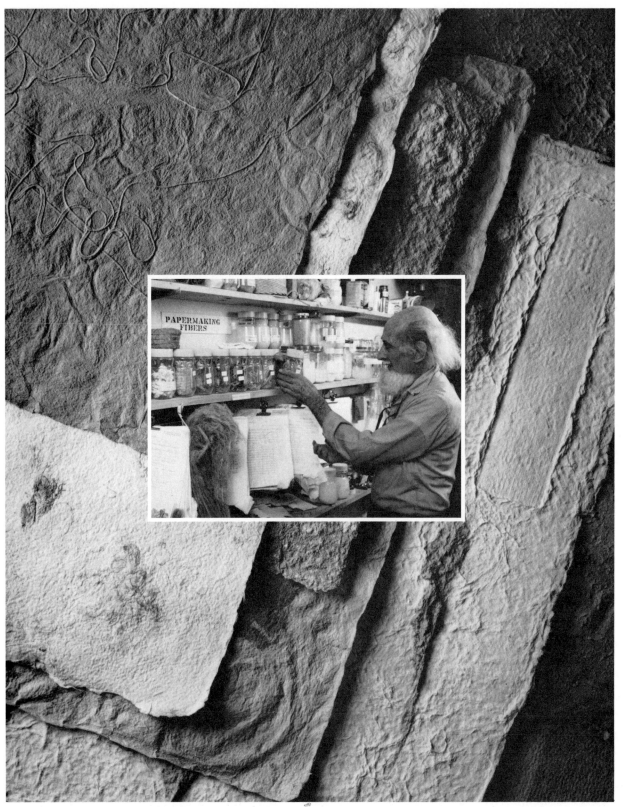

88. Papermaking. Flax and linen sheets.
Inset, Douglass Morse Howell in his Riverhead, N.Y., studio.

Printing Techniques

The ancestor of printing was the early practice of stamping carved seals in the form of clay cylinders or rings into damp clay. Babylonians stamped the names of their kings on bricks, and Roman wine dealers stamped their names on wine jars. The Chinese cut pictures and characters in relief on wood blocks, which they inked and stamped, or printed, first on fabric and then also on paper in multiple copies. Anticipating modern commerce, they used copper plates to print bank notes, which were provided with inserts for changing the denomination.

In 15th-century Europe, **woodcuts,** made from wood blocks carved in relief, were used to print religious souvenirs and cheap playing cards. As paper became generally available and printing with movable metal type spread from Germany through Europe, handwritten, hand-painted books gave way to printed books. Some of them were illustrated with woodcuts. At about the same time, engraving and copper etching developed. Playing cards for the wealthy were engraved, while princes commissioned painted and gilded one-of-a-kind masterpieces.

In succeeding centuries commercial printing techniques for mass production developed hand in hand with artistic printmaking. Artists quickly adapted commercial techniques for their own use. Many artists today, however, still use the traditional printing techniques, which commercial printers discarded long ago as too costly and slow. Some artists continue to print their own work, while others prefer to have their designs reproduced by master printers.

In the past an artist might devote a whole lifetime to mastering a single technique, such as aquatint. Today there is much cross-fertilization of ideas and techniques between artists and between artists and printers' workshops. Since the 1960s major artists such as Robert Rauschenberg and James Rosenquist have freely shared their printing innovations developed alone or in conjunction with workshops. Run by highly skilled and trained master printers, workshops provide techniques that few artists in isolation could ever hope to learn.

The Edition Since printmaking makes use of drawing skills, it is frequently difficult for the beginner to determine whether a particular work is a drawing, a print, or a photographic reproduction. However, a familiarity with some of the most common printing techniques used by artists may be helpful in identifying prints. As part of the printmaking process, single proofs, which are sample prints, are **pulled** (printed) at various stages, or states, to determine how the image—on the broad surface (sometimes called **flat-bed**) of the block, plate, or screen—is progressing (Fig. 89). When the image is finished to the artist's satisfaction, a series is run off called **artist's proofs.** A print labeled artist's proof is retained by the artist for personal record and comparison. After the inks are properly distributed on the printing surface to the artist's satisfaction, a **printer's print** is pulled and labeled *bon à tirer* ("good to pull"), the standard by which the edition is judged. The entire edition is numbered. For example, the figure 20/100 at the lower left of the print indicates that it is the twentieth print pulled in an edition of one hundred. The artist's signature in pencil verifies its authenticity and his or her approval of its quality. After completing the edition, the artist may deliberately deface the block, plate, or screen and pull a print called a **cancellation proof** to guarantee that the edition be limited.

Printmaking was originally intended to provide thousands of copies for a mass market. Today, as in the past, many painters also work in graphics to provide fine prints for those who cannot afford their paintings. They may limit their editions to fifty prints or less, each carefully signed and numbered.

Relief Printing The oldest method of reproducing images is relief printing. The most common print types are woodcuts, wood engravings, and linoleum cuts. The artist

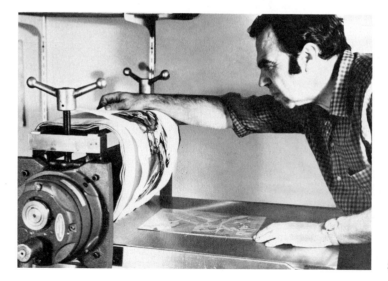

89. Stanley Kaplan at etcher's press.

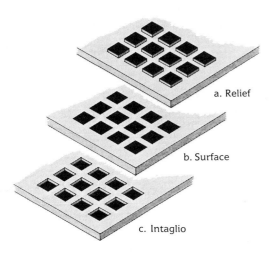

a. Relief

b. Surface

c. Intaglio

above: 90. Flat-bed printing processes.

below: 91. Katsushika Hokusai.
Fuji Seen from the Bottom of a Wave.
c. 1823–29. Color woodcut, 10 × 15″ (25 × 38 cm).
Metropolitan Museum of Art, New York
(Rogers Fund, 1914).

first transfers a design to a block. Then, using sharp gouges, he or she cuts away all unwanted areas of wood or linoleum, leaving elevated only the design area that is to be printed (Fig. 90a). Ink is then spread over the block and paper is laid upon it. The ink is transferred from the relief surface to the paper by means of pressure, usually by a press, producing a "mirrored" printed image of the original design. The technique is characterized by bold lines and strong tonal contrasts between the inked image and the paper.

In the Orient, woodcuts have been a significant art form for centuries, fulfilling a need for inexpensive art for those who could not afford hand-painted scrolls. Many Oriental woodcuts were printed with black outlines and were later colored by hand. Other woodcuts were produced by cutting a separate block for each color. Each block was carefully inked, registered over the image left by the preceding block, and printed.

The woodcut of Fuji (Fig. 91) is one of more than a hundred different views of the mountain executed by Hokusai (Katsushika Hokusai, 1760–1849). In this engaging print we scarcely perceive the tiny boats of fishermen seeking desperately to escape from the towering wave. The striking asymmetrical composition, in which the wave almost encircles the remote mountain peak, seems very different from the symmetrical work of Renaissance printmakers we have seen, such as Dürer.

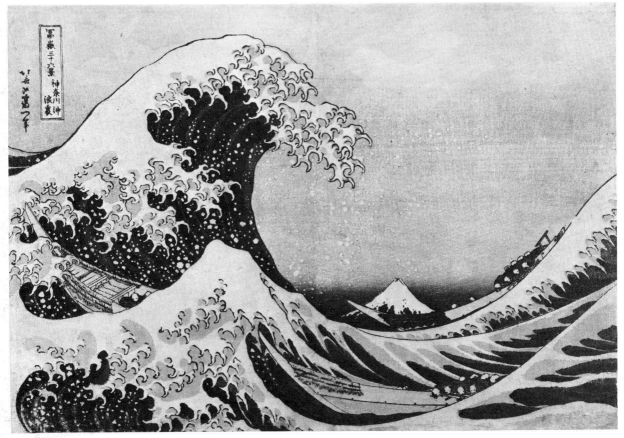

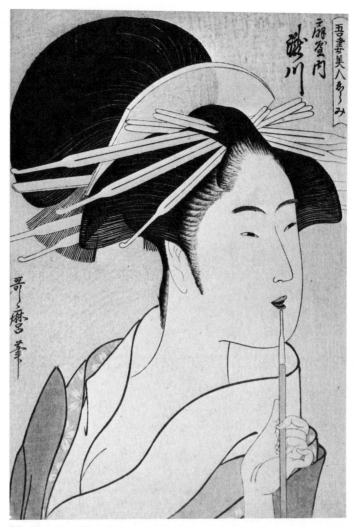

吾妻美人あ〜み

扇屋内
滝川

92. Kitagawa Utamaro. *A Bust Study of a Beautiful Girl.*
Ukiyoye School (1753–1806). Color woodblock,
13 × 8¾" (33 × 22 cm). Cleveland Museum of Art
(bequest of Edward L. Whittemore).

Japanese woodcuts reached Europe after Japan was opened to world trade in the 19th century, when they inspired Western artists in new directions. Hokusai along with Hiroshige (Utagawa Hiroshige, 1797–1858) and Utamaro (Kitagawa Utamaro, 1753–1806) (Fig. 92) were especially influential. As a result, many Western artists adapted Japanese asymmetry to their painting and some revived wood-block printing.

In Western Europe, woodcuts had been important in the 15th and 16th centuries, when religious pictures were printed in editions of thousands and sold at popular prices. People believed that because of their holy subjects the woodcuts would protect the purchaser from sickness. Similarly, cheap religious pictures have been sold in vast numbers at the shrines of the Virgin Mary at Lourdes, France, since 1858 and at Fátima, Portugal, since 1917.

Woodcut *taroc,* or *tarocci,* playing cards were widely popular. These ancestors of today's playing cards and of Tarot cards, associated by some with fortunetelling and esoteric cults, came in standard packs of 62, 78, or 97. Venetian sets copied the four Islamic suits of cup, coin, sword, and polo stick. Twenty of Dürer's pen-and-ink drawings of taroc cards, copied from a set in the Venetian style of 1462, still exist.

One of the most remarkable examples of Renaissance woodcuts is the mammoth *The Triumphal Arch of the Emperor Maximilian* (Fig. 93) by Dürer. Including the beautifully lettered explanation at the bottom, it measures about 11½ by 9¾ feet (3.5 by 2.97 meters) and is reputed to be the largest print ever commissioned before the 20th century. The work was printed from 192 separate blocks and required four separate printing shops and more than two years to complete. The **iconography,** or meaning, of the images of this fantastic design involves many means of glorification, from the simple recording of historical events to cryptic emblematic allusions. The structure can be read like a book or decoded like a cryptogram. Yet, at the same, it can be enjoyed like a collection of quaint and brilliant jewelry. The fine detail was possible because the design was probably cut on closely textured wood, such as cherry. The work is also remarkable in that the entire configuration is a product of Dürer's imagination. For the scenic representations he furnished slight sketches and supervised their execution by others. When the work of his assistants left too much to be desired, he supplied actual working drawings. When motifs had to be repeated symmetrically, he

93. Albrecht Dürer. *The Triumphal Arch of Maximilian I.* 1515–17. Woodcut (192 blocks), c. 10′ × 9′4″ (c. 3.05 × 2.85 m) without inscription. National Library of Austria, Vienna.

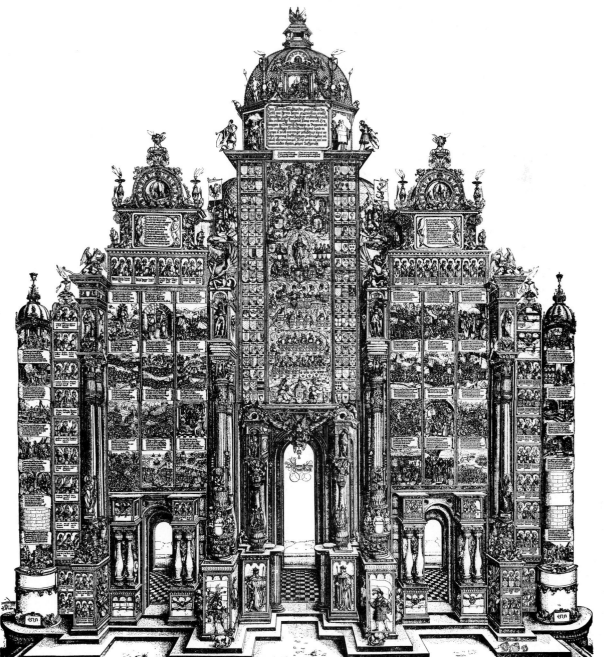

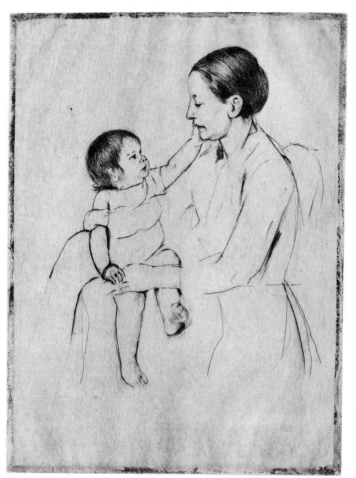

94. Mary Cassatt. *The Caress.*
1891. Drypoint, 7¹¹⁄₁₆ × 5¾″
(20 × 15 cm). Metropolitan
Museum of Art, New York (Gift
of Arthur Sachs, 1916).

furnished only the designs for half of the woodcut, leaving it to his assistants to reverse them, change minor details, and, of course, the lighting, accordingly.

Woodcuts were commercially discarded in the West in favor of copper and steel engravings, but they continued to be used in cheap books and to illustrate political handbills, particularly during the French Revolution in the 18th century and the Mexican Revolution in the 20th. Woodcut was revived in the late 19th century as a result of Japanese influence and continues to be used by today's artists.

Intaglio Printing The opposite of relief printing is **intaglio** printing, a term derived from the Italian word meaning "to cut in." In the intaglio processes of etching and engraving, the ink is forced into grooves in a metal plate with a felt-covered dauber (Fig. 90b) so that it lies below the surface. When damp paper is pressed onto the plate by a press, it picks up ink from the grooves, in contrast to woodcut, where the ink lies on the wood that has been left raised.

The differences between etching and engraving lie in the different means used to cut the image into the metal

plate. In **etching,** the plate is first coated with a waxy, acid-resistant substance, called a **ground.** The artist draws an image on the coated plate by scratching through the ground with a fine needle. When the plate is placed in an acid bath, the acid cannot reach the metal where it is covered, but along the lines where the ground has been removed it can bite, or etch, them into the bare metal. The remaining ground is then removed, the plate is inked and wiped off, leaving ink in the grooves, the paper is positioned, and the print is pulled from the plate. In **engraving,** the grooves in the plate are made by digging directly into the metal with special tools. Lines are rarely as fine as those achieved by etching, but they are sharper and clearer.

In both etching and engraving, the artist builds up areas of darks by placing many lines close together. In both processes, the ink is lifted out of the grooves by the pressure of the press, forcing the ink to stand out on the surface of the paper. The ink can be felt as a raised edge when you run your finger over it. These processes yield sharply defined images. In other methods called **mezzotint** and **aquatint,** large areas of the plate can be roughened so that the ink adheres to a whole area and is printed as a flat tone. In the drypoint etching *The Caress* (Fig. 94) by Mary Cassatt

(1845–1926), both line and aquatint are combined to create dramatic images marked by intense light and shade. Compare this work with Hogarth's engraving from *The Rake's Progress* (Fig. 24), which reveals infinite gradations and clarity in all details. Although both prints demonstrate careful draughtsmanship and love of detail, the etching is far softer and is well suited to Cassatt's preoccupation with the intimate theme of mother and child.

Engraving on copper in the 1500s was first developed as a popular commercial method and was later used for illustration by artists such as Dürer. One of the most prolific printmakers of all time, Dürer produced more than one hundred engravings, etchings, and drypoints and more than three hundred woodcuts. Editions of thousands of his prints were not uncommon. Much finer detail is possible in the engraving process then in the woodcut, which probably accounts for its popularity. Later, engravings were used for reproductions of artworks. Steel engravings of sentimental scenes were popular in Victorian homes. Few artists today, however, are as concerned with the sharp detail achieved by engraving; most, like Stanley Kaplan (b. 1925), prefer the versatility of etching (Fig. 89). Many artists, past and present, from Henri Matisse (1869–1954) and Picasso to Kaplan, have illustrated books with etchings, and all have produced limited editions of individual etchings. Using an individual approach to etching, Katinka Mann (b. 1925) has created a work of classic beauty, combining an uninked embossed image with several related motifs successively printed. Negative and positive spaces are critically interrelated in her design (Fig. 95).

Surface Printing The third printing process is planographic, or surface, printing. **Lithography** is a planographic process that depends upon the natural antipathy of oil or grease to water for the transfer of ink to paper. Limestone slabs or sensitized metal plates are used as drawing surfaces (Fig. 90c). The artist draws with greasy lithographic crayon or with a special ink called **tusche.** Next a nitric acid solution is applied to the stone or plate to make the sections that have not been drawn upon resistant to the ink. The stone is kept wet with water during the entire printing process. The greasy ink adheres only to the crayon image and is repelled by the wet areas of the stone. When the stone and paper are run through a press, the paper picks up the ink from the drawn image, reproducing the artist's work. If the stone is not kept wet, the paper will be printed solid black, as any printmaker quickly learns.

The direct drawing methods in lithography allow the artist considerable spontaneity and variety. Drawing crayons are made in varying degrees of hardness, and when stroked onto the grainy surface of the stone, they can create tones ranging from soft grays to rich, heavy darks. Crayons can be held on their edges to produce large areas of gray, while details can be drawn in with a pointed crayon or a pen dipped in tusche. In color lithography, as in color woodcuts, each color requires a separate drawing, which is printed in sequence on the one sheet faithfully following registration marks.

The lithograph by Edvard Munch (1863–1944) is one of a series on a single theme, which occupied him on and off for much of his life. The anguish of the abandoned central

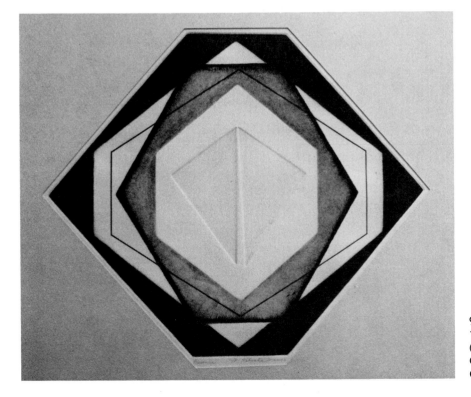

95. Katinka Mann. *Presence.* 1969. Etching, 23 × 26″ (58 × 66 cm). Nassau Community College, Garden City, N.Y.

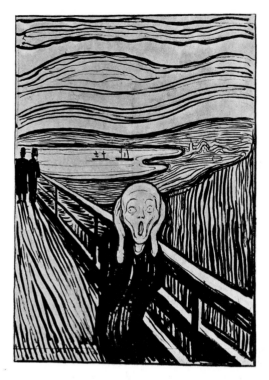

above: 96. Edvard Munch. *The Scream.*
1893. Lithograph on red paper, 14 × 10″
(36 × 25 cm). Museum of Fine Arts,
Boston (William Francis Warden Fund).

right: 97. Alan Cober. *The Forgotten Society.*
Ink, 9 × 7″ (23 × 18 cm).
Collection the artist.

figure is echoed by the land, sea, and sky, graphically demonstrated by the heavy, strident lines. The bridge on which the figures stand represents the passage of time—the human lifespan expressed with existential gloom (Fig. 96).

When lithography was invented in the 1800s, the technique became immediately popular for illustrations in newspapers and magazines since it is certainly easier to draw with crayons on a stone slab than to engrave lines into a metal plate. Honoré Daumier (1808–1879), for example, used the lithographic process on stone regularly for political and social comments. Daumier's drawings carry on the social caricatures of Goya and presage political and social works by Käthe Kollwitz (1867–1945), George Grosz (1893–1959), and Otto Dix (1891–1969), influenced by German Expressionism. For today's socially depressed, Alan Cober (b. 1935) has achieved widespread recognition with his illustrations of unforgettable pathos (Fig. 97). Cober works with most graphic media, but this drawing, the cover illustration from his book *The Forgotten Society,*

is reproduced, like our other illustrations, by mass printing methods.

A legend even in his own time, Henri de Toulouse-Lautrec (1864–1901) evolved from an illustrator (of horses) to perhaps the most trenchant satirist of the café scene. His lithograph of Jane Avril (Fig. 98) demonstrates graphic clarity, influenced by the late 19th-century exposure to the linear quality of Japanese prints, which avoid most illusions of depth provided by linear perspective (Fig. 92). His forms are flattened, the viewpoint is unusual, and the memorable imagery is designed to be quickly seen and understood, for posters are rarely given long study. The lines are economically drawn, revealing the skill of an artist who successfully produced single paintings as well as multiple works for an unlimited audience.

In our own time, a few artists maintain some involvement with both business and fine arts. The design for Lincoln Center by Frank Stella (b. 1936) was an award-winning poster (Fig. 99), yet it is clearly tied to his *Agbatana I*

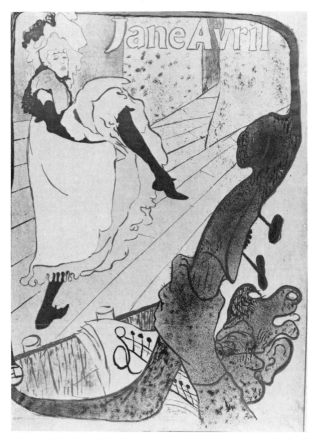

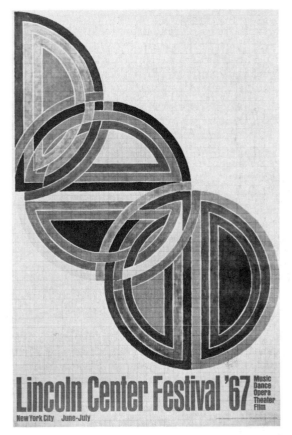

above: 98. Henri de Toulouse-Lautrec. *Jane Avril, Jardin de Paris.*
c. 1893. Lithograph, 4'2¾" × 3'⅝" (1.3 × 0.94 m).
Musée Toulouse-Lautrec, Albi, France.

above right: 99. Frank Stella. *Lincoln Center Festival '67.* 1967.
Offset lithography poster, 44¾ × 29½" (114 × 75 cm).
Museum of Modern Art, New York (gift of List Art Posters).

created the following year (Fig. 377). A very different orientation to design can be seen in the lithographs of M. C. Escher. His highly imaginative works, which border on the surrealistic, also demonstrate a delight in detail and an eye for illusions of perspective. In *Drawing Hands* (Fig. 5) we find a new dimension created through the physical and optical impossibilities which he has created.

Many artists print their own lithographs. Some alter the initial images as early proofs suggest, while others draw the image clearly at the start and maintain their original concept from beginning to end. As with other forms of printmaking, many artists relinquish their works to master printers, whom they carefully supervise.

Serigraphy is a planographic process that uses a stencil placed on a screen of fine silk. The term is the fine-arts equivalent for the 20th-century commercial printing process called **silkscreen.** Many contemporary artists adopt serigraphy because it permits more variations in the material to be printed on than other printing processes. Used com-

mercially, silkscreen can print images onto soft fabrics such as T-shirts or hard surfaces such as glasses, yielding almost unlimited possibilities. Used for fine art, silkscreen can produce prints (serigraphs) that incorporate complex images in multiple colors, which are particularly effective in large, flat areas on posters. Silkscreen, however, can also be used to achieve rich, subtle colors and varying textures.

The artist cuts a stencil from a special film, which is then fixed to the screen of silk stretched on a frame. Alternatively, the stencil may be painted directly onto the silk with glue. The stencil prevents the paint from seeping through the screen onto the paper beneath. Thus any area not covered by the stencil is printed. If the stencil is brushed on with glue, a loose, free-flowing image can result. With a firm stencil, the images are hard and sharp. The paint, which can be thick and opaque or thin and transparent, is dragged across the silk with a wide rubber squeegee and directly transmitted through to the paper. To produce multiple-color prints, the artist uses several stencils, printing each separately one over the other. The colors may be adjacent or built up in transparent layers, depending on the stencils.

Mixed Media   Prints, like paintings, can make use of mixed media. Collages made of various materials glued onto metal or wooden panels can be inked and run through a press to produce unusual textures. This new and freer way of printing is called **collography.** The potential for this technique has barely been approached and is limited only by the inventiveness of the artist. Collography can be combined with other printing methods. To achieve varied effects, prints can be given raised surfaces by printing damp papers under strong pressure onto carved wooden blocks to which textured materials such as metal scraps, screening, or heavy twine have been glued. Silkscreen and lithography have been used to print flat cutouts, many complete with slots and tabs, which can later be assembled into three-dimensional objects. Thus, the artist, instead of trying to produce an illusion of solidity through the flat image of a print, may create a printed image that will become a three-dimensional object itself.

Coco Gordon, a contemporary artist-poet who also produces her own paper, concentrates upon wit as well as the aesthetic in her work. Many of her pieces move through two- and three-dimensional space concurrently, while others are intellectual exercises, as significant for their creative concept as for the lasting work that is produced (Fig. 100). Photoprinting and other techniques have revolutionized printmaking in the second half of the 20th century. Artists are working in ways that make classification of their art impossible. For example, photographs printed on cloth may be cut out, sewn, and stuffed, becoming sculptural forms, while prints on styrofoam produce three-dimensional objects.

Many artists of the 1960s and 1970s have experimented with traditional processes and have frequently combined mass media shortcuts. For instance, Robert Rauschenberg has taken fresh newspapers and selectively transferred portions of the inked surfaces onto plates and stones. With those transfers he may combine other direct means, such as painting, to create works of fine art that are also in touch with today's mass communication processes.

Printmaking, even more than the other visual arts, is characterized by almost unlimited experimentation. A host of new processes such as photolithography, collotype, photogram collage, nonsilver photosensitive printmaking, the gum print, blueprinting, the cyanotype process, the kallitype process, GAF template, photogravure, optical and transparent imagery, Xerography, and computer art create an atmosphere of experiment and great vitality. The photomechanical processes that developed from the 1840s to the 1880s have deeply affected printmaking in the 20th century, particularly with the advent and involvement of photography. Therefore, art with the lens is the basis of our next group of studies. Where the new vision will lead, no one knows, but clearly, art will be changed radically.

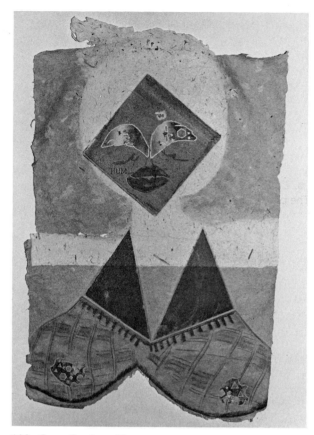

100. Coco Gordon. *Hum.*
1979. Collograph, etching,
and electric engraving on plexiglas (face),
soft-ground and brushed aquatint (collar),
on own method two-pulp linen handmade
shaped paper; 12 × 18″ (31 × 46 cm).
Collection the author.

Print Workshops

The atmosphere of today's print workshops with their invigorating smells of turpentine and ink is probably not much different from that in Renaissance shops like Dürer's. There exists today an unprecedented interest in the print process in busy art centers all over the world. A shift has occurred, away from the traditional notion of a solitary individual plying his or her craft to a community where insights and skills are shared. The practice approaches the ideal of William Morris (1834–1896) and others a century ago, when their fears for the loss of craftsmanship in an industrial age led them to encourage artists to unite skills in common interests. Print workshops are flourishing. Master printers' studios are visited by artists, who are comfortable in experimenting with new techniques and larger sizes not seen since Dürer's *The Triumphal Arch.* In the United States major artists on both coasts have taken to the printmakers' craft. The following list, though incomplete, suggests how good workshops have proliferated.

A pioneer in the workshop movement is Tatyana Grosman (1904–1982), a spiritual catalyst to many of the great artists of our time. The quotation that opens this chapter and the following remarks are based upon the author's meeting with Mrs. Grosman in West Islip, New York, in the spring of 1980. Recognizing the fine surfaces for lithography in limestone slabs no longer used in construction on their property, she and her husband, Maurice, a painter and sculptor, set up a workshop for printing on stone in limited editions. With registration of their logo, Universal Limited Art Editions, by 1956, the atelier was born. Younger artists were invited to share the facilities. The philosophy of the workshop went far beyond merely furnishing the necessary tools and presses. Work with stone was to be a revelation. Their first undertaking was with Robert Blackburn (b. 1920), an early apprentice chosen to print a work produced by a pioneering partnership (Fig. 101) of a painter, Larry Rivers (b. 1923), and a poet, Frank O'Hara. As creative novices to printing on stone they even incorporated the outlined edge of the limestone slab into their design—a practice never considered by traditional printmakers, but which made their work a unique blend of art, literature, and graphic experiment.

Everything was visual. Mrs. Grosman's personal philosophy of "glorifying existence" by inspiring artists "to do something extraordinary" brought to her door such figures as Robert Rauschenberg, Jasper Johns (b. 1930), Alex Liberman (b. 1912), Barnett Newman (1905–1970), Lee Bontecou, and Helen Frankenthaler. She established a personal level of communication with every artist, encouraging them all each time to surpass their previous work, yet allowing artists private use of the premises and the master printers. Every print is made by hand and strives to capture the spirit as expressed in the artist's design drawn the day before. There is little doubt why some artists work best with particular printers in such a milieu.

The first master print shops on the West Coast were Gemini G.E.L. and Tamarind Lithography Workshop, founded by June Wayne (b. 1918). These and subsequent master print shops provided facilities for famous artists of the 1960s. Wayne's skilled technicians created a whole new chemistry. The prints that emerged were often of a size, complexity, and degree of innovation that craftspeople with limited financial means could never otherwise have achieved.

The impetus for these American workshops doubtlessly came from the English artist Stanley William Hayter (b. 1901), who in the 1930s established Atelier 17 in Paris as a center of experimental printmaking. In the 1940s during World War II Hayter took his ideas to New York, providing inspiration to American artists. In 1968, Michael Ponce de Leon (b. 1922), using many of Howell's papers, created high-relief prints. Bongtae Kim (b. 1937) at Triad Workshop in Los Angeles is pushing these concepts still further.

As a result of such workshops all over the United States a Renaissance in printmaking has occurred. It was brought about not, as might have been expected, through the efforts of printmakers or their students, but through the finished works, which inspired a broad public. The importance of what is going on in the graphic arts, particularly in these print shops, which aim not for mass output but for creative production, is bound to be a major influence on art for many years to come.

EXERCISES AND ACTIVITIES

1. Trace the origins of paper, distinguishing between "wove" and "laid."
2. Why is handmade paper important to many printmakers today?
3. Each category of printing—woodcut, etching, engraving, stencil, lithograph, or collograph—offers a different potential for creative expression. Explain the differences between these types of printing. How does engraving differ from etching both in method and final effect?
4. Select from the prints reproduced in this book three works that appeal to you and explain your reasons for choosing them.
5. Design your own monogram and transfer it to a printing surface from which you can make a relief image. Use linoleum, styrofoam, or even a potato as a printing surface, being careful to cut a "mirrored" image so that the printed monogram can be read.
6. Design your own note cards, using a relief process. Do not concentrate on lines but focus instead on flat areas, which are easier to carve and then to print.

101. John O'Hara and Larry Rivers working on *Stones* in Larry Rivers' studio. 1958.

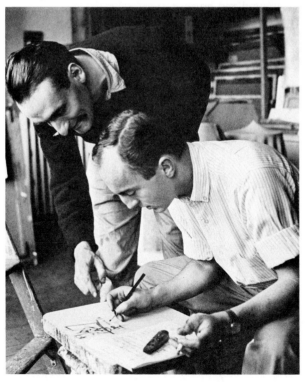

5 Arts of the Lens

*The medium, or process, of our time—electric tech-
nology—is reshaping and restructuring patterns of
social interdependence and every aspect of our personal life. . . . Everything is changing—you, your
family, your neighborhood, your education, your job,
your government, your relation to "the others." And
they're changing dramatically.*

MARSHALL MCLUHAN, *The Medium Is the Massage*

The camera lens, through its use in the media, in still photography, films, and television, has shaped our lives in the
20th century perhaps more than any other single invention. Through the photographic image we have all been
exposed to people, places, and ideas that we would never
otherwise have witnessed. Much of our understanding of
the world in which we live comes to us through the lens. In
fact, we are so completely surrounded and seduced by
photographic images that few will question the Canadian
writer Marshall McLuhan's view that "the medium is the
massage."

In this chapter, we shall explore how the camera lens
records images on film as well as how it transmits images
to the television tube. The aesthetic considerations that relate to still photography and film apply as well to the electronic medium of television, which for many people is the
dominant visual art of our time.

Photography is both a complex science and a new art
form. As a science it depends on laws of physics involving
the passage of light through a lens. Light transfers the
image "seen" by the lens onto sensitized film, and this
image is then made visible and permanent by chemical
action.

The photographic image is a product of scientific laws,
but it can also be a work of art whose impact is limited only
by the creativity and imagination of the photographer.
Though it is true that a camera more or less accurately
records what it is focused upon, the same subject can be
interpreted in as many varied ways as the many visions of
each photographer. Like all other artists, the photographer
chooses what to portray, how to emphasize or eliminate

various aspects, and what viewpoint would be most expressive. The unusual vantage point of Bill Brandt (b. 1905)
transformed conventional perspective and an unlikely
combination of a nude on a rocky beach into an arresting
image (Fig. 102).

Without a doubt, the photographer's creativity is able to
transform mere mechanical aspects of photography into
fine art, separating the snapshot and the mass of conventional photographs that surround us from the truly expres-

102. Bill Brandt.
East Sussex Coast.
1953. Photograph.

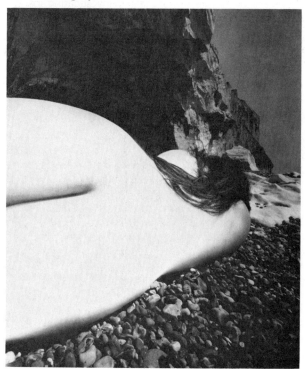

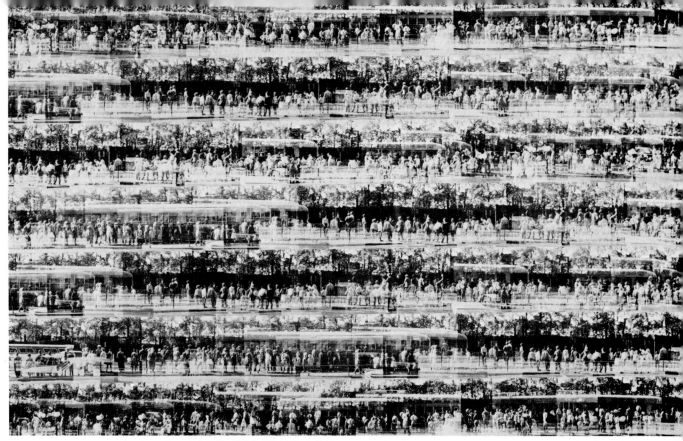

103. Ray K. Metzker. *Trolley Stop,* detail. 1966. Photograph; gelatin-silver print, work in its entirety 40½ × 35" (103 × 89 cm). Museum of Modern Art, New York (purchase).

sive photographic image. Photography is also a useful research tool for the scientist engaged in investigating space, subterranean depths, or the life of microscopic organisms. In addition, photography can act as official recorder, documenting the events, people, and places of history as history is made.

Still Photography

In still photography, the camera assures the photographer some success by assuming part of the process of recording the subject. The ease with which we can trip a camera shutter may make photography seem like a push-button art. With luck, we can expect some positive results almost from the start; but for a photographer to be able to exploit the creative potentials of photography, considerable knowledge and expertise are required. Even vast technical knowledge, however, cannot guarantee masterpieces. A work of art in photography, as in all other art forms, is the result of a combination of its creator's personal vision, technical skill, and ability to express meaning in visual images. For most photographers, a double exposure means a wasted opportunity to record two events. Not so for Ray Metzker (b. 1931) in her creative interpretation of a trolley stop (Fig. 103). Her many stills, some recording movement

and overlap of images, have produced a memorable configuration that few of us would have imagined was possible.

The principle of the camera dates at least as far back as Renaissance Italy, when artistic preoccupation with the creation of an illusion of depth on a flat surface led to the development of a device called *camera obscura,* literally "dark room." By reproducing exactly the scenes they wished to portray, artists were helped in rendering three dimensions on a two-dimensional surface. As Leonardo da Vinci described the principle, "Light entering a tiny opening in one wall of a darkened room forms an inverted image of the outside scene on the opposite wall." This view could be traced to provide the correct representation for a painting. Later, artists found that if a lens replaced the pinhole opening, a clearer image could be produced.

It was not until the 19th century, however, that a way was found to capture an image on a sensitized surface. Though Thomas Wedgewood (1730–1795) in England had earlier been able to create impermanent solar pictures, the first *fixed* camera image was probably originated by Joseph Nicephore Niepce (1805–1870) in France in 1826, and almost concurrently by Louis Jacques Mandé Daguerre (1789–1851) as well. By 1837 Daguerre had made a detailed picture of the corner of his studio using a modification of Niepce's invention. Daguerre's pioneering

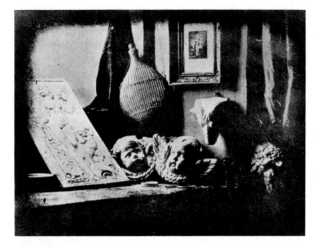

left: 104. Louis Jacques Mandé Daguerre.
The Artist's Studio. 1837. Daguerreotype.
Société Française de Photographie, Paris.

below: 105. Timothy O'Sullivan.
A Harvest of Death, Gettysburg. 1863.
Photograph. New York Public Library,
Rare Books Collection.

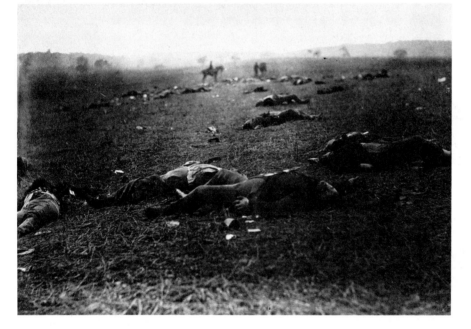

photograph is outstanding still in its artful composition, which demonstrates depth along with a range of textures (Fig. 104).

As the technique of photography improved and permanent images of people and places could be made more easily, many painters decided that their primary role in society—seen as recorders of people, places, or events—had been supplanted by the camera. Photographers began to use the new invention to duplicate art. Early creative photographers worked largely on portraiture. Despite the limitations imposed by the lengthy sittings required to illuminate slow photographic emulsions, and the delimitation of imitating painterly conventions, they produced some remarkable photographs through expressive use of pose, lighting, background, and point of view. For example, in Nadar's pensive and poetic portrait of Sarah Bernhardt (Fig. 43) much more than the actress's physical beauty is

captured. A broad range of tones, from black through grays to white, appears in the draperies, engaging our attention. After scanning the draperies, however, we return with renewed interest to the intense personality revealed in the face.

Through the technical experiments made by photographers in the mid-19th century, the picture-taking process was shortened, making it possible for photographers to record the horrors of war, which Mathew Brady (1823–1896) and Timothy O'Sullivan (1840–1882) (Fig. 105) did with great expressive power. While photographers were learning how to create photographs that resembled paintings, painters were eagerly looking for ways to work that they were convinced cameras could never duplicate. By the 1860s, French artists were experimenting with changing light and atmosphere in a style the world was soon to label Impressionism. Not much later, however, the camera,

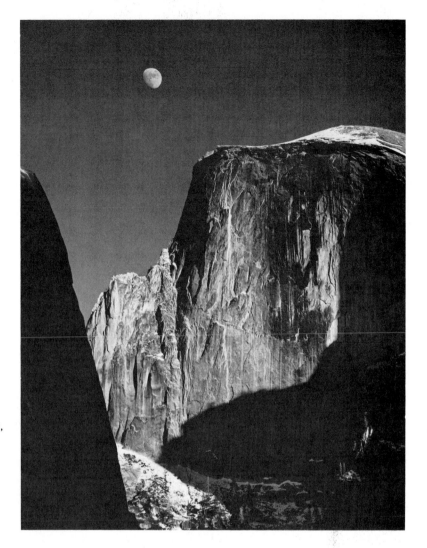

below: 106. Alfred Stieglitz.
The Terminal. 1893.
Photograph.
International Museum of Photography,
George Eastman House,
Rochester, N.Y.

right: 107. Ansel Adams.
Moon and Half Dome,
Yosemite National Park, Calif. 1960.
Photograph. © Ansel Adams
Publishing Rights Trust.

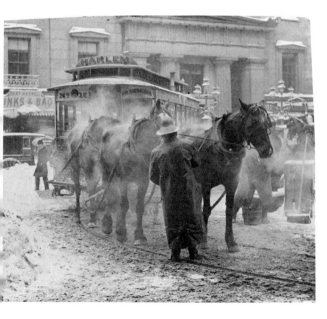

in the hands of the American Alfred Stieglitz (1864–1946), was just as successful in capturing steam and smoke in a nostalgic view of a wintry Harlem trolley scene called *The Terminal* (Fig. 106). By choosing a camera angle that leads the trolley tracks in a diagonal path into the photograph, Stieglitz produced an illusion of depth that focuses attention on both the trolley and the steam in the air.

By the end of the 19th century, photographers became less concerned with imitating painting than with allowing photography to emerge as a new field of art. American photographers such as Edward Steichen (1879–1973), Paul Strand (1890–1976), and Edward Weston (1886–1958) never viewed photographs as duplications of realistic paintings. Instead, they discovered that photography could present more expressive views of commonplace scenes. For example, Ansel Adams (b. 1902), brilliantly demonstrated the artistic potential of photography in his prints, which hint at infinity, deeply extending the range of black and white tones. His *Moon and Half-Dome, Yosemite National Park* (Fig. 107) captures a mysterious feeling of vast,

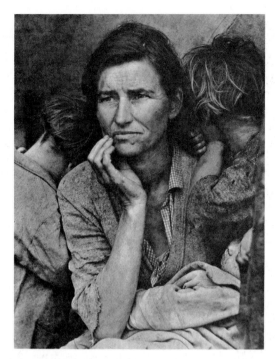

108. Dorothea Lange.
Migrant Mother, Nipomo, California, 1936.
Photograph. Museum of Modern Art,
New York (purchase).

yet confined space, illuminated by the moon, hanging in an empty sky, while black, shadowy foreground masses effectively frame and complement the textured stone cliffs.

By applying such standards of creativity, photographers extended Brady's use of the camera to document history. Dorothea Lange (1895–1966) recorded the desperate futility of a migrant farm worker in the Depression of the 1930s with a portrait that has since become a classic (Fig. 108). Her field notes describe the hopeless mother: "Camped on the edge of a pea field where the crop has failed in a freeze, the tires had just been sold from the car to buy food. She was 32 years old with seven children."

Later, Berenice Abbott and others earned international reputations as documentary photographers who creatively interpreted the events, people, and places of the world around them. The news photo has now become an important part of our lives through its ability to capture a moment of history as well as to express visually what is often inexpressible in words.

Independent of photography, innovators have explored ways to capture images through noncamera techniques. Shadow pictures called **photograms** or **rayographs** are made by placing an object on a light-sensitive material and exposing it to light. Color photograms can be made in the same way, using, in addition, color-filter modulators. Other, more specialized noncamera techniques include **holography** and **solarization.**

Basic photographic equipment consists of a camera with a lens, shutter, and diaphragm openings; films and plates; filters to control or alter lighting; papers on which the image is printed; and the chemicals needed to process the film.

Still Cameras The camera is surprisingly like the human eye, based on similar principles that enable the human eye to transmit images to the brain.

A simple box camera has a fixed lens and a nonadjustable aperture, or opening, which admits light rays. The rays are then focused on light-sensitized film at the back of the camera. The viewfinder allows the photographer to see what the final image will be. Early photographers used bulky cameras and composed their pictures through large viewfinders, which reproduced images the same size as the intended photographic print. Later the development of more sophisticated, portable cameras allowed pictures to be taken almost anywhere. The "candid" photography that resulted revolutionized the medium.

Many cameras today can be fitted with alternate lenses of different focal lengths for near, far, or detailed subjects. Some are equipped with photoelectric cells that can control the intake of light and change the shutter speed automatically. There are even some cameras capable of processing the film and producing photographs in a matter of seconds. The most complex cameras can be operated by remote control. They are designed to probe unknown areas when used in conjunction with scientific instruments such as telescopes and microscopes.

The lens components are the most valuable part of a camera. Although even a pinhole will produce an image, a good lens concentrates the light rapidly, admitting more light in less time so that even dim, moving objects can be photographed. Telephoto lenses permit detailed views of distant objects by magnifying them, while wide-angle lenses enable the photographer to focus on broad subjects in close range. Fish-eye lenses are an extreme form of

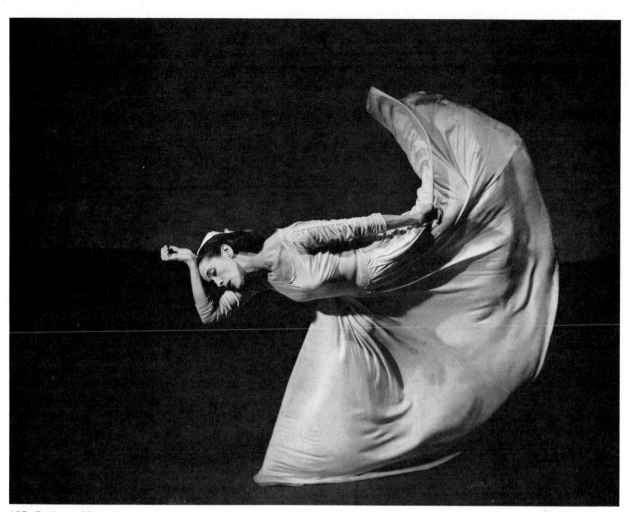

109. Barbara Morgan.
Martha Graham: "Letter to the World" (Kick).
1940. Photograph.

wide-angle lenses, which distort subjects by magnifying only the central portion of the total image.

Other important parts of a camera are the shutters and diaphragms, which control the size and speed of the camera aperture at the moment of exposure. Inexpensive, nonadjustable cameras have only one aperture size and one shutter speed. The size of the opening and the length of time the shutter is open regulate the amount of light reflected from the subject onto the unexposed film. Different lenses, focal lengths, shutter speeds, and so on, provide flexibility. With the more refined cameras, shutter speeds can range from a 2000th of a second to unlimited time exposures. The size of the aperture opening is indicated by the F-stop numbers on the lens control—the larger the F-stop, the smaller the opening.

Film Black and white film is formed from an emulsion of light-sensitized crystals (silver-halide particles) embedded in gelatin and laid upon a transparent film backing. After exposure to light and processing, the light-sensitized crystals reverse to form the negative from which positive prints can be made.

Black and white films vary in their sensitivity to dark and light values; certain films will produce stronger contrasts than others. Film speeds also vary, and the photographer must know which film to select for a particular subject and set of conditions. Moving objects must be recorded at rapid shutter speeds to stop the action and avoid blur; they require, therefore, films that are highly sensitive to light and are fast-acting. To convey the essential quality of a dance, Barbara Morgan (b. 1900) chose the full figure of Martha Graham. The merest suggestion of blur at the hemline and the arresting pose capture in a fraction of a second the emotional thrust of the entire dance sequence (Fig. 109).

Color films vary according to whether they are to be used in daylight or under artificial illumination. Some produce images that are made into color transparencies (slides); others produce color prints. Large photographic prints—whether black and white or color—are desirable for advertising or photojournalistic purposes where corrective photo retouching to clarify detail for reproduction is often necessary. As in black and white photography, the type of film selected is critical to the production of the final image.

Processing and Printing Though the processing of black and white film is not nearly as complicated as color film processing, it is not a simple procedure. Invisible chemical changes take place when light rays fall on the emulsion surface of black and white film. These rays create visual images when the film is put into an alkaline developing solution. The processed negative that results is next rinsed in an acid stop bath, which prevents further development; then it is permanently fixed in a hypo-alum solution. The more complex procedure involved in developing color films requires highly controlled conditions for both color transparencies and prints. Because film is sensitive to light, heat, and chemicals, photographic developing processes must take place in the controlled conditions of the darkroom, utilizing appropriate color filters.

The printing process requires exposure of photosensitive paper to light that is passed through a negative under darkroom conditions. Contact prints are made the same size as the negative by placing negatives and contact paper together—emulsion side of negative in contact with emulsion side of paper—and exposing both to light. Enlargements of photographs are made by projecting light through the negative and the lens of an enlarger onto sensitized enlarging paper. The distance from the lens to the printing paper controls the size of the enlargement. As in film developing, the invisible images printed on the paper must then undergo the same three baths—developer, stop, and hypo-fixative—in order to be made permanently visible.

During the enlargement process the original image may be changed and refined. For instance, by using different kinds of papers the texture or value contrasts can be increased or diminished. The negative may also be masked in order to emphasize certain parts in the final print. The image may also be darkened or lightened, or parts may even be blocked out altogether. Portions of negatives may be combined into a **montage** by exposing various sections on the same enlargement. The print itself may be trimmed to change the composition.

The variety of technical procedures available to the photographer through the camera and local controls in the darkroom allows experiment, resulting in a wide range of unusual possibilities, which may increase the expressiveness of the final print. When familiar subjects such as flowers and leaves are photographed in heroic terms, oversized and isolated from their botanical context, they can be explored for their design and structure. The magnolia (Fig. 110) reveals a gently expressed sensuous quality. By cropping her negative and focusing on the graceful curves of the petals, Imogen Cunningham (1883–1976) brings the viewer into her photograph. Light is diffused through the petals as well as on them so that they become luminous with delicate tones of gray. Such fine variations in tonality are usually rendered best with slower films. A few photographers still insist upon the purity of their original unaltered negatives, but their kind of restraint is rare today.

There can be no question that still photography has fundamentally changed our concepts of the world around us. Certainly, photography has influenced other art forms, particularly painting. And perhaps, even more important, the exploitation of still photography led to the development of the motion picture.

Cinematography

Movement is inherent in all living organisms and has always fascinated people. It is not surprising, then, that the question of how to express motion has concerned artists from the Stone Age to Duchamp and the Futurists early in the 20th century (Fig. 63) to the most advanced filmmaker today. Our delight in the pattern of splashed milk formed by a dropping ball reveals a continued preoccupation with simple movement (Fig. 111). The invention of the motion picture camera, which made possible the magic of cinema, has resulted in one of the most important and powerful forms of contemporary art.

The earliest noteworthy experiments in depicting motion through photography were those of Eadweard Muybridge in California. Setting up 24 cameras to capture successive views of a horse in motion, Muybridge in 1878 confirmed the theory that in active movement all four hoofs of a horse leave the ground, as can be seen in Figure 61. Those sequential photographs led to his invention of a piece of equipment capable of photographing a rapid succession of images. Muybridge also invented a device he termed a *zoogyroscope,* through which these images could be projected onto a screen. In 1893, an amateur photographer named Alexander Black (1859–1940) had an idea of telling a story through sequential pictures, persuading the President of the United States to be photographed at the White House. The production, called *A Capitol Courtship,* shown with a projector perfected by the American inventor Thomas Edison, was the first practical motion film to win public acceptance as entertainment. With these inventions, the film industry was born in Hollywood on the West Coast.

Motion pictures are actually made of thousands of photographic images, which produce an illusion of motion when the photographs, or **frames,** are projected in a succession of 24 frames per second. The human brain is unable to differentiate the individual images or even to see the blank screen flashed between them. This apparently single moving picture occurs because each frame differs only slightly from the one that preceded it, and each image projected lingers only briefly as an afterimage in the brain.

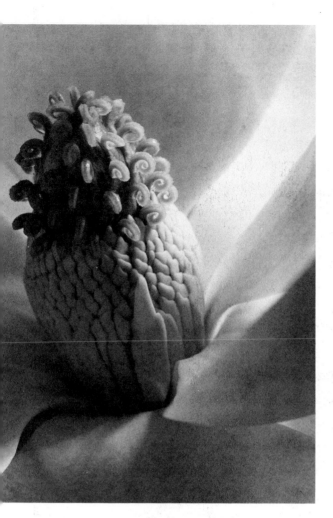

left: 110. Imogen Cunningham.
Magnolia Blossom. 1925.
Photograph.
Imogen Cunningham Trust,
Berkeley, Calif.

below: 111. Harold Edgerton.
Splash of a Milk Drop.
c. 1936.
Photograph.
Dr. Harold Edgerton,
MIT, Cambridge, Mass.

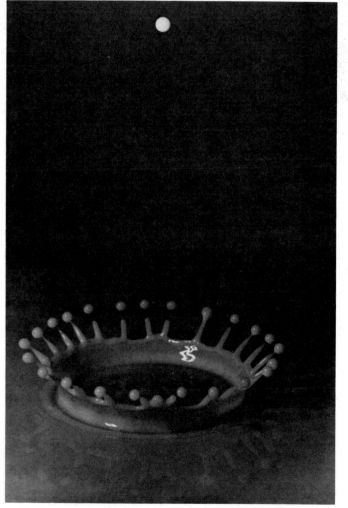

As soon as the camera was able to record motion believably, cinematographers began to experiment with a variety of space-time illusions. They soon learned that rapid movement over great distances of land or sea can appear to take place, while a brief event can be extended, because the camera is capable of accelerating, slowing down, reversing, or even holding action. A scene can be made to darken, or **fade out,** and a new sequence allowed to **fade in.** A scene can also be made to **dissolve** (merge) directly into another scene. When film scripts call for action that film codes will not permit an audience to view, such devices are invaluable. Filmmakers are thus able to manipulate our perceptions of events and people. Such techniques were developed as early as 1903 by D. W. Griffith (1875–1948) in the *Great Train Robbery* and continue to be used today.

Cinematographers discovered also that the motion picture camera can be made to imitate the human eye by scanning the overall scene or concentrating on significant details in the distant **long shot,** the closer **medium shot,** and the **close-up.** The close view creates an intense intimacy and can portray unusual views of form and texture, perhaps reminiscent of the vividness of childhood sensations when we first begin to see, feel, and touch the strange new world. Such extreme close-ups in films challenged the social conventions that have always existed regarding appropriate territorial distances between people. When such taboos were broken, the viewer became a participant in screened events, drawn into the film by the intimacy of the images, with a power akin to deities who can "see" everything. The shift from silent films ("movies") to "talkies" was brought about by the addition of a magnetic sound strip. By this revolutionary invention the gap between reality and illusion was further reduced, and another dimension was added to the cinema.

The moving picture also controls our perceptions of time. Other visual forms, such as architecture, painting, and sculpture, are restricted to the experience of the here and now. Like live theater, the cinema enjoys the benefits of extended visual experiences, but as an art form it has been most successful when the medium has rejected theatrical imitation and evolved its own kind of communication.

Visual narration has been a vital part of cinematography from early films through Sergei Eisenstein's (1898–1948) surrealistic shots in *Potemkin* (1925) (Fig. 112) to the most recent films by avant-garde filmmakers. Yet, unlike the theater where the art form unfolds through live performance, in filmmaking, editing techniques make it possible for filmmakers to use events in time creatively and to suggest rather than spell out an explicit narrative.

Concurrent with these developments in narrative cinema were experimental art films by painters such as Salvador Dali (b. 1904) and Fernand Léger (1881–1955), who created surrealistic and abstract films for small audiences in the 1920s and 1930s. Today, the underground film continues to develop almost as an independent art form, produced by filmmakers who are technically trained and alert to developments in cinema and other arts. Just as some actors such as Woody Allen have evolved their own unique film expressions, the commercial film and the art film echo other art forms as well as each other.

The Film Script Few filmgoers are aware of the techniques required to rivet the attention of an audience for 90 minutes or more. The creation of a film is a complex, communal venture, generally intended to reach vast numbers of viewers yearning to project themselves beyond the confines of their lives. The underlying structure of the film is provided by the script. Its words are translated into an analogous but quite different symbolic representation—into images that fill the screen. The filmmaker's effectiveness grows from his or her ability to visualize these images and recreate them as art.

The script is not a fixed entity but a working outline that charts the long process of filmmaking. It incorporates both the initial conceptualization of the film and the sum total of insights discovered in the process of shooting scenes. For all great filmmakers, a script that begins with one seemingly

immutable sequence may evolve through the complex process of filmmaking, requiring thousands of decisions, into something quite different. At a symposium at the 1966 Cannes Film Festival, which recognizes outstanding achievement in filmmaking, the master French short-story teller Henri Cluzot asked the filmmaker Jean-Luc Godard (b. 1930), "You agree that films should have a beginning, a middle, and end?" Godard replied, "Yes, but not necessarily in that order."

Filmmakers handle scripts differently. Ingmar Bergman (b. 1918) juxtaposes dreamlike sequences that never happened between scenes of past and present events. Federico Fellini (b. 1920), in the tradition of many Italian directors, develops his films in the company of many skilled writers. Eisenstein worked another way, filling entire notebooks with elaborate images and cryptic notations. Documentaries evolve in a still different way. The majestic procession of documentary films from *Nanook of the North* through *Woodstock* reveals a chronology unfolding in a rhythmic play of images, as, for example, the tragedy of a rich land stripped bare, tree by tree, through disastrous farming practices presented in Pare Lorentz's (b. 1905) *The River* (Fig. 113).

Cameras, Films, and Techniques The motion picture camera is based on many of the same principles as the still

112. Scene from *Potemkin,* directed by Sergei Eisenstein. 1925. Museum of Modern Art, New York (Film Stills Archive).

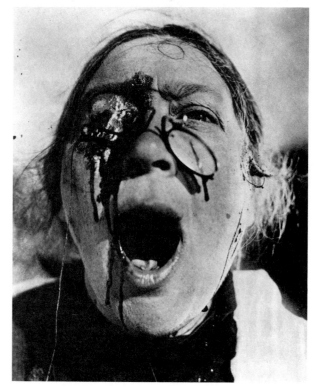

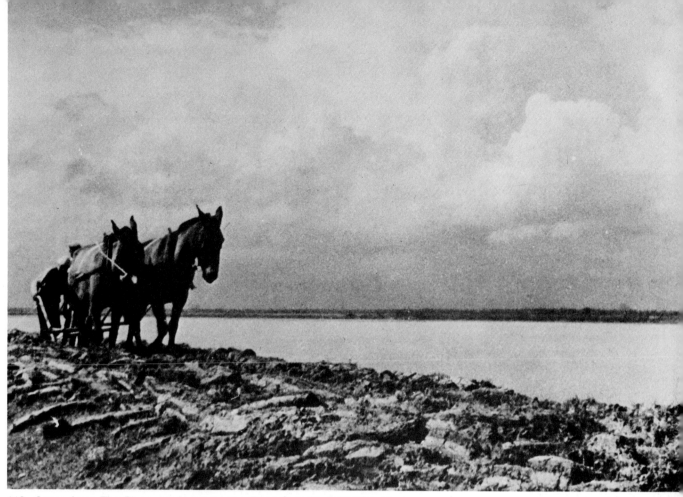

113. Scene from *The River*, produced by the Farm Security Administration. 1937. Museum of Modern Art, New York (Film Stills Archive).

camera. The difference between the two lies in the obvious fact that the motion picture camera is capable of recording a rapid succession of images. The many different specialized needs of cinematography demand varied cameras, films, and modes of operation. Camera sizes include 8 mm, 16 mm, 35 mm, and 70 mm. Generally, the smaller cameras and films are used by amateurs, while the larger, more expensive cameras used by professionals are suitable for large films that can be projected on wide screens for theater audiences.

Lenses control focal length, speed, and depth of field. For example, long focal-length lenses bring the subject closer by magnifying only a portion of the scene. The zoom lens is generally used to change focal length in a range between the extremes of a wide-angle lens and a telephoto lens, bringing subjects closer, in focus, almost instantly. A smaller lens opening permits sharp focus over a greater depth of field or distance than is possible with a wide-open lens. Moving the camera horizontally **(panning)** or vertically **(tilting)** permits a panoramic view of an area, important when a moving subject must be photographed. By focusing on the subject, the photographer is able to center

in while the remainder of the scene changes, imitating with the camera what we do with our eyes.

The process of editing the miles of filmed footage into an artistically coherent work of manageable length is the last creative step in producing a film. The editing is determined by the vision of the filmmaker, usually the director. A work print (positive film) of one or more scenes is run through an editing machine, or viewer, which consists of a lens, screen, and controls for moving the print forward and backward. When the editor decides what changes to make, frames are cut apart in the approximate places with scissors. A splicing machine glues cut frames together. Then the edited print is again run through the viewer. The process is repeated until the editor is satisfied. The sound track, which is recorded on a separate roll of tape, is finally synchronized with the film in the editing machine.

Television

Television, like cinema, has developed into a major medium for conveying information, artistic expression, and entertainment. It consists of visual images translated into

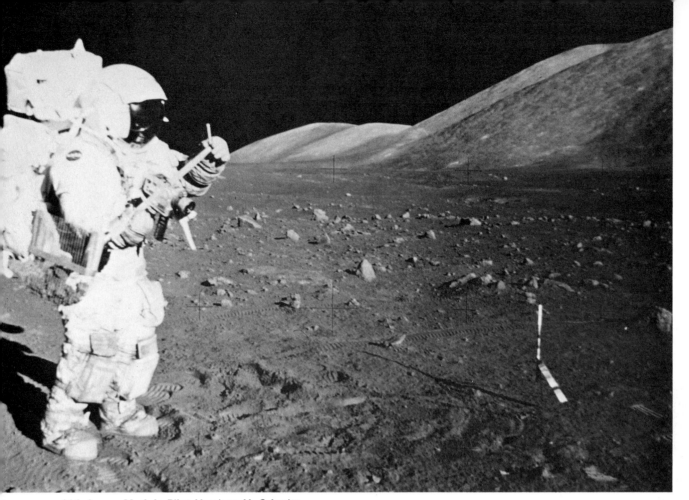

114. Lunar Module Pilot Harrison H. Schmitt
collects lunar rock samples during the Apollo 17 mission,
December 1972.

electronic signals, which are beamed through the air to a television receiver, which turns the signals back into images on the television screen. The sources of the images may be film, videotape (magnetic tape with electronic signals), or live action. Television's unique contribution is its instantaneous transmission of live events to our homes. Such live coverage of news and sports events, which gives us a sense of participation in world affairs, provides some of television's most successful programming. For instance, the whole world watched with awe and excitement the exploration of the moon and witnessed at the same time one of television's proudest achievements (Fig. 114).

Through the imagery and sound of television, events on the screen relate personally to viewers. Extreme close-ups eliminate the psychological distance between the television image and our emotions, while the immediacy of television provides us with a way to enjoy and identify with dramatic presentations or events. Crowded into large cities, people tend to become shut off from community living and isolated from other people. Yet in the tragic assassination of U.S. President John F. Kennedy, television not only heightened the impact of the event but also helped draw millions of individual viewers together in a spirit of mourning and national unity.

Television programs range widely from feature-length drama to situation comedy to musical programs, old motion pictures, interviews and panel discussions, game shows, animated cartoons, news analyses, soap operas, documentaries, and commercials. Some of these presentations are highly creative, others less so. Although panel discussions can rarely rise above the caliber of the guests, a skilled interviewer such as Dick Cavett offers the potential of memorable conversation.

Commercial television has been faulted for its tendency to program for the lowest common denominator and its apparent reluctance to experiment with new ideas. Because it is supported by businesses that buy advertising time and want the largest possible viewing audience for their commercials, the programs must appeal to the broadest possible market. Television commercials, however, have become a distinctive art form, frequently showing more creativity and sophistication than the programs they accompany.

In a videotape distributed by Castelli-Sonnabend Tapes

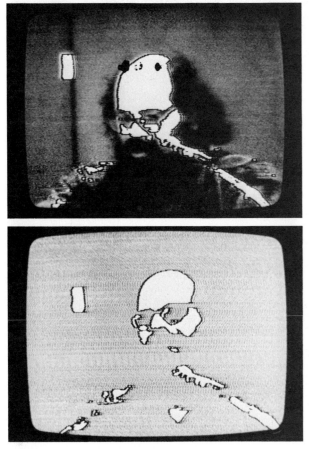

115. Nam June Paik with Shigeko Kubota.
Allen Ginsberg, from *Suite 212.*
1976. Video. Courtesy the artist.

and Films called *Television Delivers People,* Richard Serra (b. 1939) and Carlota Schoolman (b. 1947) produced a 6-minute program focusing on the political import of broadcasting as corporate monopoly and imperialism of the air. The subject of their videotape, notably video-filmed television material, is presented ironically, for their message criticizes television but uses the medium to do it. As a parody on the seduction of advertising, Muzak plays while sentences Serra has excerpted from television conferences roll down a blue background in white lettering. For instance, "The product of television, commercial television, is the audience. . . . Television delivers people to an advertiser. . . . It is the consumer who is consumed."

In contrast, noncommercial television has been freer to experiment with new expressive forms and creative approaches. Some of these shows, having first won acceptance on public-supported television, have been filtered into commercial television. Public and educational television offer creative possibilities in drama, news coverage, public-information programs, and children's programs. In

order to survive, however, and to continue creative broadcasting, public television depends on grants from corporations and foundations and on the financial support of the viewing public—us.

Some experimental video art, like film, is based upon the editing process for appeal. Nam June Paik uses the video synthesizer to alter the image of Allen Ginsberg (Fig. 115). Through electronics, he may distort, blend, and combine images, entertaining us brilliantly with a thousand fluctuating views, including the commercial, even while he reminds us of the insidious pressures exerted by television, which often seduces, persuades, and numbs our sense of values.

It is interesting to speculate on the artistic potential of cable television with its capacity for almost endless variety in programming. Another exciting innovation is the videotape cassette systems now widely available. With appropriate adapters, tapes of virtually any subject could be made available to vast audiences. Nam June Paik forecasts a not-too-distant time when loss of fossil fuels will eliminate most travel. As he sees it, knowledge will be stored on videotapes, disc-computerized for rapid retrieval, and broadcast to the public.

We have only to look around us to see some of the technical and social results of the invention of the camera. The new art forms it has produced—photography, cinema, and television—are now a part of our everyday lives. Their very familiarity should make it easier for us to evaluate just how aesthetically successful and expressive they have become.

EXERCISES AND ACTIVITIES

1. The principle of the camera was first explored in the Renaissance device known as the *camera obscura.* What was the principle on which it was based? How was it applied to later cameras?
2. Photography is both an art and a science. Explain how it can be both.
3. The operation of a camera is related to the function of the human eye. Define or diagram the relationship between them.
4. Select several photographs from a magazine or from your own collection. Which do you believe qualify as works of art? Explain your reasons for your choices.
5. Cut out magazine photographs that you like. Select those that create different moods. Analyze the way the photographer used the camera to create each mood.
6. An illusion of life can be produced thorugh the medium of the motion picture. How did motion picture photography develop out of Eadweard Muybridge's early experiments with multiple photographs? What are the advantages of cinematography and/or television over still photography? Explain the space-time concept involved in cinema and television.
7. Television commercials offer creative possibilities to the artist. Describe and analyze six commercials—three effective and three not effective. Explain their success or failure.

6 Sculpture

Sculpture is such a physical thing that you must have manipulative ability—hit a nail with a hammer—cut metal and join metal. The better you know how to make things, the better you are as a sculptor.

RICHARD STANKIEWICZ

Sculpture is a three-dimensional art form, probing space somewhat like architecture. While architectural space, however, is large enough for us to walk through, most sculpture occupies limited space. We are used to looking at statues carved upon a building's surface, set into niches, or standing free where we can walk around and enjoy them from every angle. Such forms of sculpture, whether seen only frontally or from all sides, change as the light and our angles of vision vary. The hollow spaces between sculptural masses can also become as important visually as the sculptural forms themselves. Our eyes follow the dominant lines of the work, and frequently our bodies respond as well. The human tactile response is so strong that our hands often long to touch the sculptural surfaces, to feel the smooth or rough textures. When we cannot touch sculptures, we can usually imagine what it would feel like to run our hands over the surfaces. These are all immediate sensual responses, quite separate from any emotional feelings aroused by subject matter. Some contemporary artists such as Robert Smithson work on a vast scale, involving materials of the earth and/or the seas. Their environmental sculptures seem to surround us, much like the natural environments from which each sculpture was derived (Fig. 6).

Through the ages, sculpture has fulfilled many purposes: to teach religious beliefs, to create an emotional atmosphere of veneration, to depict the gods in visual form, to record historical events, to exalt rulers, and to honor the dead. In contrast, today's sculpture is usually more concerned with communicating the individual artist's inner feelings or response to the outside world.

In addition, new ways of using traditional materials, new technical methods, and new ideas have transformed the nature of sculpture. In fact, the art has changed so radically over the last one hundred years that it is difficult to discuss much contemporary sculpture in conventional terms or to classify it in the usual way as carved wood, cast metal, or built-up clay. For example, in what category would you place a stuffed vinyl typewriter, a neon sculpture, or laser beam examples of present-day sculptures?

As we study the processes by which sculpture is made, we will see how the sculptor often uses complex techniques to create aesthetic sculptural experiences. Since a large part of the process of sculpture is problem solving on a practical level, only after sculptors become technically proficient can they concentrate on expressive aspects of their works.

Traditional Materials and Processes

Stone, wood, clay, and metal have been used in sculpture for centuries in an infinite variety of ways, each reflecting different cultural concepts. In the past, stone and wood have been carved in what are called **direct processes;** that is, the sculptor works with the actual material that forms the finished work. As a first step, a small sketch and/or model of the larger work is prepared to serve as a guide. This is then enlarged, either by eye or with a device that measures the original and marks the increased proportions on a block of wood or stone. Once the material is marked, the sculptor chips away the excess until gradually by this **subtractive process** the image begins to emerge from the block. Michelangelo used to go to the quarry to pick out the stone he wanted for a particular piece of sculpture. He believed that he could visualize sculptural forms trapped inside the stone, waiting to be released by his carving. Through a similar sense of identification with the source of their works, traditional African sculptors beseeched growing trees to give approval to those sculptures carved from their wood.

Stone   In the past, stone sculpture has varied from small fertility figures such as the *Venus of Willendorf* (Fig. 15) to the enormous sculptural bulk of the Sphinx, which was made from huge blocks of stone added to the natural rock already there (Fig. 35). Granite, sandstone, marble, onyx, and many other dense stones have been carved by sculp-

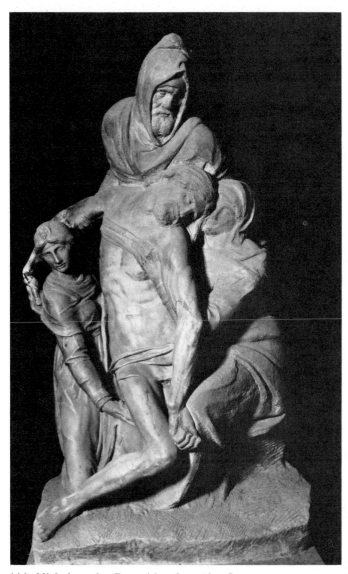

116. Michelangelo. *Deposition from the Cross.*
1548–55. Marble, height 7'5" (2.26 m).
Cathedral, Florence.

below: 117. Auguste Rodin. *The Walking Man.*
1877–78. Bronze, height 33⅛" (84 cm).
National Gallery of Art, Washington, D.C.
(gift of Mrs. John W. Simpson, 1942).

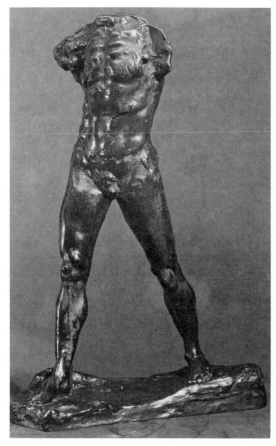

tors with tools that have changed little over the centuries. Chisels, heavy-headed mallets, rasps, and hand-finishing tools still in use by sculptors today are basically much the same as those Michelangelo used to carve the *Deposition from the Cross* (Fig. 116). But modern sculptors in stone usually also employ power tools to cut away the excess material fairly easily or to add a polish to the finished work. They may use hand tools only for the final carving and shaping, reducing to a fraction the time and effort once required for sculpture. If you were to try to chip off a few pieces of marble with a hand chisel, you would understand the difficulty of the task and the advantage electrically powered equipment has given the sculptor. The skills re-

quired, however, while somewhat different from those for hand tools, are just as demanding.

The character of the stone and selection of tools with which the sculptor chooses to work determine the appearance of the finished piece. For example, the texture of finished sculpture—highly polished or left rough—will vary depending on the type of surface worked as well as the tool with which unwanted material is eliminated. Many artists, such as Michelangelo and Rodin, have always left a small portion of their sculptures unworked to echo the original surfaces of the natural materials. If you carefully examine Michelangelo's *Deposition from the Cross* or Rodin's *The Walking Man* (Fig. 117), perhaps you can detect the virgin surfaces. In addition, the stone's special qualities, such as the veins in marble, must be respected and used expressively by the sculptor. Finally, because stone, for all its hardness, can break as it is being worked, care must be taken to choose blocks without flaws.

Wood Like sculpting in stone, wood carving is a direct technique that involves removing unwanted material until the desired form seems to emerge from the piece of wood. As with stone, the hardness and graining of woods vary. Each kind presents a different technical problem of possible breakage or splitting. Today we value the grain of the wood both from a technical and an aesthetic point of view, since the character of the material chosen by the artist affects the appearance of the final piece of sculpture. In early cultures, however, after a wood sculpture was completed, it was frequently painted or coated with fine sheets of bronze or gold, so that the texture or grain of the wood was masked by the overlying layers. For example, the mummy of the Egyptian pharaoh Tutankhamen was found in a nest of wood and gold coffins, each inner container slightly smaller than the outer. The innermost one, just fitting his body, was solid gold, but was enclosed within an oak coffin almost totally covered by layers of precious gold and inlays of semiprecious stones (Fig. 118).

Contemporary sculptors often use wood in the traditional manner, carving from solid blocks. But they also use it in new ways, such as the **additive process** called **assemblage.** Louise Nevelson (b. 1900) collects, or assembles, ready-made pieces of wood and combines them into compositions that suggest walls or niches taken from architectural settings. Her works are concerned with the play of light and shade over forms and can be looked at as symbolic spaces for retreat and protection from our plastic, streamlined world. She started by picking up scraps of wood in furniture and pattern shops. After nailing and gluing them together, she painted them all flat black, white, or gold, thus unifying the hundreds of separate pieces. Each of the small boxes is a self-contained, rectangular relief composition, recalling the intricacy of Gothic carving—a cathedral of modern times, touched with poetry and magic (Fig. 119). Newly developed processes have further increased the flexibility and versatility of wood as a material for sculpture. For example, plywood can be bent and shaped when heated and built up into almost any form; it can then be painted or left with the natural grain and color intact.

The Generals (Fig. 120) by Marisol (Marisol Escobar, b. 1930) is an assemblage formed of plywood, wood block, hair, some plastic, some paint, and several photographic details. Like all her works, it is a witty spoof of the mighty figures of our time. Charles De Gaulle and probably Erwin Rommel are portrayed as toy figures astride a rolling wooden hobby horse. Marisol has satirized the faces of the generals, leaving De Gaulle's famous oversized nose to identify him and the desert hat to remind us of Rommel's success in the Libyan desert. *The Generals* are represented

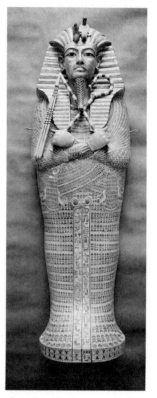

118. Sarcophagus of King Tutankhamen, second coffin, lid; Egyptian. 18th Dynasty, c. 1365 B.C. Egyptian Museum, Cairo.

by boxes and the horse's body by a barrel mounted on wheeled table legs. The comment "Have wheels, will travel," which comes to mind, becomes a private joke shared by the artist with her viewers, for certainly these generals will never be carried into battle in this play with reality and satire.

Clay Clay has been shaped into sculpture ever since human beings first discovered this material that covers much of our earth. It is a very motile substance, which is easy to model and allows for a great deal of spontaneity, especially in small sculptures. Pre-Columbian Indians in Mexico, for example, modeled lively clay figures of humans and animals for religious purposes (Fig. 121). This little figurine has a simple charm and human quality often lacking in the larger complex clay or stone figures that we normally associate with Mesoamerican cultures. Clay can also be built up into very large forms by coil and slab methods, provided that care is taken to prevent the shaped clay from collapsing prior to hardening. Such clay sculptures are generally hollow and may be built to a height of several feet.

A particular piece of sculpture may be copied one or more times by means of a plaster mold made in sections from the original. Clay is diluted with water until it has a

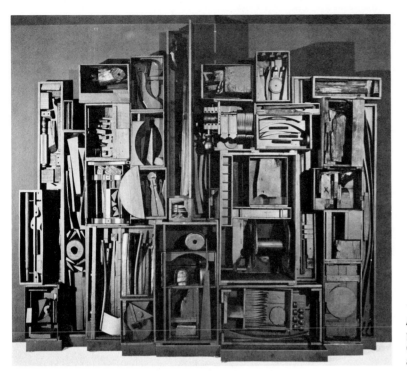

119. Louise Nevelson. *Sky Cathedral—Moon Garden + One.* 1957–60. Black painted wood, 9'1" × 10'10" × 1'7" (2.77 × 3.3 × 0.48 m). Collection Arnold and Milly Glimcher, New York.

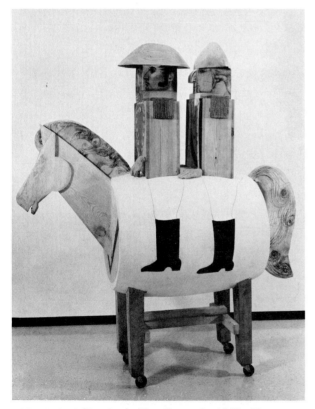

120. Marisol (Escobar). *The Generals.* 1961–62. Wood and mixed media, 7'3" × 2'4½" × 6'4" (2.21 × 0.72 × 1.93 m). Albright-Knox Art Gallery, Buffalo, N.Y. (gift of Seymour H. Knox, 1962).

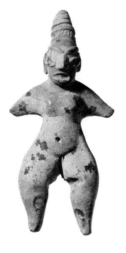

121. Figurine, from Tlatilco, Mexico (D.F.). Middle Formative Period, 800–300 B.C. Clay, height 3¾" (9.5 cm). Dumbarton Oaks, Washington, D.C. (Robert Woods Bliss Collection of Pre-Columbian Art).

creamy consistency (slip), and is then poured into the mold. When the liquid is hardened, the sectioned molds are removed from the sculpture. The molds can be used over and over again to produce many replicas of the original.

Clay can be baked in kilns heated to high temperatures to make it more durable. This firing process, discussed in the section on pottery, causes physical changes to take place in the clay, hardening it and making it nonporous. Fired clay, whether shaped by hand or cast in molds, can be decorated with paint or with *glazes,* minerals that, when fired, fuse into a glassy coating. Most Renaissance sculptors glazed their ceramic sculptures, and there is a revival of interest in the technique today. Contemporary

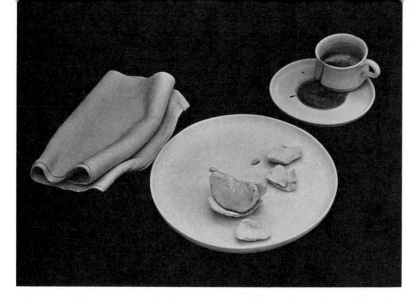

122. Lillian Dodson.
After Dinner Setting.
1980. Porcelain, life size.
Collection the artist.

artists are producing sculptural pieces using hand building, casting, or combined techniques. *After Dinner Setting* (Fig. 122) by Lillian Dodson (b. 1931) is a ceramic replica of reality. Unlike Marisol, who entertains us with a fusion of many layers of reality—some painted or photographed precisely, others clearly satirized—Dodson teases our perceptions by providing us with an illusion of verisimilitude, which is shattered under close scrutiny.

Finally, in addition to the goal of forming finished sculpture, clay has been used for centuries to make small models of large projected sculptures or to build up full-size sculptures from which metal statues are cast, as we shall see.

Metal Until the 20th century, metal sculpture, usually bronze, was cast. The same lengthy process with few changes has been used for hundreds of years (Fig. 123). Metal sculpture cannot be spontaneously produced. It takes careful planning and considerable engineering skill to foresee the problems of casting and to prepare for them.

First the sculptor creates a full-size original sculpture. This is the creative part. Most of the rest of the process is technical. The sculpture is usually made of clay, surrounding a wooden or metal framework called an **armature.** The armature, like a skeleton, keeps the clay from collapsing as it is built up, allowing the sculptor to produce slender forms and extended arms and legs, otherwise impossible with soft clay. After the sculpture is completed, a sectioned plaster or a flexible gelatin mold is made from it. Since the sculptor usually wants a hollow metal casting, which is obviously cheaper and lighter than solid metal, he makes a wax model as a hollow shell, usually by brushing melted wax onto the mold until a thin shell is built up and then filling the middle of the mold with a solid core of heat-resistant material. When the mold is removed, the wax appears as a replica of the original sculpture. Wax rods are attached to the replica to create vents and channels called **gates;** then the replica is placed upside down in a container. A mixture of plaster, silica, and clay is poured

around it. This hardens into a fireproof mold that is called an **investiture.**

The investiture is heated in a kiln and the melted wax runs out. For this reason the process is called **lost wax,** or *cire perdue.* What is now left is a hollow space, in the shape of the original clay sculpture. Molten bronze is poured into the hot investiture and allowed to harden. When the investiture and core are removed, the emerging bronze looks odd with the vents and gates sticking out from it. These

123. Bronze casting.

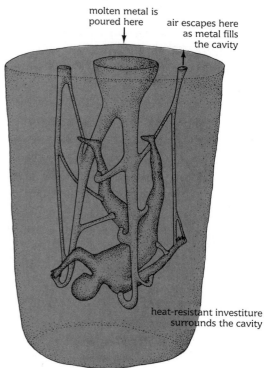

molten metal is
poured here

air escapes here
as metal fills
the cavity

heat-resistant investiture
surrounds the cavity

must be removed and the surface cleaned and finished according to the sculptor's wishes. A finish, or **patina,** is usually applied to the bronze. Depending on the chemicals used, surfaces range in color from greens to dark brown.

Renaissance sculptors usually cast their own pieces or at least directed assistants to do the work. Today most metal sculpture is cast in foundries by trained technicians. Sculptors who produce large cast sculpture may have assistants to help them to build the armature, enlarge the model, and prepare the sculpture for casting. Henry Moore (1898–1979), a contemporary sculptor whose works were often cast in bronze, made small models of his large figures, turning them over to assistants, who built them up to their final size in plaster shaped over armatures. Moore supervised their work throughout the process, refining the final plaster sculpture himself. He also completed the finishing of the bronze when it came back from the foundry.

Some sculptors today carve the original sculpture from styrofoam, a material that, like wax, melts when the investiture is baked in the kiln. Metal sculpture can also be cast with the industrial sand-mold technique. In this method the sculptor's original model is placed in a sectional metal container, and a special fine damp sand is packed tightly around it. This sand holds the impression of the original even when the metal sections are removed from the model. These sections are reassembled and clamped firmly together around a sand core suspended inside. Then liquid metal is poured into the hollow space formed between the sand mold and the core. Relief sculpture can also be cast by pouring metal into an impression made in a flat bed of sand.

Through the technique of casting, several metal sculptures can be made from original clay or wax sculpture, each reproducing the original model. Sometimes the sculptor works on the final finishing so that each piece can be considered an "original" work. However, molds can also be made from any existing sculpture, so that frequently the duplicates you see are actually reproductions, not finished by the artist. Whether the artist casts his or her own work or turns it over to a foundry, the final shape in metal exactly reproduces the handwork of the sculptor. This is particularly evident in the work of Giacometti, who intentionally left parts of his works rough or with only suggestions of details. The marks of his fingers or tools in the clay can be seen exactly reproduced in some of his bronze figures (Fig. 42). Bronze casts are still made, but today most metal sculptors build up their sculpture, using soldering and welding techniques to join and shape the pieces of metal, as in Pevsner's *Developable Column* (Fig. 41).

New Materials, New Methods, New Forms

Many of today's sculptors reject traditional materials. Even when they do use stone, metal, wood, and clay, they frequently use them in new ways. Industrial techniques, such as metal welding, lamination of wood, and the casting and vacuum-forming of plastic, are explored by contemporary artists as rapidly as they are invented. Sculptors in metal today may weld steel directly or hand hammer iron, while wood sculptors build up their pieces using techniques taken from modern furniture production and carpentry. Much sculpture today, like Marisol's *The Generals* (Fig. 120), is constructed, built, assembled, or arranged rather than cast or carved.

Constructed Sculpture Picasso was the first artist to fit objects he found around him—handlebars, bones, a feather duster—into sculptural assemblages (Fig. 20). Today, many sculptors incorporate bits and pieces found in junkyards (auto graveyards) into their work. Constructions of sheet metal, wire, or translucent plastic often replace the traditional sculptural masses with lighter shapes in which space becomes an important element, as with Pevsner's work (Fig. 41). With this new use of materials the sculptor expresses his or her concern with shaping and dividing space rather than filling it. Calder used sheet metal to produce flat-painted shapes, some of which were welded or riveted together into metallic sculptures, attached to the ground. Whenever it was possible, he placed these **stabiles** in natural settings so that the clouds and sky seen through the openings become active elements of his compositions.

Calder, a dynamic and inventive artist, has created both stable and moving sculptures. Using electrical motors to create movement in some of his works, Calder early became fascinated with the changing relationships between sections of his sculptures (Fig. 38). Some of his later **mobiles,** which depended on air currents to propel them in complex, ever-changing patterns, were even arranged to clank or ring as they moved. Clearly, 20th-century sculptors have been fascinated by the machine. Many, such as Marcel Duchamp, Naum Gabo (b. 1890), and Calder, made **kinetic sculpture** moved by mechanical means. They programmed the parts of the sculpture to move at varying speeds and through changing patterns so that the sculptured object was enriched by a new element of time.

Mixed Media and New Materials The new technique of assembling sculpture out of found objects and different materials led to what are called mixed-media combinations or assemblages, such as Kienholz's *The State Hospital* (Fig. 23). In these works, sculptors use materials that have never been considered sculptural or even aesthetic. Sometimes objects are combined with painted canvases, so that the line between sculpture and painting is at times difficult to define. For example, when Rauschenberg attaches an electric fan to a canvas (*Pantomime,* Fig. 86), in what category do you place the work—sculpture or painting—or when Picasso draws with light in space (Fig. 67)?

Three-dimensional canvases, constructed on frames and painted in the artist's individual style, are difficult to classify. Are they dimensional paintings or painted sculp-

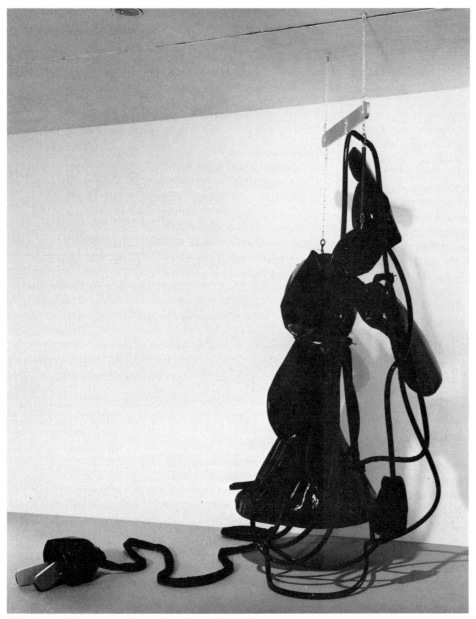

124. Claes Oldenburg. *Giant Soft Fan*. 1966–67.
Construction of vinyl filled with foam rubber, wood,
metal, and plastic tubing; 10′ × 10′4″ × 6′4″ (3.05 × 3.3 × 1.93 m).
The Sidney and Harriet Janis Collection,
gift to The Museum of Modern Art, New York.

tures? Canvases by Lee Bontecou seem to have a resemblance to primitive masks. Her technique, which involves stretching and gluing fabric over a wire-frame skeleton, is similar to early aircraft construction. Using this method, Bontecou has created openings that can be interpreted as eyes, mouths, entrances to caves, or sexual cavities (Fig. 87).

The term **soft sculpture** may seem to be a contradiction, but some contemporary sculptors create such works.

For example, many artists make stuffed fabric forms of one kind or another, and some weavers make free-standing or hanging shapes that are sculptural or environmental in form. A Pop artist such as Claes Oldenburg (b. 1929) uses vinyl, canvas, and other materials to create his soft, larger-than-life-size sculptures of electric fans (Fig. 124), typewriters, and other everyday objects. He often uses vinyls to emphasize contemporary materialism and the frequent choice of cheap plastic over natural materials.

Among the many industrial materials now also popular with sculptors is plastic, which is used in a variety of ways. Cast in solid pieces, constructed from sheets of plastic, or built up of fiberglass and resin, plastic can achieve seemingly endless effects. Lightweight and colorful, it can be made into tiny forms through which light may filter, or it can be built up over wire mesh forms or cast in solid, brilliantly colored, jewel-like forms. Sculptors have found fascinating possibilities for expression in plastic materials and in the industrial techniques used to form them. Duane Hanson (b. 1925), for example, has discovered that plastics can simulate the real thing so well that art and reality are indistinguishable. In *Self-portrait with Model* (Fig. 125) the persons on the left and right are sculpture, the artist sits in the center. The creations which have resulted are so varied that there is no single visual trait common to all.

To increase their knowledge of industrial techniques, some contemporary sculptors have spent time in the laboratories and plants of large corporations studying new methods used by engineers and technicians and collaborating with them to apply these techniques to art. Out of this joint experimentation may come aesthetic uses of industrial techniques that will not only produce works of art but may in turn influence industrial and commercial products.

For example, all sculpture involves light—natural or artificial—playing over its forms and through its spaces. But new lighting techniques have been adapted by sculptors to create spatial environments. Tubing with neon gas inside can be bent and formed into any shape. When lit, such a sculpture makes a visual statement in neon lights. Sculptors familiar with these materials could surely design signs more aesthetically satisfying than what we see around us. Plastic rods can also be used to carry light from a light source at one end of the rod, and with translucent, colored resins can be lighted from within to create sculptural objects. In Stephen Antonakos' *Red Box over Blue Box* (Pl. 8, p. 24), changing waves of colored light are programmed to play over and through the sculpture. It is apparent that light can be utilized by sculptors in new ways, which repre-

125. Duane Hanson. *Self-portrait with Model.* 1979. Polyvinyl polychromed in oil, life size. Collection the artist.

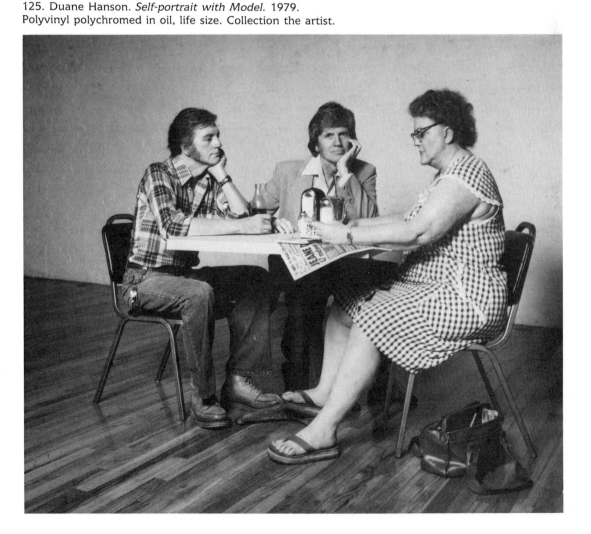

sent their individual approaches to sculpture (Fig. 67). Some works are highly organic; others, geometric; still others, mechanical.

In further explorations of contemporary technology, many artists have experimented with communications media, building rooms in which we can watch video or film images projected around us, accompanied by electric sound. Some artists have directed bulldozers to shape huge earthworks (Fig. 6), while still others have created environments intended to surround us in art. All of these are new sculptural responses to space, form, and light.

So we find the artist again often inspired by his or her era, making use of whatever timely techniques are available. Current forms evolve from the methods and materials of today, just as a Greek marble carving grew out of the materials and methods available then. Sculpture, like architecture, has accepted the challenge of new methods to create new concepts within an ancient art.

EXERCISES AND ACTIVITIES

1. Select five sculptural works from this book that appeal to you and explain why they do.
2. Although sculpture, unlike architecture, usually has no functional purpose, it serves society in other ways. List some of them.
3. The materials for creating sculpture can be found in any environment. What are the traditional sculptural materials? What materials and processes are unique to 20th-century sculpture? Discuss how contemporary and ancient sculpture differ in regard to materials.
4. Using clay, papier-mâché, soft wool, or soap, create a sculptural form that re-creates a recognizable natural object. Using any of these same materials and the same subject, create an abstract sculptural form.
5. Using 20th-century materials, create a three-dimensional form that relates to contemporary technology and also makes a personal artistic statement that expresses your own feelings.

7 The Decorative Arts

From earliest times, men and women have fashioned objects to meet their daily needs, such as telling time and serving food. People have never been content, however, with merely useful objects. Even when living conditions were difficult they have always found time and energy to refine the shape of useful objects or give them pleasing texture, finish, or decoration. In the hands of skilled craftspeople, even simple artifacts for telling time or serving food become more pleasing to see or touch. The Renaissance saltcellar in Figure 126 is a case in point. It was designed both to fill a function and please the taste of a king. Any object that both serves a useful purpose and pleases us aesthetically may be called **functional art.** The category of functional art includes handcrafts, sometimes called decorative arts, mass-produced industrial arts, and communication arts.

Functional art addresses human needs through its structure, or form. As we look about us, we see that physical structure, order, or design is basic to life. In a living thing the arrangement of cells is related to the environment and to the organism's functional needs. The functional structure of an organism, however, can also be aesthetically inspiring to humans. For example, the snail shell has fascinated scientists for centuries because as it grows to accommodate the growing animal it reveals a constant logarithmic spiral. This rate of growth, which also exists in other forms of life, appears to have been the basis for the

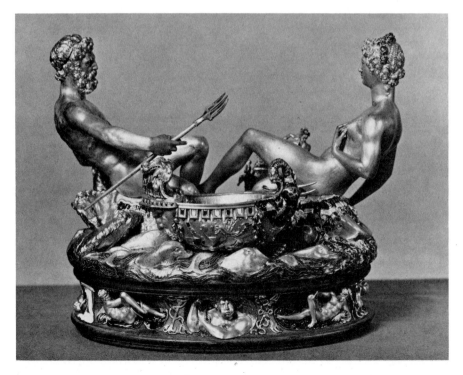

126. Benvenuto Cellini. The saltcellar of Francis I. 1539–43. Gold, 10¼ × 13⅛″ (26 × 33 cm). Kunsthistorisches Museum, Vienna.

Golden Section (Fig. 65). This rule for achieving pleasing proportion was established long ago in Greece and revived by many Renaissance artists, who also were convinced that it corresponded with the laws of the universe and should therefore apply to artistic creation as well. Whether or not we agree that art should be tied to nature's laws, we often seem drawn to artworks that embody the Golden Section.

The incredibly complex designs created by animals provide unlimited inspiration to humans. The structure of honeycombs, beavers' dams, and bird's nests all express the materials used in them and the purposes they serve. Today many designers and craftspeople believe that any article designed for use—a steel chair, a piece of power machinery, a silver pitcher (Fig. 14)—must also honestly express its materials and purposes as well as be appropriate for the time and place it is used. In addition, the elements of design, already discussed in earlier chapters, are as important in the functional arts as they are in the fine arts. Rhythm, balance, and proportion are basic to all well-designed objects; line, mass, color, and texture are critical concerns if a functional object is also to be aesthetically satisfying.

In the Old Stone Age, men and women shaped weapons and tools from available resources to fit a specific purpose. Even the earliest flint stones were differentiated in size and shape to please the eye as well as to fit a specific purpose. Missiles aimed at birds and small animals were small and finely shaped. Harpoons and hand axes intended for heavy animals might weigh as much as 6 pounds (2.72 kilograms).

A separation between beauty and usefulness in art became common only after the 15th-century Renaissance. Before then, the tools and utensils of daily living that filled homes, for example, in Classical times, were made by artists concerned with both function and beauty of design and material. They used the materials common to their region—stone, wood, wool, straw—as the case might be. The most widely available material on earth is, of course, clay, and pottery is its most familiar use. Clay may also be used, however, as a building material. Whole communities have been sheltered in adobe (sun-baked clay) houses or protected by huge, encircling brick walls.

Crafts offer a practical way for people to explore new materials and ideas. The unprecedented interest in handcrafts today amidst the abundance of machine-made products ranges from simple sewing to complicated furniture making. While schools and colleges provide studios with elaborate facilities, many private homes also have space allocated for workshops and hobbies. Public libraries are well stocked with all kinds of do-it-yourself craft books. Surely the satisfaction of making something entirely with our own hands may be matched by a corresponding rise in our levels of aesthetic appreciation.

Throughout history the needs of society have been met from available resources. Ancient flint and ivory tools, baskets, pottery, and weavings responded to the same kinds of functions served by the 20th-century synthetic and natural materials found in our pottery, steel tools, and polyester fabrics. Early in most societies the crafts of pottery and weaving developed to provide containers and clothing. As societies became more complex and sophisticated, the crafts of woodworking and metalworking appeared.

Although handmade and machine-made objects involve the same principles of design, handmade objects fulfill human needs in a more personal way. The most obvious difference lies in the touch of the creator, which is usually visible in handcrafted objects. For example, in an oversized horn ladle (Fig. 127) we can sense the handwork of the American Indian of the Northwest Coast who carved it for a village feast.

Also characteristic of handcrafts is the close relationship between the material and the form of the object. A glass vase blown from molten material looks quite different from a clay vase shaped on a wheel from wet clay. In addition, there is close contact between the artisan and the material (Fig. 128). He or she uses tools with great care and a personal concern for the object's appearance and durability, its aesthetic and utilitarian qualities.

Traditionally a handmade object was both designed and executed by the same person and so could justifiably be called one of a kind. There was also a close tie between designer and consumer. It demanded a two-way responsi-

127. Ladle. British Columbia, c. 1850–70. Horn, length 17¼″ (44 cm). Metropolitan Museum of Art, New York (Michael C. Rockefeller Memorial Collection of Primitive Art, gift of Nelson A. Rockefeller, 1964).

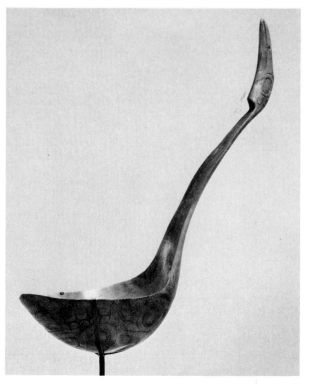

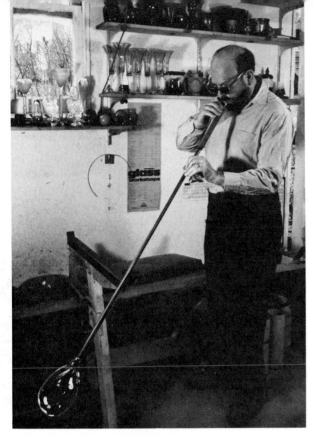

128. Julian Wolff in his glass-blowing studio.

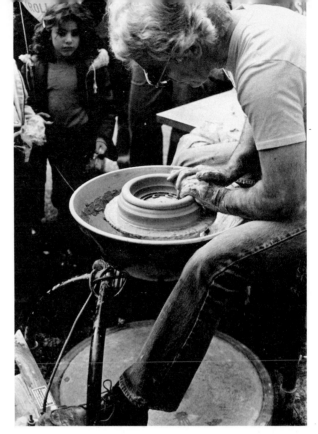

129. Potter John C. Fink at his wheel.

bility, for the artisan respected the consumer's needs, while the consumer valued the product and knew and trusted the person who made it. Modern industry does not always reveal this concern for the purchaser of its goods.

Ceramics

The making of **ceramic wares,** shaped out of damp clay and fired (baked) in a kiln, was one of the earliest crafts to develop. Clay vessels were used in most settled societies for cooking and storage. They became a form of high art in some civilizations.

There are three kinds of ceramics, depending on the kind of clay and the firing temperature. **Earthenware,** made from coarse, impure clays and fired at low temperatures (about 800° C, or 1470° F), has a soft, porous body suitable for rough pottery vessels and bricks. **Stoneware** is made from finer, purer clays and fired at higher temperatures (about 1300° C, or 2370° F), which fuse the clays into a harder, vitreous (glasslike) body. It is used for sturdy vessels. **Porcelain** is made from the finest white kaolin and other clays and fired at the highest temperatures (from about 1400° C, or 2250° F, to 1613.4° C, or 3000° F). When struck with a hard instrument, its vitreous body produces a clear, resonant sound, and when thin enough it is translucent. Porcelain makes the finest-quality vases and tableware. All three kinds of ceramics are used for sculpture.

Potters can pat and pinch clay into shape or form it into coils or slabs to build the walls of a vessel, which are then smoothed by hand or with a stone or shell. American Indians of the Southwest still make pots by these techniques. Using more sophisticated methods, potters, like John Fink, can shape clay on a rotating potter's wheel (Fig. 129), pulling the clay up from the base with the hands, or pour **slip** (a creamlike mixture of clay and water) into a mold. The wheel and mold enable them to produce more pots of greater uniformity and smoothness and more ambitious design.

The clay pot must then be dried in the air. If such **greenware,** as it is called, is to be made hard and watertight, it must then be fired to remove all moisture from the clay. Early peoples baked their earthenware pots in the coals of a fire or in covered pits. Since then pottery has been fired in special furnaces, or kilns, such as the multichambered dragon kilns with firing chambers usually stairstepped up the hillsides of southern China or in modern electric kilns.

The pot after the first firing is called **bisque.** It may then be decorated with colored stains or with slip, or it may be painted with or dipped in **glaze,** a coating of ground chemicals and water. A glazed pot is then fired a second time at a higher temperature, which fuses the glaze to the surface of the pot, making it more durable and, if it is earthenware, waterproof. Glazes range in color from muted earth tones

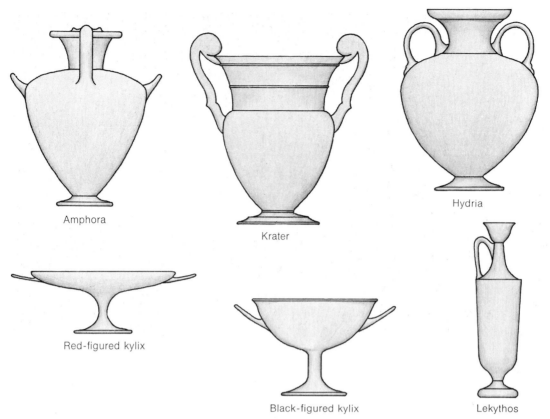

Amphora

Krater

Hydria

Red-figured kylix

Black-figured kylix

Lekythos

above: 130. Greek pottery shapes.

to brilliant primary hues, and they can produce a variety of rough, mat, and shiny textures. Additional glaze decorations can be added in subsequent firings. Each step in firing requires great technical knowledge and skill, whether it is done by an individual or a large factory. Errors can produce drastic changes in glazes or ruin pots completely.

The early Greeks and the Chinese, Koreans, and Japanese have produced some of the world's great ceramics, pieces of exceptional beauty in shape, glaze, and ornamentation. Greek potters designed graceful shapes for specific purposes. They made narrow-necked jars and bottles to hold costly wine, oil, and perfume safely and wide-mouthed bowls and cups for mixing and drinking water and wine (Fig. 130). Heavy jars had three handles to make them easier to move, dip into, or pour from. These vessels were often painted with figural scenes.

Chinese potters developed subtle shapes and a variety of glazes that depended on precise control of the heat and oxygen supply in the kiln. **Ting ware** is a delicate, creamy white porcelain from northern China (Fig. 131). It is covered with transparent, almost colorless glaze. Ting ware consists chiefly of bowls, whose rims, left raw in the firing process, are usually hidden with a copper band. Heavier kinds of porcelain, incised or smooth, are covered with gray-green celadon glazes in an attempt to give the effect of jade. **Lung-Ch'uan ware** is a particularly fine celadon

below: 131. Chinese Ting ware bowl. Sung Dynasty. Porcelain. Museum of Fine Arts, Boston (purchased from the Helen and Alice Coburn Fund).

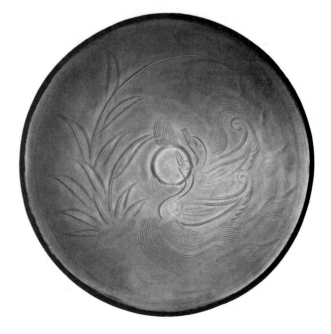

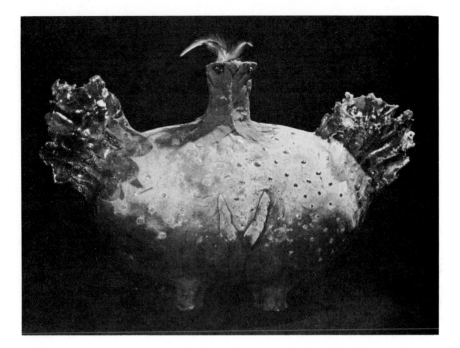

132. Nancy Baldwin. *Raku Bird.* 1974. Raku ware, length 13" (33 cm). Collection the artist.

from southern China. Chinese porcelains were widely imitated in the West in the 17th and 18th centuries.

Japanese potters were inspired by sophisticated Chinese and Korean porcelains, but they also developed a simpler, coarser earthenware and stoneware as appropriate for use in the tea ceremony, which stressed simplicity and love of nature. This **raku ware,** from the Japanese word *raku* ("enjoyment"), is modeled by hand, usually in straight-sided bowls, and often covered with runny glazes in colors suggesting nature—brown, light orange, dull green, and straw. The calligrapher and painter Koetsu (Hon-ami Koetsu, 1558–1637) made *raku* tea bowls that are highly prized by connoisseurs.

Today hand potters make use of traditional methods from many different cultures, some of which were ignored for years because of Western emphasis on industrialization. Many potters have been greatly influenced by Japanese styles—for instance, Bernard Leach (1887–1979), a pioneer in introducing Oriental skills to the West. Nancy Baldwin (b. 1928), who has achieved distinction for her porcelain, also makes *raku* (Fig. 132), rephrasing ancient techniques in contemporary styles.

Glass

The making of **glass,** a mixture of silica (sand) and other chemicals, heated and shaped, was well developed by 1500 B.C. Depending on the ingredients, glass can be thick or thin, transparent or opaque, dull or brilliant. Color is produced by adding to the mixture various minerals such as copper, cobalt, or cadmium. When the glass is heated in a furnace to a molten state, it can be blown, poured, or pressed into molds or drawn into threads. It can also be

free blown. In that technique the glassworker dips a globule of glass from the molten mixture with the end of a blowpipe. As air is blown through the pipe the molten glass forms a bubble (Fig. 128), which is then shaped with a wooden tool, calipers, and shears, the glass being reheated as necessary to keep it pliable. Modern commercial glassware is mostly molded glass made by machine.

Glassware need not be decorated, relying solely on its attractive shape, texture, and brilliance or color. But it can be ornamented by cutting and faceting; engraving, etching, or sandblasting; or painting, gilding, or enameling. Medieval stained-glass windows relied on color and transparency for their rich, luminous glow (Pl. 13, p. 202). In the 20th century many artists are exploring the possibilities of creating new forms in glass.

Enamel

In the ancient art of **enameling,** fine particles of colored glass are applied to a metal, glass, or ceramic ground and fused to it by firing. There are many techniques of applying enamel. In **cloisonné** enamel the design is outlined by **cloisons** (thin metal strips), which form partitions separating the various colors. Byzantine enamel reliquaries were cloisonné on gold. In **champlevé** ("raised field") enamel the ground is dug away to leave ridges forming the outlines of the design. Romanesque enamels in medieval France and Germany were usually champlevé on copper. Enamel may also be painted on metal or other grounds to achieve effects as varied as produced by oil painting. In the 16th century fine-painted enamel was made in Limoges, France. Cellini's saltcellar for Francis I (Fig. 126) is an ingenious masterpiece in gold and enamel in the Mannerist style. Salt derived from the sea is held in a boat guarded by Neptune; the pepper coming from the land in a little classical temple watched by Hera. Many artists work in enamel today, producing colorful jewelry, plaques, and ritual vessels.

Textiles

One of the most ancient and widespread crafts is the process of interlacing horizontal and vertical threads, called **weaving.** In the process of weaving cloth, whether by hand or machine, a loom holds taut lengthwise threads, called **warp,** and a shuttle carries crosswise threads, called **weft, woof,** or **filling,** in and out between them. Fabrics were traditionally made from natural fibers such as animal hair, cotton, linen, or silk. Today artificial fibers, including rayon, fiberglass, nylon, and polyester, are used alone or in combination with natural fibers.

Cloth The fibers used and the types of weaves determine the weight and texture of the cloth produced. There are three basic types of cloth weaves. In **plain weave,** the simplest and strongest, the filling yarn passes over one warp thread and under the next, as in broadcloth, burlap, muslin, or taffeta. In **satin weave,** or **floating-yarn weave,** the filling yarn floats over several warp threads at a time, producing a lustrous surface. In **twill weave,** which is also strong, warp and filling yarns are interlaced in broken diagonal patterns as in gabardine and denim. Other types of weave include **tapestry weave,** a plain weave in which the weft makes little irregular patches of color, and **pile weave,** in which the weft forms loops, which are cut so as to make a soft, even surface, as in velvet.

By using different kinds of threads, threading the loom in different ways, and varying the way the weft is interwoven, weavers can create an almost infinite variety of fabrics, ranging from rough, sturdy wool cloth for workers' garments to the most delicate cotton muslins and rich figured silks for the upper classes. For generations Indians, such as the Mixtec of Monte Albán, Mexico, have woven fabrics on handlooms, perpetuating the ancient geometrical motifs, which seem to accentuate the horizontal and vertical structure of weaving (Fig. 133). Renaissance Europe was infatuated with rich silks and velvets of complex design. In paintings of the period, such as *The Journey of the Magi* (Fig. 134) by Benozzo Gozzoli (1420–1497), worshipers' garments reveal finely detailed figural weaves that contrast with heavy velvets and edgings of gold or silver thread.

Hand weavers today combine some of the earliest techniques with others that have been developed over the centuries. They may use traditional fibers, new synthetic fibers, or a combination of both. Although some of the effects achieved by hand weavers can be attempted on high-speed mechanical looms, machine-made textiles are usually more aesthetically satisfying when the designer has used the machine to produce its own effects rather than trying to duplicate handwoven material.

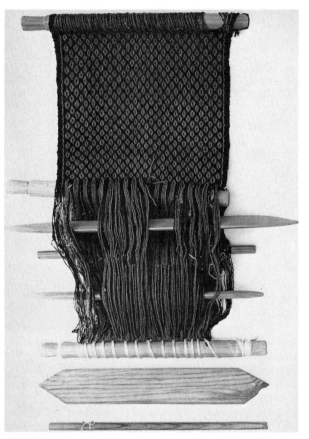

133. Fabric on hand loom, Oaxaca, Mexico. 1971. Wool, 19 × 34″ (48 × 86 cm). Collection the author.

Tapestry The tapestry-weaving technique, which dates from ancient times, has been used by some civilizations to make tightly woven, figured hangings **(tapestries)** that are considered a major art form. The silk tapestry of China and the wool tapestry made in Europe since the Middle Ages are outstanding. European tapestry weavers, working from a cartoon the same size as the projected tapestry, created intricate pictures using hundreds of colors. These tapestries, which took years to make, illustrated religious scenes and medieval and classical legends. They were used primarily to cover stone walls of chilly medieval castles and later to add richness to royal palaces. The magnificent unicorn tapestry series from the Metropolitan Museum of Art in New York is still brilliant after centuries. It depicts Christ as the unicorn, a complex 15th-century symbol (Fig. 135). In the 20th century there has been a revival of this ancient art form. Outstanding painters and sculptors design tapestries to be woven by professional hand weavers, while others design and weave tapestries themselves.

Rugs Another important textile art is that of rug making, in which short pieces of yarn are knotted around warp threads in various ways and then sheared. For centuries,

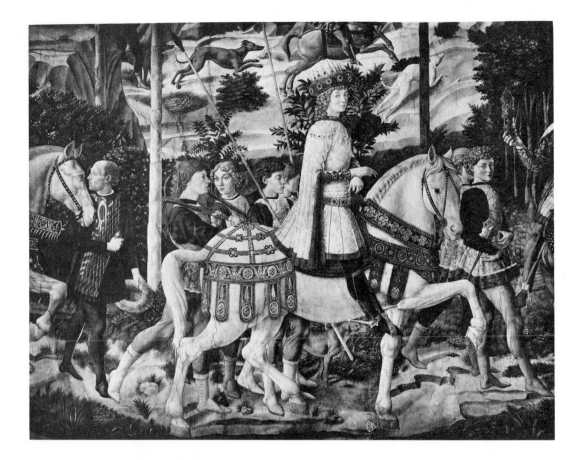

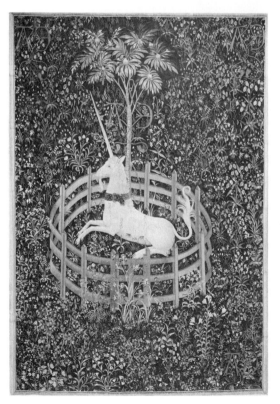

above: 134. Benozzo Gozzoli. *The Journey of the Magi,* detail. c. 1459-61. Fresco, length 12′4¼″ (3.77 m). Chapel, Medici-Riccardi Palace, Florence.

left: 135. *The Unicorn in Captivity* (*The Hunt of the Unicorn,* VII). French or Flemish, late 15th century, from the Château of Verteuil, France. Wool and silk with metal threads, 12′1″ × 8′3″ (3.63 × 2.51 m). Metropolitan Museum of Art, New York, Cloisters Collection (gift of John D. Rockefeller, Jr., 1937).

weavers in the Middle East and China have been making rugs in geometric, floral, and calligraphic designs to serve as hangings, floor coverings, and saddle bags. Persian prayer rugs of the 15th century were noted for their intricate designs and rich color. Handwoven Oriental rugs have long been highly prized in the West (Fig. 7), which has also imitated them by machine.

Applied Ornament Fabrics that do not have designs woven into them may have designs applied by embroidery, block or stencil printing, or the processes of batik and tie-dyeing. These are all ancient arts, which have persisted to the present day, though current materials and machine methods have changed them somewhat. The famous

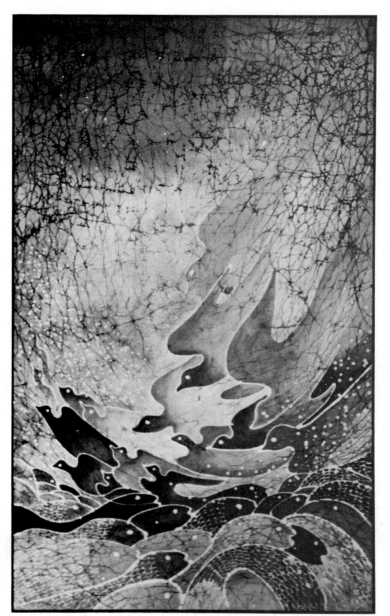

136. Helen B. Muller.
Birds and Fishes. 1973.
Batik, 4'10" × 3'
(1.47 × 0.91 m).
Collection the artist.

Bayeux Tapestry, discussed earlier, is not a tapestry but carefully embroidered linen, intended to go around the walls of a room in Bayeux Castle (Fig. 62). Embroidery was much used on household furnishings and garments in pre-industrial Europe and the American colonies.

Fabrics ornamented with hand-printed designs were made in ancient Egypt and were widely produced in India and the Orient. They were laboriously printed from carved wood blocks or from stencils. Printed Indian cottons were brought by traders to Europe and became extremely popular in the 18th century. European textile makers printed from wood blocks and engraved copper plates, but as machine printing developed, inked rollers engraved or etched with the design were substituted for the blocks and

plates. The fast presses that are in use today can print thousands of yards of fabrics for shirts, dresses, and window curtains in a short period of time. Silk-screen printing is also used.

Both batik and tie-dyeing are old methods of ornamenting fabric, which have been revived and used to create wall hangings as well as materials for clothing. In **batik,** melted wax, which resists dye, is used to block out areas of the cloth that are to remain white or light colored. Each succeeding dye bath produces deeper colors by dyeing over the lighter colors. Batik dye may also be used for painting directly over wax-blocked areas on fabric, as in a wall hanging by Helen B. Muller (b. 1922), one of a series devoted to Old Testament themes (Fig. 136). In **tie-dyeing,**

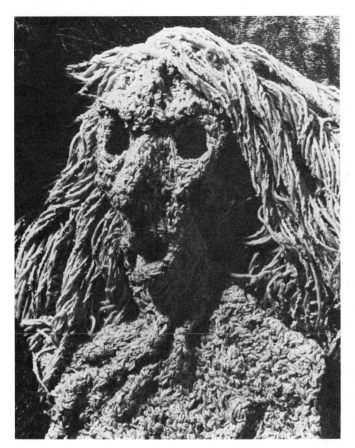

the parts of the fabric that are to remain light are tightly tied with string to prevent the dye bath from touching them.

Other Textile Arts Today artists often combine embroidery of various kinds with printing techniques, hand-weaving, and macramé. **Macramé** is the art of knotting strands of fiber together to produce a variety of openwork patterns. Originally used to make fishing nets, it is used today also to create belts, handbags, clothing, plant hangers, and wall hangings. The large macramé piece designed as body jewelry by Janna Russell (Fig. 3) is made of cross-sectioned shell, feathers, and ceramic beads, as well as intricately knotted waxed cord. Using macramé and weaving techniques, artists have created three-dimensional wall hangings, free-standing sculpture, and environments large enough to walk into.

Other old textile techniques have been revived and are used with great inventiveness. **Quilted** fabric, in which ornamental stitching holds stuffing in place, looped and knotted textiles, and the incorporation of grasses and twigs with woven fibers are some of the techniques contemporary artists use to produce interesting textures. Walter Nottingham (b. 1930) reflects the current interest in soft sculpture in his primeval figure, which uses a variety of fibers to produce a macabre effect that somehow both intrigues and disturbs us (Fig. 137).

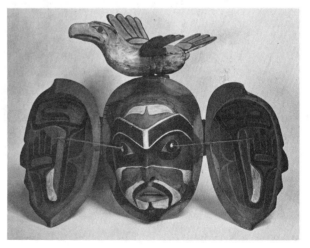

Wood

Wood has played an important role in nearly every phase of human existence. The tombs of the ancient Egyptians were full of wooden utensils and furniture put there to make the dead comfortable in the afterlife. The peoples of Africa, Oceania, and pre-Columbian America have used wood for boat decorations, sculpture, furniture, and masks (Fig. 138). Medieval cathedrals were treasure houses of carved wooden choir screens, choir stalls, and altars. In many civilizations, musical instruments, such as the famous Stradivari violins of 18th-century Cremona, Italy, were made of wood because of the mellow tones it can produce.

The great cabinetmakers of 18th-century Europe created luxurious furniture and floors for the aristocracy in which contrasting wood grains were inlaid in complex floral designs known as **marquetry** and geometric designs known as **parquetry.** Wood was also often combined with metal or inlaid with ivory or shell. In China and Japan thin wood formed the bases of bowls, boxes, and furniture coated with highly polished, water-resistant lacquer, which was then carved or painted. On the American frontier and in Shaker communities wooden furniture was simple, functional, and often aesthetically pleasing. The more refined, intricate carving, with damask seat, of the mahogany chair by Thomas Chippendale (1718–1779) in Figure 139 combines delicacy and strength. Such designs still influence contemporary furniture makers.

Artisans use wood today chiefly for furniture and accessories such as bowls, trays, and serving implements. Their work is generally characterized by emphasis on the wood grain and the patina, or finish, slowly built up. For instance, Dick Shanley (b. 1934) reveals the joy and beauty of materials in all his work. Each piece seems to rise uniquely from the wood block, as though born from the essence of the wood itself. Although all his work is functional, each piece can also be considered a piece of sculpture (Fig. 140).

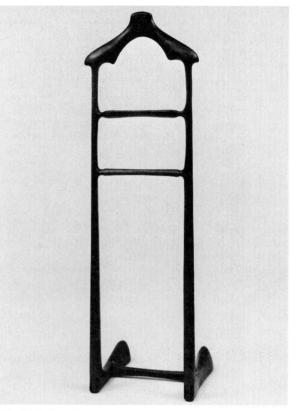

140. Dick Shanley. *Valet.* 1982. Wood, height 4′5″ (1.34 m). Collection Mr. and Mrs. Tyler Hicks.

139. Side chair. English, c. 1750. Mahogany, 38⅝ × 23 × 13⅝″ (98 × 58 × 35 cm). Metropolitan Museum of Art, New York (gift of Judge Irwin Untermyer, 1951).

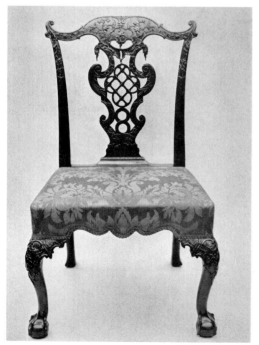

Metal

Metal has been used for jewelry, weapons, ritual objects, and household goods since ancient times, but because metalworking requires more complex technology, it developed later than ceramics and weaving. Each metal, ranging from rare gold and silver to common copper, tin, the alloy bronze, and iron, has different qualities and requires different handling, but all are worked by the same techniques—**hammering, raising** (hammering a flat shape into a hollow vessel), and casting (see Chapter 6 on sculpture). Decorative techniques include **embossing,** or **repoussé** (raised work); **chasing** (depressed work); engraving; and inlay with other metals, gemstones, or enamel. Metal can also be used to plate less expensive materials such as wood.

Chinese ritual cast bronzes of the Shang period are magnificent examples of metalwork. The vessels, used for offering food and wine to deceased ancestors, were richly covered over their whole surface with stylized animal forms that often seem to metamorphose into one another and with pictographic script. Possibly these motifs derive from religious symbolism. The wine vessel shown here (Fig. 141) combines elegant, refined detail with a powerful silhouette, perhaps inspiring awe or fear in the beholder.

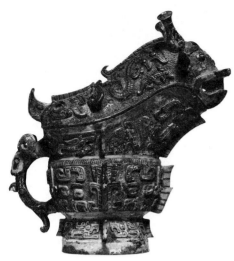

141. Ceremonial wine vessel. Late Shang Period, 12th–11th century B.C. Bronze, height 9" (23 cm). Asian Art Museum of San Francisco (Avery Brundage Collection).

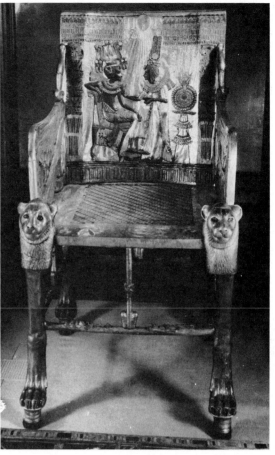

above: 142. Throne of Tutankhamen. c. 1365 B.C. Wood covered with gold leaf and colored inlays of faience, glass, and stone. Egyptian Museum, Cairo.

below: 143. Bebe Dushey. Wearable jewelry, pendant-pin. 1978. Fused, soldered, and oxidized sterling silver with large moss agate and smaller moonstone; 4½ × 2½" (11 × 6 cm). Collection the artist.

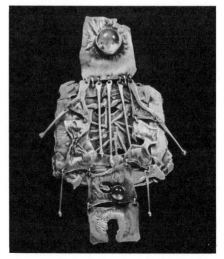

Cast coins and medals from ancient civilizations and the Renaissance often bore the portraits of rulers or other devices in low relief. Gold hammered into thin sheets was used to plate Tutankhamen's wooden throne (Fig. 142). Gold and gilded silver inlaid with jewels or enamels were used in the Middle Ages and Renaissance for jewelry, royal crowns, book covers, chalices (cups for the celebration of Mass), and secular vessels such as the Cellini saltcellar (Fig. 126). Steel armor was often engraved and inlaid with gold. Iron was hammered into hinges or elaborate grilles and gates.

Whatever metal they choose, metalworkers must consider its weight, ability to support weight, and susceptibility to corrosion. They must explore all the possibilities of shaping the metal and finishing the surface in order to create an object that serves its function as well as achieving an aesthetic effect.

The desire to enhance the human form with jewelry is universal. Men and women of the Old Stone Age decorated themselves with necklaces and bracelets of stones, shells, feathers, and bones. The jewelry of ancient civilizations involved metalwork, enameling, and cutting and polishing gemstones. Modern tastes in jewelry range from precious gold and diamonds, often regarded as an investment, to costume jewelry in artificial materials and plastic. Jewelry by Bebe Dushey (b. 1927) reflects her obvious love for the materials she uses. Each of Dushey's designs, which balance positive and negative shapes, has also been exhibited as small sculpture (Fig. 143).

Every age and society has made its own contributions to the various decorative arts. Exploring the range of materials and the ways in which artists have used them leads us to contrast handmade works with today's industrial wares. It also provokes the question, "Cannot art be produced by industry's machines if they are controlled by artists?"

EXERCISES AND ACTIVITIES

1. Many of the principles of design found in handcrafted products are based on the natural environment. Find examples in this book and elsewhere. Discuss the way these basic principles are applied to one specific piece of functional art.

2. Explain the place of proportion in the design of useful objects. What was the Greek Golden Section? Can you find an object that seems to reflect this principle?

3. Select from two to five crafts to trace from their earliest beginnings to the present. What differences, if any, do you note in those crafts today?

4. Experiment with a craft you have always admired, perhaps macramé or pottery. Use a reference text on the subject, chosen from the recommended bibliography, as a guide.

5. With a spirit of adventure, investigate a craft that is less familiar to you, such as origami. Attempt some of the earlier projects listed in a book on the subject. You may be surprised at how satisfying it is to work with your hands in a new medium.

8 Design for Industry

Form follows function.

LOUIS SULLIVAN

Design, or order, seems to be a universal principle (Fig. 144). The order of our natural world appears to inspire our designers in all the visual arts, from drawing to jewelry, as we have discovered. The design of objects for everyday use has evolved from time-honored traditions of crafts, changed somewhat by the machine, mass methods of production, and new materials.

Artists for industry design products for mass manufacture, and unlike artists in the fine and in the handcrafted decorative arts, are rarely further involved in producing what they design. Since the Industrial Revolution, however, when handwork was replaced by machines, industrial designers, whether they work in the printing, publishing, advertising, clothing, or furniture industries, must be concerned with both the aesthetic form and practical function of their design to satisfy customers. In addition, designers must respect their materials and be sensitive to the capabil-

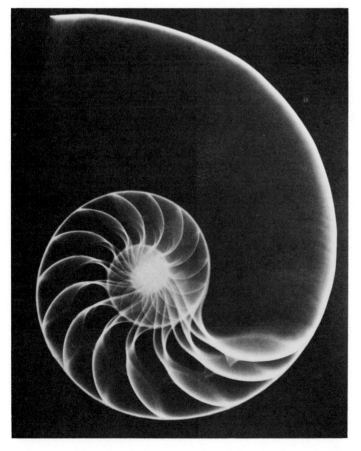

144. Nautilus shell revealed through radiography. Courtesy Eastman Kodak Company, Rochester, N.Y.

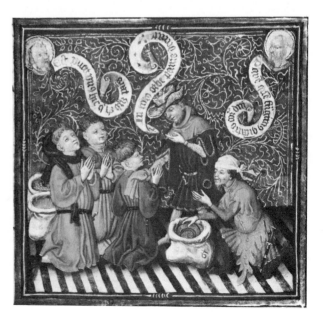

ities and limitations of the machines that transform materials into manufactured goods. Designers contribute to the complex order of our world with a view to making everyday living more efficient and gratifying to us all.

Printing Industry

The printing industry, like cinema, television, and radio, serves mass communication. Printing communicates through graphic symbols, recognized images that stand for ideas. Since earliest times societies have developed graphic symbols to communicate ideas. Some symbols are abstract, such as letters of the alphabet, Babylonian cuneiform characters representing sounds and ideas (Fig. 145), numbers, or musical notes. These are forms of written language. Other symbols are pictorial and universal, such as a drawing of a crown to symbolize royalty. Even in ancient times, symbols advertised what was for sale—for instance, a bakery in Pompeii was identified by a painting of bread. Many modern corporations have trademarks that are mainly pictorial symbols, or **logotypes,** which are usually the company's name or initials. Most Americans, for example, recognize IBM. The letters stand for International Business Machines, and their modern, squared-off computer-related style suggests the stability, accuracy, and industry that the company wishes to convey (Fig. 146).

Sometimes communication is best served through a combination of abstract, written symbols and pictures. Compare the words inscribed in the unfurled banners of the illuminated medieval manuscript page of *Solomon as the Symbol of Wisdom* (Fig. 147) with the message carried by the words in a "balloon" in any modern comic strip that you know. In the medieval work, King Solomon is distributing bread to several beggars and unfurls a banner inscribed with a quotation from Proverbs 9:5 where Wis-

above: 145. Cuneiform tablet, detail.
Sumerian, c. 2050 B.C.
Baked clay, entire tablet 3⅛ × 5⅛" (8 × 13 cm).
Babylonian Collection, Yale University,
New Haven, Conn.

below: 146. Logo for IBM. 1969.
Designed by Paul Rand.

right: 147. *Solomon as the Symbol of Wisdom,*
from the *Hours of Catherine of Cleves.* c. 1440.
Manuscript illumination, 2½ × 2⅝" (6 × 7 cm).
Pierpont Morgan Library, New York.

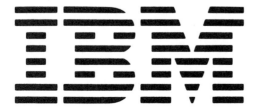

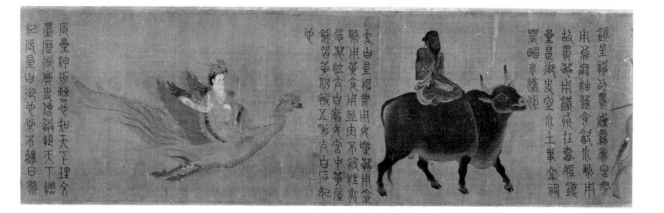

dom invites everyone to share her bread. In the corners above, the apostles Andrew and Paul unfurl banners inscribed with biblical quotations referring to the bread of the Eucharist. You can see that communication techniques have not changed substantially, although today's content and purpose are very different.

So accustomed are we to the printed page that we can easily forget that for thousands of years most words set down in permanent form were written by hand. Each book was in fact a manuscript (from the Latin words for "handwritten"), an original or a laboriously lettered copy. In China, Japan, and medieval Europe, handwriting developed into the highly decorative art of calligraphy. A study of the characters painted on a silk handscroll of the Sung dynasty reveals the pictorial quality of early Chinese writing (Fig. 148). In some examples, traces of the human figure may be seen. Later Chinese calligraphy was more abstract and, as we have noted, very close to drawing and painting (Fig. 32).

Printing began in ancient times as a way of repeating designs on fabric. By the 9th century the Chinese and Japanese were printing characters and pictures cut on wood blocks on paper. By the 14th century they were using movable wooden type many years before printers in the West. Woodcut illustrations were common in Europe in the 15th century, as we saw in Chapter 4, although books were still lettered by hand. Somewhat later Johann Gutenberg of Mainz coordinated into one process the several elements needed to make the transition from single, handwritten books to printed books in multiple copies—paper, ink, a printing press, and movable metal type. That type consisted of single cast letters that could be combined into words, locked into a form, and, after they had been printed, reused in other combinations.

Typefaces The common typefaces used today are derived from the square capital letters cut with hammer and chisel by ancient Roman stonecutters on monuments and written with chisel-ended pens on parchment by scribes. Such letters have thick and thin strokes ending in **serifs** (short lines set on angle to the stroke). Roman letters might

148. Chen Hsing (Saturn), from *The Planets and Twenty-eight Celestial Stations*. Sung dynasty, A.D. 500–550. Color on silk, height 10¾" (27 cm). Osaka (Japan) Municipal Museum.

well have been lost during the violence and unrest of the Dark Ages had not the Emperor Charlemagne in the 8th century encouraged a revival of ancient learning in the monasteries.

Over the centuries, Roman letters as copied by Carolingian scribes became modified into the angular, compressed style used in medieval manuscripts of the Gothic period. In the Renaissance Roman letters were revived by humanist scholars studying ancient manuscripts. Early designers of type were inspired by both styles. Today there are numerous typefaces to meet various requirements. They may be arranged into groups or families: Roman, black letter, script, and sans serif (often called Gothic). Italic is a sloping variant of Roman and sans serif (Fig. 149).

Roman type, with thick and thin elements and serifs, is traditionally used for books, newspapers, and other reading matter. It has two subgroups. Old Style Roman letters have graceful, sloping serifs. Modern (18th-century)

Old Style Roman

Modern Roman

Modern Italic

Script

𝕯𝖊𝖈𝖔𝖗𝖆𝖙𝖎𝖛𝖊

Sans Serif

149. Sample typefaces.

Roman faces have straight serifs and a greater distinction between thick and thin elements. Typefaces were first identified by the names of their designers, such as a **Bodoni,** Roman typeface, designed by the 18th-century Italian Giambattista Bodoni (1740–1813).

The other type families are less common. **Black letter types,** also called **text** or **Old English,** are modeled on late medieval illuminated manuscripts. Gutenberg printed the Bible in black letter. This type family is decorative but often hard to read and is used today to suggest medieval times. **Script typefaces** imitate handwriting and are therefore slanted. Just as there are many styles of handwriting, so there are many script typefaces, used almost entirely for announcements, invitations, and display heads.

Sans serif type is in wide use today. Unlike Roman, letters are of almost uniform thickness, with no serifs. Its name is French, meaning "without serifs." Sans serif types, called Gothic letters by many typographers, are chosen to give a sense of modernity and efficiency.

It is surprising to note the variety within these type families. The differences from one typeface to another often seem small and take a practiced eye to recognize, but they greatly affect readability as well as the appearance of the page as a whole. For instance, a page of this book has a light gray tone, while pages of other books, set in heavier typefaces, appear darker. Designers of printed matter, especially advertisements, must choose type carefully to give the material the desired appearance and mood. Pay special attention to advertisements, where you will often see un-

usual adaptations of the basic groups of type. Herb Lubalin (1918–1981), an internationally known type designer, created an elegant logo for *Avant Garde* magazine that has become a classic, although the magazine is now out of print (Fig. 150). He was one of the first designers to position letters almost in contact with each other.

Typesetting In general, type design has not changed radically since the earliest days, but typesetting has. For more than four hundred years, metal type was laboriously set by hand, as it still is for special headings. In the 19th century, numerous machines were invented to replace hand composition. Today two chief kinds of machines for composing metal type remain—linotype machines, which cast slugs, or lines of type, as one piece, and monotype machines, which cast individual characters. Both machines space the words to justify lines, or fill them out to the desired width.

More and more type today is being set by special typewriters as cold type or by phototypesetters, which produce photographic images of characters on paper or film. In phototypesetting, varieties of type styles are stored on small discs and can be run by computers to make printing faster and more efficient. Computers have revolutionized typesetting and are likely to induce further radical changes in the process and labor force.

Printing Processes Like typesetting, the method of impressing type on paper has changed enormously. Gutenberg and other early printers used a hand-operated torsion screw to apply pressure on a flat wooden press and were able to turn out a few hundred sheets a day. Today's mechanized rotary presses are power-driven machines, which can produce the same number of impressions in a few minutes or even seconds. The upper cylinders carry the paper—the lower ones are the printing plates, which transfer ink to paper at high speed.

There are three major printing processes, which correspond to the printmaking methods discussed in Chapter 4. **Letterpress** is printed from a raised, or relief, surface (Fig. 151a). **Gravure** is printed from an intaglio, or depressed,

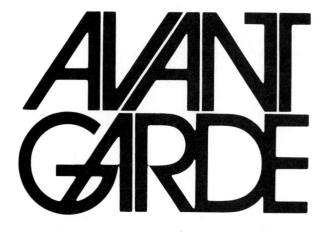

left: 150. *Avant Garde* logo, designed by Herb Lubalin.

below: 151. Mechanized rotary press printing.

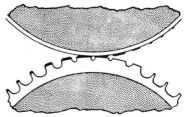
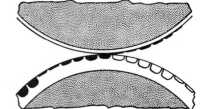
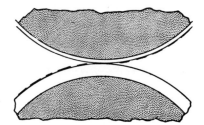

a. Letterpress

b. Gravure

c. Offset

surface (Fig. 151b). **Offset lithography** is printed from a level, or plane, surface (Fig. 151c).

Letterpress, evolving from the artist's woodcut, is the oldest and until recently the most common method of printing. Ink is applied to a raised surface and transferred directly to the paper through pressure. The ink rollers touch only the raised areas, not the lower, surrounding spaces. There are several different types of presses, but the basic principle is the same.

In gravure, derived from engraving, an image is etched below the surface of a copper plate or cylinder. The etched plate is inked and the excess ink is wiped off the surface. The ink remaining in the depressed areas is directly transferred to the paper by pressure. As with most such printing, the oily ink can be felt on the printed page. Gravure is considered to be the best method of reproducing illustrations, but since the plates are expensive to make, it is only used when a large number of impressions are to be printed. Art books and magazine sections of newspapers are mainly gravure.

Offset lithography, derived from direct lithography, is the most recent of the three printing processes. The two main differences between it and other methods are the lithographic principle that grease and water do not mix and the indirect way the image is transferred to the paper. The image, drawn in greasy material on the same level of the plate with the nonprinting areas, is inked and transferred to a rubber roller called a blanket. Then it is transferred from the blanket to the paper. One of the big advantages of offset printing is that the softer rubber blanket can produce a clearer impression on many kinds of surface.

Photomechanics The old ways of printing illustrations from handmade woodcuts, steel or copper engravings, or lithographic stones have been replaced by photomechanical processes, which transfer the image to be printed to a metal plate by photography. These processes vary somewhat for each of the major printing methods. The oldest, first used in the late 19th century, is photoengraving, which makes letterpress plates. The others are photogravure and photolithography. The cheapest and simplest kind of photoengraved plate is the **line plate,** or **line cut,** used to reproduce images made up of solid black and white lines or areas with no gray middle tones. Examples of line cut are some diagrams in this book and pen-and-ink drawings. The artwork is photographed and the resulting image on the negative is transferred to the sensitized plate by a photographic process. The plate is then etched in acid to eat away the areas that are to remain white. An effect of intermediate tones can be produced by drawing the lines close together or by using prepared screens with dots or crosshatchings. Many artists from Rembrandt to Charles White have worked in cross-hatch (Fig. 72).

Halftone plates are used to reproduce photographs, watercolor drawings, or paintings that require intermediate or continuous tones. When halftones are photographed, a screen, placed between the camera lens and the film, converts the image on the negative into dots. Like line cuts, the halftone plates are also etched in acid, and the dots remain in relief to pick up the ink. The tiny dots of fine reproductions can hardly be seen, but if you look at the pictures in a newspaper, you can see the dot patterns easily.

This complex process of printing with dots for black-and-white reproductions becomes even more critical when printing in color. The colored illustrations you see in books and magazines, like fine color prints, are made by printing several colors one on top of another. This is done by making a separate plate for each color to be printed. The plates are obtained by photographing a subject through special filters, which separate the colors of the original. Each color—magenta (red), yellow, cyan (blue), and black—is printed individually from separate plates. Alignment, or registration, is crucial for each printing; otherwise the dot patterns will not match up, and the illustration will appear fuzzy.

The many variations within the three major printing methods and different types of presses are numerous and complex. Specialized presses, inks, papers, and methods meet a variety of needs from printing metallic inks on drinking glasses to reproducing detailed colored paintings with every nuance of brush stroke. In addition, there are many new technological developments, which may change printing completely. For example, electronic engraving machines, computers that decide on the exact degree of color correction needed, and new plastics, metals, and other products are all making for faster and more accurate printing.

Commercial Art

Many professional artists, who work on commercial assignments, are paid by an industry, such as publishing or advertising. They produce graphic art. The term **graphic arts** can mean pictorial arts that are strong, clear, and linear rather than painterly. But the term today is generally restricted to pictorial arts used in printing books, magazines, advertising, posters, and other material. Commercial artists create graphic imagery that is designed to make immediate impact on the observer, perhaps to sell a product or service or to publicize an institution or event.

Illustration The professional illustrator dominates the field of graphic art. Many illustrators concentrate on editorial (nonadvertising) themes. They may illustrate books or magazines or industrial reports. A few illustrators enjoy the prestigious assignments of designing covers for books, magazines, and record albums, which may carry their signatures. Alan Cober is an award-winning graphic artist with experience in many illustration media (Fig. 97). Commercial artists also find opportunities in designing greeting cards, direct mail pamphlets, catalogs, and posters. The new medium of computer graphics expands the broad diversity available to today's graphic artists.

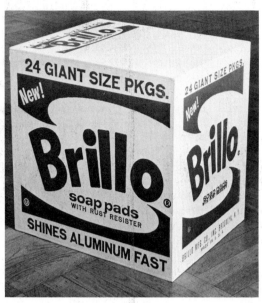

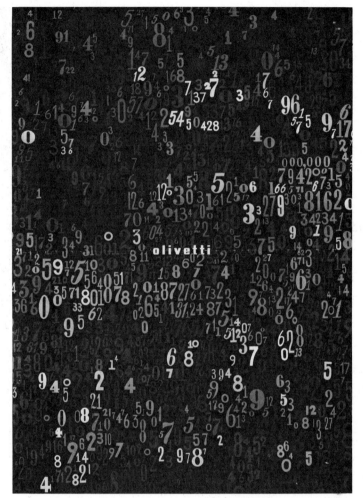

above: 152. Andy Warhol. *Brillo.* 1964. Painted wood, 17 × 17 × 14″ (43 × 43 × 36 cm). Leo Castelli Gallery, New York.

right: 153. Olivetti Corporation advertisement, designed by G. Pintori. 1947. Courtesy of Docutel Olivetti Corporation.

Advertising and Packaging In our consumer-oriented society, advertising and packaging account for a large part of the printed material in our lives. Advertising has been defined as "salesmanship in print," and the goal of most advertising art is to capture and hold the attention of potential customers long enough to induce them to buy. When we choose products in a supermarket, we are frequently led to our selections by logos and packaging details. For this reason, most advertising and packaging designs are easily understood symbols and type in bold colors.

The Pop artist Andy Warhol commented on the familiarity of these commercial images in oversized artwork such as a painted Brillo box (Fig. 152). He made the box very large in order to suggest that advertising, packaging, and marketing techniques are the dominant visual images today. His work reflects the principle that throughout history the size of images indicates their importance. Egyptian pyramids, Roman temples, and Gothic cathedrals, for example, dwarfed the individual in order to emphasize the powerful role of religion during those periods.

Although advertising art may appear deceptively simple, the process of research, evaluation, and design necessary to produce a sophisticated advertisement such as this one for Olivetti Corporation (Fig. 153) is demanding, requiring highly developed skills. Since the entire image represents symbols common to many Olivetti machines, the ad has a timeless quality that is as effective in the 1980s as it was in 1947 when it first appeared.

Most ads, however, like yesterday's newspapers, are prepared for a limited time and carefully predetermined market. Once the theme of the advertisement is selected by the client, the artist makes rough "thumbnail" sketches of the layout. They eventually result in a final, carefully prepared pasted-up assembly of artwork and type called a **mechanical,** which is copied by camera for the printing plate.

Whether working in the field of magazine, book, or advertising design, graphic artists must have a knowledge of lettering, typography, layout, reproduction methods, and printing techniques. Even more important, they must be skilled, creative, and imaginative in using the elements of design—balance, unity, line, color, and shape—that apply to all the visual arts. In the hands of a good designer, the graphic processes can be used creatively and expressively to produce visually exciting and satisfying pages. In fact, many painters such as Frank Stella (Fig. 99) and Warhol move easily into the commercial field with aesthetically pleasing results. This pen, ink, and wash drawing by Warhol, prepared for a public service campaign to deter drug abuse (Fig. 154), is a particularly arresting image.

Fabric Design

Textiles are basic to contemporary living, yet are rooted in fiber arts of the past. As we saw in Chapter 7, natural fibers have been supplemented by rayon, fiberglass, and synthetic materials, such as Orlon and nylon, which produce easy-to-care-for fabrics that are resistant to dirt, wrinkles, and mildew. Similarly, handweaving and hand decorating by wood-block printing, batik, tie-dyeing, and silkscreen have been adapted to or largely replaced by machine processes. Computers are now frequently involved in textile design. Where precise repetition of pattern is essential, few artists can operate with the speed and efficiency of a machine. Color combinations can be unlimited when the operation is computerized. Textiles that are one of a kind, however, such as those made by batik or tie-dyeing, remain the special province of craftspeople.

Textile designers, familiar with the properties of various fibers and weaves and the history and technique of designing patterned fabrics, may design textiles for furnishing or for clothing. Two major areas of clothing design are fashion and the theater.

Fashion. We usually assume that one of the basic reasons for wearing clothing is protection against the elements, but throughout history, people have also felt a strong impulse to decorate themselves and to be distinguished from (or else made to resemble) everybody else. In the past only the upper classes were privileged to wear clothes for decorative or ceremonial reasons. Today mass production has made it possible for millions to indulge their desire to be fashionable.

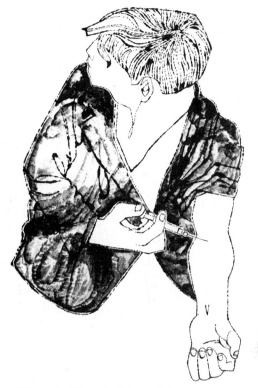

154. Andy Warhol. "Living Off the Main Line," advertisement for WCBS. 1951.
Pen, ink, and wash drawing.

The earliest wardrobes consisted not only of protective animal skins but also body paint, tattoos, headdresses, masks, and jewelry to enhance the wearer's appearance or produce magical or religious effects. Later, body scarification (Fig. 16), bloodstains, and hunting scars probably had as much social significance for the African tribal hunter as makeup had for an Egyptian noblewoman or a laurel wreath for a victorious Greek athlete. Clothing, then, was frequently linked to the wearer's status.

One of the oldest and most constant marks of status has been headgear. Even if he wore little else, the early king was distinguished by his crown. Religious leaders in all societies have been set apart by their headdresses and vestments. Other examples of status-giving clothing are the long robes and hoods worn by academics and the wigs worn by British judges. Uniforms provide instant identification for soldiers, nurses, mail carriers, the police, and Scouts. Modern athletes wear numbers and team uniforms on the field. For many young people, blue jeans have become at the same time a means of conformity and a status symbol, especially if a designer's label is affixed to the pocket. Foreign designers also now make jeans, once *the* American invention, but American jeans dominate all others on the international market.

Since the purpose of clothing is largely social, fashion in dress has been subject to as many changes as society itself, and clothing styles seem to express the social concerns of each period. Trends usually develop from the tastes of a social elite, whether that is the British aristocracy as depicted in elegant 18th-century portraits (Fig. 155) by Thomas Gainsborough (1727–1788) or the popular figures in today's entertainment world. Paris has traditionally been the center of high fashion, or **haute couture,** since the time of Louis XIV, and the semiannual showing of the latest Parisian designs continues to stimulate the fashion world. European influence, however, is not so dominant an element in American fashion today as it was 30 years ago. Now such outstanding American designers as Ralph Lauren (b. 1939), Mary McFadden (b. 1938), and (Roy)

155. Thomas Gainsborough. *Mrs. Richard Brinsley Sheridan.* 1785–86.
Oil on canvas, 7'2½" × 5'1½" (2.2 × 1.54 m).
National Gallery of Art, Washington, D.C. (Andrew Mellon Collection, 1937).

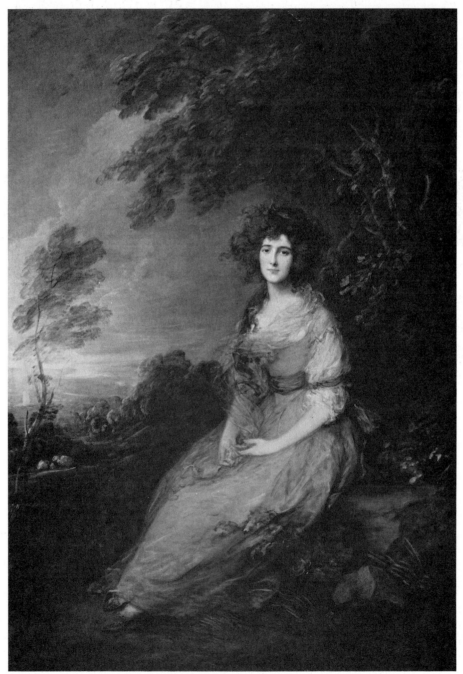

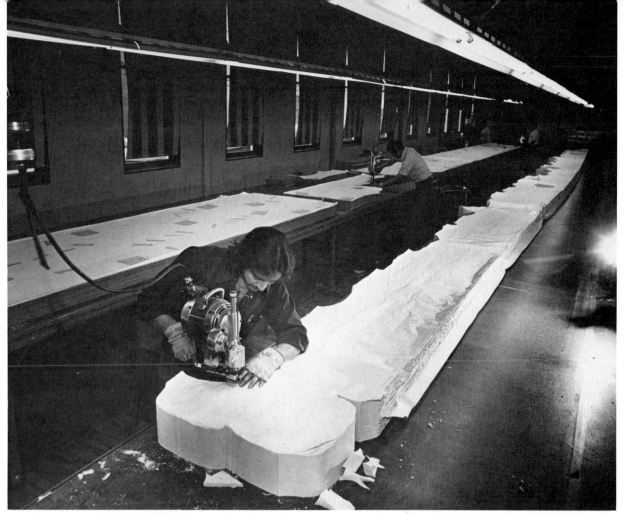

156. Cutting 400 pairs of Levis.®

Halston ([Frowick] b. 1932) have done much to replace our dependence on elegant imports with new appreciation for American styles.

A common characteristic of contemporary clothing design is that it generally conforms to the shape of the body that wears it. The awkward hooped skirts of Baroque court life find few counterparts in today's comfortable, active clothing. The same considerations of color, balance, line, and texture apply to dress as to any other well-designed article. Clothing, like sculpture, is to be seen from all sides, a fact that the designer must always keep in mind. But in addition, since contemporary clothing is seen in action, gathers of cloth are designed to emphasize the rhythmic flow of the figure.

It is interesting that there is no form of clothing worn today, with the possible exception of underwear and the jumpsuit, that cannot be found a thousand years ago. Cloaks, tunics, and sandals were worn in earliest times. Trousers were worn by ancient Persians as well as by the barbarians of northern Europe. Gloves and long (trunk) hose were a medieval creation. For this reason, knowledge of the evolution of costume is essential to every fashion designer and often provides inspiration for contemporary dress.

In the 20th century, fashion has been adapted to mass production. The latest creations of top designers, handsewn in their workrooms, are usually modified by less exclusive fashion houses and then finally produced in quantity from cheaper materials according to standardized patterns in factories (Fig. 156). The ready-to-wear fashion industry is a multimillion dollar business in the United States and depends on constant changes to provide a market for its products.

Theatrical Dress Like the fashion designer, the designer of costumes for the stage must also have a basic knowledge of the history of dress. The theatrical designer creates garments to establish the mood and character of the individual players, but they must also fit in with the total production.

Theatrical costume designs must be stylized and slightly exaggerated to carry across the footlights to the last row in the house. Often the designer has to find ways to produce historical costumes with present-day fabrics and accessories that may be quite different from the originals. Within budget restrictions the designer must create costumes that satisfy the director, meet the physical needs of the actors, contribute to the mood of the play, and interact successfully with the lighting.

Furniture

As a result of the Industrial Revolution, cheap production became the primary goal of most 19th-century manufacturers. The quality of manufactured articles was often inferior to handcrafted items. Excessive ornamentation took its place and indeed seemed to become an obsession. For instance, this chandelier, engraved around 1875 (Fig. 157), reflects the elaboration of form that a machine could achieve in seconds but that might have taken an artisan weeks to execute by hand. In reaction, William Morris and other designers in England launched the Arts and Crafts movement, hoping to lead society back to fine handcraftsmanship.

Wood   The reaction to excessive, machine-made surface ornament probably accounted for the early 20th-century style of severe simplicity called **De Stijl,** exemplified in a chair by the Dutch industrial designer and architect Gerrit Rietveld (1888–1964). An experimental design of elementary colors, of cubic forms, and a pioneering use of rectilinear, plywood planes, brightly painted in red, blue, and black, the simply joined structure of the chair is totally revealed (Pl. 10, p. 24).

The simplification of wooden shapes to **modules** (units) of standardized dimensions that can be produced in a factory has allowed the mass manufacturer to produce a maximum number of coordinated variations in furnishings with minimal effort. Purchasers can rearrange modules in varied space-saving combinations to suit their individual needs (Fig. 158). Other new industrial methods of using wood that have been applied to mass-produced furniture are laminated plywood and wood bent under heat and pressure. Plywoods, using thin layers of wood, help conserve it—important as natural materials become scarce while the demand for wood products grows.

Metal   To the traditional metals of iron and bronze, 20th-century designers have added aluminum and stainless steel for furniture and utensils. These metals can be worked by hand or machine and are particularly adaptable to mass production. An example of modern industrial craftsmanship in metal is the Barcelona chair (Fig. 159) by architect Ludwig Mies van der Rohe (1886–1969). Considered a classic for its fine design and honest use of materials, it proves again that industrially produced objects can be as aesthetically pleasing as handcrafted ones.

Synthetics   The invention of synthetic materials has opened new avenues of exploration and challenge to the designer. Probably the most important synthetic products

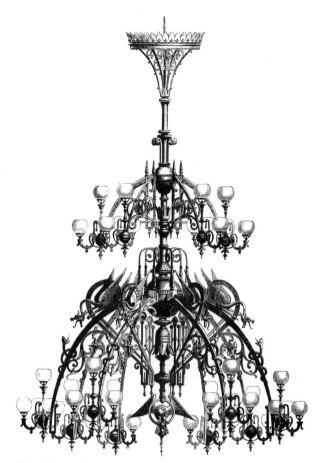

157. Chandelier, from *Household Taste,* by Walter Smith, published 1876.

are the plastic resins. Acrylic (plastic) resins make up the various types of lucites and plexiglass used for furniture and other objects. Another group, vinyl resins, are particularly adapted to tools and toys as well as to working surfaces and floors in homes and offices. All of these synthetic materials are used by designers to replace older natural materials. With these versatile plastics the industrial designer is able to quickly and economically create aesthetically pleasing designs for mass production, such as furniture (Fig. 160) by Eero Saarinen (1910–1961).

On the other hand, no way has yet been discovered to recycle plastic, and as a result we are rapidly running out of space to hold our discarded products. With the population pressures the world faces, artists and designers must consider potential use of products by vast numbers of people, as well as means of disposal, possible depletion of natural resources, and the power sources needed for production. If we are to continue to survive on this earth, we must reevaluate our goals in design and product development. What, indeed, will we leave to future generations if the industrial products we create today destroy the balance and resources of nature?

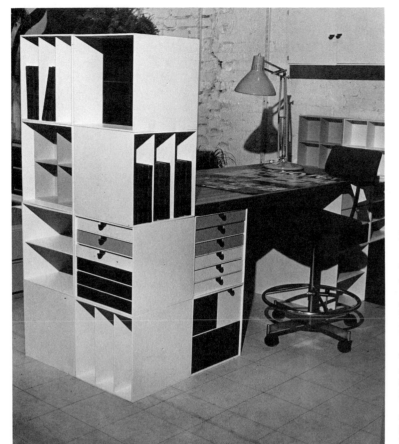

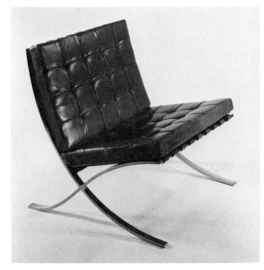

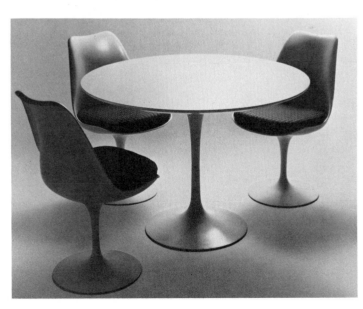

left: 158. Stackable furniture.
Ristomatti Ratia.
15½″ (39 cm) square and deep.
"Decembre" Collection,
made in Finland by Treston Oy.

below left: 159.
Ludwig Mies van der Rohe.
Lounge chair (Barcelona chair).
1929. Chrome-plated steel bars
with leather, height 29½″ (75 cm).
Museum of Modern Art, New York
(gift of the manufacturer,
Knoll Associates, U.S.A.).

below right: 160. Eero Saarinen. Table
and chairs. 1956. Courtesy Knoll
International, U.S.A.

Interior Design

Interiors need to be as carefully designed as the architectural structures that enclose them. Just as Frank Lloyd Wright (1869–1959) believed **Organic Architecture** evolves from the character of the site selected and the occupants' needs for living, so are organic interiors designed for the needs of those who occupy them. Major 20th-century architects are frequently involved in both exterior and interior design. The German Pavilion at the Barcelona World's Fair (Fig. 161) by Mies van der Rohe had a profound effect upon many later architects, including Philip Johnson (b. 1906). The original source of inspiration for both men was the traditional Japanese house, which, with its sliding screens and walls, continuously modifies interior space in relation to its occupants' needs and the outside world. Note the Barcelona chair, which made its first appearance at the Fair (Fig. 159).

The main living area of the Johnson house in New Canaan, Connecticut, is a glass box. The glass shields the interior from the weather but also makes the structure seem part of the landscape. Inside, the colors of the softly polished brick floor and leather furnishings harmonize with the grass and trees outside. The house reflects serenity and exhibits clarity of structure, beauty of proportion, and carefully refined details. Such visual spaces help shape the quality of our lives (Fig. 162).

161. Ludwig Mies van der Rohe. German Pavilion at the International Exposition, Barcelona, Spain. 1929. Photograph courtesy of Museum of Modern Art.

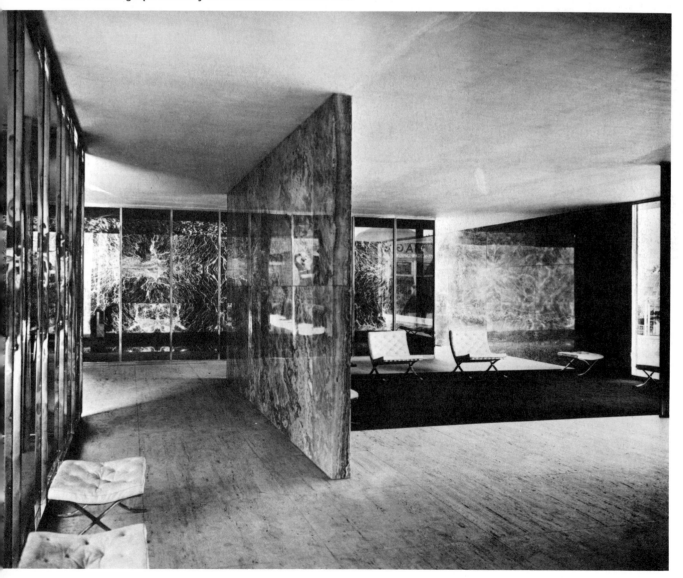

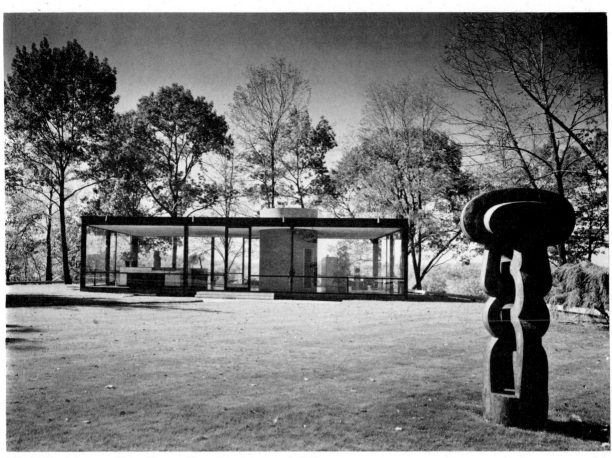

162. Philip Johnson. Glass House, New Canaan, Conn. 1949.

EXERCISES AND ACTIVITIES

1. On what basis are materials and processes usually selected for industry? Locate an example of an industrially produced object that seems honestly to express the material from which it is made. Find one that attempts to copy another material.

2. What is meant by the concept "Form follows function"? How does it apply to industrial design? Does it apply also to handcrafts? Locate one example of machine-made functional art and one of handmade functional art that seem to you to express this concept successfully.

3. How may our man-made environment be affected by industrial design? What effects may industrial design have on the ecology of our natural environment? What changes do you think could be made in our attitude toward the functional arts that might improve our environment?

4. The instinct for self-decoration is basic. What were humanity's earliest wardrobes, and what function did they serve? Pick the costume of one historical period and explain why you think it reflected the social conditions of the time. What items of apparel have developed as a result of changing life-styles in modern times?

5. Find examples of successful communication of ideas through visual means—in magazines, advertisements, and so on. What methods are used to communicate the ideas?

6. Design a logo for yourself or for a colleague. What qualities do you wish to be known by, whether on a personal or business level, that may be shown in your design?

9 Architecture

Architecture is the first manifestation of man creating his own universe. . . . The laws of gravity, of statics and of dynamics, impose themselves by a reductio ad absurdum: everything must hold together or it will collapse.

LE CORBUSIER, *Towards a New Architecture*

Of all the visual arts, architecture probably has the greatest impact upon us. Most of us spend the largest portions of our lives within walls. On the way to work or school we pass buildings, for all around us space has been enclosed and walled in. Architecture, the art of building, could as well be called the art of enclosing space in a useful and pleasing way.

What impels us to build? Obviously, the most basic reason is to provide shelter or protection from the weather or from animals or unfriendly humans. Imagine living on earth before there were buildings. What would you do for shelter? You could crawl under the branches of a tree, or—if you were lucky—you could find a cave to serve as refuge. Eventually, however, you would probably wish to create a more comfortable home.

You might make a lean-to from branches or a hut of bent sticks and sheets of bark such as those built by American Indians of the Northeast. You might weave saplings into a wall and plaster them with mud, as was done in some parts of Africa. Or you might, like people in the Middle East, shape clay into bricks, which, when dried in the sun, can be used as building units. Though these homes may seem crude, imagine the amount of time and invention needed to develop even these simple solutions to the universal requirement for housing.

After solving the problem of personal shelter, early people everywhere worked in communities to build permanent ceremonial temples to gods, fortresses for protection, and palaces and tombs for rulers. The appearance of these structures, then as now, was directly influenced by the climate, the available materials, the building site, and the needs of the people who used them.

Architectural Considerations and Plans

Architectural design involves certain basic concerns. These include (1) convenient arrangement and flow of space; (2) illumination from outside and within; (3) protection from the weather and interior climate control at all times; (4) efficient use of fuel, with possible solar alternatives. Roofs, walls, floors, doors, and windows must all be designed in the light of these requirements as well as to suit the owner and the location.

In addition, a house that satisfies its occupants goes beyond mere physical shelter and efficiency. In an age marked by standardization of materials and tastes, we appreciate houses planned and furnished with individuality. A well-designed house can provide an appropriate setting with provision for art as well as for other significant human experiences, a sense of spirituality, and a respect for the natural environment.

In the process of designing a building the architect makes many drawings, and if the design is complex, a three-dimensional model. An architect's plans may include:

floor plan: structural layout in scale, viewed from above
elevations: front, side, and rear views, in scale, showing all walls and openings
cross sections with details of electrical, heating, cooling, plumbing, and other special installations
perspective renderings: three-dimensional views, including landscaping and locations for sculpture

The architect's plans utilize a variety of materials and types of construction. Some date back thousands of years. Others are totally new materials and techniques developed during the Industrial Revolution and in the 20th century. Some architects have tried to maintain the familiar appearance of buildings while using new materials and methods, while others have designed structures that courageously reflect the new advances in construction (Fig. 163).

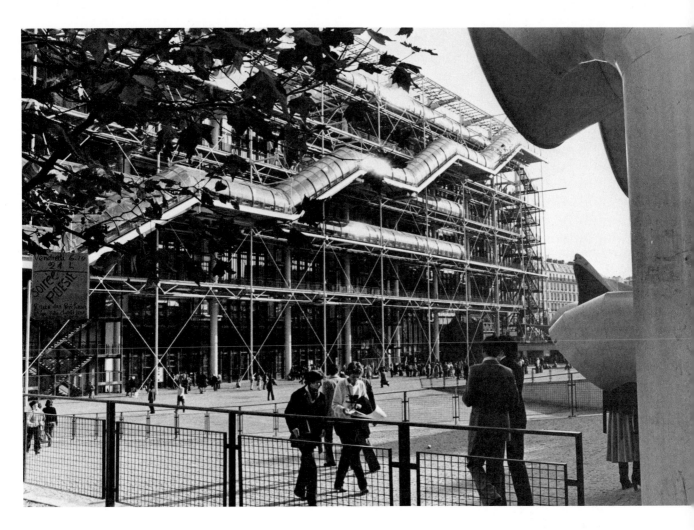

Construction Methods and Building Techniques

Over the centuries, builders have developed a number of methods of construction supporting both the weight of the building materials as well as the structures. The simplest method is the **bearing wall,** in which the whole length of the wall supports the roof. Its use is limited because the higher the roof, the heavier the wall must be. The second method is the post-and-lintel and other kinds of **frame construction.** The third is the arch and vault.

Post and Lintel More efficient than a bearing wall is a series of upright posts supporting a horizontal beam, or lintel, to form a strong rectangular frame (Fig. 164). Some lintels are placed in walls to span openings for doors and windows. The size of the opening depends on the length and strength of the lintel. Other lintels span interior space and support the roof, which may be flat in hot, dry regions or pitched (gabled) in cold, wet regions to allow snow and rain to run off. There is no limit to the size of the interior space so long as there is no objection to its being interrupted by many posts.

above: 163. Renzo Piano and Richard Rogers.
Georges Pompidou National Center for Art and Culture (Beaubourg), Paris. 1977.

below: 164. Post and lintel.

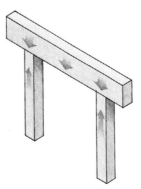

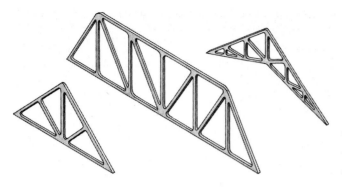

left: 165. Triangular trusses.

below: 166. Balloon framing.

bottom: 167. Steel cage construction.

The earliest post-and-lintel buildings were made of heavy tree trunks cut and fitted together, often with wooden pegs. In many ancient civilizations, temples and palaces were of post-and-lintel construction in stone. There are, however, a limited number of stones large enough to be lintels, and no stone can be very long without breaking of its own weight.

TRUSS Frame construction can span a large space without many interior posts if it uses **trusses,** or cross braces, whose members act together in tension and compression (Fig. 165). The most common type of truss is triangular. Essentially it consists of two sloping bars fastened at the top and connected at the bottom by a third bar to create a rigid triangle strong enough to support a heavy weight. Triangular trusses of wood were used under the wooden roofs of stone churches in the early Middle Ages. Later, more elaborate forms of wooden trusses developed. In the 19th and 20th centuries trusses have been made of iron and steel. Truss construction is the basis of modern A-frame buildings and of prefabricated modular systems that provide an ingenious, efficient, and economical way to span space.

SKELETON FRAME A more complex form of frame construction is the **skeleton frame.** The parts are lighter than posts and lintels and support one another to make a standing cage. In wooden construction the parts are made of light pieces of lumber nailed together, and the outside wall is nailed to the frame to increase its strength. A particularly light type called **balloon framing** developed in the 19th century when factories made iron nails in quantity and sawmills cut lumber in standard sizes. Most wooden houses today are built with balloon framing (Fig. 166). The outside walls, which used to be made of board siding, are now often sheets of plywood.

Skeleton frames are also used in iron and steel construction (Fig. 167). The parts are bolted or riveted together to make a cage that is lighter and stronger than wood and able to span large interiors with many fewer posts. The walls are attached to the cage but carry no weight and can therefore be glass or have many large windows. Such **curtain walls,** or **screen walls,** are only thin panels to keep out the weather and enclose the space. Iron- and steel-

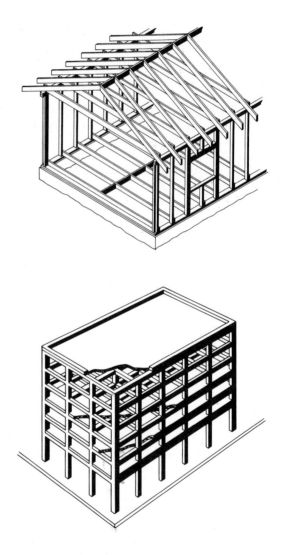

frame construction developed in the late 19th and early 20th centuries, making use of factory-made parts shipped by rail and assembled at the building site. Today steel-frame construction is all around us, as you may see in some school gymnasia and bridges and buildings under construction.

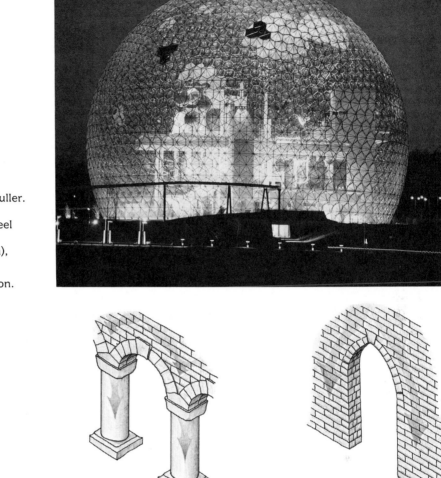

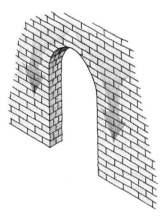

a. Corbelled arch. b. Round arch. c. Pointed arch.

GEODESIC DOME A modification of frame construction that uses the principle of the triangular truss is the **geodesic dome** invented by R. Buckminster Fuller (b. 1895) in the 1940s. It is a spherical shape consisting of a spidery framework of short struts forming a three-way grid composed of various arrangements of tetrahedrons (solids with four triangular faces). Drawing on late 19th-century discoveries that tetrahedrons are the basic structure of organic material, Fuller insisted that the tetrahedronal structure was naturally stronger than that of cubes or squares, which tend to collapse if they are not braced. The frame, usually of aluminum or other light material, can withstand pressure because it distributes stress equally among all its parts. It is covered with a skin of plastic or other light substance. Geodesic domes are made in prefabricated modular units and can be easily assembled on the site.

Fuller's geodesic dome for the United States Pavilion at Montreal's Expo '67 covered an area 250 feet (76 meters) in diameter (Fig. 168). Considered revolutionary at that time, such domes today come in all sizes and are accepted by most as a strong, efficient, and inexpensive way to enclose large areas quickly.

Arch, Vault, and Dome Still another way to span a wide opening or other large space without posts is with the **arch,** a curved line of bricks or stones. This method, which developed later than the post-and-lintel system, made possible the evolution of architecture from structures of massed materials to those of vast, open interior spaces.

The simplest form of arch is the **corbelled arch** (Fig. 169a), in which bricks or stones are built up from two sides, each projecting a little beyond the one below it, until they meet in the middle. These carefully balanced masonry units are held in place by gravity. Corbelled arches were developed in ancient Mesopotamia, where clay for brick was plentiful but there was little wood or stone.

The true arch, developed in ancient Mesopotamia and refined by the Etruscans and Romans, is an improvement over the corbeled arch because its wedge-shaped masonry units support each other through mutual pressure. In a round (semicircular) arch, such as used by the Romans, stones or bricks, shaped into wedges to fit snugly into the curve of the arch, are built up from the two sides, shoulders, or **imposts** framing the opening to meet at the **keystone,** the final wedge in the center (Fig. 169b). During construction they are held in place by wooden scaffolding called **centering,** which is removed when the keystone is in place. The wedges are squeezed together, and the weight of the wall or roof they support is sent through the arch outward and down to the ground. The sides are braced by massive **buttresses** to contain the outward pressure. Arches may also be horseshoe-shaped, as in Islamic architecture, or pointed, as in Gothic architecture (Fig. 169c), or may take other shapes.

A row of arches, side by side, forms an **arcade,** used as a wall or to hold an aqueduct, such as brought water to Roman cities (Fig. 170). A series of round arches placed one behind the other and connected by a roof produces an arch in depth called a **barrel vault** (Fig. 171a). It is used to roof a large space, as in the Roman palace of Diocletian in Spalato, Yugoslavia. It is more efficient than a wood lintel, which could burn, or a stone one, which could break. Because it is heavy, however, it must be supported by solid, buttressed walls, which can only have a few small windows.

Two barrel vaults intersecting at right angles make a **cross vault,** or **groin vault,** such as were used in Roman buildings and over the side aisles of Romanesque churches.

170. Pont du Gard, Nîmes, France. Late 1st century B.C.

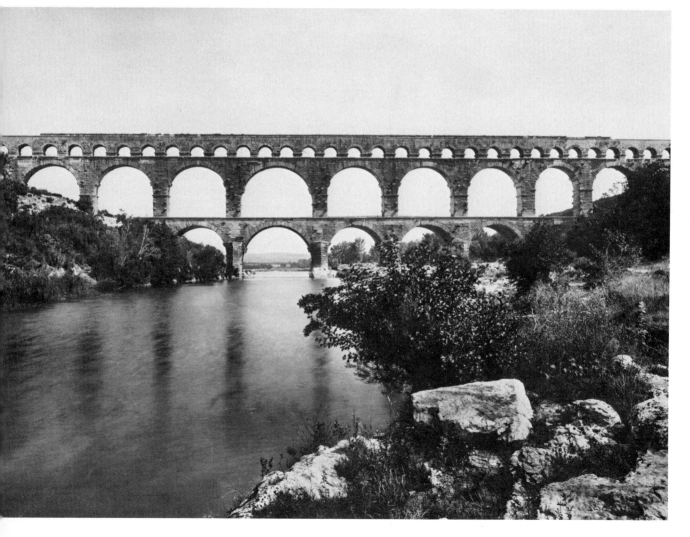

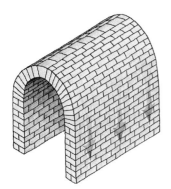

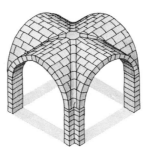

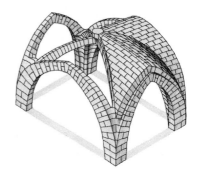

a. Barrel vault

b. Early ribbed vault with round arches covering square.

c. Gothic ribbed vault with pointed arches covering rectangle.

above: 171. Vault construction.

below left: 172. The Gothic system: cross section of a cathedral.

below right: 173. Pendentives (shaded area) supporting a dome.

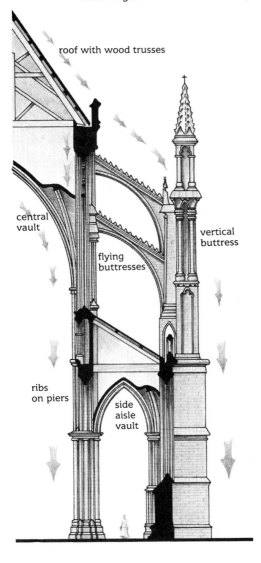

roof with wood trusses

central vault

flying buttresses

vertical buttress

ribs on piers

side aisle vault

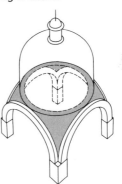

Because the two vaults support each other, they need buttressing only at the corners. The walls can be lighter and have larger windows.

A **rib vault** is a groin vault made of thin stone panels supported by a framework of stone ribs that follow the lines of the arches and joints (Fig. 171b). In Gothic architecture the ribs form pointed arches (Fig. 171c). The weight of the vaulting is concentrated along the lines of the ribs, which transmit it to the **piers** (supports) at the corners of the **bay** (the area covered by the vault). The piers in turn transfer the lateral pressure from the vaulting to buttresses against the outside walls (Fig. 172). Because the weight rests on the stone skeleton formed by the ribs and on the buttressed piers, the bays can be rectilinear, and the wall spaces between the piers can be higher and filled with lighter stone panels or large windows of stained glass. Rib vaulting, pointed arches, piers, and buttressing made possible the lofty, light-filled Gothic cathedrals (Fig. 40).

Another form of vaulting is the hemispherical **dome.** A dome, formed by stones or bricks built up in circles of diminishing size, may cover a circular or square space. Various devices such as the **pendentive** (a concave triangle) (Fig. 173) are used to make the transition between the

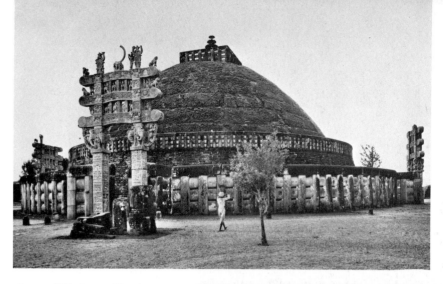

above: 174. Stupa No. 1,
Sanchī, India. 70–25 B.C.
Diameter 120′ (36.58 m).

right: 175. Gian Paolo Panini.
Interior of the Pantheon,
Rome. c. 1750. Oil on
canvas, 4′2½″ × 3′3″
(1.29 × 0.99 m).
National Gallery of Art,
Washington, D.C.
(Samuel H. Kress Collection).

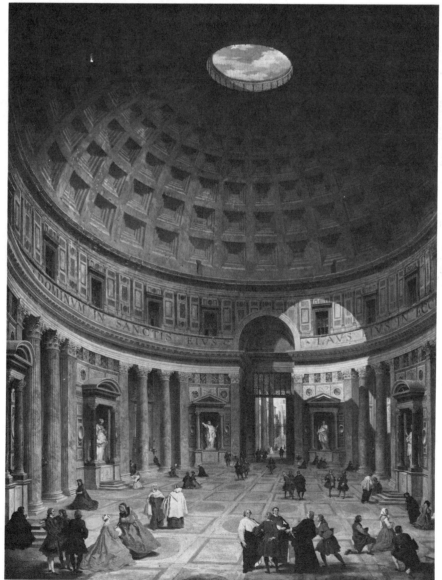

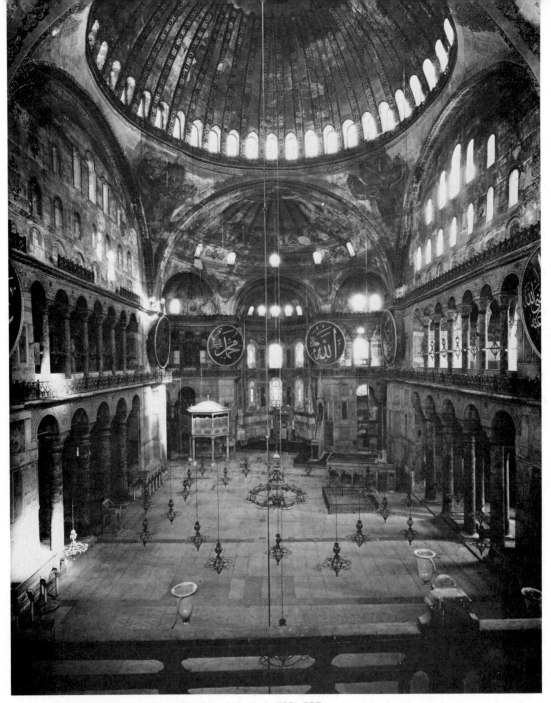

176. Interior of Hagia Sophia, Istanbul. 532–537.
Height of dome 183′ (55.78 m).

circular dome and the square space below it. The Stupa #1 at Sanchī, India, a Buddhist shrine built in the 1st century B.C., is a mound of earth surfaced by stones forming a dome (Fig. 174). A triumph of Roman engineering is the Pantheon (Fig. 175), a round brick and concrete temple built in Rome in the 2nd century A.D., which has one of the largest domes ever constructed. The dome of Hagia Sophia (Fig. 176), built as a church in Constantinople (Istan-

bul) in the 6th century, rests on pendentives. Your city hall or state capitol may have a dome inspired by Roman or Renaissance models.

In the 20th century, arches, vaults, and domes are often made of reinforced concrete. Examples are bridges and the concrete shells in such buildings as Eero Saarinen's TWA terminal at New York's Kennedy Airport (Fig. 189). Shells can also be made of metal or plywood shaped under stress.

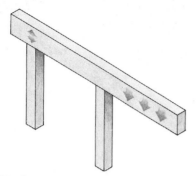

above: 177. Cantilever construction.

below: 178. Frank Lloyd Wright. "Falling Water" (Kaufman House), Bear Run, Pa. 1936–37.

Cantilever A building technique common in modern architecture is the **cantilever,** a beam or floor slab that juts out from the wall that supports it (Fig. 177). The wall acts as a fulcrum. The weight of the projecting end of the cantilever needs no posts to support it because it is balanced by the weight of the building on the interior end, much as your weight on one end of a seesaw can be balanced by that of another person on the other end. Cantilevers can also support walls, which may be hung from a cantilevered floor. Cantilevers may be wood beams, steel girders, or slabs of reinforced concrete.

Frank Lloyd Wright achieved a breathtaking effect by dramatically cantilevering the Kaufman House over a waterfall in Bear Run, Pennsylvania (Fig. 178). By making it appear to float over the water, he tied it visually to the natural environment of which it seemed to be an organic

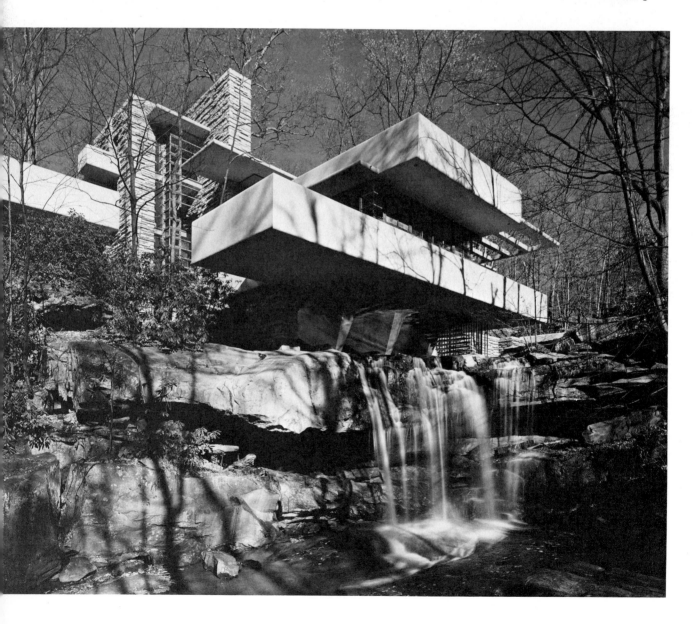

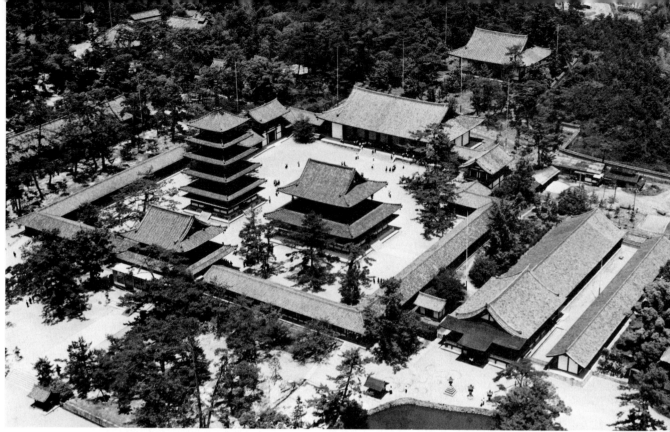

179. Five-storied pagoda, Horyuji Temple, Nara, Japan.
A.D. 607.

Construction Materials

For centuries, architects built out of wood, brick, and stone, depending on the availability and cost of the material. The Industrial Revolution introduced new kinds of factory-made building materials, such as iron, steel, and reinforced concrete, which have largely replaced the older kinds.

Wood In the forested regions of the world the most commonly used building material has been wood, which is cheap and easy to work. We know little about early wood structures because wood burns or rots, leaving us nothing to examine. We can, however, guess at their forms by studying the wooden structures built in many rural communities in more recent times. Villagers on lush, tropical Polynesian islands, for example, still use houses made from boards, posts, palm leaves, and other vegetable matter, much like those of their ancestors. In chilly, pine-covered Scandinavia, old farm buildings made of logs with mud and grasses stuffed between them, roofed with bark or sod, may still be seen. Such buildings and the log

part. The tower of Wright's Johnson Wax Building in Racine, Wisconsin, is built around an elevator shaft supporting cantilevered slab floors from which the glass outside walls are hung.

cabins built by American colonists and pioneers are probably much like the wood dwellings of early northern Europe.

These simple wooden buildings used post-and-lintel construction, which was developed into complex forms in medieval Japan. The Japanese built elaborate palaces and temples on stone bases, spanning huge spaces with wooden posts and beams fitted together in beautifully crafted joints. An outstanding example is the temple at Nara, dating from the 7th century, which is the oldest wood building in the world. It is 284 feet long and 166 feet wide (86.56 by 50.60 meters). A five-storied pagoda with up-curving roofs from the Nara temple complex demonstrates how complicated wooden post-and-lintel construction can be (Fig. 179).

In medieval Europe, builders experimented with wooden trusses for the roofs of stone churches, as we noted. These were developed into complex arrangements of triangles by such Renaissance architects as Andrea Palladio. The half-timbered houses of 16th-century England, using beams and plaster, and the clapboard houses of colonial New England, both still copied by 20th-century builders, are further examples of wooden architecture. In the late 20th century, laminated plywood shaped under stress into curved forms is used to make shells that serve as both structure and enclosure.

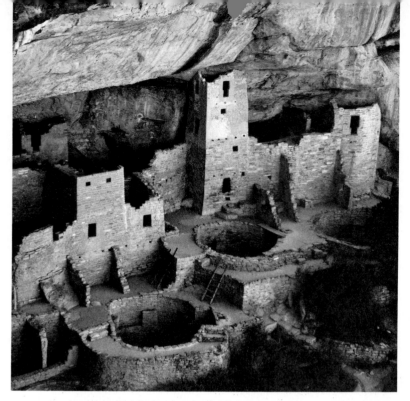

left: 180. Cliff palace, kivas and rectangular towers; Mesa Verde National Park, Colo. 12th century.

below: 181. Reconstruction drawing of Stonehenge.

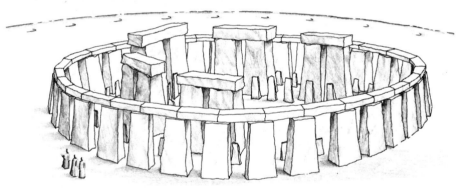

Stone Stone is one of the most widely used building materials for permanent structures. The many ancient stone buildings still standing today, such as Egyptian and Roman temples, are evidence of its durability.

Stone can support a great deal of weight, but stonework must be carefully designed or the weight will make it collapse. You may recall that as a child when you tried to build a tower out of blocks you were successful only when you placed them carefully, one on top of the other, and did not pile them too high. The earliest stone buildings were made by placing unshaped stones one above another. The downward thrust of their weight gave the structure stability. Later buildings were made of shaped, or dressed, stone. In the 12th century, Pueblo Indians built the cliff dwellings in Mesa Verde, Colorado, using the cliff as one wall and adding walls of shaped stones set in clay mortar. These multiple dwellings consisted of levels of units, each level set back from the one below to form a terrace reached by wooden ladders, an early example of apartment housing (Fig. 180). The Incas of Peru built the city of Machu Picchu of stones so skillfully fitted together that a knife cannot be pushed between them, and they do not need mortar to hold them together.

Most early stone building used post-and-lintel construction (Fig. 164). One of the earliest examples is Stonehenge, a mysterious Neolithic (New Stone Age) monument in southern England. It consists of three concentric circles of enormous vertical stones with horizontal stones as lintels (Fig. 181). How the massive stones were transported miles from the nearest quarry and raised into position is still discussed by archaeologists. The stones may have been dragged over log rollers by hundreds of workers. The stones seem to have been precisely arranged for sighting astronomical configurations.

The Egyptians, who had an abundant supply of stone, which they easily transported down the Nile River on rafts from the quarries to the building sites, built massive stone temples using posts and lintels. In the Temple of Amon at Karnak the tops of the posts (capitols) are shaped like lotus plants, probably derived from the shape of carved wooden posts in earlier structures. The immense interior space of the hypostyle hall is filled with a forest of columns, which are necessary to hold up the heavy stone lintels (Fig. 59).

The Greeks also built post-and-lintel temples of stone. We can detect evidence of earlier wood architecture in the decorative elements of their stoneworks. Despite the simplicity of post-and-lintel construction (Fig. 164), the refinements of proportions, workmanship, and detail rank Greek marble temples among the finest of architectural achievements.

The Romans built early works of stone, using posts and lintels or arches (Fig. 171b) and vaults (Fig. 171a), but later used stone chiefly as a veneer over structures of brick or poured concrete.

Most of the great churches and cathedrals of the Middle Ages were built of stone. Massive Romanesque churches had round arches and often barrel vaulting, as we have seen. Gothic churches rose to great heights supported by a cage of ribbed vaulting, piers, and buttresses (Fig. 171c).

The religious exultation of the period was expressed in the cathedral of Amiens, France, one of the tallest in the world. The vaulted nave reaches up toward heaven and is bathed in twilight pierced at intervals by light from brilliant, stained glass windows. You can sense the dynamic quality of the structure of a Gothic cathedral in which each part depends on the counterbalancing weight of every other part. The thrust moves from towers and vaults through ribs and piers out to buttresses and **flying buttresses** (half arches between buttresses and a wall) and so to the ground (Fig. 172).

Many of these cathedrals took hundreds of years to build, and it is easy to imagine the failures the builders must have experienced while trying to solve the dual problems of weight and thrust. A few cathedrals did, in fact, reach too high. That in Beauvais, France, collapsed and was never completed. Most Gothic cathedrals, however, still stand as examples of the creativity and daring of medieval builders.

Many important Renaissance churches and palaces were built of stone, usually adapting the styles of classical Rome. One of the most outstanding structures is St. Peter's Basilica in Rome (Fig. 182). Succeeding a series of earlier architects, Michelangelo drew plans for an enormous structure that was not finished until after his death. His floor plan of a

182. Façade, St. Peter's Basilica, Rome.
1601–26.

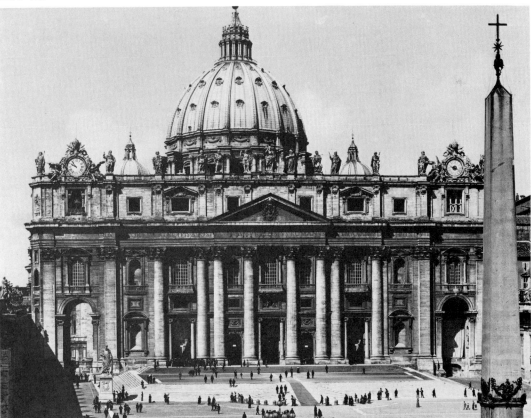

Greek cross was later modified, but his ribbed stone dome, in a slightly more elongated version, soars above the city. The upward lines of the **pilasters** (flat columnar forms) on the walls of the four massive arches that support the dome and the curving ribs reach toward the center in a restless climax. The interior of the church is so large that it is impossible to experience the whole from any one point.

Brick   In regions where wood and stone are scarce, the common building material is brick shaped out of local clay. Early bricks were dried in the heat of the sun but crumbled when exposed to rain or flood waters, as often happened in ancient Mesopotamia. Bricks fired in a kiln are hard enough to prevent such dissolution and are a tremendous advance over sun-dried ones. Bricks can be built into thick-walled houses, roofed with wooden beams, and into huge towers. The adobe brick houses built by some Indians in the American Southwest and Mexico are examples of brick architecture.

The Romans built extensively in brick and concrete, using arches, vaults, and domes to cover large areas and distances. Their basilicas (law courts), theaters, sports arenas, baths, aqueducts, and triumphal arches appeared all over the Roman world. The comfort and well-being of the Romans depended on their engineering feats. Stone or brick-faced concrete aqueducts, for instance, such as the

Pont du Gard in Nîmes, France (Fig. 170), brought water from distant mountains to supply Roman city fountains and luxurious baths and villas. Apartments up to five stories high crowded the streets of Rome and Ostia. Remains, including stairways, colonnades, light wells, and room layouts, can be seen today.

Brick was commonly used in northern Europe after the forests were cleared. Many German churches and Dutch houses were built of brick. Brick was popular for Georgian houses in 18th-century England.

Iron   Prior to the Industrial Revolution, iron was worked by craftsmen and used primarily for nails, dowels, tie rods, and hinges to fasten together parts of wood or stone structures. As a result of mechanized mass production and the development of railroads, it became an important building material, lighter, stronger, and more fire-resistant than wood and easier to work than stone. Iron was especially useful for the large, open, well-lit spaces required by factories. Expanding rail networks created the need for railway stations and bridges, which led to further experimentation with iron frames and trusses.

One of the most dramatic early examples of iron-frame construction was the Crystal Palace, built for the Great Exhibition in London in 1851 (Fig. 183). Covering 17 acres (7 hectares), it was the first completely prefabricated build-

183. Joseph Paxton. Crystal Palace, London.
1851. Cast iron and glass, width 1851′ (564.18 m).

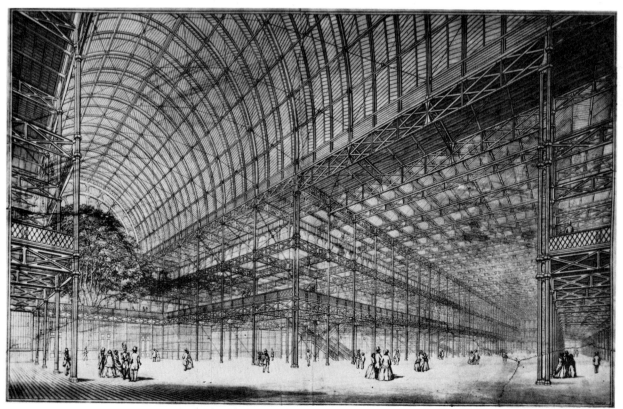

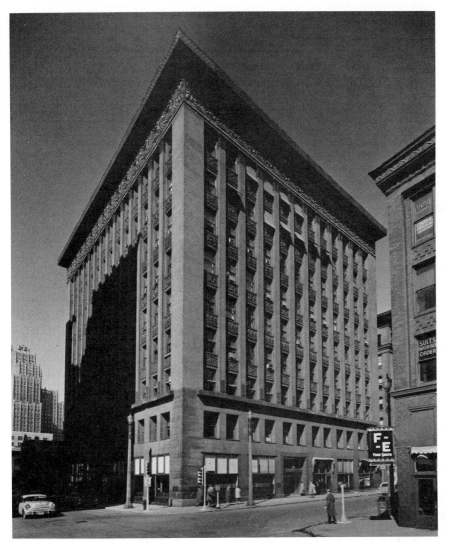

184. Louis Sullivan.
Wainwright Building,
St. Louis, Mo. 1891.

ing; all its part were made in factories and shipped to the site, where they were assembled in just six months. The weight-bearing iron frame held the largest panels of plate glass that had ever been produced. They carried no weight but only enclosed space. The enormous open interior with its high, curved, glass roof impressed viewers with its unusual approach to building.

The designer, Joseph Paxton (1801–1865), had been a gardener experienced in building greenhouses. He regarded the structural frame as an organic skeleton, commenting: "Nature was the engineer. Nature has provided the leaf with longitudinal and transverse girders and supports that I, borrowing from it, have adopted in this building." Paxton's creative vision and innovative use of materials produced completely new architectural forms, which critics of the day correctly predicted would revolutionize architecture.

A later triumph of iron construction was the 990-foot (300-meter) Eiffel Tower, built in Paris for the exhibition of 1889. Consisting of a cross-braced lattice girder, it too was made of prefabricated parts.

Steel The lessons builders learned in constructing iron bridges, factories, and other buildings provided the basis for construction in steel. Steel is stronger, lighter, more fire-resistant, and more workable than iron and holds up well under tension, where iron tends to snap. Steel-frame buildings faced in stone or brick were erected in the cities of Europe and North America, especially in Chicago, where the need to find space between the rivers that criss-cross the city led to ever higher structures. Further refinements in steel frames and the invention of the elevator made such high-rise buildings possible.

In the Wainwright Building, built in St. Louis in 1891, Louis Sullivan (1856–1924) openly used new methods and materials and designed surface ornament to emphasize the vertical (Fig. 184). Sullivan's buildings are the forerunners of modern skyscrapers.

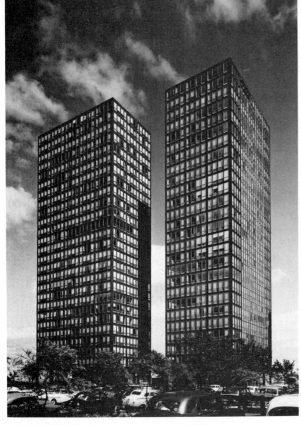

Certainly the steel cage (Fig. 167) can produce over-whelming skyscrapers that dehumanize the urban environment. Frank Lloyd Wright, a student of Sullivan, was aware of that potential problem. In his *Autobiography of an Idea* (1932) he said:

> The tall steel frame may have its aspects of beneficence; but as long as many may say, "I shall do as I please with my own," it presents opposite aspects of social menace and danger. . . . The tall office building loses its validity when the surroundings are uncongenial to its nature; and when such buildings are crowded together upon narrow streets or lanes they become mutually destructive.

In the hands of a skilled architect such as Mies van der Rohe, however, steel can create a light, elegant building. Sometimes the steel frame may be exposed to view and made to emphasize the vertical thrust of the building, as in Mies' Lake Shore Apartments in Chicago built in 1952 (Fig. 185).

Steel is also used to make cables from which girders may be suspended, as in the Brooklyn Bridge, in New York (Fig. 186), designed by the engineer John Augustus Roebling (1806–1869). Roebling invented the steel cable, which is made up of many parallel wires, and the machine to attach the cable to the two piers that hold up the bridge. Twentieth-century suspension bridges are still built by his methods. Some of them contain spans of girders almost a mile (1.6 kilometers) long. Not only do the cables support the weight of the spans but they also permit fluctuations of

above: 185. Ludwig Mies van der Rohe. 850 Lake Shore Drive, Chicago. 1950–52.

below: 186. John Augustus Roebling. Brooklyn Bridge, New York. 1869–83.

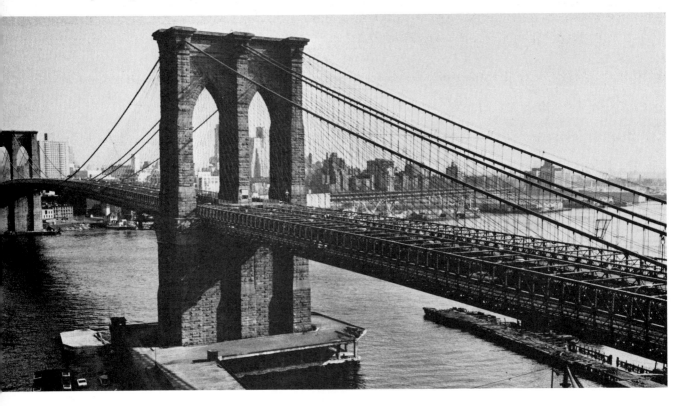

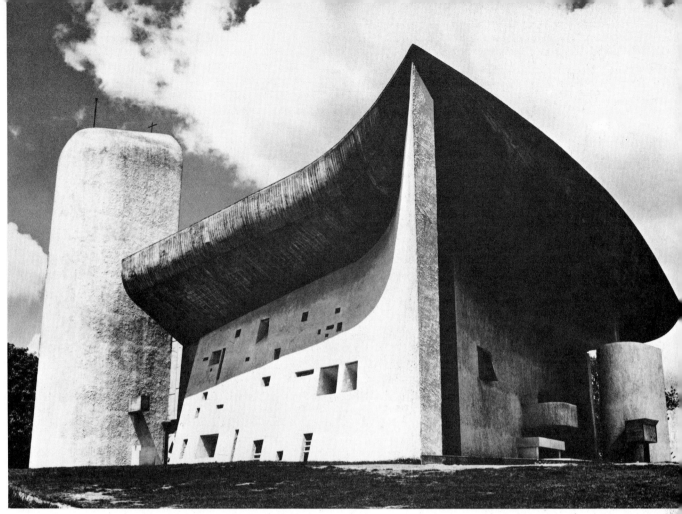

187. Le Corbusier. Notre Dame du Haut, Ronchamp, France. 1950–55.

several feet—caused by wind or load stresses—between the span and the water. Steel cables are also used for buildings. For example, pavilions for fairs and sports events often have their roofs and walls hanging on steel cables attached to central posts.

Reinforced Concrete Concrete, a mixture of sand, gravel, cement, and water, was used in Roman times for aqueducts and other large structures. Not until the 20th century when it was reinforced with metal rods or mesh was its full potential achieved. Reinforced concrete is a versatile, fire-resistant, durable material that can be molded into columns, beams, slabs, and vaults that can be self-supporting with few or no interior posts.

Builders first used reinforced concrete for factories, silos, and other utilitarian structures. As early as 1905, bridge designers in Europe used curved slabs supported on thin vertical members to create graceful arches. Since then, as technical understanding of concrete has increased, engineers have been able to calculate exactly what stresses and loads a structure can support and have experimented more audaciously. At the same time, architects have recog-

nized the aesthetic possibilities of reinforced concrete. In 1903, the French architect Auguste Perret (1874–1954) built a rectangular cage of reinforced concrete for an apartment house in Paris with walls of glass or thin panels of cast concrete. Perret made no attempt to cover the concrete, believing that decoration frequently hides errors in construction. Inside, the only immovable parts are slim columns and stairs; the rest of the space is left open for flexible arrangement of rooms. In the late 20th century, the Whitney Museum in New York and the Pompidou Center (Beaubourg) in Paris (Fig. 163) both reveal their structure while permitting infinite modification of interior space for changing art exhibitions.

Architects have used reinforced concrete for sweeping arches and vaults that are thin shells and for sculptural forms such as those in Le Corbusier's (1887–1965) chapel in Ronchamp, France (Fig. 187). The Italian architect Pier Luigi Nervi (1891–1979) developed a more efficient kind of reinforced concrete consisting of layers of fine steel mesh sprayed with cement mortar. This material is well suited to making prefabricated modular sections of shell vaults with curved rib framing. Nervi designed elegant, airy shell vaults based on complex geometry to roof vast spaces in many different types of structures, including the Palazzetto dello Sport for the 1960 Olympics in Rome (Fig. 188).

Reinforced concrete seems able to solve almost any architectural problem. Eero Saarinen's TWA terminal at Kennedy Airport, New York, as we noted, uses winglike sculptural shapes cast in concrete that are stimulating but not overwhelming. They create a large open area broken only by curving staircases, ramps, and balconies. The building, reminiscent of a bird in flight, can accommodate moving groups of people but also allows space for others to sit and watch the crowds while waiting for arrivals and departures. The movement of people increases the visual excitement provided by the architectural forms and the

spaces they define, an appropriate quality in an air terminal (Fig. 189). The building was constructed in a few months with the same number of workers, at any given time, involved in building a Gothic cathedral over several centuries.

As you review the history of architecture in the following chapters, try to remember its structural methods and materials. Look at the buildings around you today to see whether they remain from earlier periods or whether they are recent structures. If you find some that use new materials and techniques to copy traditional appearances and methods, how do they look compared with other new and exciting buildings, many of which openly reveal their materials and construction?

188. Pier Luigi Nervi.
Palazzetto dello Sport, Rome. 1960.

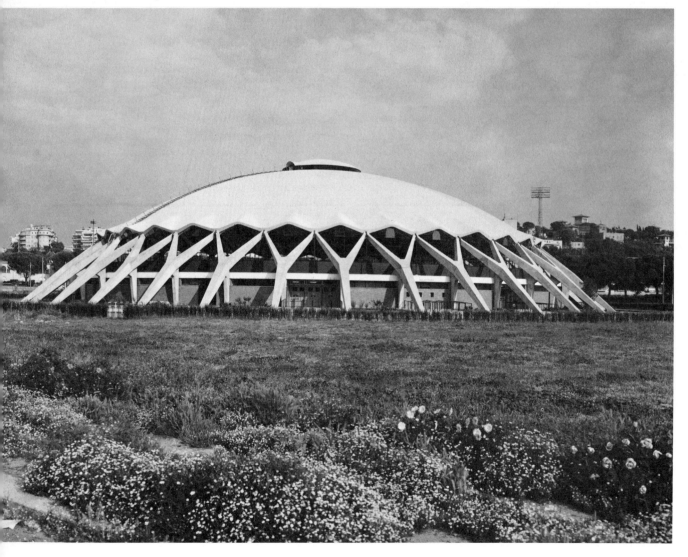

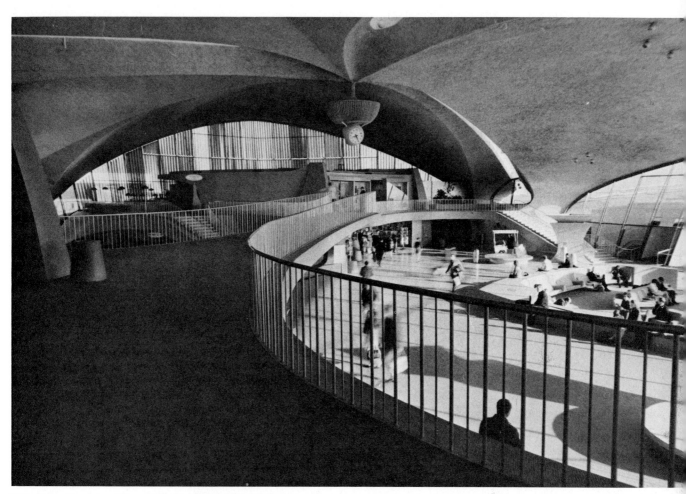

189. Eero Saarinen. Trans World Airlines Flight Center, Kennedy International Airport, New York. 1962.

EXERCISES AND ACTIVITIES

1. List several ancient and modern structural methods or building devices. Draw simple diagrams of each.
2. What qualities of 20-century construction distinguish it from past methods? List examples.
3. Locate several buildings in your community that copy historical styles of architecture, such as Gothic or Renaissance. Can you tell if old methods of building were used or if the historical detail is merely applied to the surface?
4. Locate and sketch other buildings that appear to use more contemporary structural methods. How do these methods and materials vary from the older methods you have studied?
5. Referring to a text on house construction, learn to read an architectural plan and to understand the symbols for windows, doors, solid walls, closets, steps, etc. Determine how scale is used in a plan.
6. Look at house plans in magazines. Pick out one you would like to live in and compare it with one you dislike. What features do you like about it? Are the rooms conveniently placed? What would the traffic flow be like? Do you think the house would be reasonable in cost, or are there features that probably would make it expensive to build? How would you change it to meet your needs?
7. Draw a plan of an existing school or other public building. Pick out the features you would change to make it more convenient, and draw a revised plan showing these changes.

10 **Environmental Design**

The roadside strips, the consumer products, the bill-boards, the fantasy cars, the monster junk piles are all portraits of us, not someone else. There is no "they."

GEORGE NELSON

Harmony with our environment is based on an awareness of the interdependence of all life. We have discovered that from a single cell to the billions of cells in a single human to the multitudes of people in our sprawling cities, all are liv- ing organisms whose satisfying existence depends on how each element is related. Even the smallest alteration to the ecological balance of our world makes changes we rarely predict. Yet the impulse to alter our surroundings began in prehistoric times.

Surviving from the second and first millennia B.C. (Figs. 181 and 190) are huge earthworks whose purposes we do not yet fully understand. Vast ceremonial mounds and sa- cred enclosures can be found in North and Central Amer- ica, especially in Mexico. Enormous, rectangular entrench- ments in Europe, protected by walls, seem not to have

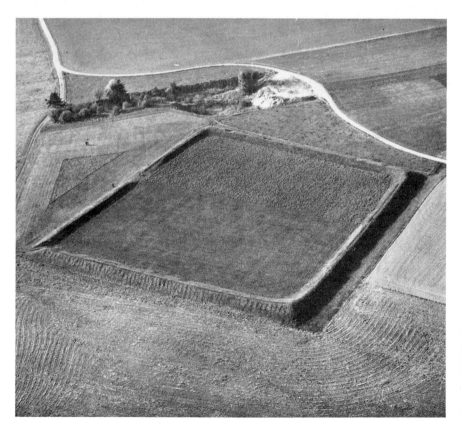

190. Aerial view of rectangular entrenchment at Buchenberg, Starnberg, Bavaria. Celtic, late La Tène Period, 5th–1st centuries B.C. Earth, 115 × 130 yards (105.15 × 118.87 m).

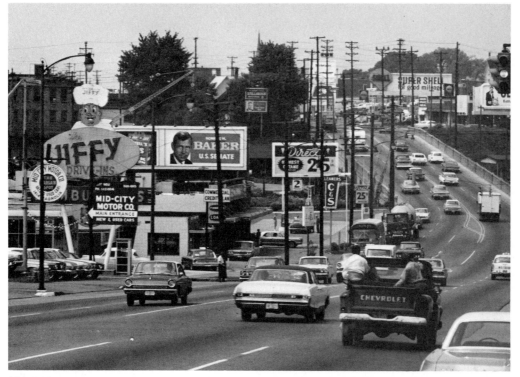

191. Urban mess.

been centers of defense or obvious worship, but, perhaps, represent an attempt to gain power over the environment by changing it.

People have also altered the landscape through the centuries by building farms and cities. Such incursions on the land were all influenced by the natural environment that existed before them. Today, however, that environment, to which our biological rhythms are still keyed, has all but disappeared. The vast forest broken by streams and meadows that once covered the eastern United States is gone, and the environment we have put in its place bears little resemblance to it. What has happened to the natural beauty of our country, and how have our communities changed from the human scale of early colonial towns to the overpowering roadscapes and skyscrapers of our time (Fig. 191)?

Faced with the anonymity of an electronic age, many people feel threatened, isolated, and at worst alienated from others, like the figures in Giacometti's *City Square* (Fig. 42). The overcrowded slum, the lonely room in a broken-down hotel, or the sterile box in a high-rise apartment—such surroundings can turn those who live in them into apathetic beings who lose the drive to live, to change things, to grow.

That people want open space is shown by the thousands who have taken up jogging, hiking, and camping. Even these activities, however, upset the ecological balance. Mountain slopes are eroded, streams are polluted, the wilderness diminishes, and animal habitats are de-stroyed. In our current concern about the environment, perhaps we can adapt age-old solutions to our universal needs for comfort and efficiency in the home, the neighborhood, and the city.

The Environmentally Designed House

Fundamental to any community design is the plan of each house in relation to its setting. In many eras, people believed that a building should stand apart from its background as a visual reflection of the architect or the client. But today's viewpoint seems to be turning toward traditions in which a structure is a natural outgrowth of its surroundings.

From the ice and snow igloos of the Eskimo to the brick and stone structures of the Pueblo Indians, our ancestors designed their houses to meet the threefold demands of land, climate, and the needs of the occupants. Frank Lloyd Wright's term "Organic Architecture" is a rephrasing of this time-honored concept. It is reflected in the work of Luis Barragán (b. 1902), Mexican recipient of the 1980 first international Pritzker prize for architectural achievement. He describes his designs as providing "shelter against the aggressions of the modern world." His major project has been El Pedregal, Mexico, a residential area on a stretch of lava left 2500 years ago. Sensitive to the lava's unearthly shapes and lush vegetation, Barragán transmuted 865 acres (350 hectares) of what was regarded as unusable

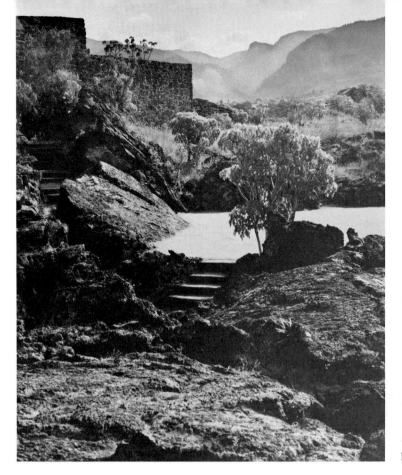

192. Luis Barragán. Garden in
El Pedregal, Mexico City. 1945–50.

land into houses and gardens (Fig. 192). Using the simplest architectural elements—abstract, geometric forms and carefully arranged planes—he achieved a modern design that profoundly respects his country's indigenous ways of building and living. Lava walls give privacy and create interior gardens, many imaginatively embellished by regenerative ponds and streams.

The basic requirements of all houses for heating, cooling, and lighting have been rapidly depleting fossil fuels since the Industrial Revolution. Today we are returning to the sun and wind for energy, yet these sources have supplied energy since ancient times. For example, climates in desert regions are noted for high temperatures by day and near-frigidity by night. The Pueblo Indians of the arid Southwest crowded their dwellings together, side by side and one atop another. This compact mass both reduced the area exposed to the sun and provided defense. The few small windows placed high in the walls allowed only late afternoon sun to enter, to be absorbed by the adobe brick walls. This "heat sink" slowly reradiated heat into the dwelling at night. A similar solar design appears in the five-story cliff dwellings called Montezuma's Castle built by the Sinaqua and Anasez Indians of Arizona in 1100 and now a national monument. The mud, stone, and other indigenous materials served as heat capacitators to absorb solar radiation for later release. In addition, the overhanging mountainside blocked high summer sun, thus cooling

the dwellings naturally. Heat collection, heat storage, and insulation are basic components of such environmentally directed Indian design (Fig. 193).

The architecture of European settlers during the colonial period solved the very different problem of retaining heat in the chilly climate of the Northeast. Stone or brick walls and fireplaces, usually in the center of early wood-frame or stone dwellings, captured and retained the heat from cooking. At the same time, the compact design of the houses reduced loss of surface heat. The sloping, one-story roof often on the north side of New England salt-box houses gave shelter from the wind, which piled up winter snow to provide natural insulation. Windows were small and usually on the southern, two-story portions of the dwellings.

Pueblo and colonial houses, using solar radiation, were perhaps intuitive responses to local climatic conditions. Japan, Israel, and Australia have long relied on sun and wind to heat domestic hot water. India, France, and the Soviet Union apply solar heating and cooling technology to both commercial and residential units. Only within the last few years has the United States directed efforts toward energy-efficient methods of heating and cooling. Drawing upon early models by native peoples, modern systems vary widely in design (Fig. 194).

Regardless of the region, four elements of climate are critical for energy-efficient heating and cooling systems—

solar radiation, air temperature, humidity, and air movement. In addition, a system requires a large collector and storage area of energy that is different from any associated with conventional heating and cooling systems. Although many houses today tap solar and wind resources (and some even incorporate greenhouses for heating and cooling as well as growing food), few are able to be totally self-sufficient. Furthermore, designs must be adaptable to all conditions because every climate variation requires a different system to maintain an ecological balance. Despite these limitations, more and more houses will be designed, doubtlessly, that are responsive to sun and wind, in natural harmony with their surroundings.

Neighborhoods

Within a city, satellite town, or suburb, a neighborhood of 5000 to 10,000 people is generally considered to be ideal for community life. Such a community should contain the services needed to support everyday life—shops, schools, a health clinic, and a library. A neighborhood must also be integrated into a larger community, which can provide schools for higher education, fully equipped hospitals, and larger and more extensive commercial and manufacturing facilities. Neighborhoods developed naturally in the past. In newer cities, however, built on a grid pattern and characterized by large apartment houses, widely spaced shopping centers, and streets full of traffic, it is almost impossible for a comfortably sized neighborhood to develop spontaneously. Also inhibiting the growth of organic neighborhoods is the segregation of people into areas based, if no longer on religion, on age, ethnic origin, or economic level.

Le Corbusier's master plan for Chandigarh, the new capital of the Punjab in India, divides the city into sections that are about the size of a village and that respect the centuries-old living patterns of the inhabitants. Each section has a market, a park, blocks of housing, paths for pedestrians, and roads for slow traffic. Because of the high cost of land, such a plan would not be suitable in more crowded areas. For this reason, apartments are often clustered in tall buildings, like the one Le Corbusier designed for Marseilles, which allow for more open space between them.

Can a sense of neighborhood be created without building a whole new city? Some designers have suggested

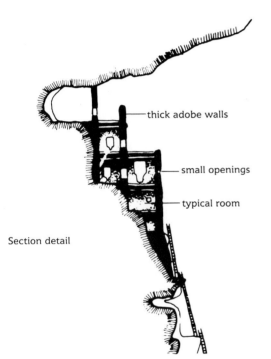

thick adobe walls

small openings

typical room

Section detail

above: 193. "Montezuma's Castle" (cliff dwelling), Camp Verde, Ariz. 12th century.

right: 194. Diagram of solar heating system.

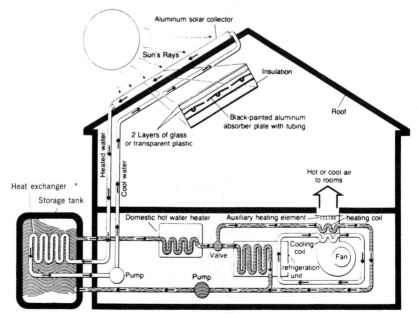

Aluminum solar collector

Sun's Rays

Insulation

Roof

Black-painted aluminum absorber plate with tubing

2 Layers of glass or transparent plastic

Hot or cool air to rooms

Heated water

Cool water

Heat exchanger

Storage tank

Domestic hot water heater

Auxiliary heating element

heating coil

Valve

Cooling coil

Fan

refrigeration unit

Pump

Pump

placing a kiosk at the intersection of several streets to provide a place where residents could pick up newspapers, cigarettes, and perhaps some groceries. Such a device would cut door-to-door deliveries and short trips by car. A tree or two and benches combined with a bus stop and a car-pool stop could make these intersections into meeting places where people might come to know one another. In New York, the residents of one block of old brownstone apartment buildings combined their backyards to create a large, shared green space. With a pleasant place to sit or play, residents developed a sense of community, something rare in the anonymous city. Since many American cities did not develop as organic communities, they have to be planned along such lines to approach the quality of urban life that exists naturally in older European cities.

Closely related to the quality of the neighborhood is the housing within it. The problem of building attractive housing to be rented or sold at a reasonable price is one of the greatest social challenges we face. The approaches to public or moderate-cost housing that have been tried so far usually have resulted in huge, inhuman structures, which have created more problems for residents and communities than they have solved. A few institutions throughout our country have established innovative housing projects at low cost.

Other examples of well-planned, low-cost housing can be found in Scandinavia, where it is built by cooperatives and trade unions as well as the government. As a result, there are innumerable pleasant city neighborhoods, towns, and, in fact, whole regions where the needs of people of all ages have been anticipated and where they can afford to live comfortably. An example is Uppsala, Sweden, where university students and urban designers are actively seeking socioeconomic solutions to housing problems. Such achievements suggest that Americans can solve the problem when they are convinced it is a vital goal.

Cities

The pueblo of the American Southwest and an unspoiled New England village share certain qualities—human scale, an ordered relationship of parts to the whole, and above all a sense of identity with a settled place. Some old European cities also have these advantages. They are generally lost in the huge, crowded cities of modern America. When did this change take place?

Growth of Cities The cities and towns of medieval and Renaissance Europe were relatively small by today's standards and were built to human scale. Many city houses had gardens with trees and flowers, while open fields and forest lay just beyond the city walls. These advantages perhaps offset the dirt, odors, and crowding in the poorer sections.

Venice, for example, is still organized in much the same way that was possible hundreds of years ago. Each neigh-

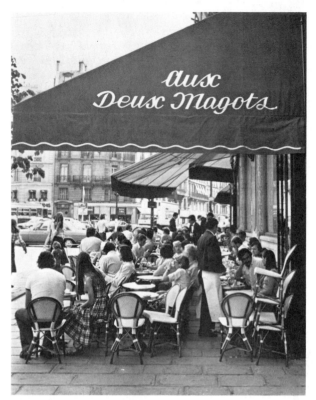

195. Outdoor café in Paris.

borhood has its own piazza, or square, which offers all the vitality and stimulus that local inhabitants need. The trees, fountain, shops, and cafés of the square are reached by streets only for pedestrians. The main arteries of traffic are the canals, where boats transport people and goods without as much noise and exhaust as cars and trucks produce. Other cities all over the world have retained neighborhoods, usually in the old part of the city, where there are small squares, narrow sidewalks and lanes, small shops, and outdoor cafés that encourage leisurely conversation (Fig. 195). New York City's Greenwich Village is a well-known example in the United States of a pocket community with common concerns.

As trade expanded during the Renaissance, and especially during the Industrial Revolution, the requirements of commerce and manufacturing gradually came to outweigh those of human comfort. Cities grew much larger and more crowded or developed around smoky factories. They were modified to facilitate the production and sale of factory-made goods. Development of city land and of suburbs was generally in the hands of private citizens concerned with making a profit. Such accelerated change brought about by the machine was difficult to fight.

City Planning Although most cities grew haphazardly as a result of private enterprise, in a few there was planned development. Inspired by belief in the power of reason and science to solve all problems and by desires for personal

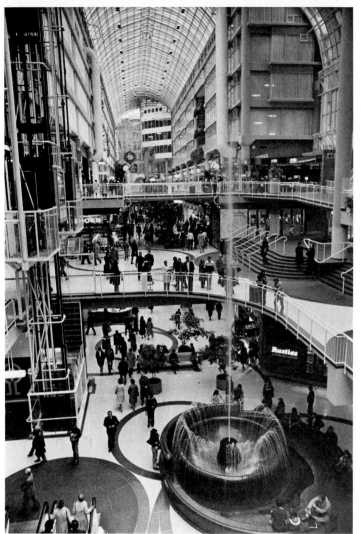

196. Eaton Centre, Toronto.

glorification, several European rulers ordered vast plans involving public buildings on large squares and the layout of streets on a grid pattern or, as in 19th-century Paris, a star pattern of radiating boulevards. Such plans provided for impressive displays of power and the rapid movement of marching troops, but the wide, tree-lined Parisian boulevards do not encourage neighborhood life any more than 20th-century freeways do.

In the United States, many towns and cities since colonial times have been laid out on the grid system, or, in the case of Washington, on the star pattern. One reason was the settlers' European-derived confidence in the power of reason. Another was their natural desire to impose human design on the frightening vastness and wilderness of a new land.

Modern city planning began in the 1890s in Britain, where Ebenezer Howard (1850–1928) and Raymond Unwin (1863–1940) rejected the assumption that individual lives were unimportant. They planned garden cities outside industrial areas, where people could live near their work, find the necessary services for daily life, but still be surrounded by greenbelts with gardens. In the United States Clarence Stein (1882–1975) and Henry Wright (b.1904) in 1928 built Sunnyside Gardens, a nonsegregated, economically mixed community on Long Island. These ventures formed models for the many "new towns" built in Britain after World War II. Unlike mass housing units in large cities, which discourage personal identity and personality, these new towns are small in scale and adapted to community needs.

In addition to providing for small-scale, local communities, modern city planners must also be concerned with large-scale design for cities. Cities can be exhilarating but also frustrating and depressing. The individual, lost in a vast area and often monotonous routine, needs to be publicly reminded of people's capacity to experience emotion in large-scale, collective circumstances. Theaters, concert halls, opera houses, sports stadiums, and pedestrian malls, such as Toronto's Eaton Centre (Fig. 196), which draw people together for recreation and employment, provide these

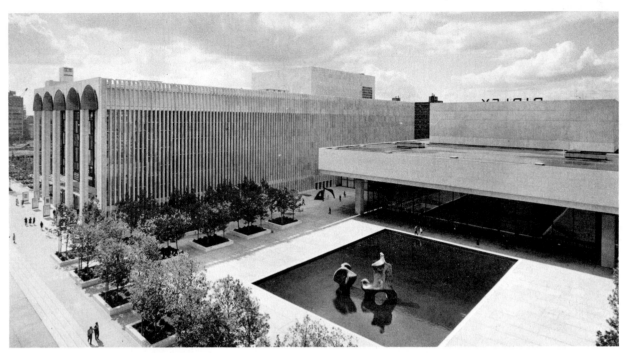

197. Lincoln Center Plaza, New York.
The Metropolitan Opera House (1966) is at the left, the Vivian
Beaumont Theater (1965) is at the right. In the reflecting
pool is *Lincoln Center Reclining Figure* by Henry Moore.

circumstances, but they also pose special problems for planners. Architects of such buildings must meet the physical needs of crowds, such as traffic flow, and also minimize occasions for confusion, inconvenience, and danger.

An example of a large-scale cultural complex is Lincoln Center in New York (Fig. 197). It consists of Avery Fisher Hall, the Metropolitan Opera House, and the New York State Theater surrounding three sides of a huge plaza with a round fountain in the center (not shown in Fig. 197). The austere, grandiose buildings create for many people an anonymous and overwhelming grouping that has little reference to human scale or familiar natural details to which people can relate. The monumentality of the buildings, instead of inviting us to enjoy them, weakens our sense of personal value. The impressive architectural scale is carried also to the interior.

By contrast, Frank Lloyd Wright designed the Solomon R. Guggenheim Museum in New York with flowing curves and human proportions (Fig. 198). The interior arrangement of the building, in which elevators carry viewers to the top so that they can walk down a sloping, circular ramp to see the paintings, is frankly expressed. The top-heavy shape would be disturbing if it were not balanced and tied to the ground by the mass of offices and library at one side. The museum, however, can be seen clearly only from across the street in Central Park. How much more inviting it would be if the space around the building could have been planned to give us glimpses of it as we approached on foot or by bus!

The Museum of Modern Art, New York's major museum of international contemporary art, recently remodeled, is a handsome building with a pleasant courtyard and garden where people can wander or sit surrounded by sculpture. It is a haven in the middle of the city, but the building itself, which invites us inside as we look through the glass front, had to be wedged between existing buildings. Individual projects like this can be a bit of relief to the otherwise deadening effect of the city.

However, architects for today's museums, whether they plan for wholly new structures or, as in this case, must add to existing structures, are bound to respect the local conditions, without sacrificing the aesthetic integrity of the museum as an active participant in the community. Public interest in traveling exhibitions requires broad spaces, while high attendance demands provision for circulation of large numbers of people. Finally, the need for income-producing facilities, including shops, restaurants, or rental space such as that in the pioneering residential tower of the Museum of Modern Art forces unprecedented demands on the limited space of an urban museum and of its designers.

Ever since the 19th century, many upper- and middle-income people have escaped from congested cities with their smoke-belching factories to live in more spacious, green suburbs. As a result, cities are today surrounded by suburbs; the inner city has been left to the poor, who cannot afford to leave, and to the rich, who live in expensive housing. Frequently, urban property is owned by absentee

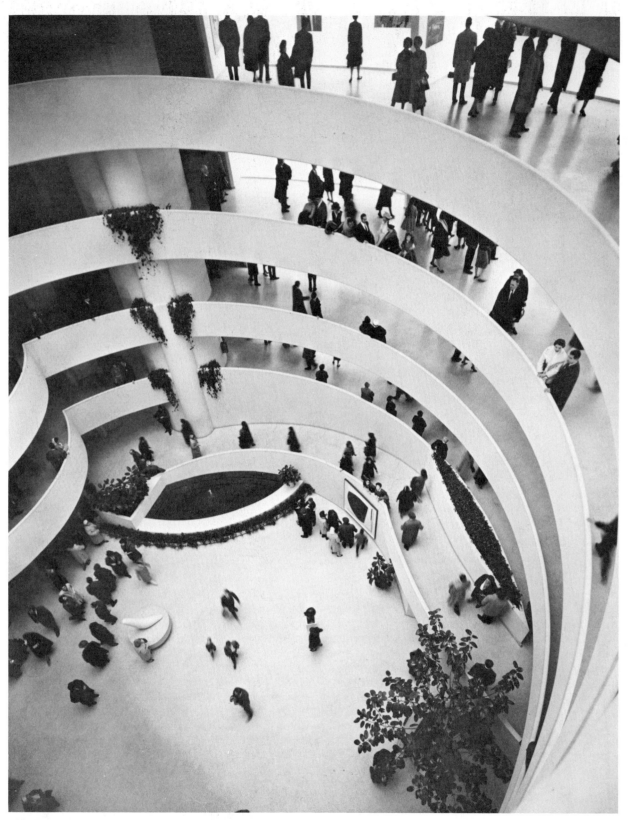

198. Frank Lloyd Wright. Ramp and reflecting pool,
Solomon R. Guggenheim Museum, New York. 1957–59.

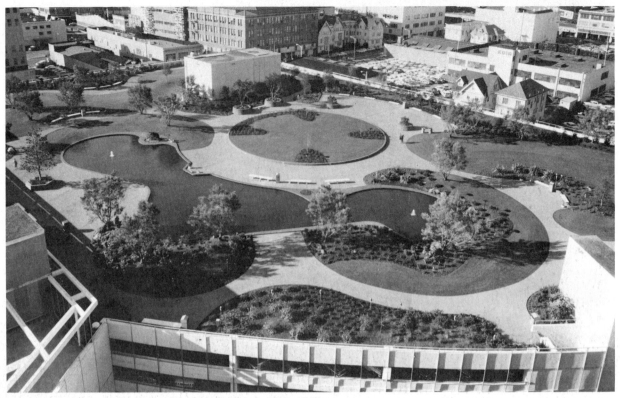

199. Roof garden of the Kaiser Center, Oakland, Calif. 1960.

landlords, who do not care about the quality of life lived by their tenants, whom they never see. The less-advantaged citizens of the central city are so busy earning a living that they have little time or energy left for the civic action necessary to bring about change. Gradually the city loses taxes and shoppers. A center for daytime office workers, it is largely deserted at night.

Nor have the suburbs turned out to be all they promised. Originally planned to provide space, light, air, gardens, and a healthy environment for families who could afford them, suburbs now are often land-eating monsters that provide some of these comforts for their residents at a price society can ill afford. The widely spaced shops, schools, and other facilities of suburbia call for two cars per family, which increase fuel consumption and pollution. Distances from the city, which increase as suburbia spreads, lead to more highways, which in turn cut up the land as well as bring more cars into the city. In addition, the similarities in economic, social, and cultural outlooks of suburban residents deprive them of the stimulus of encounters with people of different life-styles.

A radical solution to the problems of the city was proposed in the 1930s by Frank Lloyd Wright. He suggested that cities be phased out and every citizen be provided with an acre of land. He thought people should raise food even if they were employed in manufacturing. At that time there

was enough land available for the whole population of the United States, a situation that has become progressively less true. Such a solution would not be feasible in the more crowded countries of Europe, but some cities do provide inhabitants with an allotment of land outside the city where they can grow vegetables and flowers and even spend the weekend in a tiny cabin.

Automobile Traffic As a result of the growth of suburbs, combined with the appeal of theaters, museums, and other attractions of the central city, one of the greatest problems of the modern city is automobile traffic. The automobile has profoundly changed our relation to the environment. We know that the inner tempo of human beings is a biological and cosmological rhythm, keyed to the succession of night and day, the ebb and flow of the tides, the phases of the moon, and the slow changes of the seasons. The frequent changes of velocity and direction that we experience in automobiles are difficult for our systems to accept.

Moreover, in many cities, a large part of the available space is given over to the car. For example, two-thirds of downtown Los Angeles is devoted to automobiles—freeways, streets, and parking lots. Expressways form concrete barriers roaring with cars, which separate one neighborhood from another. Can we learn to balance the conven-

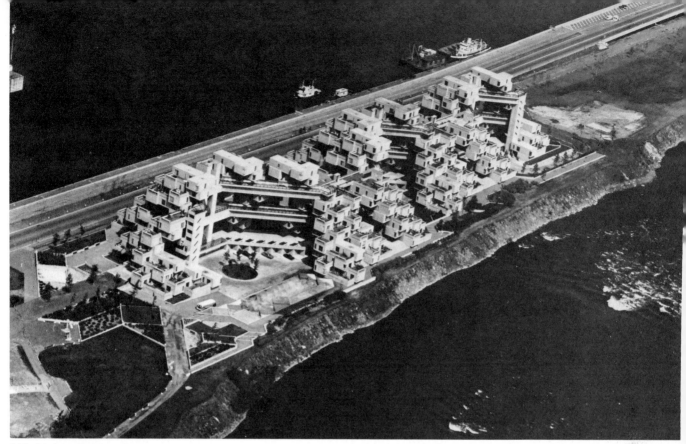

200. Moishe Safdie. *Habitat,*
Montreal. 1967.

ience that private automobiles provide against the pollution—physical and visual—that they cause? Could we not build garages around the edges of the city and provide electric transportation to carry people to the center?

Some cities have taken steps to achieve such a balance. Large office and apartment buildings provide parking on an underground level and malls and parks on another level isolated from the streets with bridges to connect the buildings or cross above the streets. Oakland, California, has built a park atop a garage to provide an open green area where people can stroll or sit (Fig. 199). Several cities have banned cars from certain areas in an attempt to restore a human scale and provide pleasant places for people to congregate. Fresno, California; Philadelphia; Minneapolis; Rotterdam, Holland; Coventry, England; and other cities have constructed pedestrian-oriented shopping areas where people can wander undisturbed by cars or can sit on quiet benches or in cafés surrounded by flowers, sculpture, and fountains. Storekeepers, who were fearful at first that such malls would hurt sales, have discovered that the pleasant new environments have been good for business.

In Portland, Oregon, miniature parks and plazas designed by Frank Lloyd Wright connect two waterfalls, creating areas for refreshment in the middle of downtown. Rockefeller Center in New York, although its buildings are huge and dehumanizing in scale, provides city dwellers

with flowers and trees and, in winter, an ice skating rink. An office building in San Francisco has placed a garden on the terrace formed by its setback where office workers can eat lunch in the sun or listen to street musicians. Small open spaces like these provide a moment or two of respite from urban turmoil.

Looking toward the Future

The appearance of cities can change if some of the new, less costly building techniques suggested by creative architects are widely adopted. Buckminster Fuller's geodesic dome, discussed in Chapter 9, is one such technique. Modules, or interchangeable sections, such as those used by Paxton in the Crystal Palace (Fig. 183) in the 19th century and by Nervi in his Palazzetto dello Sport (Fig. 188) in the 20th, are already used in prefabricated buildings, which can be fitted together quickly and easily at the building site.

The Israeli architect Moshe Safdie (b. 1938) has designed complete housing complexes consisting of modular systems that fit together in a variety of ways, providing different floor plans for individual units. Safdie's Habitat was a prototype of modular housing built for Expo '67 in Montreal (Fig. 200). Its precast reinforced concrete boxes, which were fitted with wiring, plumbing, doors, windows, and kitchens, were swung into place by a crane and attached to one another with rods and cables. Along with the obvious advantages of easily assembled units like these, Safdie's design takes other urban needs into account. These Habitat units are human in scale, allow for privacy and roof-gardens, and avoid monotony—important features for urban dwellers. Safdie also planned pedestrian malls to join the units and provided covered parking underneath. He believes that groups of Habitats could be clustered around city parks, and residents could walk on pedestrian overpasses or on paths through open spaces to reach shopping and community facilities. He has applied this principle to housing developments in Israel and other countries as well as Canada, where the original Habitat is not only in use but still in considerable demand.

Although some people fear that technological progress can result in spiritual impoverishment, Nervi is hopeful about the possibilities that it opens for us. He plans a city of tomorrow in which residential buildings, of clean and honest construction, will be made lively and cheerful through their relationship to streets, plazas, and gardens, Such a city would have a few large public buildings to serve "the highest and most significant expression of the new architecture." Indeed, we may note that the Crystal Palace in London (Fig. 183), the German Pavilion at the Barcelona World's Fair (Fig. 161), the Palazzetto dello Sport in Rome

(Fig. 188), and Habitat in Montreal were all public buildings planned for international events, which provided the opportunity for unprecedented public exposure to avant-garde design.

Still in the future are a number of visionary architectural schemes; but as space flight has passed from futuristic fantasy to reality, so perhaps some of these schemes may be worth exploring. Architects have designed cities that burrow underground, hang from poles, or seem to float in the air. Designs by the Italian-born architect Paolo Soleri (b. 1919) suggest a radical, organic architectural system called **Arcology,** frequently made of enormous vertical elements tied together by automatic transportation systems. His forms are unusual, often cylindrical or hemispherical, and totally alien to our traditional concept of cities. While other architects have suggested self-contained houses, which could be plugged into central utility masts and taken along when the family moved, few designers have aroused the devotion accorded to Soleri. At a site far out in the desert in the United States Southwest, a cult of young architects and other followers daily contribute to an *Arcosanti* in the making (Fig. 201).

Since we know that much of our environment—cities, towns, and highways—is unattractive and may actually cause us bodily and spiritual harm, we should be able to

201. Paolo Soleri. *Arcosanti,* east-southeast elevation, Arizona desert. Construction begun 1969.

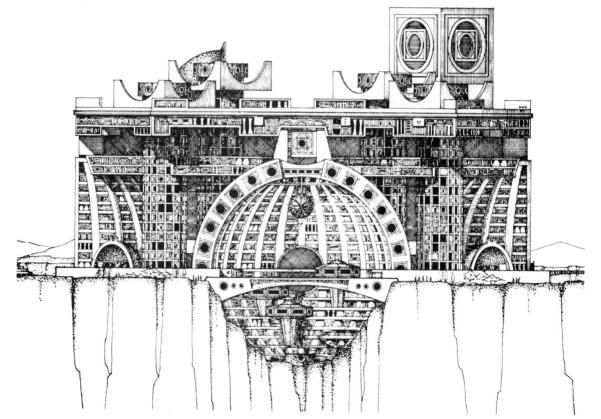

use our advanced techniques to rebuild and reshape our surroundings to make them more uplifting. To change our surroundings radically, the architects and city planners of the future, and the corporations they serve, will have to respond to people's psychological needs as much as to the needs of commerce, industry, and transportation.

Such changes are possible. The old attitude that you cannot fight city hall is out of date, for even small improvements help. To bring about alteration requires hours of effort—attending community planning meetings, telephoning, and writing letters. Changes occur only when ordinary people decide that the environment matters and that aesthetic pleasure in surroundings is necessary to personal well-being. In the final analysis, the basic materials of environmental design are not only stone, glass, and steel, or even trees, air, and fountains. The essence of such design is concern for human lives as they are enriched by the natural and human-made surroundings of our world.

EXERCISES AND ACTIVITIES

1. Study the history of your community from the point of view of the environment. Consult old photographs in the library or local historical society. Talk with long-time residents of the area to determine the extent of change. Is the community more or less attractive than it was? Which human needs are better met today, and which are neglected?

2. Choose a contemporary social or environmental problem. Write a short story or poem dealing with it or paint a picture that expresses your concern.

3. Prepare a television program dealing with a significant environmental or social problem. Present it to the class with sound effects (if possible), visual aids, and perhaps taped interviews with relevant persons.

4. Choose a natural setting in your community. Design a structure that could be incorporated into that setting without damaging the environment. Sketch the exterior, and make a plan of the interior to show the circulation pattern of the occupants and the functions it would serve.

5. Artists are either directly or indirectly involved with the culture in which they live, often furnishing guideposts for change. Select an artist whose work interests you, read biographical and critical material, and study his or her work. Analyze how the artist reflects individuality while responding to the changing currents of the time he or she lived.

6. The kind of environment we live in depends on us. What do you think that you as an individual can do to create a better environment? How would you counter resistance to your efforts?

PART III

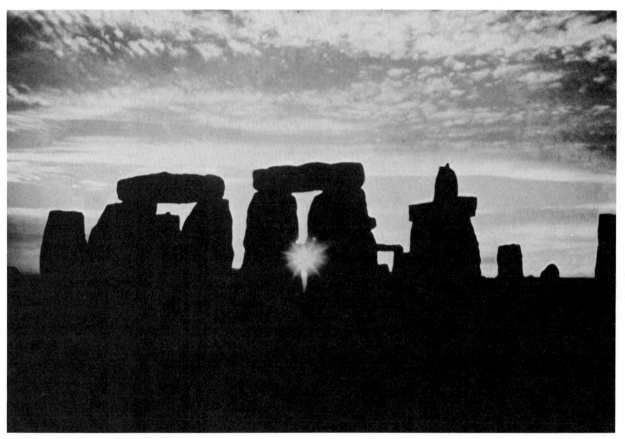

202. Stonehenge. c. 1800–1400 B.C.
Diameter of circle 97' (29.57 m),
height of stones above ground 13'6" (4.11 m).
Salisbury Plain, Wiltshire, England.

Art in Society

Art began when people first created images to express their responses to the world around them (Fig. 202). Our ancestors must have known fear and awe in the forces of nature, joy in the warmth of fire and in the taste of food, and pleasure in sexual union. Certainly, survival occupied most of their time and energy for thousands of years. These primal drives—survival, food, and fertility—run as a constant thread, and the need to express these themes in various ways was apparently common to all.

In the Old Stone Age, artists reflected concern with the capricious forces of nature. The art of later peoples expressed other universals—the crises of birth, puberty, marriage, and death. In various civilizations, artists have been dedicated to preparing for life after death; glorifying gods and rulers; and, later, depicting the growing middle class. By the 19th century, art also reflected an awareness of the machine age and its disharmony with nature. The art of our time echoes a preoccupation with technology and the environment as well.

Although we may never know just what went on in the minds of artists of the past as we try to reconstruct their society, we can better understand some of their reasons for creating art. At the same time, by examining examples of artistic expression, we come closer to understanding the life of a people or an age and needs and experiences that are universal.

In the following chapters we will emphasize Western art—that is, European and American art—because it most directly affects us as late 20th-century Americans. We can only touch on the rich artistic expression of other civilizations. Yet even in cultures beyond the influence of the West there exists a basic spirit of humanity in the art of all peoples.

11 Magic and Ritual: Prehistory and the Ancient World

To the ancients, the movement of the sun and stars was the image of perfection: to see the celestial harmony was to hear it, and to hear it was to understand it.

OCTAVIO PAZ, *In Praise of Hands*

To understand our early ancestors who first carved or painted images, we assume that most lived in an uneasy and baffling world, with little comprehension of the natural forces that affected them. Floods and fires, the migrations of the animals and birds on which they depended for food, and hurricanes and tornadoes were all inexplicable events to them. These natural phenomena must have seemed an expression of frightening forces over which they had no control. Their dwellings may have sheltered them from the wind or rain, but what could they do about other events that so intimately affected their lives? For example, how could they ensure that they would always have food or guarantee that life would go on?

The Old Stone Age

Prehistoric humans of the Paleolithic period, or Old Stone Age, apparently saw no division between objects of utility and beauty, for their world was not as specialized as ours is today. The tools and utensils they made to help them hunt, cook, sew, carve, and later build were all a part of their struggle with the powers of nature and were not separated from their everyday lives.

The oldest hand-fashioned objects were simple tools and arrowheads, which were made by flaking stones or by carving bones. Certainly the vast variety of tools were created for use, but the animals and symbols carved into some of them indicate that the need to create an image was also strong. Although the animals depicted were probably an attempt to control the outcome of the hunt through symbolic power over the prey, we can surmise that the carver also was expressing a basic artistic need in shaping the forms with such vitality. The later, more complex weapons had barbed tips, which lodged in the body of an animal, becoming more deeply embedded when the creature

struggled for freedom. Technical knowledge and artistic creativity slowly advanced as the ice-age disappeared. Humans still roamed as hunters, but their arts extended to sculptures and paintings.

Fertility Sculpture Sculptured stone figures have been found on the floors of painted caves and apparently date from about the same time as early tools. Although most of the sculptures were female, like the Venus of Willendorf (Fig. 15), a few were male, and a very few were bisexual, like the ivory hermaphroditic image in Figure 203, which looks quite different when seen from the front, side, and rear. Repetitions of bulbous shapes, which link the arms,

203. *Venus of Lespugue,* Haute Garonne, France. Late Paleolithic. Mammoth tusk. Musée de l'Homme, Paris.

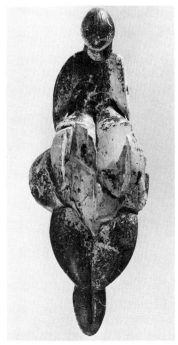

are surely sexual references. Generally considered to be fertility symbols, these images were likely used with rituals in early attempts to influence the human life cycle.

Cave Paintings   The huge boulders overlooking the caves in Lascaux, France, must have seemed overwhelming to prehistoric peoples and emphasized their helplessness in a frightening world. Trying desperately to come to terms with the unknown, they may have believed that magical painted and carved images would help them provide for their most basic needs—food and fertility.

For instance, the paintings of animals that cover the walls of caves in Spain, France, and North Africa are probably a part of magico-religious rituals (Fig. 2). When these paintings were first discovered in the late 19th century, most of the art world believed that they had been recently painted, rather than being vivid and accurate impressions of bison, mammoth, and deer made by Paleolithic artists working more than 20,000 years ago. It is now generally agreed that these works were created by early hunters who had an intimate knowledge of the animals they stalked and who used that knowledge to record their essential features with great sensitivity. Working by light from torches, deep in recessed caves, and depending on their recollection of living models seen only during the hunt, prehistoric artists must have experienced many difficulties. A visit to these caves today, now lit with electricity or powerful flashlights, is still an awe-inspiring experience.

Many game species that the hunters wished to kill were painted on those walls in realistic action scenes—often the animals were depicted pierced with arrows or spears. In the same way, aboriginal tribes in Australia today still make drawings of prey struck by arrows because they believe that symbolic killings will assure their actual success in hunting. Probably the same kind of ritual took place in the caves of the Old Stone Age. Scholars still debate the purpose of some of the images. Do they represent prehistoric scorecards used after the hunt to record success, or were they virtually painted and pierced with arrows earlier? We may never know the answer.

Parts of the caves are more fully covered with paintings than others. Possibly this is because new generations felt that the pictures painted by people who preceded them were sacred, and if more paintings were added to these areas, it might assure success for their own rituals. Perhaps that is why in the Lascaux caves images of horses were painted next to a 40-foot (12-meter) painting of a cow that was already 8,000 years old. But can you guess what the geometric symbol to the left of the leaping reindeer in Figure 2 represents? We remain unsure about many such enigmatic works.

The New Stone Age

Gradually, over several thousand years, prehistoric peoples ceased to depend solely on hunting for food and turned instead to agriculture and herding animals during the Neolithic period, or New Stone Age. They also acquired the skills of making pottery, weaving, and building. As society became more complex, the caves of the Paleolithic era were apparently abandoned. It is now believed that the paintings and tools of the Old Stone Age were not seen again for millennia, until they were rediscovered in the 19th century.

Monuments in Northern Europe   Little remains of the perishable dwellings of the New Stone Age farmers of northern Europe, but many of their impressive monuments still stand. Some of these megalithic structures, made of huge stones (**megaliths**) dragged from distant places, are set in careful arrangements and combinations, which must have served in unknown rituals. Brittany, in northern France, has thousands of **dolmens** (upright boulders with a slab for a roof, sometimes serving as tombs) and **menhirs** (single stones) set in rows. In southern England there are circles of stones such as Stonehenge, discussed in Chapter 9, built around 1800 B.C.

Although the people living in Britain at that time were less sophisticated than their contemporaries in the Middle East who had already developed distinctive civilizations, Stonehenge is evidence that its builders had precise knowledge of the movements of the sun and the stars. The exact placement of the stones in three concentric circles ensured that at dawn on June 21, the first rays of the sun would pass through the rings of stones to strike the altar in their center. Computer analysis reveals only a tenth of a degree of misjudgment. This impressive event at the summer solstice, the longest day of the year, is enhanced by the height of the stones, more than 12 feet (4 meters), which dwarf human observers. A modern photograph of Stonehenge (Fig. 202) recreates the religious mood that probably surrounded it when it was in use.

Rise of Civilizations in the Middle East   Long before civilization began in Europe, Neolithic farming villages along two river valleys developed into two great civilizations in the Middle East. The Fertile Ribbon of Egypt hugs both sides of the Nile River (Fig. 204). Though it is generally only 16 miles (25.75 kilometers) across, it is nearly 500 miles (804.67 kilometers) long, from ancient Nubia in the south to the wide delta in the north where the river joins the Mediterranean Sea. Quite different in shape is the valley between the Tigris and Euphrates rivers in Mesopotamia, called the Fertile Crescent.

Archaeological evidence indicates that both areas had active societies around 4000 B.C. By 3000 B.C. the peoples of these valleys had begun to form larger communities and to keep written records. Precise dates are difficult to establish. The details of the many dynasties that ruled Egypt and the many different peoples that controlled Mesopotamia cannot concern us here, but the main outlines of this history are clear.

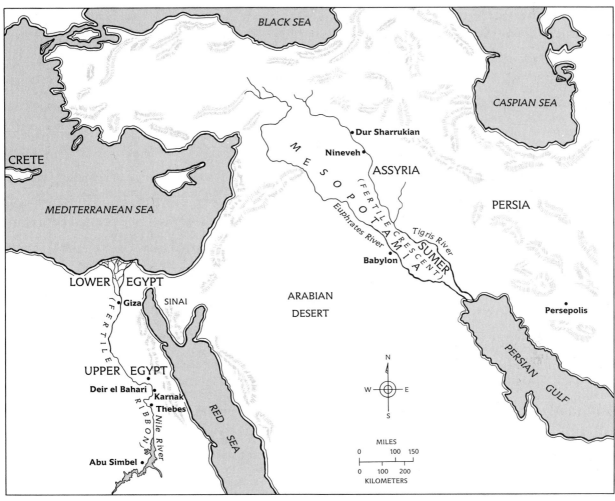

204. The ancient Near East.

Egypt

Ninety-seven percent of Egypt is arid desert, while the remaining three percent is fertile only because of water supplied by the Nile. Life was, therefore, restricted to those areas bordering the river, which could easily be nourished by the annual flooding of its waters. For this reason the Greek historian Herodotus called Egypt's civilization "the gift of the Nile." In addition to providing water for agriculture, the Nile also created a means of transportation, communication, and sanitation for the peoples living along its banks. Finally, the wide deserts on both sides of the Nile insulated and protected the Egyptians from foreign intruders, for few invaders could survive the rigors of long desert travel.

In such a favorable environment, Egyptian civilization developed a characteristic continuity over a period of nearly 3,000 years. Egyptian history is customarily divided into three main periods.

Old Kingdom, c. 2800–2000 B.C.
Middle Kingdom, c. 2000–1600 B.C.
New Kingdom and later periods, c. 1600–350 B.C.

Dynasty followed dynasty with little alteration in the customs of the Egyptians or the art forms that reflected them. For us, who live in a changing era, it is difficult to imagine so static a society, but to the Egyptians it seemed natural and desirable.

To cultivate the soil along the Nile, the Egyptians had to develop an irrigation system, which meant that many individuals and whole villages had to work together. From such communal efforts the complex Egyptian civilization arose. Cooperation also made possible the earliest monumental architecture: tombs for the important dead.

Pyramids and Other Tombs The first architectural form used for burial was the **mastaba,** a low, flat-topped mound with **battered** (sloping) sides. Several mastaba shapes of diminishing size, set one on top of another, form a stepped pyramid, such as that of the ruler Djoser (Zoser) (Fig. 205). Stepped pyramids were solid masses of rubble smoothly faced with brick or stone. The tombs of rulers were deep inside.

Stepped pyramids evolved into smooth-sided pyramids, the most famous of which were created for a father, son, and grandson of the Old Kingdom at Giza about 2600 to 2500 B.C. (Fig. 35). The power structure of Egypt centered on the pharaoh, or king, supported by the priests, who could command thousands of men to construct the huge pyramids and the temples that accompanied them. They believed that these structures would safeguard the pharaoh's immortality.

The earliest, largest, and most famous pyramid is that of Pharaoh Khufu (Cheops). Near it is that of Khafre (Chephren), which has a few limestone blocks at the top, all that remains of the limestone that once covered all three pyramids. The pyramid of Khafre, like the others, was connected by a causeway to a valley temple. Beside the causeway stands the gigantic sculpture of the Sphinx, representing a pharaoh in a royal linen headress and, before weathering and vandalism, displaying the features of Khafre. A smaller portrait statue of Khafre from his valley temple is made of diorite, a kind of stone so tough that it would quickly dull a modern steel carving tool (Fig. 206). We can only assume that the Egyptians carved with tools of a still harder stone, which would be a very slow process indeed.

Inside the pyramids, which were solid mounds of limestone, earth, and rubble, were small rooms full of the rich belongings of the pharaoh, left to provide him with what his subjects believed he would need in his life after death. Another replica of the pharaoh was set up in front of the burial chamber to hold his *Ka,* or spirit, when his body could no longer contain it. The wall paintings in the burial chambers give us a vivid view of Egyptian life and customs (Fig. 58), as do the many objects found in the tombs. Jewelry, cosmetics, toys, furniture, models of houses, pieces of clothing, figurines depicting such daily events as slaves baking bread—thousands of these have survived to tell us what life was like for a well-to-do Egyptian.

Since the images in the tombs were meant to last for eternity, they were carved and painted as clearly as possible according to strict guidelines. People, scenery, animals, and furnishings were always depicted from an angle or point of view that gave the most characteristic contour. For example, a pond or a lake was painted as if seen from above or from the side. Fish swimming underwater through the reeds and birds and trees were all drawn in profile. A table was shown from one side or from the top.

Human figures usually seem to stand in poses that even the most supple of us could never achieve. The reason for this convention was that the Egyptians represented details of the human body as a composite of its most typical shapes. They believed that since the head was most easily

seen in profile, it should be painted that way. For the same reason the eyes were shown from the front, as were both shoulders; but arms, legs, and feet were presented in profile. Egyptian art is not based on what the artists saw but on what they knew about their subjects. In somewhat the same way a 20th-century Cubist painter showed many simultaneous views of a human figure in a composite (Fig. 10).

Paintings in these tombs were detailed because pious Egyptians believed that the pharaoh could enjoy in the afterlife only what was provided for him in reality or in replica in his tomb. For example, they thought that the pharaoh would starve if foods were not depicted. Originally his descendants had brought him real meals, but they quickly found that piety is short-lived while paintings of food are durable. Similarly, birds were reproduced so accurately in tomb paintings that they can still be identified as varieties living in Egypt today.

The architects of the pyramids tried to hide their entrances to prevent the valuables inside from being stolen, but the simplicity of the exterior surface of the pyramid made concealment difficult. No matter what pains the architects took, robbers located the entrances, broke in, and stole the pharaoh's belongings. Apparently, even for those who believed that the pharaoh was descended from the sun god, the lust for worldly treasure was stronger than the fear of the divine.

New burial places had to be devised to protect the pharaoh's remains. During the Middle Kingdom, hidden tombs were constructed in cliffs, especially in those that formed the Valley of the Kings outside Thebes near modern Cairo. Tomb entrances were concealed with no monuments to mark the burial spot. Despite these precautions, most tombs were broken into by robbers. This meant more than the loss of the pharaoh's treasures; it also meant that he was deprived of the belongings he needed to exist in his afterlife.

Archaeologists have to date uncovered only one richly furnished royal tomb, that of the New Kingdom pharaoh Tutankhamen, who flourished around 1350 B.C.. When his tomb was discovered almost intact in the 1920s, the archaeologists found among other treasures a throne (Fig. 142) and a great deal of jewelry inlaid with glass and semiprecious stones. This included golden amulets of the gods, rings, bracelets, necklaces, and even golden guards to protect the mummy's toes. Small sculptures, deep-blue-glazed pottery, clothing, alabaster boxes and vases, and many ritual objects found in the tomb attested to the delicate and advanced craftsmanship of the ancient Egyptians. The royal mummy was found in a nest of four wood (Fig. 118) and gold coffins, each one smaller than the last with the innermost one just fitting his body. The delicate throne fashioned for the young king is made of wood, inlaid with gold and enamels. In a scene on the back of the throne, Tutankhamen's 15-year-old bride adjusts the lavish jewelry covering his chest by the light of the symbolic sun above. The portraits of the king and queen combine

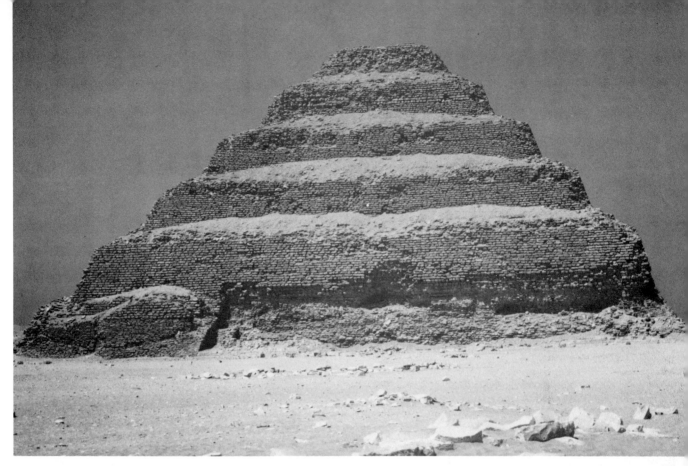

above: 205. Stepped pyramid, funerary
district of King Zoser,
Saqqara. c. 2750 B.C.

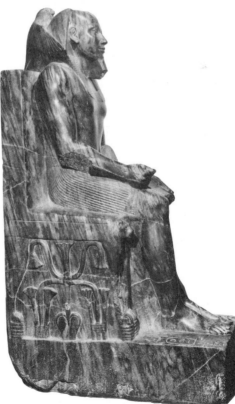

right: 206. *Khafre*. Giza, c. 2530 B.C.
Dark green diorite, height 5'6" (1.68 m).
Egyptian Museum, Cairo.

naturalism with the sensitive modeling found in fine portrait sculpture.

Temples   The pharaohs of the New Kingdom built magnificent stone temples, using post-and-lintel construction, as noted in Chapter 9. Their immense columns were often shaped like bundles of papyrus stems, which are believed to have been used in place of scarce wood in early Egyptian buildings. Other columns were topped with capitals inspired by the lotus flowers of the Nile (Fig. 59).

The exquisite funerary temple at Deir el Bahari, at the entrance to the Valley of Kings, was built about 1485 B.C. by Hatshepsut, the only woman to interrupt the male succession of pharaohs and the only one to build a temple (Fig. 207). The building, dedicated to the sun god, Amun, is carved from the living rock of the cliffs and is fronted by three tiers of colonnades connected by ramps. After an unparalleled reign of peace and trade with kingdoms as distant as legendary Punt, Hatshepsut was killed, probably by her stepson and successor Thutmose III. She never occupied any of the three graves she had carefully prepared in the Valley of Kings, and Thutmose obliterated her inscriptions wherever he could. Her story is told only in her temple and on her **obelisks,** tall four-sided monuments, which still stand proudly in the Temple of Karnak, though once walled in by Thutmose III.

A little more than one hundred years later the remarkable pharaoh Akhenaton tried to reduce the complex Egyp-

207. Mortuary temple of Hatshepsut, Deir el Bahari. c. 1485 B.C.

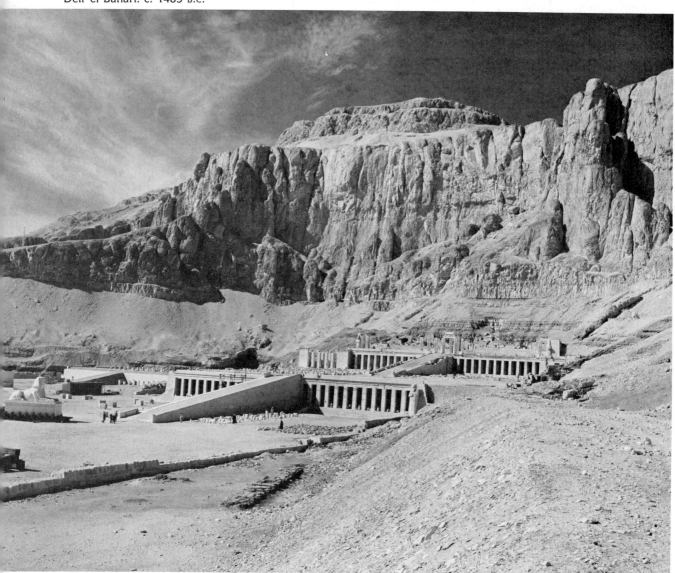

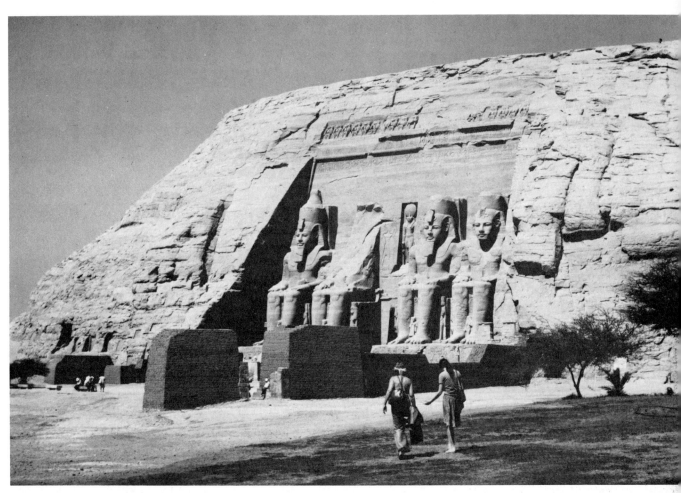

208. Temple of Ramses II, Abu Simbel.
c. 1250 B.C. Height of large statues c. 60′ (18.3 m).

tian polytheism to the simple worship of one god, the sun god Aten. He built a new temple to Aten at Amarna, which was destroyed by his successors and the priests, anxious to restore the old religion. The chief remains from his reign are some reliefs and murals in a realistic style full of movement and individuality. The portrait bust of his queen, Nefertiti, a partner in his reforms, presents her as a specific person rather than an abstract symbol (Pl. 11, p. 201).

While the Great Temple of Amun at Karnak with its hypostyle halls, discussed in Chapter 9, is characteristic of Egyptian temples, that built by Ramses II in the cliffs at Abu Simbel on the upper Nile (Fig. 208) is unique. Four colossal statues guarded the entrance. The building was so designed that twice a year, at the equinoxes, a ray of sunlight would pierce the entrance at dawn, cross the main hall, and penetrate far back to reach the tiny inner shrine containing four statues of the sun god, other gods, and Ramses. The scientific skill of these ancient Egyptian builders, shown in the temple at Abu Simbel, is staggering even when measured against today's engineering skills. When recent construction of the Aswan Dam raised the level of the Nile, the entire temple was moved to the top of the cliffs to save it from being flooded. As a result of faulty calculations, however, the sun rays at the equinox now light the inner sanctum one day late.

The complex arts preserved in the tombs and architectural remains combine to give us a picture of ancient Egypt as an aesthetically sophisticated civilization. Egyptian art, however, required a wealthy ruling class as patrons. When internal power struggles within the structured society led to the collapse of the government, Egyptian art slowly declined as well.

Mesopotamia

Like the Fertile Ribbon along Egypt's Nile roughly 600 miles away (1,000 kilometers), the Fertile Crescent, between the Tigris and the Euphrates, was flooded when the rivers overflowed in spring, and in summer it was parched by the sun. Here, also, irrigation was necessary to maintain agriculture. Unlike Egypt, however, Mesopotamia had no natural desert barriers to repel invaders and foreign influences. Therefore, over a period of thousands of years, the whole area became the home of many peoples, and its history was in constant flux. The story is confusing, with many shifts of power, especially between the empires of Babylonia and Assyria. We can, however, touch briefly on the four main societies that dominated this land.

Sumer, c. 4000–2300 B.C.
Babylonia, c. 2000–550 B.C.
Assyria, c. 1400–600 B.C.
Persia, c. 550–325 B.C.

Persisting throughout Mesopotamian civilization were the basic achievements of the Sumerians, which later peoples developed or modified.

Sumerian Art The Sumerians were great builders. Living in a land that lacked stone and wood but had plenty of clay, they built large cities, palaces, and temples out of brick. Eventually they learned to fire the bricks and glaze them to make them more weatherproof. In trying to span openings with bricks they developed the arch (see Chapter 9), a principle known but little used by the Egyptians or the later Greeks.

The characteristic form of Sumerian architecture was the **ziggurat,** an artificial mountain of packed earth surfaced with bricks, crowned by a temple to a god of an aspect of nature such as water, sky, or storm. The temple was believed to be the god's home. All that is left of the ziggurats today are eroded, truncated mounds of sun-dried clay brick, but an artist's drawing (Fig. 209) shows us how

the one in Ur may have looked, with ramps leading up from terraces on all sides through archways, past gardens and trees. The structure called the hanging gardens of Babylon was actually a ziggurat with trees and flowers planted on its terraces. From a distance the brick ziggurat blended with the dry, surrounding countryside, but the lush greenery seemed suspended in air. Mesopotamia without irrigation was dry and poor. When the inhabitants tried to imagine a more desirable existence, or Paradise, they thought of it as a garden, such as the garden of Eden described in the Bible.

The Sumerians were among the first people to have developed a written language, the cuneiform (Fig. 145). They also divided the hour into 60 minutes and the circle into 360 degrees, divisions we still use today.

Babylonian Art The Babylonians built cities and ziggurats like the Sumerians. Hammurabi, king of Babylon from about 1727 to 1686 B.C., established an empire and created the first written code of laws.

The Old Babylonian Empire founded by Hammurabi was succeeded by the Assyrian Empire, which in turn was replaced by the New Babylonian, or Chaldean, Empire, described in the Bible, which emerged about 625 B.C. The palace of Nebuchadnezzar II and the ziggurat of the great god Marduk, called the Tower of Babel, are both gone. Artists throughout history have tried to imagine how the Tower of Babel looked, but without drawings or plans of it no one can be sure. Certainly, the painting by Pieter Brueghel the Elder (c. 1525–1569), set in a 16th-century Flemish landscape peopled with workers in Renaissance dress (Fig. 210), must be far removed from the original palace.

209. Reconstruction drawing of the Ziggurat at Ur. Neo-Sumerian, c. 2100–2000 B.C.

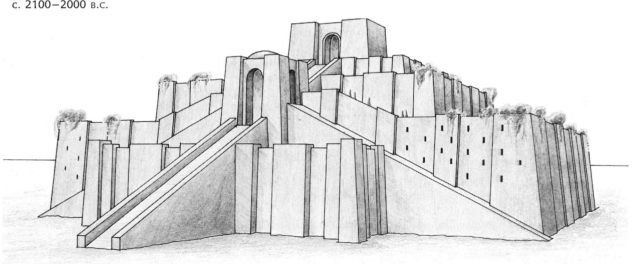

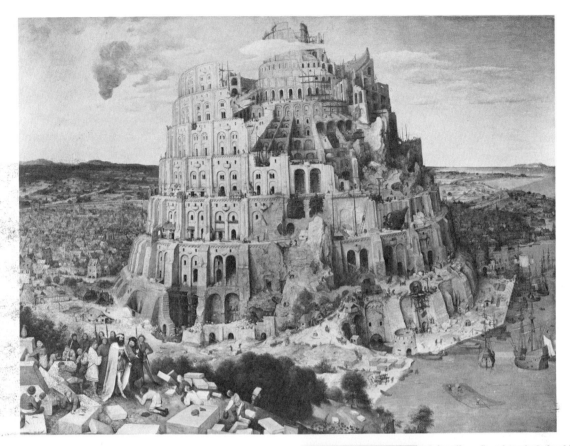

above: 210. Pieter Bruegel the Elder.
The Tower of Babel. 1563.
Oil on canvas, 3'8⅞" × 5'1" (1.14 × 1.55 m).
Kunsthistorisches Museum, Vienna.

right: 211. Ishtar Gate (restored), Babylon.
c. 575 B.C. Enameled sun-dried brick,
height 48'9" (15 m). Near Eastern Museum,
State Museums, East Berlin.

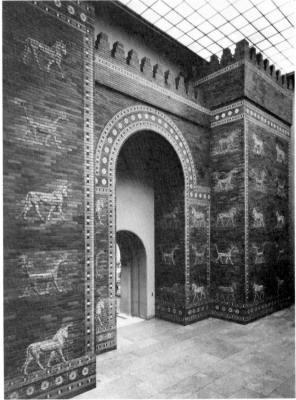

Scholars have, however, restored the Ishtar Gate of Babylon dedicated to the goddess Ishtar (Fig. 211). It is faced with glazed brick and decorated with reliefs of animals, some two-headed and some 20 feet (6 meters) long. Similar glazed brick reliefs in brilliant colors lined the Processional Way, which led to the Ishtar Gate, the only major monument remaining from this period.

Assyrian Art The Assyrians, from the upper Tigris River, established one of the world's greatest empires about 1200 B.C. At its height it stretched from the Persian Gulf in the east through Mesopotamia to Asia Minor and the Mediterranean in the west. Although the Assyrians built their own cities such as Dur Sharrukin (modern Khorsabad) and Nineveh (modern Kuyunik), Babylon remained important. The Assyrians adopted much of Babylonian civilization, to which they gave their own distinctive character.

The Assyrians introduced no new construction methods. They built highly elaborate palaces decorated with

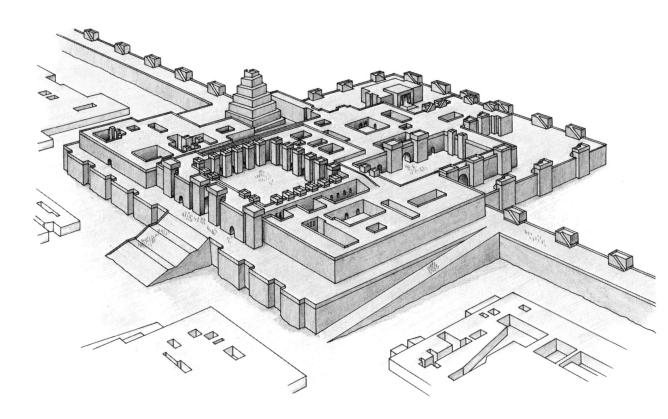

great stone slabs carved in relief. The 200-room palace-temple complex of Sargon II at Khorsabad (Fig. 212) is known to have enclosed 25 acres (10.11 hectares), including a ziggurat with a spiral ramp. Unlike the huge Sumerian Ziggurat at Ur, however, the Assyrian mountain to the gods, similar to the ziggurat form, was reduced to a small temple.

The Assyrians were primarily warriors and hunters, who commissioned their sculptors to depict expeditions, hunting scenes, and the lives of kings and the military. Some of their carvings were realistic, such as a relief decorating the palace of Ashurbanipal at Nineveh (Fig. 213). The sculptor portrays the death of a wounded lioness, showing a strong sense of action, knowledge of animal anatomy, and even a sensitivity to the pain of the animal, a concern rarely directed toward people in Assyrian art. Many animal sculptures were nonrealistic. For example, the stone guardian that stood at one of the entrances to the palace of Sargon II at Dur Sharrukin has a human head, the headdress of a god, the wings of a bird, and the body of a lion (Fig. 214). It also was made with five legs, so that when seen from the front it would appear to have four legs, and as one walked past it into the palace, it would still seem to have four legs. The extra leg represents an effort to make the animal appear as complete as possible, in the same way the Egyptians drew the human figure from several points of view in an attempt to present a total image.

above: 212. Reconstruction drawing of the palace of Sargon II, Khorsabad, Iraq. c. 720 B.C.

below: 213. *Dying Lioness*. Nineveh, c. 650 B.C. Limestone, height 23¾" (60 cm). British Museum, London, courtesy of the Trustees.

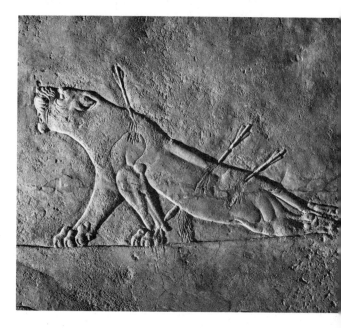

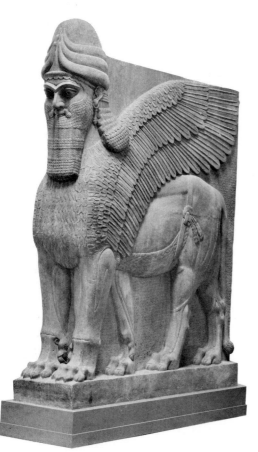

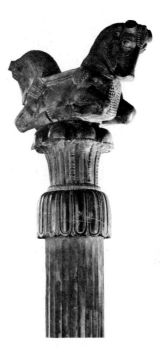

above: 214. Winged lion (guardian of the palace gate), from the palace of Ashurnasirpal II. Assyrian, 9th century B.C.
Limestone; height 10′2½″ (3.11 m), length 9′¾″ (2.76 m), width 2′1½″ (0.65 m).
Metropolitan Museum of Art, New York (gift of John D. Rockefeller, Jr., 1932.)

above right: 215. Double bull capital and column from Persepolis (restored).
Achamenid Period, 504–496 B.C. Black limestone, height approximately 13′ (4 m).
Oriental Institute, University of Chicago.

Persian Art The final period of Mesopotamian art, when the area was dominated by Persia (modern Iran), overlaps Greek civilization, and its architecture was stimulated by contact with Greece. Darius, the Persian emperor whose effort to conquer Greece was defeated at the Battle of Marathon in 490 B.C., built a massive stone palace in the city of Persepolis. Its great halls, with roofs supported on slender 60-foot (18.28-meter) pillars, show the influence of Greek architecture. Unlike earlier Mesopotamian palaces, the Persian palace did not look like a fortress; instead, it was open and inviting with many stairways and columned waiting rooms. Perhaps this huge capital with two noble bulls' heads placed back to back (Fig. 215) is symbolic of the historical role played by the Persian empire; one head looks back to the civilization of the Fertile Crescent upon which much of the Judeo-Christian tradition is based, while the other head looks toward the Mediterranean and the civilization of Greece, whose philosophy and art have so strongly influenced the West.

EXERCISES AND ACTIVITIES

1. What were the earliest art forms? What were the materials and functions of that art? Would you consider the art of our earliest ancestors to be simple and childlike? If not, in what way do you think it was skilled and expressive?
2. Locate two examples of modern art that deal with themes similar to those of prehistoric times or the ancient Middle East. How do the modern works differ from early art, and in what ways are they similar?
3. Describe the construction of Stonehenge. What structural method was used?
4. What is meant by the terms "Fertile Ribbon" and "Fertile Crescent"? How were they important? When Herodotus stated that "Egypt is a gift of the Nile," what facts did he have in mind?
5. Contrast the architecture, sculpture, and painting of Egypt and Mesopotamia from the viewpoints of material and style. Explain the reasons for the differences.
6. Do a simple painting based on a subject from everyday life, using some of the spatial concepts of the Egyptians.

12 Gods and Heroes: The Classical World

Leaving the waters of the splendid East, the sun leapt up into the firmament to bring light to the immortals and to men who plough the earth and perish.

HOMER, *The Odyssey*

Most of us in the West have been brought up to think of the Greeks and Romans as the wise ancients who developed sophisticated civilizations, which we call classical. In fact, they had the good fortune to be alive when the world was young. They had the chance to create new societies and develop new philosophies, governmental systems, and styles of art. In contrast, perhaps we in the 20th century are actually the ancients, grappling with the problems of a weary world that has made many mistakes.

Our legacy from Greece is incalculable. Drama, poetry, architecture, sculpture, experiments in democracy, philosophical concepts, a rational approach to the mysteries of nature—there is hardly a facet of our lives not affected by Greek achievements. Greek civilization was absorbed by Rome, which added its own contributions, especially in government, architecture, and engineering. Roman law, roads, arches, and the Latin language lasted for centuries after Roman political power came to an end. The combined achievements of both peoples make up the classical heritage of the West. Yet much of what we consider to be characteristic of the Greeks and Romans was in fact derived from earlier peoples.

The Aegean Background

The Aegean Sea is full of islands that provided stopping places for sailing ships. During prehistoric and ancient times, the constant trade and exchange of ideas among many peoples bordering the sea stimulated the development of Aegean civilization. The island of Crete, midway between Greece and Egypt, carried on extensive trade with Asia Minor and Egypt between 2000 B.C. and 1400 B.C. Enriched by these contacts, Crete developed a very sophisticated civilization. Egyptian post-and-lintel con-struction probably influenced the enormous palace at Knossos, which inspired the Greek legend of the Minotaur and the labyrinth. According to the story, the Greek hero Theseus found his way through a complex maze, perhaps representing the many rooms of the palace, to slay the Minotaur, a monster half man and half bull. The Minotaur myth probably developed from the Cretan cult of the bull, so vividly expressed in the palace frescoes of youths and maidens leaping over a running bull (Fig. 77).

By the mid-15th century B.C., Mycenae, in southern Greece, had grown to rival Crete as a center of culture. Gold masks, jewelry, weapons, and cups from the beehive tombs of the Mycenaeans bring to life the lusty days of the ten-year war between the Mycenaean rulers and the Trojans in Asia Minor, described in Homer's epic *The Iliad*. The lion gate stands on the hilltop citadel at Mycenae surrounded by walls of massive stone blocks fitted together without mortar (Fig. 216).

216. "Lion Gate," Mycenae. c. 1250 B.C. Relief, height 9'6" (2.9 m).

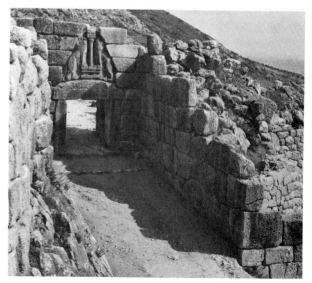

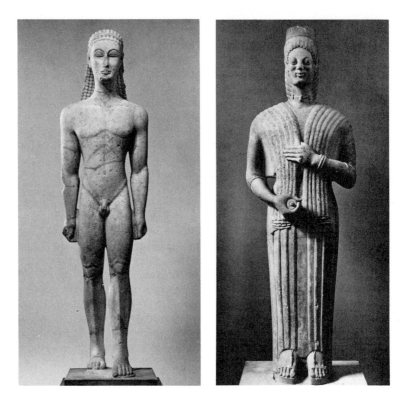

right: 217. Statue of a youth of the "Apollo" type. 615–600 B.C. Marble, height with plinth, 6'½" (1.84 m). Metropolitan Museum of Art, New York (Fletcher Fund, 1932).

far right: 218. *Young Maiden (Kore).* Early 6th century B.C. Attic marble, height 6'4" (1.93 m). State Museums, West Berlin.

Greece

Greek civilization was a blend of many influences. The Dorian Greeks, who invaded the Greek mainland, Crete, and the other Aegean islands from the north about 1000 B.C., absorbed the skills of metallurgy, pottery, weaving, and building developed earlier in Mycenae and Crete. The Ionian Greeks, who migrated from southern Greece to Ionia in western Asia Minor in the 11th and 10th centuries B.C., incorporated into their art and religion ideas from Mesopotamia. These many elements all contributed to form the distinctive Greek civilization we admire.

Greek art can be divided into three periods.

Archaic period, 7th and 6th centuries B.C.
Classical period, 5th century and early 4th century B.C.
Hellenistic period, late 4th, 3rd, and 2nd centuries B.C.

Sculpture of the Archaic Period By about 700 B.C. the basis of Greek political and economic life was shifting from agricultural villages to cities dependent on trade. Wealthy cities commissioned statues of the gods, legendary heroes, and athletes, who took part in the Olympic Games, held to honor the gods since the 8th century B.C. Although the Greeks stood in awe of their immortal gods, they also felt close to them and imagined them in human form. Greek legends and the epics of Homer presented the gods as superhuman beings entangled in the affairs of mortals.

Men and women, although weak and imperfect, were believed to resemble the gods. Therefore, Greek statues of divinities and mortals showed similarities since athletes served as models for both. Selected features of many athletes were combined in idealized sculpture, which eventually became the standard for human beauty in the West.

Rigidly posed Egyptian statues must have been the models for the early Greek representation of the nude male figure, known as a **kouros** (Fig. 217). Unlike the Egyptian artists, who made static figures to serve as eternal replicas of the pharaoh and aristocracy, Greek artists were not content with stiff poses to convey the spirit of their gods and heroes. So, although the kouros is severe, he is also full of vitality, both physical and mental, illustrating the Greek ideal of a healthy mind in a healthy body. Standing with one foot advanced, fists clenched and muscles taut, the figure seems ready to burst from its bonds of stone.

The Greeks also represented a young maiden, or **kore** (Fig. 218). Her compact figure, always clothed, stares at us with an archaic smile that may not have been so much the result of artistic design as of the sculptor's difficulty in carving the mouth. This kore holds a pomegranate, regarded as a symbol of fertility because of its many seeds.

Even in early figures of gods, heroes, and other mortals, we can perceive that quality of balance among the emotions, sensations, and intellect that became typical of later Greek art in the Classical period. Like most Greek sculpture, the kouros and kore statues were colored, and we can still see traces of their original paint.

Architecture of the Classical Period The renowned Classical period of Greece refers to a rather short time in the 5th and sometimes the early 4th centuries B.C. when Athens was the center of a rich flowering of art, literature, and philosophy. This moderately sized city-state produced in three generations such dramatists as Aeschylus, Sophocles, and Euripides; the philosophers Socrates, Plato, and Aristotle; the sculptors Phidias, Myron, and Praxiteles; and the outstanding political leaders Themistocles and Pericles (461–429 B.C.). During this period Athens and other city-states built many temples to their patron gods and goddesses. The crowning achievement of Greek architecture of the Classical period was marble temples. They adhered to the same general floor plan—a **cella,** or room housing the statue of the god, entered through a porch with columns. Some temples had also variously a porch in back, a treasure room behind the cella, and a colonnade on all four sides. Temples were set on three steps and covered with a gable roof. Every architectural element was subtly related to the whole composition.

Greek marble temples reveal Egyptian influence as well as earlier Greek temples in wood. For example, the marble columns were placed at what were originally the meeting points of wooden beams, and an **abacus,** or square form originally interposed between the capital and the beams to strengthen the joining point, was retained. Decorative details can also be traced to original wood construction.

THE ORDERS OF ARCHITECTURE Variations in temple design are mainly in the elements of the **order** of a temple. An order consists of a column, or post (including base, shaft, and capital with abacus and enchinus), and an **entablature,** or lintels, above it (including a plain **architrave,** a decorated **frieze,** and the **cornice** of the roof) (Fig. 219). All the elements were refined to create a satisfying and harmonious relationship.

There were three kinds of orders, each with its own proportions and decorative scheme. The simple, early Doric order was named for the Dorians, although it may have originated in Crete. It had an unadorned disk for a capital and a sturdy, widely **fluted** (grooved) shaft. The frieze was decorated with **triglyphs,** stone copies of the grooves in the clay tablets that once covered the ends of the wooden beams to protect them from the weather and probably to drain off rainwater. The square spaces between the triglyphs, called **metopes,** were sometimes filled

219. Orders of architecture.

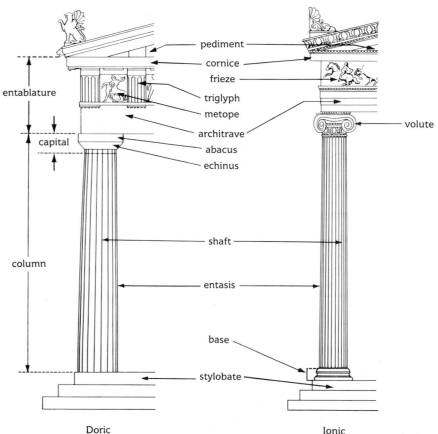

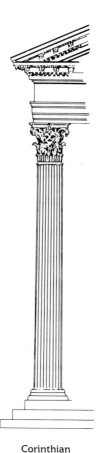

Doric   Ionic   Corinthian

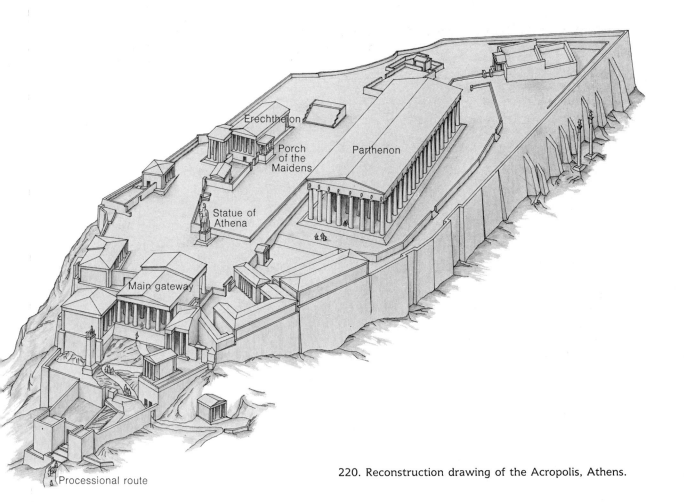

Erechtheion

Porch
of the
Maidens

Parthenon

Statue of
Athena

Main gateway

Processional route

220. Reconstruction drawing of the Acropolis, Athens.

with sculpture. The Doric order gave an air of massive grandeur to early temples.

The Ionic order, which had **volutes** (spirals) on the capitals and a slender shaft, with delicate, narrow fluting to emphasize its height, gave a temple a lighter effect that was more open and inviting. The frieze was often ornamented with sculpture. The Ionic order can be traced through Ionia to earlier forms used in Asia Minor, where spiral decoration is believed to be derived from sheaves of rushes native to Mesopotamia but unknown in Greece. Some scholars, however, believe the capital derives from ram's horns.

The later, more ornate Corinthian order had a capital shaped like an inverted bell with tiny volutes and overlapping rows of acanthus leaves. It was adopted by the Romans and eventually influenced Romanesque, Gothic, and Renaissance builders.

Since the Renaissance, Western architects have borrowed and adapted all three orders, which still can be seen. Look for them especially on libraries, courthouses, and banks, copied in wood, marble, or even concrete.

THE ACROPOLIS Some of the most famous Greek temples were built on the Acropolis overlooking Athens and the

Aegean Sea. An **acropolis** is a fortified hill, which originally provided defense in most Greek cities. This artist's reconstruction shows the Athenian Acropolis during the Golden Age of Pericles, when it was at its height as a civic and religious center (Fig. 220). Temples, a storehouse, and commemorative statues were reached through the Propylaea, a ceremonial gateway at the head of a steep, twisting path with steps.

THE PARTHENON The best-known Acropolis temple, although not necessarily the most refined, was the Parthenon. Commissioned by Pericles and designed by the architects Ictinus and Callicrates, it was dedicated to Athena during the Panathenaic Festival of 438 B.C. Its sturdy Doric form reveals the subtle architectural relationships that have influenced so many later architects. The precise proportions, the interplay of vertical and horizontal forms, the contrast of the solid cella against the many columns of the two porches and surrounding colonnade, all combine to create a harmonious design that appears simple but that is actually extremely complex.

The columns were designed to bulge slightly in the center, a distortion called **entasis** intended to counteract the optical illusion that causes parallel straight lines to appear to

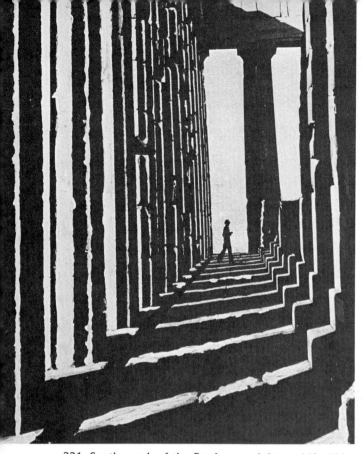

curve inward. In addition, the horizontal line of the top step of the porch and the line of the architrave were also curved slightly upward to avoid the appearance of sagging. In the space formed by the columns and architrave at the end of the colonnade we can see a graceful shape like an inverted vase (Fig. 221). Was it created by chance or by careful planning, perhaps as a symbol whose meaning is lost?

The Parthenon, like all Greek temples, was built to be visually satisfying from all sides. Its carefully proportioned form presents an impressive silhouette, which dominates the Acropolis. Let us imagine ourselves as part of a procession of Athenians making our way up the rock of the Acropolis through the Propylaea to the Parthenon. Instead of entering the temple at the near, west end, the procession will wind around to approach from the far, east end. We can look up and see the lively horses and riders carved in high relief in the metopes of the frieze above the colonnade.

Approaching the east end, we may stop to admire the sculptured figures of the three goddesses on the **pediment** (Fig. 222), the triangular space between the frieze and the gable. The quarrel between Athena and the sea god Poseidon for the patronage of Athens occupies the west pediment. The middle figures have enough space to stand erect, but as the roof slopes down, the tapering space dictates their crouched and extended poses. These pedimental sculptures, now in the British Museum, were designed by

221. South porch of the Parthenon, Athens. 448–432 B.C.

222. *Three Goddesses,* from Parthenon east pediment.
c. 438–432 B.C. Marble, over life size. British Museum, London, courtesy of the Trustees.

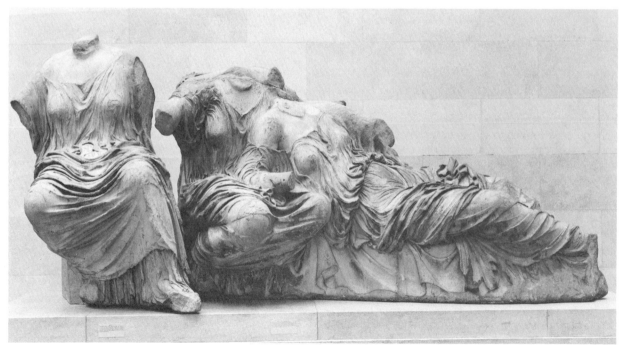

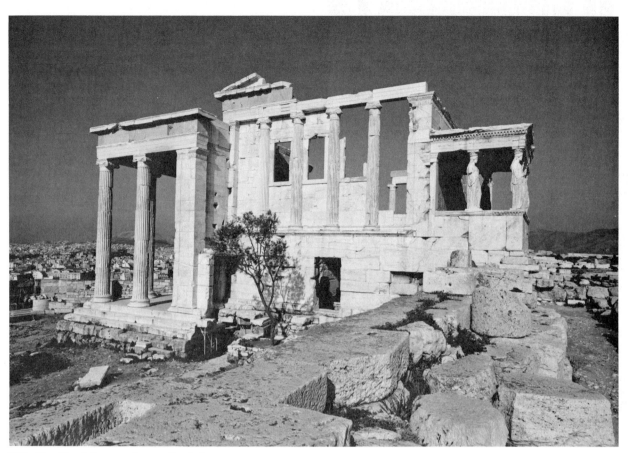

223. The Erechtheum, Acropolis, Athens.
c. 410 B.C. Height of caryatids 7′9″ (2.36 m).

Phidias, who supervised all the architectural projects ordered by Pericles. We must remember, when we are tempted to think of white marble statues and temples, that many were once brightly painted.

As we pass through the colonnade, we can see above us the low-relief frieze honoring Athena surrounding the cella depicting the Panathenaic procession held every four years. We may look for fellow-citizens represented in the frieze, but the idealized faces have a dignity appropriate to the occasion that makes them difficult to recognize. Only priests enter the sanctuary, but if we stand at the door of the cella, we may be able to glimpse the magnificent gold and ivory statue of Athena Parthenos by Phidias. Today the gold and ivory figure is gone, as well as the pediment marbles. Of Athens' foremost temple, only the basic structure and its reliefs remain.

THE ERECHTHEUM On the north side of the Acropolis is the Erechtheum, a temple built on the site of one of the most ancient shrines, sacred to Athena, the early Athenian king and snake god Erechtheus, and Poseidon. This multiple dedication explains the complicated and unusual plan of this early split-level temple. Its four levels are marked by three differently proportioned sets of Ionic columns and the **caryatids** (figures of women) that form the Porch of Maidens (Fig. 223).

Sculpture of the Classical Period Sculptors of the Classical period learned to distill the essence of beauty from the world around them, idealizing the body but retaining qualities that allow us to identify with the figures. While no particular individual is ever portrayed, enough humanity remains in the figures to express the Greek ideal of serenity. Reflecting the Greek ideal of moderation, the body is shown in a state of balance between energy and repose.

The bronze *Charioteer* from Delphi, cast about 470 B.C., stands stiffly like a kouros, but there is a lifelike quality in his head with its curly hair held by a headband and its inlaid

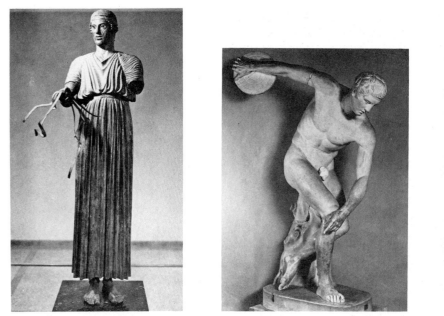

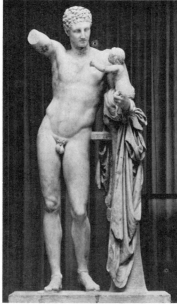

above left: 224. *Charioteer,* from Sanctuary of Apollo, Delphi.
c. 470 B.C. Bronze, height 6'11" (2.11 m). Archaeological Museum, Delphi.

above center: 225. Myron. *Discobolus* (*Discus Thrower*). Roman copy after
bronze original of c. 460 B.C. Marble, life size.
National Museum, Rome.

above right: 226. Praxiteles. *Hermes with the Infant Dionysus.*
c. 340 B.C. Marble, height 7'1" (2.16 m). Archaeological Museum, Olympia.

stone eyes (Fig. 224). Probably the statue was commissioned to celebrate the victory of a city in religious games. Whether it was a portrait or an expression of a healthy mind and healthy body is not known, but we see the beginnings of the idealization and refined proportions that characterize art of the Classical period.

Myron's bronze *Discus Thrower* (Fig. 225), cast about 460 B.C., now existing only in a Roman copy in marble, shows how far sculptors had moved from the stiff pose of the kouros. Myron successfully solved the sculptural problem of rendering movement in space by showing the athlete critically poised. We see him just as he bends down to swing his arm back to throw the discus with all his force. From whatever angle we regard the work, a rhythm develops that draws us into the sculpture and encourages us to examine it from all sides. Our eyes move from the discus to the arm, up to the head, down to the knee, and back to the heavy discus to begin the cycle again.

Hermes and the Infant Dionysus by Praxiteles is a work of the late Classical period, which prefigures Hellenistic trends. When we say that someone has the body of a Greek god, we are probably thinking of such a sculpture as *Hermes* (Fig. 226), noted for the soft, sensuous appearance of the skin and the graceful pose, which contrasts so sharply with the stiff kouros of two hundred years earlier. Hermes, messenger of the gods, stands relaxed, his weight flowing from his torso to the reversed **(contropposto)**

direction of his hips in a gentle S-curve. On one arm he holds the infant god of wine, and his missing arm probably held a bunch of grapes toward which the baby is reaching.

Painting of the Classical Period Unfortunately, the great wall paintings that adorned the temples and civic buildings of the Classical period have disappeared. We know of them only through literature. But the creativity of Greek painters has been preserved for us in the refined and expressive decorations on pottery.

Greek pottery, famous throughout the ancient world because of its varied shapes and skillful paintings, was a major export item, contributing importantly to the Greek economy. Modern divers have found pieces of Greek pottery on sunken ships as far from Greece as southern France.

Potters and vase painters were highly regarded and often signed their works. Designing specific shapes for specific functions (Fig. 130), painters imaginatively decorated pottery with myths of gods and heroes and activities of daily life. Just as sculpture evolved from the simple forms of the Archaic period to the graceful complexities of the Classical period, so vase painting developed in stages. Early pottery decoration was geometric (Fig. 29). In the Archaic period vases had lively black figures painted on red clay with details scratched through the black. In an amphora by the painter Exekias (late 6th century B.C.) we see the heroes

Ajax and Achilles sitting on stools intently bent over a game (Fig. 227). The design shows a strong sense of order, and the delicately incised lines of the hair and elaborate cloaks testify to the artist's skill. Vases in the Classical period were in a freer, more sophisticated style in which red figures stand out from a black ground and details are applied with a brush.

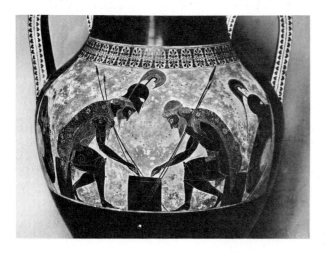

Sculpture of the Hellenistic Period In the late 4th century, Alexander the Great, a Macedonian king, forged an empire that included Greece and the lands of the eastern Mediterranean. As a result of Alexander's enthusiasm for Greek civilization and the military, Greek influence dominated this region, and continued even after his death in 323 B.C. Then, his empire was broken into small states ruled by his generals, who competed with one another in commissioning extravagant art. The art of this period, which lasted until the Roman conquest, is called Hellenistic because Greece, which inspired it, was known as the land of the Hellenes.

Sculptors of the Hellenistic period became more interested in portraying detailed specific individuals than in creating serene idealized figures. The marble group of *Laocoön* and his sons in the agony of their death is typically Hellenistic in its exaggeration of emotion (Fig. 228). According to legend, the Trojan priest Laocoön was strangled by snakes sent by the gods because he revealed to the Trojans that the wooden horse given them by the Greeks was a trick designed to defeat Troy.

Continuing the 4th-century taste for sculpture of nude women exemplified by Praxiteles was an *Aphrodite* from Melos, better known by its Italian name as the *Venus de*

above: 227. Exekias. *Ajax and Achilles Playing Draughts,* black-figure amphora. 550–525 B.C. Terracotta, height of amphora 24″ (61 cm). Vatican Museums, Rome.

right: 228. Agesander, Athenodorus, and Polydorus of Rhodes. *Laocoön Group.* c. 150 B.C. Marble, height 8′ (2.44 m). Vatican Museums, Rome.

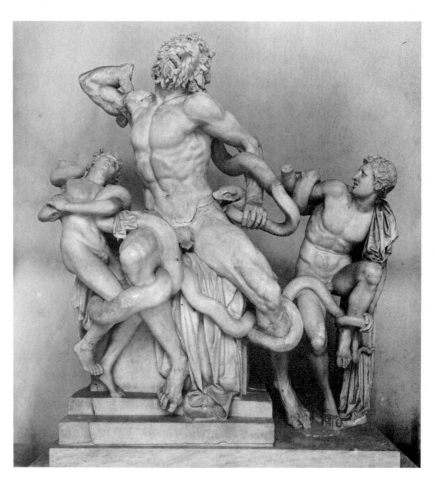

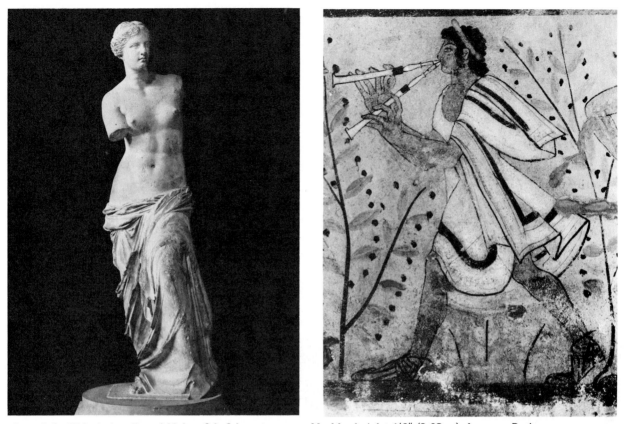

above left: 229. Aphrodite of Melos. 3d—2d century B.C. Marble, height 6′8″ (2.03 m). Louvre, Paris.

above right: 230. Aulos player, detail of fresco from the Tomb of the Leopards, Etruscan, Tarquinia, Italy. c. 470 B.C.

Milo (Fig. 229). She has captured the imagination of the public ever since she was discovered in 1820. Some scholars say she was holding a shield in which she was gazing at her reflection. Her **wet drapery,** marble carved to resemble wet cloth, reveals as much as it conceals.

Rome

Originally an Italian city-state on the Tiber River, Rome eventually ruled the greatest empire of the ancient world. The expanding Roman culture first overwhelmed the Etruscans, who had developed a civilization in west central Italy north of the Tiber, in the 3rd century B.C. Rome next absorbed the Greek colonies that had been founded in southern Italy and Sicily in the 8th century B.C., and in 146 B.C. defeated the Greeks at Corinth in their own homeland.

Like the Greeks before them and the rest of us since, the Romans borrowed ideas from earlier peoples to incorporate into their civilization. One source of ideas was the Etruscans, who had earlier absorbed elements of Greek, Mesopotamian, and perhaps ancient Italic culture. Many Roman concepts of religion and government began with the Etruscans. The Romans employed Etruscan artists and probably learned from them how to build arches, cast in bronze, and carve in stone. Roman art was also influenced

by the vigorous clay portrait figures the Etruscans placed on the lids of their coffins and the lively frescoes of banquets and festivals which they painted on the walls of their tombs (Fig. 230). Etruscan figures are generally heavier than those of the Egyptians (Fig. 58), Cretans (Fig. 77), and Greeks who preceded them.

The strongest influence on the Romans was surely Greek civilization, first encountered in southern Italy and then later as Romans studied with Greek teachers. They also commissioned Greek artists to work for them in Italy and collected Greek works. The Roman town of Pompeii was filled with art objects in the Hellenistic style. Indeed, the art of Italy in the 3rd and 2nd centuries B.C. is called Greco-Roman.

The Romans, however, added their own genius in military affairs, government, and engineering to the arts of the Etruscans and Greeks. Roman law and Roman building spread over a wider area than that achieved by any prior civilization. Under the *Pax Romanum,* or Roman Peace, the Roman army maintained law and order and assured conquered peoples of security from other invaders. Roman governors wisely allowed subject peoples to continue to worship local gods as long as they recognized the supremacy of Roman gods. Roman builders, refining the arch and the vault, provided every city under Roman jurisdiction with roads, bridges, aqueducts, temples, basilicas, forums, and baths—amenities that helped unite the empire. Temples in North Africa; the Pont du Gard, which brought water to Nîmes, France (Fig. 170); and Roman ruins in northern Britain remain as examples of their imperial expansion.

Architecture The Romans had a taste for large-scale building and lavish decoration. The Roman Colosseum, of concrete faced with stone (Fig. 231), was the largest structure for public assemblies built up to that time. It seated 50,000 spectators, who were protected by canvas awnings from the sun and rain as they watched the bloody battles between men and wild beasts. Like many other Roman buildings, the Colosseum combined columns of all three Greek orders.

Another large, richly decorated building is the Pantheon, the only temple of classical antiquity that has always remained a house of worship (Fig. 175). Originally designed to hold statues of the major Roman gods under one roof, it is now a Christian church. The building, of brick and concrete, was once faced with marble. In its huge dome, the largest of antiquity, with a diameter of nearly 140 feet (42.67 meters), we see the Romans' great skill in engineering. The walls of the building are 20 feet (6.9 meters) thick in some places to support the heavy weight of the dome, which had an open central *oculus,* or eye, to admit light. As the sun moved across the sky, it spotlighted in turn every niche holding a statue of a god.

Also large and ornate were the public baths, which included spacious halls and gardens as well as cold and hot rooms, dressing rooms, gymnasiums, open-air swimming pools, and libraries. The baths were heated by furnaces. Lead pipes, which carried the hot water, can still be seen in the ruins. The vast, cross-vaulted Baths of Caracalla in Rome, resplendent in marble, murals, and carving, are an outstanding example.

231. The Colosseum, Rome. A.D. 72–80.

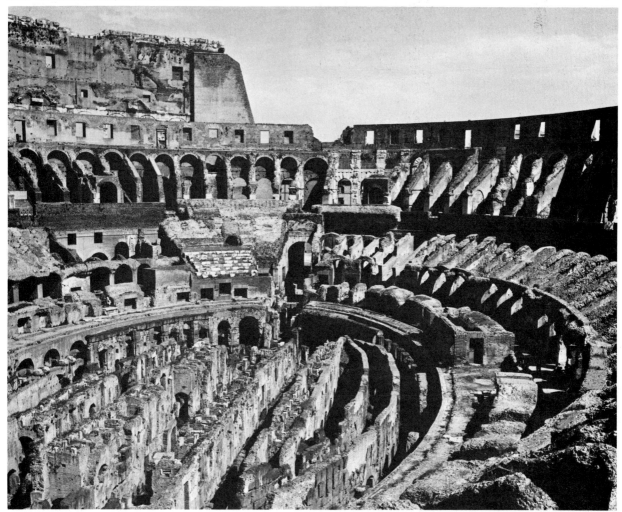

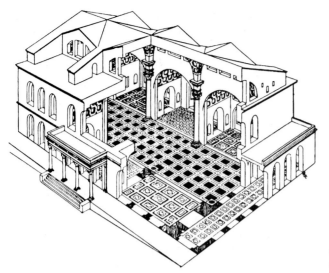

left: 232. Reconstruction drawing of the Basilica of Constantine (after Huelsen), Rome. C. A.D. 310–320.

below: 233. Arch of Constantine, Rome. A.D. 312. Height 67′7″ (20.6 m), width 82′ (25 m).

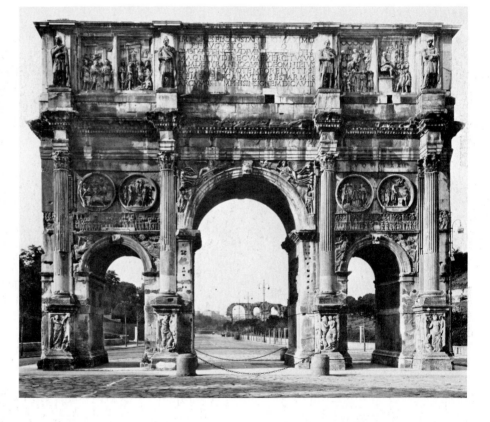

Adopting the **basilicas** of the Hellenistic Greeks, the Romans built long, colonnaded halls throughout the empire as law courts and places of assembly. Most of them had a high central nave flanked by lower aisles. They were entered from the long sides. At one or both ends was a raised semicircular area, or **apse,** where the judges sat behind an altar for the sacrifices that preceded judicial deliberations. Although many had wooden gabled roofs, the Basilica of Constantine (Fig. 232) was vaulted. Even larger than the Pantheon, it rose 114 feet (34.74 meters) and glowed inside with rich marble facing. The basilican plan was used for Christian churches, as we shall see in Chapter 13.

Typically Roman was the ornate triumphal arch, built by successful generals to celebrate their victories, and constructed in areas conquered by Rome to symbolize Roman glory. The triple Arch of Constantine (Fig. 233) was an important gateway to Rome when the city was still walled for protection. Much later, Roman arches were copied in Paris, London, Berlin, and even in Washington Square in New York.

Roman emperors, senators, and other rich citizens lived in luxurious palaces and country villas with elaborate fountains and gardens. Well-to-do city dwellers had pleasant town houses built with post-and-lintel construction around a formal court with a pool for rainwater. Many included a colonnaded rear court with a fountain and garden. The House of the Vettii in Pompeii, buried in the volcanic lava and ash that erupted from Mt. Vesuvius and now restored, shows how elegant such homes could be (Fig. 234). Urban citizens often climbed several stories to their rooms in a large apartment house, as noted in Chapter 9.

Murals Larger villas and houses were decorated with colorful wall paintings, many of which still can be seen in Pompeii. These murals give us some idea of what ancient Greek painting must have been like, for most of them were done by Greek artists. Landscapes, intimate scenes, ceremonies such as weddings, mythological figures, and still life were favored subjects, sometimes set in panels of flat color. Painted with lively brush strokes and often a sense of architectural perspective, **illusionistic** murals gave the effect of a view beyond a window.

Mosaics, made of small pieces of marble set in mortar, were also popular for wall and floor decoration, depicting battle and hunting scenes alive with exotic animals and birds from as far away as Egypt. One example shows the Nile with crocodiles, lotus buds, and a hippopotamus.

Sculpted and Painted Portraits Perhaps the most typical Roman contribution to art was portraiture. In contrast to the Greek idealization of the face, Roman portraits were

234. House of the Vettii, Pompeii. A.D. 63–79.

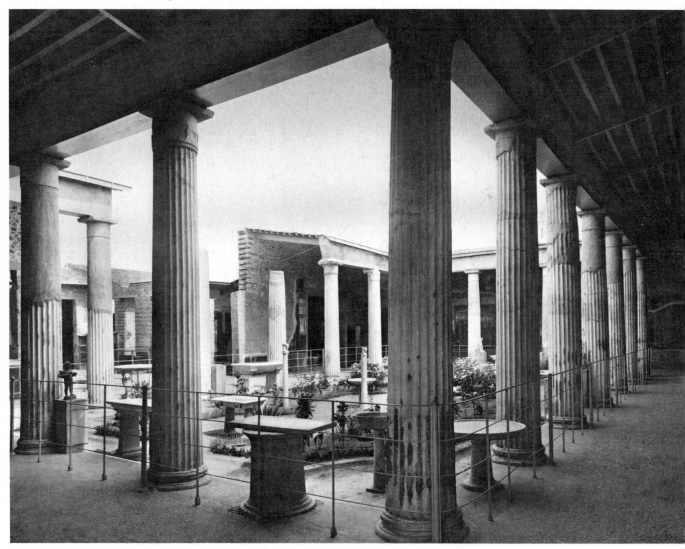

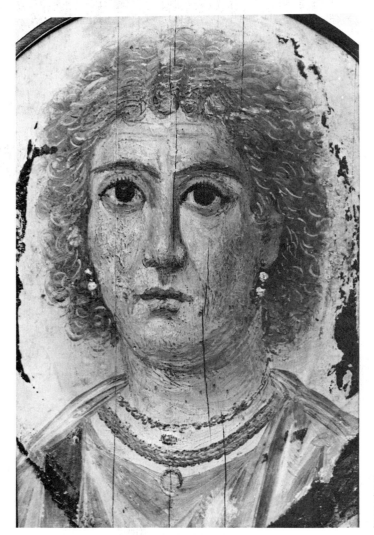

235. Mummy portrait of an elderly woman, from the Faiyum, Egypt. 1st–2d century A.D. Encaustic on panel, 14⅞ × 9″ (38 × 23 cm). Ägyptische Staatssammlung, Munich.

veristic, duplicating real people with warts, wrinkles, and other disfigurements. Realistic marble busts of stern-looking Roman generals and rulers were placed in local forums to represent Roman authority to the conquered peoples. These, along with faces depicted on Roman coins, spread the imperial image throughout the Roman world. Perhaps this ancient form of mass media contributed to the success of Roman government.

The same Roman taste for realistic portraiture appeared in a group of funerary paintings of Romans who had settled in the Faiyum district in Egypt. When they died, their bodies were wrapped in linen and a portrait of the deceased was inserted over the face, according to Egyptian custom (Fig. 235). Painted on wood panels in **encaustic,** an exceptionally durable mixture of pigments and hot wax, these informal individualized portraits are so full of life that they seem to have been painted while the subjects were still alive. Such vitality in portraiture was not to be seen again for a thousand years.

EXERCISES AND ACTIVITIES

1. Discuss the Greek architectural principles of unity and proportion that are demonstrated in the design and decoration of the Parthenon.
2. List and define the different parts of a Greek order. How do the three orders differ?
3. Explain the concept of ideal beauty in relation to Greek art, naming specific works. In what way is that ideal expressed in the sculpture and architecture of the Golden Age of Greece? How did the sculpture of the Hellenistic period differ from that of the Golden Age?
4. What features did Greek and Roman art have in common? What elements from other civilizations did the Romans incorporate into their art? What are some of the Roman engineering innovations?
5. Explain the origins of the arch, its construction, and how it was used in Rome.
6. Create in clay, cast stone, or soap a sculptural work of art inspired by Greek or Roman art.
7. Contrast Greek and Roman sculptural styles.

13 Faith: The Middle Ages

Between the city in which it is promised that we shall reign and the earthly city there is a wide gulf—as wide as the distance between heaven and earth. Yet . . . there is a faint shadowy resemblance between the Roman Empire and the heavenly city.

ST. AUGUSTINE, *City of God*

As the light of "Eternal Rome" flickered low in the 4th century A.D., in its place throughout the Mediterrean world altar lights glowed softly as the new Christian faith attracted converts. The power of Rome was fading, but images of classical times lingered on through Early Christian religious art, and were later perpetuated in Carolingian, Romanesque, and Gothic art during the period we call the Middle Ages.

Early Christian Art

For the first three centuries after the birth of Christ the Early Christians worshiped in private homes, or during times of persecution, in the **catacombs,** underground tunnels that honeycombed the soft volcanic rock, used by both Christians and pagans as cemeteries.

Christian fortunes changed markedly in the 4th century. The Roman emperor Constantine, who became a Christian in A.D. 303, in 313 recognized Christianity as one of the official religions of the empire. In 330, to strengthen the empire threatened by barbarians from the north and east, he moved the capital from Rome to Constantinople (Byzantium, or modern Istanbul) in the East. Christians, as inhabitants of the far-flung Roman empire, were already diverse in origin, language, and point of view. Some were Romans, living in the West. Some were Gauls and Goths in the North. Some were Jewish converts, Syrians, and other Eastern peoples. The shift of the capital, which resulted in a division of the empire into a Latin-speaking West and Greek-speaking East, intensified their differences. Early Christian art reflects this history.

Symbolism in Sculpture and Murals The linguistic diversity of the Early Christians encouraged them to express their common faith through visual symbols whose meaning was clear to all Christians. Symbols also had the advantage of hiding a religious message so that Romans would be less likely to persecute believers. For example, the Romans might not recognize the cross as a symbol of the crucifixion of Christ if it were combined with the Greek letters *chi* and *rho,* the first two letters of the word *Christ.* They would not know that the fish stood for Christ and the sacrament of baptism.

Early Christian art also developed symbols using classical images with new religious meaning. No pagan could object to paintings or sculpture of the Good Shepherd, for this was a popular subject in classical art; but in Christian art the shepherd surrounded by his flock symbolized Christ with his disciples or other devout followers. Posed like earlier Greek figures, Christ is beardless and wears a Roman tunic. In a fresco of *The Good Shepherd* from one of the catacombs, Christ is seen as a clean-shaven Roman youth (Fig. 236). The circle that surrounds the figure signifies eternity. Christ as a Good Shepherd also appears in sculpture (Fig. 237) and mosaic (Fig. 238).

Just as pagan festivals were reconstituted as Christian holy days, so Early Christian frescoes painted on the walls and ceilings of the catacombs used images of grapes, animals, birds, and fish, borrowed from classical art, to convey new Christian significance. For example, grapes, a pagan symbol of the cult of Bacchus, the Roman god of wine, now presented wine as the sacramental blood of Christ. The peacock, originally meaning wisdom, became a symbol of eternal life because its flesh was believed to be incorruptible.

Frescoes and mosaics on the walls and ceilings of tombs and, later, of churches were created to tell the story of Christ's life, death, and resurrection, serving as a pictorial narrative for the illiterate. Artists became progressively less concerned with realistic representations of human forms and more concerned with expressions of religious truths. As a result, images became simplified and spiritualized. Christ appeared as a middle-aged man and acquired long

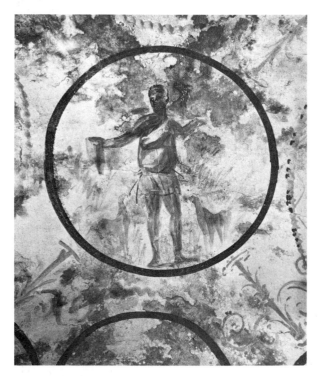

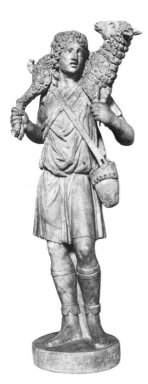

above left: 236. *The Good Shepherd.* Early 3d century A.D. Fresco. Catacomb of Domitilla, Rome.

above right: 237. *The Good Shepherd.* c. 350. Marble, height 39" (99 cm.) Vatican Museums, Rome.

below: 238. *The Good Shepherd,* from the Mausoleum of Galla Placidia, Ravenna. 5th century. Mosaic.

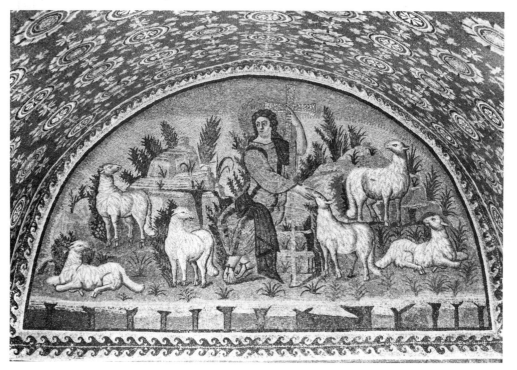

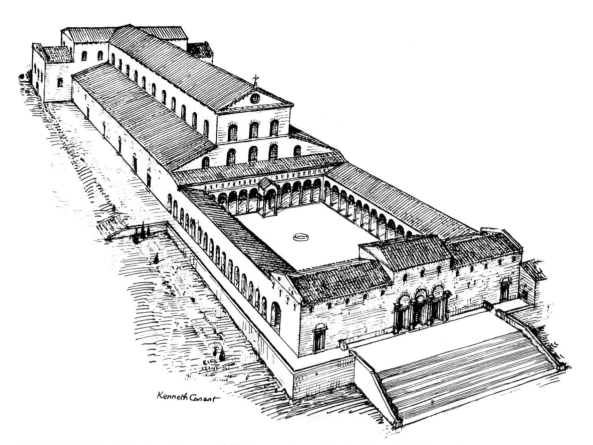

239. Old St. Peter's Basilica, Rome. c. 333. Restoration study by Kenneth J. Conant.

Middle Eastern robe and beard and a **halo,** a gold circle around his head signifying his holiness.

So he has been depicted ever since. This abstract style and the use of the halo were especially effective in mosaic, a process involving small pieces of glass set into cement and carefully placed to reflect the light that filtered through the small windows and the altar candles. The walls seemed to lose their solidity in an almost supernatural glow, well suited to express the spiritual messages of early Christianity. The shimmering gold and colored-glass pictures suggested heaven, and as the congregation entered the mysteriously lit interior of early houses of worship, they must have felt as if they were already transported there.

Architecture As Christians increased in numbers, the catacombs were abandoned and new places for worship had to be provided. These could not be modeled on pagan temples, for the ritual of the Christian Church differed fundamentally from that of ancient religions. The cella of a pagan temple was reserved for the gods and their priests. The faithful, who processed around the outside of the temple, could only glimpse the sanctuary through the doors. The sacrificial altar was placed outside where they could see it, and the exterior of the building was decorated with sculpture. In contrast, Christian ceremonies took place indoors and the congregation took part. Space was needed to allow people to participate in the mass and later to move toward the altar to receive communion.

Since Roman basilicas (Fig. 232) were large secular buildings not associated with pagan religion, they were used and copied for the new places of Christian worship. The apse, placed at the eastern end, was retained for the altar and clergy, and the main entrance was moved to the west end. This arrangement gave a powerful linear orientation, focusing attention on the altar. Sometimes the builders used columns taken from older pagan structures.

The restoration study of Old St. Peter's Basilica in Rome, an important Early Christian basilica, shows us how the needs of Christian worship were met (Fig. 239). The faithful first entered through a gateway into a walled courtyard with a pool used for baptism before entering the church, an oblong hall divided by columns into a high nave and four side aisles. The low aisles increased the floor space while allowing light to come through windows of the **clerestory,** the upper part of the walls of the nave, which could be seen from the exterior. At the east end was a **crossing** (transept), or horizontal space, that intersected the nave and beyond it the apse with an altar.

Christ had preached that riches on earth were less important than salvation. The churches symbolized this belief with plain exteriors and interiors lavishly decorated with mosaics or paintings representing the spiritual riches of the kingdom of heaven (Pl. 12, p. 201). Such interiors were suitable settings for ornate and gemstudded altar furnishings—chalices, screens, candle holders, and **reliquaries,** containers that held the relics of martyrs. Many Early Christian churches were constructed over crypts or relics of martyrs because such areas were believed by the faithful to be sacred.

Byzantine Art

Parallel with Early Christian art was Byzantine art, which developed far to the east in Constantinople in the 6th century. There the emperor Justinian launched a building program to enhance the Eastern part of the empire as the Western part declined. Architects in the East had been using domes, symbols of heaven, to roof square or cross-shaped churches for many years. In 532 Justinian commissioned the church of Hagia Sophia, or Holy Wisdom, which had a great central dome that seemed to float over the interior space (Fig. 176). The Byzantine historian Procopius, who saw it being built, said it hung "as if suspended by a golden chain from heaven." The weight of the dome, carried by four piers at the corners of the square space below it, rested on pendentives (Fig. 173), a brilliant structural innovation. The ribbon of small arched windows around the base of the dome let in a stream of light that must have been dazzling as it played over the original gold and colored mosaics.

Domes and mosaic decoration were characteristic of Byzantine architecture, as may be seen in San Vitale, a church built by Justinian in Ravenna, Italy (Pl. 12, p. 201). Octagonal in shape with a central dome, its interior was covered with marble and rich mosaics that echo the imagery of the catacomb paintings while heralding the new Byzantine style. The tall, thin, large-eyed figures, high above the heads of the congregation, added to the sense of awe and mystery that would have been felt by the worshipers. The Byzantine love of rich decoration may also be seen in the cross of Justinian, a jeweled reliquary believed to contain a fragment of the true cross, on which Christ suffered and died (Fig. 240).

Art of Northern Europe

In contrast to the sophisticated art of the Byzantine Empire, art in northern Europe during the Dark Ages of the 6th and 7th centuries was an eclectic mixture of Christian and classical elements and pagan influences from central Asia. Celtic peoples occupied central and northwestern Europe. Teutonic peoples from the east had been sweeping across the vast network of Roman roads into Europe ever since the later years of the empire. The highly civilized Romans called both groups barbarians, but the northerners' art,

though simpler than that of southern Europe, was far from unskilled.

Teutonic craftsmen worked in iron, gold, enamel, and wood, which they ornamented with stylized animals both real and mythological. The **animal style,** as it is called, originated in Asia, where it had developed among the nomads of the steppes. In northern Europe, the style was combined with elaborate patterns of interlaced elements borrowed from Christian art in Italy, Egypt, and the Byzantine Empire. The dragons on the front of this Ostrogothic iron helmet protected the wearer's eyes with magic powers, while another dragon on the top reaches down toward the nose, thereby protecting the skull (Fig. 241). The decoration was planned to guard against demons, which seemed very real to the wearer, but the helmet was clearly designed to ward off deadly sword blows as well.

Celtic craftsmen also worked in metal and enamel and carved monumental stone crosses. They mixed animal forms, geometrics, spirals, and interlacing into a richly ornamental **Hiberno-Saxon style** that reached its height in the manuscripts of the Gospels and other books, which Celtic monks laboriously copied by hand in monasteries. These manuscripts, such as the Lindisfarne Gospels (Fig. 68) and the Book of Kells, were, in a practice called *horror vacui,* or "fear of emptiness," lavishly decorated over every

240. Cross of Justinian. A.D. 527–65. Vatican Museums, Rome.

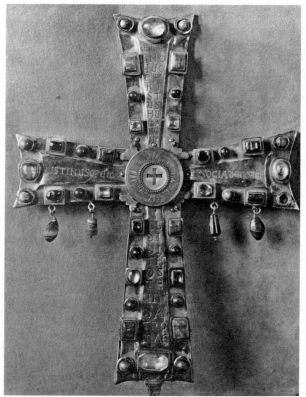

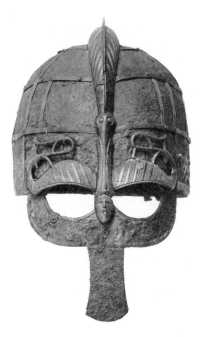

bit of space with swirling designs of plants, animals, birds, and humans that seem to merge into and out of one another. A beast may dissolve into a snake, which turns into a fish, the whole sequence perhaps forming the letter *T*.

Carolingian Art

In the late 8th century, Charlemagne, a vigorous and wise king of the Franks, tried to revive the Roman Empire in the West and to restore Roman civilization. Choosing Aachen, probably his native city, now in West Germany, as his capital, he transformed it into a cultural as well as a governmental center. There he encouraged a blend of Christian and classical scholarship, Byzantine traditions in art and architecture, and Celtic and Teutonic skills in metalwork, which fused into the **Carolingian style.** As a reward for helping the popes in Rome against their enemies, he was crowned emperor in Rome in 800.

As part of his building program, Charlemagne constructed a two-storied Palace Chapel at Aachen (Fig. 242), where he worshiped and was buried. Its massive stone walls were inspired by Roman architecture as well as

above: 241. Ostrogothic helmet. 7th century. Iron. Central Museum of National Antiquities, Stockholm.

right: 242. Interior of the chapel of Charlemagne, Aachen. c. 795.

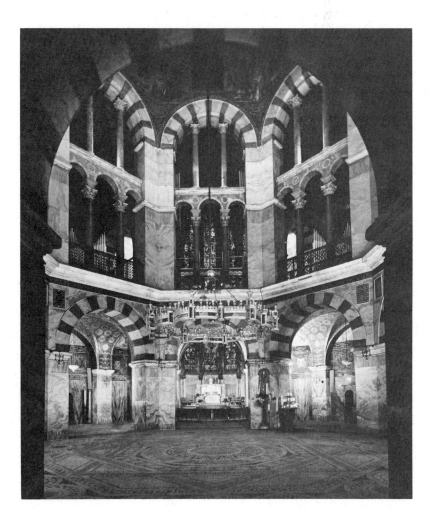

northern severity, but its octagonal central space, surrounded by an **ambulatory** (passageway) and covered by a dome, was inspired by San Vitale in Ravenna (Pl. 12, p. 201) and other Byzantine buildings. Roman influence also appeared in the barrel vaulting, the three levels of round arches enclosing the central space, and the marble Corinthian columns that divided the arches of the upper levels into three sections. The columns themselves had come from Ravenna.

The richly decorated surfaces echoed Byzantine influence, and the contrasting colors of the stones in the uppermost arches were typical of Islamic art in Spain (see Chapter 15). The emperor's throne was in the second storey gallery, where Charlemagne appeared to the congregation below as a representative of Christ on earth. From that position he was close to the Lord, pictured in a mosaic in the dome above. In its energetic combination of these different elements, the Palace Chapel embodied the Carolingian style. This and other churches sponsored by Charlemagne were an important influence on later architecture.

Charlemagne also encouraged the building of monasteries. Including a church, living quarters for the monks, workshops, guesthouse, hospital, and surrounding farms, monasteries were large, self-sufficent communities. Originally founded as quiet retreats in a turbulent world, they became bustling centers of learning and the arts. In **scriptoria,** or writing rooms, in monasteries or the palace school, copies of Christian and classical manuscripts, which might otherwise have been lost, were made. These manuscripts were illustrated with miniature paintings influenced by Byzantine art and richly ornamented with covers of gold, gems, and carved ivory.

Romanesque Art

During the Romanesque period, about 1050 to 1200, after pagan Viking invaders had settled and been converted and after Christians recovered Spain from the Muslims, art and architecture flourished. A new Romanesque style emerged, so called because it was inspired by Charlemagne's revival of Roman styles. Romanesque architecture blossomed quite suddenly when a medieval prophecy foretelling the end of the world in 1000 failed to come true. Many Christians emerged from caves where they had hidden and, as one medieval historian put it, showed their gratitude by covering Europe with a "white mantle of churches."

These churches varied in local detail according to whether they were built in Italy, Spain, Germany, or France, but they all shared a similar floor plan—the central nave and side aisles that originated in the Roman basilica and were adapted by Early Christian churches. Builders used Roman techniques of masonry and adopted the Roman vocabulary of arches and barrel vaults. These stone vaults spanned large areas and lessened the danger of fire, which destroyed so many wooden roofs, but they required heavy walls to support them. As a result, Romanesque churches were often dark because windows were few and

small to avoid weakening the walls. S. Ambrogio, Milan, is an early example.

Sometimes walls and vaults were brightened by murals, and columns were also often painted. Many columns had elaborately carved capitals, which depicted Bible stories or portrayed the constant battle between Christians and evil demons representing the seven deadly sins. In the **tympanum** (semicircular space) over the entrance doorways, sculpture often depicted the Last Judgment, as in the church in Vézélay, France. A large figure of Christ dominated the smaller figures of virtuous Christians rising to heaven and sinners falling to tortures in hell (Fig. 243). Eventually the entire church became a sermon in stone.

Gothic Art

As Europe's population grew, many people moved from sparsely populated rural areas dominated by local barons and monasteries into towns. Town dwellers, or **burghers,** usually organized into guilds, took part in lively commercial exchange of goods and ideas. Travel became easier, and Crusaders, who went to rescue the Holy Land from the Muslims, brought back new ideas from the Middle East. Universities in cities such as Paris, Bologna, and Padua attracted students from all over Europe. Teaching was in Latin, the universal language of educated men and women in the West. Pilgrims moved freely from town to town on their way to visit shrines, while burghers competed for their business. At the same time, ambitious bishops planned impressive cathedrals whose vaults rose to awesome heights.

These new Gothic cathedrals expressed not only local ambition but also the pious desire of Christians to strive toward the kingdom of heaven. They were soaring, towered structures whose interiors were filled with an unearthly light filtered through stained-glass windows.

The requirements of this style led builders to experiment with higher vaults and other ways than walls to carry their weight. Groin vaults were strengthened with ribs, which transferred the weight of the vaults to piers at the corners of the bays and thence to the ground, as we saw in Chapter 9 (Figs. 171b, 172, 171c). Buttresses against the outside walls, positioned where the ribs met the piers of the wall, provided a counter-thrust against the pressures of the vaults, while pointed arches made it possible to roof spaces that were not squares.

These elements—pointed arch, ribbed vault, and buttress—used independently in Romanesque churches, were combined for the first time in the rebuilt abbey church of St.-Denis outside Paris in the mid-12th century by the dedicated Abbot Suger. At the head of the nave Suger added a new **choir** ringing the apse, surrounded by columns with an ambulatory from which radiated seven wedge-shaped chapels. Although St.-Denis was rebuilt after more than one fire, Suger's design of ribbed vaults, pointed arches, thin interior columns, and exterior buttresses was adopted throughout the church (Fig. 40). The nonsupporting walls

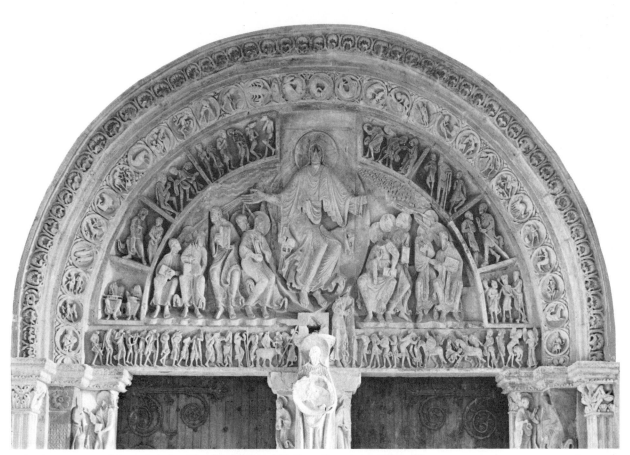

243. Tympanum, abbey church of La Madeleine, Vézélay, France. c. 1120–32.

between the buttresses of the choir were filled with glass, and were described by Suger as a "string of chapels, by virtue of which the whole [church] would shine with the wonderful and uninterrupted light of the most luminous windows, pervading the interior beauty."

And so the Gothic style was born. It spread throughout Europe during the next two hundred years and in time became more ornate. The late Gothic style is called **Flamboyant** because the stone **tracery** separating sections of windows was elaborated into curved, flamelike patterns that masked the basic structure. Because cathedrals often took a hundred or more years to build, their plans frequently changed. One section, for example, might be in the early Gothic style and another in the Flamboyant style.

Despite local variations in design and detail and stylistic changes over time, all Gothic churches used the same self-supporting system of ribs and buttresses to frame large stained-glass windows. The windows were made of small pieces of glass colored in the molten state, given details with a paint brush, fitted together with lead strips, and placed in an iron frame. Like Romanesque murals, they told biblical and other Christian stories. Particularly fine

windows were made for the cathedral of Chartres (Pl. 13, p. 202).

The exterior of churches was decorated with deeply carved sculpture. The great portals through which the congregation entered were flanked by statues of biblical figures and saints. The tympanum, no longer dominated by Romanesque preoccupation with the Last Judgment, heaven, and hell, showed a broader range of subjects, such as scenes from the life of the Virgin. Greater emphasis on the Virgin led to gentler treatment of figures in general with softer, more graceful poses and drapery.

The Gothic cathedrals were communal efforts in which all the devout participated in whatever way they could—carrying stones, cutting them into shape, hauling them up to the masons working on the high scaffolds, or contributing money. Skilled craftsmen who could carve the stone sculpture and wooden choir stalls and fashion gold and enamel reliquaries were in great demand. Their combined efforts produced magnificent structures towering over the houses and shops huddled at their feet.

Inside, the vaults soared into a dim blue twilight representing heaven, the windows sparkled like jewels, and on

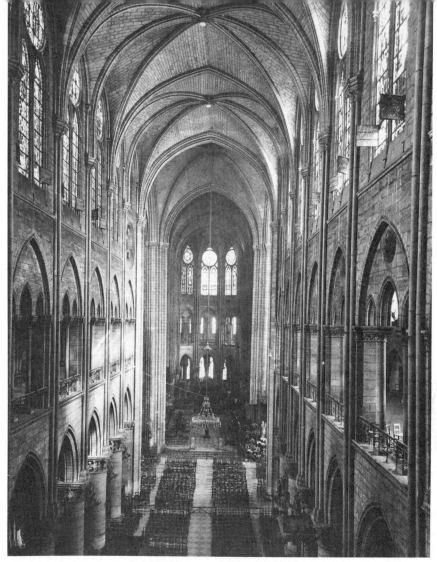

244. Interior, Cathedral of Notre-Dame, Paris. c. 1163–1250.

feast days, hundreds of candles glowed on the gold and jewels of altar screens, chalices, and candlesticks and on the gold-embroidered vestments of the priests. This vision of holiness (Fig. 244), enhanced by the singing of the liturgy, must have uplifted worshipers from the harsh realities of daily life and transported them to new realms of devotion. Yet it was at this time, when the Church dominated almost every phase of life, that the forces which led to a totally different spirit in a new era were already at work.

EXERCISES AND ACTIVITIES

1. Give the historical reasons why Early Christian art incorporated so many cultural influences. Give examples of images that derived from other cultures and were absorbed into Christian art.

2. Using colored chalks to suggest the effect of a fresco, sketch some Early Christian symbols.

3. Cut out tiny squares from magazine illustrations, searching for varied colors and textures. Paste these small pieces on cardboard to form a mosaic of geometric designs or human figures. Notice how you must simplify forms in order to represent them with mosaic squares. Study an Early Christian mosaic and see how form was developed.

4. Locate old dishes and bottles of different colors. Wrap them in many newspapers and break them into fragments with a hammer. Glue them onto a wooden surface in a satisfying mosaic design.

5. Explain how the Romanesque style of architecture originated and whether it varied throughout Europe. What earlier structural systems influenced it?

6. Draw a diagram of the Gothic structural system. Name and explain the function of the parts.

7. Using pieces of colored tissue paper, paste up a design for a stained-glass window. Use this as a guide to make a window from colored glass and leading available in craft shops.

8. Locate examples of Romanesque and Gothic Revival churches in your community. Describe how they use the elements of these styles. Sketch a floor plan of one and compare it with a plan of an actual Gothic or Romanesque church.

14 The Crossroads: Renaissance, Baroque, and Rococo

Thy will is free and whole and upright and now it would be wrong to rein it in. Be thine own Emperor and thine own Pope.

DANTE, *Divine Comedy*

History does not unfold conveniently in chapters, and the Gothic Age had not dramatically vanished when the Renaissance appeared. The Church still dominated much of medieval life, but urbanization and commerce gave rise to the self-confidence expressed in Dante's poem. Similarly, the new Renaissance humanism led to the turbulent, theatrical spirit of the Baroque Age, and the intimate Rococo period that followed.

During the late Middle Ages trade in Europe and with the East continued to increase. The merchants and bankers from prosperous cities of Italy and Flanders (modern Belgium) formed a well-to-do middle class that threatened the declining authority of the Church. The cities situated on trade routes competed as textile centers. At the same time, intellectuals began to abandon medieval scholastic philosophy. Instead they adopted a humanist view, which emphasized the abilities of the individual and the importance of life in this world. With these humanist eras, **Renaissance, Baroque,** and **Rococo** art turned from its base in religion to the modern focus of man who saw himself as an important part of the universe.

Forerunners of the Renaissance

We can see this change reflected in the work of three 14th-century artists. In Italy the Sienese painter Simone Martini (1284–1344) retained the Gothic spirit in his *Annunciation,* with its Byzantine gold background and decorative detail. But he depicted the Virgin, for the first time, as a real woman, startled by the appearance of the archangel with his fateful message (Fig. 245).

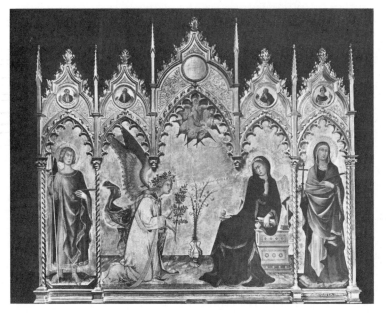

245. Simone Martini. *Annunciation* (saints in side panels by Lippo Memmi). 1333. Tempera on wood, 8′8″ × 10′ (2.64 × 3.05 m). Uffizi, Florence.

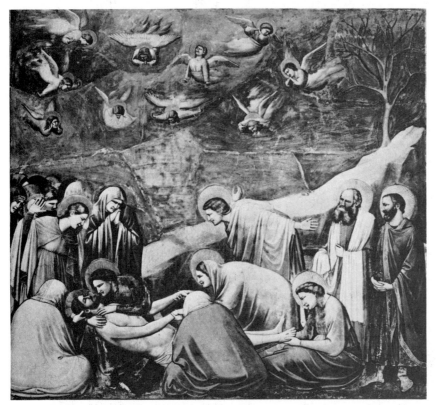

above: 246. Giotto. *Pietá* (*Lamentation*). 1305—06. Fresco, 7'7" × 7'9"
(2.31 × 2.36 m). Arena Chapel, Padua, Italy.

below right: 247. Byzantine School. *Enthroned Madonna and Child.* 13th century.
Tempera on wood, 32⅛ × 19⅜" (82 × 49 cm). National Gallery of Art,
Washington, D.C. (Andrew W. Mellon Collection).

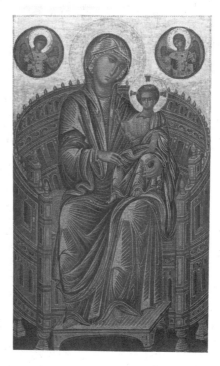

The Florentine painter Giotto (c. 1266–1337) also illustrated religious subjects, but his brush brought the warmth
of humanism into these Christian works. In his frescoes of
the *Life of Christ* in the Arena Chapel, Padua, and the *Life of
St. Francis* in the church in Assisi he expressed human
emotions in a new and striking manner. If we compare the
lifelike figures in his *Pietà* (Fig. 246) with those in an altarpiece in the Byzantine style (Fig. 247), we can see how the
drapery in Giotto's work suggests the solid shape of the
body beneath. The low horizon, the grief-stricken mourn-
ers, the frantic angels, and the severely descending slope of
the hill all direct us to the lifeless figure of Christ and the
somber Virgin.

The impact of that drama is heightened by Giotto's
daringly original approach. No wonder that, a generation
later, the poet Petrarch, accustomed to stylized Byzantine
painting, claimed that Giotto depicted nature so faithfully
that his paintings could be mistaken for reality. About the
same time, the poet Giovanni Boccaccio, familiar with classical art, hailed Giotto as the artist who has "restored to
light this art which has been buried for many centuries."
Indeed, Giotto is still regarded as the father of a new era
in art.

The third artist to foreshadow the change in art style was the Northern sculptor Claus Sluter (1380–1406), who worked at the court of the Duke of Burgundy. In his notable *Well of Moses* (Fig. 248), he portrayed the biblical prophets as real human beings expressing individual personality. Sluter's deep piety belongs to the Middle Ages, but the striking illusion of life that he created points to the Renaissance. Sluter was also the first important sculptor to abandon the tradition of placing sculpture in an architectural setting, such as above the door of a church (Fig. 243), and to produce free-standing sculptures of monumental size. His innovations influenced later sculptors.

Renaissance in Italy

The term "Renaissance" means rebirth. It refers to the renewed interest in classical learning, philosophy, and art that developed in Italy in the 14th and 15th centuries and later spread throughout Europe.

During the Gothic period, France had been the spiritual and intellectual center of Europe. Italy, where classical tradi-

248. Claus Sluter. *Well of Moses*. 1395–1406. Marble, height of figures approximately 6′ (1.83 m). Chartreuse de Champmol, Dijon, France.

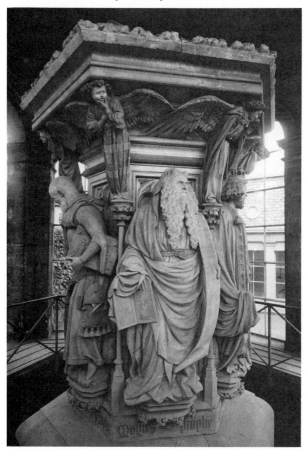

tions and monuments still remained, generally resisted the extremes of Northern religion and Gothic architecture. The humanistic spirit of the Greeks and Romans never quite faded, and Italian Gothic architecture never lost some sense of classical proportion and balance. In the 14th century enthusiastic Italian humanist scholars, joined by artists and princes, "rediscovered" ancient Rome by locating classical manuscripts and digging in ruins to find precious lost statues. These Italians were acutely aware that Rome had once been the center of power in the Western world. The Middle Ages seemed like a barbaric interlude to those who longed for "the glory that was Rome."

Early Renaissance   Italian Renaissance art first flowered in Florence, a mercantile and banking city. Rich families built fine palaces and churches and commissioned paintings and sculpture to decorate them. The most prominent was the Medici family, who gained control of the city and the surrounding territory and founded a powerful dynasty of princes to rule it. The Medici were great art patrons, maintaining courts that employed poets, scholars, musicians, and artists. They commissioned Benozzo Gozzoli to enrich their family chapel with frescoes of *The Journey of the Magi* (Fig. 134), in which their own portraits appear.

No longer was art the expression of unknown artists dedicated to the Church. Private patronage combined with the individual artist's own sense of accomplishment to open a new era. From the time of Giotto on, we will be able to trace the history of individual artists.

ARCHITECTURE   Italian Renaissance architecture, related to a human scale like Greek and Roman structures before it, was more concerned with the aesthetic questions of proportion, balance, and unity than with developing innovative construction methods.

The young Florentine architect and sculptor Filippo Brunelleschi (1377–1446) and the sculptor Donatello (1386–1466), fascinated by ancient art, traveled to Rome to find buried temples and ancient sculpture or columns. On his return to Florence, Brunelleschi was chosen from many applicants to complete the city's Gothic cathedral. Inspired by the Pantheon of Rome (Fig. 175), he awed Florence with the design and completion of a giant dome over an area so large that no one in the hundred years of the church's construction had dared to undertake the assignment. In the dome and other designs, he incorporated classical columns, pilasters, and arches to achieve balance and symmetry. Also a theorist, Brunelleschi tried to explain the world in a scientific manner, sought laws of mathematical proportion, and discovered the laws of linear perspective (see Chapter 2). His work helped bring about the change from Gothic to Renaissance style in both architecture and painting.

After the death of Brunelleschi, Leone Battista Alberti (1404–1472), well educated in classical literature, philosophy, and law, became the foremost architect of Florence. The first man of his time to study Roman buildings in

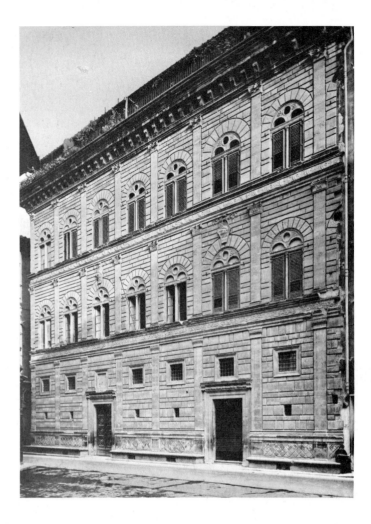

right: 249. Leon Battista Alberti.
Palazzo Rucellai, Florence. 1446–51.

below: 250. Lorenzo Ghiberti.
The Annunciation, detail of the north
doors of the Baptistry, Florence.
c. 1435. Gilt bronze, 31¼″ (79 cm).

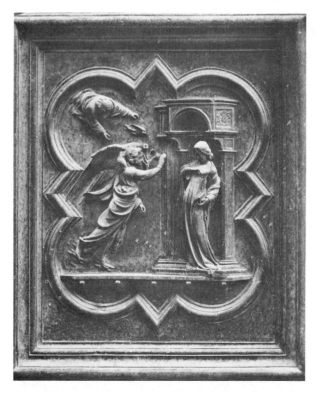

depth, he wrote the famous *De re aedificatoria,* in which he discussed the rules of proportion envisioned by Brunelleschi. This treatise on architecture was one of the most influential works of the Renaissance. Inspired by the Colosseum in Rome, Alberti designed a façade for the Palazzo Rucellai (Fig. 249), which consisted of three horizontal bands decorated with pilasters freely adapted from the Greek orders (Fig. 219). This was perhaps the first time an architect had applied an ornamental classical system to the outside of a nonclassical building.

SCULPTURE The Renaissance spirit of individualism was exemplified by a contest in 1402 to design the bronze doors on the north side of the Baptistry of Florence. Lorenzo Ghiberti (1378–1455) described his victory triumphantly: "To me was the honor conceded universally and without exception. . . . I had at that time surpassed the others." For an artist to have expressed this kind of self-congratulation would have been unthinkable when cathedrals were built by humble, unknown Christians. Ghiberti's design consisted of a series of panels depicting biblical scenes in low relief (Fig. 250). In *The Annunciation* he used aerial per-

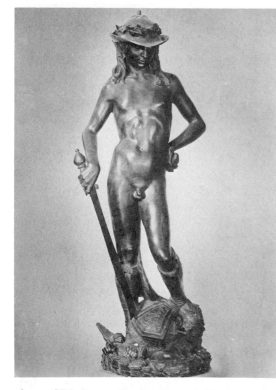

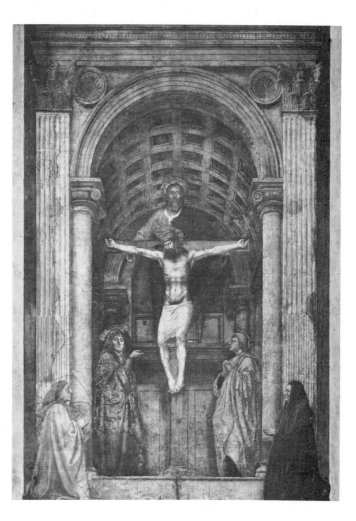

above: 251. Donatello. *David.* c. 1430–32.
Bronze, height 5′2¼″ (1.58 m).
Museo Nazionale, Florence.

right: 252. Masaccio. *The Trinity with
the Virgin, St. John, and Donors.* 1425.
Fresco, 21′10″ × 10′5″ (6.68 × 3.18 m).
Sta. Maria Novella, Florence.

spective, in which forms become fainter the farther away they are from the viewer, to give a greater sense of depth than had ever been achieved before in such a shallow space.

It was Donatello, however, who made a complete break with medieval traditions by founding a new aesthetic rationale. Following the lead of the Greeks and Romans he admired, he studied the human body carefully and sculpted from models in his studio. In this way, he created the bronze *David,* perhaps his most revolutionary achievement (Fig. 251). Donatello chose to represent David, the first life-size nude statue since antiquity, as a young Italian boy rather than as a fully developed Greek athlete. Looking at a crucifix sculpted by the more intellectual Brunelleschi, Donatello is said to have remarked, "To you is given to make Christs, . . . to me peasants." Perhaps this explains the shepherd's hat and boots worn by David.

PAINTING Departing from medieval spiritual preoccupations, painters following Giotto were fascinated with the problem of representing three-dimensional objects in flat space. Influenced by Brunelleschi's discoveries of the laws

of perspective, they applied them to painting (see Chapter 3, p. 66).

One of the first painters to employ the laws of perspective was Masaccio. He astonished his fellow-Florentines by representing space in *The Holy Trinity* (Fig. 252), a fresco in Sta. Maria Novella, as realistically as if the Crucifixion were taking place in one of Brunelleschi's chapels. Shown kneeling outside the chapel, the wealthy donors are as prominent as the religious figures and so lifelike that we feel we can almost touch them. The grandeur of scale, the solid masses, and the simple draping of garments on the figures show the influence of Roman architecture and sculpture on Masaccio. His vision was of the new Renaissance man who saw himself as an important part of the universe. The three-dimensional solidity of Masaccio's figures (Fig. 60) remind us both of Giotto and of early Renaissance sculpture. The relationship between sculpture and painting was important throughout the Renaissance.

As part of their effort to understand and portray the real world, Renaissance painters learned how to show the human body by **foreshortening,** or contracting its forms. They also studied anatomy in order to depict figures more naturally. Their paintings of saints and other religious characters show them as real men and women unlike the stylized and symbolic figures of earlier medieval painting. Frescoes by Andrea Mantegna (c. 1431–1505) for the Ovetari Chapel in Padua illustrating the life of St. James show the influences of Donatello, Masaccio, and classical sculpture. His boldly foreshortened figures, such as in *The Dead Christ* (Fig. 253), inspired many later artists.

Italian painters were interested not only in observing and portraying the world around them but also in making formal compositions of almost mathematical precision. Artists such as Piero della Francesca (1420–1492), who worked at Arezzo, found beauty in the relationship of each part to the whole, according to the Golden Section of the ancient Greeks (Fig. 65).

As Christians and classicists, Italian painters chose both religious and mythological subjects. Sandro Botticelli (1444–1510), who worked for the Medici, painted madonnas and goddesses. He was not, however, so much interested in giving an illusion of reality as in suggesting an unearthly quality. Influenced by Byzantine and Gothic painting, such as that of Simone Martini, he used elongated shapes to suggest the ethereal quality of his figures. He also expressed in his work the platonic view, originating in Greece, that everything on earth participates in an ideal form. His *The Birth of Venus* (Pl. 14, p. 202), which presents the goddess stepping from an enormous shell that has been blown to shore by wind gods amid a shower of roses, is intended to represent the entry of divine beauty into the world.

By this time, Italian painters had learned from Flemish painters how to work with oil glazes (see Chapter 3). In addition to working in fresco on plaster walls, they painted in tempera and oil on wood panels and canvas.

253. Andrea Mantegna. *The Dead Christ.*
c. 1490–1500. Oil on canvas, 27 × 32″ (69 × 81 cm).
Brera Gallery, Milan.

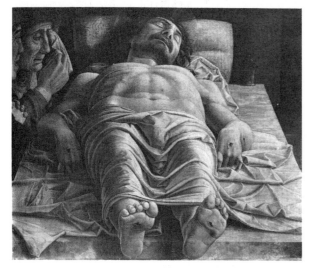

The High Renaissance Most scholars consider the High Renaissance to have lasted for about twenty years in the early 16th century, although some may include the late 15th century. It is characterized by order, balance, and symmetry.

PAINTING Leonardo da Vinci, who demonstrated vast scope as both artist and scientist, came to symbolize the Renaissance ideal of the universal man. Filling many notebooks with his findings, he investigated scientific subjects from hydraulics to war machines to botany. He became an accomplished musician and a brilliant engineer. After a career of painting at the court of Milan, he spent his last years on court assignments for Francis I of France.

Beyond his scientific interest, Leonardo was concerned with humanity. He drew a man at the heart of the universe, represented by a combined square and circle (Fig. 66), reflecting the humanist view that man is the measure of all things. His largest extant work is the life-size *The Last Supper* on the walls of the monastery of Sta. Maria delle Grazie in Milan (Fig. 52). Near ruin today as a result of his technical experiments, it was commissioned by a patron who wished to be in the company of the Lord while joining the monks at dinner. The painting reveals the individual personality of each man as Leonardo deduced it from biblical accounts, achieving the Renaissance ideal of harmony, balance, and beauty through carefully developed intellectual and technical means.

If *The Last Supper* is Leonardo's best-known religious work, the *Mona Lisa,* or *La Gioconda,* a picture of the wife of a Florentine banker, is probably the world's favorite portrait (Fig. 9). Here, Leonardo, the intellectual who claimed there was no science that could not be translated into mathematical symbols, has painted one of the world's most intriguingly poetic paintings and possibly the earliest psychological study. Some say that the soft play of light and shade that models the woman's face accounts for her cryptic smile. But since Leonardo was a master of his art and a similar smile appears in others of his portraits, it is likely that he intended to paint the mysterious expression just as it appears.

Michelangelo, twenty-three years younger than Leonardo, paved the way through the High Renaissance to the Mannerist and Baroque periods that followed. During his 89 years he created masterpieces of painting, sculpture, and architecture in Florence and Rome. Apprenticed at 13 as was the tradition, he learned essential skills from his master, the accomplished mural painter Domenico Ghirlandaio (1449–1494). By the time Michelangelo was 30, his reputation had attracted the attention of Pope Julius II, a worldly prince of the Church. Julius selected the young Florentine to carry out the ambitious plans for marble sculpture for the pope's tomb. When the work was scarcely begun, however, Julius persuaded Michelangelo to undertake an even more exacting commission.

The ceiling of the Sistine Chapel, built earlier by Pope Sixtus IV in the Vatican, was unpainted, although the walls

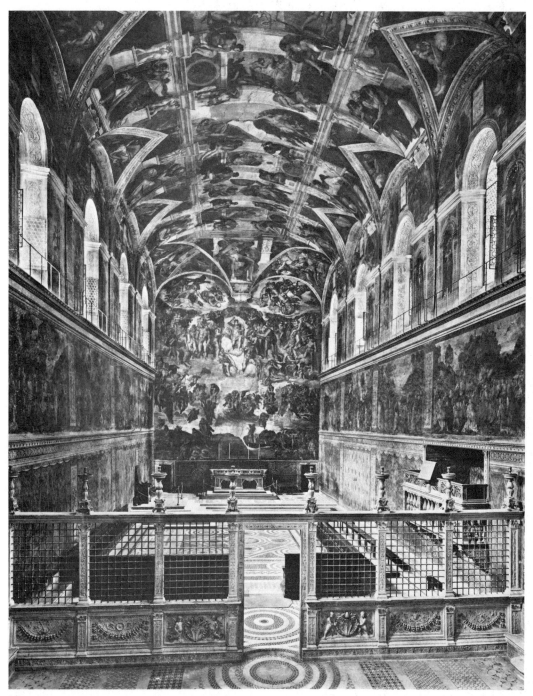

254. Sistine Chapel, view toward Michelangelo's *Last Judgment* over the altar. 1473–80. Height of ceiling 68' (20.73 m). Vatican, Rome.

held murals by earlier artists. The pope asked Michelangelo to vault the ceiling with religious frescoes. Reluctantly agreeing, Michelangelo, who until then had considered himself more sculptor than painter, refused any help and spent the next four years almost in solitude on his back on a scaffold creating hundreds of figures 60 feet (18.28 meters) above the floor (Fig. 254). In this huge work, figures of Old Testament prophets alternate with oracles of classical mythology. As a practicing sculptor, Michelangelo believed that the more painting resembled sculpture the better it was. He therefore accentuated the volume of his figures to create the effect of biblical reliefs ranging from the book of

Genesis to the Flood. We may note that in the spirit of humanism, Michelangelo placed the figures of God and Adam almost facing each other as if on equal terms. As Adam awakens from sleep and gazes directly at God the Father, we sense energy vibrate between their outstretched fingers (Fig. 1).

While Michelangelo was painting the Sistine ceiling, a young rival, Raphael, was completing a series of frescoes in the Vatican. Deeply concerned with the universality of human experience, he tried to find a balance between the religious and profane aspects of the High Renaissance. He set on opposite walls of the Stanza della Segnatura theological themes in the *Disputà* and classical subjects in *The School of Athens* (Fig. 255), creating a deep, three-dimensional space as a setting for the figures. Famous classical teachers with their pupils are grouped around symbols by which we can recognize them; Plato and Aristotle are silhouetted against the sky framed by a central arch. The

formal, one-point perspective lines lead our eyes to their figures, while the assembly of philosophers and pupils is split into two groups representing the Platonic and Aristotelian schools. In his short lifetime he became famous for these large, formal, intellectual paintings, and many consider Raphael the most typical artist of the High Renaissance.

Another great center of Italian art, second only to Florence, was Venice, a wealthy maritime power since medieval times. Classical ideals of form and proportion had never taken hold in the floating city built on canals. Instead, glowing mosaics such as those of the Byzantine cathedral of San Marco, ornate Gothic palaces, and the dazzling colors and sensuous textures of fabrics imported from the Orient dominated Venice. The city produced some fine painters, such as Giovanni Bellini (1430–1516), Giorgione (c. 1475–1510), and especially their pupil, Titian (1477–1576). A great colorist, Titian reflected the secular spirit of the Ren-

255. Raphael. *The School of Athens.*
1510–11. Fresco, 26 × 18′ (7.92 × 5.48 m).
Stanza della Segnatura, Vatican, Rome.

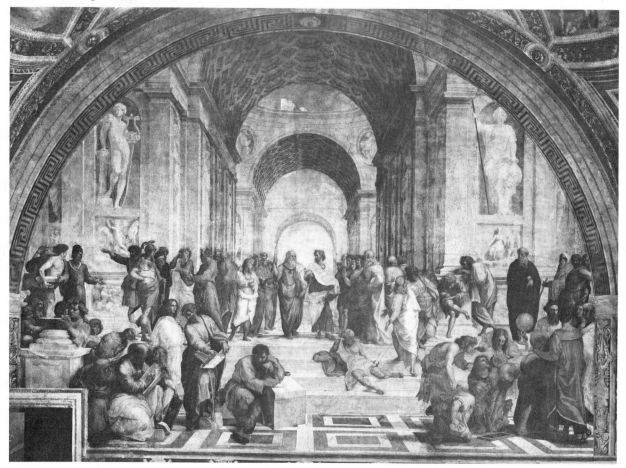

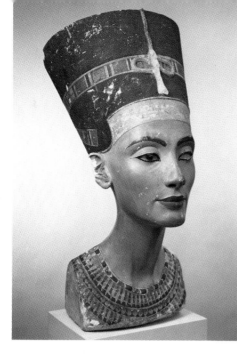

left: Plate 11.
Queen Nefertiti. c. 1355 B.C.
Painted limestone,
height 20″ (51 cm).
State Museums, West Berlin.

below: Plate 12.
Choir and sanctuary,
San Vitale, Ravenna, Italy.
c. 530–548.

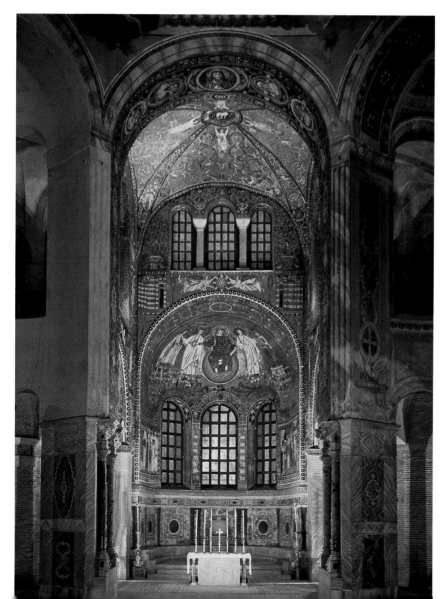

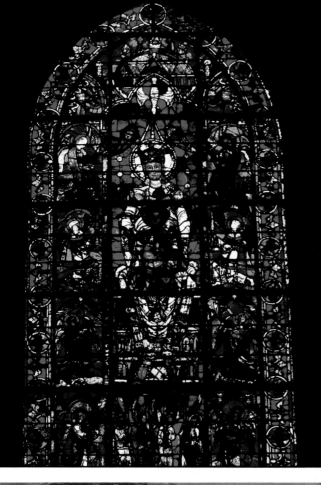

left: Plate 13.
Notre Dame de Belle Verrière,
Chartres Cathedral.
Early 13th century.

below: Plate 14. Sandro Botticelli.
The Birth of Venus. c. 1480.
Tempera on canvas,
6′7″ × 9′2″ (2.01 × 2.79 m).
Uffizi, Florence.

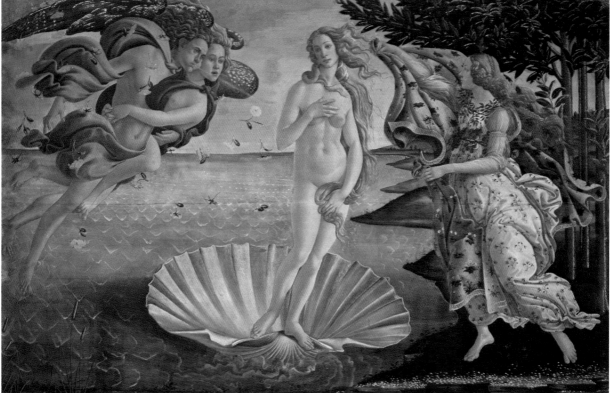

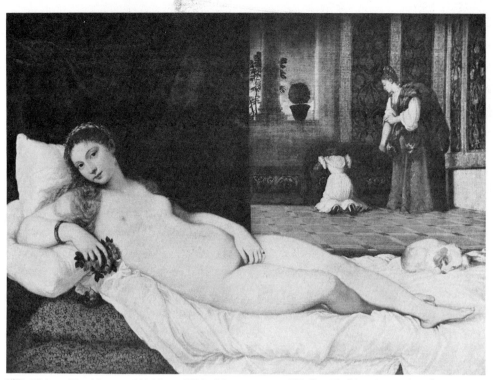

256. Titian. *The Venus of Urbino*. 1538. Oil on canvas, 3′11″ × 5′5″ (1.19 × 1.62 m). Uffizi, Florence.

aissance in *The Venus of Urbino* (Fig. 256), a worldly version of an earlier work by Giorgione.

The rhythmically ordered stability of Renaissance painting usually depended upon a tri-part division of space, which placed the subject in the foreground, against a strongly architectural middle ground, framed by a distant background. Breaking away from such limitations Titian introduced a new diagonal thrust into many of his works. For example, although our attention lingers on the idealized form of the Duchess of Urbino, our eyes flicker to the maid and the garments positioned not, as was customary, behind the central figure, but diagonally off center. Also, Titian portrayed gods and goddesses as distinctly mortal, such as this languid nude, who awaits the assistance of her maid to dress.

SCULPTURE AND ARCHITECTURE After Michelangelo finished the Sistine frescoes, he continued to work on Julius' tomb, for which he carved the mighty Moses. He also carved tomb figures for the Medici in Florence and the *Deposition from the Cross* (Fig. 116) for his own tomb. In some works the figures seem to struggle to release their stretched and contorted limbs from the stone. At the same time, the tension between those opposing forces and the larger-than-life scale of the sculptures increases their sense of power and movement. Such characteristics influenced many later Baroque artists, who often exaggerated the scale and movement of their works.

Michelangelo's last great undertaking was the continuation of work on St. Peter's in Rome, notably the dome (Fig. 182). The overpowering scale and the strong contrasts that exist between its diverse architectural elements mark this church as one of the most significant monuments of the High Renaissance and a herald of the Baroque era.

Mannerism and the Late Renaissance The 16th century was a period of contradiction and stress during which Italy was invaded by foreigners. In this changing world the equilibrium of the High Renaissance, like the Classical period in ancient Greece (see Chapter 12), was difficult to maintain. Even Leonardo and Michelangelo, typical as they were of the High Renaissance, signaled in their work the approaching Mannerist style. For example, Leonardo's preoccupation with light affected the balance of his compositions, and Michelangelo distorted his figures for expressive purposes (Fig. 116). By the 1530s the formal boundaries within which Leonardo and Michelangelo had produced their greatest works had broken down. The unrest of the time was reflected in the work of artists, who consciously altered the ideals of the High Renaissance, evolving an exaggerated, theatrical **Mannerist** style.

PAINTING Mannerist painters were not interested in the logic of real space. They experimented with elongated proportions like those of Botticelli's goddesses, the twisting forms preferred by Michelangelo, and asymmetrical com-

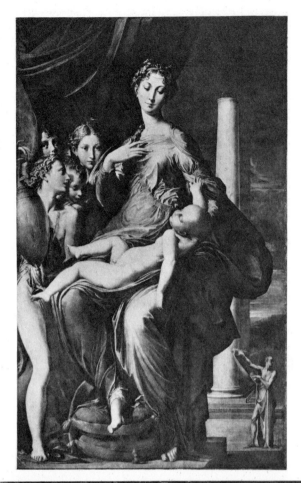

positions often used by Titian. Such effects were probably as startling to 16th-century Italians as the works of experimental 20th-century painters are to the public today.

Parmigianino (1503–1540) shocked his fellow-citizens of Parma with the elegance of *The Madonna with the Long Neck* (Fig. 257). The Madonna, her squirming baby, and attendant angels are crowded on one side, leaving a row of unfinished columns on the other. The contrast between the tightly compressed space and the open, abruptly receding space gives us a sense of instability.

The Venetian painter Tintoretto (1518–1594), influenced by Titian, altogether discarded the laws of classical structure. Tintoretto increased the sense of motion and contrast in his compositions to give the effect of floating masses lit by flickering light. His most famous work is *The Last Supper* (Fig. 258), which provides a striking contrast to Leonardo's mural of the same subject (Fig. 52). Gone is the classical ideal of balance expressed by Leonardo's one-point perspective and symmetrical composition. Tension and drama now dominate. Judas has been set aside in the shadows, while the remainder of the painting is filled with lights and half lights. This striking interpretation portends the dramatic Baroque style.

left: 257. Parmigianino. *The Madonna with the Long Neck.* c. 1535. Oil on canvas, 7′1″ × 4′4″ (2.16 × 1.32 m). Uffizi, Florence.

below: 258. Tintoretto. *The Last Supper.* 1594. Oil on canvas, 12′ × 18′8″ (3.66 × 6.69 m). San Giorgio Maggiore, Venice.

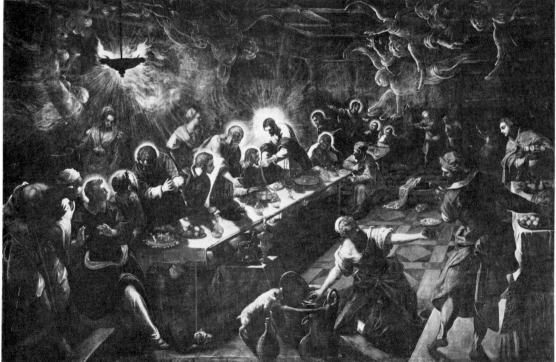

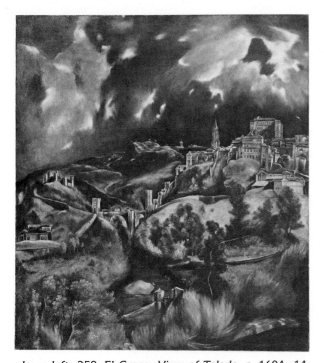

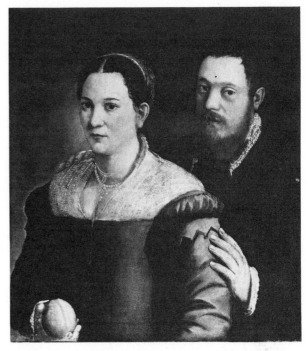

above left: 259. El Greco. *View of Toledo.* c. 1604–14.
Oil on canvas, 47¾ × 42¾" (121 × 108 cm). Metropolitan Museum of Art, New York
(Bequest of Mrs. H. O. Havemeyer, 1929, H. O. Havemeyer Collection).

above right: 260. Sofonisba Anguissola. *Husband and Wife.*
Oil on canvas, 28¼ × 25½" (72 × 65 cm). Galleria Doria Pamphili, Rome.

One of the most important Mannerists was Domenico Theotocopulos, known as El Greco (c. 1548–1614). Born on the Greek island of Crete, he was familiar with **icons** (panel paintings of holy subjects) in the Byzantine style. Traveling to Venice, he studied the achievements of Titian and Tintoretto in using light, shade, and rich color. But he retained the elongated figures of Byzantine art and developed his own strong colors to create an unreal world unlike that of other Venetian painters. After a period in Rome, he settled in Spain, where his personal style was in keeping with Spanish piety. His tall figures of saints in swirling drapery of violent rose, blue, and yellow maintain a link with the Byzantine style. He painted the city of Toledo (Fig. 259) illumined with the eerie light of an impending storm. The acrid green landscape is charged with emotion as dramatic clouds contrast with jagged hills and deep river valleys. In this work the Renaissance ideals of formal balance are totally rejected.

By the late 16th century a few women, usually born into families of painters, were becoming artists. Among the first to attract attention was Sofonisba Anguissola (c. 1528–1625), one of six sisters all trained as artists. Sofonisba is noted by the 16th-century historian Giorgio Vasari for her skill in portraiture, a favorite subject of the Renaissance. Her *Husband and Wife* (Fig. 260) is a good example. Despite the simplicity of the composition, the psychological rapport between the two subjects is remarkable for this period. Perhaps this quality and her conservative, sensitive observations account for Sofonisba's favored position at the court of Philip II of Spain.

SCULPTURE AND ARCHITECTURE Mannerism's concern with effect rather than content or intellect was typical of the work of the Florentine goldsmith and sculptor Cellini. His lively autobiography reveals expert craftsmanship and extreme egotism. Cellini was clearly delighted with his own virtuosity, displayed in the gold and enamel saltcellar he made for Francis I (Fig. 126). He wrote of this feat:

> The Sea, fashioned as a man, held a finely wrought ship which could hold enough salt, beneath I had put four sea horses, and I had given the figure a trident. The Earth I fashioned as a fair woman. . . . Beside her I placed a richly decorated temple to hold the pepper.

Such novelty appealed to princes and other rich patrons.

Similarly, architects such as Andrea Palladio (1518–1580) were determined to display inventive skill as well as classical knowledge. His Villa Rotonda, near Vicenza, was intended to duplicate ancient Roman styles, but there is no classical counterpart to this square mansion distin-

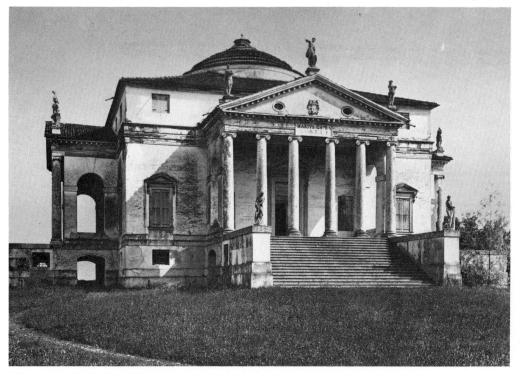

261. Andrea Palladio. Villa Rotonda, Vicenza. Begun 1550. 80′ (24.38 m) square, height of dome 70′ (21.34 m).

guished by four identical porches grouped around a central hall (Fig. 261). The low dome, however, is reminiscent of the Pantheon. Details of other Palladian buildings—columns, pediments, and three-window groupings—influenced later architecture in Italy and the 18th-century Georgian style in England. Even wooden copies of Georgian-style houses in far-off New England were often graced with Palladian windows.

Renaissance in the North

By the 15th century, the cities of Flanders, part of the duchy of Burgundy, were developing a wealthy middle class. Bankers and merchants made fortunes, guilds of tapestry weavers and other skilled craftspeople prospered, and women began to appear on guild lists. Gradually through increased trade and travel between North and South and the development of printing (see Chapter 8), the Flemish absorbed some of the artistic heritage of Rome and humanism.

Fifteenth Century Flemish painters made revolutionary technical discoveries in oil painting (see Chapter 3). By underpainting in black or brown and white tempera, drawing details in white, and overlaying thin oil glazes in color, they evolved a new technique that combined the precision of tempera with the depth of oil. It was ideally

suited for rendering the rich fabrics and shining brass furnishings of the comfortable houses of Flemish burghers and the soft blue depth of Flemish landscapes used as background.

Such painters as the Master of Flémalle (Robert Campin, 1406–1444) and Jan van Eyck (?1370–?1440), who worked for the Duke of Burgundy, depicted religious and secular subjects in the new technique, often combining realistic detail with medieval religious symbolism. Van Eyck, in his *Arnolfini Wedding,* shows the Italian silk merchant and his shy Flemish bride surrounded by symbols of the religious aspects of marriage (Fig. 262). The solitary lighted candle in the chandelier represents the presence of God, placed to remind the couple that their vows were made before Him. They stand on hallowed ground, their shoes discarded. The fruit on the windowsill represents the delights of lost paradise, while the dog symbolizes fidelity and possibly fertility. This Flemish room, therefore, had a deep meaning to those who understood its symbolism. The artist himself can be seen in the mirror, which repeats the uncompromising reality of the scene. He also inscribed in Latin above the mirror, "Jan van Eyck was here," a witness to the marriage!

Sixteenth Century By the early 16th century the states of Germany were in transition from medieval piety to Renaissance humanism and the new Reformation teachings of

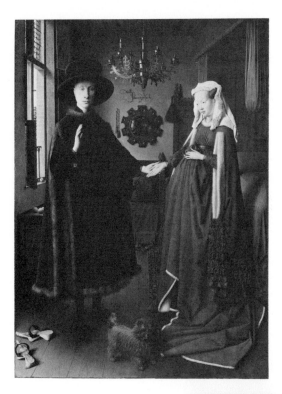

Martin Luther and other Protestant leaders. The basic spiritual conflicts produced an intensity of emotion, typified in Matthias Grünewald (1470–1528). His monumental Isenheim Altarpiece was Gothic in spirit and, like most medieval religious art, preached a visual sermon. When the wings are closed on the central panel, we see the *Crucifixion* (Fig. 263), a stark scene of suffering. Christ's dying body, painted in heroic scale, is distorted by his wounds, and his pain is reflected in his mother's face. In contrast to this scene of suffering, in an expression of hope for the world the opened panels reveal the *Annunciation,* the *Virgin and Child with Angels,* and the *Resurrection*. These scenes are filled with mystical beauty and radiant light. In this work, Grünewald stepped beyond his medieval tradi-

left: 262. Jan van Eyck. *Giovanni Arnolfini and His Bride, Giovanna Cenami.* 1434. Oil on panel, 33 × 22⅓″ (84 × 57 cm). National Gallery, London.

below: 263. Matthias Grünewald. *Crucifixion,* central panel of exterior of Isenheim Altarpiece. Completed 1515. Oil on panel, 8′9⅞″ × 10′7⅞″ (2.69 × 3.07 m). Musée d'Unterlinden, Colmar, France.

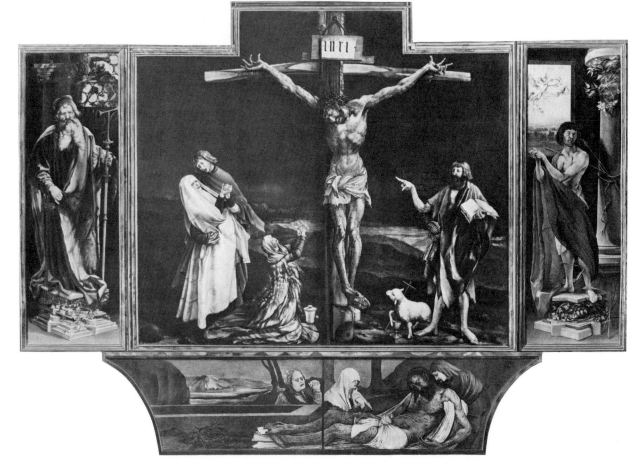

tions, and through his use of solid forms and dramatic expression of personal emotions, influenced many later painters.

Albrecht Dürer showed Northern painters with his portraits and landscapes how to adapt Italian Renaissance ideas without losing their own traditions. As an apprentice to his goldsmith father, then to a painter and an engraver, he developed the meticulous draftsmanship that characterizes all his work. Already familiar with the paintings of van Eyck, Dürer traveled to Italy, where he saw works by Mantegna and Michelangelo. He brought back to Germany the Renaissance concern for science and wrote treatises on perspective and anatomy.

In printmaking, however, Dürer truly excelled. The development of printing in the previous century had increased the demand for woodcuts and copper engravings, as we saw in Chapter 4. In these media he showed his mastery of light and shade and his devotion to the traditional faith. The classical architectural detail of the enormous *The Triumphal Arch of Maximilian* also reveals a strong Renaissance interest in ancient Rome even in Germany (Fig. 93). The emperor Maximilian, convinced of the value of art in service to the crown, cleverly entrusted Dürer with celebrating his royal deeds in a woodcut on paper rather than commissioning an architect to work in costly stone.

Other artists were less comfortable with the new ideas. For example, Lucas Cranach (1472–1553) illustrated pagan myths with nude figures of German beauties self-consciously acting the part of classical goddesses. In his jewel-like, decorative color surfaces Cranach is closer to 15th-century Flemish traditions. His spiritual conflicts between pagan morality and the religious teachings of the Reformation appear in the awkward forms and poses of his figures (Fig. 264).

While 16th-century Italians were delighting in light, color, texture, and experiments in perspective and composition, Northern Europeans were undergoing the Reformation, which discouraged the visual arts. Because the Protestant churches were opposed to religious paintings as idolatrous and the mercantile class had little interest in classical myths, Northern artists sought more prosaic subjects. Since no interest existed in large altarpieces or church frescoes, they painted on small panels, "in-hand" paintings, which could be hung on the walls of a patron's home. Landscape made its appearance as an important subject at this time. Another theme was portraiture. However, for the strictest Calvinists, all decorative objects were considered dispensable luxury, which left only portraits, small panels, and book illustration through which most artists could make a living.

A unique example of religious panel painting is the work of the late medieval painter Hieronymous Bosch (1450–1516), who drew upon his imagination to point out a moral lesson in *The Garden of Earthly Delights* (Fig. 265). On the left panel, fantastic creatures inhabit the Garden of Eden. On the right panel, fearsome demons—half animal,

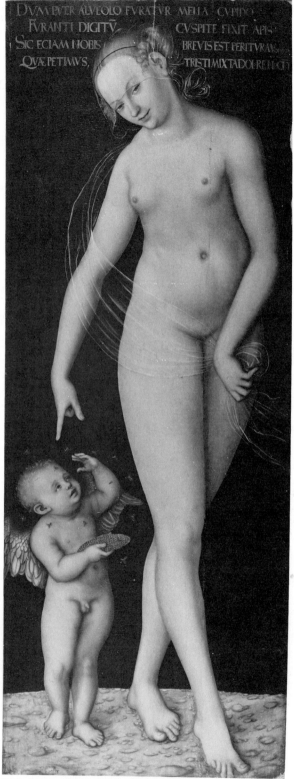

264. Lucas Cranach the Elder. *Venus and Cupid.* c. 1531. Wood, 5'8⅞" × 26" (1.75 × 0.66 m). Art Gallery of the National Museum of Prussian Culture, West Berlin.

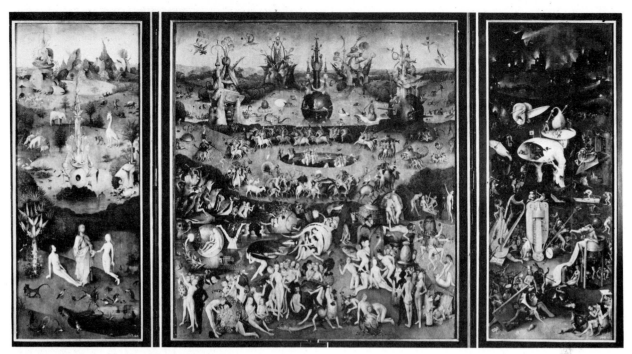

265. Hieronymus Bosch. *The Garden of Earthly Delights*. c. 1500. Oil on panel; center panel 7'2⅝" × 6'4¾" (2.2 × 1.95 m), each wing 7'2⅝" × 3'2¼" (2.2 × 0.97 m). Prado, Madrid.

half machine—punish sinners in hell. In the center, nude figures innocently enjoy sexual pleasures in a garden that may represent earth or paradise.

One of the foremost Northern portraitists was Hans Holbein the Younger. Born in Augsburg, Germany, he went to England, where he became court painter to Henry VIII. There he completed many portraits of the English nobility and was among the first to combine the Northern interest in the precision of tempera and oil glaze with the Italian interest in perspective and rich color. In his glowing portrait *Sir Brian Tuke* (Fig. 81) every detail of shape and texture has been painstakingly recorded. Often Holbein included in his portraits objects that symbolized various aspects of the subject's life.

Such scenes of the everyday world of kitchen or tavern and still life themes consisting of tables stocked with food and flowers were favored by Dutch painters. Brueghel set even biblical stories, such as the *Tower of Babel* (Fig. 210), in the local Dutch countryside populated with peasants going about their daily activities. For all his apparent taste for country-bumpkin humor, Brueghel was really a sophisticate who had traveled to Italy. In his landscapes, humans are depicted as tiny figures, conveying the lesson of human insignificance in the scheme of the universe. While many of his paintings are religious allegories, they also reveal his personal joy in nature—in the hot sun on hay fields, and in frozen, snow-covered fields at dusk.

Baroque in Italy

The extraordinary achievements of the Renaissance were, perhaps, possible only at a time when traditional religious beliefs still had meaning and artists in a new spirit of inquiry and observation found fresh means to express them. During the Age of the Baroque, the 17th and early 18th centuries, the religious unity of Europe was destroyed, and the increasing scientific spirit of the new age encouraged a secular outlook. It was a period of confusion and longing for a more perfect world that beckoned out of reach. Artists of the Baroque period went beyond the limits set by the Renaissance in their desire to express fresh ideas in unusual ways. Sometimes their individualism spilled out of strict stylistic categories, but their innovations foretold similar developments in later times.

By the 17th century the exodus of converts from Catholicism to Protestantism had been halted, while the Roman Catholic Church sustained a period of renewal called the Catholic or Counter Reformation. Much-needed Church reforms were made, and in Italy a great program of renovation and rebuilding was launched to make Rome once again the center of the world. This program continued in the Baroque period. The papacy spared no expense to proclaim the authority of Rome and authorized architects to build palaces and churches and to lay out piazzas, fountains, and gardens on a grand scale. Paintings and sculptures were commissioned to decorate the architecture.

Much of this art was intended for the aristocracy, but some, such as the piazza in front of St. Peter's, added a new dimension to the life of the ordinary citizen.

The word "Baroque" originated from a Portuguese derisive term used to mean "absurd" or "grotesque" because many considered Baroque art a degeneration from the restraint of the High Renaissance. In Baroque painting and sculpture emphasis was placed on light and dark contrasts, turbulent compositions, and exaggerated emotion. In Baroque architecture classical elements were freely handled to create the effects of painting and sculpture. Dramatic and mysterious effects were preferred.

Painting One of the first to work in this new style was Annibale Carracci (1560–1609), a member of a family of painters from Bologna. Distrustful of Mannerist distortion, in his frescoes for the ceiling of the Farnese Palace in Rome he combined a sense of realistic anatomy and foreshortening with dramatic light and energetic movement.

The Carracci family founded an academy of art in Bologna, the very first art school. Later, as other academies appeared, aspiring artists no longer were apprenticed to a master painter but could enroll for instruction to study art.

Also opposed to Mannerism but more strikingly dramatic than the Carracci was Michelangelo Merisi da Caravaggio (1573–1610), who used highly exaggerated lighting to dramatize biblical stories in ordinary settings of his day. In *The Conversion of St. Paul* (Fig. 266) traditional images are gone. St. Paul is shown as an armored man flat on his back, almost trampled beneath his horse. The striking perspective and extreme contrasts of dark and light draw us into the event. It is obvious why many of Caravaggio's conservative contemporaries were appalled by this work, which presented sacred figures in such untraditional ways.

The foremost woman painter of the Baroque period was Artemisia Gentileschi, the daughter of a painter. Influenced by Caravaggio, a friend of her father, she painted biblical scenes, portraits, and nudes. Her first major work, *Judith Beheading Holofernes,* portrays a heroic woman performing an atrocious duty with quiet courage (Fig. 12). The range of color and tonal effect are impressive. The strong diagonals all lead to the sword blade from which drops of blood brilliantly contrast with the snow white bosom of Judith. Gentileschi chose to outdo all her predecessors by showing the ferocity with which Judith destroyed the general who was attacking her beloved city.

Sculpture and Architecture The most outstanding sculptor-architect of the Baroque period was Giovanni Lorenzo Bernini (1598–1680), who is probably best known for his extraordinary *The Ecstasy of St. Theresa* (Fig. 267), influenced by emotional Hellenistic works. This sculpture of religious mysticism epitomized the spirit of the Baroque. In the saint's own words, at the moment of ecstasy she felt such a great love of God that "the pain was so great that I cried out, but at the same time, the sweetness which the

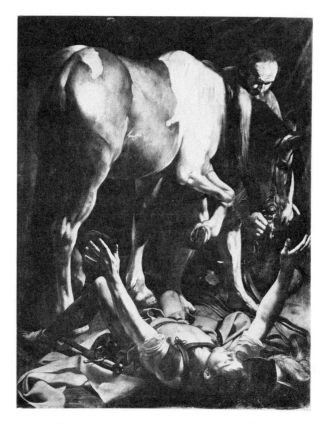

above: 266. Caravaggio. *The Conversion of Saint Paul.* 1601–02. Oil on canvas, 7'6½" × 5'9" (2.3 × 1.75 m). Cerasi Chapel, Sta. Maria del Popolo, Rome.

below: 267. Gianlorenzo Bernini. *The Ecstasy of Saint Teresa.* 1645–52. Marble, stucco, and gilt bronze; life size. Cornaro Chapel, Sta. Maria della Vittoria, Rome.

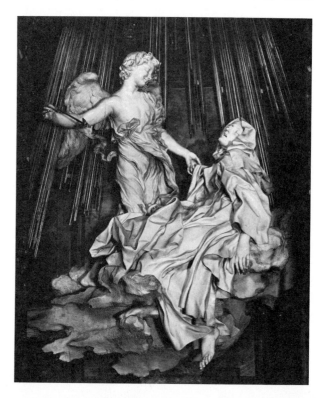

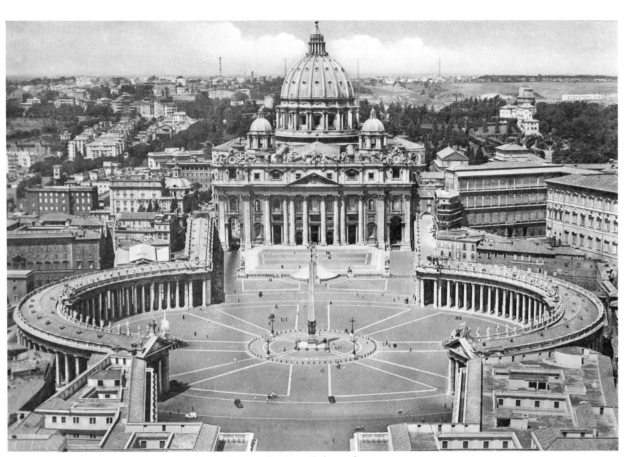

268. St. Peter's Basilica and the Vatican, Rome. Apse and dome by
Michelangelo, 1547–64; dome completed by Giacomo della Porta, 1588–92;
nave and façade by Carlo Maderno, 1601–26; colonnades by
Gianlorenzo Bernini, 1656–63.

violent pain gave me was so excessive that I could not wish
to be rid of it."

The drapery falling in a cascade of agitated folds rejects
the solidity of the marble from which it was carved, revealing Bernini's technical skill and preoccupation with detail.
His religious intensity led him also to create a spectacular
design for the piazza of St. Peter's Basilica in Rome (Fig.
268). Designed to hold crowds of worshipers at Easter and
Christmas time, the piazza is said to accommodate two
million people. Bernini intended the two curving colonnades to represent the arms of the Church, which "em-
brace Catholics to reinforce their belief, heretics to reunite
them with the Church, and agnostics to enlighten them
with the true faith."

Baroque in Spain and the North

Born in Italy, the showy Baroque style soon spread to
Spain, France, Germany, the Low Countries, and England.
In each country, Catholic or Protestant, it was modified by
local circumstances. Princes and nobles competed to build
magnificent palaces and gardens, redesign cities, and

amass works of art. Even functional objects soon acquired
Baroque curves and elaborate decoration.

Spain   With the immense wealth derived from their colonies in the New World, the kings of Spain maintained an
impressive court in keeping with the role in which they
saw themselves, as divinely appointed rulers of their people
and representatives of the Church in Spain. Continuing the
16th-century practice of commissioning works from foreign painters, such as El Greco and Titian, they also favored
Spaniards.

The most illustrious Spanish court painter was Diego
Velázquez (1599–1660), who excelled in portraiture and
grandiose historical scenes. Although influenced by Caravaggio's lighting and by Titian and the Flemish Baroque
painter Peter Paul Rubens (1577–1640), Velázquez evolved
his own personal style. His canvases are Baroque in color,
depth of space, and light and dark contrasts, but he applied
his paints in separate brush strokes that presaged 19th-
century Impressionism. With this technique, Velázquez
could recreate the play of light over the rich garments of his
royal subjects and the luxury of their palaces. In *Las*

Meniñas, he painted his own portrait standing next to the tiny *Infanta* surrounded by her maids of honor (Fig. 269). Tiny portraits of the king and queen, who came to watch the artist at work, appear in the mirror behind him. He must have indeed felt secure as court artist to record himself more prominently than his royal employers.

France The most outstanding example of French Baroque art was the Palace of Versailles (Fig. 270), built by Louis XIV outside Paris to reflect France's position as the major power in Europe. The king assembled a team originally consisting of the architect Louis Le Vau (1612–1670), the landscape architect André Le Nôtre (1613–1700), and the painter and decorator Charles Lebrun (1619–1690) to integrate all aspects of the design. Although a new wing for the old Louvre Palace in Paris had been a collaborative effort, Versailles was the first design and construction of such tremendous scope to be a group effort.

In its magnificent scale Versailles resembled Bernini's piazza in Rome (Fig. 268), but its restrained, intellectual style defined characteristic qualities of French Baroque. Unlike most Italian Renaissance palaces, which looked inward on central courtyards, Versailles' long, windowed galleries overlooked broad terraces and formal gardens full of pools, splashing fountains, and marble statuary in the classical style. The palace with its gardens and park covered about 20 acres (8.9 hectares). A small city in itself, it held a thousand brilliantly dressed courtiers and their servants.

Louis, who expected all French culture to serve the state, was responsible for the founding of royal academies of literature, science, and the arts. Other rulers founded similar institutions. These powerful, conservative state academies set official standards and dispensed honors only to those who followed their dictates. Artists who opposed their rigid rulings usually had a difficult time finding work. We will see later how 19th-century artists rebelled against the restrictive influence of academic art.

Low Countries Rubens, a prolific painter trained in Flanders and Italy and a worldly, well-traveled ambassador at home in many European courts, helped spread the Baroque style. During his years in Italy he learned to make full use of color and light. Huge, movement-filled canvases reflect his delight in painting rich drapery, the sheen of armor and jewels and the glowing skin tones. His work, such as the *Garden of Love* (Fig. 271), was tremendously popular, bringing him great wealth and a studio in Antwerp with many assistants. He kept such tight control over the artwork, however, that when a painting was almost com-

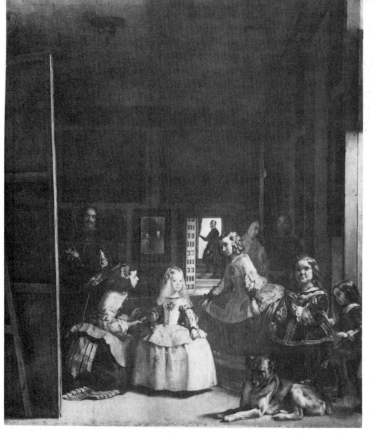

269. Diego Velázquez. *Las Meniñas* (*The Maids of Honor*). 1656. Oil on canvas, 10′5¼″ × 9′3¾″ (3.18 × 2.76 m). Prado, Madrid.

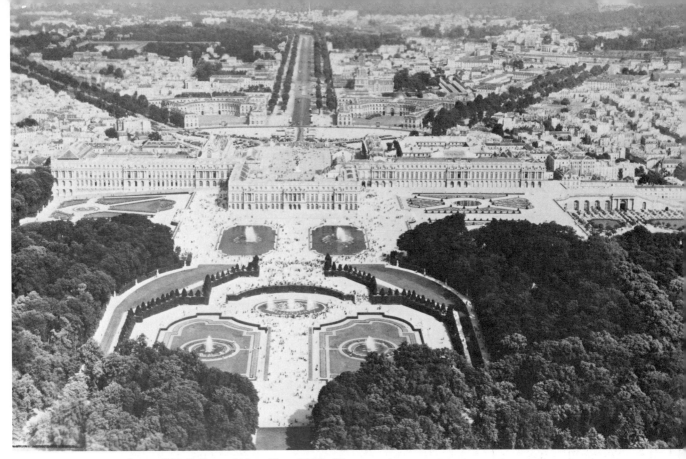

above: 270. Palace of Versailles. 1669–85.

below: 271. Peter Paul Rubens. *The Garden of Love*. c. 1632–34.
Oil on canvas, 6′6″ × 9′3½″ (1.98 × 2.83 m). Prado, Madrid.

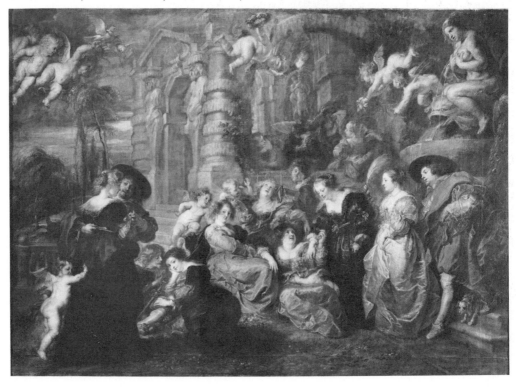

plete, he had only to take a brush to a detail here or there to make the painting his own. In only four years, he painted twenty-one murals for the Luxembourg Palace in Paris, a work rivaling in magnitude Michelangelo's Sistine ceiling. Rubens' theme is the history of Marie de' Medici told through a mixture of myths, history, and allegory—a combination much favored by the aristocracy.

Meanwhile, Dutch painters were producing for a Calvinist merchant class unassuming works that emphasized middle-class daily life. Frans Hals, a Protestant from Haarlem, was a popular portraitist of Dutch burghers, whom he often depicted in official group paintings such as the *Women Regents of the Old Men's Home at Haarlem.* He was innovative in his method of finishing his paintings in loose, distinct brush strokes. In *The Bohemian* (Fig. 82) he catches a momentary expression to give the impression of quick work, which was in fact the product of long, calculated effort. Hals's rough naturalism is, however, quite different from the smooth naturalism of Caravaggio's *The Conversion of St. Paul* (Fig. 266).

Hals greatly influenced his fellow-citizen Judith Leyster (1609–1660), whose substantial body of work is somewhat similar in style. Several of her paintings, such as *The Jolly Companions* (Fig. 272) and *The Jolly Toper,* which has her monogram, were sold as the work of Hals. Although the themes of the two artists are similar, there are differences in their work. Leyster's compositions are generally more intricate, the brush work more sensitive, and the mood less exuberant.

While Hals and Leyster painted their subjects as if caught in a passing moment, Rembrandt, working in Amsterdam, studied his subjects with psychological penetration, searching for the essential core of each one. His portraits reveal such depths that at times we turn from the embarrassing intimacy of his insights. To find authentic models for his biblical works, he frequented the Jewish quarter of Amsterdam.

Rembrandt used strong contrasts of light and shade like Italian Baroque painters, but with more restraint. His unconventional approach to group portraits is evident in *The Night Watch,* in which he strengthened the overall composition with light and shadow at the expense of detailed likenesses (Fig. 71). So titled because darkened layers of varnish made it look like a night scene until it was cleaned in the 1940s, *The Sortie of Captain Frans Banning Cocq's Company of the Civic Guard,* as it is properly called, actually represents a volunteer military company called together to honor visiting royalty.

Rembrandt was also a master at graphics. He preferred etching to engraving because etching gave him more freedom to change a plate in preliminary states. With only a few lines he could express the essence of a scene, a gesture, or a pose.

In contrast to Rembrandt's uncluttered, deep-shadowed works, paintings by Jan Vermeer of Delft appear clearly detailed. He portrayed the interiors of Dutch households with loving concern for meticulous accuracy, using

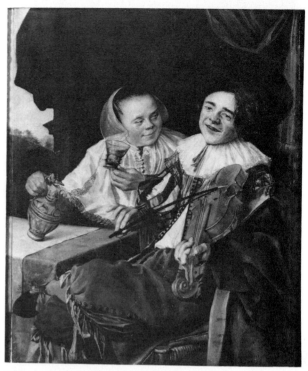

272. Judith Leyster. *The Jolly Companions.* 1630. Oil on wood, 26¾ × 21¾" (68 × 55 cm). Louvre, Paris.

mellow colors that reflect Dutch Baroque taste. The strong compositions brought attention to the sensuous colors and textures of everyday objects (Fig. 39). If the paintings were reduced to abstract shapes and flat colors in the 20th-century style of Mondrian (Pl. 3, p. 22), we could see the careful plan of the composition. Vermeer's skill in framing his scenes with draperies, combined with his innovative device of cutting off figures at unusual levels, presaged a different way of depicting the world.

England Separated from the mainland of Europe by the English Channel and conservative tradition, England was slow to accept Renaissance and Baroque art. English Baroque, exemplified by two London buildings, the Banqueting Hall at Whitehall by Inigo Jones (1573–1652) and St. Paul's Cathedral by Sir Christopher Wren (1632–1723), is not so ornate or luxurious as Italian Baroque. Jones was influenced by Palladio. Wren's restrained forms link St. Paul's more closely to Italian and French Renaissance styles than to exuberant Italian Baroque (Fig. 273). The dome and façade were probably influenced by the late Renaissance St. Peter's in Rome (Fig. 182), and the double row of paired columns are reminiscent of the classical Louvre in Paris.

St. Paul's was the largest of many churches that Wren designed after the Great Fire of London in 1666. Their pillared porches, classical pediments, and single, slender steeples, imaginatively combined to give an effect of dignity and strength, influenced 18th-century churches in the English colonies in North America.

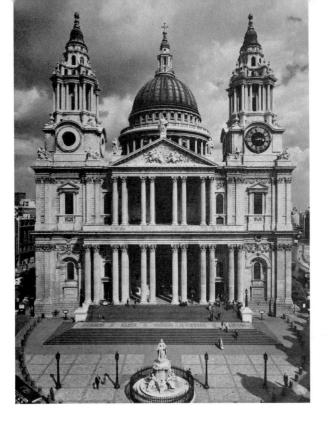

above: 273. Christopher Wren. St. Paul's Cathedral, London. 1675–1710.

below: 274. Jean Antoine Watteau. *The Embarkation for Cythera.* 1717. Oil on canvas, 4'3" × 6'4½" (1.3 × 1.94 m). Louvre, Paris.

Age of Reason

The restless Baroque period passed quietly into the Age of Reason. Sir Isaac Newton had discovered laws of physics that led to a Scientific Revolution in the 18th century. Later, writers such as the French Voltaire expressed questions about the gap between the brilliant court life of the aristocracy and the poverty of the masses. Reflecting the times, art also underwent changes. Whereas the Baroque taste had favored theatrical arts of sensuous color and huge scale, French designers now created an intimate **Rococo** style, smaller in scale, and characterized by subtle colors and a profusion of curved ornament. Palaces and country estates were soon filled with paintings, tapestry, porcelain, and silver, intricately decorated.

Rococo Painting Painters in the new style chose as subjects classical divinities and the aristocracy, in classical or rich court dress. Their palette was light—white, gold, pink, blue, and other clear hues. The work of Antoine Watteau (1684–1721), who, like most court painters, was also an interior designer, shows us the Rococo style at its best. He was especially successful at recording the open-air entertainments so popular at court, making quick sketches at the scene and then painting the event in silvery tones in his studio. *The Embarkation for Cythera* (Fig. 274), a dreamy landscape peopled by courtiers on the mythological island of love, may have been inspired by a court fête. Adapting painting techniques from Rubens' more robust works, Watteau also borrowed ideas from the theater. His subjects, who included actors, seemed to act out their parts like tableaux in a stage setting as artificial as their lives.

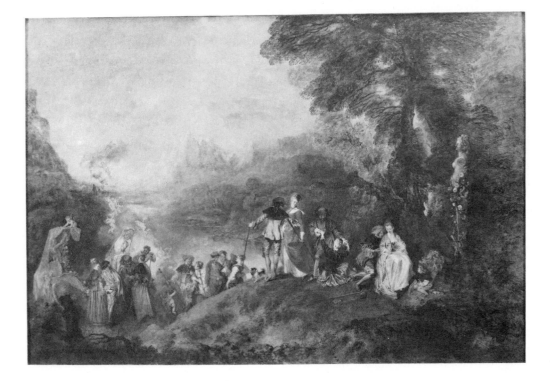

François Boucher (1703–1770), painter to Louis XV's mistress Madame de Pompadour, was also known for allegories. Typical of his sprightly fantasies is *The Toilet of Venus* (Fig. 275). Jean Honoré Fragonard (1732–1806), a pupil of Boucher, was equally adept at painting scantily clad gods and goddesses surrounded by cherubs. The works of both men were filled with pretty faces on supple bodies in coy poses. Titles such as *The Stolen Kiss, The Bathers,* and *The Fountain of Love* give us an idea of what aristocratic patrons chose to decorate the walls of their salons and boudoirs.

Portraiture One of the most popular subjects of Rococo painters was portraiture. Rosalba Carriera (1675–1757) gained a reputation for life-size and miniature portraits in her native Venice. Many were in pastel, a new medium, which she introduced to Paris on a trip there in 1720. Her pastels, which range from simple studies to complex group compositions, illuminate the character of her subjects. They were so popular with Paris society that she was elected to the French Royal Academy of Painting and Sculpture. Her self-portrait (Fig. 276) is a typical example.

Another member of the Royal Academy was Elisabeth Vigée-Le Brun (1755–1842), the daughter of a painter. Of the more than twenty portraits to her credit, the best known, a self-portrait with her daughter, Julie, is a rhythmic composition well suited to aristocratic demands (Fig. 277). In fact, she pleased royal tastes so well that Queen Marie Antoinette sponsored her election to the Royal Academy.

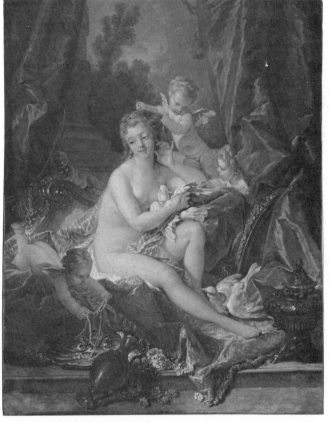

above: 275. François Boucher. *The Toilet of Venus.* 1751. Oil on canvas, 42⅝ × 33½″ (108 × 85 cm). Metropolitan Museum of Art, New York (bequest of William K. Vanderbilt, 1920).

right: 276. Rosalba Carriera. *Self-Portrait, Holding Portrait of Her Sister.* 1715. Pastel, 28 × 22½″ (71 × 57 cm). Uffizi, Florence.

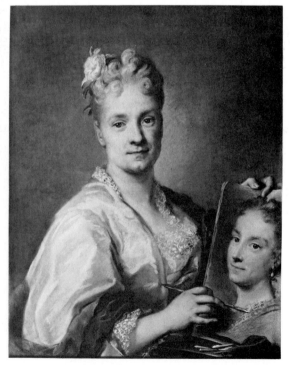

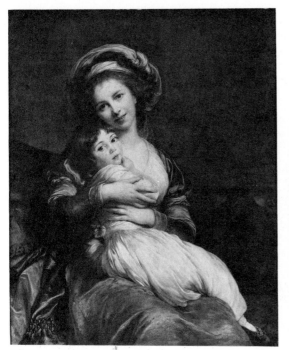

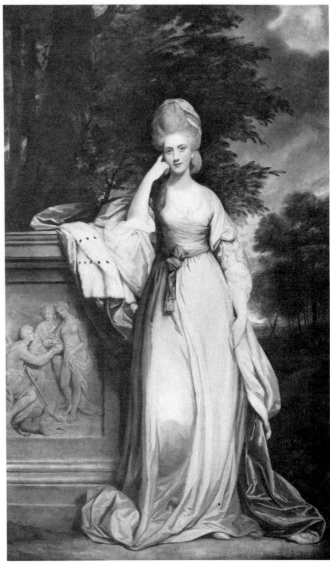

above: 277. Elisabeth Vigée-Le Brun.
Self-Portrait with Her Daughter. Oil on wood,
51⅛ × 37″ (130 × 94 cm).
Louvre, Paris.

right: 278. Joshua Reynolds. *The Marchioness
of Townsend.* c. 1780. Oil on canvas,
7′11″ × 4′10″ (2.41 × 1.47 m).
Fine Arts Museum of San Francisco
(gift of the Roscoe and
Margaret Oakes Foundation).

The art of portraiture flourished especially in England. One of the foremost portraitists of his day was Sir Joshua Reynolds (1723–1792), who had studied in Italy. As co-founder and first president of the Royal Academy in London, he laid down rules governing the creation of art in accordance with Italian and French academic principles. Although his writings on art were somewhat pompous, his portraits have grace and dignity. Flattering to their subjects, they appealed to aristocrats and set a style in fashionable portraiture (Fig. 278).

In contrast to Reynolds' formal compositions are the freer works of Gainsborough, which point forward to the Romantic style. He had a talent for posing his subjects with an easy grace (Fig. 155), set before a landscape suggesting their luxurious estates. His colors are delicate, and his light-filled canvases sparkle with an elegance that evokes aristocratic life.

Genre and Still Life The middle classes, like the aristocracy, also enriched their surroundings with art. Some chose

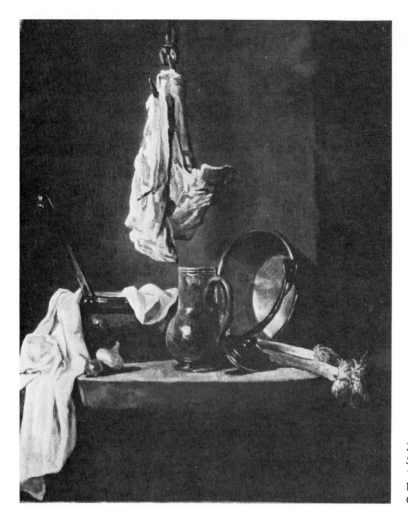

279. Jean Baptiste Siméon Chardin. *Still Life*. c. 1728–30. Oil on canvas, 15¾ × 12⅜″ (40 × 31 cm). Norton Simon Foundation, Pasadena, California.

allegories by Boucher, Fragonard, and others, but many preferred subjects that reflected their own world—comfortable household scenes and boisterous drinking parties or tables laden with food and flowers. In short, their tastes were much like those of 17th-century Dutch burghers.

The foremost French painter of genre and still life was Jean Baptiste Chardin (1699–1779). His refined arrangements of food and cooking implements (Fig. 279) reveal subtle color harmonies and textures, and, despite the simplicity of the subjects, they satisfied even the most conservative patrons. Through his ability to infuse a quiet dignity in domestic scenes, he reminds us of Vermeer (Fig. 39). Chardin's paintings were even enjoyed by the aristocracy, who liked to play at living a simple life.

Still-life painting, called *nature morte* ("dead nature") by the French, did not, however, rank high by the standards of the academies, which insisted that narrative content was a painting's major justification. Since few women were encouraged to try their hands at "noble narratives," or were admitted to the academies for the requisite training, still-life subjects, and in particular flower painting, had obvious appeal for them. One of the great still-life painters

of the time was Anne Vallayer-Coster (1744–1818), the daughter of a goldsmith. She reveals a delight in her subject, even in such early work as *The White Tureen* (Fig. 280). The composition is masterful, the silvery tones quite sensuous, but it is likely that her skill in portraying texture determines the appeal of the work.

Life in the 18th century had its problems, even among the privileged. The unpleasant side was told by William Hogarth in bitingly satirical works such as *The Harlot's Progress* and *The Rake's Progress* (Fig. 24), a moralizing series of engravings narrating the downfall of a young man and woman. The rake comes to a pathetic end as a raving maniac in Bedlam, London's insane asylum, where his demented companions include a grimacing fiddler and a schizophrenic wearing an impromptu crown. Engravings had become a popular and inexpensive form of art, and a series like this reached large audiences. With Hogarth, the graphic arts had become an important propaganda tool for arousing indignation against social injustices, the vices of the rich, and the uneducated tastes of the new patrons. As the century progressed, the rising tide of democratic ideals presaged a new age.

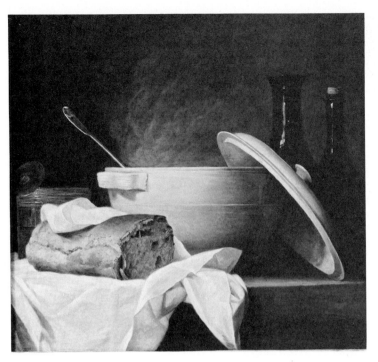

280. Anne Vallayer-Coster.
The White Tureen. 1771.
Oil on canvas, 19⅝ × 24½" (50 × 62 cm).
Private collection, Paris.

EXERCISES AND ACTIVITIES

1. What factors were responsible for the development of the Renaissance attitude? How was it reflected in art? Describe one example of Renaissance sculpture, painting, or architecture, and contrast it with one work of art from the Middle Ages.
2. How was Renaissance architecture influenced by Greek art? Cite specific examples. Find a building in your community that has Renaissance details and sketch some of them.
3. How did the Renaissance discovery of the mathematical laws of perspective change the character of Western art? Using examples from this book, discuss the effect of this discovery of perspective on painting and on relief sculpture. How did the Italian concern with perspective and idealized form affect the art of northern Europe?
4. Analyze the use of perspective in a Renaissance painting or print from northern and from southern Europe. Trace the work, and make a diagram of its perspective, using paper wide enough to incorporate both right and left vanishing points. Can you see differences in the way southern and northern Europeans used perspective?
5. Select a Renaissance work such as Raphael's *School of Athens*. Using colored chalk or pens, create a new composition from it in which Renaissance colors are changed and the subject is reorganized in the Baroque style.
6. What was the relationship between the Mannerist styles of El Greco, Tintoretto, and Parmigianino and earlier artists, such as Titian? Mention details of their work that show this relationship.
7. How does the Baroque style in painting, sculpture, and architecture differ from that of the Renaissance? Compare specific works of both periods.
8. What is meant by the statement "Michelangelo was born with one foot in the Renaissance and the other in the Baroque era"? Cite examples of his work that support this statement.

15 The World Beyond the West

The society of the masks is the whole world; and when it bursts out in some public place it dances . . . the system of the world.

OGOTOMMÊTE

Our Western culture is so firmly embedded in Judeo-Christian concepts and the classical ideals we have discussed that many of us find other arts and ideologies bewildering. Yet ever since the Middle Ages, and especially since the 19th century, Western art has been influenced by Middle Eastern cultures and by the Far East and Africa. Moreover, today, in a time of instant communication, the cultures of remote peoples are no longer distant from us. It is important for the West to be exposed to what may be called non-Western art because most of the world is composed of non-Western peoples, whose cultures have increasing impact on ours.

Many differences exist in the visual images of other societies because of varying geographical and religious conditions, but the visual arts of all people—Western or non-Western—speak to us across time and space. In the limited pages of this book we will glimpse fleetingly their riches. Other books listed in the bibliography will direct us further.

Africa

The art of northern Africa is predominantly Islamic and is closely related to that of the Middle East. It is the art of sub-Saharan, or black, Africa that we consider to be traditionally African, the site where many believe human life began.

Most paleontologists agree that the oldest human skeletal remains found have come from northeastern Africa. The huge continent, three times larger than the United States, with almost one thousand different languages, has yielded numerous art styles.

Before 3000 B.C. Africans of the Old Stone Age painted animated scenes on rocks in the Tassili region of the Sahara and in the south. They illustrated hunters pursuing their game (Fig. 281) and also their religious beliefs. One scene of a creation myth depicts the first man mating with the

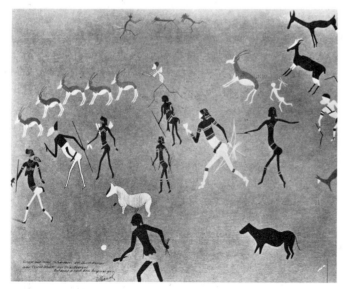

281. The White Lady of Brandberg. Bushman cave painting, Nambia, South West Africa.

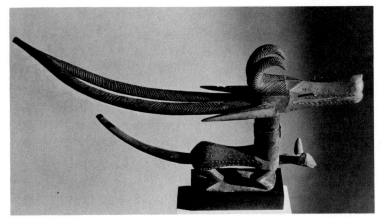

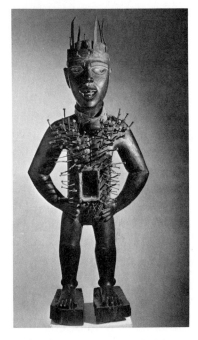

left: 282. Antelope headpiece, from Mali. 19th century. Wood, length 24¾" (63 cm). Whereabouts unknown.

below: 283: Nail fetish, from Zaire. 19th century. Wood, height 32¼" (82 cm). Whereabouts unknown.

morning and evening stars to produce all the creatures of the earth.

Traditional African Culture Many Africans today live much as they have for centuries. They are grouped in **extended families,** consisting of several generations and many cousins, on whom they depend heavily for support. Important in Africa and other traditional societies, the extended families are parts of clans united by blood ties in devotion to their ancestors. The clans in turn form groups that share a common language and culture. Today one or more such groupings may be combined into a nation.

Africans who continue a traditional way of life live in villages of a few families, raise crops for the community, and believe in an animistic religion. They think of the world around them and the forces of nature—sun, rain, fertility of crops and humans, and death—as determined by powerful spirits, or divinities. These spirits seem very real and are encouraged or soothed as occasion demands. African art expresses human responses to those forces with great emotion and vitality.

The Western division between fine and functional art never existed in traditional African (or any other preindustrial) society. Some art objects, such as masks and head pieces (Fig. 282), were created for religious ceremonies held by secret organizations, so our knowledge of their use is scanty. Houses and furnishings were decorated with carving and color. Africans also enhanced their own bodies with paint, tattoos, and scars (Fig. 16), both as decoration and as symbolism. For the Africans, as for the ancient Greeks and many other peoples, art was an important part of life.

Expressing an emotional response to the world was vital to African artists, who usually considered realism in art an infringement on the powers of the divine. Therefore, they emphasized and exaggerated the characteristic shapes of humans, animals, or imagined spirits, sometimes so strongly as to startle Western eyes. Perhaps that is why many 20th-century artists looking for new approaches found African art so appealing.

Wood Sculpture In Africa as in the West, the human figure has been a constant source of inspiration. Sculptured forms, usually carved from wood, range in height from 6 feet to 3 inches (1828.8 to 76.2 millimeters). Most figures were left uncolored or painted solid red or black. Some present-day Yoruban art from Nigeria and sculpture from East Africa is multicolored. Male and female figures were carved from tree trunks for ancestor rites as commemorative statues or as mendicant figures holding bowls for contributions (Fig. 17). Many of these figures were status symbols made for the well-to-do in each community.

Like Christian sculptures of religious figures, African images evoke ancestors and gods. Some of the sculptures are fetishes, which were designed both to make contact with the gods for help and to ward off evil spirits. For example, in this fetish from Zaire (Fig. 283), each nail represents an attempt to reach a divinity. If there had been no rain for weeks, a priest might drive a nail into the figure to attract the power of the rain god. Or if someone were ill, a fetish would be used to reach a spirit for help in effecting a cure. An unsuccessful fetish would soon be discarded. Such rituals might be distantly compared with Christians lighting a candle before an image of a saint in a plea for help.

Besides figures, African sculpture includes ceremonial stools, neck rests, masks, and other furnishings. Most were

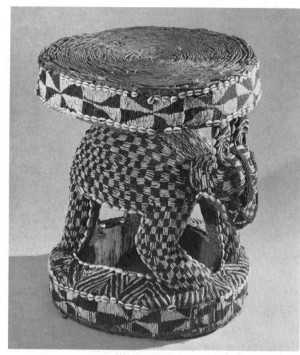

left: 284. Animal stool, Bamum Tribe, Cameroon. 19th or 20th century. Wood, glass beads, cowrie shells, burlap, and cotton cloth; height 19⅛" (49 cm). Metropolitan Museum of Art, New York (Michael C. Rockefeller Memorial Collection of Primitive Art, gift of Nelson A. Rockefeller, 1964).

below: 285. Akua'ba statue, from Ghana. Ashanti. Wood, height 11" (28 cm). Segy Gallery for African Art, New York.

bottom: 286. Bayaka mask (front and back views), from Lower Congo. 19th century. Painted wood, 13 × 12 × 9" (33 × 30 × 23 cm). Collection the author.

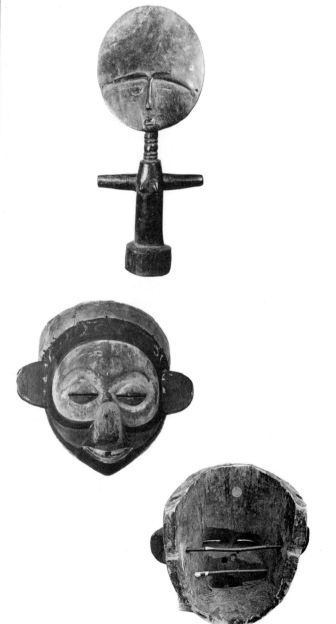

ornamented with carving, paint, or materials such as feathers, shells, hair, and stones. Typically, a wooden stool from the Cameroon was completely covered with a geometric design of beads and cowrie shells (Fig. 284). Stools were important to Africans. In some regions people believed that a person's soul occupied the stool that he cherished during his lifetime. In other regions, certain stools were reserved for important personages. The Ashanti people of Ghana preserved a myth about a golden stool that fell miraculously from heaven and brought good fortune. Royal Ashanti stools were often covered with gold, once so abundant that Europeans called Ghana the Gold Coast. Neck rests were used to support the head of a sleeping person without disturbing an elaborate hair style. Most decorations on these rests were geometric, but designs differed from place to place.

Sculptural styles and decorative patterns varied widely. Often certain objects were unique to an area. An example from Ghana is the disc-headed Akua'ba figure similar to those worn by young Ashanti girls as fertility charms to ensure a good marriage with children (Fig. 285).

Masks African ritual masks played an important role in community life. Elaborate masks were worn in ceremonial dances to heighten the emotional effect on the spectator as well as to draw power from the spirits. Masks also emphasized the strong emotional ties that exist among humans, animals, and nature. Some masks were made to fit on top of the head, others to cover the face, and still others to fit over the head and shoulders. In order to help dancers keep their masks on, they were often fitted with a bar inside for the wearer to grip with his teeth (Fig. 286).

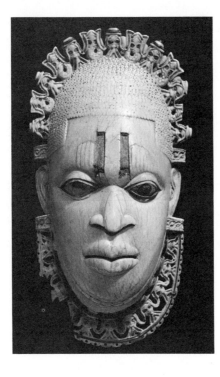

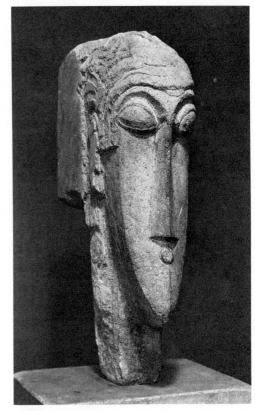

In addition, the body of the masked dancer was usually decorated with paint or costumed in feathers, skins, cloth, or vegetable fibers. Representing a particular god or spirit, masked ritual dancers often felt themselves to be psychologically identified with the power of the spirit. And, in turn, they were identified as that spirit by the community. Similarly, masks for identification and emotional effect were used in ritual dances in Oceania and pre-Columbian (before Columbus) North America and in Chinese and Japanese theater.

Many African dance masks were designed to celebrate the rites of passage through life—particularly birth, puberty, marriage, and death. Since ancestor worship was strong in African cultures, death was a constant preoccupation, and masks reflected its importance. Thus, a white mask might be worn to attract the power of ancestral spirits because white symbolized dead flesh. In this Bayaka puberty mask from the Congo (Fig. 286), the color white signifies the death of the child and the initiation of the young adult in community life.

Sculpture in Clay, Metal, and Ivory Although most African sculpture is wood, Africans also used other materials. The earliest sculptures are small clay heads from Nok in Nigeria, made about 2000 years ago. Metalworking was known about 500 B.C. From the 14th century A.D. rulers in the kingdoms of Ifé and Benin in Nigeria commissioned cast bronze and brass relief plaques and portrait heads. These were realistic representations of rulers. The Benin people also worked in ivory. If you closely examine this 16th-century ivory miniature mask for a belt, you will see tiny heads of Portuguese soldiers in the scalloped beard and

above left: 287. Belt mask, from Nigeria. c. 1400. Ivory, height 9⅜" (24 cm). Metropolitan Museum of Art, New York (Michael C. Rockefeller Collection of Primitive Art, gift of Nelson A. Rockefeller, 1972).

above: 288. Amedeo Modigliani. *Head.* c. 1915. Limestone, 22¼ × 5 × 14¾" (57 × 13 × 37 cm). Museum of Modern Art, New York (gift of Abby Aldrich Rockefeller in memory of Mrs. Cornelius J. Sullivan).

pierced headdress. Thus with typical wit and inventiveness, the African artist created a work of art in which he expressed his feelings about the Portuguese invasion of his homeland in the 15th century (Fig. 287).

African Influences on 20th-Century Art In the 19th century, European traders began to bring African sculpture home with them. Artists in Paris soon discovered these exotic objects. Searching for new ways to depict the world and express their emotions, they were impressed by the uncanny ability of African sculptors to emphasize the essentials of a subject while simplifying and distorting it. Picasso, Braque, and Fernand Léger (1881–1955), influenced by African sculpture, developed Cubism. Some of the distorted figures of Picasso's *Guernica* (Fig. 22) certainly derive from African masks and figures. Few artists were more deeply moved by African art than Modigliani, who deliberately abstracted and elongated his stone heads and figures (Fig. 288).

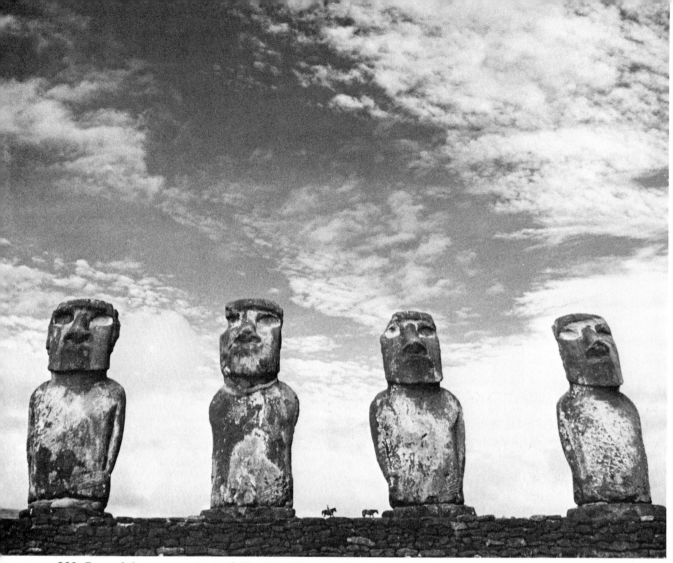

289. Four of the seven statues of Ahu-Akivi, Easter Island.

Oceania

The islands of the south Pacific Ocean are grouped into three cultural areas: Micronesia (including the Caroline and Marshall Islands), Melanesia (including New Guinea), and Polynesia (including Hawaii, New Zealand, and Easter Island). Sometimes Australia is considered part of Oceania. Although each area and island had a distinctive culture, many elements were common to all.

Most Oceanic peoples came originally from the Asian mainland and traditionally belonged to extended families and clans. They farmed and fished for a living and worshiped their ancestors and other spirits. Since wood was plentiful, it was the most common material for building tools and war implements, often fitted with blades of shell or stone. Each island had its particular form of war club, all of them lethal. Wood was also used for carved stools, house posts, and figures of the gods.

Oceanic art objects, such as carved and painted shells, reflect the constant warfare between the islands. Many

were part of elaborate religious ceremonies. Most art was made to be seen in action—masks moving with the rhythms of ceremonial dancers, weapons wielded in battle, the carved paddles and prows of Maori canoes moving over water.

The famous heads on Easter Island, made from volcanic tufa, are an exception to the liveliness of most Oceanic art (Fig. 289). These large, brooding sculptures, originally set on ceremonial stone platforms, were discovered on Easter Sunday by 19th-century missionaries. The islanders had then lost all recollection of the origins of the sculptures, and archaeologists are still uncertain of the religion they served.

Pre-Columbian America

In prehistoric times Asian nomads crossed the land mass (now the Bering Straits) into the area of modern Alaska and gradually filtered down into North, Central, and South America. In the pre-Columbian period the Eskimo and the

Indians developed distinctive cultures shaped by geographic conditions. They created civilizations in the most prosperous regions, including what are today Mexico and Peru. The arrival of Europeans in the 16th century resulted in the destruction of most Indian traditions.

North America Eskimo in the North lived by hunting and fishing, moving from one area to another with the seasons and the migrations of game. Life was hard, yet artists found time to carve utensils and imaginative masks from driftwood and small figures and harpoon heads from ivory, bone, and stone.

Indians along the Pacific Northwest Coast lived in settled villages. Abundant supplies of fish, wild plants, and berries allowed them some leisure to build large wooden plank houses and carve boats, masks, and furnishings. Each family or clan had a set of songs and myths and a heraldic crest, or **totem,** which was displayed on its possessions. Tree trunks were carved in the shapes of these animals to form poles, which told the lineage of the family, somewhat like a family tree or a house directory (Fig. 290).

Dugout canoes, so important to a fishing and whaling economy, were shaped with stone tools and sometimes decorated with carved figures of protective spirits. The complex multiple masks of the Northwest Coast are among the most arresting in the world. Often they illustrated myths enacted by the dancers who wore them. Some were sophisticated masks within masks. During a

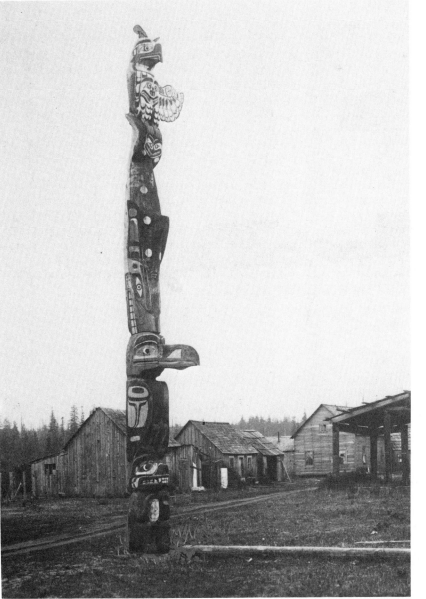

290. Totem pole, Cape Mudge,
Vancouver Island,
British Columbia.
Early 20th century.

dance, the wearer could expose several images, one after the other, by pulling the strings that operated the hinges. Other masks had moving parts that made noises. Most of these carved and painted masks were designed to be seen in ritual by the light of a flickering fire to heighten their effectiveness (Fig. 138).

The Northwest Coast Indians also carved utensils such as the oversize ladle (Fig. 127) used in a community potlatch ceremony. These unique gatherings were ritual occasions for feasting, poetry, and dancing at which a person of rank gained prestige by giving food, drink, blankets, tools, and utensils, sometimes to an entire invited village. While the custom inspired much art, it also ruined village economies.

Indians in the West, relying mainly on hunting and gathering, wove delicate baskets in intricate patterns that, like geometricized textiles, reflected the weaving process (Fig. 291). The Navajo in the Southwest, who herded sheep brought by the Spanish, wove distinctive blankets.

Indians in the Southwest settled in communities called pueblos and irrigated fields of maize. The pueblos, as we saw in Chapter 9, were cliff dwellings (Fig. 180) or freestanding adobe buildings built on mesas or near riverside fields. Each one had a **kiva,** or underground sacred room, symbolizing the underworld, where the Indians believed their ancestors originated and they themselves would return. Part of the kiva ritual included sand painting, done by pouring different-colored sands on the floor in traditional patterns. Such ceremonies reaffirmed the contact of people to the earth and the brevity of the human lifespan. After every ritual the sand painting was destroyed.

Each pueblo also had its own distinctive pottery. San Idelfonso, for example, produced black pots painstakingly polished with a stone while slightly damp and then fired. Other pueblos made red pottery with intricate geometric designs painted in black and white. After the arrival of the Spanish, the Pueblo and Navajo Indians learned to make silver and turquoise jewelry, artworks by which they are still known today.

Mesoamerica In much of Mexico and Central America, a region usually referred to as Mesoamerica, a number of distinctive civilizations developed from the 6th century B.C. to the 16th century A.D. Basic ethnic similarities among cultures suggest that they all derived from common racial stocks, among which was the Olmec civilization in eastern Mexico between 1000 and 600 B.C. Fertility figures with details similar to those on Oriental artifacts have been found that date from 1000 to 600 B.C. (Fig. 121). Somewhat later are enormous Olmec stone heads.

Peoples of Mesoamerica included the Toltec in the north, the Maya in the southeast, the Zapotec and Mixtec in the southwest, and the people of Teotihuacán and the Aztec, the last best known because of their dramatic conquest by Spain, in the central Valley of Mexico. All their economies were based on growing maize. Since there are extremes of climate throughout the region, the Indians probably felt overwhelmed by the forces of nature, personified as gods, on which their crops depended. Their efforts to appease the gods directed their social, political, and artistic life.

Most of these peoples built walled stone courts for highly competitive ritual ball games in which the ball symbolized the sun. To encourage the sun god to make his daily journey across the heavens, Aztec priests made sacrifices of prisoners of war to supply him with human blood. The rain god was also important. Some groups believed that his attention could be attracted by the tears of sacrificed children. The Toltec and Aztec worshipped Quetzalcoatl, a symbol of the life force represented by an image that combined the beautiful feathered quetzal bird and the coatl serpent.

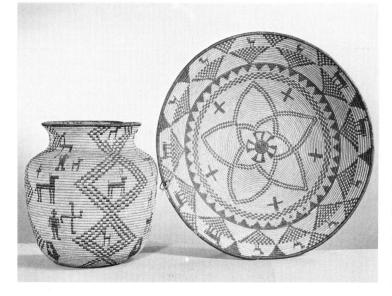

291. Apache basket and tray. c. 1899. Coiled basketry; basket: height 13½″ (34 cm), width 13½″ (34 cm); tray: height 4″ (10 cm), width 22½″ (57 cm). American Museum of Natural History, New York.

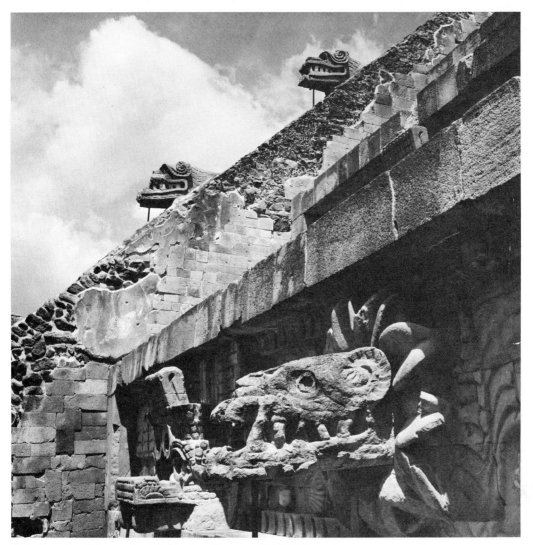

292. Temple of Quetzalcoatl, Mexico City. A.D. 300–700.

ARCHITECTURE The Indians of Mesoamerica were not so much concerned with enclosing space as with building impressive stepped pyramids with a temple on top as the focus of religious rituals. The pyramids were faced with stone that was often ornately carved or covered with painted stucco. The pyramids stood in the midst of ceremonial centers surrounded by palaces for official functions. The masses probably occupied simple adobe houses on the outskirts. Teotihuacán, however, near present-day Mexico City, covered more than 20 acres (8.9 hectares) and supported a large population. Its most imposing structure is the 300-foot- (65-meter-) high Pyramid of the Sun, still standing. The city flourished for about six hundred years, attracting sculptors, painters, potters, and other artists.

All these Mesoamerican groups followed a similar calendar based on cycles of 52 years. The Maya kept annals for hundreds of years. Each cycle usually was celebrated by building, usually a temple or pyramid over an already existing one. Memorial stelae were set up in the plazas to mark the time of dedication, as modern cornerstones date Western buildings. The Spanish conquerors, following Indian practice, built their churches over Indian holy places. By digging through layers of construction, archaeologists have been able to trace a history of Mesoamerican architecture. Scholars have correlated the Mesoamerican calendar with that of the West so we can study Mesoamerican architecture in relation to our own dating systems.

SCULPTURE AND OTHER ARTS Much Mesoamerican sculpture was architectural—reliefs of gods and priests and geometric designs on pyramids and temples as in the Temple of Quetzalcoatl at Teotihuacán (Fig. 292). There were also small stone and clay figures of gods, humans (Fig. 121), and animals. Filled with vitality, they give us a glimpse of

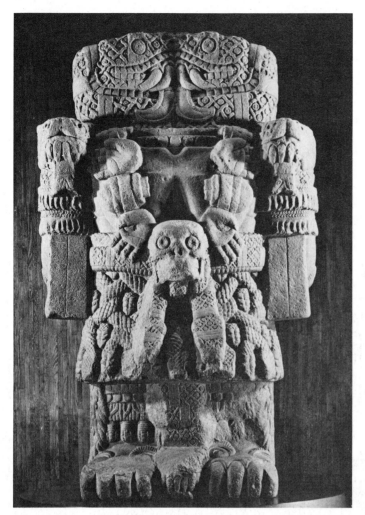

293. Coatlicue (goddess of earth and death). Aztec. 15th century. Basalt, height 8'3" (2.51 m). National Museum of Anthropology, Mexico City.

the daily life of the people. Arresting is a figure of the ferocious Aztec earth and death goddess, which reflects the warlike Aztec's belief in the need for human sacrifice to satisfy the sun god. Her head consists of two serpents facing each other. She wears a necklace of hands and hearts with a pendant skull, and her skirt is made of intertwined skulls and serpents (Fig. 293).

The Maya and other peoples painted murals of warriors and religious scenes inside palaces and tombs. Other forms of painting were pottery and accordion-folded, bark paper books (codices). Beautifully designed jewelry of gold and jade and ritual objects of inlaid shell, turquoise, and other stones attest to the great skill of Mesoamerican craftsmen. They also wove fabrics (Fig. 133) and made elaborate feather mosaic headdresses and cloaks for priests and nobles.

South America In the Andean region of South America other Indian peoples were raising maize and building ceremonial centers with pyramid temples before 800 B.C. Somewhat later, pottery, weaving, and goldwork reached a highly sophisticated level. The Paracas and Nazca peoples and their descendants on the south Peruvian coast wove and embroidered magnificent garments with colorful stylized patterns of animals and divinities. To the north, Mochican potters made clay vessels molded in the shapes of people and animals or painted with animals or scenes. Mochica, Quimbaya, and Chimú craftsmen made fine gold jewelry set with turquoise, and gold cups. The Chimú and the Inca built great cities, such as the 15th-century Inca stronghold of Machu Picchu high in the Andes (Fig. 294). The Incas, who ruled a large empire at the time of the Spanish conquest, constructed large plazas, temples, and palaces of massive stone blocks.

Although the Spanish disrupted the pre-Columbian civilizations for centuries, many present-day artists work close to the artistic mainstream of their ancestors.

The Islamic World

The vast area of North Africa and the Middle East is dominated by Islam, the religion founded by the prophet Mohammed in Arabia in the early 7th century A.D. In its first forty years the new faith spread through the Mediterranean world, drawing more converts than Christianity had won in the previous six centuries. Devout Muslim warriors occupied Spain in the 8th century and in the 16th and 17th centuries controlled northern India. Medieval Christian Crusaders, who drove the Muslims from Spain and fought them in the Holy Land, learned much from their highly civilized adversaries.

Architecture Throughout the Islamic world the Muslims built **mosques** as houses of worship. A mosque usually consisted of a courtyard and fountain for ritual washing and a spacious columned or vaulted hall where men knelt on rugs in prayer. Most mosques had **minarets,** or towers, from which the faithful were called to prayer five times a day. In the great 9th-century mosque built by the caliph Mutawakkil in Samarra (in modern Iraq), the largest ever

294. Machu Picchu, Peru. c. 15th century.

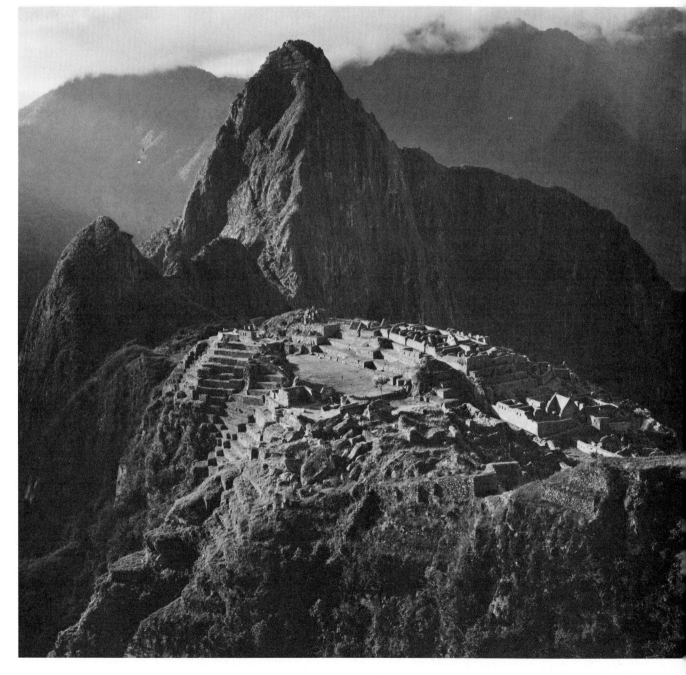

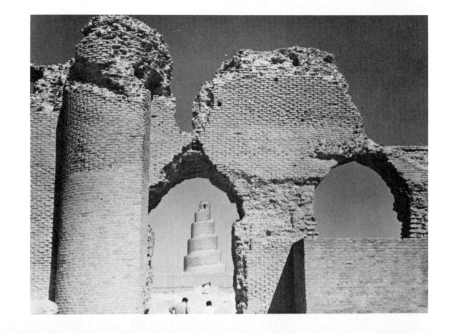

right: 295. Mosque of
Mutawakkil,
Samarra, Iraq.
A.D. 848–52.

below: 296. Court of the
Lions, Alhambra, Granada,
Spain. 1309–54.
115 × 66′
(35.05 × 20.12 m).

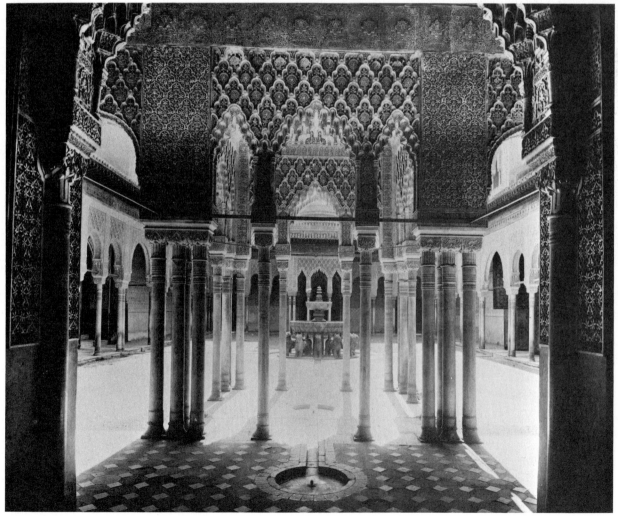

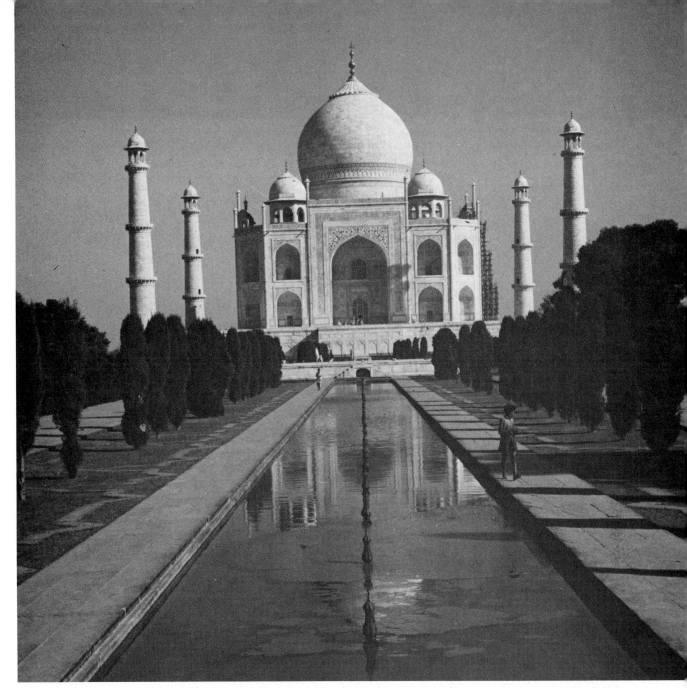

297. Taj Mahal, Agra, India. 17th century. 186′ (56.69 m) square, height of dome 187′ (57 m).

built, you may recognize the influence of the ancient Mesopotamian ziggurat (Fig. 209) in the minaret, which is encircled by a steep ramp (Fig. 295).

The Muslims also built religious schools, palaces, and tombs. One of the most magnificent palaces is the 14th-century Alhambra, or red castle, in the Moorish city of Granada in southern Spain. Its lion court (Fig. 296), enlivened by a fountain, is surrounded by brilliantly tiled walls and an arcade of slender columns supporting high arches in a lacelike wall. The Alhambra set a style copied throughout the Islamic world.

Probably the best-known Islamic structure is the Taj Mahal in Agra, India, built in the 17th century by the Mughal emperor Shah Jahan as a loving memorial to his favorite wife (Fig. 297). The onion-domed, white marble tomb, standing on a square platform with slender minarets at each corner, seems to float above its reflecting pool.

Other Art Forms Because orthodox Muslim tradition forbade representation of the human figure in religious art, there is little Islamic sculpture. Most figure painting in delicate miniature illustrated secular books by Persian court

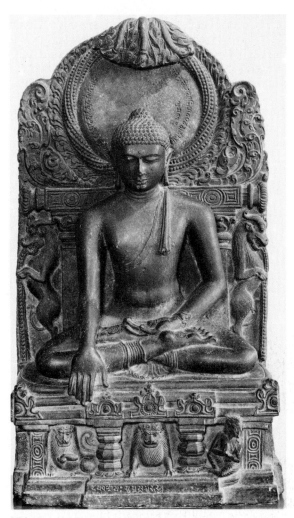

298. Seated Buddha. Bihar, India; Pāla period, 9th century A.D. Chlorite; height 33″ (84 cm), width 17½″ (44 cm). Asian Art Museum of San Francisco (Avery Brundage Collection).

artists. The Muslims excelled, however, in nonrepresentational decoration, which appeared on mosques and other buildings, in copies of the Koran, and on glazed pottery and tile, metalwork, glass, and rugs. Some motifs were geometric; others were flowing abstractions of flowers and plants called **arabesques.** Much favored were inscriptions in Arabic from the Koran (Fig. 7).

India

Indian art was influenced by Muslim art, but it had a strong native tradition as well. Civilization flourished in Mohenjo-Daro on the Indus River in the Indian subcontinent as early as 3000 B.C. Indo-Aryans from the northwest invaded the area about 1800 B.C. They brought with them the Vedic religion that is at the root of later Brahmanism and Hinduism. Common to all three religions is the view that men and women are part of nature, which leads to the Brahmanist belief that everyone must go through cycles of re-

birth but that all beings are ultimately one. Such an outlook permits enjoyment of the senses, a view that is reflected in the art of Hindu India.

Buddhist Art In the 6th century B.C. Prince Siddhartha gave up wealth and family to seek the enlightenment that would release him from the cycle of rebirths. Having become the Enlightened One, or Buddha, he preached that only through renouncing worldly attachments could a person escape rebirth and win salvation, or Nirvana. His saintly teaching inspired an order of monks, who wandered through India begging in symbolic identification with the Buddha.

Early Buddhists built stupas, domed monuments holding relics, such as Stupa No. 1 at Sanchī (Fig. 174). Stupas stood on platforms surrounded by walls or railings and large gateways. On top of the domes were finials, like small umbrellas, signifying royalty. The rails and gates were often carved with reliefs of scenes from the Buddha's life.

They never portrayed the Buddha himself but used symbols such as his footprint or the wheel of the laws of conduct that he taught.

Over the centuries many Buddhists came to believe that Buddha was divine. They built cave temples in his honor and carved free-standing statues, showing him teaching or in meditation (Fig. 298). His gentle smile and halo suggest saintliness. His long ear lobes show how attentively he listens to the secrets of the cosmos, and the jewel in his forehead represents the third eye of inner vision. The figure is serene, far beyond sensual pleasure and other attachments. As Buddhism spread to Southeast Asia and north to Tibet, China, and Japan, painters and sculptors adapted this Indian concept of the Buddha in their own images.

Hindu Art Although Buddhism became a major world religion, it did not persist in India. Hinduism, which fused with Brahmanism and incorporated some features of Buddhism, had much greater appeal, perhaps because of its delight in the physical world, which dominates Hindu imagery.

The Hindus built large temple complexes, which included a cella, or chamber, for the god surmounted by a tower, assembly halls, ritual baths, and loggias (Fig. 299). These structures were often completely covered with miles of relief sculpture of intertwining human, animal, and floral motifs expressing the rhythm of life. Leaving no surface undecorated, the sculptors carved a lavish testament to their belief in the unity of all living forms. Because sexual

299. Hindu temple compound. 8th–13th centuries A.D.

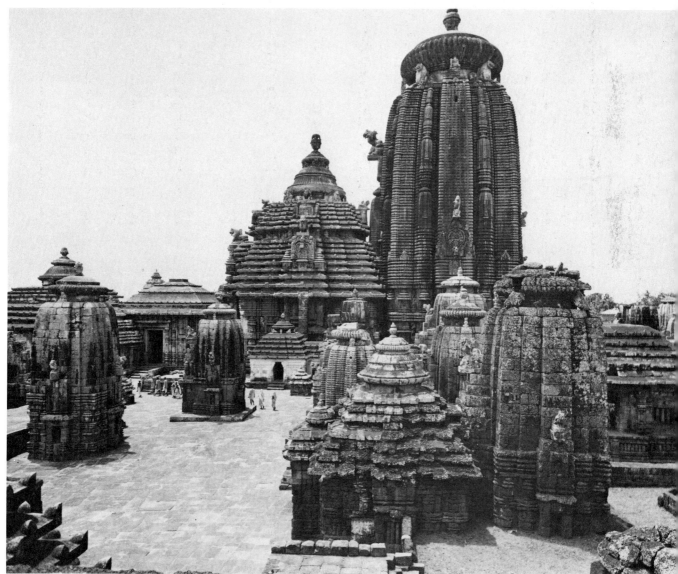

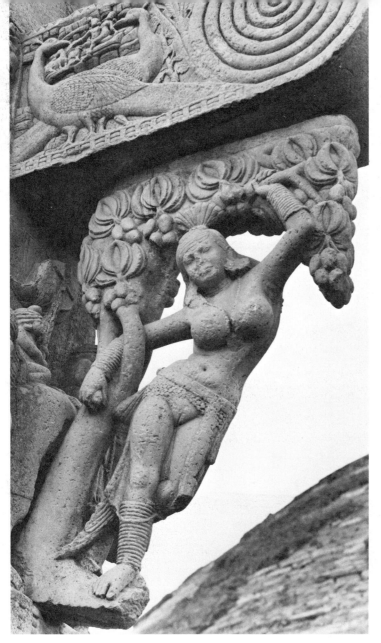

300. *Yakshi* (tree goddess),
from the East Gate of the Great
Stūpa, Sānchi, India.
Early Andhra period,
1st century B.C.

desire was a revered part of life and physical union was believed to be one way to attain unity with the gods and the universe, erotic subjects were frequent. The exaggerated curves of a Hindu tree goddess also express the rhythm that pulses through creation (Fig. 300).

China and Japan

Because Chinese civilization greatly influenced that of Japan, we will review Chinese and Japanese art side by side. In both countries, society was structured into rigid classes controlled by the emperor. Daily life was ruled by the extended family, respect for the ancestors, and custom. With this conservatism, art styles remained much the same for long periods. Artists intentionally copied past work. A

detail from a scroll of the five planets and twenty-eight constellations is an 11th- or 12th-century copy of a 6th-century masterwork (Fig. 148).

Architecture   Traditional buildings of the Far East used post-and-lintel construction and were made of wood. Conservative architecture changed little over the centuries. Chinese temples, palaces, and houses, as we know from clay models found in tombs of about 200 B.C. and from later paintings, consisted of a complex of low buildings built around a series of courts. Each building stood on a masonry platform. Columns topped by brackets, all carved and painted, supported the tiled roof. The curtain walls of plaster over bamboo could be adjusted according to climate. Multistoried pagodas, originally used as watch-

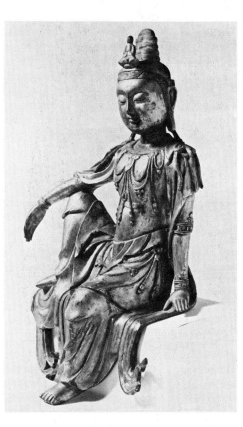

301. Seated *Shui-Yüeh* (Water-Moon).
Kuan Yin. Late Yüan or early Ming,
14th century A.D. Gilt bronze;
height 13″ (33 cm), width 8″ (20 cm).
Asian Art Museum of San Francisco
(Avery Brundage Collection).

towers, became Buddhist shrines. At first of wood, then of brick, they had spires based on the finials on Indian stupas. Monumental gates recalled stupa gates.

Japan accepted Chinese architecture along with Buddhism imported from China via Korea in the 6th century. Japanese temple complexes such as the Horyuji in Nara include pillared halls, a pagoda (Fig. 179), and wooden gates. Japanese craftsmen developed wooden architecture to its finest expression. The house or palace with its sliding paper screens for walls, opening onto a deep porch and garden, permitted great flexibility in interior design and the integration of indoor and outdoor space. Through the work of Frank Lloyd Wright, who built the Imperial Hotel in Tokyo in the 1920s, concepts of Japanese domestic architecture influenced the modern glass and steel architecture of the West, as in Mies's German Pavilion (Fig. 161) and Philip Johnson's glass house (Fig. 162).

Sculpture Chinese and Japanese sculpture was generally religious. Early examples were related to tombs. The Chinese carved reliefs on tomb walls and later in the 7th and 8th centuries filled tombs with lifelike glazed pottery figurines of courtiers, horses, and camels. Early Japanese tombs of about the 3rd to 6th centuries were guarded by large hollow clay Haniwa figures of people and animals set into the ground.

Buddhism and its accompanying Indian mythology was a major influence. From the 5th to the 8th centuries the

Chinese carved Buddha figures in the walls of caves, some of them 70 feet (21 meters) tall. Their austere attitudes emphasized the other-worldly qualities of the Buddha. Sculptors made smaller, more graceful images in gilded bronze or wood for temple altars. Some were of **Boddhisattvas** (Buddhas to be). One Boddhisattva developed into Kuan Yin, the Chinese goddess of mercy, who shares many of the same warm qualities of the Christian Madonna and is often shown with a child in her lap (Fig. 301). The Japanese made Buddhas of wood and bronze and realistic wooden portraits of guardian spirits and priests.

Painting The Chinese and Japanese considered painting and calligraphy the most important forms of artistic expression. Both arts demanded great skill with the brush, requiring years of training. In calligraphy the quality of the brush strokes and the formation of the characters became as important as the story or poem they conveyed (Fig. 32). Most Chinese painters were also poets (Fig. 148).

Except for early murals in caves and other temples, most Oriental paintings were on vertical or horizontal scrolls. The latter, held in the hand and unrolled a little at a time, allowed the viewer to travel through the painting, moving from scene to scene. Some Oriental paintings depicted the natural world, often in Japan verging on cartoons. Others, under the serene influence of Buddhism and Chinese Confucianism and Taoism, were more philosophical. They were less concerned with details of outward reality than with the essence of an object or a scene in order to arouse a response in the viewer.

Chinese scroll painting, which began in the 4th century and flowered in the 7th and 8th centuries, included elegant scenes of court life, realistic horses, and the first landscapes. In the Sung dynasty in the 12th and 13th centuries many gentlemen retired to the country where they painted soft, poetic landscapes inspired by the Taoist search for unity in nature. In their watercolor scrolls tiny human figures seem overwhelmed by the grandeur of mountains, forests, and seas. Sung painters worked in gray ink washes and a few spontaneous, brisk brush strokes, reflecting the Ch'an ideal of flashes of sudden enlightenment after meditation. The oneness of the universe was also a theme of Ch'an (better known as Japanese Zen) Buddhism. "The branch drooping in the fog, the butterfly on a blossom, the beggar in the filth of the courtyard—they are all Buddha," said the painter Hsia Kuei (c. 1195–1224).

Japanese painting shows strong Chinese Buddhist influence but is infused with a native vitality and decorative quality all its own. Scrolls of the 9th to 12th centuries, inspired by Chinese art, depict Buddha in a delightful but quite worldly Western paradise surrounded by lovely Boddhisattvas playing musical instruments and dancing. Other scrolls portray terrifying Buddhist guardian deities. Later scrolls present colorful scenes narrating tales from Japanese history or literature or social satires. In the 14th to 16th centuries, Japanese Zen Buddhist painters, influenced by Chinese Ch'an art, used a few quickly splashed lines and washes of ink to express their responses to the natural world and their experiences with Zen. The landscapes of Sesshu (Fig. 32), noted for strong brush work, brilliantly sparse imagery, and consummate artistry in handling ink on paper, show us why he holds such a high place in Japanese art. Expressive Japanese brush work and calligraphy influenced the 20th-century American painters Mark Tobey (b. 1890) and Franz Kline (1910–1962). In the 16th century, decorative folding screens in bold designs and vivid colors used as room partitions were a distinctively Japanese art.

Woodcuts The art of printing from wood blocks developed in China in the 6th century. Inexpensive images of the Buddha were printed for popular distribution. Japan transformed the technique in the 8th century into an expression of its own culture. From the 17th century on, wood-block printing was a mass medium all could afford. Illustrations of folktales appeared in widespread inexpensive editions, revealing humor and love of landscape. Eighteenth-century woodcuts portrayed figures of the entertainment world, especially actors and courtesans. Utamaro's stylized versions of courtesans (Fig. 92) were as unrealistic as many of today's fashion illustrations. Eighteenth-century artists such as Harunobu (1724–1770), Hokusai, and Hiroshige developed the woodcut to a high level of artistic expression while turning out hundreds of prints of genre scenes and landscapes to satisfy the public demand for the latest nov-

elty (Fig. 91). The popularity of the woodcut depended on the styles of the moment, and a new hairstyle could suddenly outdate a whole edition of prints. When these woodcuts reached Europe in the mid-19th century, their flat shapes and diagonal composition profoundly affected French Impressionist painters such as Monet, Pissarro, and Degas. They also affected Toulouse-Lautrec and the American James Abbott McNeill Whistler (1834–1903).

Decorative Arts In addition to its painting, sculpture, and architecture, the Far East has a long tradition of decorative arts of the highest quality. Pottery and porcelain, silk brocades, ivory and jade carvings, lacquer, and metalwork have been treasured in the Far East for centuries and later also in the West.

Chinese bronze ritual vessels are alive with stylized animal forms. The background and figures are often decorated with **lei-wen,** spiral designs signifying the clouds, thunder, and water necessary to an agricultural people. The vital designs engage the Westerner.

Ceramics evolved into a high art in both China and Japan. From earliest times, clay pottery in China was associated with religion. The bowl or jar, made from "divine earth" and hardened by "divine fire," itself became a religious expression. From a Neolithic earthenware pot decorated with spirals to subtle monochrome Ting (Fig. 131) celadon platters to elegant blue-flowered white porcelain vases of the Ming period in the 14th century, Chinese ceramics have shown extraordinary sensitivity to shape, color, glaze, and decoration. Japanese potters adapted Chinese techniques and designs. Oriental porcelains were imitated by Western potters from the 17th century on.

The Japanese also developed a rough, simpler pottery, influenced by Zen Buddhism, as we saw in Chapter 7. Its spontaneous shapes, variety, earth-colored glazes, and quickly brushed-on decoration has appealed greatly to 20th-century potters in the West (Fig. 132).

Because Zen Buddhists considered ordinary living to be as important as the spiritual, many took delight in the process of making pots, stressing that uniformity and repetition were fatal to imagination. The Zen tea ceremony, a religious ritual, traditionally takes place in a simple teahouse designed to recreate the peace and purity one might feel alone by a mountain waterfall. Everything used in the ceremony is intended to induce serenity. The subtle response of the tea drinker to the shape of a bowl, the sound of the bamboo whisk stirring the tea, or the color of a flower in a vase characterizes for us the essential difference between the art of the Far East and the art of the West.

By the 19th century, after two thousand years of largely Greek and Roman inspiration, many Western artists began to question their goals. The spiritual essence of much Oriental art profoundly affected Western concepts, while from Africa came part of the Cubist impulse for Picasso and the others. Beyond the Church and our classical heritage existed a whole world we knew little about. The art of our 20th century took part of its legacy from that other world.

EXERCISES AND ACTIVITIES

1. Explain why the term "primitive" does not accurately describe the cultures of Africa, Oceania, and pre-Columbian America. Working with wood, clay, or stone, create an artwork that echoes the work of one of these areas.
2. Discuss the impact of African art on the art of the Western world. Give examples of this influence.
3. Describe African artists' use of certain types of exaggeration and abstraction for expressive purposes. Create a carving, a papier-mâché mask, or a piece of jewelry using similar expressive tools.
4. On a simple loom made from a picture frame with yarn stretched between nails, weave a wall hanging using American Indian designs.
5. Fashion a clay pot using the coil method. If a kiln is not available, air dry the pot and paint it with poster paints using designs inspired by Indian motifs.
6. Create in clay or soap a three-dimensional figure reminiscent of the art of the Orient.

PART IV

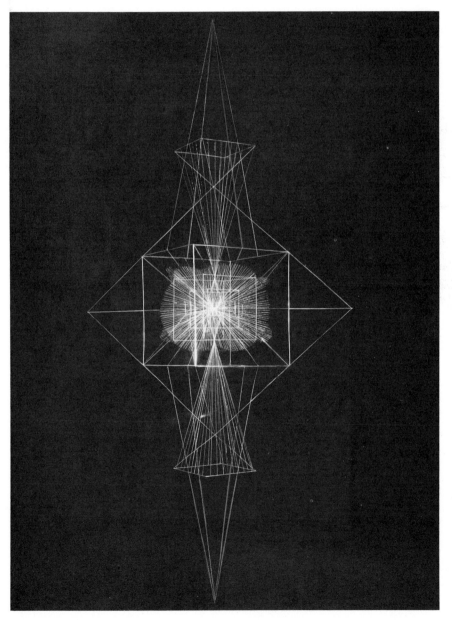

302. Richard Lippold.
*Variation Number 7:
Full Moon.* 1949–50.
Brass rods, nickel-
chromium, and stainless-
steel wire; height
10 × 6′ (3.05 × 1.83 m).
Museum of Modern Art,
New York (Mrs. Simon
Guggenheim Fund).

The Modern Age

The Age of Reason promised to resolve all problems through the application of a scientific approach. With the growing revolutionary spirit in Europe and America, the modern world was born.

Confidence in science and progress ran high. Industrialists and the growing middle class lived comfortably side by side. The United States survived a Civil War. For the lower classes, however, industrialization often meant low wages, uncertain employment, and disagreeable living conditions in crowded, dirty factory towns. The traditions of a rural society and the comforts of religion were often destroyed for them, and socialism, anarchism, and labor movements provided poor substitutes.

As the 20th century replaced the 19th, world war, economic exploitation, and dehumanizing labor enveloped many who crowded into smoky towns. The rate of change has accelerated enormously over the last eighty years. Advances in technology reflected in our art (Fig. 302)—airplanes, cinema, television, and computers—follow so quickly that we reel from the shock of rapid change. Our slow biological rhythms are upset by the speed of modern transport and communication. The mass media help to create a society to which millions are persuaded to conform, while their survival is threatened by its pace. Much of the world still faces famine. Wealthy countries find that they can no longer deny entire nations or races an equal share in the profits of their labor. Our natural resources are being depleted, and even remote areas are affected by our abuse of this earth. For example, penguins in Anarctica have been found with insecticide residues within, while satellite photographs show huge smudges of smog covering continents. Against this background of change we will view the art of modern times.

16 Revolution and the Modern World

Revolution is the larva of civilization.

VICTOR HUGO

By the mid-18th century, absolute monarchies ruled almost everywhere. Aristocrats were insulated from the real world where most people lived in abject poverty. But the farther the wealthy retreated to their country estates, the stronger a revolutionary spirit grew through Europe and the New World. The modern age began with revolution.

Age of Revolution

As the 18th century drew to a close, the French ruling classes retreated from signs of the shaky monarchy and isolated themselves from the needs of their subjects. Despite the example of the American Revolution against British rule in 1776, most were unprepared for the violence of the French Revolution in 1789, which cost the king and scores of nobles their lives. A new spirit of democracy and reform was sweeping the land, to which many artists were sympathetic.

Neoclassicism Long before the Revolution, Rococo art was displaced by another style. Rediscovery of the buried cities of Pompeii and Herculaneum in the 1730s and 1740s and their study through archaeology led to renewed interest in classical Greece and Rome. The **Neoclassical** movement emerged, which, combined with the new scientific approach, appealed to intellectuals, who believed in the power of reason to uplift society. The style eventually became associated with the republican ideals of the Revolution and the early career of Napoleon Bonaparte.

The Neoclassical style stressed straight lines and classical ornament in architecture and decorative arts. Neoclassical paintings emphasized balanced formalism, precise linear drawing, and often classical subjects. In England, Neoclassicism appeared in Georgian architecture and in the interior decoration of great houses by Robert Adam (1728–1792), who made his own interpretation of classical motifs. The Swiss-born Angelica Kauffman (1741–1807) painted sentimental scenes in Adam houses. Neoclassicism also affected American architecture, for example, Monticello, Thomas Jefferson's home in Charlottesville, Virginia (Fig. 303), and most government buildings in Washington.

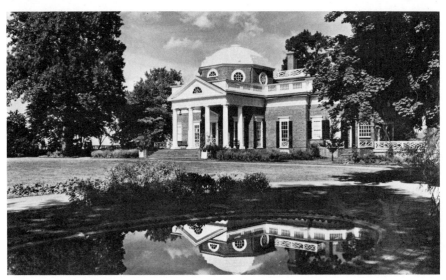

303. Thomas Jefferson. Monticello, Charlottesville, Va. 1770–84; 1796–1809.

The most prominent Neoclassical painter was Jacques Louis David (1748–1825), who celebrated in his work the French Revolution and the rise of Napoleon. David portrayed classical themes as dictated by the Academy while expressing republican ideals and the moral strengths of Greece and Rome. In *The Death of Socrates* (Fig. 304) he retold the self-sacrifice of the ancient Greek philosopher who preferred to die than to give up the freedom to teach what he believed. In a formal composition he shows Socrates addressing his followers in prison. Vertical and horizontal shapes dominate the rigidly composed painting, giving it a structured quality of shallow space that may not seem revolutionary by our standards. David, however, felt that these classical forms were the best way to express the ideals of liberty, equality, and fraternity that were the watchwords of the Revolution. His emphasis on two-dimensionality became increasingly important in later 19th-century painting.

Goya Belonging both to the Age of Reason and the Age of Revolution was Francisco Goya, one of the greatest painters of all time. He was a skillful portraitist in the tradition of Velázquez, adept at depicting both the personality and fine costumes of the Spanish aristocracy and the court. He was most popular with his subjects, who apparently did not realize that beneath the elegance of his paintings he was commenting on court vanity and corruption.

Goya witnessed Napoleon's invasion of Spain in 1808. The artist depicted the violence and human capacity for evil in a series of etchings, *The Disasters of War,* which presented an uncompromising view of slaughter, rape, and destruction. Some of his paintings delved into the same themes, such as *Execution of the Madrileños on May 3, 1808* (Fig. 33), which marks an incident of the war. This work strongly influenced Edouard Manet (1832–1883) in France a half century later.

Disillusioned in his last years, Goya lived in seclusion and produced dark images of horror and despair. They might be taken as indications of the greed of the court feeding on its children, the masses (Fig. 305); or possibly as works of the artist's old age, they were an allegorical reference to time, which consumes all.

Romanticism Reacting against the early 18th-century confidence in reason and the artificiality of court life was the **Romantic** movement, which began in the late 18th

304. Jacques Louis David. *The Death of Socrates.* 1787. Oil on canvas, 4′3″ × 6′5¼″ (1.3 × 1.96 m). Metropolitan Museum of Art, New York (Wolfe Fund, 1931).

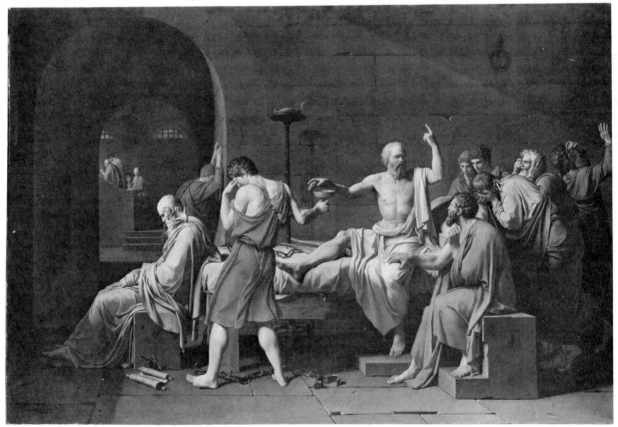

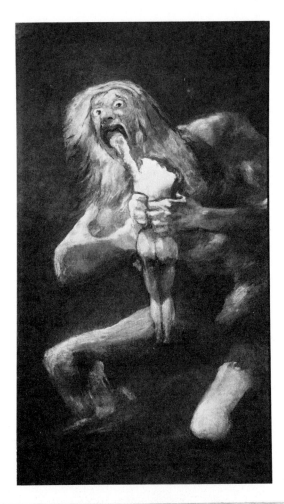

century and continued into the 19th century. It was characterized by the great value placed on strong emotion and a fascination with untamed nature, country folk in natural settings, and picturesque or exotic themes.

ENGLISH LANDSCAPE Romanticism flourished in England, which was not torn by revolution and had little need for an art of propaganda. John Constable (1776–1837) devoted himself to the study of nature. His quiet English landscapes, painted in rich earth tones, shocked people accustomed to pretentious academic art. Constable said he wanted to capture the "light—dews—breezes—bloom—and freshness" of the English countryside. He sketched outdoors, and his quick studies are bolder than the paintings that he later composed in his studio. Nevertheless, he tried to keep the freshness of nature in his work and to portray what he saw, without contriving compositions to fit academic rules. *The Haywain* (Fig. 306), typical of Constable's rural subject matter, was painted with a real love of the countryside and an ability to show atmospheric effects with a free brush stroke. The idea of landscape without allegorical or religious references attracted other artists, and the technique paved the way for the Impressionists, at midcentury.

left: 305. Francisco Goya. *Saturn Devouring One of His Sons.* c. 1821. Fresco detached on canvas, 4′9½″ × 2′8⅛″ (1.46 × 0.83 m). Prado, Madrid.

below: 306. John Constable. *The Haywain.* 1821. Oil on canvas, 4′2½″ × 6′1″ (1.28 × 1.85 m). National Gallery, London, courtesy of the Trustees.

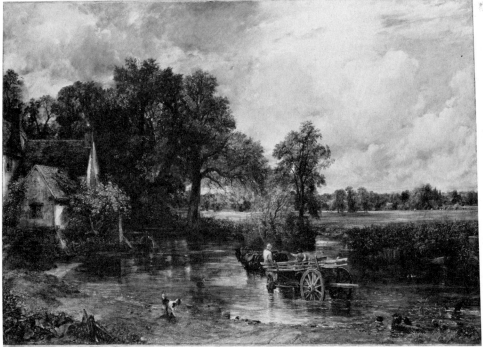

Another landscape painter, Turner, had visions of painting the "unpaintable" and was possessed with a determination to record the changes of nature's atmosphere. In many ways, Turner was ahead of his age, reducing air, water, and even fire to undetailed color arrangements. When Turner watched the fire that destroyed the houses of Parliament in 1834, he was inspired to paint a series of remarkable pictures of the disaster. Images of flames, smoke, reflections in the river, and crowds of people watching all dissolve into one another. Occasionally applying paint with a palette knife, Turner suggests turbulence with spontaneous, bold streaks and dabs, as in his scenes of Venice (Fig. 79).

Turner was a forerunner of the Impressionists and was rediscovered by two of them, Pissarro and Monet, after his death. But Turner was concerned with the poetic quality of light, with more interest in abstract patterns than were the Impressionists, mainly concerned with the effects of light on objects. A poem by Turner about Switzerland, where it was fashionable for English artists and lords and ladies to go to contemplate the grandeur of the Alps, tells us a good deal about his attitude toward nature.

> . . . its pine clad forests
> And towering glaciers fall,
>   the work of ages
> Crashing through all: . . .

FRENCH ROMANTICISM In the spirit of Romanticism the French painters Théodore Géricault (1791–1824) and Eugène Delacroix chose faraway and exotic subjects. Géricault's *The Raft of the "Medusa"* (Fig. 307) was also an indictment of mismanagement and corruption in the French government, which sent a shipload of emigrants to North Africa. Géricault depicts in realistic detail the makeshift raft crowded with desperate, starving, shipwrecked passengers and crew. But the protest went unheeded. Instead, the public was outraged by the artist who used naked figures in unclassical poses to convey his message. This was a revolutionary painting in its dramatic championing of a current political cause and in the use of colors and composition to intensify emotion. Compare its complex arrangement of turbulent forms with David's Neoclassical painting (Fig. 304) to see how strongly Géricault was rebelling against academic constrictions.

307. Théodore Géricault. *The Raft of the "Medusa."* 1818. Oil on canvas, 16′1¼″ × 23′6″ (4.91 × 7.16 m). Louvre, Paris.

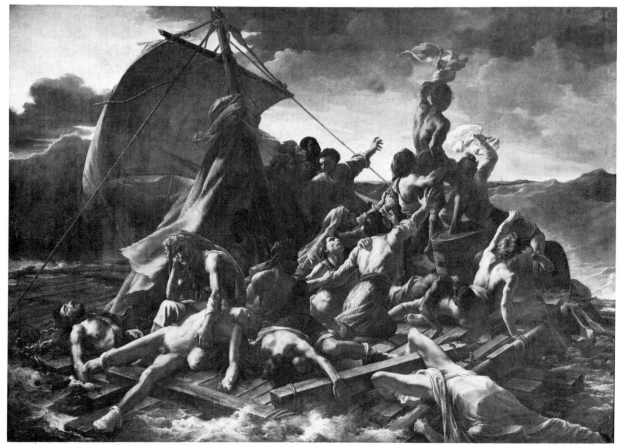

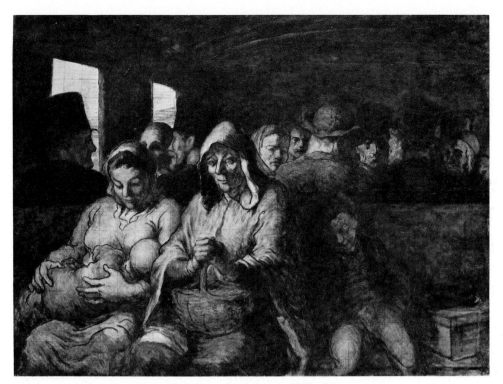

308. Honoré Daumier. *The Third-Class Carriage*. c. 1862. Oil on canvas,
25¾ × 35½" (65 × 90 cm). Metropolitan Museum of Art, New York
(H. O. Havemeyer Collection; bequest of Mrs. H. O. Havemeyer, 1929).

Also rebelling against tradition was Rosa Bonheur, daughter of a painter, who studied at the École des Beaux Arts. From her childhood, Rosa had adopted masculine dress, which freed her to travel (and paint) in public places. Her reputation as a painter was established by *The Horse Fair* (Fig. 25), which won her the rank of Chevalier de la Légion d'Honneur. Although animals and flowers were considered suitable subjects for women, as, for example, Beatrix Potter's (1866–1943) charming illustrations of animal stories in the early 20th century, Bonheur's work was outstanding for its power and scope.

Realism and Social Protest During the 19th century the Industrial Revolution encouraged a capitalist economy in which hard-driving entrepreneurs used the productivity of workers for personal gain. Peasant families crowded into industrial towns to find work and settled in cheap housing near factories, which quickly became slums. Even children were forced to work long hours in factories and mines. Although the British abolished the slave trade early in the 19th century and slavery was ended in the United States by the Civil War, the exploitation of industrial workers continued.

Newly rich industrialists and bankers, if they bought art at all, chose academic, Neoclassical paintings such as those of David or of Jean Auguste Dominique Ingres (1780–1867), whose portraits and exotic scenes show his mastery of line and classical composition. Few were interested in the social criticism of Géricault or of the political commentator and satirist Daumier, who earned his living as a cartoonist and illustrator. His lithographs were sympathetic to the poor and disadvantaged while presenting brutal caricatures of the ruling classes. Criticisms of the French political, judicial, and police systems, these prints appeared in newspapers, where they influenced political cartooning for years to come. In addition to his graphic work, Daumier painted the slum dwellers of Paris in their squalid surroundings. His *The Third-Class Carriage* (Fig. 308) and its companion *The First-Class Carriage* make strong statements about the gulf between the rich and the poor. At the same time, the three generations represented in the third-class coach, all trapped in the economic system, reflect Daumier's view of the power of the proletariat.

Another French painter who rejected the standards of the Academy was the independent Gustave Courbet (1819–1877). His paintings did not depict graceful poses or rich textures, but, like those of Caravaggio two centuries earlier, were realistic portrayals of daily life. He gathered students to him and even brought a bull into the studio for them to draw.

Refused entry to the Paris Exposition of 1855, Courbet set up in a nearby wooden shed his own exhibit entitled "Réalisme, G. Courbet." His most ambitious painting, *The Studio: A Real Allegory of the Last Seven Years of My Life*

(Fig. 309), was featured. Among the figures were a nude, Courbet himself at the easel, a small boy, famous critics, and a cadaver. Courbet issued a *Manifesto of Realism* supporting this work. Thus he addressed an issue central to avant-garde artists as they struggled against the rigid control of the Academy. Accused of socialist political activities, Courbet was exiled in 1873, but his independent spirit continued to influence young artists.

Other Views of Reality In the mid-19th century two influences altered artists' traditional ways of viewing reality. One was Japanese woodcuts. The other was the camera.

Japan had isolated itself from Western contact since the 17th century. When the American Navy forced it to open its doors to the West in 1853, Europeans excitedly bought the newly discovered art of Japan. From these Oriental art objects and from Japanese woodcuts, which were used like newspapers to wrap them for shipping, artists in the West discovered a new way of representing form in space. In a woodcut showing an unusual view of Mt. Fuji, Hokusai created a bold composition in which a huge wave curls up and breaks in the foreground, dwarfing the distant mountain (Fig. 91). A traditional Western landscape artist would likely have emphasized the mountain, not the off-center wave, and would have shown Mt. Fuji in realistic perspec-tive. The Japanese approach to portraiture, which reduced form to flat images, also appeared strange, though fascinating to Western eyes (Fig. 92).

As a result of the invention of the camera, a 19th-century Western painter, trained to believe that the purpose of art was an imitation of nature, faced a new dilemma. Because the camera could capture a sitter, an event, or a scene more quickly and more realistically than could the painter, no artist was needed to transcribe reality. Relieved of having to transpose solid forms onto a flat surface, many painters were forced to find new outlets for artistic expression.

Edouard Manet faced this dilemma creatively, and instinctively combining many influences, he transformed them into a new style. Schooled academically, he was, however, a Romantic in his choice of exotic subjects and use of rich color and texture. He often chose Spanish themes in paintings that show his admiration for Velázquez (Fig. 269) and Goya (Figs. 33, 305), and he was fascinated by the flat areas of color in Japanese art. His broad areas of paint, reminiscent of early photographic effects, and his occasional spots of brilliant color shocked a public accustomed to academic painting. In addition, Manet was attacked as a heretic because he did not follow the traditional method of modeling forms, going back to the time of Giotto, by painting dark values, middle values, and then

309. Gustave Courbet. *The Studio: A Real Allegory of the Last Seven Years of My Life.* 1855. Oil on canvas, 11'9¾" × 19'6⅝" (3.6 × 5.96 m). Louvre, Paris.

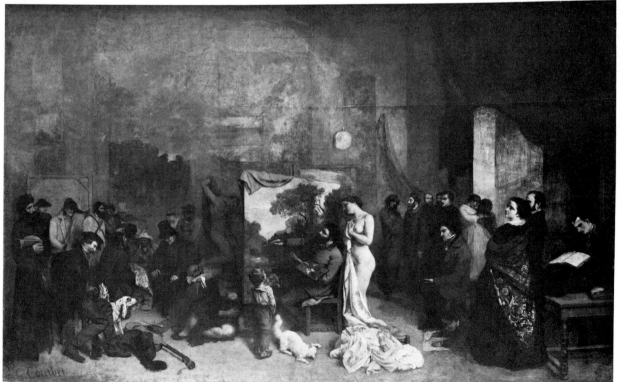

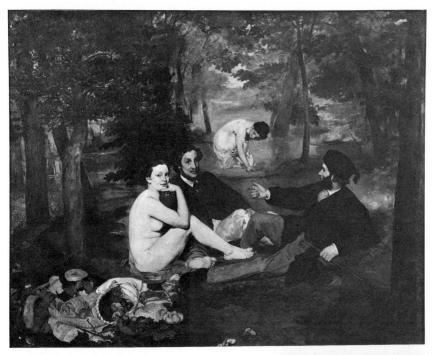

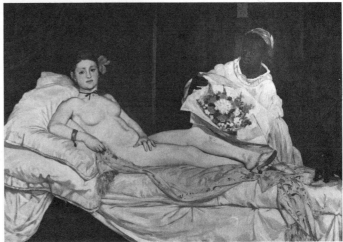

above: 310. Edouard Manet.
Le Déjeuner sur l'Herbe. 1863.
Oil on canvas, 7'¾" × 8'10⅜"
(2.15 × 2.7 m). Louvre, Paris.

right: 311. Edouard Manet. *Olympia.*
1863. Oil on canvas, 4'3¼" × 6'2¾"
(1.3 × 1.9 m). Louvre, Paris.

building up lights and reinforcing darks. Instead, he adopted a radical approach of trying to duplicate sunlight by preserving the natural brilliance of the primed canvas and gradually adding darker tones.

Manet's large painting originally titled *The Bath* and dubbed by critics *Luncheon on the Grass* presented a nude woman picnicking with two fully clothed men in a woodland glen (Fig. 310). The painting was a reworking of the Renaissance painting by Giorgione, *Sacred and Profane Love,* an allegory referring to the Muse, who must be present to inspire art. Manet included a figure bathing in a pool in the background to justify his posing nudes outdoors and used a well-known courtesan as a model, presenting her as a naked picnicker gazing boldly at the viewer. The public

was scandalized. Moreover, his painting of skin tones under strong natural light was not considered sound academic practice. The Academy refused to exhibit his painting in the official Salon of 1863. The protests of Manet and other rejected painters led to the government's forming a separate *Salon des Refusés,* which eventually broke the hold of the Academy upon artists.

In 1865, Manet's masterpiece, *Olympia* (Fig. 311), today a favorite in the Louvre Museum, created an even greater scandal than *The Luncheon* and was considered pornographic by some of the artist's contemporaries! Actually, Manet based *Olympia* on Titian's *The Venus of Urbino* (Fig. 256), but Manet's figure does not appear goddesslike. Obviously a courtesan of the Paris demimonde, she lies on her rumpled bed, with no signs of modesty when her maid brings an admirer's flowers. Although figures of goddesses were traditional subjects, Manet's suggestion in *Olympia* that Venus was an ordinary woman was badly received by the public. The flat silhouette of her body further shocked traditionalists. Manet never hesitated to paint as he believed, but he disliked the criticism that came his way, and he rejected for himself the term Impressionist, which his followers were beginning to apply to him.

Impressionism   Several young artists were influenced by Manet's attempts to capture the immediacy of a moment, his use of flat areas of color, and his efforts to depict natural light. Rejected by the official Salon of 1874, these rebellious painters organized their own exhibit in the studio of the photographer Nadar (Fig. 43). They considered the location appropriate because they believed that photography was a vital new art medium as they hoped their own work marked a new direction in painting. The name **Impressionism** was provided by a journalist who laughed at a painting exhibited by Monet entitled *Impression: Sunrise* (Pl. 15, p. 267). The critic's statement that "these are not artists, they are Impressionists" seemed to describe the common trait in their work. Although it was meant as an insult, the painters adopted the label for their new style.

THEORY AND TECHNIQUE   The Impressionists were more interested in the fleeting light and color reflected from an object than in form or content, and they had little interest in storytelling. To capture the effects of movement and atmospheric vibration over landscape and figures, Monet and other Impressionists such as Pissarro, Degas, and Auguste Renoir (1841–1919) painted *en pleine air* ("in the open air"). This practice, begun by the Barbizon painters in the 1830s, was a radical departure from the academic custom of making only sketches outdoors and developing them traditionally into paintings in north-lighted studios. Another departure was the Impressionists' determination to paint directly on primed canvas without the traditional underpainting in an umber (brown) tone. Also revolutionary was the Impressionists' use of the **broken-color** technique, in which they painted with pure colors taken directly from the tube. Instead of, for example, mixing blue and yellow on their palettes to make green, or yellow and red to make orange, they placed small brush strokes of these analogous colors (Pl. 4, p. 22) next to each other, intending the eye to mix them. They also juxtaposed strokes of complementary colors to intensify their effect (Pl. 5, p. 23). When viewed from a distance, these areas of color became images of trees, flowers, figures, and buildings. Such techniques enabled the Impressionists to produce works that seemed to vibrate with color.

Broken colors, emphasis on visual sensation, flat shapes, and unusual perspective, the last two borrowed from the Japanese, were common traits of Impressionism, but individual painters varied considerably in their styles. Some, such as Monet and Pissarro, remained dedicated Impressionists all their lives. Others, Cézanne, Gauguin, and van Gogh, for example, began as Impressionists but developed different approaches later.

PAINTERS   Most typical of the Impressionists was Monet. He was chiefly concerned with the appearance of objects in changing light. Intrigued by the dancing patterns of sunlight through mist on the water at dawn, he created the controversial *Impression: Sunrise* (Pl. 15, p. 267). Influenced by Hokusai's 100 views of Mt. Fuji (Fig. 91), he explored the effects of light at different times of day in 26 canvases of Rouen Cathedral. As Monet continued to refine the broken-color technique, he became more and more absorbed in light. Saying that he wished he had been born blind so that he could regain his sight and paint objects without knowing what they were, he painted solid forms that dissolved into mists of color. Monet produced hundreds of studies of the shimmering surface of water and light on the shiny leaves and delicate blossoms of the water lilies of the Japanese-style pool in his garden at Giverny. In his last, large paintings just before his death, the water lilies are almost completely abstract (Fig. 312). These loose, much-admired paintings, like his Japanese garden, have become aesthetic environments that were forerunners of the large field paintings of Jackson Pollock (Pl. 2, p. 21) and other Abstract Expressionists in the 1950s.

Academic tradition was also questioned by Pissarro in such works as the *Boulevard des Italiens, Morning, Sunlight* (Fig. 19), when he captured a busy Paris street scene on canvas. According to the Academy, beauty was achieved through the careful, rational rearrangement of nature and the elimination of the accidental. But Pissarro, influenced by the unusual perspectives of Japanese prints, chose the reality of a bird's view of a boulevard from his room under the roof. The critics condemned *Boulevard des Italiens* as having no center of interest; no foreground, middle ground, or background; no ordered path through which the eye could travel. They also criticized Pissarro's technique because one could see the strokes of color. Today, we find it difficult to imagine that people once found it shocking, but we must remember that we have become used to the Impressionist way of looking at the world.

Renoir, who was first apprenticed to a painter of Rococo ornament and flowers on porcelain cups and plates, loved color, flowers, beautiful women, and charming children. He sincerely wished to please himself and his viewers. Because Renoir would not undertake commissions from those he found unappealing, all his works show similar delight in their aesthetic subject.

The traits we identify with Impressionism can be seen in Renoir's *Le Moulin de la Galette,* a painting of a Parisian outdoor dance hall (Fig. 313). The scene is informal. Color is broken. The vertical and horizontal shapes, such as the pavilion in the background, are emphasized so that our eyes stay on the surface of the painting, for depth in space was not important to Impressionists. We may compare this shallow space with the deep space in a Renaissance paint-

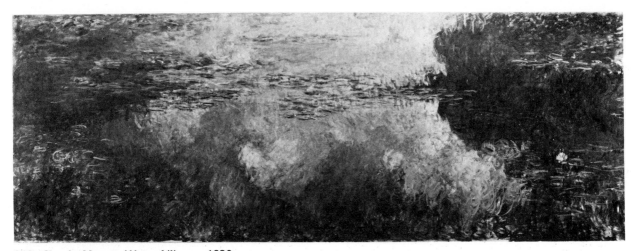

312. Claude Monet. *Water Lilies*. c. 1920.
Oil on canvas, 6'6½" × 19'7½" (1.99 × 5.98 m).
Museum of Modern Art, New York
(Mrs. Simon Guggenheim Fund).

313. Auguste Renoir. *Le Moulin de la Galette.*
1876. Oil on canvas, 4'3½" × 5'9"
(1.31 × 1.75 m). Louvre, Paris.

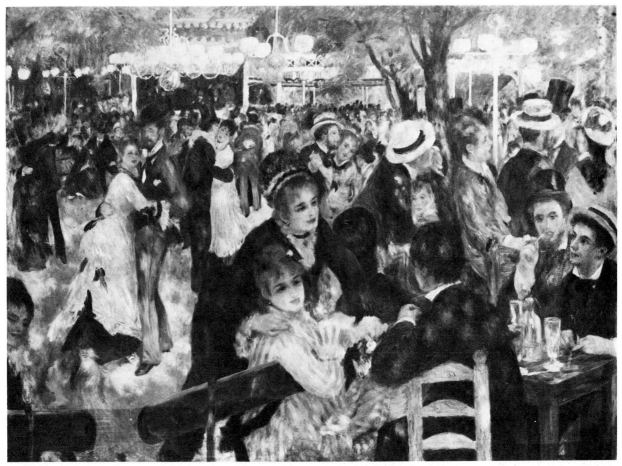

ing such as Leonardo's *The Last Supper* (Fig. 52). In spite of his early dedication to Impressionism, Renoir, like Degas, was concerned with composition in his paintings, and his later canvases, especially those of bathers, were influenced by Titian and other Venetian painters.

Degas carried the idea of painting figures in momentary poses even further than Manet. Like most Impressionists, he was intrigued by movement, and horses and dancers were among his favorite subjects. He liked to catch ballet dancers in unusual positions or moments of action on stage, lit by bright footlights (Fig. 314). His paintings appear to capture movement like the candid shots of photography, with which he experimented. Inspired by Japanese prints, he also depicted his subjects from unusual views.

Degas, however, was deeply concerned with composition and worked out his paintings carefully in sketches and studies. While he exhibited with the Impressionists, he never considered himself one of them because of his formal interest in composition. He supported Impressionist efforts to change the rules of the Academy primarily because he believed in the right to question restrictive attitudes. He could afford to give them his support, for he was a wealthy aristocrat by birth, had been trained in the tradition of the Academy, and had been accepted to exhibit in the Salon. Set apart from the Impressionists also because of his concern for faithful draftsmanship, Degas might have become one of the greatest portraitists of his day. But he would paint only friends with whom he felt empathy.

Also responding to the influence of Japanese art, Whistler was particularly impressed by the apparent simplification of planes and colors, which he identified in Oriental woodcuts and paintings. As an ex-patriate American who from an early age was exposed directly to European art, he managed somehow to detach himself, like Degas, from the Impressionist movement around him. Rejecting the brilliant colors of his Impressionist friends, Whistler used muted grays and subtle harmonies with only touches of gold and red. He called his paintings "nocturnes," "symphonies," and "arrangements" to emphasize his belief in the importance of the abstract qualities of painting, which he compared to music. Unlike artists such as Pissarro and Monet, who painted the momentary light effects they saw before them, Whistler believed that "Nature contains the elements, in colour and form, of all pictures, as the keyboard contains the notes of all music." Form and color, rather than subject matter, were elements he considered important. He called his famous portrait of his mother *Arrangement in Gray and Black No. 1* (Fig. 315) because he saw no reason why the public should be interested in the identity of the sitter. Whistler's concept of a painting as an arrangement of color, value, and shape had an important influence on later painters and upon the development of abstract painting in the 20th century.

We have seen the number of women in the art world gradually increase since the Renaissance. Although they were often denied entrance to the academies for instruction, some of them traveled to distant lands to paint the exotic scenes popular during the Romantic period.

The youngest of the Impressionists was Mary Cassatt. After a comfortable childhood in a rich Philadelphia family, trained at the Pennsylvania Academy of Art, she studied in Europe. Although she is best known for her sensitive paintings of women and children (Fig. 94), it is in her etchings and aquatints that she is most original and free. They show the influence of Degas, whom she greatly admired, and the unusual perspective, reminiscent of Japanese prints.

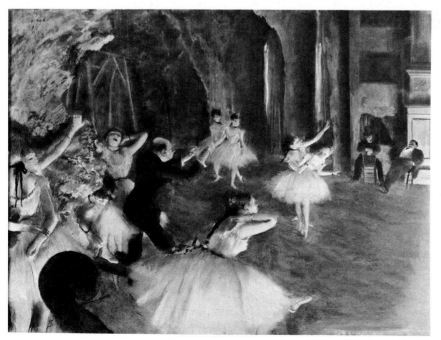

314. Edgar Degas.
The Rehearsal on the Stage.
1878–79.
Pastel over brush-and-ink drawing on paper,
21 × 28½" (53 × 72 cm).
Metropolitan Museum of Art, New York
(H. O. Havemeyer Collection; bequest of
Mrs. H. O. Havemeyer, 1929).

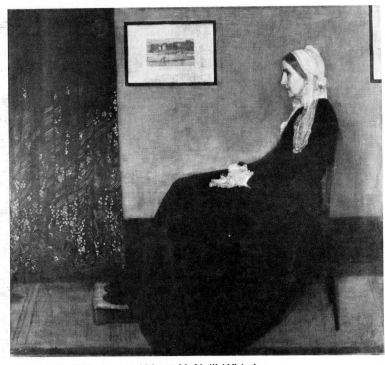

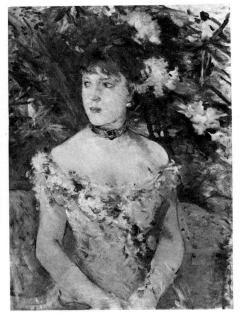

above left: 315. James Abbott McNeill Whistler.
Arrangement in Gray and Black No. 1 (The Artist's Mother).
1871. Oil on canvas,
4′9″ × 5′4½″ (1.45 × 1.64 m). Louvre, Paris.

right: 316. Berthe Morisot. *Young Woman in a Ball Dress.* 1879–80.
Oil on canvas, 28 × 21¼″ (71 × 54 cm). Louvre, Paris.

An important figure in the Impressionist group was Berthe Morisot (1841–1895). She began early to experiment with the technique of capturing fleeting impressions. Her portrait of a young woman with its sketchy brush strokes (Fig. 316) shows characteristics similar to Monet's later work. Dedicated to Impressionism, Morisot tried to keep the early group functioning while continuing the style after most had abandoned it.

Applied Arts As a result of the Industrial Revolution with its cheap, overdecorated, factory-made goods (Fig. 157), men such as the critic John Ruskin and the painter and designer William Morris campaigned for a new attitude toward art and crafts. Attempting to reinstate the traditional skills of the medieval guilds, they turned toward stained glass, decorative wall paintings, and handcrafts. They were associated with a group of painters who called themselves Pre-Raphaelites because they were inspired by the forms of art created just before the High Renaissance of Raphael. Morris, who was also a writer and social reformer, was a Romantic in his desire to return to the Middle Ages, but with his competent technical knowledge he inspired a revival of interest in handmade ceramics, jewelry, weaving, and book printing. Genuinely appalled at the ugliness

of the pompous furniture and household implements exhibited at the Crystal Palace (Fig. 183) in 1851, he designed the Morris chair in an attempt to simplify furniture and make it more functional. Although his approach to wallpaper, fabrics, and glassware looked toward the past, Morris was progressive in his belief that useful objects should emphasize function and materials, not decoration. His campaign bore fruit in the 20th century when Germany's Bauhaus school applied these principles to industrial products.

Architecture Nineteenth-century architecture at first continued the Neoclassical style exemplified by Jefferson's Monticello (Fig. 303). Soon a nostalgia for all things past produced an eclectic mixture from Assyrian to Gothic. Revivalists built banks, stock exchanges, and government buildings patterned on Greek and Roman temples. Engineers, however, were using their new prefabrication skills, introduced in Joseph Paxton's Crystal Palace, to build bridges, railway stations, and monuments such as the Eiffel Tower. By the end of the century, some architects were following their lead. The pioneer American architect Louis Sullivan, despite his traditional training, turned to the new structural systems in his designs (Fig. 184). His ideas led the way to the skyscrapers of the 20th century.

Sculpture In contrast to the static academic sculpture at this time, Rodin restored sculpture to a major art form while creating a style leading to Expressionism. Born in a working-class quarter of Paris, Rodin first earned his living as a goldsmith and a maker of plaster decorations for buildings. When he visited Italy, he was influenced by the sculpture of Donatello and Michelangelo. Fascinated by the human body in action, he made quick drawings and clay sketches of dancers to catch their momentary poses. In this way he became familiar with the natural movements of the nude human body instead of repeating the stiff stances approved by the Academy. Rodin's rather Romantic figures are often carved or modeled so that the solid stone or bronze appears like living flesh. The influence of Impressionism can be seen in the way the light plays over the textured surfaces so that they seem to vibrate (Fig. 117). He himself called sculpture "quite simply the art of depression and protuberance."

Post-Impressionism By the mid-1880s, the Impressionists were accepted as serious artists by critics and a large portion of the public. But many of their colleagues and younger followers came to feel that in the search for momentary sensations of light and color, traditional elements of picture making had been neglected. The **Post-Impressionists,** as they came to be known, all worked for more solid structure in art, which each, in his or her own way, found by a method essentially personal.

One of the most important of these artists was Cézanne, who exhibited in early Impressionist shows, although he disagreed with their aesthetic theories. He thought that Impressionistic works were brilliant renderings of natural light and color, but lacked clarity and order. He determined "to make of Impressionism something solid and durable like the art of the museums." By emphasizing horizontal and vertical shapes and other classic devices of composition, he brought formal order to his paintings. To further his knowledge, he studied great paintings of the past, stating that a museum is "the book in which we learn to read." Cézanne very early discarded the idea of capturing transient light effects. His paintings, although colorful, are made up of forms that exist in a timeless light rather than in the glancing sunlight seen by Monet or Renoir.

In order to develop solidity, Cézanne modeled his masses in a series of planes of color. This approach made him one of the most innovative painters of the 19th century and led directly to the art of the 20th-century Cubists. "Treat Nature by the cylinder, the sphere, the cone," he wrote, applying this rule to his painting by breaking down the most complex objects into geometric-like forms. In his later paintings Cézanne treated masses in small planes of color, using warm yellows and oranges to bring planes forward and cool blues, violets, and greens to push them away from the viewer. He also distorted perspective and shapes to achieve the composition he wanted, disregarding realistic appearances. Deliberate and careful, he painted Mont Sainte-Victoire near his home in the south of France over and over again, gradually abstracting the familiar view (Pl. 16, p. 267). The mountain, valley, trees, and houses in his later paintings of the mountain are no longer treated as recognizable themes but become simply planes of color. In essence, he diminished the subject's importance to stress the objective character of his art.

Thus Cézanne, although he lived in the 19th century, was one of the strongest painters of the modern period, and from him we can move easily into the daring art of the early 20th century. We have only to compare *Mont Sainte-Victoire* with a loose, Romantic landscape such as Constable's *The Haywain* (Fig. 306) and with later geometric, Cubist paintings by Picasso (Fig. 10) to see how important Cézanne was as a bridge between the old and new ways of looking at the world. Without the influence of Cézanne's experiments, the radical 20th-century view that art need not imitate nature could never have developed.

While Cézanne searched for new ways of depicting form, Seurat was also trying to develop more ordered compositions than those of the Impressionists. Seurat extended earlier ideas of broken color into a scientific process called **Divisionism,** or **Pointillism** (Pl. 5, p. 23). He studied scientific theories of light and color in order to separate colors, trying to analyze the exact amounts of each color complement. Then he meticulously placed dots of complementary colors side by side on the canvas, letting the eye blend them. Seurat was also concerned with the silhouettes of objects, simplifying them into simple shapes. He assembled his figures into large compositions, which, despite the vibrations of the color, appear stable because of the quiet shapes and poses. This reduction of form and strong composition, even more than his use of broken color, make Seurat historically important.

A young, enthusiastic Dutchman, painting in the blazing sunlight of southern France, also searched for new color techniques. But, unlike Cézanne and Seurat, who had used color to define planes in space, van Gogh used color to express his very personal, emotional response to the world. Van Gogh was deeply religious, concerned about all of humanity. Indeed, at the start of his painting career he had lived with coal miners and had painted their poverty in dark, depressing colors. He had also hoped, with the help of his brother, Theo, to establish a community of artists dedicated to spiritual values, in rebellion against the commercialism produced by the Industrial Revolution.

In a frenzy of creation, van Gogh painted the grandeur of nature (Fig. 4) and the simple objects of his daily surroundings. Primarily concerned with his personal response to these objects, he used bright color to intensify the mood of joy and somber for pain. A painting of his bedroom (Fig. 317) shows how strongly color can affect us. He wrote about this bedroom: "I had a new idea in my head and here is the sketch to it . . . this time it's just simply my bedroom, only here colour is everything."

Along with many 19th-century painters influenced by Japanese prints, van Gogh, like Cézanne, was unconcerned with linear perspective. However, his interest was

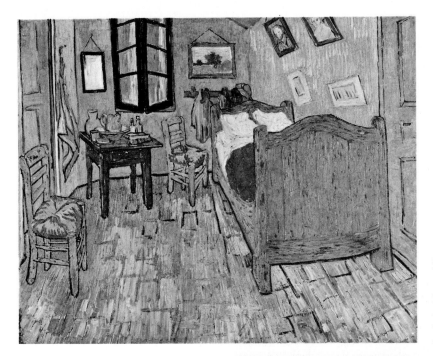

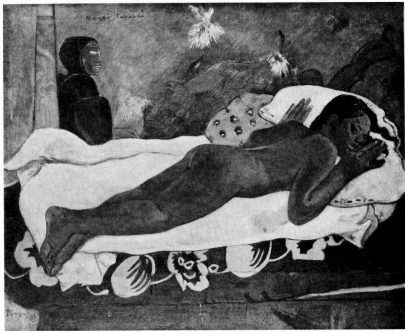

not in portraying the structure of objects as was Cézanne's. Van Gogh saw the outer world in deeply personal terms, which he expressed with strong, slashing brush strokes and brilliant color. In this approach he was a forerunner of 20th-century Expressionism.

Distrustful of conventions in art and impatient with academic emphasis on technical skills, Gauguin was as idealistic as van Gogh. To escape the harsh realities of an indus-

trial society, he retreated to the island of Tahiti in the South Seas. There Gauguin sought the simplification of reality that he believed could exist only where life was stripped to its essentials. Many were attracted to such remote cultures, believing they could lose themselves and avoid worldly problems. We, as viewers of their exotic works, are also momentarily diverted from our daily pressures. In *The Spirit of the Dead Watching* (Fig. 318) we can vicariously experience a simple life-style in a romantic setting. The drama is heightened for us by a juxtaposition of tropical flowers with the dark figure from the spirit world.

Gauguin was influenced by Japanese prints, and he also studied the art of Polynesian craftspeople in the village where he lived. He developed a decorative style of painting, making use of flat areas of pure, often unrealistic, color. Gauguin believed that the Impressionists used color without freedom, constrained by the needs of reality and probability. He simplified the outlines of figures and objects to make them often appear unrealistic or symbolic. He believed that a painter should study the silhouette of every object—as he saw it—for distinctness of outline comes from sure knowledge. Aside from their own beauty, Gauguin's paintings are important also for their influence upon later Expressionists.

Another noteworthy Post-Impressionist was Suzanne Valodon (1865–1938), a former model and mother of the **Fauvist** painter Maurice Utrillo (1883–1955). She had no formal art training but great skill in drawing. She worked in the spirit of the Impressionists, especially Degas, although she painted at the beginning of the 20th century. The heavily defined contours, simplification of form, and non-representational colors of her vigorous paintings link her also to Gauguin and the Expressionists.

The dissatisfaction of van Gogh and Gauguin with Western society was a point of view shared by others at the end of the 19th century. Many artists seemed preoccupied with decadence and despair. Henri de Toulouse-Lautrec, an artist of great talent, led a dissolute life on the fringes of society, illuminating the café scene in the flat, patterned Japanese style he so much admired. Jane Avril is a superb example of his work (Fig. 98).

Edvard Munch, a Norwegian with a tragic sense of human isolation, expressed alienation, anxiety, and despair in both paintings and prints. His remark, "I hear the scream in nature," is vividly illustrated in *The Scream* (Fig. 96). The open mouth of the central figure suggests howls of fear or pain, while the anonymous silhouettes on the bridge portray the coldness and indifference of the world. The torment of the lonely figure fills the atmosphere with expanding waves of terror, which are repeated in the water and sky. Munch's figures, isolated from one another and caged in their separate terrors, are ageless, sexless, classless symbols of late 19th-century humanity.

The Age of Revolution had signaled the growing movement toward freedom for personal expression in the subject matter, technique, and style of art. The styles of Post-Impressionism, with which the century closed, anticipate the bold individuality of art in the 20th century.

EXERCISES AND ACTIVITIES

1. Select a passage from the *Discourses* by Sir Joshua Reynolds that seems particularly relevant to today's world. Explain your reasons for choosing that passage.
2. Locate some buildings or photographs of buildings that show Palladio's influence on architecture.
3. How were such artists as Goya and Turner influenced by the earlier works of Velázquez and Rembrandt? How were they affected by the new spirit of the age?
4. Discuss some art movements of the 19th century that expressed the conflict between industrialization and nostalgia for the past. Analyze two art works.
5. The Impressionist painters of the 19th century developed a technique that created the illusion of light, color, and atmosphere. How did it differ from earlier painting techniques? Give examples.
6. Draw a still life in outline. Using poster paints, create an illusion of light on the objects, applying dabs of pure color next to each other. See if your eye mixes the dots to form an area of color. If it does not, alter the proportions of the colors until you achieve the effect you wish.
7. Sketch a view of part of a room. Paint it, using dabs of poster, oil, or acrylic paint.
8. In the spirit of Whistler, organize a cityscape in charcoal based upon a division of space, respecting the Golden Section. Does this principle apply to a composition of houses and sidewalks?

17 The Great Divide: 1900

One of the main causes of our artistic decline lies beyond doubt in the separation of art and science. Art is nothing but humanized science.

GINO SEVERINI

As we approach the art of our own time, the pace quickens and diversity becomes the rule. Changes occur so rapidly that despite the perspective of almost one hundred years we are shaken by the explosion of styles.

The 1920s and 1930s were a period of broad disillusionment and unrest. Nineteenth-century promises of peace and prosperity had resulted in World War I and the Great Depression of the 1930s. Numerous writers and artists saw this era as one of mass exploitation, dehumanization, and irrational political leadership. Social confusion led to considerable artistic experiment. It was a period when modern art flourished, and some critical artists even produced works that were anti-art.

The spirit of artistic freedom that had developed in the 19th century with the efforts of Courbet and Whistler to choose their own styles, subjects, and titles of works increased in the 20th century. By the second and third decades a half-dozen or so manifestos were issued, and artists, who generally resisted grouping, had developed several art currents. In addition, different styles originated in different countries. By the early 1930s, however, the many confusing styles or "-isms" could be sorted out into the following general trends, which have persisted to the present time: formalism, Expressionism, fantasy, and realism.

Formalism refers to an intellectual approach popular in the modern period that is more concerned with form—the spatial arrangement of such elements as line, shape, and texture—than with content.

Expressionism refers to a concern with the intensity of the artist's emotion as opposed to the representation of reality, an approach that often results in distortions of color and shape. The term was perhaps first applied to the art of van Gogh.

Fantasy refers to art derived from the artistic imagination. It may be expressed either realistically or with abstract symbols.

Realism refers to the artist's use of light, shade, color, and perspective to reproduce as closely as possible the appearance of objects in nature. As proposed by Courbet in the 19th century, the trend never took hold in most of the European world, yet it never quite disappeared in America.

If we remember that the many styles and "-isms" discussed in Chapters 17 to 20 are loosely grouped within these general trends, perhaps the first decades of modern art will be easier to follow.

Formalist Painting

For centuries artists were concerned with how to paint the illusion of three-dimensional objects in deep space on a flat, two-dimensional surface. The Greeks and Romans used a limited form of linear perspective, which Renaissance painters developed into a science. They held up a mirror to nature and then surrounded the painting with a frame, making the painting a window on reality. This concept prevailed until the mid-19th century when the invention of the camera released Western artists from the need to reproduce nature. Cézanne and Gauguin began to take advantage of this freedom, as we saw in Chapter 16.

The public is always slow to change. Few people in 1910 understood the new views of the world, and many artists continued to cling to tradition, comfortable as skillful recorders of society. But in the early 20th century, avant-garde artists plunged ahead to explore new horizons, especially in styles of formalist painting. Their work in **Cubism, Futurism, Nonobjectivism, De Stijl,** and **Suprematism,** all of which we shall now examine, has come to be recognized for its outstanding creative achievement.

Cubism The young painters and sculptors who gathered in Paris from all over Europe from the 1880s on discussed Cézanne's efforts to reduce volume and space to simple cones, cylinders, and planes to make objects appear to be seen from several vantage points (Pl. 16, p. 267). Many of these young rebels also looked to the arts of Africa (Fig. 285), with their exaggerations and simplifications of forms, as an escape from the binding rules of the Academy as well as from the Impressionists' preoccupation with fleeting light. Under these major influences two young artists, Braque and Picasso, developed a new kind of pictorial space in which objects were presented as if seen from several angles. Some observers believe that they also added a temporal dimension to space by representing objects in sequential moments of time. A startled critic gave the name **Cubism** to this new style. Braque and Picasso later said, "We had no intention of creating Cubism but simply of expressing what we felt inside."

Leaving Cézanne behind, in 1907 Picasso explored the essential elements of Cubism in a major experimental work, *Les Demoiselles d'Avignon,* or *The Young Ladies of Avignon* (Fig. 319). In this painting artistic rebellion became outright revolution. First planned as an allegory of vice and virtue, the painting became intense and stark. The figures and faces of the women are distorted in angular, jagged forms. The girl on the left is depicted in a series of overlapping planes; the central figure has eyes that look directly at us, but the nose is in profile; and the faces of the figures on the right are like African masks. *Demoiselles* attacked long-held Renaissance concepts of space and the idealized nude and had a tremendous effect on the course of 20th-century Western art.

319. Pablo Picasso. *Les Demoiselles d'Avignon.* 1907. Oil on canvas, 8′ × 7′8″ (2.44 × 2.34 m). Museum of Modern Art, New York (acquired through the Lillie P. Bliss Bequest).

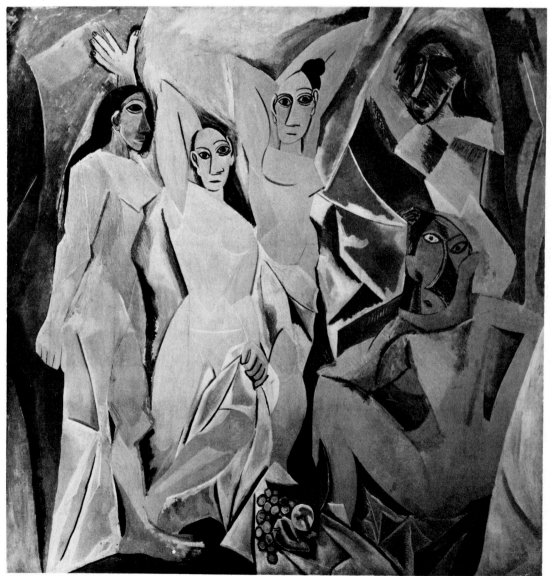

Both Picasso and Braque recorded the world in a startling way, as if they echoed the weakening in social patterns and the uncertainty of the new age. Just as the political radicals tried to find a new order to restructure an unjust society, so too did the Cubists search for a new way to rearrange visual images. Familiar objects—tables, wine bottles, violins, sheet music, and the human figure—were reduced to geometric abstractions, simplified, and then restructured. Picasso said, "We have kept our eyes open to our surroundings, and also our brains." The Cubists abandoned conventional linear perspective, replacing it with a new surface perspective that does not create a sense of depth in the canvas but rather seems to advance from the frame. A comparison of *"Ma Jolie"* (Fig. 10) with Leonardo's *The Last Supper* (Fig. 52) demonstrates the revolutionary manner in which these young painters handled perspective.

The Cubists painted not only what they saw but also what they knew was there. For instance, a wine bottle might be painted as seen from the side, back, and top; all these views organized into a single, complex, intellectually analyzed composition in muted colors. Because of the intellectual and disciplined nature of these paintings, the early stages of the style are described as **Analytical Cubism.**

320. Pablo Picasso. *Girl Before a Mirror.* 1932. Oil on canvas, 5′3³⁄₄″ × 4′3¹⁄₂″ (1.62 × 1.31 m). Museum of Modern Art, New York (gift of Mrs. Simon Guggenheim).

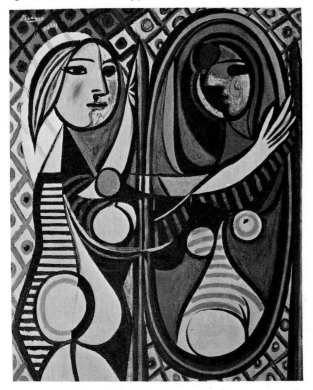

Gradually, however, the object itself was lost, and the Cubists became more interested in the design formed by bright-colored, overlapping shapes in a shallow space. This mingling of the decorative aspects of an object by taking its various parts and combining them into compositions that may only remotely resemble their origins is described as **Synthetic Cubism.** Picasso's *Girl Before a Mirror* (Fig. 320) is a remarkably direct Synthetic Cubist work. It presents a psychological study of a young girl considering her impending sexual maturity with apparent fear and anticipation. Her arm, stretched into the mirror, forms a bridge from the present time to what will be.

Along with Cubist paintings, Picasso, Braque, and others made collages (Fig. 47) and, then, paintings that looked like collages (Fig. 57). The colors, shapes, and volumes of the language of Cubism were used more inventively and expressively, often with humor. The rules of academic art were totally shattered. Even painters who used the academic devices of perspective and light and shade to create the illusion of three dimensions used them more freely. Art was never again the same.

Although Picasso was one of the founders of Cubism, he also worked in a number of different styles. Cubist, Expressionist, Neoclassical, Surrealist—any of these labels suit some of his work, but none could describe it all. Born in Spain but working in France, Picasso was an artist of vitality and inventiveness. In his long life he produced thousands of paintings, drawings, etchings, lithographs, sculptures, and ceramics in a rich and varied outpouring of artistic expression (Figs. 10, 20, 319, 320). In his work, lush colors alternate with muted soft tones, sketchy images of bullfights contrast with amusing ceramics or play with light (Fig. 67). But it is probably for his large painting *Guernica* (Fig. 22) that he will be best remembered.

Guernica was painted during a few weeks in the spring of 1937 after German planes supporting General Francisco Franco attacked the village of Guernica in a test run of saturation bombing. The village was totally destroyed. Picasso's 26-foot-long (7.92 meters) black, white, and gray mural was his memorial to those who had perished—his agonized protest against senseless destruction of human lives. The many studies that Picasso made for the painting (Fig. 21) show the gradual evolution of the images—from three-dimensional drawings of distorted, screaming mouths and fragmented bodies to the flat, abstracted shapes of the final painting. In the finished work a mother clutches a dead child, a woman falls from a flaming house, and a horse dies from the thrust of a spear. The bull, sometimes a symbol of evil and sometimes of resurgent Spain in many of Picasso's etchings, stands triumphantly over the dead and dying villagers, while a single glaring light bulb stares down like a cold eye on the scene of death. It is difficult to experience from reproductions the full impact of one of the strongest antiwar statements of our century. Universal in its images, this painting could represent a village in Vietnam, the Middle East, or Northern Ireland—anywhere the horror of war destroys the innocent.

Picasso summed up the confused reactions to Cubism (and to all his art) by saying, "Everyone wants to understand art. Why not try to understand the song of a bird?" Spontaneously creative, he could paint a charming young girl in a lyrical Neoclassical style, capture the pathos of starving beggars with a few lines, and then assemble a bicycle seat and handlebars into a humorous bull (Fig. 20). With such works, Picasso introduced playfulness and humor into art that was a refreshing change from the stuffy gravity of David's academic painting (Fig. 304) and the intellectualism of Analytical Cubism. But the impact of Cubism on painting was so powerful that it affected sculpture and architecture as well, as we shall discover shortly.

Futurism   In 1908 the American inventor Wilbur Wright flew across the English Channel at about the same time that Ettore Bugatti was designing racing automobiles in Italy. Many artists were intrigued by concepts of motion, and a group of young painters anxious to escape tradition founded the **Futurist** movement. In their painting and sculpture they tried to reconcile the human being with the new machines and to express their joy in the glorious speed of steam engines, automobiles, and airplanes. Influenced by the Cubists, some of these artists reduced forms to planes and painted almost abstract canvases with titles such as *Dynamism of the Automobile*. Robert Delaunay (1885–1941) and his wife Sonia Terk-Delaunay (1895–1979) experimented with the mechanics of light, merging Pointillist techniques with Cubist and Futurist forms.

Others, such as Gino Severini (1883–1966), who painted multiple images to show movement, may have been influenced by the new art of the motion picture. In *Dynamic Hieroglyphic of the Bal Tabarin* (Fig. 321), for instance, Severini expressed the swirling movements of cancan dancers in a brilliantly colored painting whose forms have been broken down into Cubist planes. Only the dancers' ringlets and red lips remain recognizable; added touches of painted lace and real sequins suggest their costumes. The Futurist movement broke up under the stress of World War I, but Futurist influence continued in works by Fernand Léger (1881–1955), Marcel Duchamp (Fig. 63), and later machine-oriented painters. Duchamp's Cubistic, machinelike walking nude parodies the idealized Venus figure of Renaissance art.

First affected by the Cubists, Léger moved slowly toward a style that related human beings to machines. In his paintings he turned city buildings, smoking factories, machine parts, and human bodies into simplified cylinders, rectangles, circles, and cubes, painted in brilliant blue, yellow, and red against stark white and black. His figures are static robots surrounded by machine parts. The colors and forms of Léger's painting directly influenced furniture design and advertising art in the United States in the 1940s, for his simplified forms lent themselves well to graphic poster art (Fig. 322).

De Stijl and Other Nonobjective Art   During the years of World War I the neutral Netherlands remained

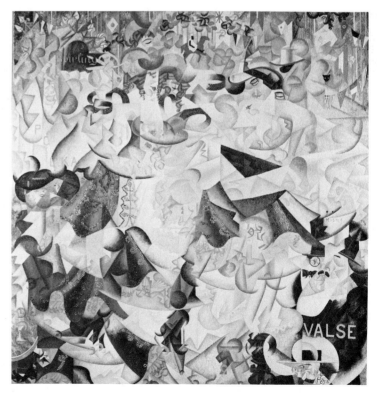

321. Gino Severini.
Dynamic Hieroglyphic of the Bal Tabarin.
1912. Oil on canvas, with sequins;
5′3⅝″ × 5′1½″ (1.62 × 1.56 m).
Museum of Modern Art, New York (acquired through the Lillie P. Bliss Bequest).

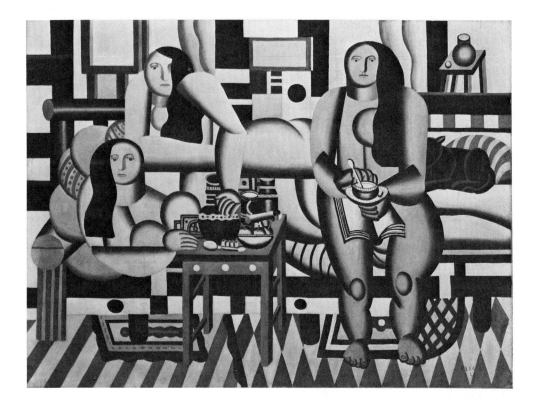

above: 322. Fernand Léger.
Three Women (Le Grand Déjeuner). 1921.
Oil on canvas, 6'1¼" × 8'3"
(1.84 × 2.51 m).
Museum of Modern Art, New York
(Mrs. Simon Guggenheim Fund).

right: 323. Theo van Doesburg.
The Cow (series of 8 pencil drawings).
c. 1916–17.
Nos. 1, 2, 4, 5, 6, 7: 4⅝" × 6¼"
(12 × 16 cm); nos. 3, 8: 6¼" × 4⅝"
(16 × 12 cm). Museum of Modern Art,
New York (purchase).

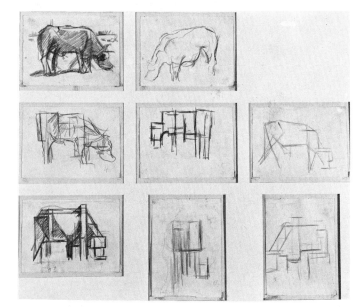

one of the few countries where creative design and construction could continue uninterrupted. As a consequence, this country became a center of innovation. The architect Gerrit Rietveld and the painters Theo van Doesburg and Piet Mondrian worked closely together and in 1917 evolved a movement they called **De Stijl** ("The Style"). Convinced that realistic or even semiabstract images had no place in the machine age, the painters of De Stijl re-duced their images to simple shapes and horizontal and vertical lines. Later, van Doesburg's studies of a cow reveal clearly the process of abstraction (Fig. 323). In most canvases by Mondrian (Pl. 3, p. 22) and van Doesburg, the object that may have originally inspired the works has completely disappeared, leaving only flat rectangles of color and strong dark lines placed in harmonious compositions. Applied to painting, architecture, and all areas of design, De Stijl affected creative expression in many countries for decades, as evidenced by Rietveld's chair (Pl. 10, p. 24).

Another painter who helped develop nonobjective art (see Chapter 2) was the Russian Wassily Kandinsky (1866–1944). Studying in Munich and visiting Paris, he was exposed to various kinds of avant-garde art. He painted his first nonobjective work, a watercolor of pure color and line, in 1910, about the time he became also a leading figure in Expressionism. He claimed that what is most important in art is what the viewer feels while under the effect of the combinations of form and color in a painting. Like Whistler before him, he wanted painting to approach pure music. He called his compositions "improvisations" to emphasize their lack of literal subject matter. His later works in the 1920s and early 1930s, when he was teaching at the Bauhaus, became entirely geometric (Fig. 324).

Nonobjective art was also being developed in Russia about the time of World War I by such men as Kasimir Malevich (1878–1935). In 1913 he exhibited a painting of a black square on a white background. Describing this work Malevich stated, "It was not just a square I had exhibited but rather the expression of nonobjectivity." Malevich spent years exploring squares and their relationships to each other. In 1918 he painted *Suprematist Composition: White on White* (Fig. 325) in which he believed he had attained the ultimate in purity of art. Many agreed.

In Russia at this time nonobjective painting and other experimental art were encouraged by the Communist

325. Kasimir Malevich.
Suprematist Composition: White on White. c. 1918.
Oil on canvas, 31¼″ (79 cm) square.
Museum of Modern Art, New York.

party, which came to power in 1918. By 1920, there were more museums of abstract art and more artists working in a nonobjective manner in Russia than anywhere else in the world. As with Courbet in France, political radicalism was again linked with artistic radicalism. Soon, however, the new regime outlawed experiment and insisted on realistic works that glorified the state. Avant-garde artists had to choose either to stay in an environment that was hostile to innovation or to leave the country. Kandinsky, for example, who had taught in Russia during World War I, left in 1921 and joined the faculty of the innovative Bauhaus school.

Expressionist Painting

Also innovative but quite different in their approach to art were the Expressionists, who worked in France and Germany. Of course, emotional expression has existed as long as art. Certainly Romanesque sculptors expressed religious emotion (Fig. 243). In the 19th century, Goya expressed his horror at the cold-blooded murder of hostages by Napoleon's troops (Fig. 33). Later, Géricault, in *The Raft of the "Medusa,"* protested against the callous disregard of the authorities for human life (Fig. 307). Van Gogh poured his emotions into his vigorously brushed, vibrantly colored paintings (Fig. 4). Munch expressed his personal distress in woodcuts (Fig. 96).

Troubled by the dehumanized and materialistic world they saw around them, many early 20th-century painters worked in a variety of styles that are loosely classified as Expressionist. Those in France are known as the **Fauves.** Those in Germany are called **German Expressionists.**

324. Wassily Kandinsky. *Black Relationship.* 1924.
Watercolor, 14½ × 14¼″ (37 × 36 cm).
Museum of Modern Art, New York
(acquired through the Lillie P. Bliss Bequest).

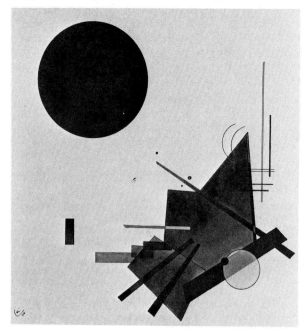

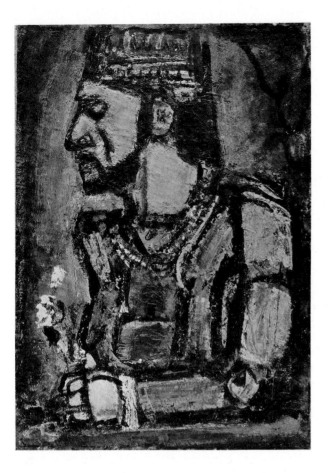

326. Georges Rouault. *The Old King*. 1916–38.
Oil on canvas, 30¼ × 21¼″ (77 × 54 cm).
Museum of Art, Carnegie Institute,
Pittsburgh (Patrons Art Fund, 1940; purchase).

The Fauves In 1905 a new movement burst on the Paris scene with an astonishing exhibit by Henri Matisse and eleven other artists. Among the rooms filled with brilliantly colored canvases a bewildered critic noticed a small bronze sculpture in Renaissance style, which, he remarked, was like "Donatello among the wild beasts." Consequently, the term *les Fauves* ("the wild beasts") was applied to artists of this movement. It lasted only three years or so, but had far-reaching effects.

Matisse's innovative use of color and strong, simplified forms was startling. For example, in his *Madame Matisse* (*The Green Line*) (Pl. 17, p. 268) he arbitrarily painted one of his wife's cheeks a warm yellow-ochre, the other a cold pink, and then separated them with a wide line of green down the middle of her face. Here he used color with minimal reference to reality, and, like other Fauves, in its fullest intensity. The features were simplified into a mask.

Throughout his long life, Matisse showed an impressive ability to put colors together successfully in unusual ways. As an accomplished pictorial designer, he could define space by overlapping planes of flat color. As a master of anatomy, through extreme simplification and elimination of detail, he, unlike many other Expressionists, represented a serene world where line, color, and shape could be enjoyed independently of the subject matter.

The Fauve painter Georges Rouault (1871–1958) was haunted by the poverty and misery of his day. His paintings depicted the degradation of prostitutes and tragic circus clowns as symbols of the cruelty of people toward each other (Fig. 326). Deeply religious, Rouault also painted many biblical characters and Crucifixions. His youthful apprenticeship to a maker of stained glass is reflected in the glowing colors and black outlines of his paintings. As an experimental printmaker, commenting on the horror of war, Rouault developed daring graphic techniques. For instance, he combined etching and engraving in one print and worked on the plate with files, sandpaper, and anything else that would mark it. This free approach helped expand the limits of 20th-century printmaking.

An Expressionist painter and sculptor who lived in Paris but was not a Fauve was the Italian-born Modigliani. He used the distortions of African art as well as strong, often somber colors to express the restlessness of his life. Handsome, poor, dissipated, and dying of tuberculosis, he nevertheless carved fine, abstract figures (Fig. 288) and painted portraits and nudes that echoed the work of Botticelli in their graceful elongation of the female form.

German Expressionists Before World War I, Dresden, Munich, and cities in northern Germany were centers of artistic innovation, where avant-garde artists formed groups to promote their Expressionist ideas. They used harsh, brutally simplified forms and strong, clashing colors to express the intensity of their inner sense of conflict, violence, and tragedy.

Paula Modersohn-Becker (1876–1907), a gifted and strongly motivated painter, joined the Expressionist colony in Worpeswede and fell in love with her teacher, Otto Modersohn. After marriage she was torn between her artistic aspirations and her maternal responsibilities. Of all her 259 paintings, many of them intense reworkings of images of motherhood (Fig. 327), she sold only one. She died with the birth of her last child, at 31.

The German Expressionists used distortion and exaggerated color not only to convey their own feelings but also as symbols of emotion. Emil Nolde (1867–1956) in his violent religious and moral paintings distorted the physical features of his figures to the point where they resemble animals, driven by greed, anger, or grief (Fig. 328). Franz Marc (1880–1916) pushed the color symbolism, already used by Gauguin (Fig. 318), beyond reality, painting horses sometimes red and sometimes blue, referring to symbolic meanings of those colors.

The German Expressionists may have reached their greatest heights in their prints. Inspired by Japanese prints and perhaps drawing on their own medieval graphic tradition, they began to experiment with woodcuts, often using color in conjunction with strong black and white. They distorted figures to bring intense emotion to printmaking. Käthe Kollwitz made drawings and lithographs chiefly in black and white (Fig. 329). A champion of the poor and exploited, she poignantly depicted agonized mothers clutching starving children and peasants revolting against rapacious landlords. Ernst Kirchner (1880–1938) and George Grosz screamed their hatred of social apathy, militarism, and corruption in their prints. Thus the Expressionists continued the tradition of social protest introduced by Goya and Daumier a century earlier.

Fantasy in Art

During World War I and in the uneasy years afterward, when Europe was gripped by political tension, anxiety, and fear of revolution, many intellectuals and artists became disillusioned by traditional values. While Cubists, Futurists, and Expressionists sought different ways to represent the world and their feelings, others reached nihilistic conclusions. Their rejection of the world took the form of **Dada, Surrealism,** or other expressions of fantasy.

Dada The movement known as Dada arose among European poets, experimental writers, and artists arriving in neutral Zurich in 1915. To express their rebellion at the uselessness of war and the meaninglessness of all past art they called their movement Dada, meaning nonsense like the babble of babies. The word was supposedly found by opening a dictionary at random, but probably it was carefully chosen. The founders were laughing at the pompousness of traditional artists such as David and at the society that supported them. Unlike artists of the past, who presented viewers with images from their own culture, which they were expected to understand, Dadaists did not care to be understood. They felt they were living in an incomprehensible world bound for destruction. Nevertheless, they published the periodical *Dada* in 1917. Dada also flourished in New York, where European artists had settled during the war, and later in Paris. The movement ended in the 1920s, but its influence continued in Surrealism.

One of the founders of Dada in Zurich, who was later a Surrealist, was the painter and sculptor Hans (later Jean) Arp (1887–1966). He created artworks by tearing or cutting paper and allowing the rectangular pieces to drop onto a sheet of paper. He also favored paintings and thin wood reliefs of amebalike forms with curving contours, mushroom-shaped heads, and round-dot eyes or simplified egg or navel shapes. He abhorred contrived art. To him, art was "a fruit which grows out of a man like a fruit out of a plant or like a child out of a mother." In *Objects Arranged*

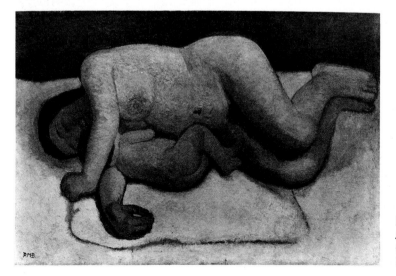

327. Paula Modersohn-Becker.
Mother and Child. 1907.
Oil on canvas, 7 × 9⅜″ (18 × 24 cm).
Ludwig-Roselius Collection, Bremen.

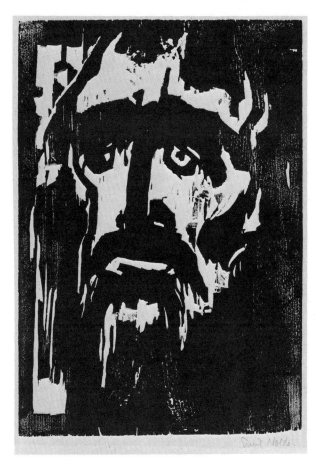

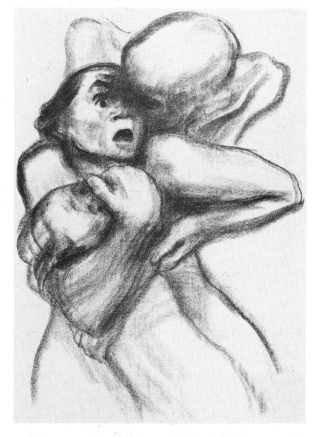

above: 328. Emil Nolde. *The Prophet.* 1912.
Woodcut, $12\frac{3}{4} \times 9''$ (32 × 23 cm).
National Gallery of Art, Washington, D.C.
(Rosenwald Collection).

above right: 329. Käthe Kollwitz.
Death Seizes a Woman. 1934. Lithograph,
$20\frac{1}{16} \times 14\frac{3}{8}''$ (51 × 37 cm). Fogg Art Museum,
Harvard University, Cambridge, Mass.
(Frances Calley Gray Fund, purchase).

right: 330. Jean (Hans) Arp. *Objects Arranged
According to the Laws of Chance or Navels.*
1930. Varnished wood relief, $10\frac{3}{8} \times 11\frac{1}{8}''$
(26 × 28 cm). Museum of Modern Art,
New York (purchase).

According to the Laws of Chance or Navels he used flat,
organic shapes of painted wood to make a small construction (Fig. 330). His love of nature is perhaps best expressed
in his later stone sculpture, influenced by Surrealism, with
its sensuous and organic forms as smooth and simple as
water-worn rocks. Arp's free-form shapes have inspired
contemporary industrial design such as that of cocktail tables, but they have been so much modified that much of
their early impact has been lost.

Working with similar motifs from her paintings, Sophie
Taeuber-Arp (1889–1934), wife of Hans Arp, also created a
prodigious range of works, including weaving, embroi-

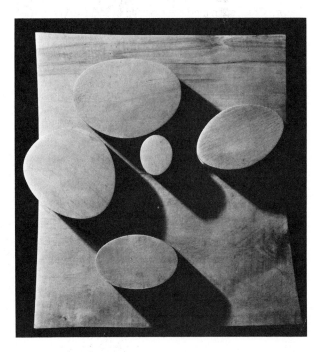

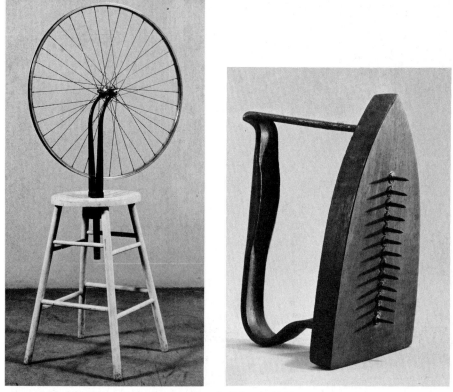

above left: 331. Marcel Duchamp. *Bicycle Wheel.* 1951
(third version after lost original of 1913). Assemblage; metal wheel,
diameter 2'1½" (0.65 m), mounted on painted wood stool,
height 1'11¾" (0.6 m), height overall 4'2½" (1.28 m). Sidney and
Harriett Janis Collection, gift to the Museum of Modern Art, New York.

above right: 332. Man Ray. *Gift* (*Cadeau*). c. 1958
(replica of partially destroyed original of 1921).
Painted flatiron with metal tacks, 6⅛ × 3⅝ × 4½" (16 × 19 × 11 cm).
Museum of Modern Art, New York (James Thrall Soby Fund).

dery, stained glass, collage, and wood reliefs. She and her
husband shared a creative relationship that inspired productivity in both.

A leading contributor to Dada who worked both in
New York and in Paris was Marcel Duchamp. According to
him, "Dada was a way to get out of a state of mind, to get
away from clichés—to get free." He had left behind his
Cubist- and Futurist-inspired paintings such as *Nude Descending a Staircase (No. 2)* (Fig. 63) to comment on the
results of the machine age. Like Picasso and Braque, he also
worked in collage. In 1913 he had glued string onto a canvas and combined it with paint and varnish to recreate the
childhood memory of a chocolate-grinding machine titled
The Bride Stripped Bare by Her Bachelors Even. Out of
such experiments he combined ordinary mass-produced
objects into constructions, which he called ready-mades.
His first construction consisted of a bicycle wheel fastened
to a kitchen stool so that the wheel could be spun easily—a
spoof on activity (possibly referring to the government)
that goes nowhere, ending where it starts (Fig. 331).

With this new method of absorbing actual objects into
compositions, painters had moved away from the mere
representation of reality. The question became, "Where
does reality end and art begin?" Dadaists believed art was
created by the very process of the artist's selection.
Duchamp's ready-mades emphasized his belief that there
is no boundary between life and art, and his constructions
expressed his disgust with the assembly-line production of
material goods. In bringing together everyday experiences
and common objects in new combinations, Duchamp was
reflecting on the absurdity of human attachments to the
mundane in a world he saw as illogical. He considered the
creating of art the only rational act.

Mocking human attempts to find salvation through
materialism, the New York Dadaist Man Ray (1890–1976)
transformed a flatiron into a work of art by gluing a row of
tacks to it (Fig. 332). Here, a useful object in the hands of a
Dadaist becomes nonfunctional, leading us to consider
whether people today may also become nonfunctional
because of dependency on machines. Dadaist objects like

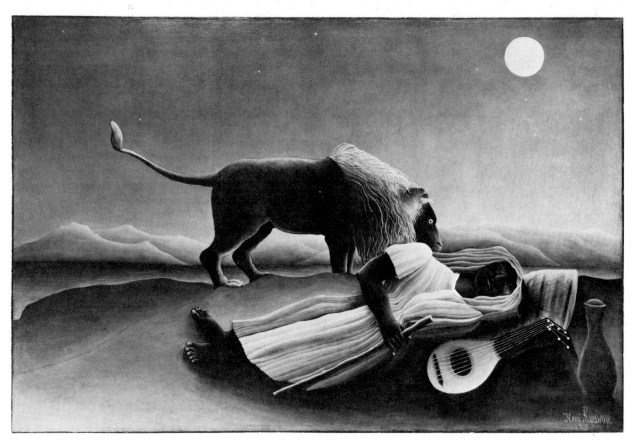

333. Henri Rousseau. *The Sleeping Gypsy.* 1897. Oil on canvas, 4'3" × 6'7"
(1.3 × 2.01 m). Museum of Modern Art, New York (gift of Mrs. Simon Guggenheim).

these also posed another question—whether a culture that produces masses of material goods has provided for disposal of that mountain of junk society soon discards.

The outstanding German Dadaist was Kurt Schwitters (1887–1948), who deliberately threw out traditional notions of beauty as a gesture against artistic authoritarianism. He collected crumpled trash to make collages that hint at the disintegration of our civilization and perhaps of our personal values. In his home in Hanover about 1925 he built the first of three *Merzbau.* It was a spatial environment of little grottoes, assembled from refuse, which filled a whole room and the one above. Titled a "cathedral of erotic misery" and dedicated to his friends, it even incorporated bits of their discarded clothing cast in plaster.

Surrealism In Paris in the 1920s a few Dadaists such as Picabia and Max Ernst (1891–1976) and avant-garde writers such as André Breton brought their ideas together in a new literary and artistic movement called Surrealism. According to Breton's *Manifesto of Surrealism* (1924), the movement was based on the conviction that dreams and other nonrational mental processes were the most important way to deal with life.

Influenced by the Austrian psychologist Sigmund Freud and the Swiss psychologist Carl Jung, Surrealist poets and painters tried to strip away the façades that often conceal our unconscious desires. They advocated spontaneous or automatic scribbles, doodles, or drips as a means of bringing such desires to light, and they gloried in the unexpected, the contrary, and the element of shock for shock's sake. In 1925 the Surrealists held their first group exhibition, including works by Max Ernst, Jean Arp, Man Ray, Picasso, Giorgio de Chirico (1888–1978), Paul Klee, André Masson (b. 1896), and Joan Miró. Not all these men continued to paint in the Surrealist manner, and others such as Kandinsky joined Surrealism later, but these painters formed the core of the movement.

Long before the appearance of Surrealism as a recognized style, people were interested in art inspired by dreams and the subconscious, as depicted in the Renaissance *Garden of Delights* (Fig. 265). Later in the 19th century the self-taught artist Henri Rousseau (1844–1910) painted an enchanted dream world. A customs inspector, unspoiled by exposure to traditional artistic conventions, Rousseau painted exotic canvases, such as *The Sleeping Gypsy,* which anticipated the limitless space of Surrealist paintings (Fig. 333). We delight in the paradoxical relationship of the man and the animal.

An early 20th-century forerunner of Surrealism was the Italian poet, novelist, and Metaphysical painter Giorgio de

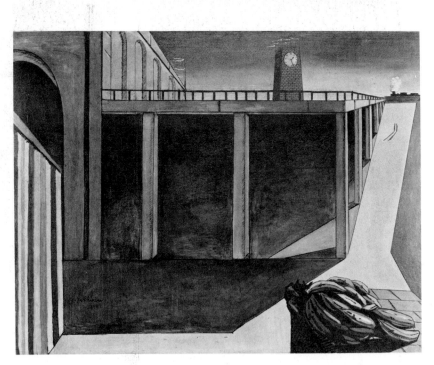

above: 334. Giorgio de Chirico. *Gare Montparnasse* (*The Melancholy of Departure*). 1914. Oil on canvas, 4'7⅛" × 6'5⅝" (1.4 × 1.84 m). Museum of Modern Art, New York (fractional gift of James Thrall Soby).

right: 335. Paul Klee. *Twittering Machine*. 1922. Watercolor, pen and ink; 16¼ × 12" (41 × 30 cm). Museum of Modern Art, New York (purchase).

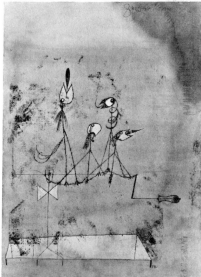

Chirico. He wrote, "Everything has two aspects: the current aspect we see and the ghostly which only rare individuals see in moments of clairvoyance and metaphysical abstraction." Strongly affected by the classical architecture of his homeland, De Chirico believed that an understanding of architecture was vital to the painter and that a landscape enclosed in an arch acquired "a greater metaphysical value, because it is solidified and isolated from the surrounding space." He frequently used arches in his urban scenes to suggest timelessness. These works also convey a sense of loneliness and menacing supernatural power. In *Gare Montparnasse* distorted linear perspective creates an eerie space, broken only by shadows cast by empty buildings, with tiny figures, a train, and a clock ticking off the minutes before departure (Fig. 334). These same images are repeated in other works where a distant horizon and empty city express the infinite time and space of the subconscious mind.

The Swiss artist Paul Klee, who taught at the Bauhaus, combined nonobjective tendencies, Expressionistic color, and elements of fantasy and humor that link him with Dada and Surrealism. He believed there is a kind of laughter that "can be put on the same dignified level as higher lyrical emotions." Certainly his watercolor *Twittering Machine* (Fig. 335) and his many etchings make us smile with a sense of delighted discovery.

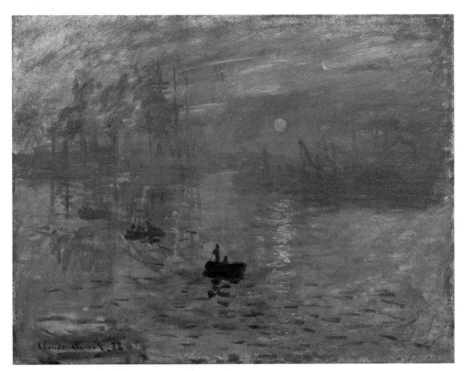

left: Plate 15. Claude Monet.
Impression: Sunrise.
1872. Oil on canvas,
19½ × 24½" (50 × 62 cm).
Musée Marmottan, Paris.

below: Plate 16.
Paul Cézanne.
Mont Sainte-Victoire.
1904–06. Oil on canvas,
27⅞ × 36⅛" (73 × 92 cm).
Philadelphia Museum of Art
(George W. Elkins Collection).

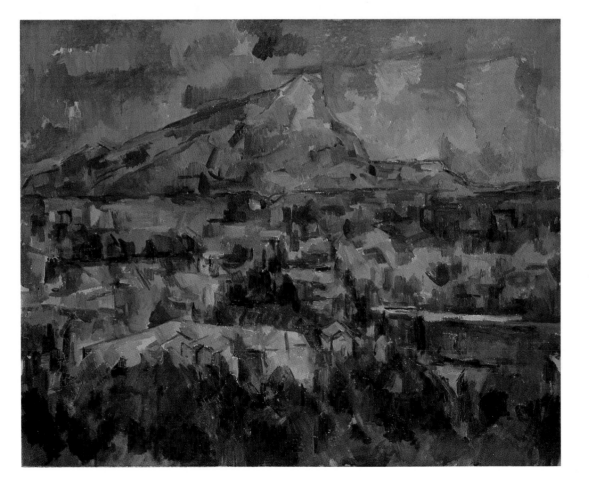

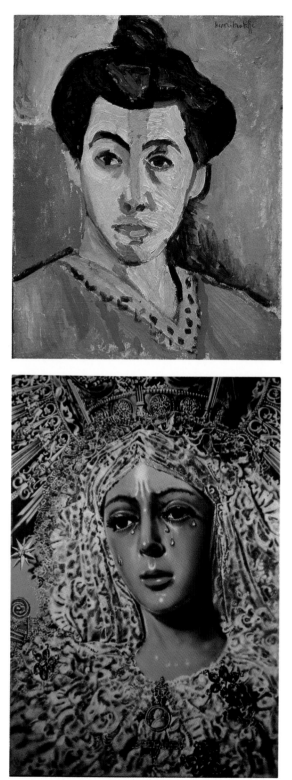

As a Surrealist, Klee believed in the importance of intuition as opposed to analysis. He tried to avoid the burden of historical styles by dipping into the art of children and "primitives," that is, people without art training. He wrote, "Everything vanishes around me and good works rise from me of their own accord. . . . It is not my head that functions but something . . . more remote." To keep in touch with his subconscious, Klee left himself open to new associations throughout the painting process. He rarely knew at the start of a work what might emerge, but developed in a splash of color or a line images as they suggested themselves. He titled the work only after he had finished it.

The Spanish painter Salvador Dali, whose explanations of his paintings are purposely enigmatic, declared, "All men are equal in their madness." His paintings reflect this view. Brilliant and arrogant, Dali is a master at publicizing himself and is, therefore, the best known of the Surrealists. He joined the movement late, and many consider him too theatrical to be taken seriously. Technically skilled, he creates precisely delineated, dreamlike landscapes filled with unexpected images. In *The Persistence of Memory*

(Fig. 336), time wilts in a limitless desert; ants cavort in an empty watch case; and a warped headlike image in the foreground, said to be a self-portrait, suggests the last remnant of a vanishing humanity.

Another Spaniard, Joan Miró, uses abstracted images in his inventive, poetic paintings, which Surrealistically combine humor and horror. Some of the images are recognizable, while others are strange forms, which he said he saw in hallucinations as a starving young artist. About *Carnival of Harlequin* (Fig. 64) he wrote, in flamboyant Surrealist prose,

> The ball of yarn unraveled by the cats dressed as Harlequins of smoke . . . throbbing like the throat of a bird at the contact of a woman . . . at this period I plucked a knob from a safety passage which I put in my eye like a monocle . . . which dives into the phosphorescent ocean after describing a luminous circle.

Miró was trained in Spain in the academic tradition, and there is nothing undisciplined about his seemingly childlike paintings. Although he was anti-intellectual, pas-

336. Salvador Dali. *The Persistence of Memory.* 1931. Oil on canvas, 9½ × 13″ (24 × 33 cm). Museum of Modern Art, New York (anonymous gift).

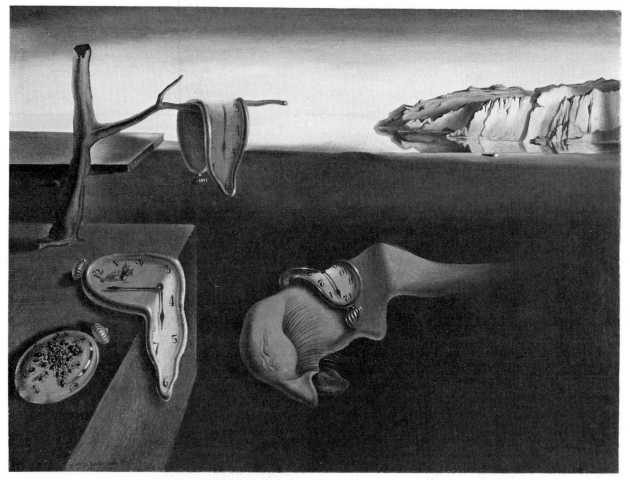

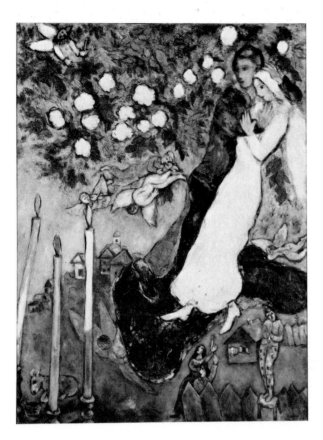

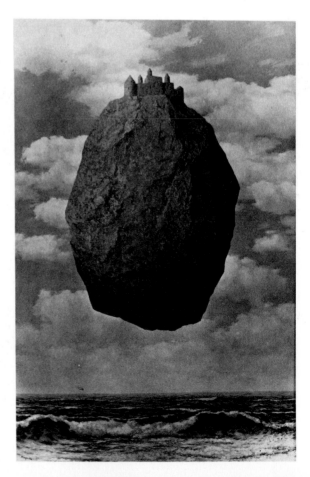

sionately fond of color, and hostile to tradition, he produced paintings, sculpture, lithographs, and ceramics that are subtle and brilliantly composed. He was also active in theater and ballet, designing sets and costumes for the famous ballet company of Serge Diaghilev, and it is from this period that *Carnival of Harlequin* dates. Of all the Surrealists, Miró perhaps had the strongest influence on painters of the later Abstract Expressionist movement.

Instead of expressing Surrealist anxiety and pessimism, Marc Chagall painted his feelings of joy, festivity, and love with a sensuous delight in color and texture. His works, based on memories of his childhood in a Russian Jewish family, are steeped in folklore and the mystical Hasidic tradition. He filled his canvases with fiddlers, Talmudic scholars, peasant women, and floating cows and roosters. In his fantasies, Chagall is close to Henri Rousseau, and his works are richly personal. His portrait of himself on the shoulders of his wife expresses the perennial euphoria of love (Fig. 337).

The Belgian Surrealist René Magritte used unexpected and disturbing images in his paintings. Heavy rocks float lightly through soft blue skies (Fig. 338); or a room as perfect in scale and detail as a van Eyck interior (Fig. 262) may contain a huge apple, which almost reaches the ceiling. A closet full of discarded clothes may bulge with invisible human forms, becoming a chronicle of past events. Painted in a meticulous, realistic style, most of Magritte's works present the incredible as an accomplished fact.

Alternating truth with illusion, Magritte makes us suspicious of both the painted and the real world. In a painting of 1964 he depicted a room with a broken window. Through the window we can see a sunset as well as a landscape, which is repeated on the broken windowpane propped against the interior wall. Which of the two landscapes really exists? Reflecting on the 17th-century philosopher René Descartes' radical statement about reality, "I think, therefore I am," Magritte presents us with a world in which we see his dreams become real objects and his objects become dreams.

Meret Oppenheim (b. 1913) emphasized the Surrealists' sense of the absurd. She created a fur-covered cup and saucer that mocked a pretentious society whose products could no longer function (Fig. 339).

The Surrealist current continues in the paintings of the Irish-born Francis Bacon (b. 1910), who uses the past as a basis for his works but transforms them through his own inward vision of personal torment. As part of a series of works on the Crucifixion, one of his characteristic themes, he painted a *Magdalene* (Fig. 340). The figure's solid form recalls Giotto. Under an umbrella and veil the gaping

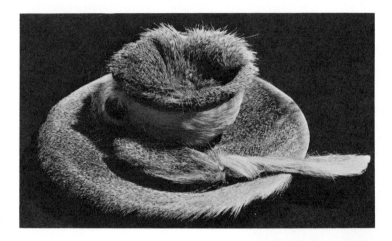

above: 339. Meret Oppenheim. *Object* (fur-covered cup, saucer, and spoon). 1936. Diameter of cup $4\frac{3}{8}''$ (11 cm); diameter of saucer $9\frac{3}{8}''$ (24 cm); length of spoon $8''$ (20 cm); overall height $2\frac{7}{8}''$ (7 cm). Museum of Modern Art, New York (purchase).

right: 340. Francis Bacon. *Figure Study II* (previously known as *The Magdalene*). 1945–46. Oil on canvas, $4'9\frac{1}{4}'' \times 4'2\frac{3}{4}''$ (1.45 × 1.29 m). Kirklees Metropolitan Council, Huddersfield, West Yorkshire, England.

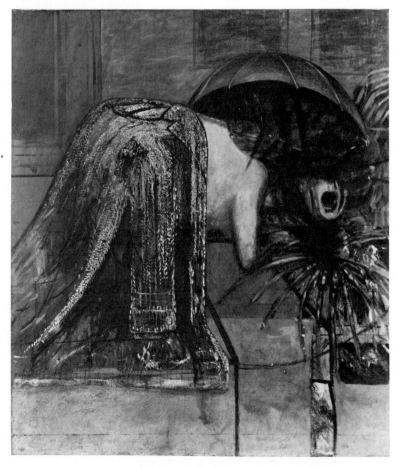

mouth howls in grief. This work reveals Bacon's superb skills as a painter, his foundation in tradition, and the acute sense of the horrors of his world.

A different personal vision inspires the work of the Afro-American artist Eldzier Cortor (b. 1915). Exposed to African art at Chicago's Art Institute, he seems to merge African and Surrealist influences in the distorted figures and extended vistas of paintings such as *Trio V* (Fig. 341).

341. Eldzier Cortor. *Trio V.* 1959.
Oil and tempera on wallboard,
$36\frac{1}{2} \times 17\frac{1}{8}''$ (93 × 43 cm).
Collection Margaret Parry, Elkhart Lake, Wis.

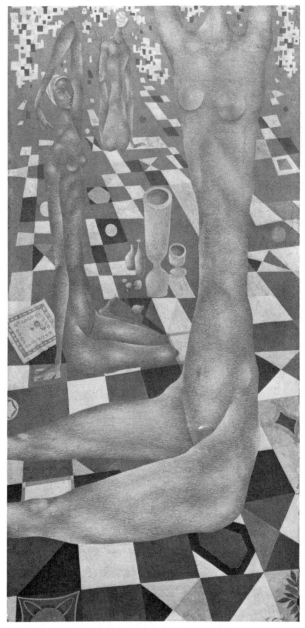

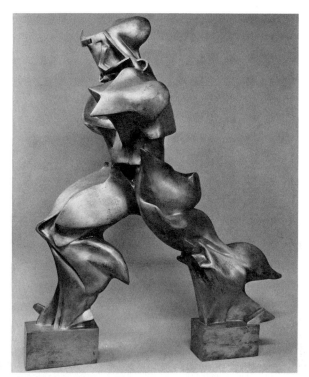

342. Umberto Boccioni.
Unique Forms of Continuity in Space. 1913.
Bronze, height $43\frac{1}{2}''$ (101 cm).
Museum of Modern Art, New York (acquired through the Lillie P. Bliss Bequest).

Sculpture

Until the 20th century, sculptors had carved or cast figures that relied on visually solid volumes surrounded by space. At the beginning of the century, many sculptors continued that tradition, exemplified by Rodin. In the new age, however, the changing concepts of space and motion that affected painting also affected sculpture. Avant-garde sculptors reached for different images, techniques, and materials, as we saw in Chapter 6.

One of the first sculptors to break with the past was Umberto Boccioni (1882–1916), whose *Manifesto* of 1910 announced Futurism. His *Unique Forms of Continuity in Space* (Fig. 342) depicts a figure rushing forward in violent motion. Expressive as it is, with strong, forward-thrusting diagonals, the cubistic figure is impersonal. Boccioni was interested in movement in the abstract and arranged the shapes to convey the impression of action.

Cubism The Cubist movement freed many sculptors from traditional imagery. Jacques Lipchitz (1891–1973) at first created flat forms that seemed to be almost literal translations of Cubist paintings into sculpture. Later he developed a personal style in which he combined Cubist simplification with his own ideas about birth, growth, and death. Also affected by African art, he searched for a way to reconcile human forms with the new geometry of the machine. His bronze, robotlike *Figure* (Fig. 343) of 1926–1930 is composed of biomorphic (organic) shapes, yet in its stark simplicity suggests an ominous, machinelike force.

An academically trained Rumanian, Constantin Brancusi joined the radical young artists working in Paris. Although he was concerned with the machine age, African art, and Cubism, he never gave up his deep involvement in the natural world. His famous *Bird in Space* (Fig. 344) deals

with organic subjects at the same time that they explore Cubist simplification of masses.

Constructivism An even more radical break with tradition was Constructivist sculpture. No longer dependent on carving, modeling, or casting but moving into a new technical area, these sculptures consisted of constructions, or assemblages, of pieces of wood, metal, plastic, or other

343. Jacques Lipchitz.
Figure. 1926–31.
Bronze, height 7′1¼″ (2.17 m).
Museum of Modern Art, New York
(Van Gogh Purchase Fund).

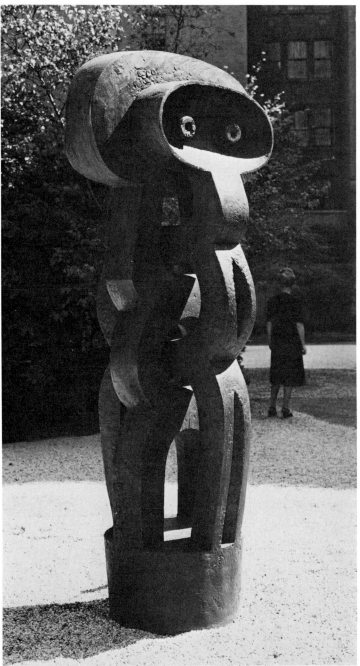

344. Constantin Brancusi.
Bird in Space. c. 1928. Bronze (unique cast), height 4′6″ (1.37 m).
Museum of Modern Art, New York
(anonymous gift).

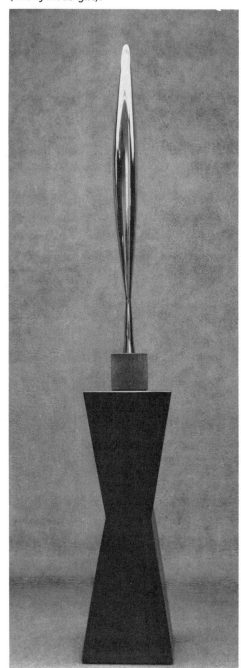

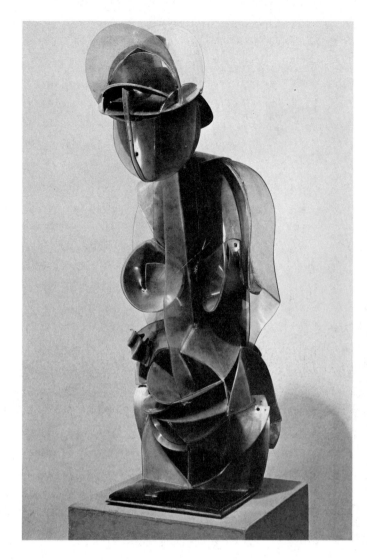

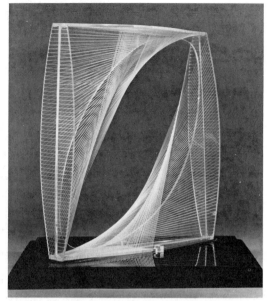

left: 345. Antoine Pevsner. *Torso.* 1924–26. Construction in plastic and copper, 29½ × 11⅝" (75 × 30 cm). Museum of Modern Art, New York (Katherine S. Dreier Bequest).

above: 346. Naum Gabo. *Linear Construction No. 1 (Smaller Version).* 1942–43. Plexiglas and nylon thread on plexiglas base, 12¼ × 12¼ × 2¾" (31 × 31 × 6 cm). Hirshhorn Museum and Sculpture Garden, Smithsonian Institution, Washington, D.C.

materials. Constructivist space between solid forms and seen through transparent planes was composed as carefully as the forms themselves.

Constructivism began in Russia where two brothers, Naum Gabo (1890–1977) and Antoine Pevsner, were attracted to the analytical approach of Cubism and to new areas of technology. In 1920 they wrote a *Realistic Manifesto,* in which they declared that sculpture must no longer describe reality but must be in harmony with engineering technology. When the Soviet government insisted on a return to conservative art, they, like Kandinsky, left for the West, where their ideas were well received by avant-garde artists. Pevsner's *Torso* (Fig. 345) used Cubist-inspired planes to recreate the concave and convex forms of the human body out of sheets of copper and plastic. The transparency of the plastic denied the solid aspects of traditional sculpture. Even more revolutionary was Gabo's *Linear Construction No. 1* (Fig. 346), which consisted of a plastic frame threaded with nylon. Like Cubist painters, both

sculptors were concerned with overlapping and combining multiple views of the same, usually geometric, subject as well as with the relation of mass and interior and exterior space.

Both Cubism and Constructivism influenced the work of the outstanding British sculptor Barbara Hepworth (1903–1975). Using highly polished marble, wood, and bronze, she sculpted abstract geometric forms, which were usually pierced or hollowed out in order to incorporate space within their design. Her *Single Form* (Dag Hammarskjöld memorial) (Fig. 347) is a fitting testimonial to her powers. She wrote of it:

I had to work to the scale of twenty-one feet and bring into my mind everything . . . taught me about stress and strain and gravity and wind force. Finally all the many parts were got out of St. Ives safely, and when assembled, . . . they stood in perfect balance. This was a magic moment.

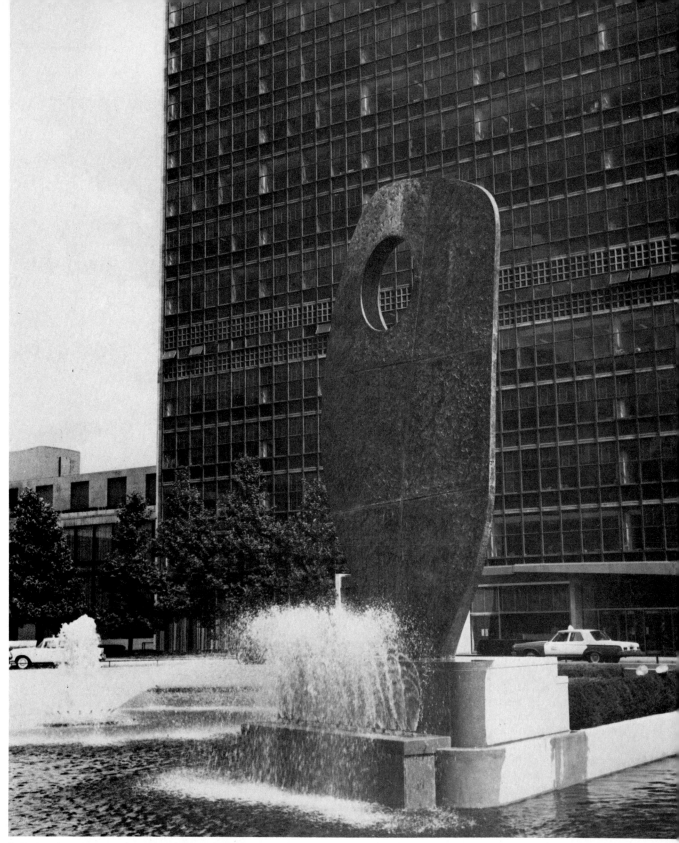

347. Barbara Hepworth. *Single Form*. 1964.
Bronze, height 21′ (6.4 m). United Nations Plaza, New York.

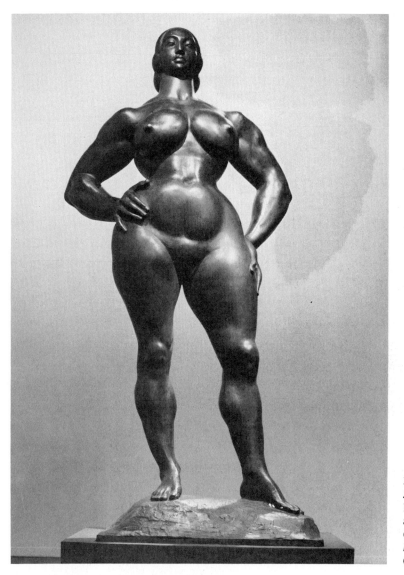

348. Gaston Lachaise.
Standing Woman. 1932.
Bronze; height 7'4" (2.24 m),
at base 3'5$\frac{1}{8}$" × 1'7$\frac{1}{8}$"
(1.04 × 0.48 m).
Museum of Modern Art, New York
(Mrs. Simon Guggenheim Fund).

Realism The human body has been the main subject of figurative sculpture since ancient times. It has been treated in a variety of ways. Egyptian sculptors carved massive stone statues (Fig. 35), abstracted in form and exaggerated in scale, to glorify their rulers and gods. Classical Greek statues of gods and heroes, subtly elegant examplars of moderation, show the body in a state of balance between energy and repose (Fig. 224). Medieval sculpture, chiefly for the Church, portrays the human figure symbolically (Fig. 243) in conflict between yearning for heaven and earthly temptation. The open sexuality of an Indian goddess was intended to remind the viewer of his oneness with the universe (Fig. 300). In 19th-century Europe, Rodin's sculpture expressed his interest in psychology and movement (Fig. 117).

In the 20th century, the concept of the figure changed radically, as we have seen. Reflecting the machine age, the body was abstracted and almost dehumanized by Cubist sculptors and ignored by Constructivists. Other sculptors, however, remained closer to the figurative tradition.

The fertility symbol first seen in the prehistoric *Venus of Willendorf* (Fig. 15) reappears in the work of Gaston Lachaise (1882–1935). Throughout most of his career he was obsessed by the image of the female nude. He modeled her as a gross, maternal figure with mountainous breasts and thighs, but her delicately tapered arms and legs give her an almost classical elegance. She sits in a chair, floats on a high pedestal, or stands (Fig. 348).

One of the most creative of the figurative sculptors is Henry Moore (1898–1981), the son of an English coal miner. Unlike the work of his friend and colleague Barbara Hepworth, Moore's work is highly organic. He is interested in the biological structure of the body and the connections between its forms and the natural world. He explored these relationships in wood, stone, and bronze, handling each with a deep sensitivity to its innate characteristics.

Moore developed his style to express an association of the body with the universal mystery of life and to separate it from the emotions of the individual. Often he reduced the head, concentrating instead on the shafts and terminals of the body structure, which is often shown reclining (Fig. 349). Like the Constructivists, he brought space into sculpture. He created great hollows in the middle of his figures, sculpting strong rhythmic volumes and spaces that suggest the openings of the living body and emphasize

sexual associations but may also recall caves, and holes in rocks and trees.

These forms reflect one of the most pervasive influences in his work, the *Chac Mool* (Fig. 350), a massive pre-Columbian stone figure of a rain god from Mexico, which lies on its back and has a hollowed out abdomen. Related to his figures and groupings are the drawings he made of families taking refuge in air-raid shelters and underground stations during the bombing of London in World War II. Their simplified forms suggest timeless mountains as well as the solidity of the bony structure under the flesh.

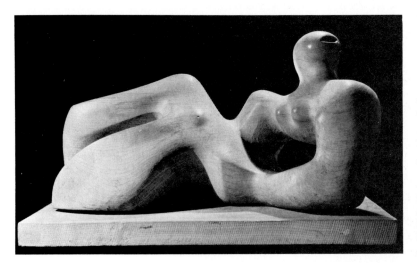

left: 349. Henry Moore. *Reclining Figure.* 1935. Elmwood, 19 × 35 × 15″ (48 × 89 × 38 cm). Albright-Knox Art Gallery, Buffalo, N.Y. (Room of Contemporary Art Fund).

below: 350. *Chac Mool*, rain god, from Chichén-Itzá, Mexico. Mayan-Toltec, 10th–11th century. Limestone, height 42⅛″ (107 cm). National Museum of Anthropology, Mexico City.

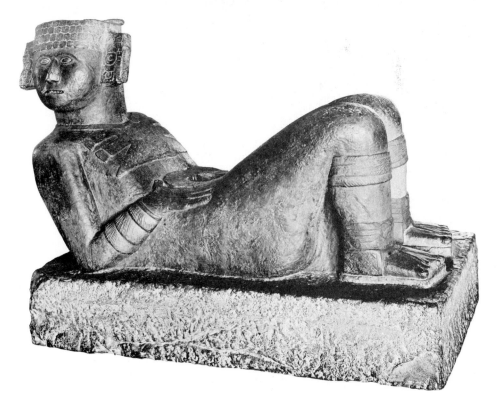

Two influential Continental sculptors, Marino Marini (b. 1901) and Alberto Giacometti, have used the human figure expressively to comment on human isolation and fear. In the tradition of Rodin, both emphasize surface textures. Having absorbed Surrealist attitudes as well as influences from early Italian figure sculpture, their styles are nonetheless quite personal.

Although Marini's subjects include female figures and portraits, he is known for his bronzes of men on horses—forms that seem linked to the Etruscan sculpture of his native Tuscany. The sense of isolation and fear projected by these anonymous riders is not accidental. Marini watched Italians fleeing from wartime air raids. The frightened way they looked upward to watch the sky for bombers became an important gesture in his sculpture—expressing human helplessness (Fig. 351). In recent years his images have become increasingly violent. The stumplike vestiges of feet and hands suggest mutilation of bodies by war and make his figures appear even more isolated and mute.

Giacometti, the son of a Swiss painter, created a new human image in his emaciated bronze figures that stand so stiffly and face us so directly. The attenuated forms in *City Square* (Fig. 42) appear almost like shadows that float across the flat plane of the street. The five figures, captured in a momentary encounter, seem unable to experience any real interchange. Large or small, in groups or by themselves, Giacometti's forms seem lonely and alienated. He has exaggerated the distance between subject and viewer by erasing the nonessential details of the body, thereby increasing its sense of isolation.

Architecture

We saw in Chapter 9 how consideration of structure, function, and space were related to the development of new building materials and engineering methods in the 19th century. Louis Sullivan, who used new techniques in his tall, steel-frame buildings (Fig. 184), made a statement that widely influenced 20th-century architecture: "Form follows function." That is, an architect should consider the function of a building and then design a form to suit the function rather than deciding on a Neoclassical temple design, for example, and forcing a modern bank to fit into it.

In the early 1900s in France, Auguste Perret was using reinforced concrete frames and nonsupporting, or curtain, walls, which left building interiors free to be divided into a

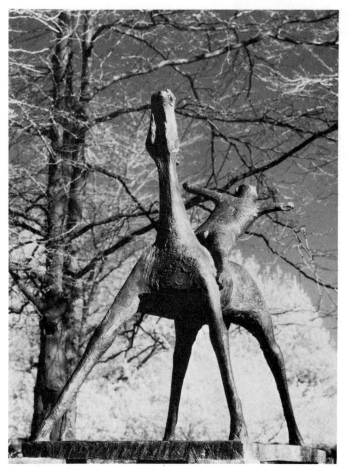

351. Marino Marini. *Horse and Rider.*
1952–53. Bronze, 6′10″ × 6′9″ × 3′10½″
(2.08 × 2.06 × 1.18 m).
Hirshhorn Museum and Sculpture Garden,
Smithsonian Institution,
Washington, D.C.

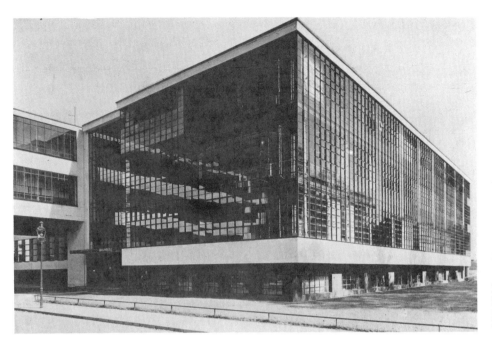

352. Walter Gropius.
Bauhaus Building,
Dessau, East Germany.
1925–26.

combination of rooms. In Germany, Peter Behrens (1868–1940) and Walter Gropius (1883–1969) were using the same technique to construct functional buildings with clean, almost mechanical lines. Gropius in collaboration with Adolf Meyer (1881–1929) carried a curtain wall of glass windows out to the corners of the Fagus Shoe Factory in Alfeld-an-der-Leine. This device made possible simultaneous views of the interior and exterior, as in the shifting planes of a Cubist painting, and at the same time achieved an appearance of lightness. In the United States, Frank Lloyd Wright was experimenting with functional buildings, Cubist planes, and cantilevering (Fig. 178). This ferment of new ideas in architecture influenced artists, who in turn influenced architects. In fact, architects, artists, and designers knew one another or were familiar with one another's published works.

The Bauhaus and the International Style Many of these ideas flourished in the Bauhaus, a school of design founded by Gropius in Weimar, Germany, in 1919 from two earlier schools of arts and crafts. Here art, technology, and business were brought together in an attempt to apply principles of good design to industrial production. Artists from Germany, Russia, the Netherlands, and Switzerland joined the faculty to develop an **International Style** of architecture and design, which gradually spread throughout the industrialized world.

Fundamental to Bauhaus teaching was Sullivan's principle that form follows function and William Morris' belief that utility and aesthetics could be integrated. Rather than returning to old craft-guild concepts, however, the school looked forward, embracing modern technology and materials. It explored new approaches to printing, metalwork,

weaving, pottery, and stagecraft as well as architecture. The faculty included such prominent figures as the painters Kandinsky, Klee, and Albers; and the designers and architects Ludwig Mies van der Rohe, Marcel Breuer, and Laszlo Moholy-Nagy (1895–1946). Gropius declared:

> We want to create a clear, organic architecture whose inner logic will be radiant and naked, unencumbered by lying façades and trickiness; we want an architecture adapted to our world of machines, radios, and fast motor cars, an architecture whose function is clearly recognizable in the relation of its form.

A structural base of the new style was the use of a weight-bearing cage, or frame, on which the outer, non-weight-bearing walls could be hung. These curtain walls could be made of any material that would serve to enclose space. As a result, windows and doors could be enlarged almost indefinitely, while the reduction of interior supports allowed the inside of the building to be rearranged at need. Fundamental to the new International Style was an avoidance of applied decoration. Gropius believed that aesthetic satisfaction in a building could be achieved through a balance of solids and spaces. Nothing more was needed to make a building beautiful.

When the Bauhaus was moved to Dessau in 1925, new administrative offices, classrooms, studios, workshops, a library, and living quarters for faculty and students were needed. Instead of attempting to fit these varied areas into a group of Gothic or Neoclassical buildings, Gropius designed a new building, using new engineering methods, that honestly served its varied functions and reflected them in its design (Fig. 352). Beginning with an open box as the basic unit, Gropius varied its volume according to its potential use and then grouped the boxes into a pleasing three-dimensional composition that suggested the crisp rectangles of a Mondrian painting.

Mies van der Rohe, who became director of the Bauhaus after Gropius, refined the International Style, bringing it an elegance through the use of light-reflecting materials and subtle detail. His German Pavilion at the International Exhibition in Barcelona in 1929 (since destroyed) was the archetype of the International Style (Fig. 161). The long,

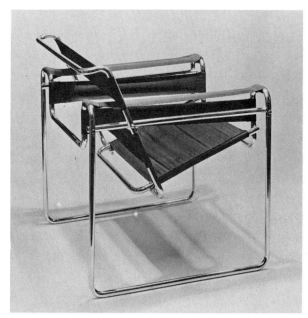

above: 353. Marcel Breuer. Armchair. 1925.
Chrome-plated steel tube and canvas,
height 28″ (71 cm). Manufacturer: Gebrüder Thonet A.G., Germany. Museum of Modern Art, New York (gift of Herbert Bayer).

below: 354. Frank Lloyd Wright. Robie House, Chicago. 1909.

low, open building conveyed a quality of serenity through its clean lines, refined details, and sensitive use of materials. Its interior spaces were defined, without being isolated, by chrome-plated steel supports, glass walls, and marble panels. These surfaces contrasted with one another and with the open expanse of the pool in the court. Mies's famous Barcelona chair (Fig. 159), designed for this pavilion, can be seen through the glass wall, expressing the Bauhaus ideal of carrying good design through all aspects of a building.

When Hitler closed the Bauhaus in 1933, many faculty members went to the United States, where they taught Bauhaus principles and continued to work in the International Style. In his buildings for the Illinois Institute of Technology in Chicago, his Lake Shore Apartments in Chicago (Fig. 185), and the Seagram Building in New York, Mies integrated concrete, steel, and glass into refined, rational compositions. Gropius and Breuer designed low, cubistic houses. Breuer's tubular metal chair (Fig. 353), first made in Germany, and Mies's Barcelona chair were mass produced, as were lamps and other objects that showed Bauhaus influence. Herbert Bayer (b. 1900), also from the Bauhaus faculty, influenced typography and advertising design.

Frank Lloyd Wright An American pioneer in early 20th-century architecture was Frank Lloyd Wright. Although he affected the International Style, he despised it and developed a personal style that never fit into any category. Brilliant, rebellious, and innovative, he was influenced by Sullivan, with whom he studied. Even in his early years he opposed any architecture that borrowed styles from the past. Like Sullivan he believed that buildings should openly reflect the functions they are intended to perform. He deplored, however, the ferroconcrete boxes produced by the International Style. He designed the Imperial Hotel in Tokyo around an open court, adapting Oriental decorative details. He also built it according to a structural system that enabled it to withstand the devastating earthquake of 1923. It was razed in 1968 to make way for a larger hotel.

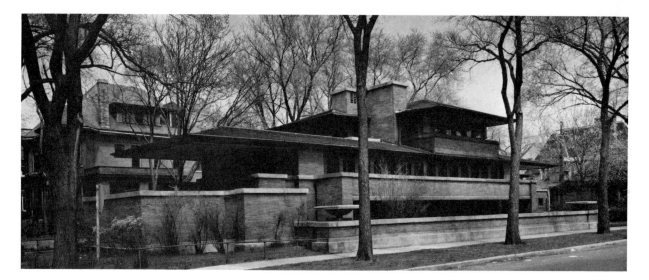

Wright also believed that a building should reveal the materials with which it is constructed. For example, stone should look like stone and be used as a means of support rather than to conceal modern structural systems. In the same way, ferroconcrete building blocks should not pretend to be anything else.

In addition, Wright was always concerned for natural surroundings and people's spiritual needs. Rejecting the European idea that buildings should be machines, he believed that a house should provide for the spirit as well as the body. Strongly influenced by Japanese architecture, he was convinced that people must keep alive their relation to the natural world. Therefore he gave his houses an organic quality by often using wood and stone, and he designed them to fit into their natural surroundings. The long, low lines of the early ranch-style Robie House in Chicago (Fig. 354) are integrated with the flat site, and the later Kaufman House in Bear Run, Pennsylvania, is cantilevered over a waterfall (Fig. 178).

Wright's designs evolved over the years. In the 1920s, for example, his buildings were massive rectangular forms as a result of his experimenting with poured concrete and patterned concrete blocks. Decorative elements were provided by the texture of the materials and the interplay of blocklike masses and open space. The glass and cantilever construction of the Kaufman House suggests the machine-oriented International Style. Nevertheless, his basic philosophy was maintained.

Wright was once asked by a student how to develop an original personal style. He responded briefly, "You can't. I invented the new architecture at the turn of the century. All you can do is learn its principles and work them." Despite the arrogance of the statement, Wright's buildings radically altered the course of architecture in the 20th century.

Le Corbusier In France, Le Corbusier, who had worked with Behrens, was also designing innovative, functional buildings in the International Style. He used his knowledge of modern engineering techniques to open up his buildings and introduce light, air, and sun. He saw a house as "a machine for living in." In his influential book *Towards a New Architecture* (published in French in 1923), he urged architects to move away from an architecture stifled by custom and to study ocean liners, airplanes, and automobiles instead. His Villa Savoye in Poissy, France (Fig. 355), one of the outstanding examples of the International Style, illustrates these beliefs.

355. Le Corbusier. Villa Savoye, Poissy-sur-Seine, France. 1929–30.

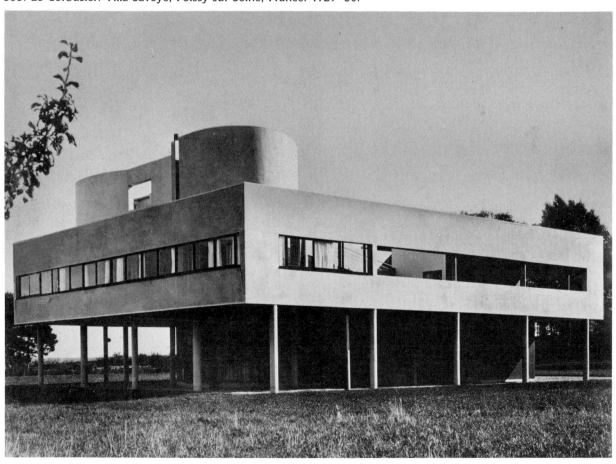

The concrete and glass structure is close to the purist ideals of Mondrian, and the combination of its curved forms and rectangles suggests Le Corbusier's interest in ocean liners. The Villa Savoye has none of Wright's respect for site; instead, raised on posts, it seems to float above the earth, suggesting the rootless, transient quality of modern life. Many of its features, such as the posts and the windows in horizontal strips, were adapted by later architects. Wright derisively referred to Le Corbusier's buildings as "boxes on stilts," but they may have influenced his Kaufman House (Fig. 178).

Le Corbusier's influence on architecture was immense, but perhaps in the long run he will be remembered best for his social philosophy. He believed that not only the rich, who could afford houses like the Villa Savoye, but *all* human beings are entitled to live in buildings that will surround them with space and beauty. Dedicated to this ideal, he planned groups of inexpensive, mass-produced houses made of reinforced concrete. These houses were designed to provide comfortable living in units, which could be divided inside according to the needs of each family. As the movement of population to cities progressed and space became scarce, he gave up his early row-house concept and built vertical apartment towers surrounded by open space. These structures are discussed in Chapter 19.

The work of these internationally active architects, and others who adopted their philosophies, has profoundly affected our lives. Thousands of useful objects and buildings in the last several decades have been influenced by them. Out of the chaos of changing needs, changing materials, and changing art of the 20th century, these creative minds brought a measure of logical order, through architecture, into our world.

EXERCISES AND ACTIVITIES

1. Trace the growth of one new style of art that emerged during the first two decades of the 20th century. Discuss in detail two artists who worked in that style.
2. Explain in what way exposure to African art was an important force in the development of 20th-century art; give examples. Explain what aspects of Oriental art influenced 20th-century artists.
3. Draw a composition in the style of Cubism, superimposing in one drawing at least three views of an object. Include interior and exterior aspects and top, side, and front views, presenting a familiar object in a new way.
4. Search for and quote passages of poetry or fiction that deal with the same themes as those that appear in Surrealism and Dadaism.
5. Create a construction of objects emphasizing nonart values.
6. The creation of the illusion of deep space has appeared throughout art history. What Surrealist painters used this technique? Create a composition in color or in black and white using perspective, changing hues, and values to create an illusion of deep space, but using images from the world of dreams and fantasy.
7. What is the International Style? How did the style start, and how did it influence painting, architecture, sculpture, and the industrial arts?
8. Using poster paints, create a simple still life in at least two of the styles that developed in the first quarter of the 20th century.
9. One of the most powerful architectural forces of this century was expressed in the philosophy of Frank Lloyd Wright. What was his philosophy, and how did it influence other architects? What was the influence of the architectural ideas of Le Corbusier?
10. What was the Bauhaus? How did it influence 20th-century art? Cite examples.

18 America in Ascendancy: 1925–1945

At a certain moment the canvas began to appear to one American painter after another as an arena in which to act.

HAROLD ROSENBERG

After a brief euphoria following World War I, the world slid into the Great Depression of the 1930s. Paris, where the arts had continued during the international conflict, resumed its position as the art capital, but an ocean away, America's growing isolation had led our artists to develop their own art forms. As bankruptcy gripped much of the country, social problems multiplied. In response, the arts in the United States became more socially conscious, increasingly realistic, and often nationalistic. The diversity of European art did not exist in this country. We can identify for the most part, however, the same basic trends that characterized European art—realism, derived from what already existed in traditional American art; Expressionism with strong emotional overtones comparable to the European currents; formalism with a concentration on design and color; and fantasy.

Realist Painting

During the first decades of the 20th century, conservative American artists continued to follow the rules established by academies of art. These American academies were modeled after their European counterparts, where many Americans studied.

The Ash Can School and Its Influence In the 19th century, realist painting had been developed to a high degree by such artists as Thomas Eakins (1844–1916) and Winslow Homer (1836–1910). Painters of the **Ash Can school** in the early 20th century carried realism much further. Possibly drawing upon their experiences as journalists, they found themes for art in backyards, city streets, and bars. John Sloan (1871–1951) produced paintings and etchings illustrating the lives of working people in New York. George Bellows (1882–1925) painted portraits and vigorous scenes of prizefights and other New York subjects.

Edward Hopper (1882–1967), perhaps influenced by the Ash Can school, adhered to American realistic traditions, commenting on human isolation with paintings of empty city streets and lonely houses. Hopper, who supported himself for years as a commercial artist, insisted that his aim in painting was always "the most exact transcription possible of my most intimate impression of nature." While that may have been true, his sensitive eye carefully selected and reorganized colors, forms, and light patterns in order to convey a sense of poignancy. His point of view is that of a traveler who stands in the street watching the lives of other people through the windows of all-night cafés and of empty-looking, flatly lit rows of apartments. In *Early Sunday Morning* (Fig. 356), without seeing a single person, we sense the desperation of individuals caught in their own cycles of life and death. Each area of the painting is reduced to the essentials, and the bare windows and empty shops are organized into a quiet, almost formal vertical and horizontal composition which implies, rather than depicts, the loneliness behind drawn shades.

Social Protest and Other Forms of Realism With the Depression, Americans turned inward, frightened and disillusioned by the failure of the economy. The stock-market

356. Edward Hopper. *Early Sunday Morning.* 1930. Oil on canvas, 2′11″ × 5′ (0.89 × 1.52 m). Whitney Museum of American Art, New York.

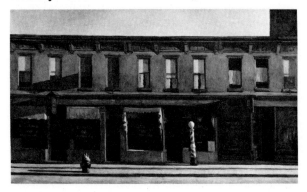

crash of 1929 meant that people could no longer depend on limitless material progress to provide security. Businesses failed and unemployment spread. Artists stood with factory workers in bread lines. To give some artists employment the Works Projects Administration commissioned them to paint murals in public buildings. This was the first broad governmental program of support for the arts in U.S. history.

Many artists turned to social issues for their subject matter. Before the 1930s, most artistic expressions of political and social criticism in the United States had been limited to cartoons. But the Depression inspired the first American movement that combined serious art with social protest in the tradition of Goya, Daumier, and Picasso. One artist involved in this movement was Ben Shahn (1898–1969), whose work powerfully expressed the tragedy of human degradation and social injustice. Experienced as a mural painter and illustrator, he depicted isolated city dwellers, victims of official inequity, and the starving wives and children of coal miners. Shahn, like other American artists, incorporated the influences of Cubism and Expressionism into his protest paintings. In *The Passion of Sacco and Vanzetti* (Fig. 357) he condemned the execution of two Italian immigrants who he, and many other Americans, believed were victims of personal and political prejudice.

From a strongly personal viewpoint, Ivan Le Lorraine Albright (b. 1897) used an almost microscopic form of realism to express his response to the disintegration of the individual in a hostile world. Of *Poor Room* (Fig. 358), which shows a clutter of Victorian decadence seen through a broken basement window, Albright said as a title, *"Poor Room—There is No time, No end, No Today, No Yesterday, No Tomorrow. Only the forever and forever and forever without end."* The sense of decay and rotting flesh that pervades Albright's still lifes and figure paintings turns them into intense statements about the impermanence of material possessions and of life itself.

Isolationism was especially strong in the Midwest, where a combination of erosion, caused by years of poor farming practices, and prolonged drought created dust-bowl conditions in many areas. At first, Midwestern artists depicted the world around them with a satirical eye. As the Depression wore on, they became more nationalistic, turning their anger toward foreign influences rather than toward the absurdities of provincialism and conservativisim. Many rural and small-town Americans viewed European culture with distrust, even though their own ancestors had come from the Old World. Fearful that what they had worked so long to achieve might be lost in the Depression, they clung to their possessions and their beliefs. Grant Wood (1892–1942) in *American Gothic* (Fig. 359) combined humor with a respect for the hardships of farm life. He depicted a farmer and his spinster daughter as solemn, suspicious provincials.

Georgia O'Keeffe (b. 1887), who taught in western Texas and eventually settled in New Mexico, painted barns, mountains, and bleached bones characteristic of the

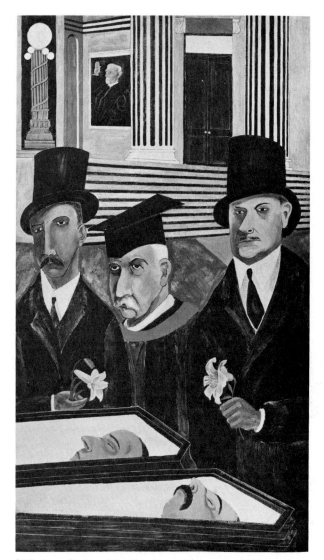

357. Ben Shahn. *The Passion of Sacco and Vanzetti.* 1931–32. Tempera on canvas, 7'½ × 4' (2.14 × 1.22 m). Whitney Museum of American Art, New York (gift of Edith and Milton Lowenthal in memory of Juliana Force).

harsh, barren landscape of the Southwest. Other subjects included flowers, New York skyscrapers, and clouds seen from a jet plane. Well-acquainted with European art currents, she presented all these objects, manmade and natural, from a distinctive point of view and in a precise personal style that gives them fresh meaning (Fig. 360). The natural smoothness of her technique, the extreme perspective and enlarged scale of the objects tend to convert most of her work into almost abstract images, which may be terrifying in their starkness and intensity.

A painter who balanced realistic recording of the world with poetic invention is Loren MacIver (b. 1909). Whether her themes are urban life or ephemeral aspects of the natu-

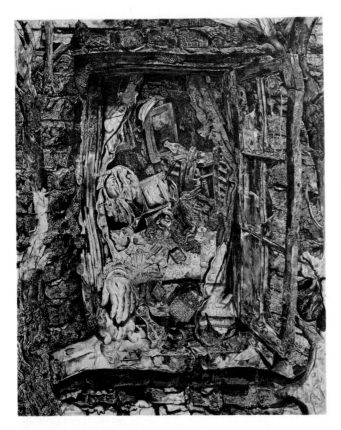

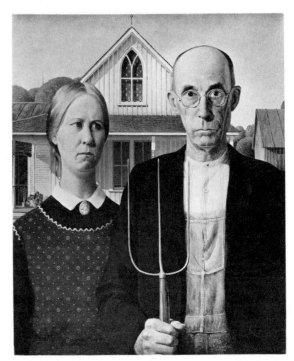

above left: 358. Ivan Albright. *Poor Room.* 1941–62. Oil on canvas,
4' × 3'1" (1.22 × 0.94 m). Art Institute of Chicago (loan).

above right: 359. Grant Wood. *American Gothic.* 1930. Oil on beaver board,
29⅞ × 24⅞" (76 × 63 cm). Art Institute of Chicago
(Friends of American Art Collection).

below: 360. Georgia O'Keeffe. *Calla Lily with Red Roses.* 1927.
Oil on canvas, 2'6" × 4' (0.76 × 1.22 m). Private collection.

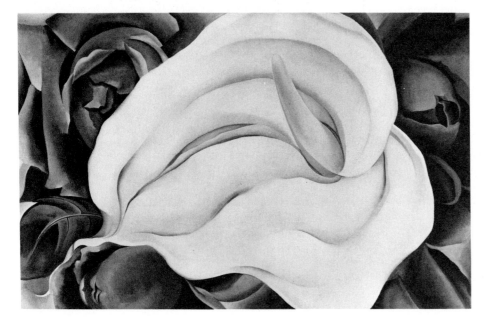

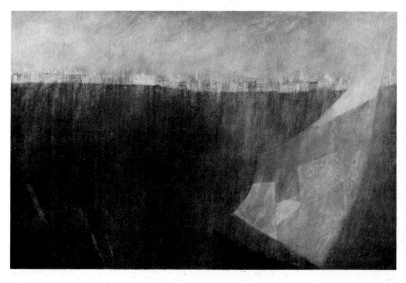

361. Loren MacIver. *Venice.*
1949. Oil on canvas,
4'11" × 7'9" (1.50 × 2.36 m).
Whitney Museum of American Art,
New York.

ral world, her work reveals both formal sophistication and control and expressive delicacy and pictorial suggestion. *Venice* (Fig. 361), for example, implies transparent views of sails and, perhaps influenced by Cubism, projects the exhilaration of light and movement through water.

Black American Art

The art of North America includes more than European contributions. We have read about the ancient arts of Indian peoples in Chapter 15. The art of black Americans of African descent began in the colonial period. Many blacks were anonymous craftspeople. Others, such as Scipio Morehead (18th century), Joshua Johnston (active 1796–1824), Patrick Reason (c. 1817–1852), and Robert Douglass (1809–1887), were established itinerant portrait painters, like their white counterparts, moving from town to town or plantation to plantation.

In the mid-19th century the landscape painter Robert S. Duncanson (1817–1872) was able to study art in Europe through the support of antislavery societies. His example encouraged other black painters. Edward M. Bannister (c. 1828–1901) was the first black artist to receive major recognition in a national competition for his *Under the Oaks.* Henry Ossawa Tanner (1859–1937) studied with Thomas Eakins and in France, where he spent most of his life. The son of a bishop, he was a leading painter of religious subjects. His rich, realistic work influenced other black artists.

Not until the 1920s and 1930s did black artists develop an art based on appreciation of their own heritage. They were part of the **Harlem Renaissance,** a cultural movement which flourished in the Harlem section of New York City and included writers, jazz musicians, and entertainers as well as painters. Black artists of the Harlem Renaissance took pride in their roots and expressed that pride in their work. For example, Archibald Motley (b. 1891), Marilou

Jones (b. 1905), who painted in France and Haiti, and Hughie Lee-Smith (b. 1914) dealt with African themes. Aaron Douglas (b. 1899) combined African simplification of forms with a personal symbolic style in his murals for a Harlem branch of the New York Public Library. His paintings were emotional stylizations, employing extreme elongation, distortions, and circles of mystical light to honor his racial heritage (Fig. 362). In 1925 Douglas collaborated with the author Alain Deroy Lock to produce *The New Negro,* an illustrated anthology of writings by black sociologists and political scientists. That book encouraged the African orientation of American blacks.

The rediscovery of African culture inspired many black American artists, who cultivated a close kinship with it. Douglas was soon followed by Charles Alston (b. 1907), Charles White (Fig. 72), Richmond Barthe (b. 1901), Sargent Johnson (1888–1967), and Elmer Brown (1861–1934). These men, sponsored by the Works Project Administration, contributed significantly to the development of American art of the 1930s. Hale Woodruff (1900–1980) evolved a highly personal style, which resulted from many influences—his studies of Cézanne in Paris, his work in Mexico with Diego Rivera (1886–1957), and, of course, African art. By the 1940s and 1950s, Woodruff's work had achieved a lyrical abstraction (Fig. 363). Other artists such as Beauford Delaney (b. 1901) and Joseph Delaney (b. 1904), sons of a circuit preacher; Norman Lewis (b. 1909); Romare Bearden (Fig. 26); Eldzier Cortor (Fig. 341); and Richard Mayhew (b. 1924) were inspired by what they knew best—their own experiences and dreams.

By 1941, Jacob Lawrence had emerged as a vigorous artist who drew material from the historical background of his race as well as from everyday life. His subject matter, his flat, vividly colored shapes, and his originality established him as an exceptional painter. In his gouache painting *Going Home* (Fig. 80) the drooping shapes of the fatigued train travelers contrast with strong horizontal and

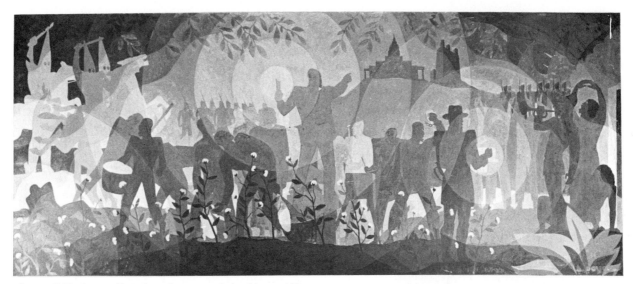

above: 362. Aaron Douglas. *Aspects of the Negro Life,*
detail. 1934. Oil on canvas, entire work 5 × 11'
(1.52 × 3.35 m). Schomburg Center for Research
in Black Culture, New York Public Library, Astor,
Lenox and Tilden Foundations.

right: 363. Hale Woodruff. *Shrine.* 1967. Oil on canvas
with gold leaf, 20 × 40" (51 × 102 cm).
Collection Mrs. Edwina Ferguson, New York.

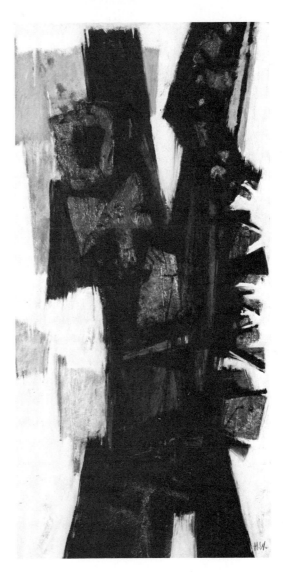

vertical lines. The only active figure is the man reaching
hurriedly for his suitcase as the train nears the station.

Only in the 1960s and 1970s have blacks achieved fuller
access to the art world. Many remain concerned with aid-
ing their people in their struggle for justice. Elizabeth Catlett
(b. 1919), for example, expresses what seems to be the
conclusion of many blacks, that art is important only to the
extent that it helps black liberation. Marie Johnson (b.
1920) creates painted plywood constructions that portray
black hopes and frustrations. Tom Lloyd (b. 1928), formerly
an instructor at Sarah Lawrence College, is today a militant
black, whose work is highly intellectual and abstract and
may cut across color lines. In a recent exhibit he made
geometric combinations of colored glass lights and plastic,
which the viewer could reprogram, experientially, with a
computerized keyboard. Benny Andrews (b. 1930), cur-
rently teaching at Queens College, is best known for his
painted collages such as *Trash,* dealing with themes of
black oppression. Ben Jones (b. 1942) is also concerned.

Other black artists, like most minorities, are part of the
mainstream of American art, exploring many creative avenues. Sam Gilliam (b. 1933) hangs, shapes, and molds his
unframed, paint-stained canvases as wall suspensions that
gain meaning, with the light and gallery space around the
canvas. Richard Hunt (b. 1935) works with found objects in
direct-metal, open-form sculptures. His welded steel pieces
are menacing yet elegant echoes of insect and plant forms,
closely observed. Robert Carter (Fig. 76), Dana Chandler (b.
1941), William T. Williams (b. 1942), and countless other

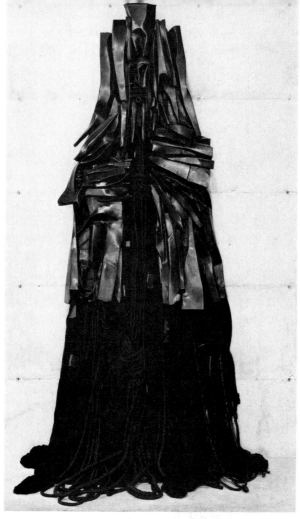

364. Barbara Chase-Riboud. *Confessions for Myself.*
1972. Bronze, painted black, and black wool,
10′ × 3′4″ × 1′ (3.05 × 1.02 × 0.30 m).
University Art Museum, Berkeley. Purchased with
funds from H. W. Anderson Charitable Foundation.

blacks have found creative outlets. An example is Barbara Chase-Riboud (b. 1939), whose sculptural compositions have African connotations but use modern materials, including bronze and silk, bronze and wool, steel, or aluminum and synthetics. In *Confessions for Myself,* she indicates her goal: "To salute that power that exists in all beings in the form of Illusion. Reverence to Her, All Reverence to Her. Reverence . . ." (Fig. 364).

Mexican Protest Art

The Spanish conquistadors had brought with them to the New World the typical colonizer's attitude that the only worthwhile culture came from their homeland. Consequently, Mexican colonial art since the 16th century was generally modeled on that of Baroque Spain. The vitality of the Indian tradition, however, contributed to the rich deco-

ration of Mexican churches. The culture of the Mexican people was influenced by pre-Columbian traditions. Such artists as Jose Guadalupe Posada (1852–1913) were passionate in their support of working-class Mexicans against an oppressive dictatorship, combining fantasy, humor, religion, and protest. Their art formed a direct link between Indian culture and the painting of the three great Mexican protest muralists, who flourished in the late 1920s and 1930s—Diego Rivera, José Clemente Orozco and David Alfaro Siqueiros (1898–1974).

Rivera studied in France, where he encountered Cubism, and traveled in Italy, where he was deeply affected by the frescoes in the churches. In fact, he was responsible for the rebirth of the fresco technique in North America, where his frescoes show the influence of Renaissance art in their formal composition.

Rivera's murals for Mexican public buildings—the National Palace, the Secretariat of Public Education, and the University of Mexico, all in Mexico City—took art from galleries and museums to places where it could be seen by large numbers of people. Convinced that his countrymen needed to develop a pride in their past, he painted scenes that chronicled the life of the peasant and drew on Mexican legend and folk custom as well as on revolutionary social and political themes (Fig. 365). Thus he used murals to teach Mexican heritage in the same way that the medieval church used art to make the Bible a familiar part of everyday life. Although his murals were decorative and at times rigid in composition, they brought a sense of community to the Mexican people.

Orozco's works are more powerful, brutal, and political than those of Rivera. Trained in architecture as well as painting, Orozco created huge murals in which surging masses of peasants and workers struggle against tremendous odds of steel bayonets in their unceasing striving to reach their revolutionary goals. His figures echo the violence and cruelty of ancient Aztec religious practices and the conquering Spaniards, which continued in Mexican folk tradition. There is also an element of folk fantasy, for Orozco's skeletons and the tortured forms of the oppressed relate to the candy figures traditionally sold in Mexico for the Day of the Dead.

Orozco covered the walls of government buildings in Mexico with his dramatic works. Those in Guadalajara are so exaggerated in scale, so violent and twisted in form, and so savage in their masses of figures that they seem to burst from the walls. His murals at Dartmouth College in Hanover, New Hampshire, create a panorama of the history of Mexico in brilliant colors and striking symbols. The overpowering figures tell stories of the feathered-serpent god, Quetzalcoatl, and of the coming of the Spaniards. The murals also protest the destructive forces of war and the machine age. Their climax is reached in an overwhelming figure of a militant, flayed Christ, who destroys his cross, calling on oppressed peoples everywhere to arise (Fig. 366).

Siqueiros, like Courbet, a half-century earlier in France, was as involved in political activities as he was in painting

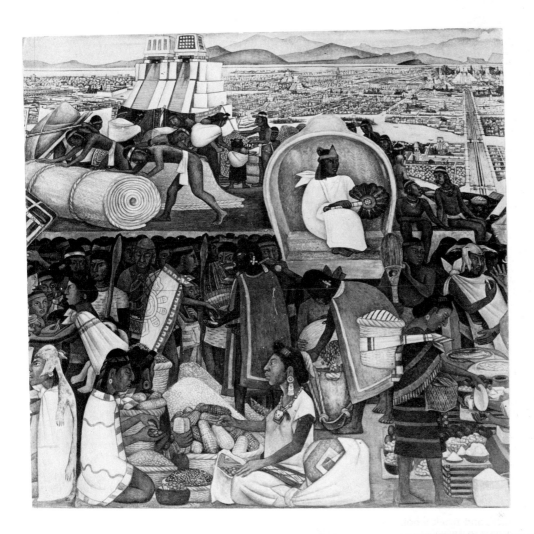

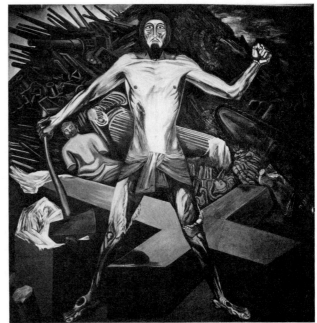

above: 365. Diego Rivera. One of a series of murals, National Palace, Mexico City.

right: 366. José Clemente Orozco. *The Modern Migration of the Spirit.* 1932–34. Fresco, 10′5″ × 10′ (3.18 × 3.05 m). Dartmouth College, Hanover, N.H. (by permission of the Trustees).

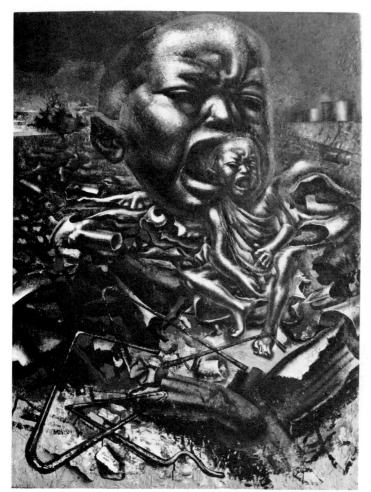

367. David Alfaro Siquiros.
Echo of a Scream. 1937. Duco on wood,
4 × 3′ (1.22 × 0.91 m). Museum of Modern Art,
New York (gift of Edward M. M. Warburg).

and was later imprisoned for his Communist beliefs. He led the organization of the Syndicate of Technical Workers, Painters, and Sculptors, which contributed much to the development of art in Mexico. Siqueiros' murals, more visionary than those of Rivera and Orozco, use Surrealist images to protest social injustices. Compare his *Echo of a Scream* (Fig. 367) with Picasso's *Guernica* (Fig. 22) and Munch's *The Scream* (Fig. 96) to see how the three artists employed strident images in different ways to express inhumanity and horror. Siqueiros, like Jackson Pollock (Pl. 2, p. 21) also experimented with materials, using industrial enamels for his outdoor murals, which he hoped would expose his ideas to the largest possible number of people.

Artists in the United States became more interested in fresco painting in the 1930s through exposure to the works of Rivera and Orozco. Supported by the Works Projects Administration, many, such as the Dutch-born Willem de Kooning (b. 1904), traveled around the United States, painting murals on post offices and other government buildings. Most of the paintings were conservative, and few approach the impact of their Mexican counterparts as expressions of social protest.

The New York School

During the Depression and World War II, New York became a center for the kind of discussion and stimulating exchange that had formerly made Paris so attractive to creative people. Artists came to New York from all over the country, from Mexico (Orozco and Rivera), and from Europe (Mondrian, Chagall, Ernst, Dali, and Léger). Whether they settled in New York or only visited, they are all loosely classified as the **New York school** because they shared a common center of artistic concern. Their work showed no uniform style. They issued no manifestos. A few of these artists were realists, such as Hopper (Fig. 356), but most explored highly personalized nonobjective painting. Many developed a free-flowing style that was described by critics as Abstract Expressionism.

Abstract Expressionist paintings are generally nonobjective, without obvious reference to reality. Many have a raw, tough strength that is remote from the grace and finesse of the early nonobjective formalist paintings of Kandinsky (Fig. 324), Malevich (Fig. 325), and Mondrian (Pl. 3, p. 22). Abstract Expressionist works may be grouped in two broad divisions. In **Action painting,** the physical traces of the artist's actual gestures are explicit and emphatic. In the other, known as Color-Field painting, the emphasis is on large planes of color. Action painting dominated the 1950s. The formalist painting of color areas developed more gradually until it emerged as one of the significant movements in the 1960s, as we will see in Chapter 19.

When we look at Action paintings, our own muscles respond with awareness of the movements of the artist's body. The canvases are very large because traditional, easel-size paintings seemed too small to contain the artist's energies. The artist had to reach beyond restrictive borders to enormous areas in which to work out his or her drives. To feel this physically expressed energy we must see the paintings themselves, for their huge scale intensifies the impact, forcing us to become involved in the work.

European influences on Abstract Expressionism were the powerful transitions of color developed by such 19th-century painters as Turner (Fig. 79) and Monet (Pl. 15, p. 267; Fig. 312) and the various forms of Expressionism of the early 20th century, such as Emil Nolde (Fig. 328). Abstract Expressionism drew also on Oriental sources, notably calligraphy and Zen Buddhism. According to Zen belief, when the mind and body are in accord, or centered, the hand becomes free to serve a deeper purpose, allowing inner vitality to be released. This attitude, which inspired much of Chinese and Japanese painting for centuries (Fig. 32), proved congenial to many Abstract Expressionists.

From these currents, Abstract Expressionism evolved in the late 1940s. It had a vitality that was typical of much American painting of the 20th century no matter what its style. It seems that American artists tackled art frontiers with the same fresh excitement with which their ancestors had tackled the physical frontiers of the New World.

We may consider Arshile Gorky (1904–1948), who painted abstract expressive works that recalled his childhood in Armenia, an early Abstract Expressionist. He evolved his paintings in the automatic manner of the Surrealists, who used doodles to suggest images, drawing and painting according to impulse. In their random brush marks the Surrealists would see suggestions of a figure, which they would then encourage to emerge into a more definite image. Gorky's organic forms and erotic fantasies were influenced by the Surrealist works of Kandinsky (Fig. 324), Miró (Fig. 64), and Picasso (Fig. 22). He brought to his painting a love of texture and especially of richness of paint. Compare, for example, Gorky's lively, free brush strokes (Fig. 368) with the tight, smooth surface of American Realistic painting exemplified by Grant Wood (Fig. 359).

The free-flowing style of Gorky and other abstract organic painters was also characteristic of Hans Hofmann (1880–1966), a German-born artist whose art school in

368. Arshile Gorky. *Agony.* 1947. Oil on canvas, 3'4" × 4'2½" (1.02 × 1.28 m). Museum of Modern Art, New York (A. Conger Goodyear Fund).

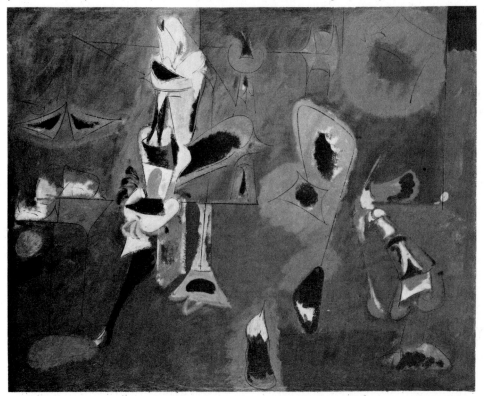

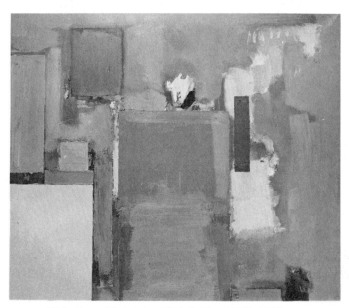

369. Hans Hofmann. *The Golden Wall*. 1961. Oil on canvas, 5' × 6'½" (1.5 × 1.84 m). Art Institute of Chicago (Mr. and Mrs. Frank G. Logan Purchase Prize Fund).

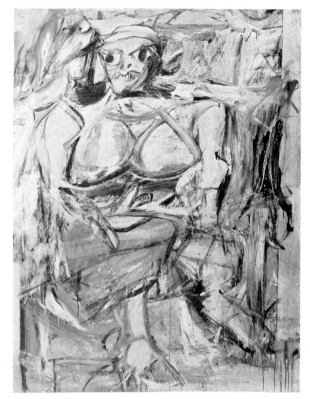

370. Willem de Kooning. *Woman, I*. 1950–51. Oil on canvas, 6'3⅞" × 4'10" (1.93 × 1.47 m). Museum of Modern Art, New York (purchase).

New York became a center of Expressionism and abstraction. The apparent spontaneity of his brush strokes was based on an unusual combination of painterliness and abstraction. In *The Golden Wall* (Fig. 369), rectangles of rich color are contrasted with areas of thick, loosely brushed paint. Hofmann's glowing color expresses his joyful attitude toward life. He considered the actual process of looking at a painting to be an important part of the act of art. He felt that if this process is successful, the painting and the viewer will establish a relationship based on spontaneous feeling.

Two painters became the focal point for the new style—Willem de Kooning and Jackson Pollock (Pl. 2, p. 21). In direct opposition to the carefully composed geometric painting of Albers (Pl. 1, p. 21) and Mondrian (Pl. 3, p. 22), they brought to their work an immediacy of emotion that made the process of painting an important part of the artwork itself. For several years de Kooning painted in a broadly Abstract Expressionist style, angrily slashing wide, violent strokes onto his canvas. Later, in the 1950s, he became almost obsessed with the image of a female (Fig. 370). These paintings seem conceived in horror and depict a sense of desperate rage that was physically expressed in the brush strokes. This use of the larger muscles of the

body, typical of Abstract Expressionism, brought great energy to painting.

Pollock said, "I believe the easel picture to be a dying form and the tendency of modern feeling is toward the wall picture or mural." Because he felt the public was not ready for murals, he painted on large canvases, which he considered to be a transitional step toward wall painting. Pollock's drips, splashes, and spills appear to have been painted in an intense and undisciplined fury of action. His paintings, however, actually are carefully textured and organized. Each of his active strokes appears balanced by an opposing one. His color combinations are subtle, and the structure of each painting develops through the rhythm of his movements. Pollock, who often used industrial enamels and metallic paints, spread his canvases on the floor and dripped his paints from buckets, using sticks and large brushes. The concentration of paint on the canvas from the path of his hand forces us to note the importance of the artist's association with his materials.

Pollock's passages of color lead our eyes into the painting to wander through the canvas, finding refreshment by following the myriad paths of the paint as they build up a weblike surface. Through the involvement of our eye movements, his paintings become environments that sur-

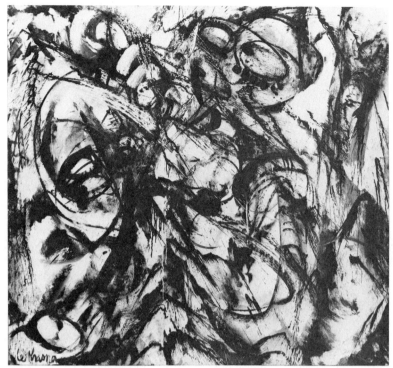

right: 371. Lee Krasner.
The Guardian. 1960. Oil on canvas,
4'5" × 4'10" (1.35 × 1.47 m).
Whitney Museum of American Art,
New York (gift of Uris Brothers
Foundation, Inc.).

below: 372. Franz Kline.
Two Horizontals. 1954.
Oil on canvas, 31⅛ × 39¼"
(79 × 100 cm). Sidney and Harriet Janis
Collection, gift to the Museum of
Modern Art, New York.

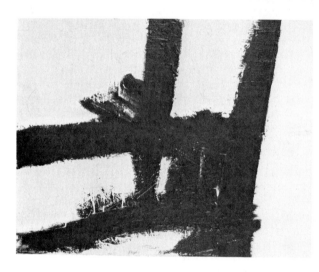

round us. Perhaps subconsciously expressing the fears and hopes of midcentury, Pollock extended his painting to limitless horizons, bringing together the near and the far, the important and the trivial, to merge into a broad cosmos. Through his work we sense the tensions of all people trapped by the 20th century, as well as Pollock's own explosive personal frustrations as an artist living in a hostile world.

Lee Krasner (b. 1908), who studied and worked with Hofmann and married Pollock, assimilated Surrealism, Fauvism, Cubism, Oriental Zen, and Action painting. Her images suggest movement, flux, and growth, reflecting energies essential to life. The rhythmic flow of her paint and the density and transparency of her surfaces identify her as an Action painter, but it is the monumental concept of even her small-scale work that marks her contribution as significant (Fig. 371).

The Oriental calligraphic element is particularly strong in the work of Mark Tobey (b. 1890), Robert Motherwell (b. 1915), Bradley Tomlin (1899–1953), Morris Graves (b. 1910), and Franz Kline (1910–1962). Kline painted enormous black shapes, somewhat like enlarged Chinese characters. His large strokes of black drawn across the white surface of the canvas create tensions to which we respond physically—a pull we can feel (Fig. 372). Both Kline and Motherwell are concerned with tensions and balances of positive and negative space.

The youngest of the original Abstract Expressionists, Motherwell wrote in *The New Decade:* "I happen to think primarily in paint. . . . If a painting does not make a human contact, it is nothing." The act of applying paint to canvas alone dominated the Action painters. They did not represent their emotions but enacted them in their works.

Still Photography and Films

The same spirit of freedom that inspired painters to break away from academic and realistic representation led artists and others to experiment with still photography and film in both Europe and America. Film became a big business in America as well as a major art form, often fulfilling the role of fantasy.

Still Photography Classical American photographers such as Weston and Adams explored form and light in their still lifes and landscapes (see Chapter 5). The artist Alvin Langdon Coburn (1882–1966) experimented with mirror-multiplied photographic images he called Vortographs. Skilled also in rotogravure (see Chapter 4), he made the plates used to print four of his books. Moholy-Nagy, who founded the New Bauhaus in Chicago after the closing of its namesake in 1933 in Berlin, was convinced that photography is an indispensable tool of this century. He created photographic shadow prints and micrographs of rare scientific beauty and educational value.

During the 1930s photographic technology improved greatly. New lighting methods and more sophisticated lenses made for greater flexibility. Magazines such as *Life* that featured photojournalism became popular. The Farm Security Administration of the federal government used skilled photographers to record the life of rural America during the Depression years. These sensitive and perceptive photographers produced prints that are unquestionably fine art. Dorothea Lange, in particular, commented on the tragic plight of the farmers who were driven from their homes in Oklahoma by dust storms. Her photographs of women and children from this period are classics. Realistic and objective, she never used unusual angles or lighting to increase the expressiveness of her work. *Migrant Mother* (Fig. 108) is much more than a mere recording; the faces and poses speak eloquently of hopelessness and despair.

Film In the early 20th century, avant-garde painters and writers alike were fascinated by the potentials of filmmaking. In Paris, Duchamp made a natural progression from the painting *Nude Descending a Staircase (No. 2)* (Fig. 63) to using ready-made objects (such as the wheel) that moved (Fig. 331) to his moving picture *Anaemic Cinema* (1926). Léger developed his interest in machines into moving images in his film *Ballet méchanique* (1924), and Dali expressed his theatrical and Surrealist viewpiont in films. French filmmakers created art films in an Impressionist style that brought cinema into the stream of modern art. René Clair's (b. 1898) stylized, fanciful films commented on the absurdities of our machine-dominated lives. During the 1920s filmmakers in Sweden and Germany made experiments in visual design that made possible new intensity of emotion, unity of mood, and fuller expression of character. The Soviets developed a new system of editing by montage, which allowed unprecedented evolution of ideas.

Despite these achievements in Europe, the "movies" are more closely identified with the United States than with any other country. When Europe was involved with World War I and America was still neutral, Americans gained several years' lead in filmmaking. In contrast to European "art films" for elite audiences, Hollywood produced films for the mass market, ranging from the epic pageants of D. W. Griffiths, culminating in *Birth of a Nation* (1915), to the disciplined lunacy of Mack Sennett (1884–1960) and British-born Charlie Chaplin (1889–1977) comedies, to the classic romances starring Greta Garbo, Gloria Swanson, and others. The classic Western film such as *Stagecoach* introduced by John Ford in 1939 presents an historic image of America by which much of the world still identifies this nation. The ability to appeal to a wide variety of tastes, plus American business skills of mass production and distribution, established the American motion picture as a great commercial success and an influential art form. *Birth of a Nation* grossed an estimated $50 million, making it the top money maker until recent years.

The major breakthrough in cinema was signaled on October 6, 1927, when Warner Brothers presented *The Jazz Singer* with Al Jolson, the first feature film with synchronized music, speech, and other sounds. Their Vitaphone system used disc recordings, which were mechanically synchronized with the projector. At the end of the 1920s there was no doubt that synchronized sound films would be the film form of the future.

In commercial cinema, the need for mass escapism during the Depression led to slick, sophisticated comedies and elaborately staged singing and dancing shows. Charlie Chaplin, however, continued to produce satirical comedies. He commented on the world of machinery (Fig. 373) or on the rising European dictatorships in such films as *Modern Times* (1936) and *The Great Dictator* (1940). These films describe the loneliness and isolation of those who refuse to conform to the dictates of the world around them—whether it be a factory or an oppressive political regime.

Chaplin's creativity was echoed in the remarkable American phenomenon of the animated cartoon. The need for food for the spirit and escape in fantasy from daily reality perhaps explains the desire of millions to return to an adolescent state through the art of Walt Disney (1901–1966) and other animators. Mickey Mouse, imaginary subject of many short Disney cartoons, became for many people a symbol of America. The importance of music to Disney led him to create *Fantasia* (1940), a feature-length film composed of seven episodes of animated ballet set to classical music. In visual style *Fantasia* ranges from total abstraction as a background for music by J. S. Bach to romantic cartoons for most of the film. Mickey Mouse himself appears as the hapless servant in the *Sorcerer's Apprentice,* by Paul Dukas.

Disney's art was determined, perhaps most significantly, by his creative organization of skilled technicians, whom some consider pioneering artists. In their hands, color is used expressively rather than illusionistically. It is bright and flat. All the best Disney films use line rather than modeling to present an image. One can recognize in them the influence of Picasso, Matisse, and even Modigliani. The Disney films can convince us that art can also be entertainment and storytelling can be art.

Film seems to have given us a universal language. While cartoons can amuse people, documentaries can influence public opinion. Such films as *Nanook of the North* (1922) and Pare Lorentz's *The River* (1937) (Fig. 113), dealing with farmers in the Mississippi Valley, made audiences feel close

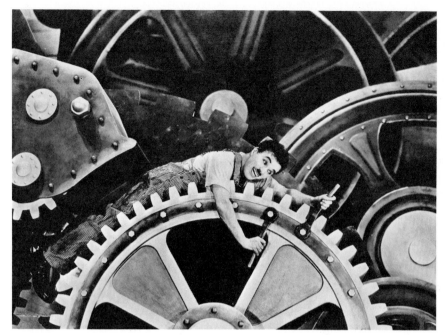

373. Film still from
Charlie Chaplin's *Modern Times*.
1936. Museum of Modern Art,
New York (Film Stills Archive).

to people struggling for existence in two difficult natural environments. Techniques developed in these films were used in army films during World War II and have continued to influence documentaries.

The American contribution to film—in comedy, fantasy, drama, or documentary—is obvious. We will consider recent developments in cinema and the effect of television in Chapters 19 and 20.

EXERCISES AND ACTIVITIES

1. Abstract Expressionism was an important force in art in the 1950s. Compare and contrast the work of Jackson Pollock and Willem de Kooning. Analyze how their works are similar and how they differ.
2. Create in oils, acrylics, or enamels a painting in the style of Pollock. To get the full impact of the muscular involvement in his work, you will need a large area of paper or canvas.
3. The traditional fresco technique was revived by Mexican painters to serve a particular purpose. Why was the technique particularly appropriate to their work? How did they use it? How did their art influence painting in the United States?
4. Describe your reaction to a work of Orozco and to Picasso's *Guernica*.
5. How did a changing approach to the human body affect sculpture of the 20th century? Give examples.
6. How did technology affect the art of the 1930s? Select two artists and discuss their work from this viewpoint.
7. How was photography used as a means of social protest?
8. Read a novel of protest that describes the social conditions existing between World War I and World War II. Discuss the art of the period in relation to the book. Does the art mirror in visual form the conditions described in the book? If so, how?
9. Select a modern artwork of black social protest. How did the artist use the elements of design to communicate a message?

19 The Mid-Century World

The future of art no longer seems to lie with the creation of enduring masterpieces, but with defining alternative cultural strategies.

JOHN MC HALE

World War II marked the end of European art leadership. The flow of art directed for hundreds of years by European academic tastes was now firmly centered in America, and the shift in power surprised very few. The United States dominated so many aspects of living overseas—from American hamburgers, Coca Cola, and blue jeans to the heavy industries we have set up all over the world. Other factors contributed toward centering the art world in America. Several major artists had spent the war years here—Mondrian, Chagall, Ernst, Dali, and Léger—joining Duchamp, de Kooning, and other artists, writers, and critics already on the East Coast.

It seems that few areas could compete with the stimulation of New York. Poetry, aesthetics, and the philosophies of Zen, Jung, Sartre, and Kirkegaard provoked heated discussions among artists, while exhibitions at the Museum of Modern Art and the Solomon R. Guggenheim Museum provided on-the-spot stimulation. The pioneering New York school of Abstract Expressionism had established a strong medium for individualism and, in so doing, was rejecting most traditional art conventions that might inhibit "modern art." Many postwar artists became engrossed in highly personalized interpretations, such as de Kooning's involvement with the female figure (Fig. 370). Antibiotics, computerization, electronic transistors, and the prospect of an atomic age all portended a fresh world.

Against this background of ferment, it is still possible to view 1950 through 1970 within much of the framework we have seen before—formalism, modified realism, Expressionism, and fantasy.

Formalism
Since the 1950s, as we saw in Chapter 18, America has taken the lead in avant-garde art all over the world.

While the more emotional side of Abstract Expressionism, called Action painting, had dominated the art world at mid-century, many artists turned to cooler, more intellectual, nonobjective art whose formal aesthetic depended mainly on color, shape, and texture.

Color-Field Painting Some Abstract Expressionist painters in the 1950s had been more interested in planes of color than in gestural brush strokes. Their interest developed into a form of **Postpainterly Abstraction** called **Field painting,** or **Color-Field painting,** a dominant style of the 1960s. Color-Field painting avoids subject matter in order to concentrate on color relationships (see Chapter 2 on color). Often a painting is a huge canvas consisting of large, nonobjective areas of color on a flat-colored or white ground. One brush stroke may be as large as a conventional easel painting or even as large as the viewer. Although a large area of color may have smaller shapes floating on it, they do not completely break up the larger area.

Color-Field painters usually created oversized works so large that they are not meant to be seen all at once. Widths of 10, 12, or even 40 feet (3.04, 3.65, or 12.19 meters) are not unusual. Such paintings are designed to overwhelm us. To appreciate them as the artist intended, the viewer must stand close enough to the canvas to be surrounded by the field of paint and visually led into it.

Many Color-Field painters used acrylic paints (see Chapter 3), which came into general use in the 1950s. Although they have not replaced oils, they are applied in new ways, giving painters an opportunity to create new effects. Acrylics can be used to fill in flat areas by creating a smooth surface that is glossy or matte according to the vehicle used. Since acrylics flow easily onto the canvas and dry quickly, they are more suitable than oils for painting sharp edges on forms next to each other. Also, acrylics can be thinned to give a transparent, watery look; and if used on absorbant, unsized canvas, they will sink into the fabric and produce soft edges.

A Color-Field painter who used acrylics in this way is Morris Louis (Fig. 85). His pigments interact with the canvas, becoming part of it, rather than remaining on the

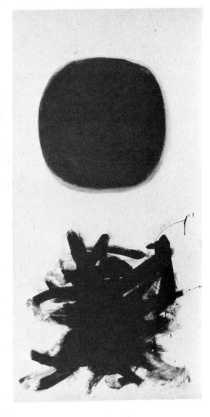

surface. This technique gives depth to the color, reducing the reflective quality of the painting and producing a very different effect from that of oils. Like Louis, Helen Frankenthaler (Pl. 9, p. 24) often allows her colors to soak into the canvas. Like Pollock, she lays her huge canvases on the floor, pouring and pushing her paints into the fabric until the color arrangements satisfy her.

Works such as *Number 19* by Mark Rothko (1903–1970) have great impact based on color sensation and large size (Fig. 374). Rothko placed vaporous, rectangular patches in front of one another, and his color, unrestrained by drawn lines or hard edges, spreads from one shape to the next. Often the color areas are extremely close to each other in value. Sometimes Rothko soaked and stained the canvas with transparent paint, and sometimes he brushed on opaque pigment. Color provides both the form and the content; it is the sole carrier of his ideas, capable of endless variations.

In a series of large paintings, Adolph Gottlieb (1903–1974) produced images that remind us of explosions (Fig. 375). In *Blast II* the two main forms are separate, placed one above the other. The brilliant color and the rounded form of the upper shape may represent the sun or a nuclear explosion, while the somber colors below remind us of the earth. No matter what these forms may suggest to us, however, their opposition creates a visual tension in the viewer.

Hard-Edge Painting Other artists who came to maturity in the 1950s, turned away from Action painting in favor of a form of Postpainterly Abstraction known as **Hard-Edge painting.** Their works are comprised of flat areas of color, confined within precisely delineated boundaries. In formal investigations of color and design, many approached painting methodically, using masking tape, triangles, and rulers to make straight edges. Within this climate of technical precision, the contribution of Albers is prominent.

After leaving the Bauhaus, Albers continued his preoccupation with color in the United States. For more than fifteen years he worked on a series of one hundred paintings called *Homage to the Square* (Pl. 1, p. 21). Of approximately the same outer dimensions, each consists of squares that vary in size, in color, and in their relationship to each other. Albers experimented with innumerable combinations of warm and cool, muted and intense color. The simplicity of the square shapes intensifies the visual relationships of the colors, exploiting their optical effects fully. Albers recognized that in visual perception a color is rarely seen alone but usually in relation to the colors around it. As a simple demonstration of this, look at the corner of a plainly painted room. The slight variation in the intensity of the light that hits the two walls will show some difference in the color of the two surfaces. One wall may appear nearer, while the other looks distant. If a warm light hits one wall and the other is in cool shadow, the tension between them will be further increased.

376. Alice Trumbull Mason. *Shafts of Spring*. 1955. Oil on gesso board, 27 × 29″ (69 × 74 cm). Collection the author.

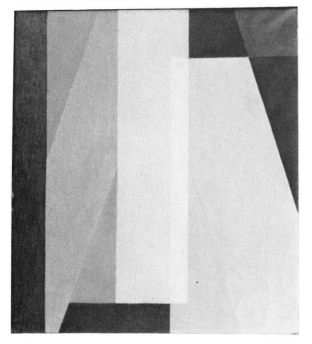

The variety in Albers' series of squares depends not only on the combinations of colors but also on how the colors change in relationship to each other, the amount of each color used, and the number of squares. Albers also makes use of the physical phenomenon of afterimages to cause vibrations in our eyes. For him, color experiments enrich the visual experience, and since he believes that the eye is an important part of the mind, he also believes that his paintings have intellectual as well as visual content.

Two other Hard-Edge painters who were color purists were Alice Trumbull Mason (1904–1971), descendant of the American historical painter John Trumbull and a charter member of the American Abstractionists, first exhibiting as a group in 1937, and Ad Reinhardt (1913–1967), who claimed to be following her lead. Both worked mainly in a geometric style since the 1930s. Mason's canvases have a haunting, poetic lyricism, which she sometimes produced with a limited range of colors (Fig. 376). She studied with Gorky and the graphic artist Stanley Hayter at his Atelier 17 and produced a large body of significant works that are recognized today more than in her lifetime.

Like Mason, Reinhardt gradually reduced his paintings to areas of muted tones, close in intensity and value. In the late 1960s he worked only in dark monochromes, creating areas of paint on canvases as large as 5 by 5 feet (1.52 by 1.52 meters). His goal was the refinement of painting to a single, all-consuming experience. A small reproduction cannot convey the response that viewing painting does (Pl. 18, p. 268). Experiencing such a work, we feel drawn into its depth and may have a physical sensation of floating in a lightless, soundless void. As in many Color-Field paintings, his canvas surfaces cease to exist, leaving a mysterious infinity of visual and spatial effects created by color. Paintings such as these are closely related to the Minimal, or Primary, painting of Ellsworth Kelly (b. 1923).

Other Color-Field painters, such as Kenneth Noland (b. 1924) and Frank Stella, also depend on large scale and color to offer a visual experience of total immersion. The concept of expanding and contracting intervals of color arranged in hard- or soft-edge stripes is dominant in their work. As in his graphics (Fig. 99), Stella painted complex patterns of stripes separated by light lines. He also used unconventionally shaped canvases for his paintings, fitting the pattern of the stripes into the shape of the canvas or contrasting them to set up an opposing tension (Fig. 377). Avoiding the individualization of Action painting, the clean-cut outlines and flat surfaces of these large, bright Minimalist paintings often suggest the anonymity of mass-produced industrial products. Other Hard-Edge paintings are created by repeating hundreds of small shapes, such as in the Optical Art we will examine next.

Optical Art Art has used optical illusions since the Old Stone Age. Without illusion, we would not accept foreshortening or use linear perspective to create a three-dimensional representation of a two-dimensional surface.

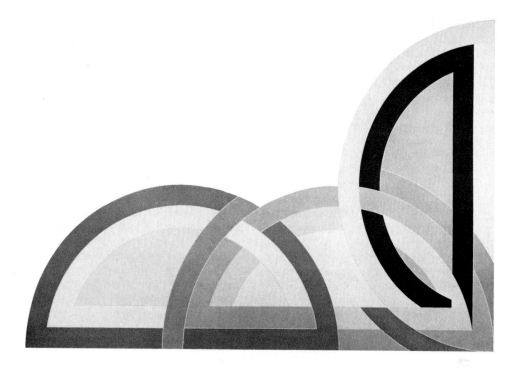

The Op artists of the 1960s made such illusions the basis of their work. The Israeli-born artist Agam (Yaacov Gipstein, b. 1928) devised works that appear to change as we view them. Possibly inspired by moving billboards, which change their images by means of mechanically turning louvers, Agam incorporates similar, though fixed, projecting louvers in some of his paintings (Fig. 378). Looking at an Agam creation from one side of a room, we see what appears to be a flat painting with simple, nonobjective shapes. But if we observe the same painting from another point in the room, it looks like a different work.

Bridget Riley also depends on optical illusions for the impact of her black and white paintings (Fig. 36). These illusions suggest movement where none exists and produce an intense, sometimes uncomfortable sensation as we view the works. Modular shapes fit together into an allover pattern of color in the paintings of Hungarian-born Victor Vasarely (b. 1908).

Direct-Metal and Primary Sculpture A logical progression from the work of early 20th-century Constructivist sculptors (Fig. 41) was the **direct-metal** and **Primary sculpture** of the 1950s and 1960s. Rejecting the traditional representation of the human figure, sculpture became an extension of physics rather than a reflection of humanity. Architectural space became an arena for exploration by means of welded metal sheets, rods, and wires.

Richard Lippold (b. 1915) extended the spatial concepts of Constructivism. Using taut strands of metal wire as lines that reflect light, he suspends a series of interconnecting geometric units in space. Sometimes light is focused at the heart of the structure, as in *Variation Number 7: Full*

above: 377. Frank Stella. *Agbatana I.* 1968. Synthetic polymer on canvas, 10 × 15′ (3.05 × 4.57 m). Whitney Museum of American Art, New York (gift of Mr. and Mrs. Oscar Kolin).

below: 378. Agam (Yaacov Gipstein). *Double Metamorphosis II.* 1964. Oil on aluminum, 8′10″ × 13′2¼″ (2.70 × 4.02 m). Museum of Modern Art, New York (gift of Mr. and Mrs. George M. Jaffin).

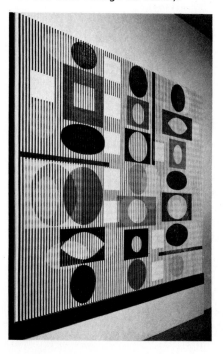

Moon, a creation of luminescent beauty 10 feet high (3.04 meters) that seems to float in space (Fig. 302). The shimmering quality of its overlaying squares is evidence of Lippold's detailed planning, mastery of the material, and careful execution. He has produced even larger works of wire and metal strips that probe space in diagonal thrusts and are designed to relate art to architecture. In such works, light seems to pulsate over the geometric forms much as a musician might create subtle variations on a basic theme. Perhaps Lippold's work suggests the positive aspects of our technological age.

David Smith (1906–1965), who had welded tanks in a war factory and studied the direct-metal sculpture of Picasso and other Europeans, made complex linear steel constructions in a Surrealist vein. In later work, using painted steel plates, he explored the human figure in Cubist terms. (Fig. 379). Jason Seley (b. 1919) welded discarded automobile bumpers to form strong spatial constructions.

The new inquiry into space led to a gradual reduction of nonessential details until sculptors reached a vocabulary, or system, of simple, basic geometric volumes. Their works are called **Primary, Minimal, ABC,** or **Systemic sculpture.** The shapes are usually so depersonalized that the artists can turn over their drawings to a workshop to do the actual construction. As a reflection of materialistic anonymous society, the surfaces of the shapes are mechanically finished, and they are assembled in multiples.

Primary sculpture may be placed on the floor or against the wall, suspended from the ceiling, or placed outdoors on a lawn or sidewalk. Such work enjoys the same freedom in three dimensions that nonobjective painting occupies in two. Although the physical presence of the viewer is not part of the design, his or her perceptions and responses to spatial openings, volumes, and enclosures concern the artist. Most significantly, the spectator is often invited to become part of the scene, to wander under, around, and through the sculpture.

Primary sculptors range from engineers who design by equation and computer to sculptors who create intuitively. David Smith belongs to the latter category. Just before he died he created the *Cubi* series, which may be considered Primary sculptures in the stark simplicity of their forms and in the economy of their flat surfaces. Using only cubes and cylinders of stainless steel, he created works of endless variety, welding and finishing them himself with great technical control and sensitivity (Fig. 379). The British sculptor Anthony Caro (b. 1924) used industrial steel girders and sheet metal to produce powerful structures. Often monumental in size, simple in their planes, and occasionally painted in brilliant colors, these sculptures remind us of primary paintings.

Isamu Noguchi's (b. 1904) bold red *Cube* is a Minimal sculpture that engages our attention and creates tension by the questions it raises about balance (Fig. 380). Its ap-

379. David Smith. *Cubi* series. Stainless steel. Left: *Cubi XVIII.* 1964. Height 9′8″ (2.95 m). Museum of Fine Arts, Boston. Center: *Cubi XVII.* 1963. Height 8′11¾″ (2.74 m). Dallas Museum of Fine Arts, The Eugene and Margaret McDermott Fund. Right: *Cubi XIX.* 1964. Height 9′4¾″ (2.84m). Tate Gallery, London.

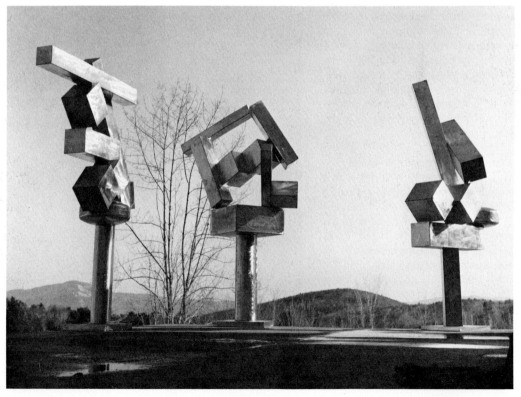

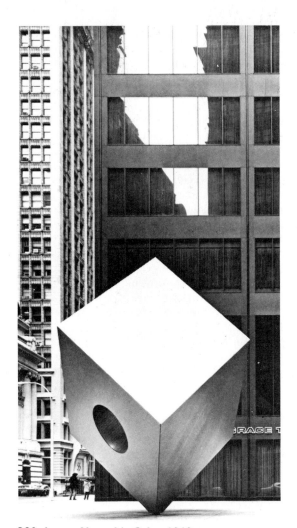

380. Isamu Noguchi. *Cube.* 1968.
Painted welded steel and aluminum,
height 28′ (8.53 m). 140 Broadway, New York.

ancestors. Motion is essential to life, even if it is the slow, almost imperceptible motion of a germinating seed thrusting a shoot through the earth. Today, however, we live in an age of motion unlike any the world has ever known. The speed with which our space vehicles rush toward other planets is almost beyond comprehension, while here on earth jets travel at velocities never dreamed possible. It is no wonder, then, that 20th-century artists have been fascinated with motion and have attempted to respond to it in their art.

The concept of combining sculptured figures with mechanical motion is not new. Turkish sultans had elaborate mechanical figures built for their amusement, probably inspired by Oriental creations. In medieval Europe, the bells in many clock towers were struck by mechanical figures, and during the Renaissance Leonardo designed figures for royal festivals which were moved mechanically.

The machine-oriented Futurist Boccioni expressed motion in his sculpture as early as 1913 (Fig. 342). Brancusi's *Bird in Space* of 1919 (Fig. 344) minimized the material limitations of solid mass by its soaring form. But it was the Constructivist sculptor Gabo who, in 1920, designed the first motorized sculpture, a tall shape that vibrated. Works of this kind, moved by a motor, are called **kinetic sculptures.** At the Bauhaus, Moholy-Nagy built the first light-and-motion sculptures, which were activated by the sun and called light modulators (Fig. 381).

381. Laszlo Moholy-Nagy. *Light-Space Modulator.* 1923—30. Metal and plastic, height 4′11½″ (1.51 m). Busch-Reisinger Museum, Harvard University, Cambridge, Mass.

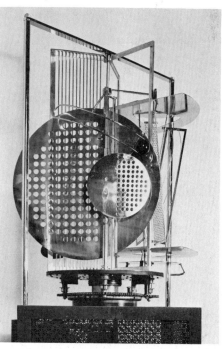

parently precarious position, poised on one corner, startles and disturbs us, while its huge geometric mass forces us to see it in relation to the surrounding architecture.

Tony Smith's (b. 1912) oversized black cube simply titled *The Box* reduces to the ultimate any exploration of space. It makes no statement beyond its very real, dull, black volume. Investigation confirms that the form expresses nothing more than itself. It *is* a box. The next step is the *idea* of a box. Some sculptors conveyed the idea of their work by no longer fabricating solid structures but by merely showing us the plans, drawings, or even written outlines of works that would never be built. The concept of the idea itself being the art led inevitably to Conceptual art, which flourished in the 1970s.

Motion in Sculpture Like all animals, we are fascinated by motion. The driving rain, waving branches in the wind, the crash of waves onto a beach intrigue us as they did our

Since the 1930s Calder constructed moving sculpture from industrial materials such as sheet metal and wire. Although he added motors to some constructions to make them move, he preferred to leave their motion to the unpredictability of air currents. The result was a totally new sculptural form called a mobile by his friend Duchamp (Figs. 37, 38). The cheerful elements of his mobiles remind us not of machines but of fish, animals, plants, and sometimes planets. Arranged in carefully balanced systems, they are set in motion by a passing breeze, the hot air of a furnace, or even the movement of someone walking past.

Each element moves independently but within a prescribed orbit. Some strike each other like gongs and bells, adding an element of noise to the sculpture. Many of Calder's largest pieces are balanced on bases anchored to the ground, and movements of their heavy forms are slow and stately. He also built some pieces of sculpture that do not move, called stabiles. Influenced by Calder, George Rickey (b. 1907) is also interested in motion and balance. He groups long, tapering strips of stainless steel into such delicately balanced compositions that the slightest air current sets them into slow, quivering vibrations. Thus, over the last fifty years, motion has become an important feature of works of art.

Kinetic sculptures often consist of nonfunctional machines, their movement existing only to provide a visual experience. Some of these machines perform complex operations perfectly, but at the same time they amuse us with their somewhat ridiculous uselessness. In our mechanistic society, a machine that can do nothing but move seems laughable.

Such movement is expressed uniquely by the Swiss sculptor Jean Tinguely (b. 1925), who creates machine-powered kinetic sculptures that perform a series of actions. *Homage to New York* (Fig. 382) was constructed of assorted discards found in dumps or secondhand stores. It made music with a battered piano, issued reports from an old typewriter, and gave birth to machine offspring. Finally one memorable evening in the garden of the Museum of Modern Art in New York, under the baleful eye of a New York City fireman and before an enthralled audience, *Homage to New York* with some frantic help from its inventor committed suicide in a flurry of movement, sound, and smoke. Its demise echoed the absurdity of Dada as it parodied modern, self-destructing society.

Another example of kinetic sculpture is the work of Ernest Trova (b. 1927). All his pieces consist of an armless, sexless, featureless figure that is apparently helplessly thrust

382. Jean Tinguely. Fragment from *Homage to New York*. 1960. Painted metal, 6'8¼" × 2'5⅝" × 7'3⅞" (2.04 × 0.75 × 2.23 m). Museum of Modern Art, New York (gift of the artist).

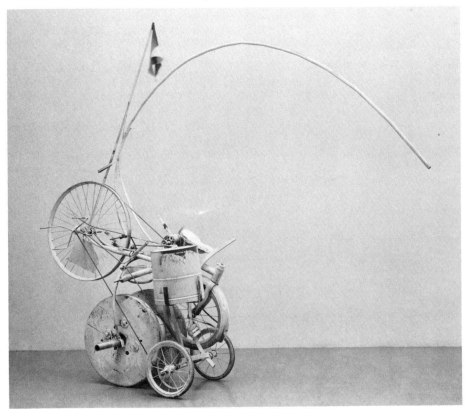

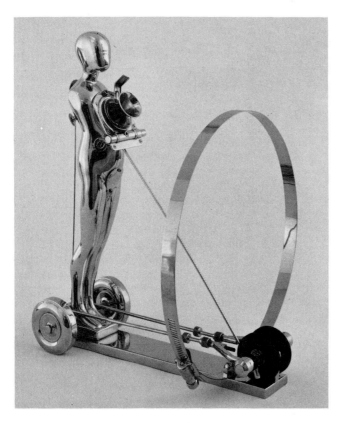

383. Ernst Trova.
Falling Man, Study No. 53. 1968.
Nickel-plated bronze, 13 × 10 × 9¾″
(33 × 25 × 25 cm). Pace Gallery,
New York.

by modern technology in a machine that threatens to destroy it or perpetuate it, unknowing, unfeeling, operating in a void, as in *Falling Man, Study No. 53* (Fig. 383).

Some sculptors work with moving objects to create varying effects. Robert Breer (b. 1926) designs motorized aluminum tanks that crawl along the floor, frightening viewers by their inexplicable changes of direction. Len Lye (b. 1901), a pioneer filmmaker, created whirling metal strips that scream through the air in a frenzy of activity. But in *The Fountain,* the metal becomes a delicately balanced mobile whose rods sway gently, simulating the gentle flow of water.

Expressionism and Realism

The emotional trend in art, identified with Expressionism in the 1940s, has all but disappeared. Briefly, the Feminist movement became a passionate cause for some, combining personal feelings with a response to the real world.

Women Artists and Feminist Art The Feminist movement, which gained new strength in the 1960s, led to a re-examination of women's achievements in the visual arts. In the past, as we have seen, most women unrelated to artists had little opportunity for training or art patronage. Nonetheless, it has been discovered that many swelled the ranks of medieval craft guilds and later worked in the great tapestry manufactories of the Baroque era. There has

been painstaking research and increased recognition of those few who became artists, whom we have noted. Early in the 20th century the legions of women artists working untouched by public furor far outnumber all the early pioneers and include the Britons Gwen John (1876–1939), Vanessa Bell (1879–1961), and D. Carrington (1893–1932), the Frenchwoman Marie Laurencin (1885–1956), and the Americans Romaine Brooks (1874–1970) and Isabel Bishop (b. 1902).

Unusual sculptors include Edmonia Lewis (1843–1900), daughter of a free black and a Chippewa, noted for Neoclassical pieces such as *Forever Free* and others on ethnic and Feminist themes, and Malvina Hoffman (1887–1966), who excelled in realistic portraiture. Among contemporary sculptors are the political satirist Marisol (Fig. 120), whose work we discussed as a form of Pop Art, Louise Nevelson (Fig. 119), and Lee Bontecou, discussed in Chapter 6. Bontecou's art often incorporates paradoxical images, such as one based on a concept of teethed sexual openings (Fig. 87).

Like Bontecou, French-born Louise Bourgeois (b. 1911) also works in a variety of media, including wood, plaster, and marble. She traveled extensively from her childhood in Paris and taught at the Louvre and elsewhere. Her first exhibition, in New York, was an extraordinary assemblage of forms. Wooden constructions with knobby heads stood together in clusters. A 6-foot-tall (1.83 meters) group of beams, painted purplish red and joined at cranial level by one wooden lintel, clumped unsteadily across the bare

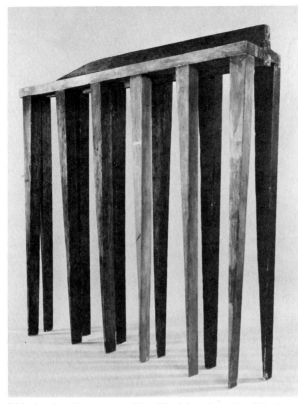

384. Louise Bourgeois. *The Blind Leading the Blind.*
1949. Painted wooden stakes 7′ × 7′ × 7″
(2.13 × 2.13 × 0.18 m). Detroit Institute of Arts
(Founders Society Purchase, Mr. and Mrs.
Walter Buhl Ford II Fund).

floor, a comment on modern-day witch-hunts (Fig. 384). It was named *The Blind Leading the Blind* and perhaps recalls Brueghel's similarly titled work, which satirized the religious cults of his day. Also a sculptor beginning in clay, Mary Frank (b. 1933) has poetically and musically transformed all materials she touches into personal statements that suggest an optimistic world.

As we review the works of these women, it appears that women's experiences, although different from men's, do not make women's artworks similar to one another in style. Most women artists, in fact, seem to find affinity with other artists of their own **milieu** (environment) and period and work within the general mainstream of art.

In the 1960s, however, women's cooperative galleries mushroomed, and a few commercial dealers in art by women appeared. They have succeeded in directing some women toward an awareness of a ground-breaking role as women artists. Some women seem to derive their art from the Feminist movement. Niki de Saint-Phalle (b. 1930), for instance, has produced in a brief ten years half a dozen styles all based on sexist themes. Her best-known works are huge, playful papier mâché "Nana" figures, which somehow never threaten us by their size. For an exhibit in

Stockholm she constructed an enormous figure called *hon* ("she"), which visitors could enter and therein be surrounded by a sexual world.

Judy Chicago (b. 1939), an ardent Feminist, uses hard-edge imagery to communicate Feminist intuitions about female nature. While she taught at the California Institute of the Arts, she initiated a Feminist art program that was highly successful in politicizing the female art community. Together with Miriam Schapiro (b. 1923), she worked on projects such as Womanspace, the first cooperative women's art gallery on the West Coast, which became the Woman's Building, still functioning as a busy art center in Los Angeles. Her best-known work is *The Dinner Party* (Fig. 385), the archetypal Feminist work. Five years in the making, it was assembled by the collective skills of 400 women who executed Chicago's design. The format of the work is a huge triangular table with 13 place settings on each side, referring to Christ and his disciples at the Last Supper. All 39 place settings, named in honor of famous women, consist of plates, goblets, and flatware, with each one decorated with female sexual symbols. They repose on hand-worked place mats. The triangular ceramic floor bears the names of 999 other cultural heroines. *The Dinner Party* has been exhibited to packed crowds and, like many frankly sexist works, has received mixed criticism.

Fantasy

Fantasy, like formalism, was partly a reaction to the emotional aspects of Abstract Expressionism. It pervades Pop Art, assemblage, and the improvisational art experiences known as **"happenings."** Two important transitional figures who drew on Abstract Expressionism but were forerunners of Pop Art were Robert Rauschenberg and Jasper Johns.

Rauschenberg, as we saw in Chapter 3, combines collage, the commercial silk-screen process, Action painting technique, and ready-made objects such as an electric fan to create combine art (Fig. 86). The prevailing theme is often nonmeaning, or like Dada, art of the absurd.

Johns painted familiar objects such as American flags and beer cans. In *Studio I* (Fig. 386) he follows the Renaissance tradition of the artist painting his own studio (Fig. 39), while also referring to the Romantic Courbet's painting of his studio (Fig. 309), an assertion of freedom of artistic expression. Johns's piece, consisting of several canvases nailed together to which a string of his paint cans is attached, is another early example of **combine art.**

Pop Art   A movement of the 1960s that combined both fantasy and realism was Pop Art. It began in London in 1956 when the Independent Group, a small group of artists, architects, sculptors, and art historians who were studying the symbolism and imagery of the art of mass society, staged the exhibition "This Is Tomorrow." It included a provocative work by one of the members, Richard Hamilton (b. 1922), entitled *Just What Is It That Makes*

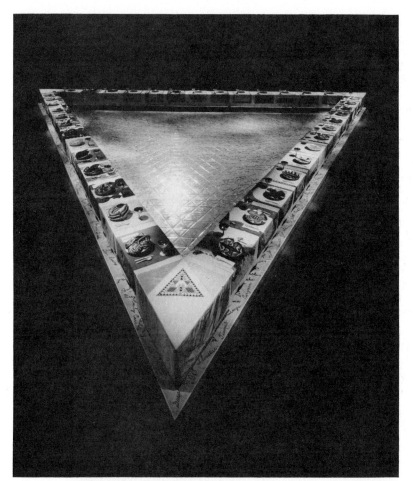

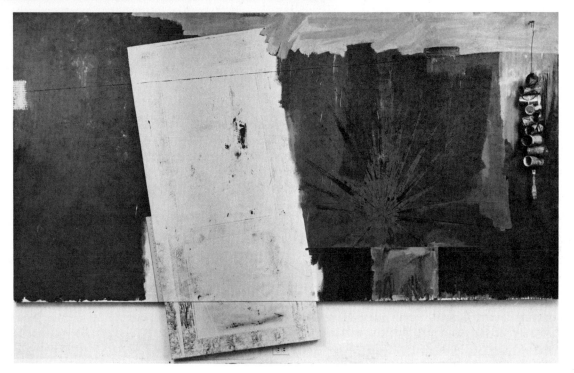

left: 385. Judy Chicago.
The Dinner Party. 1979.
Mixed media,
each side 47′ (14.34 m).

below: 386. Jasper Johns. *Studio I.*
1964. Oil on canvas with objects,
6′1½″ × 12′1″ (1.87 × 3.68 m).
Whitney Museum of American Art,
New York.

Today's Home So Different, So Appealing (Fig. 387). It was unclear whether the public was expected to consider as art this montage of ready-made motifs culled from many nonart sources and explicitly connected to Dada.

However, the content of Hamilton's work could also be compared with a 17th-century Dutch painting whose genre theme is brought up to date—a couple at home, served by an upstairs maid standing before a window view of an urban scene beyond. The name for the new style may be expressed in the oversize Tootsie Pop held by the head of the house. In any event, this work ridiculed the banalities of daily life and the fantasy world depicted by mass media. The popular culture represented at this exhibition was identified as **Pop Art** by the British critic Lawrence Alloway, a member of the group.

Pop Art focuses on movies, billboards, machines, comic books, and advertising. Pop artists examine our everyday world and report it directly, with neither satire nor antagonism, but with such intensity that the spectator frequently becomes conscious for the first time of what he or she sees every day. Pop Art depends on large scale to increase its impact, thrusting forward in monumental size aspects of our culture we have chosen to ignore. Another characteristic of Pop Art is the repetition of images in patterns reminiscent of the rows of mass-produced packages seen in the supermarket, an emerging phenomenon at mid-century.

In the United States, Andy Warhol was a pioneer in using multiple images and in container art as well. He made use of his commercial training and early career in advertising in his paintings. Since 1961, his subjects have included soup cans, Brillo boxes (Fig. 152), Marilyn Monroe (Fig. 18), and a bottle of Coca Cola. Some of his pieces are paintings on two-dimensional surfaces, but many are sculptures executed in mixed media such as commercial lithography and silk-screening. For example, the Brillo boxes are made of plywood with silkscreened labels. In this way Warhol has removed the artist's touch from the art, not scientifically like Seurat (Pl. 5, p. 23) but by the techniques of industry. He believes that "painting is essentially the same as what it has always been. . . . All painting is fact, and that is enough; the paintings are charged with their very presence."

Warhol is not the only Pop artist to have used the Coke bottle as an image. Charles Frazier (b. 1930) comments on both the universality of Coca Cola and the influence of Hollywood in a sculpture shaped like a "feminine" bottle of Coke.

The work of James Rosenquist (Fig. 8), who initially was an outdoor-sign painter, performs the same function as the work of Warhol—magnifying images and forcing us to look at the carbon-copy quality of our lives and at the endless assemblyline products of which we have become a part. In *F-111* he covers all four walls of a room with blown-up images of food, automobile tires, spaghetti, a mushroom cloud, and a little girl being initiated into the rites of grown-up artificiality. Roy Lichtenstein, however, may best represent Pop. He has seized standardized im-

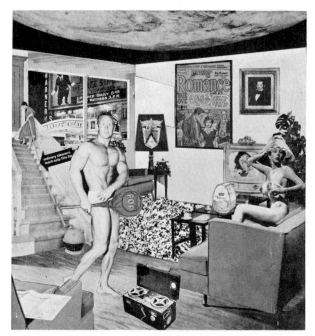

387. Richard Hamilton. *Just What Is It That Makes Today's Home So Different, So Appealing?* 1956. Collage on paper, 10⅛ × 9¾" (26 × 25 cm). Kunsthalle, Tübingen, West Germany. Collection Professor Dr. Georg Zundel.

agery of sentiment and violence in our popular comic strips and greatly enlarged its impact while faithfully transcribing every detail (Fig. 388). Like the carefully lettered message which amplified the medieval illustration page of the *Symbol of Solomon as Wisdom* (Fig. 147), Lichtenstein's caption pinpoints his story.

Jim Dine's art, like that of Rauschenberg and Johns, draws on Abstract Expressionism (Fig. 74). Retaining the stock accessories of theater—stage-set colors and actual props—Dine uses paint and modeling materials to remind the spectator of commonplace objects. His work combines anti-art objects with the immediacy of Action painting. For instance, in one of his assemblages, Dine set a lawnmower against a canvas painted green and permitted the paint to drip off the canvas onto the mower as if art must include not only paint and canvas but also anything attached to the canvas.

Anonymity is another feature of Pop Art. Robert Indiana (Robert Clark, b. 1928) exhibits paintings of stenciled signs that reveal nothing about the artist except what can be read into his choice of subjects. Indiana is absorbed by word images that suggest the stark simplicity of flashing neon signs. The words *eat, love,* and *die* are rendered in clashing, precise, hard-edged colors. His *Love* (Fig. 389) has become so much a part of the popular American scene that few are aware of its source. Many other Indiana word images are bitter indictments of modern life. Thus Pop Art echoes the bland character of our commercial surround-

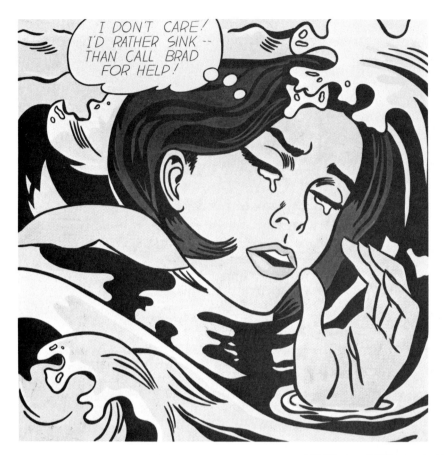

above: 388. Roy Lichtenstein.
Drowning Girl. 1963. Oil and synthetic
polymer paint on canvas.
5'7⅝" × 5'6¾" (1.71 × 1.70 m).
Museum of Modern Art, New York
(Philip Johnson Fund and gift of
Mrs. Bagley Wright).

right: 389. Robert Indiana. *Love.*
1968. Aluminum, 12 × 12 × 6"
(30 × 30 × 15 cm). Whitney Museum
of American Art, New York
(gift of the Howard and Jean
Lipman Foundation, Inc.).

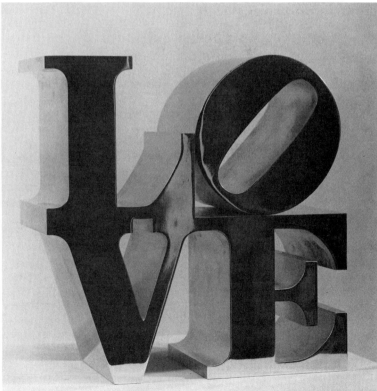

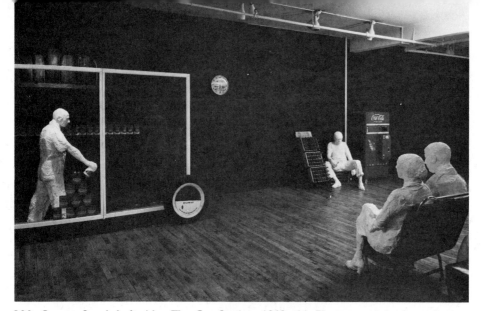

390. George Segal. Left side: *The Gas Station*. 1963–64. Plaster, metal, glass, stone, and rubber; 8 × 22 × 5′ (2.44 × 6.71 × 1.53 m). National Gallery of Canada, Ottawa. Right side: *The Bus Riders,* detail. 1962. Plaster, metal, vinyl: 6′2″ × 4′ × 9′ (1.9 × 1.2 × 2.7 m). Hirshhorn Museum and Sculpture Garden, Smithsonian Institution, Washington, D.C.

ings as contrasted with the highly individualized creations of traditional art.

The most impressive sculptor associated with Pop Art may be George Segal (b. 1924), who, like Edward Kienholz (Fig. 23), will also be discussed as an environmental sculptor. After working on happenings with Allen Kaprow (b. 1927), Segal turned to building real environments into which he placed sculptured people (Fig. 390). These works, often assembled from junkyard materials, are filled with machines, oil cans, and other Pop images. But the figures are always taken directly from life. Replicas of nondescript people, they are cast from the live model into plaster as if they could be produced in multiples, like beer cans or soap boxes.

Marisol has created her own style, which uses wood, plaster, paint, photographs, and accessories. Her works are studies of modern personalities, mocking the stuffed-animal figure of the hero, an empty image of leadership, which the public demands. Her portrait *President Johnson* is a devastating satire on his need to be loved by the masses, since the smiling head is designed to nod continuously. *The Generals* (Fig. 120) ridicules past military heroes.

In his sculpture, Claes Oldenburg calls attention to the character of ordinary objects by taking them out of context and changing their scale. His *Hamburger,* the symbol of American fast food, made of painted plaster-of-paris and enlarged to four times normal size, had a wide influence on the art of the 1960s. Similar painted plaster food and other products filled his *Store,* a New York establishment rented in 1961. Explaining his role as storekeeper, Oldenburg said of his pieces that galleries are "not the place for them. A store would be better." Everything he sees becomes saturated with meaning, and he has turned things inside out or upside down or changed their substance. For example, he

reproduced an electric fan in soft, stuffed vinyl as a satire on our dependency on material objects (Fig. 124). Art critic Max Kozloff observes:

> With Claes Oldenburg, the spectator's nose is practically rubbed into the whole pointless cajolery of our hard-sell, sign-dominated culture. Oldenburg may even be commenting on the visual indigestibility of our environment by his inedible plaster and enamel cakes and pies.

Assemblages The refuse of our industrial culture possesses great variety and appeals to many artists as a substitute for traditional materials. They combine debris— the rind of an orange, bits of advertisements, and found objects such as pieces of old cars—with paint to create collages and assemblages. Early examples are Cubist collages and assemblages such as the *Merzbau* of Kurt Schwitters. Jean Dubuffet's (b. 1901) statement that "anything can come from anything" explains the attitude of artists who create assemblages. Neither painted nor sculpted in the traditional sense, and not expected to last, they are made of whatever appeals to the artist.

Joseph Cornell (1903–1972) made memorable contributions to assembled sculpture. Perhaps inspired by penny arcade fortune-telling machines, he concentrated on boxes, creating glass-fronted containers crammed with odds and ends redolent with personal associations. Occasionally they included Cubist forms and multiple images. Often containing mirrors, his assemblages suggested intimate, magical dream worlds (Fig. 391). Alice Aycock (b. 1946) also makes assemblages. She builds complex wooden constructions such as *Studies for a Town,* which incorporated references to Roman amphitheaters, medieval walled towns, and modern shanty towns.

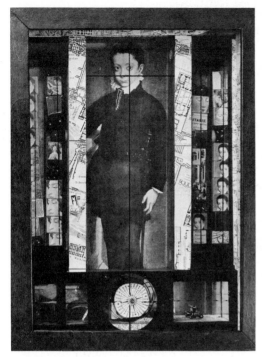

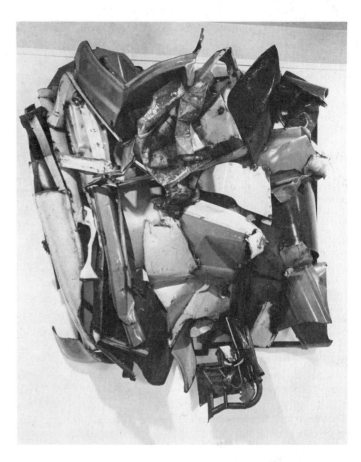

above: 391. Joseph Cornell.
Medici Slot Machine. 1942. Construction,
15½ × 12 × 4⅜" (39 × 30 × 11 cm).
Private collection. Location unknown.

right: 392. John Chamberlain. *Essex.*
1960. Automobile body parts and other
metal, relief; 9′ × 3′4″ × 3′7″
(2.74 × 2.03 × 1.09 m). Museum
of Modern Art, New York (gift of Mr.
and Mrs. Robert C. Scull and purchase).

Destruction is the dominating theme of John Chamberlain's (b. 1927) assemblages. In such works as *Essex* (Fig. 392) he builds bent and welded remnants of dead automobiles from junkyards into sculpture. These rusted, crushed, or fragmented forms have a macabre fascination for us, allowing us vicariously to experience destruction. Tinguely's self-destruction machine had a similar appeal. In many of us there seems to be an element that enjoys seeing buildings torn down, cars crashing in a movie, or a piano being torn apart, as the comedian Jimmy Durante used to stage nightly. The author Edmund Feldman concludes, destruction must be attractive to many people or there would not be so much of it.

Happenings When the distinctions that separate art from reality blur, the fabricated object may no longer be our major concern. If the medium really has become the massage, then the actual making of art may become the focus of interest. The staged happenings of the 1960s might have occurred anywhere, on the streets or in the supermarket. Allen Kaprow, an assemblage sculptor who

was one of the first to stage such events, believes that the "gallery has given way as a place for staging happenings to a craggy canyon, an old abandoned factory, a railroad, or the oceanside."

Happenings were performed without a real script or even a rehearsal. Participants were selected for their suitability to the plan, and props and costumes were gathered. The excitement when a planned sequence jelled and one event led to the next often gave the happening, like improvisational theater, a thrilling, unpredictable potential. Happenings were an art, sometimes closer to life than to theater. They were briefly a part of the American art world, perhaps because they reflected the sense of chaos many of us still observe in society.

Environmental Art

The term *Environmental Art* refers to constructions that often combine painting and sculpture in architectural settings. Built on a large scale, many surround the viewer with visual sensations, totally immersing him or her in the art

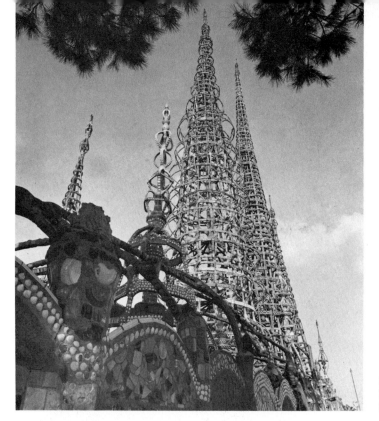

393. Simon Rodia. Watts Towers,
Los Angeles. c. 1921–54
(now partially destroyed).

experience. As such they may be called **Experiential Art.**
By extension the term may include art that reworks the
natural environment.

Architectural Environments. To create an architectural environment requires multiple skills. Its combination
of assemblage and other techniques is another indication
of the merging of the arts after centuries of separation.
Most of them permit the viewer to walk inside them, and
many are rooted in the artist's response to social concerns.

In their commentaries on contemporary culture, the
Pop artists Kienholz and Segal are inheritors of the social-
protest paintings of the 1930s. Kienholz's tableaux (Fig. 23)
place us in the role of peeping Toms, and our own macabre
fascination with what we see provides an added element
of discomfort. Like Kienholz, Segal also creates groupings of
people in environments (Fig. 390), but instead of presenting dramatic incidents, he reveals their banality. Segal may
be reporting the nondescript aspects of our lives so that we
may either more fully enjoy day-to-day living or find a way
to transcend its tedium.

Calder created an architectural environment in the
form of a 60-foot-high (18.29 meters) direct-metal sculpture, which guided automobile traffic in Spoleto, Italy. He
also designed an accoustical ceiling for an auditorium in
Caracas, Venezuela, in which tremendous, free-form
shapes seem to float above the seats. Before Calder, architectural sculpture had been obviously attached to the
building; in this work, it appeared to be a suspended element of the environment.

Working with wooden found objects and other materials, the assemblage sculptor Louise Nevelson (Fig. 119) is
most often identified with the large environmental works
discussed in Chapter 6. The art critic Cindy Nemser has
said of them, "All the rubbish of Manhattan is transformed
by this artist into phantom architecture." Working in a
different manner, closer to Schwitters, Clarence Schmidt
(b. 1923) created a series of grottoes within a cavelike
house in Woodstock, New York. A little-known, self-taught
artist, he lived in his creation as he burrowed into the earth.
Similarly, an Italian-born tile setter named Simon Rodia
designed the Watts Towers of Los Angeles, California.
Emerging from Rodia's tiny backyard like the towers of a
medieval city, the steel, mesh, and mortar spires are lovingly covered with broken tiles and other discards (Fig.
393). Rodia's environment has become a living echo of
himself. Here again the line between art and reality is difficult to find.

Architecture

The essence of the International Style (1930–1950) was its
conviction that architecture could produce the millen-
nium—a perfect society instituted by architects. The famous dicta followed in profusion: "Form follows function,"
"The house is a machine for living in," "Less is more," and
so forth. By mid-century, Le Corbusier (Fig. 355) and others
had persuaded us that there could be no civilization without cities. Mies van der Rohe (Fig. 185) claimed that the
essence of modern buildings was "skin and bones"—the

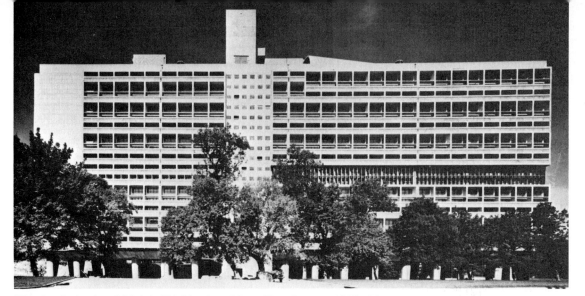

394. Le Corbusier. L'Unité d'Habitation, Marseilles, France. 1947−52. Length 550′ (167.64 m), width 79′ (24.08 m), height 184′ (56.08 m).

skin of glass, the bones of steel or concrete. And Walter Gropius (Fig. 352) had persuaded us that the "building team" was the only effective expedient for the creation of modern construction.

If any one building sums up mid-century philosophy, it is Le Corbusier's *Unité d'Habitation* (Fig. 394) in Marseilles. *Unité* is one of the most famous structures of the postwar world. It was to be the model for a series of complexes that Le Corbusier planned to build across France to house, without resorting to urban sprawl, the four million French families made homeless by the war. In its design he evolved unusual combinations of past traditions and new ideas—the pillars on which it stands taper toward the bottom, the gardens are on the roof, the streets are inside and in the air, the shopping center is on the seventh floor instead of connected to the commercial center of Marseilles.

Critics were numerous. Jane Jacobs condemned the shopping center for being too far from the center of the city. Lewis Mumford criticized the long apartment units as being too much like halls. Siegfried Giedion complained that the internal streets were all dark corridors, and journalists attacked the notion of one thousand people holed up in a vast, anonymous beehive. Nevertheless, *Unité,* efficiently constructed of precast concrete, achieved a balance of positive goals: (1) 23 different types of apartments for all family sizes, (2) absolute privacy, (3) isolation from traffic fumes and noise, and (4) 26 communal facilities. Because of such work in urban architecture, Le Corbusier was asked to apply his ideas on urban design to Chandigarh, the new capital of India. His beliefs are still an inspiration to city planners.

Despite Le Corbusier's far-reaching goals in *Unité,* this gargantuan design has not provided Utopia to its inhabitants. Can it be the loss of personal identity in an autonomous living center? Or, isn't it likely that the human animal depends to some degree upon natural environments for survival? Certainly, we may recall that Moshe Safdie *was* able to achieve in *Habitat* (Fig. 200) a large communal facility, apparently so desirable that even now the supply of available apartments never equals the demand for them. And Buckminster Fuller (Fig. 168) *was* able to provide efficient climate control in the U.S. Pavilion at Expo '67 and elsewhere, unlike *Unité,* which was designed before universal awareness of ecoenvironmental balances required to accommodate efficient energy consumption.

The world of the seventies and the eighties will demand a different set of architectural priorities, as we shall soon see, and our designers will have to develop solutions to effectively meet these needs.

EXERCISES AND ACTIVITIES

1. What are some of the major mid-century movements, grouped as to formalism, Expressionism, realism, and fantasy?
2. Can you think of other popular slogans as significant as the *LOVE* theme of Robert Indiana? Create a work of art in paint, sculpture, or any combination that uses Pop images or slogans?
3. Create a work of art in which motion—either natural or mechanical—is an important element.
4. Modifications of earlier geometric abstraction and nonobjective art can be seen in Op Art. Using graph paper or your own ruled squares, experiment with small units of color. Create an illusion of three dimensions by varying the sizes and colors of the units. Superimpose three-dimensional louvers made of paper or cardboard to create more exciting visual effects.
5. Explain how the approach of many women to art changed in the 1960s.
6. How does the art of assemblage reflect our growing concern with the wastes of our society?
7. Create a work that recycles the materials of industry.
8. Environmental art can be found in painting, sculpture, and architectural design. What are the common features in all three media? What are the differences?

20 Our Own Time

There are more artists creating more works of art (of some sort) than ever before in our history.

HILTON KRAMER

The accelerating rate of change that pervades our lives today is clearly reflected in the art of the seventies and eighties. Many artists feel liberated from traditional rules and free to follow any line of exploration. Art styles constantly shift, while artists develop their styles into new forms. Categories of art become blurred. Painting, for example, often merges with sculpture in assemblage. The line between art and craft hardly exists as sculptors crochet, quilt, blow glass, or weave environments and painters use the dye techniques of crafts. New categories emerge that use light, the natural environment, or pure ideas. Today almost any art form is acceptable.

The flow of new art has been accompanied by an increasing awareness of art on the part of the general public. Unprecedented numbers of museums and galleries are eager to show both the new and different as well as the art of the past. Publications on art (along with art reviewers) have mushroomed. Fad and fashion, nurtured by mass media, exert insidious pressure on artists to try to capture attention. A few have become national figures overnight, only to be forgotten when the smoke cleared. Most artists, however, are not widely known, and earn livings at jobs that leave them too little free time in their studios. Yet, they are nonetheless committed to producing art that satisfies their own creative needs.

As we have traced the history of art through the centuries, we have often been rewarded with artistic expressions that affect us today as strongly as they moved observers at the time they were created. No less significant is what we may learn from history about the pattern of artistic development. Many of us might anticipate a flowering in our time of all the currents we have examined, as if art, like science, were to evolve from past experience toward a glorious new age. For others it is tempting to think that as Western society has moved in cycles in the past, today it

moves faster and in wider circles. And yet we cannot be sure that either of these views is accurate. Without the distance that time provides, it is difficult to sift through the rich variety of today's art to distinguish the significant from the merely novel.

Art historians and critics are pressed to point out guideposts to align in comprehensible segments the disorderly jumble of present styles. Some historians have noted remarkable similarities between the Mannerist period—when artists rejected traditional views of reality, ideal Renaissance form, and balance in favor of stylistic effects, imbalance, and restlessness (Chapter 14)—and the present time—when many artists are less concerned with the correlation between art and life than with the nature of painting itself. If the mechanical aspects of art become for many artists their preoccupation if not their goal, historians may be justified in labeling some late 20th-century experimental work manneristic.

We may observe, beneath the surface variety that characterizes present-day art, a general continuation of the tendencies that we have already perceived. The formalist trend is found in abstract paintings and sculptures—mostly cool, nonemotional works that depend on design, color, and technique. Realism includes artists who attempt a verisimilitude perhaps comparable to the verism of late Roman sculpture (see Chapter 12). Expressionism can be found mainly in European art and young American artists for whom the real world remains an opportunity for personal emotional interpretation. Art as escape from this imperfect world through fantasy also continues, chiefly in the form of television and film. These photographic art forms, which dominate our world as never before, sometimes provide us with an imaginative existence that may explore dionysian modes or regions once considered taboo. The multiple image, whether on film, video, or graphics, predominates, relating mechanical duplication to the repetitious electronic aspects of our world. The intellectual planning process also dominates in Conceptual art and some Environmental art, which is planned to disappear after it is made.

Formalism

Painting With the 1970s, formalistic painting moved from Color-Field abstraction to utilization of color in a new phase of complexity and paradox. Building upon the celebrated acrylic-stained paintings composed of parallel bands of stinging colors by Kenneth Noland and others, later huge works consisted of innumerable widely differentiated bands, each section as important as the whole design. Many works are composed of hundreds of tiny elements, each unit carefully painted onto a grid, as seen in paintings and drawings by Agnes Martin (b. 1912). Color codes are increasingly analytical. Many optical artists appear to have codified the color relationships in their works by computers.

Sculpture Carl André (b. 1935) is an innovative and controversial sculptor who often works with multiple units, stacking up planks or carefully arranging firebricks or metal squares. He has also arranged natural objects such as rocks. Richard Serra (b. 1939) creates monumental sculptures consisting of such materials as heavy metal sheets, arranged in piles, scattered at random, or mostly buried in the earth. Sol Lewitt (b. 1928) has built modular wood or aluminum structures based on cubic frames that are intellectual spatial arrangements of uncommon beauty. He has also drawn mathematical series of squares directly on gallery walls.

By placing modular repeats in a straight line, Donald Judd (b. 1928) eliminates variables, or human qualities. The predictability of his sculptures, which make no reference to past traditions, reduces emotional overtones to zero. What remains is only a real construction in real space (Fig. 395). If we find such sculptures disturbing, it may be they remind us of manufactured environments that cannot fulfill human needs. Another sculptor who commented

on the synthetic quality and similarity of many lives is Eva Hesse (1936–1970), who has arranged plastics and other synthetic materials in endless repeat patterns.

Light Art Obviously, light is involved in all art. But in recent years artists have become aware of the potential of light itself as a theme (Fig. 67). Light has become a recognized medium since the late 1960s, and light artists use their material with the same skill that other artists apply to color and paint.

Thomas Wilfred (1889–1965) was one of the first artists to conceive of light as an independent aesthetic experience. His experiments in the early part of this century led to the development of the *Clavilux Lumia,* an instrument on which he performed publicly as early as 1922. From the spectator's viewpoint, the *Lumia Suite* presents a continuously changing pattern of fading and regenerating colored light, which produces a hypnotic effect similar to that of some Color-Field and Optical paintings.

One of the most innovative light artists working today is West German-born Otto Piene (b. 1928), who created a light ballet that toured Europe in 1961. Piene has designed light installations of thousands of individual bulbs programmed to coordinate with activity onstage. Many light artists combine light and motion, and some have used light along with water to create moving compositions that delight the eye with artificially lighted waterfalls and fountains and gratify the ear with the sound of rushing water.

Larry Bell (b. 1939), a light artist of deep sensitivity, sets glass cubes on glass cases. Lit from within and coated with a translucent substance that acts as a prism, the cubes create delicate effects of light and color that change depending upon the position of the viewer. The simplicity of the cubic forms adds to the impact of the changing color.

Another light artist, Greek-born (Varda) Chryssa (b. 1933), combines theatrical skill with technical precision in

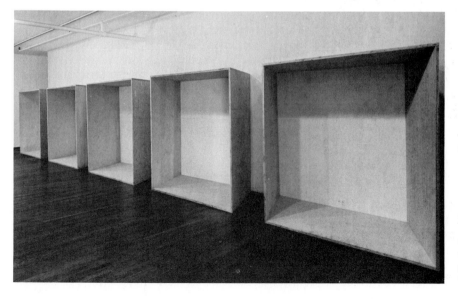

395. Donald Judd. *Untitled.* 1972. Plywood; five boxes, each 3'5" × 6' × 6' (1.04 × 1.83 × 1.83 m), spaced 1'7" (0.48 m) apart. Private collection.

blinking neon sculpture, enclosed in simple shapes. Her inventive work comments on today's industrialization, while at the same time it suggests the ever-expanding frontiers of science and technology. Like many of today's experimental artists, Chryssa has explored some aspects of environmental art by combining theatrical and technical elements in an aesthetically exciting spectacle. Her work is reminiscent of the glaringly lighted environment of Times Square in New York City (Fig. 396) or the Strip in Las Vegas. For example, under the sponsorship of Intermedia 68 and the Museum of Modern Art, she created an electromagnetic environment in which vibrating color and light was designed to envelop the participants.

Light sculpture uses some of the same theories explored by Optical painters and Color-Field painters. Stephen Antonakos' recent neon sculpture investigates continuous planes of light by using an industrial method of joining neon tubes (Pl. 8, p. 24). By juxtaposing these tubes he interrelates space, time, and light, and his art extends our concepts of what our future environment may be like.

396. Chryssa. *Fragments for the "Gates to Times Square."* 1966. Neon and plexiglas, 6'9" × 2'10½" × 2'3½" (2.06 × 0.88 × 0.7 m). Whitney Museum of American Art, New York (gift of Howard and Jean Lipman).

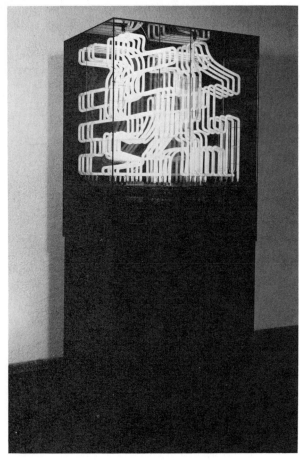

Realism

Realism has been a strong current in American art since the 18th century. Even during the great enthusiasm for Abstract Expressionism, when it was almost impossible for realistic painters to find galleries in which to exhibit their work, painters such as Andrew Wyeth continued to paint recognizable people and objects in rural America.

Painting Wyeth's approach to realism can be seen in *Christina's World* (Fig. 78), a painting in which he illuminates the hardships and isolation of the handicapped. His precise tempera technique establishes a matter-of-fact world, yet he imbues his subject, a crippled girl, with pathos. However realistic the painting appears to be, Wyeth uses exaggerated perspective in the high horizon and the wide vista of the sky to increase the sense of distance between Christina and the house. A visual tension is developed, which expresses the physical struggle of her inching progress toward home. The impact of Wyeth's work is heightened also by the stark simplicity of the composition and by the frequent suggestion of forces beyond the minute, factual details he presents.

Magic Realism, or **Superrealism,** is a realistic style in which the painter exploits our camera-oriented responses but takes us beyond them. At first glance, an oil painting by Philip Pearlstein (b. 1924) may strike us as a mere copy of a photograph (an aid he never uses). His painting demonstrates in its light and shadow the harsh quality of a snapshot. But on deeper scrutiny we see that, with this kind of lighting, Pearlstein achieves a sharper, heightened reality, which emphasizes certain features of the model to produce a desired emotional effect, usually a rather heavy, melancholy mood, heightened by the downward glance of the eyes and the drooping hand (Fig. 397).

Also working with traditional materials and techniques is the unconventional Alice Neel (b. 1900), an outspoken Feminist who is probably best known for her portraits. Her paintings on the theme of mother and child are incisive, sometimes shocking, transcriptions of her subjects, devoid of any sentimentality. A recent self-portrait shows her in a rocking chair, naked but for her glasses.

Photography, especially the Polaroid camera, has become the realist artist's ultimate research tool. Photographed sketches, often with the aid of the airbrush, originally a tool for commercial illustration, are translated into **Photo Realist** paintings. Richard Estes' (b. 1936) camera provides detailed images of urban environments, which he then painstakingly reproduces with oils on masonite. Like Hopper, he is more concerned with physical evidences of our society than with the people who created it. His particular interest in recent years has been scenes of storefronts, in which he carefully lays complex street reflections over detailed, meticulously rendered shop-window displays.

In the hands of an expert such as Audrey Flack (b. 1931), the airbrush can simulate fine (photographic) detail, making a painting almost indistinguishable from camera art. In her travels through Spain, Flack came upon a life-size

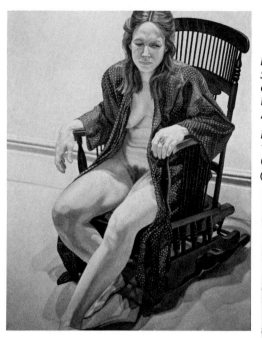

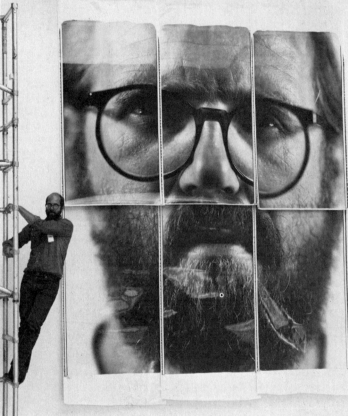

Baroque terracotta and wood sculpture made in the 17th century by Luisa Roldán. Flack's oil painting of the Roldán *Macarena* is a tribute to the unrecognized genius of the Baroque sculptor as well as to her own skill (Pl. 19, p. 268).

A pioneer among artists who use photographs as a source of imagery, Chuck Close (b. 1940) is noted for huge, photographically precise black-and-white portraits. From a distance, they seem monumentally scaled blowups of his original photographs. At closer range, they assume alter-identities as fields of dots, brush marks, or fingerprints. Confronting his portraits is a direct experience. Of vast scale and sober countenance, their fixed, hypnotic stares are riv-

eting. Recently he has turned to six-panel photographic montages produced only from Polaroid prints (Fig. 398).

Sculpture A certain amount of American sculpture, like painting, is an effort to imitate reality. Somewhat conventional forms are created with unconventional materials, such as polyester reinforced with fiberglass and wood. Surfaces are dense and opaque, and the figures are often painted and slick. Occasionally, they are placed on real props, creating a juxtaposition of art objects within real environments. Examples are George Segal's early white plaster figures of ordinary people seated in real chairs or in

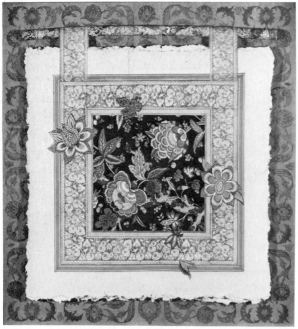

399. Charlotte Brown. *Wildflower.* 1982.
Xerography; Chine colle 3M color process on hand-made paper and wood, 42 × 45 × 5″ (107 × 114 × 13 cm). Collection the artist.

a gas station (Fig. 390). John de Andrea (b. 1941) and Luis Jimenez (b. 1940) reveal similar influences.

By contrast, Duane Hanson, a sculptor who feigns reality with polyresins and synthetics, cultivates the banal. His groupings are so lifelike that visitors who see them in museums are uncertain as to which figures in the crowd are Duane Hanson's and which are alive. Neatly avoiding most stereotypes of beauty, Hanson's overweight, middle-class subjects are placed in everyday situations such as a bus stop or a fast-food restaurant (Fig. 125).

Ceramic sculptors such as David Gilhooley (b. 1943) and Lillian Dodson may bypass more profound themes in exchange for scrutiny of the simplest items of singular beauty rendered with unsettling verisimilitude; a crate of Dodson's oranges may be stoneware, and a succulent meal, porcelain (Fig. 122). In a world of imitation reality, her ceramic sculptures comment on the originals, sometimes with humor and always with uncanny skill.

Graphics

There have been great changes in the graphic arts in the last few decades. The unprecedented vitality in the production of prints can be accounted for, in part, by the growing numbers of painters (and sculptors) enthusiastically joining the ranks of printmakers in all branches of the medium. The infatuation with advertising images, first perceived by Pop artists such as Richard Hamilton (Fig. 387), who carefully chose and composed the materials of his montages, has persisted through the 1970s.

Changes in size and format of printed works are as extreme as changes in imagery. The advent of large sheets of paper was simultaneous with increasing concern for the quality of paper. As the craft grew, artists inevitably were introduced into the papermaking process.

While it seems a long way from the hand techniques of making fine prints to the industrial techniques of commercial reproduction, artists successfully use both. The fascination of photocopying machinery for so many artists, perhaps beginning with Rauschenberg, has led them to investigate light-activated processes for multiplying their images. Ozalid, blueprint, 3M, and the ultracomplex technology of xerography are all being explored. Uncommonly handsome works in black and white and in color are being produced by **Xerography,** a medium that also permits the translation of solid objects into printed images. A pioneer in machine-involved art, Charlotte Brown uses a 3M color copier. Through an electrostatic technique she has developed, Brown transfers images chosen from textiles and printed papers onto handmade paper, fabric, and clay, creating tapestry-like patterns. In her 3-dimensional *Wildflower,* suspended from fabric-covered wood, she has combined floral prints onto squares, embellished with delicate clay blossoms (Fig. 399). Xerography offers unlimited implications for the future.

The computer, which has revolutionized so many spheres of activity, has formed a bond with art in the field of graphics. With a keyboard or electronic tablet, an artist can form a pattern on a monitor such as a television screen, enlarging or contracting the whole design or sections of it as desired. The effect is described as drawing with electronic light on a display terminal, a possibility barely suggested by Picasso's early experiments with light (Fig. 67).

Another way of displaying computer graphics is through a plotter on paper. By suitable programming techniques, an artist can easily draw directly all the effects created on a display unit. Artistic forms can also be developed by high-speed, computer-programmed printing and spacing of characters. Whatever method is used, the performance of the computer depends solely on the instructions of the artist. With AARON, a computer designed and programmed by Harold Cohen (b. 1928), a stylus moves up and down and across a 22- by 30-inch sheet. Shapes appear that suggest spatial inhabitants of a future world (Fig. 400).

Photographic Arts

Conservativism seems to underlie the photographic arts of the last two decades.

Still Photography   Photography has finally been accepted as an art form by leading museums, critics, and collectors. As painters become fascinated with photography and some try to create imitation photographs on canvas, they cause an identity crisis for photographers. In reaction, some photographers tend more toward the combine

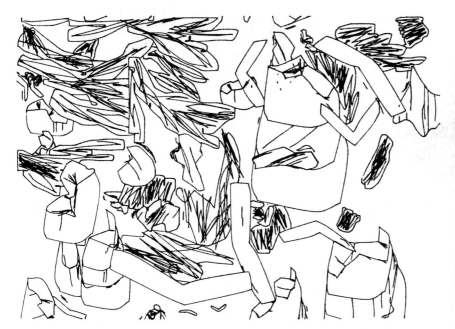

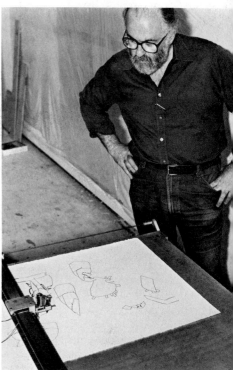

400. At left is a drawing produced by AARON, a computer built and programmed by the artist Harold Cohen. 1982. At right Harold Cohen and a computer-driven machine of his own design producing a drawing generated by his program. 1982.

paintings of Rauschenberg (Fig. 86) and his followers than toward the classicism of Edward Weston or Ansel Adams (Fig. 107). Many are interested in handwork on photographs. Others, however, make new use of ideas and techniques taken from the photographic past. After a quarter century of dependence on the 35-millimeter camera, many are returning to the large-format, stand camera used by many early 20th-century photographers. Such developments may lead photography back to an era of careful preplanning, creativity, and control of scientific, photographic techniques.

Film and Television America dominates the cinema. Perhaps most important is the element of fantasy that films provide. Audiences can escape the everyday world through the fantasy of the classic romance or of science fiction, as in Stanley Kubrick's (b. 1928) *Dr. Strangelove* (1964), an omniscient reference to hypocrisy in high places, and the ground-breaking *2001: A Space Odyssey* (1968). Anticipation builds from the start of the title sequences, linked by designers to the film that follows. The kaleidoscopic opening of *Around the World in Eighty Days,* a brilliant sequence designed by Saul Bass (b. 1920) is a case in point. Bass in his own 1970s film *Why Man Creates,* a compendium of unusual animation and live photography, illumines the process of creativity, fundamental to all the arts and indeed to life itself. Designers like him and Steven Spielberg (b. 1947) with their technical wizardry are changing the face of the films we see.

Tron (1982) follows by more than a decade the revolutionary *2001* and is an electronic odyssey into tomorrow by Disney Studios, exploring special effects hitherto never seen by camera or eye. More than half the film's 93 minutes of running time was generated by computers that simulate the impossible. Objects pass through one another, metamorphosize from one thing to another, and appear to move with the speed of light while live photography is daringly overlaid with electronic animation created without pen, pencil, or brush. The dramatic effects of machine-made worlds with limitless landscapes, sunsets, and moons offer a glimpse of what the computerized future holds in the arts.

Most conventional American films continue to provide escape through action and adventure. Although the American cinema is the freest in the world, and the vast sums involved in production have resulted in more specialized films by smaller film companies, the sky-rocketing costs of film-making allow less opportunity for experiment and risk today than there existed in the film industry's infancy. The effect on cinema of television has already been felt. What changes cable television and cassette and disc recordings of motion pictures will make remain to be seen.

American film directors, however, have worked with originality and distinction. Alfred Hitchcock (1899–1980), creator of suspense films, earned increasing respect for achieving deeper intensity and increased control. Francis Ford Coppola (b. 1939) in *The Godfather* (1972) and its successor may be pointing out the all-too-frequent gulf between what we say and what we do in our supposedly moral society. Other directors of the 1970s such as Arthur Penn (b. 1922) of *Bonnie and Clyde*, Robert Altman (b. 1925) of *Butch Cassidy and the Sundance Kid* and *M∗A∗S∗H*, Martin Scorsese (b. 1942) of *Taxi Driver*, and Michael Cimino (b. 1943) of *The Deer Hunter* have made important statements about the value systems inherent in the periods explored in their films. The future of film, despite fewer pictures and smaller audiences, may lie with present-day directors who can survive the uncertainties of the art to create serious works that question our lives.

Television continues to play a large part in many people's lives. Over-the-air television generally serves a mass market, as we have noted. The increasing popularity of cable television makes possible a wider variety of programs and greater specialization.

Conceptual Art

Over the last hundred years, struggling Western artists have gradually won release from many restraints society imposed on creativity. Impressionism in the 19th century and nonobjective art in the early 20th century were steps in this struggle. In the late 1960s **Conceptual Art,** claiming that art exists as ideas rather than as objects to be permanently displayed and evaluated, took a further step toward freeing the artist from any restrictions. Similar to a theatrical or musical performance, which leaves no art object after it is over, Conceptual Art may involve a process, but it leaves no material art object. The idea itself or the process is sufficient reason for its being.

Social problems concern many Conceptual artists. Les Levine (b. 1936) comments on the American Coke culture. To show his contempt for our transient, die-stamped, machine-produced culture, he creates disposable art, which calls for no commitment. One of his most celebrated early works, sponsored by the New York City Parks Department, consisted of removing 10 sheets of plastic from a vacant lot, in stages, over a period of 30 days. On the last day the ground on which they had lain was dug away for a building. According to Levine, the rationale for this process was the breakdown of spiritual values in today's society and our preference for disposable synthetic goods. Once our rituals are over, nothing of worth is left.

In 1972, to bring attention to the political strife in Northern Ireland, Levine recreated certain aspects of it in a multimedia exhibition in five parts called *The Troubles: An Artist's Document of Ulster*. One part, called *High Noise Torture Chamber*, was a darkened room in which participants could hear the noises used during interrogations of prisoners to isolate them from communication with others and, thus, to break their wills.

Inspired by a documentary television series on an American family, Vito Acconci (b. 1940) created a three-week series called *Following Pieces*. For each he chose a figure in the art world at random and followed him for one day. His written report of his findings, which he mailed to art critics, was the only record of his activity. In another event he persuaded a woman in a nearby room, through an electronic intercom, to wrap 50 yards (45.72 meters) of rope around her body until she was fully imprisoned. Apparently his goal, to establish interaction between himself and his subject, was reached.

Many Conceptual artists, influenced by aerial views of the world provided by planes, spaceships, and satellites, create works that can be seen or photographed only from the air. For example, Walter de Maria (b. 1935) made a huge drawing in the sand of the Mojave Desert, California, that was eroded by winds within a month of its completion. The only record of the drawing is a photograph taken from a plane. De Maria's work echoes Indian sand paintings, which are destroyed at the end of the ceremony for which they were created. In our world of paper, plastics, and tapes, future archaeologists will find few evidences of permanence to illuminate our culture.

Endowed with a sense of the theatrical, the Bulgarian-born artist Christo (Christo Javachef, b. 1935) wanted to find an arena where art could happen within a specific time period by means of his own choosing. He planned to hang a 250,000-square-foot (22,500-square-meter) curtain across a 1,250-foot (375-meter) valley between two mountains in Colorado. His giant *Valley Curtain* (Fig. 401) hung from five steel cables suspended from two specially constructed towers. A reaction to the Iron Curtain separating Soviet-dominated Europe from the West, it was intended to conceal the other side from view and to bar traffic. *Valley Curtain*, however, confronts us with a paradox, as so many Conceptual works and earthworks do. It seemed to be functional but in fact served no practical purpose because it was translucent, allowing light to come through, and was hung to allow space for traffic to pass. More important, instead of acting like a theatrical curtain to unveil or hide a spectacle, Christo's curtain was the spectacle itself. In the same spirit he wrapped cliffs in Little Bay, Australia, in cloth and constructed a 24-mile (38.62-kilometer) cloth fence in the western United States. Instead of making containers for works of art, he has made the packaging become the art.

Immersed in Conceptual Art and fascinated with numbers and the alphabet, Karen Shaw (b. 1942) devised a transliteration system not too distant from the *gematria*, a Cabalistic method of interpreting Hebrew scriptures. By assigning a numerical equivalent to each letter of the alphabet, she transformed such varied material as the poems of the 20th-century German Rainer Maria Rilke and the Gospel according to St. Matthew into personal artistic statements. Her system never fails to yield unexpected rewards for the viewer (Fig. 402) while it turns literary expressions into machine- or computer-type language, which Shaw identifies with the current world.

Other forms of Conceptual Art are thinkworks and nihilworks. **Thinkworks** yield only information. The medium thus becomes the message. Joseph Kossuth (b. 1945), for example, imparts ideas by transfering a negative photostat of words such as *water* or *nothing* to canvas. He

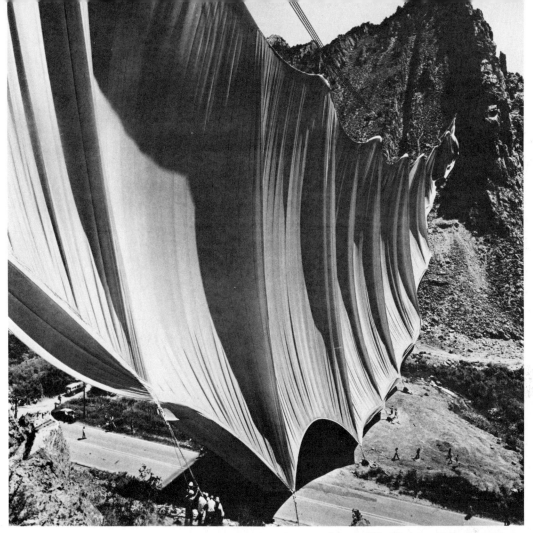

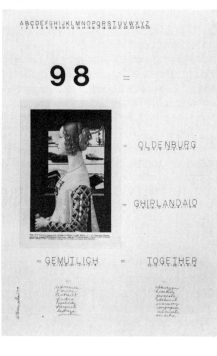

above: 401. Christo. *Valley Curtain,*
Grand Hogback, Rifle, Colo. 1971–72.
200,000 square feet of nylon polyamide,
110,000 pounds of steel cables; width
1250–1368' (381.25–417.24 m), height
185–365' (56.43–111.33 m).

left: 402. Karen Shaw. *Equations:* 98. 1979.
Collage, ink, pencil, and Letraset on paper,
23 × 15" (59 × 38 cm).

said that "what is seen is the presentation of the information. The idea exists only as an invisible ethereal entity."

Nihilworks destroy themselves, like Tinguely's self--destructing machine (Fig. 382). At Alfred University, Robert Smithson investigated accounts of the legendary lost continent of Atlantis and from his research roughly determined its imagined silhouette. He had students collect large, smooth, round rocks, which were positioned on a quicksand bed in the approximate shape of the continent. Slowly they sank out of sight. This type of art raises questions about permanence. Was the event still authentic art after the stones were no longer visible? Can a work of art be justified if someone only remembers it? For example, did the possessions of an Egyptian pharaoh lose their value

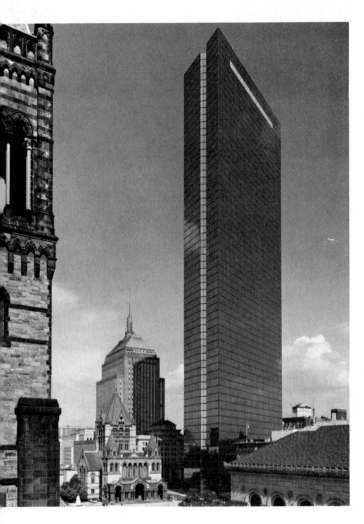

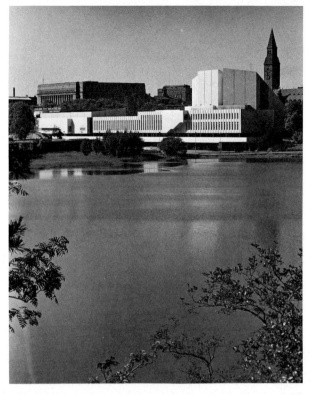

left: 403. I. M. Pei and Associates. John Hancock Building, Boston. 1974.

above: 404. Alvar Aalto. Finlandia Hall, Helsinki, Finland. 1967–71.

when they were buried in his tomb, to be concealed forever? Much of what has been going on in the art world in recent years raises questions such as these.

Earthworks Art forms that involve some significant, often enduring change in the natural environment are called **earthworks,** a term that may refer to alterations to the sea and sky as well. They are related to Conceptual Art, which is essentially an idea rather than an object, but are often more permanent.

Throughout history, artists have interacted with their environment; today the interest in large-scale art has reached a climax in earthworks. Artists such as Michael Heizer (b. 1944) and Robert Smithson use the natural world itself as a medium. Like engineers, architects, or farmers, they want to change the face of the earth. They may dig trenches in a dry lake, redirect streams of water, pile up embankments of earth, or merely photograph natural geological sites. They seem to be protesting against artistic traditions and also human tampering with fragile ecosystems. Like happenings, many earthworks are too vast or too transient to be experienced permanently by many people, and they are limited by the economic resources needed to support them.

Smithson, a major innovator of earthworks, was interested in spirals, which he saw as moving from a path as close to us as our own cells out to the vastness of a spiraling nebula in space. In *Spiral Jetty* (Fig. 6) he fused the concept of the spiral with his dedication to nature:

> My works have been based on a dialogue between the outdoors and the indoors. . . . I'm not interested in reducing art to a set of ideas. I prefer making something physical, and the world is a part of the process. . . . Art will become less isolated and deal more in relationships with the outside world, out of the white room of the gallery into spaces that are natural.

An example of a more ephemeral earthwork, and thus one closer to Conceptual Art, is *Annual Rings,* executed by Dennis Oppenheim (b. 1938). It consisted of concentric rings the width of a snow shovel cleared on a section of the frozen St. John River at Fort Kent, Maine. Of course, this drawing in the snow could last only until the spring thaw.

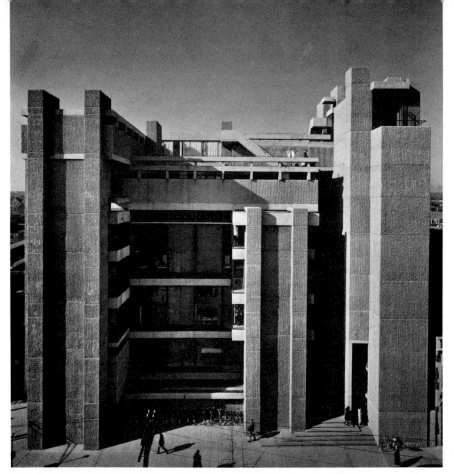

405. Paul Rudolph. Yale University Art and Architecture Building, New Haven, Conn. 1958–64.

Architecture

Central to the International Style that dominated the architecture of the early and middle 20th century was the belief that the architect could bring us Utopia, that properly designed buildings could influence social change. That principle pervaded the art of the Russian Revolution and of the Bauhaus designers both in Europe and later in the United States. It was fundamental to Le Corbusier's city planning for Paris in 1920 and for Chandigarh in the 1950s.

The principle has not, however, worked out as planned. The unadorned grid structure with curtain walls, first advanced in its newness and purity by Mies van der Rohe (Fig. 185), was repeated all over the United States during the building boom of the 1950s and 1960s. In the process it was debased into rubber-stamp construction, impersonal and lifeless. As Wright once said, "Doctors bury their mistakes, but architects can't." The architect Peter Blake (b. 1920) described the American scene in his book *Form Follows Fiasco* (1977):

All around the environment we have built over the past century or so, with supreme confidence, is literally collapsing: the walls of our buildings are crumbling . . . literally; the finest public housing projects to be found anywhere in the world, and designed according to the noblest precepts, are turning into enclaves of murder, rape, mugging, and dope addiction . . . literally. Something or somebody isn't quite up to snuff somewhere in the exalted regions of our architectural establishment.

Certainly the master builders of the 20th century whom we have studied so far—Gropius, Mies van der Rohe, Le Corbusier, Wright, Fuller, Saarinen, and Breuer—have made great contributions to their field. Others have also created outstanding works—Philip Johnson, mentioned in Chapter 9, I. M. Pei (b. 1917), Alvar Aalto (1898–1976), Paul Rudolph (b. 1918), and Louis Kahn (1901–1974).

Pei, formerly a partner of Johnson, built such varied structures as the towering John Hancock building in Boston (Fig. 403) and the triangular east wing of the National Gallery of Art in Washington, D.C. Aalto, a Finnish architect, has been particularly esteemed because he evolved a rich, expressive style of understated humanism as opposed to the prevailing extremes of sterile, glass-box rationalism and curvilinear flamboyance. Each of his designs appears new, yet all share a spatial flow, are warmed by textural modifications, especially through the use of wood and brick, and are scaled to their human occupants. The concert hall of a cultural center in Helsinki, his last major work (1967–71), is an irregularly shaped structure of white marble. The classically simple form of Finlandia Hall is an appropriate climax to a revolutionary architect who was dedicated to humanizing the architecture of the 20th century (Fig. 404).

The influences of Wright and Le Corbusier are revealed in the composition and detail of Rudolph's Yale School of Architecture building in New Haven, Connecticut (Fig. 405). Its spatial organization on 28 different levels is subtle and its handling of light, texture, and form remarkable. Every detail has been studied with loving care, including the imposing façade, a dominant element in all Rudolph's designs. Kahn's beliefs that the architect must respect the materials and function of the building and must not hide its heating and ventilating systems are expressed in his Richards Laboratories for the University of Pennsylvania in Philadelphia. He also designed government complexes in Dacca, Bangladesh, and Amedhabad, India.

We seem today to be close to the end of one architectural epoch. Glass-box houses are becoming things of the past. The direction future builders will take is not clear. It is to be hoped that they will recognize the need for designs that are energy efficient and on a human scale.

Looking to the Future

Today it is more than ever apparent that avant-garde artists have lost their traditional power to shock even die-hard conservatives. In the last few decades such new trends as Optical Art, combine paintings, kinetic and light sculpture, Environmental Art, and Conceptual Art have exploded accepted ideas of what art should be. It is the very nature of the current scene that no single style or point of view predominates. If the categories of art, styles, and artists we have just surveyed seem overwhelming, perhaps it is because we live in a world of multiplicity, which the world of art often illumines.

We may observe certain trends. The popular taste for photographic verisimilitude is unparalleled in the modern period. The experiences of being black and being a woman are social phenomena reflected in black and Feminist art. Museums, galleries, and critics have begun to accept minority artists as professionals. In the 1980s, however, most artists create as individuals rather than as members of groups.

There was once a time when art was an important element of everyone's life, not just the artist's personal preoccupation. Today we realize that art can again become a part of everyday life, enhancing the buildings in which we live and work and even the highways on which we drive. To bring art into our daily lives involves choice, commitment, and support—not only from the dedicated artists but also from citizens who care—those of us who appreciate the art in our world.

EXERCISES AND ACTIVITIES

1. Some artists use their art as the vehicle of social protest, while others are concerned only with form and style. Select examples of these two approaches from the artists discussed in this book, giving reasons for your choices. Is one approach more valid than the other?
2. Today the pace of change in every area of life has accelerated. How does art reflect that acceleration?
3. Light art, Conceptual Art, earthworks—all have their followings. Realistic painting also exists in the style of Magic Realism. Discuss two of these movements. What were their predecessors in earlier styles, if any? List prominent artists and their works.
4. The public usually has resisted the most pioneering artistic efforts. How do you account for public mistrust and lack of interest in the works of experimental artists? In view of the general resistance to innovative art, how do you account for the popularity and acceptance of other new media, such as cinema, radio, and television?
5. Plan and outline a Conceptual artwork.
6. Many individual and regional styles exist in art today. No one style is dominant. Create an artwork in any medium, based either on a familiar style or in your own personal style.
7. The major architectural achievements of every civilization identify its primary concerns. Evaluate today's world on the basis of its major structures. How does our architecture suggest the directions in which we might grow?

Glossary

ABC sculpture See *Minimal art*.

abstract art Art not primarily concerned with representation of nature; the artist selects and exaggerates certain aspects of reality in order to provide a visual experience by means of *line, color,* and *form*.

Abstract Expressionism A painting style, also called the *New York School,* developed after World War II, combining spontaneous personal expression with abstracted or nonobjective shapes painted on large areas of canvas. The action of the artist in flinging, brushing, and dribbling the paint, using the large muscles of the body, led to the term *Action painting*. Pollock was an early Action painter.

Academy Derived from the Greek *Akademeia,* a grove where Plato lectured. The official school of art in France in the 18th century, which set forth rules dictating the style in which artists could work, controlling art by refusing to exhibit any work that did not follow these rules. The term "academic art" is now used to describe conservative art, adhering to traditional rules.

Acropolis A Greek word meaning "hill town" or "fortified hill," applied to the upper section of a Greek city that usually contained the temples. The Acropolis at Athens is the best-known example.

acrylic paint A synthetic resin paint which, along with *polymer* paint, is frequently used by artists today in place of traditional *oil paint*. Quick drying and durable, it can be used on a great variety of surfaces. Helen Frankenthaler and Morris Louis are painters who use acrylic paints.

Action painting See *Abstract Expressionism*.

additive primary colors Red, blue, and green—colors that produce white when projected onto a single area.

additive process Building up objects from plaster, clay, wood, or metal fragments, joined mechanically or by adhesives. See also *assemblage*.

aerial perspective See *atmospheric perspective*.

afterimage The illusion of an *image* persisting after the original visual stimulus is removed.

aesthetic Having to do with beauty as opposed to usefulness or moral or emotional content.

airbrush A small, precision spray gun, used to produce soft lines and fine graduations of paint.

altarpiece A screen, a series of painted panels, or a sculpture placed on or behind the altar in a church. Usually decorated with religious subjects.

ambulatory The apse aisle of a church, such as the gallery aisle behind the altar.

analogous colors *Hues* that are close to each other on the *color wheel,* such as blue, blue-violet, and blue-green.

Analytical Cubism See *Cubism*.

aperture In photography, the opening that admits light into the camera. The size of the aperture controls the amount of light that reaches the film.

apse The semicircular or polygonal area at the end of a building. First used in Roman *basilicas,* later copied by Christian church builders. The apse of a Gothic cathedral was roofed with complex *vaults* and often had small chapels opening off it.

aquatint A *print,* or an area in a print, which is textured by coating the metal plate, from which the print is made, with rosin dust. The plate is then heated and etched with acid, producing an allover textured tone. See *mezzotint*.

arcade A series of arches supported by *columns,* standing free or attached to a wall for decoration. First used by the Romans, later incorporated into Christian churches and *Renaissance* buildings.

archaic The earliest period of Greek art, from the 8th to the 6th centuries B.C. Also used to describe the early stages of art in any civilization.

architecture The art of building with solid materials, enclosing space in a useful and pleasing way.

architrave The lowest division of an *entablature*.

armature An internal metal or wood support for clay, plaster, or wax to be modeled into sculpture.

artist's proof The first *print* to be *pulled* that satisfies the artist's criteria.

Ash Can school Early 20th-century American artists, who produced realistic art concerned with unpretentious subject content.

assemblage A work of art composed of materials, objects, or parts originally intended for other purposes. See also *additive process*.

atmospheric perspective Also called *aerial perspective*. A method of creating an illusion of three-dimensional depth on a two-dimensional surface, using *color, light,* and *shade*. Objects painted in intense, warm colors with strong contrasts of dark and light appear close to the viewer. Light, cool colors with less contrast make objects appear farther away.

balance The visual balancing of *colors,* shapes, or masses to create a sense of equilibrium.

balloon framing A lightweight wooden frame of milled lumber nailed together to support the walls, floors, and roof of a building. Developed during the 19th century and still used today.

baptistery A building used for baptism in the Christian church, usually circular or polygonal in shape. The baptistery in Florence, Italy, is a famous example.

Baroque A style of art in Europe during the 17th century known for its dramatic light and shade, violent composition, and exaggerated emotion. Caravaggio was a Baroque painter.

barrel vault A roof over a square or rectangular area consisting of a continuous round arch of stone or brick that spans the space between the walls. Widely used in Romanesque churches.

base In architecture, the lowest part of a *column.* Made of stone in ancient temples, it protected the wood from the moist ground.

basilica A rectangular Roman assembly hall containing rows of *columns* that divided it into aisles, usually with a raised platform and semicircular area at one end. Early Christian churches were based on the basilica.

batik A method of producing a design or image on cloth. Wax is painted on the cloth, and the material is immersed in dye. When the wax is removed, the areas that had been covered by it retain the original color of the material.

battered Sloped, as in *battered* walls.

Bauhaus School of design Founded in Germany by Walter Gropius, fostering learning by working with professional painters, designers, and architects.

bearing wall The wall that supports a superstructure, such as a roof or an *entablature.*

binder The material used in paint that causes *pigment* to adhere to the surface.

bisque Ceramics that have been fired at a low temperature, usually in preparation for receiving a *glaze.*

broken-color Application of pure tube colors onto a painting surface, intending for the eye to mix the colors. See *Impressionism.*

buon fresco See *fresco.*

buttress A solid *masonry* support, usually square, built against a wall to counteract the outward thrust of the wall and roof. Used extensively in *Romanesque* and *Gothic* churches. See also *flying buttress.*

Byzantine art Styles of painting, *design,* and *architecture* evolving from Byzantium, now Istanbul, involving round arches, massive *domes, mosaics,* stylized elongated figures, and rich use of color, especially gold.

cage construction Self-supporting steel frame used for skyscrapers and other many-storied structures. A system used by pioneer architect Louis Sullivan. See *steel cage.*

calligraphy The art of writing, or controlled, flowing *line* used in a decorative manner. Oriental characters that are written with a brush.

camera obscura A device developed during the *Renaissance* to project an image through a small hole onto a surface from which it could be traced. Forerunner of the modern camera.

cancellation proof The proof of a *print* that is *pulled* after the block has been intentionally defaced by the artist, to signify the end of the edition.

cantilever A structural method in which beams or sections of a structure project beyond their support and are held in place by weight on the attached end.

capital The top part of a *column,* usually wider than the upright section, usually carved. Different civilizations used a variety of decoration on capitals. See also *Greek orders.*

Carolingian style The era of Charlemagne, 8th–10th cent. Devoted to restoration of Classical culture.

cartoon A drawing that is used as a guide for a large artwork, usually drawn the same size as the finished work. Also a humorous or satirical drawing.

carving A sculptural method in which the image is formed by removing material from a block, using sharpened tools. The opposite additive method builds up or adds material to create the sculpture.

caryatids Whole female sculptured figures supporting the roof of a building. The most famous are in the porch of the Erechthion in Athens.

casting The process of pouring a liquid material into a *mold,* causing it to take the shape of the mold when it hardens. Used for metals, clay, and synthetic materials. An important method in metal sculpture.

catacombs A series of subterranean tunnels used for burial. Those in and around Rome were used by the early Christians for worship; they contain many paintings.

cella The main room in an ancient Greek temple, containing the ritual image of a god or goddess.

centering The method of supporting an arch in construction. Once the *keystone* is in place and the arch becomes self-supporting, the centering is removed.

ceramics Any object formed of clay, hardened by baking. Ceramic sculpture, pottery, tiles, and building materials may be built up by hand, formed on a *potter's wheel,* or in *molds.*

champlevé A style of *enamel* decoration in which areas to contain colors are dug away and bounded by ridges.

charcoal A drawing material made from charred wood. Used since prehistoric times for drawing on a variety of surfaces.

chasing A technique for decorating metal by embossing or gouging it.

chiaroscuro (kee-a-roh-skoo-roh) An Italian word meaning "light and dark." In painting and drawing, the use of light and dark areas to create the illusion of light and shade.

choir That part of the church separated from the *nave* and altar, often designated for the singers and/or musicians during a religious service.

cinematography The art of expressing emotion or communicating meaning through moving images made with a motion-picture camera.

cire perdue See *lost wax* process.

Classical In general, the art of ancient Greece and Rome. In particular, the art of Greece of the 5th century B.C. It can also mean any art that is based on a carefully organized arrangement of parts, with special emphasis on balance and proportion. See *Neoclassicism.*

clerestory That part of a building that rises clear of adjoining roofs, and whose walls contain windows to light the central area below.

cloisonné An enameling technique in which color or design areas are separated by wire strands fused to the metal base.

collage Generally two-dimensional works made of pasted paper pieces, cloth, or other materials.

collography A method of printing from a flat surface onto which a variety of materials has been attached. When damp paper is pressed against the surface, a print with indented areas is produced.

color What we perceive when our eyes sense the waves of visible light reflected from a surface. As the light hits the object, our eyes absorb certain colored rays, while others are reflected. These reflected rays cause us to see the hue of that wave, such as red, yellow, or blue. Color is also formed by coating a surface with a *pigment* that reflects certain rays. See also *spectrum, hue, value,* and *intensity.*

Color-Field painting A style of painting of the 1960s and 1970s, using large areas, or fields, of color to surround the viewer with a visual experience of color.

color wheel An arrangement of the *hues* of the *spectrum,* usually twelve. They are placed in a circular pattern, with *complementary colors,* such as yellow and violet, opposite each other.

column An upright, usually cylindrical, support for a roof or upper portion of a building. In *Classical* architecture it was made up of a *base*, a *shaft,* and a *capital,* and generally was made of stone. Today a column may be made of reinforced concrete or metal.

combine art A combination of media, usually painting and diverse objects, such as an electric fan in *Pantomine* by Robert Rauschenberg. See also *assemblage.*

complementary colors The *hues* that appear opposite each other on the *color wheel,* such as orange and blue, red and green, yellow and violet. When mixed in equal amounts, these hues form a neutral gray.

composition The ordered grouping of *line, color, shape,* or *mass* in the visual arts. Composition implies an effort on the part of the artist to organize the parts into a whole, whether the result appears carefully organized or free and spontaneous.

Conceptual Art A work of art or an event conceived in the mind of the artist, sometimes produced in visible form, but often merely presented as a concept.

constructivism An art movement, overlapping *Cubism* and *De Stijl,* based on the use of nonobjective, often technological, shapes and new materials. In sculpture the artwork was constructed rather than being cast or modeled. Naum Gabo and Antoine Pevsner were the best known of the constructivist group.

content The theme or story of a work of art.

contour The edge of a form or group of forms in painting or sculpture.

contrapposto The counter position of the upper and lower parts of the body, as when the weight is unevenly distributed in an active pose. The hips and shoulders are counterbalanced in nonparallel directions.

corbelled arch A method of spanning an opening by placing each stone or brick so that it projects slightly beyond the one below it.

Corinthian One of the Greek orders of temple architecture, which used slender columns topped by elaborate *capitals* decorated with carved leaves. Copied extensively in Roman and *Renaissance* times.

cornice The horizontal section crowning a *facade* or a roof.

crayon A stick of white or colored chalk or wax impregnated with a *binder.*

cross-hatching A system of lines drawn in close parallel order, crossed at an angle by other lines, which produce changes in tonality. Shading or volumes so indicated can be reproduced as *line art,* or a *linecut.*

cross vault See *groined vault.*

crossing The point of intersection where one passage crosses another, as when the transept crosses the *nave* of a church.

Cubism A style of painting developed in 1908 by Picasso and Braque, who built up *still lifes* and figures with cubelike shapes. Joined by other artists, the Cubists later depicted objects with flat, often transparent areas, frequently showing several views of the subject in one composition.

cuneiform A form of writing with wedge-shaped characters carved in stone or pressed into clay tablets. Used in ancient Assyria, Babylonia, and Persia.

curtain wall A nonload-bearing wall, also called a *screen* or *skin* wall.

Dada An early 20th-century anti-art movement ridiculing contemporary culture and conventional art. Many of its adherents later became *Surrealist* artists.

daguerreotype An early photograph in which the photographic image is fixed on a base (plate) of metal.

decorative arts See *functional arts.*

De Stijl An art movement started in Holland during World War I, using nonobjective geometric shapes. Piet Mondrian introduced this style with Teo Van Doesburg.

design The organization, structure, or *composition* of a work of art or object of use. Industrial or commercial design refers to the activity of planning and designing objects for factory production and commercial use; graphic design applies to design for printing. Also used to describe the decoration applied to objects.

diptych A double-paneled altarpiece.

direct-metal Constructed art in metal, as contrasted with sculpture cast in metal or modeled in stone.

direct painting A painting method in which undiluted paint is applied directly to the canvas instead of being built up in layers of transparent *glazes.*

direct process In sculpture, the creation of the final work by removing wood or stone from the original block. See also *subtractive process.*

Divisionism See *Pointillism.*

dolmen An upright boulder.

dome A hemispherical roof supported on *columns* or walls. The Pantheon in Rome, the Church of Santa Sophia in Constantinople, and the *Stupa* of Sanchi in India are famous domes.

Doric The oldest Greek order of temple building, in which the *column* has no *base,* is heavy, and is topped with a simple flat *capital.* The Parthenon in Athens is the best-known Doric temple.

drypoint A type of *printmaking* in which a sharp needle is used to cut a groove into the metal plate. The rough edge of the groove catches the ink, giving the printed line a soft edge.

earth colors Paint *colors* derived from colored earth. Usually browns, reds, and yellows.

earthenware A type of rough *ceramic,* used for pottery and some sculpture, fired at a low temperature.

earthwork Sculpture involving the moving of earth in large amounts to shape it into an image or *composition*.

easel painting Any painting that is small enough to be painted on an artist's easel, as opposed to a large wall painting.

eclectic A style of art, particularly of *architecture*, in which parts are chosen from earlier styles and combined into a new whole.

edition In *printmaking*, the number of prints taken from one block or plate, usually numbered consecutively.

emulsion A suspension, usually in a viscous vehicle—such as photographic silver salts in gelatin—coating plates, films, and so on.

enamel The method of applying ground glass to metal, fusing it with heat into a shiny, colored surface.

encaustic A method of painting with *pigments* in wax. Used by the Romans for funeral portraits.

engraving The process of making grooves in a material either to decorate it or to create an image from which prints can be made. Also the *print* that is made by pressing paper onto an inked wood or metal engraving.

entablature In *Classical* architecture, the horizontal section between the *columns* and the roof.

entasis In Greek architecture, the slight swelling of a column *shaft* to counteract the optical illusion that makes a series of vertical columns appear to curve inward.

Environmental Art Art that forms or represents a total visual environment, usually large, and frequently combining light and sound with paint and sculpture.

etching An *intaglio* printmaking process. An *image* (or area) applied to a metal plate that is coated with a resist and removes the resist from those sections, allowing them to be exposed to acid. The resultant grooves can be inked and printed. The finished print is also called an *etching*.

Experiential Art Works that require audience participation.

Expressionism A style of art important at the beginning of the 20th century, dominated by German artists and emphasizing an artist's expression of personal emotion. Also applied to art of any period that is particularly concerned with the expression of group or individual emotion.

façade The front exterior of a building, usually containing the main entrance.

fantasy Art that is irrational, mystic, or "make-believe."

Fauvism A style of painting in the early 20th century characterized by the use of large areas of brilliant, strong color, often with violent, distorted shapes. The name comes from the French word for "wild beasts." Henri Matisse and Georges Rouault were well-known Fauvist painters.

ferroconcrete A building material consisting of concrete with metal rods or mesh embedded in it. Also known as *reinforced concrete*.

fetish Art believed to have magical powers.

Field painting See *Color-Field painting*.

fine arts Arts whose primary concern is *aesthetic*.

fisheye lens A lens used in photography to achieve a distorted image in which the central portion of a circular image is magnified.

fluting Grooving, as in the shaft of a *column*.

flying buttress A *masonry* arch used on *Gothic* churches to counteract the outward thrust of the *vault* of the *nave* by carrying the force to a vertical support.

focus A point of convergence or center of attention. In photography, the degree of sharpness of an image.

foreshortening A method of representing an object on a two-dimensional surface so that it appears to be projecting toward the viewer. Developed by *Renaissance* painters.

form In two-dimensional art, any defined area on a picture surface, whether flat or creating the illusion of solid, three-dimensional mass. In three-dimensional art, any solid part of the composition, or the overall shape of the composition.

formalism Art prescribed by rules of color, design, or other specific intent.

forum In the Roman world, the marketplace or public place of a city, the center of judicial business.

frame construction *Cage construction* in which all parts of a design support one another, as in a *skeleton* and *balloon frame*.

fresco A painting technique in which pigments are brushed onto wet plaster, drying to become part of the surface of the wall.

fresco secco Fresco painting in which *pigments* mixed with a *binder* are applied to dried plaster. The result is less durable and brilliant than *buon fresco*.

frieze In *Classical* art, the central portion of the area between the columns and the roof, usually decorated. Any horizontal area of decoration.

functional art Any art that fills a utilitarian need and is aesthetically satisfying. See also *decorative* and *minor arts*.

Futurism A style of painting and sculpture in the early 20th century that represented and interpreted modern machines, particularly those that moved. An attempt to represent movement and speed with nonmoving materials.

gates Vents or channels allowing air to escape in metal casting.

genre art The casual representation of everyday life and surroundings.

geodesic A structural system based on tetrahedrons; developed by Buckminster Fuller as an alternative to, and improvement on, cube structure. Used to create *domes*.

gesso A mixture of glue and chalk painted on panels or canvas as a base for *tempera* and other paints. It may be pure white or tinted.

glaze In painting, a thin, transparent coat of pigment. Traditionally used in *oil painting* since the 1500s; now possible with synthetic paints. In *ceramics*, a mixture of minerals painted onto clay that fuses into a glasslike substance when fired in a kiln.

Golden Section A ratio for determining pleasing proportions in art; the size of the smaller part relates to the size of the larger part as the larger part relates to the whole (A:B = B:c). Originally used by the Greeks, it was employed by *Renaissance* and later artists.

Gothic A style of architecture that spread throughout most of Europe between the 12th and 16th centuries. Characterized by an interlocking system of stone *arches, vaults,* and *buttresses* that carried the weight and thrust of the building, enabling buildings to reach great heights. Gothic cathedrals were constructed by communal efforts and expressed the religious faith of the time.

gouache (goo-ahsh) A form of *watercolor* paint in which the *pigments* are made opaque by adding zinc white, in contrast to pure *watercolor* paint, which is transparent.

graphic Descriptive of art involving line or flat tones. "Graphic art" usually refers to printed art, such as advertising, packaging, and editorial art.

gravure A form of commercial printing from an *etched* plate. The ink is transferred to the paper from the depressed areas of the plate, as opposed to *letterpress* printing, in which the raised areas of a plate transfer the ink to the paper.

Greek orders Three types of architectural structure developed by the Greeks: the Doric, Ionic, and Corinthian. Although the orders varied in proportion and decoration, they all consisted of a vertical *column, capitals,* and a horizontal *entablature* between the columns and the roof. Copied and changed by later architects, they have been used in various forms throughout Western *architecture*. See *Doric, Ionic,* and *Corinthian.*

greenware Clay objects that have been air dried and are ready for the first, low-temperature firing in a *kiln.*

groin(ed) vault A structural method of roofing a square area. Two *barrel vaults* of the same dimensions intersect at right angles, producing edges called "groins." Introduced by the Romans and used by Romanesque church builders.

ground A preliminary base applied to a support in preparation for drawing or painting. *Gesso* is the usual prime. Also the preliminary coating—a waxy, acid-resistant substance—applied to a plate before *etching.*

halftone A metal plate used for reproducing illustrations in commercial printing. The image is photographed through a grid that breaks down the areas of tone into various-sized dots. The plate is *etched,* leaving the dots raised. When inked and run through a press, the plate transfers the *image* to paper with all the gradations of tone of the original image.

happening An event, generally unrehearsed and without predetermined script, produced by artists. It may include light, sound props, and costumes and may involve audience participation.

Hard-Edge A mid-20th century art style depicting geometric form, meticulously rendered.

Harlem Renaissance Black movement involving jazz, literature, and art which flourished in Harlem around 1930, and featured the black cultural heritage.

haute couture Unique or limited editions of highly styled fashions designed for the trendsetters of society.

Hiberno-Saxon style Medieval style in which profuse geometric and animal forms are decoratively interlaced.

high key Area consisting primarily of pale or light *values.*

highlight The lightest area of a painting. Usually refers to the spot where the brightest light is reflected from an object or figure.

holography The production of images using laser beams to record on a photographic plate a diffraction pattern from which a three-dimensional image can be seen or projected.

horizon line In *linear perspective,* the imaginary level toward which all the parallel lines receding into the picture seem to converge. Along the horizon line there may be several *vanishing points.*

hue An identifiable color on the *color wheel* or spectrum. Also, the element of a particular color that separates it from others.

humanities Branches of culture, especially the classics, as contrasted with science or religion.

icon An *image* of symbolic significance, often sacred.

iconography Visual *images,* conventions, and *symbols* used by a culture or religion.

idealization The representation in painting or sculpture of objects or figures in a simplified, perfected style, particularly characteristic of Greek sculpture of the 5th century B.C.

illuminated manuscript Any decorated manuscript, particularly those of the *medieval* period, in which religious scenes, daily life, animals, flowers, and humans were favorite subjects.

image A visual representation of an object, figure, or event in painting, sculpture, photography, or any visual art.

impasto Thickly applied paint.

Impressionism A style of painting developed in the last half of the 19th century that tried to capture the quality of light as it plays across landscapes and figures. Its followers used small strokes of contrasting color placed next to each other to create the illusion of vibrating light.

inlay Any material set into another material, particularly wood or metal set into the surface of an object to decorate it.

intaglio A *printmaking* technique in which lines and areas to be printed are recessed below the print surface. See *etching.*

intensity The degree of purity or brilliance of a *hue.* Also called *saturation.*

International Style Geometric architectural style, developed in Europe between 1910 and 1925 and relating to De Stijl; structural system emphasizing massive horizontals, based on functional design, devoid of ornament.

investiture The outer, fire-resistant *mold* used in the process of metal casting in sculpture.

Ionic One of the Greek styles of temple architecture; characterized by slender, fluted shafts and capitals decorated with carved spiral shapes.

keystone The central wedge-shaped stone in an *arch,* the last one to be put in place. When the keystone is inserted, the temporary supports holding up the arch may be removed, and the pressure of the wedge-shaped stones against each other will hold the arch in place.

kiln An oven in which clay objects are baked to harden them. Simple outdoor kilns are fired with wood, while complex gas and electrical kilns are capable of reaching extremely high temperatures under closely controlled conditions.

kinetic Art that incorporates movement, usually motor-driven, into a composition.

kinetic sculpture Sculpture that includes movement as part of the composition, whether provided by air, motors, or human muscles.

kiva A ceremonial American Indian structure, mainly subterranean.

kore Greek for "maiden." An archaic sculpture of a standing female, usually fully clothed.

kouros Greek for "youth." An archaic sculpture of a standing nude male.

lacquer A clear, hard-finish resin used to coat wood or metal. May also be mixed with *pigment* to give brilliant colors. Oriental artists used coats of lacquer over wood in furniture and sculpture as well as in dishes.

laid paper Distinctly patterned paper made on a mold composed of intersecting wires of different weight. See also *wove paper.*

lens The part of the camera that gathers and concentrates the light to produce an inverted image on light-sensitive film.

letterpress A method of printing in which the ink is transferred to the paper from raised type or from a raised image etched on a plate, as opposed to *gravure,* which uses grooves to hold and transfer the ink.

line A mark made by a moving point, pencil, brush, or pen. Also, the edge between two forms, or the silhouette edge of a form.

line art *Images* created by lines or dots.

linear perspective A method of determining or representing the size of objects as they recede in space. Imaginary parallel lines drawn at right angles to the viewer appear to converge at a *vanishing point* on the *horizontal line.* Widely used by painters during and after the *Renaissance* to create the illusion of space on a two-dimensional surface. Oriental art and much contemporary art may not be concerned with linear perspective.

linecut In printing, a metal plate used to reproduce images that consist only of lines, such as drawings, *woodcuts,* or architectural plans.

Linotype A machine that casts type for printing in the form of slugs of one-piece lines, already spaced for printing.

lintel A structure member that spans a rectangular opening between two posts, *columns,* or walls.

lithography A method of *printmaking* based on the antipathy of grease toward water. The image is drawn with a greasy crayon on a grainy plate or stone, which then is chemically treated so that it will accept the printing ink only where the crayon has been used. The image is transferred under pressure from the stone to damp paper.

local color The natural color of the subject of an *image.*

logo (logotype) Two or more letters symbolizing a product, company, or an institution.

lost wax A method of casting in which wax is used to form the sculpture. Heat-resistant material is built up around the wax to form a *mold.* When this mold is baked, the wax runs out, leaving a hollow space that reproduces the original. See also *cire perdue.*

low key Areas consisting primarily of dark values, as occur in night scenes.

Lung-Ch'uan ware A fine *porcelain* from southern China.

macramé A fiber technique, achieving form by knotting strands into patterns.

Magic Realism See *Photorealism.*

Mannerist A style of art in Western Europe in the 16th century that rejected the classic balance and moderation of *Renaissance* art and was characterized by exaggerated, distorted, and highly emotional images.

marquetry Complex floral designs of contrasting woods in furniture and floors. See also *parquetry.*

masonry Stone or brickwork used in building.

mass A three-dimensional form that has actual physical bulk. Also, the illusion of weight and bulk created on a two-dimensional surface.

mastaba Arabic term for "bench"; applied to earliest Egyptian burial monuments, from which the design of the great pyramids evolved.

mausoleum A large and elaborate tomb, usually for a person of great importance.

mechanical A pasted-down assembly of the parts of an advertisement or other pieces of art, ready for printing.

medieval Characteristic of the Middle Ages in Europe, between the 4th and late 15th centuries A.D.

medium The material, method, or techniques used by an artist to create a work of art. Also, the material used to dilute paint, such as water or turpentine.

medium shot The medium-range equivalent of a cinematographic *long shot.*

megalith A huge boulder.

menhir A single large stone, usually set with others in formation.

mezzotint A variant of *etching* and *engraving* in which large areas of the image are roughened to produce flat tones.

minaret A tower outside a *mosque* from which Moslems are called to prayer.

Minimal art Painting and sculpture of the simplest contours, surfaces, and colors. The precision of machining may dominate. *Primary, ABC, Systemic,* or *Minimal* sculptures are largely comprised of depersonalized geometric forms.

mixed media The use of several different materials, methods, or techniques in one work of art.

mobile A sculptural construction incorporating motion. The parts of the construction are moved by currents of air or by motors.

module A unit that is standard in size and can be fitted into another, similar unit to form a larger composition. Used in building and in furniture.

mold The hollow form or cavity in which a liquid or pliable material is shaped or cast to create sculpture, jewelry, or *ceramics.* Also, the sieve through which the mash of fibers is poured in papermaking.

monochromatic A color scheme that uses only one hue in varying degrees of light and dark.

montage An arrangement of pictures, or parts of pictures, previously drawn, painted, or photographed.

mosaic A surface decoration made of small pieces of glass, tile, or stone set in plaster or mortar. Used widely throughout history for decorative floors and as wall decoration.

mosque A Moslem religious building, usually incorporating towers, pools, and fountains, as well as a central hall.

mural A wall painting, usually large, which may be painted with any kind of paint. Often confused with *fresco,* which refers only to a painting done on a wet plaster ground.

nave The central aisle of a church. In *Gothic* cathedrals, the nave was much higher than the side aisles. Amiens cathedral has a well-known example of a Gothic nave.

negative space The background in a work of art; the space surrounding the main defined areas or *shapes.*

Neoclassical A style of art in the 18th century that revived the *Classical* art of Greece and Rome in painting, sculpture, and *architecture.* Many government buildings in Washington, D.C., such as the Lincoln Memorial, are Neoclassical.

New York School Artists in the New York area who shared a common center of artistic concern during the 1940s and 1950s.

niche A recess in a wall, usually containing a piece of sculpture.

nonobjectivism A style of art in which no object is represented. It became an important force in art in the early 20th century and continues to be so today. Piet Mondrian, Jackson Pollock, and Ad Reinhart represent different types of nonobjective painters.

nonrepresentational art See *nonobjective art.*

obelisk A tall, four-sided monument, sometimes covered with carved inscriptions.

oil painting A method of painting developed in the 16th century in which *pigment* is combined with one of a number of oil mixtures. Applied to a surface, it dries to form a continuous film. Oil paint is still widely used today.

one-point perspective *Perspective* viewed from directly in front of a subject. Only on *vanishing point* is apparent.

Optical art Also called Op art. A style of art in the late 1960s and 1970s characterized by flat shapes of contrasting colors or values, placed next to each other to cause vibrations in the eye.

Organic Architecture Building system developed by Frank Lloyd Wright, which satisfies in design the needs of the occupants in relationship to the site. Such constructions "grow" like living organisms.

palette A range of colors; the surface on which an artist mixes paint.

palette knife Knife with a small, flexible wedge-shaped blade, used to mix colors on the palette; sometimes used to apply paint to an art work.

panning Moving the cinematographic camera horizontally. See also *tilting.*

parquetry Geometric designs of contrasting woods in furniture and floors. See also *marquetry.*

pastels Sticks of pure *pigment* with a minimum of gum *binder.* A favorite *medium* of the *Impressionists,* because of its freshness and brilliance.

patina The finish applied to a metal sculpture. Also the finish applied to wood sculpture and furniture.

pediment The triangular space forming a gable of a double-pitched roof.

pendentive A triangular construction serving to transfer weight from a *dome* to a *pier.*

perspective See *linear perspective* and *atmospheric perspective.*

photogram A photographic technique in which an object is placed on light-sensitive material and exposed.

Photo Realism An art style of the mid-20th century in which objects or people are depicted with photograhic precision.

pier A heavy *masonry* support, usually square.

pigment A dry coloring material, made from a variety of organic or chemical substances, which is mixed with some form of liquid and a binding material to form paint, ink, crayons, or pastels.

pilaster A decorative nonweight-bearing column attached to a wall.

pile weave A form of weaving in which loops are left on the surface and are cut to form a soft texture. Ofted used in rugs.

plain weave The simplest form of *weaving,* in which the *weft* passes over one *warp* thread and under the next. Broadcloth and burlap are examples.

plan In *architecture,* a view of the layout of space in a building, drawn as if looking down on it.

plane Any flat or level surface.

plastic Synthetic materials with varying qualities that are used in the *functional arts* as well as in painting and sculpture. Also used as a general term to describe any of the visual arts. Also, any material that has the characteristic of being easily formed or manipulated, such as clay.

Pointillism A technique of applying tiny dots of color to painting; especially referring to the work of Georges Seurat.

polymer See *acrylic paint.*

polyptych A multipaneled altar painting usually employing *tempera* on wood.

Pop Art A style of painting and sculpture in the 1960s that used popular and commercial symbols and images as subject matter.

porcelain A form of thin, delicate *ceramic,* created from fine clays and baked at an extremely high temperature. The potters of the Orient have produced porcelain for centuries.

post and beam A type of wooden construction using two upright posts and one horizontal beam to span a space.

Post-Impressionists A group of artists active in the late 1800s who painted in varying personal styles and were linked mainly by their rejection of *Impressionism.* Some, such as van Gogh and Gauguin, were most interested in personal expression, whereas others, such as Cézanne, were more concerned with composition and structure.

Postpainterly Abstraction Art style developed in the mid-20th century, in which forms are meticulously depicted and separated; also known as "hard-edge painting."

pottery The art of making utensils and vessels of clay. See *ceramics.*

potter's wheel A circular metal, wood, or stone disk that revolves by foot or motor action on which a potter shapes wet clay into a vessel.

Pre-Columbian art Art produced in North and South America before the European invasions of the 16th century.

prehistoric art Art created before written history: the only record of many early cultures. Cave paintings and rock paintings in Europe and Africa, carved implements, and statuettes are examples of prehistoric art.

primary colors The *hues* that can be mixed to produce all other hues. In painting, the primary colors are red, yellow, and blue.

Primary sculpture See *Minimal art.*

print A multiple impression made from a wood block, a *lithographic* stone, or by *etching* a plate. Usually signed by the artist.

printer's proofs The *prints* that form the *edition* of the print.

printing A method of producing *images*—verbal or pictorial—by transferring the ink on a master surface to another surface.

printmaking The process of making *prints,* generally done by the artist or under his or her careful supervision. Also called "graphics."

proportion The relationship of one part of a work of art to another and of each part to the whole. See *Golden Section.*

pull To remove a *print* from the printing plate.

quilted fabric A puffed fabric, in which ornamental stitching holds a stuffing in patterned shapes.

raku ware Rough, dark glazed ware, low-fired, as in Japanese raku ware.

raising Hammering a flat shape of metal into a hollow vessel.

rayograph See *photogram.*

ready-made *Dada* works that combined several manufactured objects into one construction. A method of working developed by Marcel Duchamp.

realism Mid-19th-century art style, developed by Gustave Courbet in opposition to contrived *Academic art.* Art style depicting subject matter, true to its appearance.

reinforced concrete See *ferroconcrete.*

relief sculpture Sculpture in which the three-dimensional forms are raised from a flat background, as contrasted to free-standing sculpture. The relief may be low, called bas-relevé, or high (haut-relevé), in which the forms are raised far above the background.

reliquary A small box, casket, or sculptural object that contains a religious relic.

Renaissance The period in Europe between the 14th and the 16 centuries; characterized by a rebirth of interest in *Classical* art and philosophy. A scientific attitude dominated, and art expressed balance, harmony, and the importance of individual humans.

repoussé A process, raising a relief *image,* usually metal, by pushing out areas from the back surface to the front.

representational art Art that reproduces reality with little or no change or distortion.

rhythm The repetition, either regular or varied, or visual elements, such as *lines, shapes,* or *colors.* As in music, visual rhythm is an expressive tool, important in the creation of an aesthetically pleasing work of art. The repeated *pilasters* on the Colosseum in Rome are an example of rhythm in *architecture,* while the figures in Michelangelo's *Creation of Adam* show the use of a more subtle rhythm in painting.

rib vault A groin construction that follows the line of the arches and joints of the *vault.*

Rococo A style of art, popular during the 18th century, in which delicate colors, curving shapes, and sinuous lines created ornate decoration on interior surfaces, silverware, and furnishings. Paintings of the period were elegant and pleasant, reflecting the life of the aristocracy.

Romanesque A style of *architecture* and its art prevalent in Europe between the Roman and *Gothic* periods. Characterized by the round *arch* and use of *piers, columns, arcades,* and *vaults.*

Romantic movement A style of art lasting from the mid-1700s into the 19th century, emphasizing individual emotions expressed in a dramatic manner. Exotic subject matter and scenes of distant places were common, and the movement rebelled against the established art of the times.

sans serif A letter, especially in printing, that has no cross strokes at top or bottom.

satin weave Weave in which the *weft* passes over several *warp* threads at a time, producing a lustrous surface.

saturation See *intensity.*

scale The size, or apparent size, of an object relative to other objects, people, or its environment. In architectural drawings, the ratio of the dimensions to the full-size building: for example, "one inch equals one foot."

scriptoria The rooms in *medieval* monasteries where manuscripts were copied and decorated.

secondary colors Three *hues* on the *color wheel* formed by mixing the *primary colors* in equal amounts: green, violet, and orange.

serif A fine line or cross-stroke at the top or bottom of a letter.

serigraphy See *silkscreen.*

sfumato The hazy blending of light and dark tones in a painting, creating soft and indefinite edges.

shade A color that is low on the value scale; a dark color.

shaft In *architecture,* the upright portion of a *column,* usually cylindrical.

shape Any area defined by *line, color,* tones, or the edges of forms.

silkscreen Also called *serigraphy.* A process of *printmaking* in which *stencils* are applied to silk that is firmly stretched across a frame. Paint is forced through the unblocked portions of the screen onto the paper beneath.

silverpoint A drawing technique in which a fine-pointed silver tool inscribes lines on paper coated with white or tinted *pigment.*

simultaneous contrast The contrast formed when *complementary colors* are placed side by side.

skeleton frame See *frame construction.*

slip A creamlike mixture of clay and water, mainly used in *mold casting.*

soft sculpture Sculpture made with fabric forms or woven free-standing or hanging shapes. A technique used by *Pop* artists such as Claes Oldenberg.

solarization The reversal of gradations in a photographic image by intense or continued exposure to light.

spectrum A continuous sequence or range of colors, from the shortest (red) to the longest (violet) wavelengths.

stabile Sculpture of flat (painted) construction, attached to the ground. Technique developed by Alexander Calder. See also *mobile.*

steel cage Also called steel frame. A structural method in which steel supports, placed in a post and *lintel* system, are connected to produce a strong self-supporting framework. Nonsupporting walls, floors, and roof are attached to the frame. Used extensively in contemporary construction.

stele A free-standing upright stone or pillar, usually bearing an inscription or relief decoration.

stencil An image or design cut out of a still material. Paint is forced through the holes in the stencil to reproduce the cut image. Used for hand printing on cloth, paper, or walls, and in *silkscreen* printing.

still life A painting of ordinary objects such as bottles, flowers, or fruit. Also the arrangement from which such a painting or drawing is made.

stoneware A type of coarse *ceramics* fired at a high temperature.

stupa The earliest type of Buddhist religious building, probably derived from the Indian funeral mount. Erected in places made sacred by a visit from the Buddha. The stone roof was in the form of a *dome.*

style The characteristic approach an artist takes to his or her theme.

subtractive primary colors Cyan (blue), magenta, and yellow, colors that produce black when white light is projected through them.

subtractive process Process through which form is created by removing, cutting away, or carving out unwanted materials. See also *direct process*.

successive contrast The appearance of a *complementary color* in neutral gray when the gray is placed next to a *primary color*.

Superrealism See *Photo Realism*.

Suprematism Geometric, nonrepresentational art style derived from *Cubism*.

Surrealism A style of painting that developed in the early 20th century; based on subject matter from dreams, fantasy, and the subconscious. Its images often appear unrelated and startling. Max Ernst was a Surrealist painter. Many artists incorporate some Surrealist qualities into other styles.

symbol An image or sign that stands for something else, or the visible sign of something invisible.

Synthetic Cubism See *Cubism*.

Systematic art Art based on a mathematical system of unit repeats that might be infinitely expanded. See *Minimal art*.

tapestry Tightly woven hangings, carrying patterns and *images*.

tapestry weave A weave in which the *weft* makes patterns only in specific design areas.

tempera A *medium*, binding *pigments* with egg yolk, gum, or casein. Usually applied to wood first coated with a *ground* of *gesso*.

texture The tactile quality of a surface.

three-point perspective An extension of *linear perspective* in which three different *vanishing points*, widely separated, provide the effect of great depth.

tie dye Process of hand-dyeing fabrics with ties and knots to create resist areas that will not absorb dyes.

tilting Moving the cinematographic camera vertically. See also *panning*.

Ting ware Delicate creamy white *porcelain* from northern China. The *glaze* is transparent and almost colorless.

tint A light *hue*, or a *color* with a large amount of white mixed in it.

totem A symbolic *image*, usually defining blood lineage.

tracery Decorative stone openwork in the head of a Gothic window.

trompe l'oeil The illusion of form, light, space, and texture, contrived so that the observer confuses the image for reality.

truss A framework of beams, bars, or rods arranged in triangles. Used to span the space between post or walls, supporting floors, or roofs. Triangular construction is more rigid than that using only right angles.

tusche A greasy black liquid used to paint images on a *lithographic* stone or plate in preparation for printing.

twill weave Weave in which *warp* and *weft* yarns are interlaced in broken diagonal patterns, as in gabardine and denim.

two-point perspective *Perspective* viewed when an object is observed from an angle. There are two *vanishing points*.

tympanum A recessed space, arched or triangular, spanning an arch or above a *lintel*, often decorated with sculpture.

typography The art of composing printed characters; a variety of typefaces of wood or metal have been designed since early Roman times.

unity The arrangement of a work in which all parts seem interrelated.

vacuum forming A method of shaping sheet plastic into sculpture. The plastic is heated and softened, then pulled against a mold by a vacuum machine, which causes the plastic to take the shape of the mold as it cools. An industrial technique adapted to art.

value The measure of lightness or darkness of a color.

vanishing point The point on the *horizon line* at which parallel lines appear to converge.

vantage point The position from which a viewer regards the object.

vault An arched covering spanning two walls, constructed of a series of continuous arches.

vehicle A liquid or emulsion used as a carrier of pigments in a paint; used interchangeably with the term *medium*.

verism Art style that includes the displeasing truth as well as the beauty of a subject.

video The visual aspect of the television medium; *videotape*, a prerecorded television presentation.

visual arts Arts appealing to the optical sense—painting, drawing, *printmaking*, photography, sculpture, *architecture*.

votive statue A statue dedicated to a god or goddess in fulfillment of a vow or promise. Many Greek statues were originally votive statues.

warp The lengthwise threads in a loom—a machine for *weaving*. See also *warp*.

wash A thin, transparent layer of paint. Wash drawings combine wash and *line*.

watercolor Any paint that uses water as a medium. Generally applied to paint formed of *pigments* mixed with a gum *binder* and diluted with water to form a transparent film, as opposed to *gouache*, which is opaque.

weaving The forming of fabrics by interlacing lengthwise threads (the *warp*) with crosswise threads (the *weft*).

weft The crosswise threads in a loom—a machine for *weaving*. See also *warp*.

woodcut A *print* made from an image cut into a block of wood. The ink is transferred from the raised surfaces onto the paper.

woof See *weft*.

wove paper Smooth, virtually patternless paper made on a mold composed of fine, smoothly woven wires of even weight.

Xerography Late 20th-century art medium, utilizing a photocopy technique, in black, white, and color, derived from a process developed by the Xerox Corporation.

ziggurat Mesopotamian mountain to a god. Terracotta-surfaced pyramidal-shaped mound of rubble.

Bibliography and Suggested Readings

CHAPTER 1 CREATION AND RESPONSE

Berenson, Bernard. *Seeing and Knowing*. Greenwich, N.Y.: Graphic Society, 1968.

Ehrenzweig, Anton. *The Hidden Order of Art*. Berkeley and Los Angeles: University of California Press, 1967. Interesting insights into the creative process and the psychology of the artist.

Elsen, Albert. *Purposes of Art,* 4th ed. New York: Holt, Rinehart and Winston, 1981. An engaging, personalized viewpoint, introducing art history in terms of the universal themes of the artist.

Fuller, Buckminster. *Ideas and Integrities*. Englewood Cliffs, N.J.: Prentice-Hall, 1963. A leading and innovative architect of the last quarter-century shares his philosophy in readable prose.

Gombrich, E. H. *Art and Illusion,* 12th ed. London: Phaidon, 1972. Fascinating configurations that illustrate ambiguities in human perception.

Hauser, Arnold. *The Social History of Art*. 4 vols. New York: Vintage, 1957–1958. An important sociological approach to art history.

Samuels, Mike, and Samuels, Nancy. *Seeing with the Mind's Eye: The History, Techniques and Uses of Visualization*. New York and Berkeley: Random House, Inc., and The Bookworks, 1975. Fresh approach to age-old beliefs.

CHAPTER 2 EXPLORING THE ARTIST'S LANGUAGE

Albers, Josef. *Interaction of Color*. New Haven, Conn.: Yale University Press, 1971. A lifetime of devotion to color experiments discussed by the Bauhaus authority on color.

Bevlin, Marjorie Elliot. *Design Through Discovery,* 4th ed. New York: Holt, Rinehart and Winston, 1984. Excellent survey of design with many fresh perspectives.

Birren, Faber. *Color, Form and Space*. New York: Reinhold, 1961.

Itten, Johannes. *The Art of Color*. Translated by Ernest Van Haagen. New York: Reinhold, 1961.

Judd, Deanne B., and Wyscewski, Guner. *Color in Business, Science, and Industry,* 2d ed. New York: Wiley, 1963.

Kepes, Gyorgy. *Language of Vision*. Chicago: Theobold, 1944. Pioneer Bauhaus artist presents his view of design.

Ocvirk, Otto G., et al. *Art Fundamentals: Theory and Practice*. Dubuque, Iowa: William C. Brown, 1968. Survey of elements of design with step-by-step illustrated projects to supplement analysis.

CHAPTER 3 DRAWING, PAINTING, AND MIXED MEDIA

Periodicals

Art in America

Art News

Arts Magazine

Chaet, Bernard. *An Artist's Notebook*. New York: Holt, Rinehart and Winston, 1979. Survey of drawing and painting techniques—traditional to contemporary.

Goldstein, Nathan. *Painting: Visual and Technical Fundamentals*. Englewood Cliffs, N.J.: Prentice-Hall, 1979. Emphasis upon traditional materials and techniques.

Mayer, Ralph. *The Artist's Handbook of Materials and Techniques,* 3d ed. New York: Viking, 1970. Complete survey of materials and techniques.

Mendelowitz, Daniel M. *A Guide to Drawing,* 3d ed. New York: Holt, Rinehart and Winston, 1982. Comprehensive yet compact drawing analyses with excellent illustrations—traditional to contemporary.

Read, Herbert. *A Concise History of Modern Painting*. New York: Praeger, 1959. Selective survey.

CHAPTER 4 PRINTMAKING

Artist's Proof: The Annual of Prints and Printmaking. New York: Pratt Graphics Center and Barre Publishers. Annual review.

The Complete Woodcuts of Albrecht Dürer. New York: Dover, 1963. Works by one of the greatest printmakers of all time.

Heller, Jules. *Printmaking, Today,* 2d ed. New York: Holt, Rinehart and Winston, 1972.

Mayer, A. Hyatt. *Prints and People*. New York: The Metropolitan Museum of Art (Dist. New York Graphic), 1971. Excellent analysis and survey.

Narazake, Munishige. *Hokusai Sketches and Paintings*. Palo Alto, Calif.: California Kodansha International, 1969. Works by a major Oriental artist influencing the East.

Peterdi, Gabor. *Printing Methods Old and New*. New York: Macmillan, 1959. A pivotal 20th-century printmaker defines the art of prints.

CHAPTER 5 ARTS OF THE LENS

Bourke-White, Margaret. *The Photographs of Margaret Bourke-White*. Greenwich, N.Y.: Graphic Society, 1972. Memorable gallery of works, prefaced with biographical notes.

Feininger, Andreas. *Successful Photography*. Englewood Cliffs, N.J.: Prentice-Hall, 1954. Successful teacher-photographer's text on know-how for the student.

Gernsheim, Helmut, and Gernsheim, Alison. *The History of Photography*. New York: McGraw-Hill, 1969. Full account of photographic history to the mid-20th century.

Halas, John, and Manville, Roger. *Technique of Film Animation*. New York: Hastings, 1968. Clear and well-organized text.

Johnson, Nicholas. *How to Talk Back to Your Television Set*. New York: Bantam Books, 1970.

Karsh, Yousuf. *Karsh Portfolio*. Toronto: University of Toronto Press, 1967. Gallery of famous subjects by the well-known photographer; biographical summaries with each portrait.

Lyons, Nathan. *Photographers on Photography*. Englewood Cliffs. N.J.: Prentice-Hall, 1966. Many of the major 20th-century photographers share their views.

MacDonnell, Kevin. *Eadweard Muybridge*. Boston: Little, Brown, 1972. Still views and multiple photographs.

McKowen, Clark, and Byars, Mel. *It's Only a Movie*. Englewood Cliffs, N.J.: Prentice-Hall, 1970.

Morgan, Douglas O., and Morgan, David Westall. *Leica Manual*, 15th ed. Dobbs Ferry, N.Y.: Moran and Morgan, 1972. Complete information for the 35 mm enthusiast.

Ross, R. J. *Television Film Engineering*. New York: Wiley, 1966. Lucid and well-organized text.

Souto, H. M. R. *Technique of the Motion Picture Camera*. New York: Hastings, 1967. Like the others of the series, this text is clear and complete.

Steichen, Edward. *A Life in Photography*. Garden City, N.Y.: Doubleday, 1963. Magnificent illustrations include portraits of famous personalities, with Steichen's notes on each entry.

Wooley, A. E. *Photographic Lighting*, 2d ed. New York: Amphoto, 1971.

CHAPTER 6 SCULPTURE

Itten, Johannes. *Design and Form*. New York: Reinhold, 1964. The foundation course of the Bauhaus school.

Kepes, Gyorgy, ed. *The Nature and Art of Motion*. New York: Braziller, 1965.

Moholy-Nagy, Laszio. *The New Vision*. New York: Wittenborn, 1967. Bauhaus pioneer in design presents his innovative approach.

Read, Herbert. *A Concise History of Modern Sculpture*. New York: Praeger, 1964. A selected presentation in readable style.

Seitz, William C. *The Art of Assemblage*. New York: Museum of Modern Art, 1961. The museum curator defines a typical medium at mid-century.

CHAPTER 7 THE DECORATIVE ARTS

Periodicals

Craft Horizons. Monthly periodical dealing with craft design.

Design Quarterly. Highlights of fine design.

Jenkins, Luisa, and Mills, Barbara. *The Art of Making Mosaics*. Princeton, N.J.: Van Nostrand, 1957.

Karasz, Mariska. *Adventures in Stitches and More Adventures, Fewer Stitches*. New York: Funk & Wagnalls, 1959.

Kenny, John B. *Complete Book of Pottery Making*. New York: Chilton, 1949. Clear, comprehensive, leading text for decades.

Meilach, Donna Z. *Contemporary Batik and Tie-Dye*. New York: Crown, 1973.

——. *Contemporary Leather: Art and Accessories*. New York: Crown, 1971.

——. *Macramé: Creative Design in Knotting*. New York: Crown, 1971.

——. *Papercraft*. New York: Crown, 1967.

Meilach, Donna Z., and Erlin, Snow Lee. *Weaving Off-Loom*. New York: Crown, 1973. Crown's Arts and Crafts Series are all lucid, well-organized, and excellently illustrated texts.

Nelson, Glenn C. *Ceramics: A Potter's Handbook,* 5th ed. New York: Holt, Rinehart and Winston, 1984.

Rottger, Ernest. *Creative Wood Design*. New York: Reinhold, 1961.

Von Neuman, Robert. *Design and Creation of Jewelry*. Philadelphia: Chilton, 1972.

CHAPTER 8 DESIGN FOR INDUSTRY

Periodicals

Advertising Age. Weekly newspaper for the trade.

Design Quarterly. Highlights of fine design.

Interiors. Furniture and interior design.

Vogue. Fashion magazine leader.

Women's Wear Daily. A must for the fashion trade.

Baker, Stephen. *Advertising Layout and Art Direction*. New York: McGraw-Hill, 1959. Excellent survey of the advertising art field.

Brewster, Arthur J. *Introduction to Advertising*. New York: McGraw-Hill, 1954. Principles and practices of advertising.

Fitz-Gibbons, Bernice. *Macy's, Gimbel's and Me*. New York: Simon & Schuster, 1967. An outstanding advertising executive writes a swiftly paced account of her rise in the industry.

Frey, Albert Wesly. *Advertising*. New York: Ronald, 1970. Good, clear account of the advertising process.

Kleppner, Otto. *Advertising Procedure*. Englewood Cliffs, N.J.: Prentice-Hall, 1973. Leading reference for many years; voluminous survey of advertising.

Lester, Katherine Morris, and Kerr, Rose Netzorg. *Historic Costume*. Peoria, Ill.: Bennet, 1967. Excellent summary of the history of costume; good illustrations.

Mottley. *Designing and Making Stage Costumes*. New York: Watson Guptill, 1964. Interesting text; beautiful illustrations.

Payne, Blanche. *History of Costumes*. New York: Harper & Row, 1965. A complete history from ancient times to the 20th century.

Quant, Mary. *Quant by Quant*. New York: Putnam's, 1966. Readable book by the British designer.

Rottger, Ernest. *Creative Wood Design*. New York: Reinhold, 1961.

Schiaparelli, Elsa. *Schiaparelli*. New York: Dutton, 1954. Autobiography by the grande dame of the fashion world.

CHAPTER 9 ARCHITECTURE

Periodicals
Arts and Architecture
Architectural Record
Progressive Architecture

Conrads, Ulrich, and Sperlich, Hans. *The Architecture of Fantasy.* New York: Praeger, 1962.

Giedion, Sigfried. *Space, Time and Architecture.* Cambridge, Mass.: Harvard University Press, 1963.

Gropius, Walter. *The New Architecture and the Bauhaus.* Boston: Branford, 1937. Classic study by the founder of the Bauhaus.

Hamlin, Talbot. *Architecture through the Ages.* New York: Putnam's, 1953. Classic survey of architecture.

Le Corbusier. *Towards a New Architecture.* New York: Praeger, 1970. Leading 20th-century architect explores his philosophy.

————. *The Modular.* Cambridge, Mass.: MIT Press, 1968. An approach to architecture, based on a universal human scale.

Wright, Frank Lloyd. *The Natural House.* New York: Horizon, 1958. Pioneer architect defines the organic system.

CHAPTER 10 ENVIRONMENTAL DESIGN

Blake, Peter. *God's Own Junkyard.* New York: Holt, Rinehart and Winston, 1964.

Halprin, Lawrence. *Cities.* New York: Reinhold, 1972.

Jacobs, Jane. *The Death and Life of American Cities.* New York: Random, 1961. A controversial view of city planning.

Mumford, Lewis. *The City in History.* New York: Harcourt, 1961. Comprehensive survey of cities throughout history.

Neutra, Richard. *Survival through Design.* New York: Oxford University Press, 1954.

Rudofsky, Bernard. *Streets for People.* Garden City, N.Y.: Doubleday, 1969.

CHAPTER 11 MAGIC AND RITUAL:
PREHISTORY AND THE ANCIENT WORLD

Aldred, Cyril. *Development of Ancient Egyptian Art.* London: Tiranti, 1962.

Childe, V. Gordon. *The Dawn of European Civilization,* 6th ed. London: Trubner, 1958.

Frankfort, Henri. *The Art and Architecture of the Ancient Orient.* Baltimore, Md.: Pelican, Penguin, 1955.

Ghirshman, Roman. *The Arts of Ancient Iran from Its Origins to the Time of Alexander the Great.* Translated by Stewart Gilbert. New York: Golden Press, 1964.

Lange, Kurt, and Hirmer, Max. *Egypt.* New York: Abrams, 1956.

Leroi-Gourhan, André. *Treasures of Prehistoric Art.* New York: Abrams, 1967.

CHAPTER 12 GODS AND HEROES:
THE CLASSICAL WORLD

Arias, Paolo. *A History of 1000 Years of Greek Vase Painting.* New York: Abrams, 1963. Comprehensive, well-illustrated work.

Beazley, J. D., and Ashmole, Bernard. *Greek Sculpture and Painting to the End of the Hellenistic Period.* New York: Cambridge University Press, 1966.

Dinsmoor, W. B. *Architecture of Ancient Greece.* London: Batsford, 1950. The standard work on the subject brought up to date.

Lawrence, Arnold. *Greek Architecture.* Pelican History of Art. Baltimore, Md.: Penguin, 1957. A basic text.

Richter, Gisela. *A Handbook of Greek Art,* rev. ed. London: Phaidon, 1960.

————. *Sculpture and Sculptors of the Greeks.* New Haven, Conn.: Yale University Press, 1950.

————. *Archaic Greek Art.* New York: Oxford University Press, 1949. Lucid, well-organized, and illustrated. These texts and all others by her have remained invaluable aids since their first publication in 1929.

Robertson, D. S. *A Handbook of Greek and Roman Architecture.* New York: Cambridge University Press, 1954.

CHAPTER 13 FAITH: THE MIDDLE AGES

Beckwith, John. *Early Medieval Art.* New York: Praeger, 1964. Lucid, well-organized text.

Frankl, Paul. *Gothic Architecture.* Translated by Dieter Pevsmer. Pelican History of Art. Baltimore, Md.: Penguin, 1962.

————. *The Gothic.* Princeton, N.J.: Princeton University Press, 1960.

Grabar, André. *The Beginnings of Christian Art.* Translated by Stewart Gilbert. London: Thames & Hudson, 1967.

————. *Byzantium: Byzantine Art in the Middle Ages.* Translated by Betty Forster. London: Methuen, 1966.

Panofsky, Erwin. *Abbot Suger on the Abbey Church of St. Denis and Its Art Treasures.* Princeton, N.J.: Princeton University Press, 1946.

————. *Gothic Architecture and Scholasticism.* New York: Meridian, 1957.

Rice, David Talbot. *Art of the Byzantine Era.* New York: Praeger, 1963.

Swift, Emerson. *Hagia Sophia.* New York: Columbia University Press, 1940.

CHAPTER 14 THE CROSSROADS:
RENAISSANCE, BAROQUE, AND ROCOCO

Bazin, Germain. *Baroque and Rococo Art.* New York: Praeger, 1964. Good general text.

Berenson, Bernard. *Italian Pictures of the Renaissance.* London: Phaidon, 1957. The long-established text on the subject of Italian painting.

Friedlander, Walter. *The Age of Poussin.* New York: Abrams, 1964.

————. *Caravaggio Studies.* Princeton, N.J.: Princeton University Press, 1955. Both studies are perceptive views of significant Baroque painters.

Huyghe, René. *The Larousse Encyclopedia of Renaissance and Baroque Art.* New York: Putnam's, 1964. Excellent general treatment of the subject.

Kitson, Michael. *The Age of Baroque.* New York: McGraw-Hill, 1968. Survey text.

Kubler, George, and Soris, Martin. *Baroque Art and Architecture in Spain and Latin America.* Baltimore, Md.: Penguin, 1959. Good regional study.

Marle, Raimond van. *The Development of the Italian Schools of Painting.* 19 vols. New York: Hacker, 1971. Comprehensive treatment of the subject.

Milton, Henry. *Baroque and Rococo Architecture.* New York: Braziller, 1961. Clear introduction to the subject.

Pope-Hennesy, John. *Italian Renaissance Sculpture.* London: Phaidon, 1958. Good, complete survey of sculpture of the period.

Portoghesi, Paolo. *The Rome of Borromini.* New York: Braziller, 1968. Brilliant study.

Rosenberg, Jakob, Silve, Seymour, and Kuile, E. H. *Dutch Art and Architecture.* Baltimore, Md.: Penguin, 1966. Excellent regional study.

Rykwert, Joseph, ed. *Alberti's "De re Aedificatoris."* Ten Books on Architecture. London: Tiranti, 1955. Invaluable source book of the time.

Thompson, Daniel. *Cennino Cennini.* New York: Dover, 1954. Translation of Cennini's handbook for the craftsman-artist. Original document of the period.

Vasari, Giorgio. *The Lives of the Most Eminent Painters, Sculptors, and Architects.* New York: Simon & Schuster, 1959. Fascinating chronicle and source book of the day.

Wittkower, Rudolph. *Architectural Principles in the Age of Humanism,* 3d ed. London: Tiranti, 1962. Intriguing, scholarly exploration of harmonic ratios in music and architecture.

———. *Art and Architecture in Italy.* Baltimore, Md.: Penguin, 1958.

———. *Gian Lorenzo Bernini.* London: Phaidon, 1955. Penetrating specialized study of the exponent of Baroque sculpture and his age.

Wölfflin, Heinrich. *Principles of Art History.* 1932. Reprint. New York: Dover, n.d. Classic comparison of the Renaissance and the Baroque.

CHAPTER **15** THE WORLD BEYOND
THE WEST

Boas, Franz. *Primitive Art.* New York: Dover, 1955. Classic study of non-Western art; reissued and translated into English.

Dockstader, Frederick. *Indian Art in America,* 3d ed. Greenwich, N.Y.: Graphic Society, 1968. Comprehensive approach to American Indian art.

Douglas, Frederick H., and D'Harnoncourt, René. *Indian Art of the United States.* New York: Museum of Modern Art, 1970. Introduction to Indian Art.

Drucker, Philip. *Indians of the Northwest Coast.* New York: McGraw-Hill, 1955. Interesting presentation of Indian art with historical background.

Fraser, Douglas. *Primitive Art.* New York: Doubleday, 1967. Incisive survey.

Inverarity, Robert B. *Art of the Northwest Coast Indians,* 2d ed. Berkeley and Los Angeles: University of California Press, 1967. Thorough treatment of the subject.

Lee, Sherman E. *A History of Far Eastern Art.* New York: Abrams, 1964. Comprehensive introductory survey of the scope of Oriental art.

Leuzinger, Elsy. *Art of Africa.* New York: Crown, 1967. Broad survey of African art; profusely illustrated.

Linton, Ralph, and Wingert, Paul S. *Arts of the South Seas.* 1946. Reprint. New York: Museum of Modern Art, 1972.

Rowland, Benjamin. *Art and Architecture of India.* Pelican History of Art series. Baltimore, Md.: Penguin, 1970.

Sickman, Laurence, and Soper, Alexander. *Art and Architecture of China.* Pelican History of Art series. Baltimore, Md.: Penguin, 1971.

Wingert, Paul S. *Primitive Art.* New York: Oxford University Press, 1962. Pioneer scholar in African art surveys the field.

CHAPTER **16** REVOLUTION AND THE
MODERN WORLD

Brion, Marcel. *Art of the Romantic Era.* New York: Praeger, 1966. Well-illustrated study.

Canaday, John. *Mainstreams of Modern Art.* New York: Holt, Rinehart and Winston, 1959. Fascinating personalized chronicle of the Romantic period through 1900.

Friedlander, Walter. *From David to Delacroix.* Cambridge, Mass.: Harvard University Press, 1952. Definitive text for the period.

Rewald, John. *The History of Impressionism.* New York: Museum of Modern Art, 1967.

———. *Post-Impressionism.* New York: Museum of Modern Art, 1962. Fundamental survey.

Reynolds, Sir Joshua. *Discourses on Art.* Edited by Robert Wark. San Marino, Calif.: Huntington Library, 1959. Founder of the British Academy discusses his philosophy of art.

CHAPTER **17** THE GREAT DIVIDE: **1900**

Arnason, H. H. *History of Modern Art.* Englewood Cliffs, N.J.: Prentice-Hall, 1969. Comprehensive survey to the present.

Arp, Hans. *On My Way.* New York: Wittenborn, 1948. Sculptor-painter discusses his art of Surrealist imagery.

Barr, Alfred Jr. *Fantastic Art.* New York: Arno, 1969. Museum of Modern Art curator covers the art of dreams and the irrational world.

Bayer, Herbert, Gropius, Walter, and Gropius, I. *Bauhaus, 1919–1928.* Boston: C. T. Branford, 1959. Written by founders of the Bauhaus; based on the Museum of Modern Art exhibition in 1938.

Canaday, John. *Mainstreams of Modern Art,* 2d ed. New York: Holt, Rinehart and Winston, 1980. *The New York Times* art critic presents a fascinating account of art from the late 18th century through the 19th century.

Crespelle, Jean Paul. *Principles of Neo-Plastic Art.* Greenwich, N.Y.: Graphic Society, 1968. Proponent of abstraction-nonobjective art discusses his philosophy.

Haftmann, Werner. *Painting in the Twentieth Century.* 2 vols. New York: Praeger, 1961. Comprehensive overview.

Hamilton, George H. *Painting and Sculpture in Europe 1880–1940.* Baltimore, Md.: Penguin, 1972. Covers Western modern art to World War II.

Kandinsky, Wassily. *Concerning the Spiritual in Art.* New York: Wittenborn, 1947. Pioneer abstractionist explores his philosophy.

Mondrian, Piet. *Plastic Art and Pure Plastic Art.* New York: Wittenborn, 1945. Leader of the De Stijl movement illuminates his theories.

Motherwell, Robert. *The Dada Painters and Poets.* New York: Wittenborn, 1951. Insights into the nonart movement and philosophy; essays and poetry.

Raymond, Marcel. *From Baudelaire to Surrealism.* London: Methuen, 1970. Commentary on the literature of the period.

Rickey, George. *Constructivism: Origins and Evolution.*

New York: Braziller, 1967. Innovator in kinetic art traces the development of the style.

Rubin, William. *Dada and Surrealist Art.* New York: Abrams, 1969.

Selz, Peter. *German Expressionist Painting.* Berkeley and Los Angeles: University of California Press, 1959.

————, and Constantine, M. *Art Nouveau and Design at the Turn of the Century.* New York: Museum of Modern Art, 1959. Surveys of the movements.

CHAPTER 18 AMERICA IN ASCENDANCY: 1925–1945

Brown, Milton. *American Painting from the Armory Show to the Depression.* Princeton, N.J.: Princeton University Press, 1970. Survey of realistic art.

Butcher, Margaret Just, and Locke, Alain. *The Negro in American Culture.* New York: Knopf, 1956. Ethnological background material.

Catlett, Elizabeth. *The Negro Artist in America.* American Contemporary Art, April 1944. Seen from the perspective of a black artist.

Dover, Cedric. *American Negro Art.* Greenwich, N.Y.: Graphic Society, 1969. Good survey; many illustrations.

Fine, Elsa Honig. *The Afro-American Artist: A Search for Identity.* New York: Holt, Rinehart and Winston, 1973.

Geldzahler, Henry. *American Painting in the Twentieth Century.* New York: Museum of Modern Art, 1965. Interesting survey of American painting.

Hughes, Langston, and Meltzer, Milton. *A Pictorial History of the Negro in America,* rev. ed. New York: Crown, 1972.

Janis, Sidney. *Abstract and Surrealist Art in America.* New York: Arno, 1944. Traces the abstract movement in the United States.

————. *They Taught Themselves.* New York: Dial, 1942. Discusses black self-taught artists. Well illustrated.

Locke, Alain. *The New Negro.* New York: Arno Press, 1968. Anthology of the period with illustrations by Aaron Douglas.

Sandler, Irving. *The Triumph of American Painting.* New York: Praeger, 1973. Good accounts of individual movements.

CHAPTER 19 THE MID-CENTURY WORLD

Gardner, Helen. *Art through the Ages,* 5th ed. New York: Harcourt, 1970. This text remains a favorite for students of art appreciation and art history.

Greer, Germaine. *The Obstacle Race.* New York: Farrar Straus Giroux, 1979. Subjective survey of women painters and their work.

Janson, Horst W. *History of Art.* New York: Abrams, 1969. The definitive text for art history students and an excellent foundation for the beginning student in art.

Knobler, Nathan. *The Visual Dialogue,* 3d ed. New York: Holt, Rinehart and Winston, 1980.

Kozloff, Max. *Renderings: Critical Essays on a Century of Modern Art.* New York: Simon & Schuster, Clarion, 1969. Essays on art and artists.

Munro, Eleanor. *Women Artists, Originals.* New York: Petersen and Wilson, 1976. Succinct summary of the achievements of women in art.

Scully, Vincent. *Modern Architecture,* rev. ed. New York: Braziller, 1974.

Vasarely, Victor. *Vasarely.* Neuchatel: Editions du Griffon, 1965. Study of Op art by a pioneer Op artist.

CHAPTER 20 OUR OWN TIME

Blake, Peter. *Form Follows Fiasco.* Boston: Little, Brown, 1977. Provocative review of much modern architecture with devastating criticisms.

Crowther, Bosley. *Vintage Films.* New York: Putnam's, 1977. Starting with 1929 *Broadway Melody* to 1980 *Godfather II,* film critic provides easy-to-read summaries and many photographs.

Ellis, Jack C. *A History of Film.* Englewood Cliffs, N.J.: Prentice-Hall, 1979. Early film discoveries, good treatment of regional European and Hollywood productions, third-world cinema, re-emergence of American films.

Greenberg, Clement. *Art and Culture: Critical Essays.* Boston: Beacon, 1961. Facinating philosophy of a leading contemporary art critic.

Jencks, Charles. *Modern Movements in Architecture.* New York: Doubleday, 1977. Compact analyses.

Langer, Susanne K. *Problems of Art.* New York: Scribners, 1957. Fine subjective work.

Lippard, Lucy R., ed. *Six Years: The Dematerialization of the Art Object from 1966–1972.* New York: 1975.

Lucie-Smith, Edward. *Art in the Seventies.* Ithaca, N.Y.: Phaidon, Cornell Press, 1980. Nonchronological analysis of modern movements.

Read, Herbert. *Art and Alienation.* New York: Viking, 1969. The role of the artist in society.

Reichardt, J. *The Computer in Art.* New York: Van Nostrand, 1971.

Rose, Bernice. *Drawing Now MOMA.* New York: 1976. Illuminating unexpected works.

Rosenberg, Harold. *Art on the Edge: Creators and Situations.* New York: Macmillan, 1975. Critical essays.

Index

References are to page numbers. **Boldface type** identifies pages on which illustrations appear. (Pl.) following a boldface number indicates a color plate and the page on which it can be found. Works of art are listed under the names of their creators, when known; otherwise under their titles. Many technical terms are included in the index, with references to their text definitions. For a more complete list of terms, consult the Glossary.

Photographic credits The author and publisher wish to thank the custodians of the works of art for supplying photographs and granting permission to use them. Unless listed below, photographs have been obtained from sources noted in the captions.

AR: Art Resource, New York
A/AR: Alinari/Art Resource, New York
BPK: Bildarchiv Preussischer Kulturbesitz, West Berlin
Caisse: Caisse Nationale des Monuments Historiques et des Sites, Service Photographique, Paris
G: Giraudon, Paris
H: Hirmer, Munich
HB: Hedrich-Blessing, Chicago
LCG: Leo Castelli Gallery, New York
NM: Nick Manley, Oyster Bay Cove, N.Y.
PR: Photo Researchers, New York
RMN: Service de Documentation Photographique de la Réunion des Musées Nationaux, Paris
SPR: Photographs by Stella Pandell Russell

References are to figure numbers.

Cover: Photo by © Jake Rajs/The Image Bank, New York

Color Plates 7: NM. **11:** BPK. **12:** Scala/AR. **13:** Photo by Wim Swaan, New York. **14:** Scala/AR. **19:** Photo by Edwin S. Roseberry, Charlottesville, Va.

Chapter 1 1: A/AR. **6:** Photo by Gianfranco Gorgoni, Contact Press, New York. **9:** RMN. **11:** G. **12:** A/AR. **14:** Georg Jensen Silversmiths—Denmark, New York. **16:** American Museum of Natural History, New York. **17:** SPR.

Chapter 2 20: RMN. **27, 28:** Photo, Philadelphia Museum of Art. **35:** Egypt Tourist Authority, New York. **37, 38:** Photo by Herbert Matter, New York. **40:** Photo by Loomis Dean, Life Magazine © 1960 Times Inc. **44:** Photo by Norman Katz. **48, 51, 53:** A/AR. **54, 55:** Rockefeller Center, Inc., New York. **59:** H. **60:** A/AR. **61:** Photograph Collection, Prints & Photographs, Astor, Tilden & Lenox Foundations, New York Public Library. **62:** G. **66:** A/AR.

Chapter 3 67: Photo by Gjon Mili, Life Magazine © 1950 Time Inc. **75:** Photo by Eric Pollitzer, Hempstead, N.Y. **76:** Photo by D. James Dee, New York. **82:** RMN. **86:** Photo, LCG.

Chapter 4 88: Photo by David Riley, New York. **89:** Photo by Stanley Kaplan, Levittown, N.Y. **97:** From the show The Forgotten Society, 1975–1980. **100:** Photo by Coco Gordon, Huntington Bay, N.Y. **101.** Photo by © Hans Namuth, 1983, New York.

Chapter 5 102: PR. **105:** From A. Gardner, Photographic Sketchbook of Wash. [1865–1866], pl. 36. **107:** Ansel Adams Publishing Rights Trust ©. **110:** The Imogen Cunningham Trust, Berkeley, Calif. **114:** NASA, Washington, D.C.

Chapter 6 116: A/AR. **118:** Photography by Egyptian Expedition, The Metropolitan Museum of Art, New York. **119:** Photo by Al Mozell/Pace Gallery, New York. **122:** Photo by Stanley Twardowicz. **125:** Photo by © Harvey Stein, New York.

Chapter 7 129: Photo by Leah Fink, Northport, N.Y. **132:** Photo by Leo Lewis. **133:** NM. **134:** A/AR. **137:** Photo by Bob Hanson, New York. **140:** Photo by Bill Tytus. **143:** Photo by Kahan/Kirsher-Image l.

Chapter 8 147: Photo by Charles Passela. **151:** Mergenthaler Linotype Company, Melville, N.Y. **156:** Photo by Bill Owens, Livermore, Calif. **160:** Photo by Herbert Matter, New York. **161:** Photo, The Museum of Modern Art, New York. **162:** Photo by Alexandre Georges.

Chapter 9 163: © Centre G. Pompidou, Paris. **168:** Buckminster Fuller Archive, Philadelphia. **170:** H. Roger-Viollet, Paris. **174:** Photo by Eliot Elisofon, Life Magazine, © Time Inc. **176:** H. **178:** HB. **179:** Consulate General of Japan, New York. **180:** Photo by William Current, San Francisco. **182:** A/AR. **183:** Engraving by RP Cluff; British Architectural Library/RIBA, London. **184, 185:** HB. **186:** Bernard P. Wolff/PR. **187:** George Holton/PR. **188:** A/AR. **189:** Trans World Airlines, New York.

Chapter 10 190: Holle Bildarchiv, Baden-Baden. **191:** Van Bucher/PR. **192:** Photo by Armando Salas Portugal, Mexico City. **193:** From Solar Dwelling Design Concepts, U.S. Department of Housing and Development, Washington, D.C. Published by Sterling Publishers, Inc., New York, 1977. **194:** Aluminum Association, Washington D.C. **195:** French Embassy Press & Information Division, New York. **196:** Photo by Terry Kirk, Financial Times, London. **197.** Photo by Bob Serating, Lincoln Center for the Performing Arts, Inc. **198:** Photo by Robert E. Mates. **199:** Photo by William Wasson, Kaiser Aluminum & Chemical Corporation, Oakland, Calif. **200:** Canadian Government Office of Tourism, Ottawa, Ontario, Canada. **201:** From Arcology: The City in the Image of Man, by Paolo Soleri. M.I.T. Press, Cambridge, Mass., 1969.

Chapter 11 202: SPR. **203:** Photo by J. Oster. **205:** SPR. **206, 207:** H. **208:** SPR.

Chapter 12 216: TAP Service, Athens. **221:** NM. **223, 226:** H. **227, 228, 229, 230:** A/AR. **231:** George Holton/PR. **233, 234:** A/AR.

Chapter 13 236: A/AR. **238:** Photo by Leonard von Matt, Buochs, Switzerland. **240:** A/AR. **242:** Photo by Ann Münchow, Aachen, West Germany. **243:** Bulloz, Paris. **244:** Jean Roubier/PR.

Chapter 14 245, 246: A/AR. **248:** Caisse. **249, 250, 251, 252, 253, 254, 255, 256, 257, 258:** A/AR. **260, 261:** A/AR. **263:** Photo by O. Zimmermann. **264:** BPK. **266, 267:** A/AR. **270:** French Embassy Press & Information Divisioin, New York. **272:** G. **273:** Photo, National Monuments Record, London. **274:** G. **276:** A/AR. **277:** G.

Chapter 15 281: South African Information Service, New York. **285:** Photo by Ladislas Segy. **286:** © Eugene Gordon 1982/PR. **290:** Photo, Museum of the American Indian, Heye Foundation, New York. **292:** Fritz Henle/PR. **294:** Photo by Edward Ranney. From Monuments of the Incas, New York, Graphic Society, 1982. **296:** Linares, Yale Arts & Architecture Library Photograph Collection, New Haven, Conn. **297:** Government of India Press Information, New York. **299, 300:** Photos by Eliot Elisofon, Life Magazine © Time Inc.

Chapter 16 303: Thomas Jefferson Memorial Foundation, Charlottesville, Va. Photo by Edwin S. Roseberry, Charlottesville, Va. **307, 309, 310, 311:** G. **315:** RMN.

Chapter 17 341: Pannier Photography, Plymouth, Wisc. **347:** Photo, United Nations, New York. **352, 354, 355:** Photos, The Museum of Modern Art, New York.

Chapter 18 360: Photo, Hirschl & Adler Galleries, Inc., New York. **365:** AR.

Chapter 19 376: NM. **379:** Courtesy of Candida Smith and Rebecca Smith. Photo, Archives of American Art, Smithsonian Institution, Washington D.C. **380:** Helmsley-Spear, Inc. New York. **385:** Photo by Michael Alexander/Through the Flower Corp., Benicia, Calif. **386:** Photo by Rudolph Burckhardt/LCG. **390:** Photo by Rudolph Burckhardt, New York. **391:** Photo, Guggenheim Museum, New York. **393:** Photo by © Seymour Rosen, 1983, Los Angeles. **394:** Photo by Lucien Hervé, Paris.

Chapter 20 395: Photo by Eric Pollitzer/LCG. **398:** Photo, Walker Art Center, Minneapolis, Minn. **400:** Photo by Becky Cohen, Leucadia, Calif. **401:** Photo by Shunk Kender, New York. **403:** Photo by Gorchev & Gorchev, Woburn, Mass. **404:** Consulate General of Finland, New York. **405:** Photo by Joseph W. Molitor, Valhalla, N.Y.

Works by Escher, Mondrian, Rietveld: © BEEIDRECHT, Amsterdam/VAGA, New York, 1984, Collection Haags Gemeentemuseum—The Hague. Works by © Rosenquist, Warhol, Shahn, Rauschenberg, Wood, Lichtenstein, Chryssa, Flack, 1984. Works by Picasso, Nadar, Rodin, Le Corbusier, Monet, Renoir, Matisse, Watteau, Rouault, Dali: © S.P.A.D.E.M., Paris/VAGA, New York, 1984. Work by De Chirico: © S.I.A.E., Italy/VAGA, New York, 1984. Work by David Smith: © Estate of David Smith, 1984. Works by Arp, Braque, Brancusi, Calder, Cassatt, Chagall, Duchamp, Giacometti, Kandinsky, Léger, Magritte, Miro, Modigliani, Severini: © ADAGP, Paris, 1984. Work by Klee: © ADAGP, Paris & COSMOSPRESS, Geneva, 1984.

616